THE
CHILD IN AMERICA

THE
CHILD IN AMERICA

≻≻≻≻≻≻≻≻≻≻≻≻≻ • ≺≺≺≺≺≺≺≺≺≺≺≺≺

BEHAVIOR PROBLEMS AND PROGRAMS

≻≻≻≻≻≻≻≻≻≻≻≻≻ • ≺≺≺≺≺≺≺≺≺≺≺≺≺

WILLIAM I. THOMAS

AND

DOROTHY SWAINE THOMAS

≻≻≻≻≻≻≻≻≻≻≻≻≻ • ≺≺≺≺≺≺≺≺≺≺≺≺≺

NEW YORK · *ALFRED·A·KNOPF* · MCMXXVIII

TO
MRS. W. F. DUMMER

PREFACE

THE examination of child study here presented is based in part on visits, in some cases repeated visits, to cities and institutions in the United States and Canada where important or typical programs are in operation.

No attempt has been made to present a survey in the sense of a complete enumeration of programs. In general we have attempted to select for emphasis superior examples of work. In order, however, to represent the present distribution of attention in the whole field and to secure a basis of comparison we have in some cases given a rather extended representation to certain types of program and approach which in our opinion have an inferior value.

We wish to express our thanks to the many directors and research workers who have coöperated with us in the preparation of this study. With hardly an exception we have been given access to the records of work and have been permitted to publish here, when it seemed to us desirable, descriptions of methods and results before they have otherwise appeared in print.

Because of the technical nature of some of the research procedures we have added an explanatory appendix.

W. I. T.
D. S. T.

Contents

PREFACE   vii

INTRODUCTION   xi

PART I. VARIETIES OF MALADJUSTMENT

I. VARIETIES OF MALADJUSTMENT   1

PART II. PRACTICAL PROGRAMS

II. THE TREATMENT OF DELINQUENCY   95

III. PSYCHIATRIC CHILD GUIDANCE CLINICS   144

IV. COMMUNITY ORGANIZATIONS   166

V. THE TREATMENT OF MALADJUSTMENT
      IN THE SCHOOLS   219

VI. CHARACTER EDUCATION IN THE SCHOOLS   273

VII. PARENT EDUCATION   295

VIII. THE PSYCHOMETRIC APPROACH   330

PART III. PROGRAMS

IX. THE PERSONALITY TESTING APPROACH   370

X. THE PSYCHIATRIC APPROACH   435

CONTENTS

XI. THE PHYSIOLOGICAL - MORPHOLOGICAL
APPROACH 468

XII. THE SOCIOLOGICAL APPROACH 505

XIII. THE METHODOLOGY OF BEHAVIOR STUDY ... 553

APPENDIX: EXPLANATION OF TERMS 577

INDEX .... *follows* 583

THE
CHILD IN AMERICA

Introduction

As THE RESULT *of rapid communication in space, movements of population (concentration in cities, immigration), changes in the industrial order, the decline of community and family life, the weakening of religion, the universality of reading, the commercialization of pleasure, and for whatever other reasons there may be, we are now witnessing a far-reaching modification of the moral norms and behavior practices of all classes of society. Activities have evolved more rapidly than social structures, personalities more rapidly than social norms. This unstabilization of society and of behavior is probably no more than a stage of disorganization preceding a modified type of reorganization. When old habits break down, when they are no longer adequate, there is always a period of confusion until new habits are established; and this is true of both the individual and society. At present, however, it is widely felt that the demoralization of young persons, the prevalence of delinquency, crime, and profound mental disturbances are very serious problems, and that the situation is growing worse instead of better.*

In this general connection there have been developed in recent years various types of standpoint, organization and program directed toward the study and control of behavior. It is a significant fact that these activities, as will appear in the course of the volume, are so largely of extra-academic origin. Psychologists, educators, and sociologists have not been directly confronted with the problems of personal demoralization, and the procedures which we are here outlining frequently had their origin in the practical problems of the court, the school, and the street — situations which could not wait upon the findings of the learned institutions, even if these proved eventually available and applicable. Consequently the juvenile court, the court psychiatrist, the social worker, the teacher, eventually the visiting teacher, public-spirited persons, have been more directly instrumental in the formation of practical programs. In the meantime problems have arisen in these practical programs concerning mental deficiency, emotional instability, habit formation, special disabilities, family relationships, leisure-time activities, gang life of children, etc., and the academic psychologists and sociologists have linked up their research and speculative work with these practical programs. One of the interesting results has been the development of a somewhat new approach in the form of organizations (more especially the child welfare institutes), having as main objective the development of scientific techniques as related directly to the practical problems.

It is the purpose of the present volume to examine these practical programs and scientific techniques and make some appraisal of them as means of prediction and control.

PART I

CHAPTER I
Varieties of Maladjustment

O UR study is not limited to the maladjustments of children, but
since all child studies have ultimately in view the control of behavior and a happy adjustment it is convenient to provide as a background some picture of the types of problems arising in the life of the
child. The cases are not designed to represent the proportions of the
different maladjustments among themselves but merely the important
varieties.

Viewed in one way the organism is a mechanism for the release of
energy. The child will naturally respond to stimuli impulsively, pro-
miscuously, pleasurably. The parents, on the other hand, and the older
members of society, are interested in having these expressions of
energy assume certain conventional behavior patterns. They desire a
selection of response on the basis of conformity, regularity and utility.
From the adult standpoint, therefore, the impulsive behavior of the
child will in part be judged as "mischievous," "disorderly," "per-
verse," "incorrigible," and eventually "delinquent." This struggle
between impulsive behavior (pleasure selection) and inhibited behavior (utility selection) is the oldest and most persistent conflict
between the individual and society.

The first case below is an item representing the release of physiological tension, spontaneous behavior in immature children:

1. Laura was given a large mama doll at Christmas. The mother left Laura
and Nancy playing with it while she went on an errand. When she came back
the doll was torn to pieces, the head broken and they had attempted to burn
it in the stove. Comment: The doll was apparently broken in rough aimless
play and then they attempted to hide the results by burning it.

They were each given a set of tin dishes for Christmas and burned them up. Laura got into the closet and emptied a whole bottle of oil. Nancy slopped buckets of water all over the kitchen floor. Nancy used all the freshly ironed clothes to mess in the water. Comment: The dishes were not burned up wilfully but were put on the hot stove, pretending to cook. Laura was trying to polish the furniture with oil as she had seen her mother do. Nancy was trying to wash the kitchen floor and didn't have the judgment to handle the water. Nancy wanted to wash clothes and grabbed whatever she could get. Both children were beaten for these things.

I tried to make the mother see that it was not naughtiness but misdirected energy and a real desire to help. I asked her if the children could not have clothes and broom of their own and a place to keep them. She said she had bought brooms but that they were carried outside and soon lost. I urged that she get more things, such as brooms, etc. That she show them patiently the right way to do the things they wanted to do to help. That she show them how to play, to use a chair for a stove, etc., and give them *a place* to keep their things and see that they put them there when through with them.[1]

In case 2, where the girl is " old enough to know better," there is a resistance to social patterning, a rather amiable conflict with society, which has gone on for nine years. An examination of the extensive record shows that the girl is open to all types of response, both good and bad. We are not raising at this point the question whether the girl's behavior is motivated by the evident " mental conflict " but presenting an example of promiscuous and random spending of energy without regard to social patterning:

2. Margaret Eytam. April, 1918: Chronological age — eight years, four months. Mental age — eight years plus. . . .

Margaret is described as a very nervous, emotional type. Could not sit still for even one minute. Clasps her hands; looks around, and says she is tired. Will give no reason for stealing. Says sometimes she will do as her mother bids, and at other times will not. . . .

November, 1918: Patient returns for re-examination. . . . The day of the examination . . . took $5.00 from the purse of a guest in the home, spending $2.50 of this before discovery. Mother was angry and " beat patient unmercifully," although she realized that this was not the proper method of training. Mother seems helpless in the present situation, and wants patient placed. Patient seems devoted to the new baby sister born in June, 1918. . . .

---

[1] Caldwell, Grace M.: Records of the Boston North End Habit Clinic. Manuscript.

Patient works about the house, helping mother, but will not work alone. She forgets as soon as mother leaves her. She is good-natured and kind. Restless; does not like to stay inside the house any length of time. Father humored patient and gave her all that she wanted. For six months previous to father's commitment mother had to work out and father had entire charge of patient. She has been more difficult to manage since this time. Father gave her absolute authority and responsibility in the house, to buy food for the meals. She had practically entire charge of Robert, who was then a baby, giving him his bottle and caring for him. When father was committed to Chicago State Hospital, and mother stayed at home again, she first noticed patient's tendency toward frequent taking of money. . . . She never spends the money that she steals, alone; always shares it with other children. Patient is very tricky in stealing. In taking the $5.00, she went out on the street with playmate; suddenly stooped and apparently picked the $5.00 from the sidewalk, half of which she gave to playmate. Patient spent her half treating the neighborhood children. Patient is always ready with a story when questioned. Is never at a loss to reply. " Makes up one lie after another," without stammer or blush; looks right at mother while doing this. . . . Father died November, 1918, at Dunning. . . .

March, 1919: Mother says that patient does not lie or steal from anyone else outside the home. . . . Is like a little mother to the other children. When mother whips them, she will cry and say, " Oh, mama, please don't! " At any time of night if one of them wants a drink, she never thinks of telling mother, but gets it for them herself. This morning the baby was sick. Patient got up, built the fire in the cook-stove, made the coffee, and set the table. " She works just like an old woman." Every day after school patient has to mind the baby until supper-time, then helps wash dishes, helps put the children to bed; then studies her lessons until 8:45. She used to go to bed earlier, but cannot now, on account of lessons. " People say I shouldn't ask her to do so much, but where could I get help, with so many children? I can't help it."

In talking with patient, she said she liked to go to school, and that the sisters were good to her except when she was late or did not go to mass. " I am punished a lot of times. Sometimes they don't let me down-stairs, and whip me a lot of times. Punish me for taking pencils and penholders from the other children. I take them and use them without asking, and then when I put them back they tell sister. I never take money from school, only from mama. I never meant to keep the penholders." Asked why she took the money from the mother, patient replied, " When I see other kids have it, I want it, and then I take it." Asked if she thought it right to do so, she replied, " No. I just wanted it." She does not know any other little girls who steal; does not know why she does it. " I take sometimes, and then sometimes I don't take." . . .

October, 1919: When left at home to look after the children, patient will go out to play and have some of the children stand watch to tell her when mother is returning, so that she can get back inside the house in time. She even did this when informant went out to get material to make a costume for patient to wear to a party. Depriving of privileges has no effect. When told that she cannot go out, she will take a book and apparently be entirely satisfied in remaining at home. . . . Patient seems to feel that she is considered a wicked child. When mother made a red crepe paper dress for her for Hallow'en, patient put it on and said, " Now, I'm a devil outside as well as inside." Mother is threatening patient by telling her that she will send her away, and patient no longer seems to care. . . .

February, 1921: Many delinquencies during early part of month. Goes to the store for her mother at two o'clock, and does not return until eight o'clock. Takes with her a five dollar bill; she does not spend any money, but does not get what her mother has sent her for. Sent to a show with William, patient wanted to take the two neighbor children, next door, but had not the money, so she went into the street, walked along the edge of the sidewalk, scuffling in the dirt, and pretending to look for something. A man passed by and asked her what she was looking for. She cried and said that she had dropped the money that was given to her to take her little sister to a show. The man immediately gave her the money for the show, and she took the neighbor's children. William told patient that he thought it was the last money that the man had, but patient was not worried over this. A neighbor left her house key at the patient's for her husband to call for. When she came home she found patient in the house looking through her things. So far as known, nothing was taken. . . .

May, 1921: As a reward for good behavior, patient and sister Ann are taken one week-end to worker's home. . . . Patient learns the names of all the children on the street during this time, and apparently plays pleasantly with them. No friction is noticed. She shows a good deal of responsibility for Ann; several times correcting her in her table manners and general behavior about the home. In the evening, worker finds both patient and Ann on their knees, praying that Ann will not wet the bed that night. Patient herself wakes up and takes Ann to the toilet two times during the night.

The next day they are taken to the movies. During the performance patient sits very still and rigid. During the feature film, where the heroine defies her husband, patient breaks into applause. On returning home she does not walk with the rest of the party, but goes rapidly ahead — a full block before the rest. She answers questions impatiently; makes no mention of the picture for about an hour, then asks worker's opinion of it. After this she shows little interest in any form of activity, and is somewhat irritable. . . .

August, 1921: Report of psychiatrist: Patient was given much sex information in 1918 by a girl at Holliday Home. The girl was older than patient. What she said made a great impression on patient, for she repeated the girl's statements word for word. . . . The first two hours of the interview were spent largely in getting enrapt with patient. Her emotional reactions to all admissions were the strongest informant had ever seen. After each admission she would give a long sigh, and the same difficulty in getting coöperation would occur again. . . .

[Admits sex experiences with four or five boys and one man. Leaves home and stays two nights with neighbor women, claiming mother has thrown her out. It is noticed that she has four or five dollars. After some fabrication to the worker], patient says: " There was $10.00 in the purse instead of $6.50." This seems to worker to be said in an impulsive manner, and worker asks patient where it is. She takes an envelope out of her bloomers in which there is $8.00. . . . Placed in Juvenile Detention Home by police officer, to whom money is turned over. She is taken in a patrol wagon, and shows no emotion at having her friends see her in the patrol wagon. Manner is pleasant and jaunty. Police officer reports as follows: Informant took Miss Sharp, who works at the library on St. Louis avenue, to the Detention Home. She identified patient as the girl she believes took her purse. At first patient denied this. Soon, however, she admitted that she took it. Informant said she showed no emotion; was " like a blank wall; " was not apologetic. Miss Sharp had noticed patient in the library in the morning, and about noon she sent her on an errand. Patient returned with the exact change. Informant remembers noticing that patient watched her very closely as she counted the bills in her pocketbook. She put her purse on the counter and left the room for a few minutes. Upon returning, the purse and patient were gone. . . .

January, 1922: Case presented at staff meeting. Decision reached that patient be placed in a girls' school. [She was placed more than twenty times. Is now married.] [2]

In the case of boys this socially unregulated activity is more frequently connected with groups and gangs, more divorced from the home, and has a more predatory character:

3. I was supposed to go to school, but Eddie said do I want to come with him. I went with him. We met Mike and went to the " Boy." I do not know his name, but Eddie had seen him out in South Chicago. The Boy, who was

---

[2] *Records of the Illinois Institute for Juvenile Research.*

about sixteen, had been in St. Charles. When we met him he was working in a wienie shop on Sixty-third. We were about twelve and thirteen then.

The Boy brought us some buns, and then we went to Jackson Park. On the way back we went to a show. When we came out, we bought some candies. We slept that night with the Boy, in a little shed. The next day we spent in the park. About four o'clock that afternoon, we helped the Boy, but we left the door of the store open so we could come back later. In the evening we went to a show. About midnight we met the Boy and came back and robbed the store. We got about $46 in there. Then we went back to our shed to sleep.

The next day we all went to Twelfth Street, where we bought tennis slippers, four hats, four mouth organs, some cuff buttons, some bananas, and some soft drinks. The Boy always held the money. Then we went down town to a show. Afterward we bought some candies. Then the Boy bought himself one of them there collars [Van Heusen].

The Boy had a train ticket and we went to Forty-third Street on the Illinois Central. We got tired of sitting down, so we got off there and walked to Sixty-third. The Boy bought a package of cigarettes. We went to Jackson Park. The Boy had some guff [golf] sticks and we started playing around on the links. Then it was about eight o'clock, and we went to the show again. We bought some candies.

That night we robbed another wienie store where the Boy had worked.

The next day we went out to Jackson Park again and went boat riding. We stayed in the park till noon, picking up guff balls and making tips for finding them. We was with another boy out there. Mike stole the guff clubs on us and ran away back to South Chicago. We went boat riding in the afternoon, and that night we went to a show in Sixty-third. That night we slept in the same shed again. The Boy had a big trunk full of stuff there.

The next morning we sneaked out and went back to Jackson Park boat riding. We went to the guff grounds again and got balls and sold them. We started out looking for stores to rob that night. In the afternoon we went to another show. That night we tried to break in the door of a store. The boy took a rock and tried to break the lock, but he couldn't. Finally the little boy grabbed it and broke through. We went in and got cigars, cigarettes, a searchlight, and a gun. We found a lot of ice-cream, but most of it was salty. We spilled all the cones out of a big box. Then we took all the gum, candy, and a lot of O'Henrys. Went back to our shed. We smoked and ate candy the whole night.

The next morning we bought two loaves of bread for breakfast. We went boating again. In the afternoon we went to White City and spent $6.00. We came from there to a restaurant and bought some meat. After playing around on Sixty-third, we went to a show. Then we went again to our shed to sleep. Our beds were some old coats and paper trash. . . .

The next morning we were up early and jumped from the shed. We went to Commercial Avenue and bought some wienies, coffee, and pop. We tried to get boats on Calumet Lake but had to come back. We hung around Commercial Avenue till about noon and then went to Eighty-ninth Street, where the Boy shot off some bullets. We went back to Commercial Avenue and bought some pie and coffee. Then we went to a quarry at Ninety-first Street to play, and finally came back to sleep in a shed by the Boy's house.

That night we robbed a grocery store. We got some money, a gun, some canned shrimps, candies, cigars, cigarettes, stockings, cuff buttons, and bananas. We slept in the store on a shelf till about five o'clock in the morning, and then got out through the back. Then we went to the Boy's brother's shed, where we fetched all the stuff. We went out again and got ourselves some eats. We went to a movie show. Then we went out to the quarry again to catch minnies with a little hook and bait. That night the Boy gave his brother a box of cigars. When his brother found he was sleeping in the shed, he asked him why he did not come home. Then his brother took all the stuff from the shed into the house and kept it.

That night we went and tried to rob an A. and P. store. We were hungry and did not have nothing to eat no more. When we got in we found we'd made a mistake and it was a barber-shop instead of the grocery.

Finally, me and Eddie and the Boy went back to his brother's shed to sleep, and Johnnie went to his own shed. In the morning Johnnie came early and waked us and said that a man from the police had been around there. The Boy got his brother's pay check, took it to the bank, changed it, and kept the money. Then we bought eats and candies. We also bought a bar of soap and went to the quarry to wash ourselves. Then we took a hike to the Calumet River.

When we were out there, two policemen went by in a flivver. They stopped and asked us what we were doing. They knew the Boy; for they had been looking for him for a long time. So the policemen robbed the Boy and found his revolver. They took it and tried to shoot into the air, but it had no bullets and was broke. Then they robbed us and got all our stuff, dice, cigarettes, and $6.00. They took us to the station, where they finally brought Eddie and Johnnie. And that was the end of our sport.[3]

4. Olaf's companionship since he was 13 has been almost entirely with boys who together make up a crowd that consists of about twenty members

[3] Boy's own story, from Thrasher, Frederic M.: *The Gang: A Study of 1,313 Gangs in Chicago* (1927), 86–88.

ranging from 12 to 16 years of age. Our information about them has been derived from accounts given us by Olaf and his mother and others belonging to the group. At first we did not recognize how many there were in this group nor the strength of the influences which permeated their association. . . . Olaf knew several of these boys when he was younger, but his real companionship with them began only when he was 13 years old.

It was never a real gang with an organization; some of its members associated somewhat with other crowds. There were no special meetings or meeting places; the boys congregated on the street corners, or in by-places, or in the neighborhood of pool-rooms. There have been no recognized leaders, although some boys have naturally had more influence than others — the boys whose exploits had been more daring or who have set them forth with most gusto. Younger boys have been recruited from time to time, but not in any deliberate or formal fashion. While they spoke of each other as belonging to the Downey Street crowd, they were boys who merely lived in the same district, not in the same street.

Not only the main, but apparently the sole bond that held these boys together has been the recounting and committing of delinquencies. The latter were practically always carried out by two or more of the crowd who would then tell their adventures to the others. The idea thus acquired would rapidly spread and be acted on. They had no other interests in common, neither secret club activities, athletics, antagonism to other gangs, or anything else.

Their delinquencies have been multifarious: Early there was jumping railroad trains, petty street stealing, staying out late nights. Then began runaway expeditions to other cities — a remarkable number of trips were taken to New York. Thieving in stores was carried on extensively, at one time by a system, groups of three or four going into a store and getting away with anything they could.[4]

It will be seen from the title of Thrasher's volume, from which case 3 is taken, that he has listed 1,313 boys' gangs in Chicago, either loose association groups or more formally organized. Shaw, of the Illinois Institute for Juvenile Research, is now analyzing the records of about 9,000 boy delinquents. One of his results shows the number of boys arrested for stealing in connection with each episode, and the striking fact appears that a single boy is involved in less than 10% of the cases, or, conversely, in over 90% of the episodes of stealing coming before the courts two or more boys were arrested. In about 30% of the cases

---

[4] Healy, W., and Bronner, A. F.: *Case Studies.* Judge Baker Foundation. Case 8, *passim.*

three or more boys were involved (this was the mode), and in some cases eight or ten or more. It is certain also that not all the boys involved in a given episode were arrested because some were not caught.[5] The results of Burgess and Shaw show also that the proportions of juvenile delinquency vary enormously in different regions of the same city. In one region 37% of the boys between 10 and 16 years may be delinquent, and in another region less than 1%.[6] A large percentage of criminal careers originate in local areas and in boy gangs.

The gang of young boys is an organization for adventure, a conflict group, and the attitude toward girls is usually one of hostility and contempt:

5. " Do you like little girls, Tony? " I asked a boy of fifteen.
" Naw! I never love no girls. I don't want to monkey around wit' girls. Dey give me troubles. I kill de girls."
He has several sisters, so I asked him if he hates them too.
" What, should I hate my sisters? Dey don't give me no troubles. Dey're my sisters." [Teacher's interview with boy]. . . .
" The leader of our gang was what is usually called a ' hard rock.' He was the leader because he was the ' hardest,' and because he had a strip clipped off through the hair of his head so that he might show the girls how little he cared for what they thought of his looks." [Statement by former member of gang]. . . .
The gang developed in the boy a distinct point of view, so that he considered it somewhat of a disgrace to play with girls. At this stage he would be the subject of derision if caught playing or even conversing familiarly with any girls except his sister. The older boys, however, became instructors of the younger boys of gang in sex matters, and in many of them a premature interest and curiosity was inculcated. There was a large amount of obscene literature and art which was circulated very freely among the boys, copied many times over and handed down to the next " generation." [Manuscript by former member of gang].[7]

There is, however, a mixed gang or free association group, composed of boys and girls, whose interest is sexual. This type of association is relatively new and has become a serious problem in the schools:

6. The main purpose of this gang was sexual, and the indications are that not only normal but many unnatural or degenerate methods of sex gratification

---

[5] Communication from Clifford R. Shaw.   [7] Thrasher: *op. cit.*, 222–24.
[6] See data in chapter XII.

were in vogue. The boys of the group were as a whole stronger or tougher than the other boys in the school and they succeeded pretty well in dominating the rest of us and playing the part of bullies.

In seasonable weather the scene of the gang's activity was a vacant lot on the South Side, or else a half-block of meadow land east of the I. C. tracks. The lot was at one time raided by the police and a number of the group were taken, but no punishment followed so far as I am able to discover. In rainy or chilly weather the gang assembled in some deserted barn. . . .

Of the fifteen or more members of the gang, some seemed to be quite normal mentally and physically while others were sub-normal or worn out by excesses. There was not much conscious organization in the group, but the biggest boy was the apparent leader. The ages of the members were from thirteen to sixteen. . . .

The only rule which the gang had, to my knowledge, was that no member should indulge in relations with outsiders. On the whole, they made no effort to conceal the nature of their activities and seemed to take pride in flaunting them before the rest of us. They possessed certain signals by which one of the boys could " ask " one of the girls while in class. These signals soon became known to the rest of us, and it is probable that even the teacher was not entirely unaware of what was going on.

The attitude of the rest of the class toward the group was largely one of disgust mingled with hatred. This was especially true of the boys, although there was a small group on the border line that looked upon the gang with admiration.[8]

7. Sex delinquency among groups of young children we have come to know of only too frequently. . . . Starting in a small way it may grow until a group of considerable size is involved, with practices continued for months, quite unknown to those who have the children under their observation daily — parents, teachers, school principals. There may be some one individual who initiates all the members of the group. Sometimes the group is organized into a club with initiation ceremonies and rites of membership. Sometimes the group is not at all organized. What transpires varies from sex talk or exhibition of pictures to actual sex practices of various kinds between members of the same sex or between boys and girls. In this instance we are particularly concerned with the latter. All that we have to say on this matter is based on facts that have been elicited during the study of actual situations. The discovery of the situation has been made in various ways, and some-

---

[8] Manuscript prepared by an observer of the gang, from Thrasher: *op. cit.*, 230–31.

times, as in this case, the group practices have not been known at all until years later. . . .

It may be instructive to say a little about some notable situations that we have known involving boys and girls. . . . Recently we studied seventeen members of a group of twenty or so, boys and girls, of ages ranging from 10 to 14 years, who had a rendezvous in a room in the back of a building where originally some of the boys had started a club among themselves. A defective boy, the oldest of the group, initiated another boy into sex practices, and then one by one others were taken in. Girls were introduced early, one of whom became a leader in drawing in other little girls. Very definite sex relations were practiced for at least four months before anyone knew anything about the affair. In another instance two sisters were the instigators in getting boys and girls to visit their home for group sex practices. The parents, while people of good reputation, gave very little supervision to their children. In another very large group known lately, children 8 to 12 years old formed definite boy and girl partnerships for sex practices.[9]

One of the forms taken by the desire for adventure, the interest in new experience, is running away. It seems to be one of the most incorrigible behavior tendencies, and usually leads to delinquency, since stealing, lying, truancy and bad companions naturally go along with it. In commenting on the first of the cases recorded below (No. 8) Healy and Bronner say: " Reviewing a group of cases of which this is a fair example, we are forced to conclude that neither we nor others have at all adequately realized the difficulties which dealing with them presents. We are astonished to find that among a dozen cases, carefully studied, we have no single success.[10] The group comprises little boys who are extreme runaways; they are normal mentally, attractive, likeable, and active, and because of their characteristics they are able to obtain for themselves pleasures away from home which are greater than their satisfactions in home and school life."

The following cases illustrate two points of importance. In both it appears that a single incident, a critical experience, is sufficient to determine a dominant line of behavior. Tom follows a parade, gets lost, gets a good deal of attention, has pleasurable experiences, and runs away habitually. Carl has an exciting experience connected with a trip to his grandparents and gets an obsession for travel and trains. Again,

---

[9] Healy and Bronner: *Case Studies*. Case 15.
[10] They have later had some successes.

new experience, exploration, curiosity, are the basis of specialized achievements, and both the boys become specialists, Tom as an artist and Carl as a scientist, if we may speak in these terms. Carl, indeed, at the age of eight, has all the peculiarities of the learned man. He seems to be the greatest specialist of his age for his age:

8. When between 5 and 6 years old Tom [now aged 8 yrs., 11 mos.] started running away by following bands and parades. Before he entered school he had already been picked up by the police a number of times. After he entered school his running away increased, now sometimes in connection with truancy. By the time we saw him he had run away so often that his mother could not give even a near estimate of the number of times, she said. However, he had never remained away over night, except when placed somewhere by the police, until a month ago. Then he was away for three nights; but it was found that he slept one night in the cellar of his own home and two nights in the alley nearby. . . .

Two years ago he had taken his mother's bag, containing thirteen dollars, when he ran away but since then has taken no money from home. He usually returns with his pockets full of small change, which he says people have given him for singing. His mother is not sure whether he ever steals any of it or not. His brother once found him in a park singing for money and took what he had in his pockets and put him on the car to go home. But instead of this the boy went to a beach resort where, after a message from the police, the mother had to go to get him. Once a man picked him up and after feeding him took him to the address which the boy said was his home. It proved a tenement occupied by Italians, but still the boy insisted that he lived there until the man became suspicious and turned him over to the police.

Sometimes Tom begs in restaurants with very good results to himself. His mother says that he is able to get into the movies without paying, and he has learned to worm his way through the turn-stiles on the elevated road. Just how he has made his boat trips down the harbor to the beach she doesn't know, but believes that it is by begging and singing. His lying has been mostly about his truancy except when he fabricates to strangers about his parents being abusive, or sick, or dead.

Tom is allowed one cup of coffee in the morning. He is not known to smoke at all, and there has not been any evidence whatever of bad sex habits. . . .

Seen several times by us we found Tom always friendly, talkative in a childish and rather nervous way, contradicting himself at times and evidently drawing on his imagination occasionally. The gist of what he told us at length in an irregular fashion is as follows:

He has lived a long time at the present place, he thinks about fifteen years. . . . " I started myself running away. Something made me start — something in my head — it might be the devil." In answer to questions he said it was his mother who said the devil got into his head. When he began to run away he only knew good boys. He was 6 or 7, he thinks. One trouble was he didn't like school and he doesn't like it now. " It's too hard." He would like it in school if they would let him draw pictures, but they only let the children draw apples and pears. The arithmetic is too hard and he doesn't like reading because he can't learn it. And again he says that's what's the trouble, he doesn't want to go to school. [But he began running away before he entered school]. . . .

Tom gave us many details about the good times he has when he is away. He has been to many parks and amusement places, and he always succeeds in making quite a little money by begging or singing. For instance he crawled under the flying horses to get a sailor's hat and he got fifty cents for it. Sailors and other people take him into places and give him a good time. He maintains that Jim first told him about the good times he could have at these places and so he started going around to them. He asks for money on the elevated trains or on boats. He has been taken to police stations a number of times when he has been away and twice has been held over night, but he always had a good time and has been well treated. . . .

Tom never worries about anything. He always has good times and is always happy. He shows us how well he can sing, and in a childish, rather sweet voice, he sings a number of melodies, particularly war songs, very well indeed.[11]

9. During the past few years the Juvenile Court of Los Angeles County has been concerned with a case presenting an unusually persistent habit of running away, combined with an obsessive interest in trains as a means of travel. The boy in question, Carl Nelson, was eleven years old in 1923 when he was committed to Whittier State School for boys. . . .

Carl began running away at the age of two and for a period of nine years he ran away from home two or three times a week. He never returned of his own accord but neither did he resist those whose duty it was to bring him home.

His parents resorted to extraordinary measures to keep him at home. Once his mother tied him for five weeks so that he could not leave the yard. She sewed signs on his overalls asking autoists not to take him for rides. His father whipped him repeatedly, and is known to have attached a window weight to the child's leg by means of a chain. All of these attempts were fruitless, he persisted in running away.

---

[11] Healy and Bronner: *Case Studies*. Case 7.

He early developed an absorbing interest in simulating a train; he played that he was an engine by shuffling his feet, making circular motions with his closed fists suggestive of the connecting rods, and by imitating the sound of the whistle. So closely did he mimic this sound that auditors were deceived into supposing that a train was actually in the distance. His concentration was so complete that he was oblivious of most stimuli. While absorbed in this train play, he frequently ran squarely into teachers who purposely placed themselves in his course. After such an encounter he would present a startled and dazed appearance, but would presently, if allowed, resume his interrupted course.

He preferred the study of road maps and time-tables to playing with other boys. Nevertheless, his contact with real affairs was by no means completely broken. As a result of his study, he worked out an elaborate system of stations patterned after actual local conditions in Southern California, and was able to name the main railway lines and give accurately the distances between stations. . . .

About seven months after Carl's birth, Mrs. Nelson . . . and her two sons went to visit relatives in Allentown, Pennsylvania, where they remained for ten months. During that period Carl was extremely happy, and the pet of all his relatives whom he won by his frequent charming smiles. After his return to Los Angeles Carl often expressed the desire to go back and see his Aunt Gertrude. . . . In speaking of this period the mother remarked, " Carl thought the big engines were fine." She added that he afterward preferred trains to any other toys, and that he expressed a wish to go around the world in a train some day. In this connection it is interesting to note that in the mental examination of 1922, upon being asked by the psychologists regarding his birthplace, he answered, " back east by the train-track." . . .

Carl began to run away from home in 1914 just after he returned from his visit to his mother's relatives. . . . Before he was three years old he had gone as far as Culver City, a suburb about six miles from his home. . . . By the time he was eleven his wanderings had extended to Fullerton, Santa Ana, San Bernardino, San Diego, and other cities of Southern California . . . and he had been twenty-eight times in the detention home. . . .

He has never been known to steal. On February 13th, 1923, his probation officer reports that he was acquiring the serious habit of telling imaginary stories and of begging from the people whom he met. . . .

Carl was a boy of a single drive with an otherwise colorless temperament — a disposition that showed little emotion no matter in what circumstances he was placed. He merely accepted things as they were and then did the best he could to further his only drive.

He was quite languid in all of his responses until his dominant interest was aroused and then he worked persistently and vigorously. Moreover, he became skilful and exacting in one phase of this interest — drawing and interpreting maps.

He had a tendency to be reclusive. He did not brood nor become sullen when his plans were thwarted, he simply started immediately to make new ones. On the whole he was submissive and obedient, except in the matter of his persistent fugues.

Carl was a day dreamer. At times his vivid imagination led him completely to sever his connections with reality . . . while on other occasions it seemed to be of a constructive nature that caused him, for example, to make a miniature California of his playground, taking great care to locate each station correctly on his " railroad." . . .

A school report in 1923 states that " he was not interested in school lines " — only in trains — and although other reports state that he was inclined to play train at recess to the exclusion of all else yet there is no evidence that this interfered directly with his work while in the school room.   In fact the final report states that " from the time Carl entered the school door he tried to coöperate with his teachers in every way." . . . Another teacher states that his work would have been average if it had not been for his irregular school attendance. . . .

From the time he was six years old, when questioned concerning his vocational plans, Carl has with one exception expressed an intention of being a " car-man," or (later) engineer. He has shown a few other interests, closely allied to this basic one of trains and travel. His mother reports that as a child of about eight years when taken by her to town he used to ask for time-tables and maps, and would upon his return home study these in preference to play with other children. She states also that geography was one of his outstanding school interests. He was interested in the electric interurban trains and on one occasion in the detention home was made very happy by the gift from the son of a conductor of a bundle of punched transfers. . . . " He is happy when given paper and pencil to write names of stations, using them in playing trains. His companions join him, hands on shoulders, making ' choo-choo ' sounds and shuffling feet around the court. Face lights up when asked about trains. Not interested when group is read to or other games are played." He can read maps as few grown people can do.[12]

There are sometimes behavior disturbances which seem directly due to the physiological expansion and reintegration accompanying pubescence. Dr. Bronner [13] has assembled a number of cases where the

---

[12] Knapp, Pearl M.: "An Habitual Truant Who Has Developed an Obsession for Railway Travel," *Journal of Delinquency,* 10:368–86 (1926).

[13] Bronner, Augusta F.: "Effect of Adolescent Instability on Conduct," *Psychological Clinic,* 8:249–65 (1915).

heredity was good, home conditions good, behavior good up to a certain period, then restlessness, running away, abandoning positions, etc., difficult behavior traits for a time, and presently a return to settled behavior. While recognizing a multiple causation of maladjustment, she thinks that in these cases the physiological changes of adolescence are mainly responsible. Healy has frequently emphasized the same point and has successfully treated adolescent boys by sending them to ranches where their physiological energy is engaged in motor activities.[14]

Omitting examples of this kind, we give below a case where the physiological maturation, the adolescent revolt and release of tension are accompanied by a single idealism (love of pretty things) and a crude conception of self as person, desire to be released from conformity to authority, to play a rôle and provoke response to self. The sex experience is subordinate to the social experience and the pretty clothes are an adjunct of personality:

10. For the last few months Tillie [13 yrs., 11 mos.] had been very insubordinate, untruthful, and dishonest. She had stayed away from home over night several times. . . . Just now the girl had returned after being away ten days, her whereabouts being quite unknown. . . .

The father and mother are both religious and have brought up the children carefully in this respect and in the ways of obedience. Church attendance has always been quite regular with them and, of late, closer church connections have been established through a church benevolent organization. There has been an attempt to cultivate at home a religious atmosphere with family prayers and strict observance of the Sabbath. . . .

Tillie progressed uneventfully through the grammar grades in the public school. Her mother states that she always had good reports. She graduated at 13½ with a report of doing passable work only — clearly there had been a great change in her attitude toward school during the last year. She lost interest in her studies, was defiant, and caused considerable disturbance in petty ways in school. She was persuaded to enter high school at the beginning of the following term, but attended only for the first few days. She was then formally expelled for non-attendance; not that she had made any attempt to return.

When younger she was apparently satisfied with her school and home life; she had no outside interests except in her Sunday school; she belonged to no settlement or other clubs. She was a great reader and her mother thought

---

[14] E.g., Healy, William: *The Individual Delinquent* (1915), 242–43.

her a very clever girl because she liked to discuss various questions of the day; she read the papers and kept well informed. But within a few months she has lost all interest in reading, and ceased to be helpful in the house. She often appears " as if her mind was not on her family, but was somewhere else." She is very fond of the " movies " and for a time went as often as two or three times a week because she could get passes from one of the neighbors.

Formerly she had many friends, girls who, to the mother, seemed entirely respectable. She had never shown interest in boys. But beginning with last summer she did not go any longer with her former companions; she told her mother that she had met sailors and soldiers. The fact is that her family do not know with whom she has been going these last few months.

The main trouble with Tillie began just as soon as she entered high school in February. Several weeks later she applied at the office of the aiding organization and asked for money for school supplies, saying she was out of school that day because of the principal's death. Inquiry showed that she had not attended school for a week. Just before this Tillie had taken three dollars from her father and refused to say how she spent the money, but later she was found to be wearing silk stockings. At about the same time she took fifteen dollars from her brother, and told tales of ill treatment by her family to the neighbors. Then, following her expulsion from school, for weeks she said she was looking for employment, and she would frequently not return home till late at night, at first giving excuses, but later becoming defiant. . . .

After . . . weeks of misbehavior and effort to get her straightened out, Tillie, one day, dressed unusually carefully and said she was going to get a position. Nothing was heard of her for almost two weeks. Her mother received a letter from her saying that by the time this letter arrived she would be dead; that she was pregnant by a sailor and would kill herself before giving birth to an illegitimate child. A warrant was got out for her, but nobody found her, until one morning her mother met her on the street near their home and asked her to come back. Tillie seemed glad to do so.

Tillie appeared quiet, unconcerned, with an expression of considerable humor concerning the situation. With her broad face and thick lips, rather homely and rather sensuous, she looks the part of a good natured country girl. . . . Closely observed on account of the peculiarities of the situation; no indications whatever of abnormality could be discovered, — indeed there seemed to be unusual poise, good orientation and emotional control, in particular there was no haziness or cloudiness of consciousness. . . .

Girl's Own Story. . . . Tillie says that she lied about where she was working a time ago because she didn't want the agency visitor to know what she was doing — " she tried to make a fool of me." But she only worked in that place a few days, and the woman gave her five dollars to go out and buy something and she never went back. She wanted the money to get some shoes. Her mother had told her to go to the social agency about her shoes, but Tillie did not want to do this. Tillie also tells about stealing the three dollars from her father and fifteen dollars from her brother. She claims not to know exactly what she did with the money, but, " I must have spent it on something to wear; I like pretty clothes."

She says she would not have stayed away from home such a long time if she had been in her right mind. She was living in a room with a sailor who was on a furlough. She got tired of it after three days and would have come home, but she was afraid. " I went to the Charles River to commit suicide a lot of times, but I didn't have the courage." She finally went home because she didn't care what would happen to her. She supposes she will be sent away somewhere.

When she was 12 years old and living on R. Street she heard a lot about sex things. In their tenement there was always a lot of quarreling, and, in particular, Mr. Royer, one of their neighbors, used to accuse his wife of having relations with other men. She also heard a lot of bad stories from the girls around there, but none of this, at that time, bothered her at all.

Then when they moved to G. Avenue, where they lived before moving to their present nice apartment, she met Mildred W. This girl talked to her much about boys and introduced her to " some bums," and through Mildred she also met Helen M., who had been out a good deal with men. The latter part of last summer Tillie had a chance, through the agency, to go out to the country for a vacation (to a very beautiful place where working girls are invited for a couple of weeks at a time). There she talked a good deal to a girl who told her much about picking up sailors and soldiers. " She told me how warm you get when a man touches you."

After she returned she met some sailors in the park and on the streets after school and walked around with them. But she never made any real engagements with them until she met Jim. She liked him very much and used to meet him almost every Thursday and Saturday. After she had known him for a few weeks she spent the night with him, and after this did so several times. Besides she was often with him late at night. He paid her for living with him. At first she refused to take the money, but later didn't care, because she could buy pretty things. . . .

[Placed in foster homes and not treated very well there but permitted to attend high school where she completed the first year with good marks and showed no marked interest in boys], she has worked steadily, now nearly two years, for one firm. Her employer considers her very capable and has twice raised her salary. All of her money she turns over to her mother. She has grown responsible in every way and her mother depends on her much for advice. Tillie is interested in the younger children, and especially in the welfare of her sister Eva, about whom she has consulted the agency visitor in an endeavor to get her carefully placed in business following her graduation. The family is on the up grade. . . . During the more than three years on parole, her attitude toward boys and men has seemed altogether normal; she has neither shunned them nor seemed unduly attracted by them. . . .

Notes: . . . Apparently her earlier hearing of sex talk did not disturb her at the time. This was probably because she was then younger, preadolescent, and her sex curiosity not yet awakened, but no doubt this earlier experience formed a background that later added to her sex consciousness and sex interest . . . [but] having reached the adolescent period, Mildred W's confidences became dynamic influences. And then there was, too, the actual introduction to a poor sort of young men, " bums." More especially important was the type of information imparted at the vacation camp at a time when Tillie was already so alive to sex matters. The reaction to living with Jim is noteworthy — the quick satiation was perhaps due to Tillie's youth, for it is very likely the physical sex urge was not nearly so great as the hold of ideation that centered about sex life.[15]

" Pretty things " are the most prominent item in the repertory of the young girl for getting favorable notice and " being somebody." " Bloss um etwas zu gelten " (just to amount to something) was the reply of a Viennese shopgirl to the judge when asked why she had posed as the betrothed of a Rothschild and promised her employer patents of nobility from the Kaiser. At the other end of the list of devices to be attractive which could be enumerated in this field we have cultural accomplishments, artistic skills, scientific attainments and professional careers. Negatively we have frustrations, inferiority feelings, subterfuges, pathological lying, stealing, delusions of persecution, etc. Thus the desire for recognition, the struggle of the young person to be a personality, to play a rôle, to have respect, status, distinction, is expressed in more and less sophisticated ways and represents lower and higher levels of social values, but the underlying psychology is the same. In the case of Abigail, following this, we have a more elaborated and we may say thoughtful schematization of behavior in her effort to play a rôle and be somebody, though her efforts are still, at first, in the region of delinquency:

[15] Healy and Bronner: *Case Studies.* Case 9.

11. Abigail Hardell: (16 yrs., 6 mos.; born in Vermont. Both parents of old New England stock). November, 1917: Abigail had been well known for over four years to the staff of " Boston People's Institute," an educational and recreational institution for young people. She had been a great favorite there, was herself very fond of the Institute and its workers, and had at times been given some responsibility in the purchasing of supplies and in handling the money involved. In this she had been considered very faithful. They themselves and the girl's mother, however, now sought the advice of the judge of the juvenile court because a large sum of money had disappeared and it seemed plainly indicated that Abigail had taken it. Not only this, but the girl had been suspected the summer before of purloining a piece of valuable jewelry and other articles from a shop where she worked at a seashore resort. The Institute people had not believed this about her at the time, but just now she had confessed to taking some of these articles and they had come to the conclusion that she had been lying excessively then, just as she had lied about this last stealing. . . .

[The father drank heavily, the mother went away to work, leaving the children, but eventually taking them to Boston, where the total income was very small]. This has meant that the children have had almost no spending money and very little for clothing. Abigail has worn made over things obtained from various people interested in the Institute. . . . So far as known she was never in the least influenced towards delinquency by any companions. During the last year Abigail had developed a great fondness for pretty things, especially pretty clothes. No bad habits of any kind were noted. . . .

Abigail's immediate and most serious delinquency is concerned with her larceny, which she does not deny, of about $200 in cash from the Christmas Savings Club at the Institute, a club made up of young people who put aside money during the year. She is known to have spent a large part of this sum on clothes for herself; she has lied much about the details of her purchases. It has also been discovered that recently she has made some small false charges for supplies. . . . Abigail had also certainly stolen some articles of clothing and, perhaps, jewelry from the shop last summer. Soon after leaving there she had telephoned, assuming the voice of the other sales girl, inquiring if the things had been found.

Abigail is a very neat, cleanly, and altogether healthy, wholesome-looking girl of strong posture, rather attractive features, well shaped head and decidedly responsive expression. Although normally girlish, she has a notably direct way of looking at one and a firm manner in speaking. . . .

In general Abigail must have been honest, for the accounts at the Institute had in the past always checked up correctly, and the only lying that the Institute workers knew of when they started the inquiry was done in self defence. But it came to light that to her companions and in the school room Abigail had been indulging in well concocted fabrications. She had told tales of rich relatives, of an uncle who had a large estate near Manchester, Vermont, where so many wealthy people live, and of how sometimes he drove down to Boston to see them, always putting up at the Copley-Plaza. And to some she declared she was engaged to a young Vermonter who was an officer in the army and wealthy. Once she came home with a bouquet of violets and orchids (this was about the time when she had the stolen money) and said that it had been given to her at a party where she was the guest of honor. In the school room one day she burst into tears and gave a graphic description of the heroic death of her father at Ypres. He had, she said, earlier had training in the militia and joined the Canadian army soon after the beginning of the war.

Girl's Own Story: She remembers her home in Vermont. She is quite sure that she was in no trouble when she was little. The only wrong thing she did that she remembers was when she was five years old she spent for candy a penny with which she was to buy a newspaper. She is perfectly sure that she has never stolen from then until this past summer. . . .

This summer she was working at M., a seashore resort, in a shop where an older girl of about 24 was also employed. They sold beautiful laces, jewelry, and women's apparel. This other girl used to talk a great deal about how unfair it was that wealthy people could buy all these things. She used to say that they had everything and didn't care at all about others; that the poor people who had to work hardest had the least. Sometimes when a customer would buy many things she would say that it was absolutely wrong that one person should have so much. Abigail told her about the household where she had lived the summer previously; how many fine things the woman of the household had. She knew this because in her laundry sometimes there were clothes that belonged in Mrs. L. She used to return these, but in this way saw how many pretty things Mrs. L. had.

The girl this summer put the ideas of injustice into her head and once in a while they would seem to be true. She recalled the family of last summer; they were really very kind to her and she liked them very much, but she remembered how much more they had than they needed. Abigail thinks that these ideas must have been in her mind the day she took the things at the shop. She maintains that she took them all on the same day. She didn't wear these things, and many a time after taking them she felt worried and wondered how she could get them back. She denies absolutely that she took the brooch which it is claimed she stole.

After she came back home this fall she had no temptations whatever to steal. She had been going regularly to the N. High School. She has never taken a thing there. She hadn't planned the stealing at the Institute. That afternoon she was in and out of the room where the Christmas Fund was kept. During the afternoon the worker who had charge of the money was counting it and had later put it away in Abigail's presence, stating that she would, the following day, deposit it in the bank. As Abigail was leaving to go home she went into the room to get her wraps and " it flashed into my mind that I wanted the money." The idea came very suddenly, without any thought of what she wanted it for. Without hesitating she took the money and hurried out of the building, and when she was half way home she began to think of what she could do with it. After she had considered a number of things which she could buy she became rather frightened and thought only of getting rid of it.

She hid the money at home and the next day after school came in town and bought expensive clothes, a handsome pin which she had monogrammed with the initials of the older girl friend of whom she was so fond. The clothing which she bought she had sent out in her own name but in care of this girl friend.

Until this year she went to a Boston high school where she knew most of the girls because she had gone to the same grammar school with them. She always stood near the top of the class and took part in all the class activities. In the high school in N. she has not been at all happy. The girls have not made friends with her; she feels strange; has had no part in the social life there, and she has felt all along that she would rather be somewhere else. She has never had any association with anyone who stole, and the earlier talk about stealing, she insists, " never got on my mind." Long ago in Boston she first heard about sex affairs and it was at first a " dreadful shock." She thought about it a good deal because it seemed very terrible to her for a time, but although she has never talked to any adult about it she has long since got over her first shock and she is quite sure that for a long time now she has never thought about such things. She knows a good many boys, especially those who come to the Institute. She likes them all well enough for friends, but she isn't at all boy crazy and is never bothered in the least by sex ideas or sex feelings. . . . She remembers her father; knows that he and her mother didn't get along. She doesn't feel unhappy about this or ever worry about her father; why should she, he didn't worry about them. Sometimes she does feel badly about the way she has to dress. She thinks she looks as nice as the average girl in school. But she would like new things that she herself selected. . . .

[Given a suspended sentence by the judge and ordered to pay restitution, still befriended by the Institute and placed with an interested family, she worked and attended night school]. She completed her restitution, including the amount she owed her mother. In the fall of 1922 she was accepted into a kindergarten training school of excellent standing in New York and her record there has been splendid. . . .

From the school, from her friends at the Institute and from the M's, where she spends her holidays and week-ends, come reports that she is a very attractive, steady, stable young woman who shows no evidences of fabricating or even of boasting and who has a serious, satisfying purpose in life. . . .

Interesting to a student of the psychology of conduct is the gradual evolution of this girl's character tendencies from attempted ego satisfactions, through phantasy and dishonest acquirement of possessions, to satisfactions derived from reality as she has found it possible, through outside help and through her own efforts, to obtain a place for herself in the world.[16]

In another of their admirable studies Healy and Bronner present a case (No. 12) in which a girl, conceiving a personality for herself not possible in the miserable family of her birth, deserts the family and improves her situation while the condition of the family deteriorates still further on account of her desertion. This is not the usual outcome when a girl repudiates her family. The young rebellious girl who goes alone usually runs into trouble. But while the outcome of the case is rare, in view of the hostility between girl and family and her headstrong course, the type of behavior, the detachment from family, is now the normal course of individualization and establishment of careers, whereas the historical family was a unit where all the members went either up or down together:

12. Stasia (18 yrs. old; born in U. S.; parents Polish). . . . Her mother originally complained to the Polish worker for girls in the nearby settlement that her daughter was nervous, excitable, and so strange in her behavior that she was sure there must be " something wrong with her head; " she was afraid to leave the other children alone with her. Then, before we could see her, Stasia left her home and took a room in the neighborhood. . . .

Though short in stature, Stasia is well nourished. She is very attractive, impressing one at once with her neatness and good taste in simple dress. Her features are refined, her expression responsive and open, and her manner quiet and friendly. . . .

It is reported that Stasia forms friends normally; when younger she associated regularly with school girl companions. Recently she has had a nice girl chum. She has shown little interest in boys. She is fond of reading,

---

[16] Healy and Bronner: *Case Studies.* Case 12.

especially stories of romance and adventure, and when younger she read many fairy tales. She enjoys moving picture theaters; recently she joined a girls' club which has general sociability as its aim. . . .

Mother's Story: . . . Her oldest girl Rosa has never given them any trouble. She is a fine girl, " an angel," ambitious, good to her parents.

Stasia is altogether a different kind of girl. She never gave a great deal of trouble until she was about 14 years old, but since then she has been very ugly at home, making sarcastic remarks, and being mean to all of them. Sometimes when the children talk to her she doesn't answer. She slams the doors behind her. She is worst of all to her father. This, her mother thinks, is because he made her leave school to go to work. But they needed the money. Stasia wanted to go to day school and she has borne her father a grudge ever since. She showed that she disliked him. If she saw him coming she would say, " Oh, he's coming already! " . . . Stasia has always been very neat and clean about herself. " She loves to bathe herself often." Of all the children she has taken the most interest in trying to keep the house looking nice. . . .

Stasia's Story: She has never been happy at home. She doesn't understand herself just why she has always had such a feeling of grudge and dislike for her father. It infuriates her sometimes just to see him. . . . " He wants to be the king in the household; he wants to boss us all. I think it's because he's a failure, and he wants others to be, too, so that they won't be better than he is. Anyway, he should have made good. He's got enough sense and education." . . .

In the evening the father sits at the table and reads the Polish papers to her mother and if she or one of the others makes a comment he tells her it is not for her to talk but to listen. She has never been able to give in to him as the others have. . . .

Asked what is her earliest memory of any incident that she resented, Stasia tells us that she thinks it was something that occurred when she was about five. She loved to go with her mother on shopping expeditions because she was usually given candy or some treat. Once when she was very good and her mother had promised to take her, her father forbade it for no special reason. When she cried through disappointment he beat her in front of some customers in the shop. From that time on she avoided him; if he tried to whip her she would hide and lock her door, which aggravated him exceedingly. Then they disagreed about her likes. She was always fond of dancing around the house and waving her arms about. This made him furious because he has a sister who was on the stage and whom he says she resembles. When she would dance and sing at home her father would forbid it, telling her she would have a bad end. . . .

Of her school career she says she was not a success and not a failure. She has always been most fond of drawing, gymnastics, and dramatics. . . .

Asked about outside influences, she says she doesn't think there have been many that have shaped her life. She never was a hero worshipper and had only one teacher whom she admired. Reading has been a much greater influence than people. She remembers that at 8 years she lied about her age to get a library card and she has had one ever since. Then she read many fairy stories and day-dreamed a good deal, imagining herself a princess. At about 12 she became interested in love stories and read so many that she became sick of them. Now she likes mystery stories, although she reads some better books and current fiction. During recent years she has indulged very little in day-dreaming, and never romances to herself. She is quite sure that bad companions have been no influence. She is rather ashamed of her attitude about sex matters, being afraid she will be thought too good and smug about this. To tell the truth she has never been interested in sex things at all. . . . She has always had girl friends and some boy friends. She goes now with a group of six girls who occasionally give little affairs to which they invite boys. The club in the settlement to which she belongs has debates of which she is very fond; she likes to argue. They occasionally give dances and plays. . . .

Subsequent History: During the three and a half years since this family was first known to us they have continued to live in the same place under conditions in the home that have become steadily a little worse. . . .

The home itself has been neglected, until now there is only slight semblance of order and cleanliness. The mother has become somewhat erratic and increasingly complaining. Recently our visitor found her moving about the room putting things in one place and then in another in a purposeless way. The house itself was dirty, the floor strewn with papers and bits of cloth, the bathroom so neglected that it seemed impossible that it could be used, and the beds were covered with dirty linens. The mother said that since Stasia had left no one had cared whether the place were orderly or not. Rosa is uninterested in such things. The curtains have not been washed and put up for a long time — it was Stasia who used to look after such matters, and the mother alone cannot cope with the situation. The income has been very irregular. . . .

Stasia has remained away from home, living for a long time with the same friends with whom she was when we first saw her. Through the worker in the settlement who was interested in her she obtained a clerical position in a publishing house with which she was much more contented than she had been with factory work, and which she retained for about eight months. During this time she not only cared for herself and saved, but regularly gave money to her mother. . . . With her mother she has been friendly, but the feeling between herself and her father has never been overcome, and she has not been on very friendly terms with her sister or brothers. She has kept up with her club interests. It was on one of her summer vacations that she met the young man whom she has married. Although she took him to her home to introduce him to her family she refused ever to bring him for a visit and she did not invite her family to the wedding, solving the matter by being married by a justice of the peace. Largely through her influence, her husband, who is reported to be an ambitious and industrious young man, has found employment in Philadelphia and they have started housekeeping there, Stasia making it distinctly plain to her family that she wishes to live her own life according to her own ideals and standards.[17]

The clinical records contain many cases where the misbehavior is the result of a sense of social misplacement and personal inadequacy. It is an " inferiority feeling," not, however, usually sexual as is assumed in the Adlerian standpoint (see chap. X), and the misbehavior is a compensatory activity:

13. In analyzing the histories of sixty stealing cases studied in the child-guidance clinic, it was found that in nearly half of them the stealing and associated activity were related definitely to feelings of inadequacy which had their roots in various factors in the life situation of the child. Common among these factors were physical characteristics which stamped the individual as being different, such as obesity, speech defects, undersize; mental defects of varying degrees; certain habits, such as enuresis and masturbation; racial prejudices; presence of more attractive and gifted brothers and sisters; immorality and desertion of parents; economic factors; failure to achieve a healthy emancipation from parents; and repressive discipline. Each of these factors occurs more than once in this small series of cases.

These were some of the factors that brought about a sense of being different, inferior to others in the group. They placed barriers in the road to healthy attainment of self-respect and self-confidence. The delinquent activity was part of the compensatory effort of the individual to overcome these handicaps. The operation of [some of] these factors is illustrated by the following case:

A boy of fourteen embezzled a considerable sum of money from his employer and was using the money for making a big splurge at a local amusement park. Previous to this serious offense, he had stolen small amounts at home. The main sources of the difficulty in this case were:

1. A very over-solicitous mother who insisted on treating this boy as an

---

[17] Healy and Bronner: *Case Studies*. Case 17.

infant. Before company he was always introduced as " my baby." She super-vised all the details of his clothing and dressing, she gave him spending money only as he needed it, and in many other ways prevented him from growing up.

2. The father, a large, masculine type, was very stern and rather repressive in his handling of the boy, and somewhat inclined to scorn his lack of virility and his rather infantile type of personality. This discrepancy in the attitudes of his parents was having a very destructive effect upon the self-respect of the boy.

His decision to leave school at fourteen to go to work was a significant gesture of the boy to test himself. He felt very insecure about himself, par-ticularly in relation to the somewhat older adolescents whom he met in his work and at school. The desire to establish himself was a very keen one, but his background had given him very little confidence in his ability to do this in a normal way. The stern and awe-inspiring discipline of the father, com-bined with the coddling of the mother, did not make a very firm foundation upon which the boy could stand when placed on his own. The quickest way to gain his goal and to compensate for his obvious immaturity was to get money. He proceeded to do this and to make the impression that he felt was necessary if he was to become a " regular fellow." It was also an opportunity to prove to himself that he could do something unsupervised by his mother.

[This boy] . . . had to have a chance to free himself from the dependent relationship that had been fastened to him and to gain a healthy degree of confidence in himself. To bring about this result and change the methods and attitudes of the parents so that it might be achieved seemed almost impossible while they were all together. A plan was finally worked out between the parents and the boy which enabled him to go away to a boys' school for a period of a year and a half. This removed him from the chief source of his difficulties, yet gave him sufficient supervision and expert guidance to enable him to work out a healthy sense of his own individuality which we hope will carry over when he returns to his own home.[18]

The following case shows the feeling of " self " in small children and the effect on their behavior of discrimination and disesteem:

14. Two sisters, Rose and Mary, came into the care of the Children's Bureau [of Philadelphia] November 12, 1919, when Rose was eight and a half and Mary just five. . . . They were placed in a home selected in ac-cordance with the very best home finding standards, of about the same social

---

[18] Allen, Frederick H.: " Psychic Factors in Juvenile Delinquency," *Mental Hygiene,* 11:768–73 (1927).

status as that of the children's own people. The foster mother, middle-aged, left alone with her husband by the marriage of her two children, eager to have a child for company, seemed to be a kindly, common-sense, conscientious person, who although limited in intelligence and education, had done a good job on her own children and might easily provide the right kind of home for two children like Rose and Mary. She was known as a good housekeeper, a great church worker, and a favorite with children. Except for such general knowledge, the placement was largely a matter of chance, as too little was known of the personalities involved to make any prediction as to their effect on each other. It was merely the putting together of an ordinary home and two apparently ordinary children.

It took six or eight months for this foster mother to become sufficiently discouraged to give up the problem. Rose was the stumbling block. Mary, although not perfect, she would have kept. Throughout this period reports came in from time to time of Rose's unreliability and of her distressing habit of enuresis at night and occasionally in day-time. The good housekeeper revolted against such behavior and a variety of punishments were resorted to. Once a diaper was put on. This was effective for the time being. In a letter the foster mother tells of dressing Rose up in Mary's clothes to make a baby of her and shame her. She also pinned on her dress a sign, " I wet the bed." " I only wish," she writes to the visitor, " you could have happened in and seen her — you know she sucks her thumb." On the same occasion Rose was exhibited to a small nephew who came in as the foster mother's baby. Her behavior, at first not unusually bad, grew increasingly troublesome. She was disobedient, resisted authority, told sensational stories with only the faintest relation to fact, denied any misdeed even in the face of proof, took ten cents from the foster mother's purse, would not come home promptly from school or when sent on an errand. She responded to scolding by sinking into a sort of dumb apathy from which it was not easy to rouse her. School reports were satisfactory.

The younger sister, Mary, while influenced by her sister and reported once for telling stories and taking change when sent to the grocery store, was a much more lovable, responsive, docile child and found favor with the foster mother who would have kept her except for the difficult Rose. . . .

[A psychometric test was given]. The placement visitor was reassured as to the children's normal intelligence and was advised to try separating them as it seemed probable that Rose was suffering from comparison with Mary, who was getting all of the praise and attention from the foster mother, besides being *in fact* brighter, prettier and more lovable. Rose was to be returned for further study. It developed that Rose's eye defect was serious in the extreme, but for some reason had escaped the attention of the previous medical examiner. There was good cause to believe that Rose might become a serious problem and was in need of intelligent foster home care. There seemed no particular reason to consider Mary difficult as children go.

On April 18, 1921, Rose was placed in an untried foster home simply as a temporary arrangement, until a suitable home could be obtained. This home, consisting of a fairly young married couple, crude, not well educated but well to do, promised nothing except kind-hearted ignorance and good physical care.

Mary was placed at the same time with a refined, better educated, more intelligent man and woman who had an almost luxurious home and wanted a little girl as a companion to their own five-year-old, adopted by them when a baby. They were eminently respectable, adored their adopted child, had the happiest kind of marital relationship, and gave every indication of providing what Mary needed as a permanent home, a home which would give her advantages and intelligent care. These foster parents had worked out a health problem with their adopted child most successfully and were recommended by all the references as just the people to care for a child conscientiously. Nearly a year has passed and the picture presented by the two placements is almost humorous if it were not so serious an indication of the blindness of our best plans.

Rose, taken in as an only child by the warm-hearted, but uneducated childless couple, has flourished as a green bay tree — not a report of misbehavior has been received. She has been given pretty clothes, she has begun music lessons, her foster parents help her nightly with her lessons, they are in touch with her school, they take her to visit their relatives, she spends a summer at the shore, they receive her aunt with open arms. At no time in this period, despite many annoyances put upon them by the interference of Rose's own father, and despite her failure to make a brilliant record at school and all the ups and downs of a first experience with a strange child, is there the slightest lessening of their whole-souled acceptance of Rose as their child, worth the trouble she causes. Rose as a problem seems to have vanished into thin air. She has been transformed into a spontaneous, happy child. The attachment of the foster parents has become so genuine and Rose's response so appealing that although they never intended to adopt so old a child, they cannot bear the idea of the separation and will adopt her rather than run the risk of having her snatched away at the father's whim.

Mary, on the other hand, has gradually lost ground and is just beginning to look like a problem. The foster parents report that she is utterly unresponsive and unappealing, seems to care for no one. Recently on two occasions she has been discovered in a theft. They have tried to treat her fairly, giving her every material advantage which their adopted child has, but cannot help feeling that she is inferior to their own in every way and would not consider keeping her permanently. So little is she a part of their lives that the foster mother complains of the time it takes to bring her to the doctor for earache. The child herself appears unhappy and repressed.[19]

Up to this point the behavior difficulties which we have illustrated by the cases have had to do with lack of conformity to socially sanctioned patterns. The misbehavior of very small children is " mischievous " and merely amoral — not moral because of lack of maturity. The other cases represented appetites, exploration, physiological expansion, and we have just considered some cases of more or less conscious protest and revolt. In these cases there have been points where questions of mental deficiency or emotional instability might have been raised — whether the child was constitutionally inferior and unable to react in normal ways to social situations. We now present some materials which bear more directly on these questions.

Inability to conform to social patterns of behavior on account of mental deficiency has perhaps received more systematic attention than any other problem relating to the child, and we treat the theoretical and experimental side of this question in chapter VIII. At this point we outline some cases representing types of mental deficiency and inadequacy as related to the curriculum of the schools and to habit formation in general.

Our conception of mental deficiency must be viewed partly in its relation to the history of our culture and our concept of values. Our learning process, especially on the formal side (the schools) has developed on the assumption that all members of society are gifted with the power of employing abstraction and symbolism in their mental life. And this power is, in fact, the only clear intellectual mental endowment which man has in distinction from the other animals. A gentleman once asserted that he had a dog who could think. On one occasion when the sponge with which they bailed out the rowboat was missing, the gentleman made a gesture and told the dog to go to the house and get the sponge. The dog did so and this was called " thinking." It would have been abstract thinking if the dog, failing to find the sponge, had brought a dipper, or a bed blanket, or coffee-sack, or a brace and

[19] Taft, Jessie: " The Need for Psychological Interpretation in the Placement of Dependent Children," *Child Welfare League of America, Bulletin,* 6:3–7 (1922).

bit and cork, with the idea of making a substitution — boring a hole and plugging it. Replacing an element (a sponge) in a familiar situation is " association through contiguity," but the other is " association through similarity," and it would take a bright boy to do this. Behaving " as if " one thing were another is abstraction, as when a stick is used as if it were a hand. And Köhler's apes were capable of this. Language and numbers are important organized fields dependent on this power. We react to the letters composing the word " fire " as to a conflagration, and a little black loop on paper, or reversed loop, as if it were 6 or 9 objects of this or that kind. Total inability to do this in the human child at a certain point of maturation would be idiotic. At the same time, it is a troublesome acquirement, as can be seen in the history of the learning process of the deaf, dumb and blind girls, Laura Bridgeman, Helen Keller and Marie Heurtin. These children possessed the nervous machinery for the task but owing to the sense defects it was difficult to get the problem stated. At one time when Dr. Howe gave the abstract problem to Laura: " If you can buy a barrel of cider for $1.00, how many can you buy for $5.00," she gave the concrete answer: " I would not buy so much. It is sour."

In cases where the child is unable to conform to the usual routine of mental life, particularly to the organization of learning in the schools, we call him feebleminded, or where the deficiency is not very great a moron. The whole procedure of mental testing, which has assumed so great proportions, has grown out of the realization that children have unequal constitutional mental endowment, and that this is an important factor in school retardation and in delinquency. In the beginning mental testing assumed in the main that disability was due to hereditary organic defects, but there is at present a full realization of the fact that social conditions, defects in the learning process, the dropping out of essential steps through adventitious circumstances, play perhaps a greater rôle than heredity. Furthermore, experience has shown that we have been speaking of " normal " and " abnormal " with reference to a rigid process of learning based on the printed page, whereas a multitude of children are manual and motor minded, able to learn through activities more readily than through symbols. In backward children we have frequently not an " abnormality " but a special distribution of abilities.

Case 15 (from a report of a clinical demonstration by Dr. Witmer) gives a good conception of what may be involved in the question of feeblemindedness or mental deficiency, and cases 16 and 17 are descriptions of school troubles arising from this source:

15. As he appeared before the class, Arthur was a well-nourished boy of nearly eleven, good looking, neatly dressed, and respectful in manner. He sat quietly at the table while doing the form-board and cylinder tests. . . . He did this kind of work very well, using trial and error method to some extent, but performing the test mainly by the exercise of a high degree of distributed attention and space perception. He noticed instantly if a cylinder was too long or too short for its socket, taking it out and putting it in the right place, which he found quickly by looking for it. As far as concerns this kind of test, he " looks " very efficiently.

Dr. Witmer asked him to write his name on the blackboard, and his age. Arthur wrote his name and the number 10.

Q. Ten? Ten what? Arthur made no answer.

Q. When I ask you how old you are, what do you answer? A. Ten years old.

Q. You write *years* then. Do you know how to write it? Do you know what begins it? Now I will tell you how to spell it, but don't put anything down there until I finish. You spell it y-e-a-r-s, write that.

After some hesitation Arthur wrote y, then stopped. Dr. Witmer had him come to the further edge of the blackboard and write the letters s, r, a, and e, one under another. Arthur wrote them correctly; then Dr. Witmer rubbed them out.

Q. Now what was the word you were to write on the board? A. Years.

Q. And I told you it began with a y, and you put the letter on the board. Now put down the rest of the word *years*.

Arthur hesitatingly added an s to the y, and stopped again.

Q. What's the second letter you have got there? S? All right, y-s. Do you know any word that you spell y-s? Don't know any such word? Then why did you put that down? Can you guess how the word *years* is spelled, — years, ten years (pronouncing it very slowly with the full sound of each letter). Can you guess how that is spelled? Can't guess at all? Now I'll tell you once more how it is spelled. You rub out what you have down there. That word is spelled y-e-a-r-s, years.

Arthur wrote ye, and stopped again.

Q. Y-e, now what was the next letter that I told you? Arthur could not tell.

To the class Dr. Witmer said, — Now observe that that word has five letters in it. He knows how to make each one of the five letters, so that it isn't that he doesn't know the letter and can't write it down; but if you give him five letters in succession, he is not able to repeat them in the same order. That is a memory span test, and my demonstration today has the object of showing you the importance of the memory span. The memory span is fundamental in school work. Now we will see if we can find out something about Arthur's memory span.

Q. Do you know how to spell the word *cat?* All right, put that down. Arthur wrote it on the board, and also the word *dog* from dictation.

Q. Right, can you spell horse? He wrote ho, and then paused.

Q. All right, you can't spell that, very good. Can you spell *desk?* Again Arthur wrote the first two letters of the word, and paused.

Q. Can you spell *girl?* Try *girl,* write it down.

Arthur wrote gar, and stopped. While writing he fumbled with his left hand toward the eraser and loose pieces of chalk at the bottom of the blackboard, a clear betrayal of his state of uncertainty.

Q. Can you spell *cow?* Right. Can you spell *boy?*

He wrote *bog,* rubbed it out, wrote b, and then stopped.

Q. That's very good. Now I'm going to tell you the spellings of some words. *Boy* is b-o-y, write it down.

Arthur wrote *bay.*

Q. What have you put on the board? Did you put b-o-y on the board? You have got b-a-y. I want b-o-y. Right. Now write g-i-r-l.

Arthur innocently wrote *goil,* to the uproarious amusement of the class, and looked around in wonder to see what they were all laughing about.

Q. Do you remember the spelling I gave you? I will spell it again for you, g-i-r-l. .

This time he wrote *giol.*

Q. What did I say? Girl? I know, but how did I spell it? You write *girl.* At last Arthur got it right.

Q. That's good. Now you can write *desk.* You write it. Let me see you write *desk.* Write on the board d-e-s-k. That's right. Can you write the word *horse?* Can't do that, can you? Know how to spell that? Now you write on the board what I tell you, h-o-r-s-e.

Arthur wrote *hose,* omitting the r.

Q. What's that word, spell it, h-o-s-e? What does h-o-s-e spell? What was the word that I spelled for you a short time ago, the whole word? A. Desk.

Q. Desk was one word, but what was the word you were trying to put on the board now? A. Horse.

Q. Yes, that was the word, *horse.* Know what a horse is? A. Animal.

Q. Animal, yes. Seen one today? What color was it? A. Brown.

Q. Now *horse* is spelled h-o-r-s-e. Try it again.

Arthur got it right on the second attempt. . . .

Q. Put down a few numbers for me. Put down 1, 2, 3. Right. Put down 9, 5, 8. Right.

Arthur wrote the numbers as he did the separate letters, one below another in a vertical column. For 7, 3, 9, 2, he wrote 7932; for 8, 4, 6, 1, he wrote 8642. Series of three numbers, as 9, 4, 2, and 8, 5, 7, he wrote correctly. For 7, 4, 8, 3, he wrote 7432.

Turning again to the class Dr. Witmer continued, — Now you see here a very limited memory span, and you get the distinction between intelligence and certain other qualities which are necessary for intellectual development. I haven't been able to produce any evidence this afternoon that this boy has a memory span of more than three. He has a memory span which seems adequate for three, but not for four digits or letters. Now the first time he did the Healy completion test, he put all the blocks in the right places. That is a test of imagination, a test to show what sort of images he has, what ideas he has. In the same way I gave him a completion test when I asked him what *horse* meant, and he answered all right. The test here is mainly in the reasons that are given, first the correctness and then the reasons. He gave good answers for all his placements, and that is a test which is sometimes not satisfactorily performed by twelve-year-old children. . . .

The general indications are that Arthur's deficiencies in associability and memory are rather limited to language. . . . He seems to have good sense when you ask him ordinary questions. His understanding is good. He understood these tests right away. His power of attention is good. It would appear, therefore, that it was limited entirely to the field of memory for language and number, the two important branches of school work. But you understand that the number work is based upon language, so it may be in his case a specific defect of language memory. . . . We have got evidence here today that this boy has a congenital verbal amnesia, a defect of memory which is something inherent in his brain. Just as one boy hasn't got an ear for music, because he hasn't got the kind of brain which stores up musical tones, so this boy hasn't got the kind of brain which stores up memories of words and letters and sentences that are spoken to him. In his case it is probably a congenital verbal amnesia.

We are finding that these conditions exist in some children. Take this boy, for instance. The principal of the school writes to me, " We consider him very slow mentally, but not feebleminded." He doesn't make the impression upon the principal of being feebleminded. He doesn't make the impression here today of being feebleminded. He does the mechanical tests correctly. But so far as his standing goes, he is in the feebleminded class, and probably as he grows older and falls further and further behind, he will probably be diagnosed as feebleminded, not socially competent to get on with others of the same age. . . . We saw a couple of years ago an extremely able mechanic, doing very high grade work, who didn't know how to write. He had gone to school and had never learned to write. He came to us to learn why it was he had not learned to write, although he had tried to do it. Apparently he had congenital aphasia, or congenital alexia. When he asked us that question we had to explain to him, " You are in the position of the person who has no ear for music, who can't learn to sing." [20]

The following case typifies what is perhaps the most frequent cause of failure to make a good school adjustment. There is sufficient ability but it is not distributed in a way to meet the requirements of the curriculum:

16. Kenneth McGregor [was] . . . a well set-up youngster of thirteen, endowed by nature with the ever-alluring combination of red hair and freckles, and overflowing with vitality and mischief. . . . In the seven years of his school life he had attended five different schools. But while frequent changes might account for some of his earlier repetitions of grades they could not explain those of the last two years. In brief, Kenneth had repeated 1A, 2B, 3A, 3B, and 4A, and was now repeating 4B. According to his teacher he was quite capable of doing the work of this grade or even of a higher one, but he would not apply himself. His written work was particularly bad, almost illegible, in fact. He seemed to make no effort at all. Though she kept him after school till five o'clock and made him rewrite his exercises ten times, he did them no better than at first. [He created amusement in class, appropriated pencils and pads and lied about it, and played truant]. . . . The psychological examination . . . revealed in Kenneth a general inferiority of intelligence which ranked him as a definitely dull child, with a mental age of 10 years, 7 months and an intelligence quotient of 81. On educational tests he did especially badly, showing a decided distaste for school subjects; indeed, he was clearly bored by all the tests except those requiring manual manipulation. It appeared that, despite his many repetitions, he was correctly placed in 4B, his present grade.

Very different, however, were the findings on the supplementary tests designed to bring out mechanical ability. These tests he seemed thoroughly to enjoy. On one of them he made only an 11-year score, but in two others he made 13-year and 14-year scores, while on still another he made a record surpassed by only five per cent of boys of his age. He was clearly weak in

[20] Witmer, Lightner: " Congenital Aphasia and Feeblemindedness — A Clinical Diagnosis," *Psychological Clinic*, 10:181–91 (1916).

auditory learning powers, but he showed a decided ability in visualizing and in perception of space relations. It was thus evident that he had definite ability along mechanical lines which was not being utilized or cultivated in his present school setting. . . . He had no complaints of special injustice, indeed, when asked if he thought his treatment fair answered, " Yes, I think they are fair to me — they don't treat me any different from the other boys." He said that he disliked his teacher and she him, but he did not attribute his failure to be promoted to any other cause than his poor work. Spelling and writing were, according to him, his weakest points. He admitted freely that he gave a good deal of trouble in the classroom. . . .

In the discussion of Kenneth's school problem a fact of some significance in explaining his difficulties came to light for the first time. The boy was left-handed, but from the beginning of his school life had been compelled to use his right hand. This forced transfer had evidently upset him, for he said, " When they made me use my right hand I couldn't write well, and when the teacher wasn't looking I would use my left hand." . . .

The great event of December, from Kenneth's point of view, was the obtaining of his own newspaper route. This meant afternoon deliveries on every week-day and on Sunday mornings, and a Saturday morning devoted to collections. The young business man entered upon his duties with the utmost enthusiasm, determined to surpass his brother's achievements at every point. He met with certain annoyances, as when some youthful bandits on a certain street raided his cart while he was making a delivery, but these only served to give him further exercise in his favorite art of fighting. Altogether the boy's entire personality appeared to be called into play by this work as it had never been in school, and his pride and pleasure in the new undertaking were engagingly evident. . . .

[Transferred to another school, Kenneth was anxious to improve his writing in order to keep a legible account-book in connection with his business, and practiced assiduously, but his teacher still complained of his papers]. He admitted that the fault was partly his, as sometimes when his left hand grew tired and he fell back on his right. One of his outstanding problems was that he wrote slower than the other children and was always behind. He said, " My teacher often hollers at me about this. I've tried to tell her about my writing but she won't leave me alone." . . . He said it took him twice as long to write a composition or test as it took the other children and this was probably not much of an exaggeration, since when asked to write his name he spent a minute and a half of painstaking effort in producing a signature. This poor coördination of the muscles involved in writing meant, of course, that he had to spend far more time on his evening work than the average child, and as Kenneth's outstanding trait was his desire to get through things quickly, this meant a constant burden of irritation to be borne.

Only in regard to business was the boy's report a happy one. He was still enthusiastic over his paper route and proud of the fact that he had recently earned a prize of $1.00 for getting new customers. . . .

[Contact interrupted by vacation]. Early in September relations between the McGregor family and the Bureau were renewed. Kenneth had been transferred, it appeared, to a "vocational class" at another school, but had not yet put in an appearance, though his family supposed he had been attending school for three days. The social worker at once got in touch with him, and by picturing the new class in attractive colors roused his interest so that he promptly reported at school. . . . Three features of the new school situation appear to account for the boy's satisfaction in it, which has continued unabated to the date of writing. First, he liked his teacher. Only a woman capable of taking a genuine interest in retarded, difficult children would be likely to be placed in charge of an opportunity class, and the teacher in question was clearly of this type. Second, he had two periods of carpentry during the week, each of two hours' duration. Third, the new class, by some mysterious legerdemain, ranked as a 7A grade. The exhileration, to a boy who had failed in 5A the year before, of finding himself at this lofty pinnacle, may be imagined. . . .

Discussion of the case by Professor Henry C. Morrison: . . . Kenneth is a pupil who is not at all uncommon in school. He is an extreme instance of a type which in varying degrees constitutes perhaps a distinct majority of all who go to school. We may describe his particular type as that of the direct-learner. Such pupils seem to live in such a world of vivid reality that they can conform only with difficulty if at all to the lesson-getting type of learning. Usually, they tend to flock to manual work, because in the typical cut-and-dried lesson-assignment kind of school that is the only department in which direct-learning is possible. Others are able to conform to the round-about way of learning implied by the daily lesson. It is interesting to note that perhaps half of the latter never acquire anything more than the ability to get lessons. So long as they can grind out lessons they shine; deprived of this routine, they fail. The other half succeed in learning by learning lessons, and they are the ones upon whom the school has to rest its case. In a recent test in a group of city high schools it was found that only about ten to fifteen per cent belong to this lesson-transfer type. The others were sheer lesson-learners, or vague approximate learners of the passing grade type who make up the bulk of our high school and college graduates. The Kenneth type usually gets eliminated before reaching high school. They appear later either as successes in life and lasting reproaches to education; or as criminals or semi-criminals, depending probably upon their individual types of inherited instinctive equipment.[21]

In the above record some emphasis is placed on the point that Kenneth is left-handed. A good deal of attention is being given at present to handedness, some investigators holding that this is associated with nervous structure and that a left-handed person forced to right-handed writing is thrown into confusion. The important comment made by Professor Morrison, however, is from another standpoint.

There are cases where the nervous structure is all right and the distribution of abilities corresponds sufficiently to the curriculum, but the mental backwardness or pseudo-feeblemindedness results from the failure to form some important habit at the usual age level and the appropriate stage of maturation. The development of mind and personality is a stepwise process in which the later stages are dependent on the earlier ones. If, for example, arithmetic is not learned the higher mathematics is completely out of the question. Or if the teacher fails to make plain the concrete meaning of the abstract proposition, " let X equal the unknown quantity," the subject will then be classed for his whole life as a case of " mathematical disability." Omission to form the reading habit is the most serious handicap of all, because all the higher levels are dependent on it. In the case of Arthur (No. 15) we had a constitutional reading disability. In the case of Mildred below we have apparently not a reading disability but a failure to learn to read:

17. Mildred Martin was brought to the Bureau of Children's Guidance in the spring of 1922, a tragic figure of school failure. Transferred at the age of eleven from a church school to a public school, she had speedily been found wholly unequipped for work in her proper grade, the sixth. A psychologist to whom she was taken reported her mentally fitted to do average work in the fourth grade, but she proved unable to do even that of the first, and had to be put back into 1A. In the three months that followed, though tutored and given every encouragement the school could offer, she had succeeded in advancing only one grade.

Thus at twelve years — an unusually tall girl for her age, stoop-shouldered but otherwise well developed — Mildred was stranded in a room full of tiny children, hardly more than half her age or height. Standing to recite, she

---

[21] *Three Problem Children: Narratives from the Case Records of a Child Guidance Clinic.* Joint Committee on Methods of Preventing Delinquency, Publication No. 2:77–124, *passim.*

towered above the others and seemed to shrink up in an effort to be inconspicuous. Either as a result of these destructive school experiences, or for other reasons, the child had developed a profound state of intimidation, embitterment, and withdrawal from contact with others. Things had reached a pass where even her tutor, to whom she had at first responded well, could not, on certain days, elicit a word, a smile, or a gleam of interest in her work. Apathetic, unsocial, sullen, she seemed to have retired into an inner world of her own to such a degree that those who observed her had become seriously alarmed about her mental state. . . .

In the absence of a report from the child's former school the mother's account was the only one available, though this was later supplemented by details gathered from Mildred herself. She had entered the church school at six; her five years there had, however, been much interrupted by illness. She made no progress, apparently — at all events did not learn to read — but was promoted from year to year nevertheless. Much of the time she was used as an errand girl and assistant cleaner. . . .

Regarding Mildred's present school situation, Mrs. Martin took an even more discouraged view than did the school itself. She stated that Mildred had a wonderful memory and she believed that the child often fooled her teachers, making them think she was reading when she was merely repeating passages that she had heard the other children read. Often when the mother pointed to separate words in something Mildred had read, the child could not tell her what they were, or would say some altogether different word. Her mother did not believe that she could read at all. . . . Mrs. Martin recalled that up to the time of beginning school the child had been bright, sociable and friendly, apparently quite normal. Some time after her start in school a change began, and this became more marked as the years passed, Mildred's disposition growing progressively worse until Mrs. Martin began to feel that the girl " would go crazy " if something were not done. . . .

Inasmuch as sex practices and imaginings are found often to be a source of trouble with children presenting problems, the Bureau worker enquired upon this point, but learned that, so far as the mother knew, Mildred had no bad sex habits [but had inherited syphilis]. . . .

Mildred showed very clearly her unhappiness over the fact that she was so much larger and older than the other children with whom she was associated in grade 2A. She could read only a very few words such as " the," " a," " boy," " girl," " ball," but wrote well and made fine figures, much better than those of the average 14-year-old child. She did first, second and third grade arithmetic correctly, and addition in fourth grade work.

Her stock of general information was fairly good, and her powers of association fair. Her auditory attention and memory were excellent. Her visual memory for form was good, but owing to her inability to read, it was impossible to test her visual memory for words. She defined abstract words intelligently, and handled concrete material well. In other tests she showed varying abilities, but on the whole her performance was an intelligent one. . . .

We have here a child with an intelligence that is clearly normal and a body that, in spite of inherited constitutional disorder, and of failure to outgrow one of the weaknesses of babyhood [enuresis], seems essentially sound. At least neither mentality nor physique, so far as the most highly skilled technique of analysis can reveal, offers any explanation of this child's failure to respond successfully to the demands of her environment. Yet here she is, at twelve years, weighed down by an experience of complete school failure, and suffering from a resultant bitterness and despair that has evidently been exaggerated many fold by the circumstance of having a much younger sister, free from all her handicaps, drawing ahead and exulting in the fact. . . .

[Through tutoring, visits to museums and theaters, membership in the Girl Scouts, attendance on summer school, acquiring the art of pendant making, the treatment of her venereal disease, her difficulties were cleared up, her enuresis vanished, she overtook her younger sister, was promoted seven times in one year, and became " alert, interested and keen "].[22]

There is a type of inability to conform to the acceptable social patterns which is not at all related to mental or emotional disability nor to any defect of the organism, but simply to the failure of opportunity to come into contact with the patterns in an intimate and continuous way. The situation of Gregory in case 18 represents this psychic isolation. He is an immigrant boy, his mother is dead, his father is very intimately devoted to him but in an unusual way, sparing him all responsibility, talking to him in a cultural-historical way, and magnifying the glories of Greece. This seems to be the source of a rare idealism in the boy, the desire to be a clever dialectician like Socrates or Demosthenes, but as this tendency is displayed in school it appears merely as argumentative and impertinent. He was offensive also in his claims of Greek superiority. This was all very well in Sir Henry Maine, whose phrase, " Nothing moves in the modern world that is not Greek in its origin," has been quoted thousands of times, and Sir Francis Galton could afford (very foolishly) to argue that the average intelligence of the Athenian Greek of the age of Pericles was as much superior to the

---

[22] *Three Problem Children*, 11–42.

average white intelligence of today as the latter is superior to that of the negro, but such attitudes seemed preposterous in a dirty Greek brat. This type of situation in which the person fails in the accomplishment of a projected rôle is even more important for the interpretation of the psychoneuroses than of the delinquencies. In a less serious way the psychology is the same in the case of the social parvenu who, however assiduously he may imitate and rehearse the social gestures of the superior classes, always gets them wrong:

18. For the last two years Gregory [born in Greece, in U. S. 7 yrs.] had been in foster homes carefully selected and believed to be suited to his needs. From each of the four homes in which he had lived for varying periods there came, after a time, the same complaints and demands that he be removed at once. Too impudent to be tolerated, too conceited to be amenable to ordinary family life, he was lazy, hot-tempered, generally dirty, and he was forever asserting the superiority of his own race and of communistic ideas.

When, two years earlier, the court had asked that he be placed out, Gregory already had quite a career of delinquency. At eleven years he first appeared in court for petty larceny, and there followed repeated appearances for begging, stealing, staying away from home for days at a time, truanting, petty burglary, and receiving stolen goods. . . .

All observers have remarked the deep devotion of the father to his boys and particularly to what he has thought to be Gregory's best interests. . . . In his efforts to be good to the children he has really been extremely over-indulgent all through these years. He himself has done all the cooking, cleaning, and even the washing of the clothing of all three of them — never asking even the boys to take any share in the duties of their little household. He says that he has preferred to do it himself — " Let them go on with their studies and work." . . . He interested himself in the boy's school work, although he had no relations with the school people. It must be remembered that the father spoke very little English. Himself a great reader earlier for a man of his opportunities, he has discussed with Gregory the story of the Iliad, the Odyssey, modern Greek history, and what he has read of the political ideas of Pericles, Aristotle, and modern writers of the liberal school. He says that he has tried by this to inculcate patriotism. . . .

In the five years between the ages of nine and fourteen, Gregory had no contact with women other than his teachers. The distant relatives in this country have had practically nothing to do with the family. . . .

Gregory had no games at home and the most meagre of boyish possessions. His father would not permit him ever to handle his few tools, because he did not wish him to develop an interest in hand work. He wanted him to be educated. " Why did I send him to school? "

There was much discussion at home, even of some classical literature (as told above), and Gregory early showed an interest in history and in argumentation. Even his father said, " He likes to talk better than anything else." There were no books at home — his father had done his reading in the old country — but Gregory made use of the nearby branch of the public library. He was not a very great reader, but really liked a better class of books. By the time he was fifteen his favorites were the King Arthur stories, the " Arabian Nights," and " Don Quixote." . . . He was taking a commercial course in the first year high school in his fourth home placement at the time he was studied. In this last school he was doing very poorly, his marks averaging only 67. But the principal, who characterized the boy as dirty, disobedient, and uninterested in his work, quite anomalously stated that he believed him worthy of a high school education. The visitor, investigating why his marks should be so poor, felt that [there] was considerable in the fact that the teacher had made fun of him before the class, with such remarks as, " Here is a Greek friend who does not know a thing." . . .

Gregory was [first] placed in a family consisting of Mr. and Mrs. A. and a nineteen year old son. . . . Gregory got into no delinquencies here, but he did not fit into the household, being particularly argumentative and somewhat impertinent when Mr. A. and his son were at home evenings. They kept him for a year, but when they were going to move they made this an excuse for not keeping him longer. Their complaints altogether were of his disobedience, hot temper, " demanding things as his right, deliberately trying to annoy, staying out late." The visitor felt that the boy's mental life and ideas had been made fun of in this home; that he had not been encouraged in self-expression; and that in answering back the boy did not know when fun stopped and seriousness began. . . . [In another home there was complaint] that he was forever extolling the Greeks as models and " holding Americans in contempt as easy marks." When told to do something, would say, " Do it yourself." When in the heat of argument would shout, " You lie." . . .

Boy's Own Story: . . . His father always took good care of the children and was always very good to them. " He would eat what we didn't like so we could have the best. He wasn't the kind who was always hitting, but when things were bad enough he would punish." He remembers that very early his father used to talk a great deal to him and his older brother about Greece. He knew all about Greek history. " And I didn't want him to put it over me, and so I began to read other histories, Roman and American, and I would tell my father about it and we would argue about which was the best." His older brother didn't care much about such things. " He is not as smart as me.

He isn't interested in history; he likes art things better." . . . All of the homes in which he has lived have been very good ones; the people have been good to him. The greatest trouble was in his second home. " That man was pretty smart. He knew a lot about cows. He used to be called all over the neighborhood to examine the cows; but he was smart in other ways too." They used to argue much together. " He made me mad. He called me a Wop. He said the Wops were no good, and then I would say that they were better than the English and that would get him mad. I used to keep it up just to get his goat and to have some fun. I knew it made him mad. I used to tell him to look it up in the books. I always wanted to be the right one. I didn't want to let any one else put something over on me. Of course I haven't always been in the right, but I would like to be, and I always think I am until I find out better." . . .

He has never been truant since he was placed out. He really likes school and wants to get an education. He is fond of reading. He doesn't care for love stories; he likes books of adventure and travel. " I don't read many books, but I read good things." He doesn't know what he wants to be when he is grown. " I want to be everything. When I was about twelve I smoked every butt I saw; now I just smoke once in a while to show off. That's what's the trouble with me. A good many of the troubles I get into is because I want to make others think I am wise. You do lots of things to make others think you are a great fellow." . . .

[Gregory wrote in his diary]: " I used to think about how a man became great and what he did that made him great, etc. Those things used to impress me very much. Some times those thoughts used to make me ambitious. I used to try to make plans, then I'd see my position and I would forget." [23]

In the last four cases one showed undoubted mental disability, the second a non-conformist distribution of ability, the third neglect of habit formation in the required order, and the last was a rather gifted case where the behavior was offensive and excited prejudice because it was not schematized according to the recognized social values.

The behavior difficulties having their source in the emotional life are on the whole more serious than those related to mental deficiency and we shall see in chapter IX that it is more difficult to test and classify the emotional factors. An emotionally unstable class contains those called by Professor James the " tender-minded," inclined sometimes to artistic forms of creation work on the one hand and to the insane asylums on the other. But it contains also the hyperkinetic,

---

[23] Healy and Bronner: *Case Studies.* Case I.

explosive, cruel and criminal. We find the most opposite expressions — instability with moral sensitivity and again instability with moral insensitivity — sentimentalist, artist, moral imbecile and hardened criminal. In chapter XI we shall review the work on the chemistry of the body in its bearing on the theory of temperaments. At this point, without attemping to work with the concept of types, we enumerate some of the important forms of behavior and delinquency accompanying emotional instability.

Healy has treated "mental conflict" throughout his published works and one of his volumes [24] is devoted entirely to this situation. In cases of mental conflict a reprehensible form of behavior frequently suggests itself and is inhibited, but the emotional tension is partially relieved by a less reprehensible performance:

It is true that nearly all of the mental conflicts which have been brought to our attention in girls and young women have centered on unfortunate aspects of the sex problem, sometimes, to be sure, existing only as matters of conceptual mental activity. Considering the usual suppressed attitude in these matters, following what society, and perhaps nature, would seem to regard as the part of womankind, this is not to be wondered at. In the opposite sex, it may be oftenest this theme, but there are, nevertheless, many other immediate causes of mental conflict. There are questionings of parentage, and of position in the world, and experiences of treatment by those who are bound by family ties — all of which may cause unfortunate shock, and unconscious inner strife and reaction. . . .

The conflict about sex does not always lead to sex transgressions; indeed, one of our main theses concerning this whole subject is that there are substitution delinquencies. The individual gets relief, as it were, perhaps quite subconsciously, by entering into misdeeds which may seem altogether less reprehensible than gaining experience in the manner dwelt on inwardly. This fact comes out again and again in our case studies. . . . Mental conflict as seen in our numerous cases may find expression in truancy, all sorts of stealing — the most exaggerated cases we have ever seen, sleeping out nights, running away from home entirely, display of great temper and insubordination, setting fires, and so on.[25]

19. A girl of German parentage, who when first seen was a little over 10, for two years had been engaged in much petty stealing. She had taken money

---

[24] *Mental Conflict and Misconduct* (1917).
[25] Healy, William: *The Individual Delinquent*, 353–54.

and other things, not only from her parents on repeated occasions, but also money and jewelry from neighbors, and various things from school. She had already stolen in two schools, and been expelled. In spite of much threatening of police, and reform school, and some whipping, and having been given money regularly to spend, there had been no improvement. She was said to be strong-willed, but not quick-tempered, and to lie only in the matter of stealing. Her parents, who are typical, honest Germans of the artizan class, were at their wits' end. . . .

Nothing in any way explanatory of this girl's persistent stealing at first could be obtained. She is cleanly and extremely modest, avoids vulgarity most carefully, is not quick-tempered, likes picture shows in a normal way. She has a good voice, and enjoys singing. She is very affectionate to parents. She learns games quickly and enjoys them — in all ways seems to be normal, and very bright little girl.

In an attempt, after a couple of first interviews which brought forth nothing, to get at the genesis of her stealing, very interesting situations came to light. It seems that where the family lived two years previously she had for a playmate a little boy. She spoke of him with some vehemence, and after considerable inquiry said that this boy long ago told her a lot of sex things which she has never well understood, but which have been excessively in her mind ever since. " That was a boy across the street in X, who was not a good boy, but when a fellow comes over you have to treat him nice. He swore before me and said awful ugly words. Papa threw a stick at him once. He started me on the road to saying bad words." (The latter statement was especially interesting since the parents had previously asserted she was very modest and would never say even such words of slang as were commonly indulged in by little girls.)

" He never did anything bad to me. He's awful vulgar and says bad things. I've never said bad words to other people, but I can't help thinking the words he said. He got me all mixed up. I told mama about it once, that he was not a nice boy, but that's about all I ever said. His father did not support the family, and used to just lie around. He told me bad things, or hinted them to me, and mama told me never to listen to bad things."

When asked whom she first knew that stole things she says, " He's taken many things of mine. I think that's what started me. And then up here I know a girl, and a boy goes with her, and he told her a lot of bad things and she came and told me about them right along. Oh, they are things I would not say. These things come up in my mind often. Well, when I'm in school and have that headache I told you about, and sometimes at night, and then I get all mixed up. They told me many bad things like that, but when I think of them I just start away and go away and that's the only way I can get away from them. When these things come up I forget all I'm doing and get upset and then sometimes I take things."

She assures us her papa and mama are good to her, and then tells us how she would like a chain for her neck, even if it were not a silver one, but would like one that looked like silver. She then goes on with her story, and says nobody actually taught her to do really bad sex things, and she does not do them, but it is just the idea of these things that worries her. She repeats a little piece of obscene poetry that she says comes up in her mind. The rest of the story all hinges on the same point. " These things come up to me when I am in school, and I can't study well. I got all mixed up at P. school, too." (This was the school where she stole.)

Corroboration was readily obtained from the parents in regard to her boy friend and the character of his family, and also that it was just when they came away from there that she began to steal. It was very hard for these intelligent parents to believe their little girl could be thinking of sex things when her demeanor was so exceptionaally calculated to make them believe she was entirely innocent, as they thought. They knew she was modest even to the extent of not wishing any one to see her take her bath. However, they fell quite in line and agreed to explore the whole situation still farther.

The outcome of this case has proved the point, for from the time of this exploration of the trouble there has been in the following three years a complete cessation of her old stealing. The good mother took up the question of sex teaching with her child, and found all the story to be true. Then with exploration and much reconstructive work, keeping the girl's mind active in school and at home, there has been full measure of success. The child has developed well mentally, morally and physically.

No better example of mental conflict causing delinquency could be found. There was the substitution of one form of misconduct for another; the repressed type being the one really dwelled on and obsessional, but considered as altogether too bad to be engaged in.[26]

20. In another case, strikingly similar to the above . . . remarkable evidence of the association of ideas was obtained. The dynamic quality of the associations centering about the companion who taught both stealing and the strange, new facts of sex life, is obvious in the following excerpt. . . .

" I was thinking about those words when I took the money from my teacher. My teacher was putting on her hat, school was over. There was just three girls with me. I had been thinking those words. Sometimes when I'm eating I think about Sam and I think I hear him saying those words. It was in the afternoon — we was having reading at 3 o'clock — we was reading

[26] *Ibid.,* 370–73.

about a little boy and it said Sam, and it came up in my mind about Sam S. and the words he said." [27]

21. Although Edward first appeared in court only a month ago, there has been much adverse comment recorded concerning his case. The police officer who dealt with him as a truant said that nothing in the way of discipline was too severe for him. Even when promising to improve he had in his pocket twenty dollars which he had stolen. . . .

The court people were impressed by the boy's indifference. He sat reading a newspaper when they were all talking about him. The interested teacher was told by several that certainly he would steal if placed out on a farm and any agency that took him would have to make restitution. . . .

Asked about his parents, he says that he does not remember his father, who died, he thinks, many years ago. He sees his mother occasionally. At first he says he never worries about her, or wonders why she didn't raise him. But when asked if he ever thought that perhaps she was not a good woman, he answers, " Sometimes." And when asked if he ever thought she stole, Edward with averted face blurted out, " I know it! " (Once having stated this, boy became less repressed and talked somewhat more freely).

He knows that she stole at least twice. Just before he went to his uncle's he overheard the family talking about it. Some money was missing. It was just after his mother had been to visit him, and they said they were sure she had taken it. (These facts were corroborated by the uncle, whom we questioned later). He never heard them at any other time talk about his mother's stealing, but it got on his mind after that and he thought they were careful not to talk about her in front of him. They never called her any names in his presence or said that she was bad in other ways. Just after this he was spending a week-end with her and he went in the afternoon to meet her at the store where she worked. Then, while he was waiting in the next aisle, unseen by his mother or the manager, she was discharged, accused of stealing, and when she denied it the things were brought out from her locker and she had to give them back. (Boy showed much emotion about this, tears filled his eyes). He thinks about this sometimes; it makes him feel badly. These things happened before he ever took anything. He doesn't know whether he has been thinking about this just before he steals or not, or whether he is feeling unhappy just before he steals; but sometimes he feels so discouraged that he just doesn't care. He has never spoken to any one about these things that his mother did. [28]

The following case of pathological lying disclosing the same mechanism is thus presented by Burt:

[27] *Ibid.*, 373.   [28] Healy and Bronner: *Case Studies.* Case 20.

22. Abnormal, morbid, or pathological lying is simply lying that is wholly disproportionate to any discernible end in view. In character it is usually complex, and in origin seemingly motiveless; impulsive rather than planned; and so repeated or sustained in duration, as sometimes to extend over many months or years. . . . At times the development of mendacious tendencies can be dated from some upsetting personal experience, both the upset and the experience having been repressed, or at least concealed, by the child herself. As a general rule, her nature is to brood, to nurse a grievance, to live an inner life of self-told fantasy; and her complicated fabrications are the upshot of some secret wish of a suppressed or a compensatory kind. . . .

The pathological liar is nearly always a girl, and frequently pubescent.[29] The cases that have obtained most notice are those of false accusation, sometimes against strangers, most frequently against near relatives, and occasionally against the liar herself. The sender of anonymous letters, usually more or less indecent, is a common instance of the general type. At times the falsehood is kept up by actions rather than by words, and becomes more of a hoax than a lie. Of these acted frauds the history of witchcraft and of spiritualistic prodigies furnishes the best examples. Where the family circle is disturbed by weird cries and mystic messages, where uncanny raps are suddenly heard, missiles hurled, windows smashed, tables overturned in the dark — all seemingly apart from human intervention — the simple and usual agent is an hysterical child or young woman; and a safe precept has been formulated for such cases: *Ne cherchez pas la femme, mais le tendron*.[30]

One morning in 1917, Mr. Naylor, a highly respected foreman holding a responsible position in a large electric light company, arrived at his work, and found himself suddenly confronted by two furious acquaintances, waiting for him at the gate. " Look here, Naylor," cried the first, " how long have you been carrying on with my wife? " " And I want to know the same," said the other. " Look at this." They showed him a couple of letters, scrawled in filthy language upon equally filthy sheets, addressed to each of them by name at the " Lectric Light Shop, Blank Street, Richmond." The first letter began:

" Mr. Thomas. This is to tell you your Mrs. Thomas came to our house on Saturday. That pig Naylor took her up into the bedroom; and then he . . ." The remainder contained a minute account of certain repulsive and perverted practices; and was subscribed " May Naylor." The second letter was to much the same effect, except that it trailed off into a string of

---

[29] In Healy's cases there were five males among eight cases of borderline mentality, and, among the nineteen whose mentality was normal, one male only.

[30] " Look, not for the woman in the case, but for the damsel."

foul words, ending " Amen amen and bow-wow-wow to you," with a little dog scratched in underneath.

While Mr. Naylor was protesting that he did not even know that either of the men was married, a third workman came up with an identical complaint. Now, the thing was manifestly something more than a practical joke in unwholesome taste, for Mr. Naylor had himself been receiving from the postman almost daily an interminable correspondence, scribbled in the same illiterate hand on torn and crumpled flour-bags, and signed with the same name, which was that of his only daughter. These letters contained a similar string of baseless accusations. And, two days after the foregoing incident, a long document was sent to the vicar of the parish, and a copy to the head of Mr. Naylor's firm, urging each of them to " drive this lothsum man from London." Accordingly, after consultation with his friends, Mr. Naylor put the whole affair in the hands of a detective.

The detective began with inquiries at the school. May appeared a neat, happy, inoffensive child of nine. Both at the day-school and at the Sunday-school (which she attended with punctual regularity), she bore the character of a well-behaved and even pious pupil: " the last person in the class," said her class-mistress, " who would ever use bad language." She was a careful speller, and wrote a tidy printed hand [taught at school], the very opposite of the dirty scrawls her father had received. Her mother, however, an ill-educated woman of bad repute, had been divorced two years before, when the father returned from the war; and the detective at length decided that the letters must have been composed by this woman out of spite. . . .

Nevertheless, May's stepmother (for the father had remarried) gave it as her conviction that the letters were really the handiwork of May herself, though possibly inspired or dictated by her divorced mother's malevolent mind. . . .

To me, as to everyone else, she seemed a serene, sweet-tempered, blissfully innocent child, a little sentimental, and of a distinctly neurotic strain. She was moderately clever, her mental age being a year above the actual age. She possessed great facility in English composition, strong powers of visual imagination, and a wide and refined vocabulary. Her tastes and ways were dainty, indeed, almost demure. She told me, I remember, that her favourite flower was the lily of the valley; it was " so white and pure and clean " — the exact antithesis of the writings I had just inspected. Her teachers, and all who knew her, protested that it was " a shame even to think of the child in connexion with such wickedness."

I made no mention of the letters; and put no questions to her about them: for I was at once convinced that she was the sole and secret author. My belief was corroborated, when, after a special speed-test, I found that she had committed several of the same mistakes in spelling that were sprinkled so thickly all over the disputed documents. For some months she came to see me almost weekly. She proved highly suggestible; and went easily into a semi-hypnotic state. In these dreamy moods she would chatter with freedom of her own past life. She recollected, in much detail, how, three or four years ago, strange men had visited her mother in the night-time; and it was evident that, more than once, she had witnessed scenes of a kind no uninitiated child could guess at or invent. During all these weeks, despite the strictest watch at home, the surreptitious writing still continued. It was a veritable effusion of ink and gall. New scandals were trumped up; alleged witnesses were named. Letter after letter, card after card, arrived by post, accusing the father now of theft, now of heartless cruelty, and ultimately of an incestuous assault upon the girl herself. Twice they announced, without a shred of truth, that May herself was stealing: once, that she had taken to immoral practices upon Wimbledon Common; and, on three occasions, they all but led to criminal proceedings against the father.

One evening I showed her an unopened envelope, sent on to me from her home. In her trance-like condition she could recite, word for word, every item that the letter contained. It had been written, she explained, in the lavatory; stowed away in an under-garment; and stamped and taken to the post by a triumph of manœuvring. Next week, in her waking state, she repudiated the whole thing, protesting with bitter tears that she knew nothing of it, utterly oblivious that she had already confessed all that the last communication stated and how it had been composed. . . . There were thus, by a sort of spiritual split, two minds in the same body. Behind the visible May was an invisible May; and their natures were exactly opposed. The one was frank, the other cunning; the one was affectionate, the other mean; the one was fastidiously correct and scrupulously pure, the other coarse, revengeful, and foul-mouthed. The child was, in truth, the nearest approach that I have ever known, at an age so young, to a dual personality. She seemed the living counterpart, in feminine miniature, of Dr. Jekyll and Mr. Hyde. . . .

In the course of all these discussions, the hidden roots of the child's abnormal conduct floated gradually to the surface. Her own mother, it would seem, she had always loved so much that she could never believe anything evil about her; her memories seemed like memories of a dream too frightful to be true; and she had shut them away in some back cupboard of her mind. Her father's remarriage she had, in secret, fiercely resented; and the transfer of his affection from herself and from her mother to the new wife had goaded her to jealous fury. These heated feelings she had tried to extinguish — with entire success, had it not been for what she called her wicked moods.

Why her revenge took a shape so singular was explicable when I knew more of the family and her history. Her father himself was a prolific cor-respondent; his foolscap communications to me fill a large box-file. Plainly, he pinned great faith to the written word; and, during the war, when he left home for the second time, he had insisted on a weekly note from his little daughter. If she had done anything wrong during the past seven days, she had to write and tell him; and he would send back a loving letter of advice. Some of her later notes contained small self-accusations that were wholly untrue; but they served to provoke an answer full of tenderness. Once or twice even, her distressed father, after receiving them, had travelled home, petted her, promised her toys and presents, if only she would be good. But, so long as her notes reported immaculate behaviour, he saw no reason for a prompt reply, and merely sent through the step-mother a greeting at second-hand. May's penetrating shrewdness soon taught her that in this power of correspondence she was wielding a formidable weapon, an effective instru-ment for wresting her father's attention back upon herself, and for repaying his neglect with blows more cruel than any other she could use. The letters become almost a diary of her "wicked moods," and the periodic outflow seemed to bring a consolatory relief to all the agitating memories that kept gushing up in her mind. Most of the earlier notes the stepmother intercepted; and forbore even to mention them to the father. When at last the father returned for good, the epistolary habit sank into abeyance, until the baby-brother was born. Then May's jealousy returned with an overmastering force; her worst humours revived. Not for a moment could the father credit his own daughter with composition so outrageous; and the step-mother, reproached with a prejudice against the child, kept her notions to herself. Very foolishly, however, the wounded man displayed his grief before the girl, even ejaculating one day in her hearing: " Good Heavens! Some fine morning they'll be sending letters like this to the works." And it was from exclamations such as these that she reaped much of her encouragement and inspiration.

As, little by little, May unfolded the autobiography of her soul, the bad moods and evil impulses began to diminish, and at length to disappear. But, before this final stage was reached, the detective had discovered that the first wife had long ago left England for Australia. The news by accident came to May's ear. She had one more " bad day," and ran to me, announcing that she was afraid she would murder the baby, or her father would murder her, if she stayed any longer in her own home. She begged that her maternal grandfather, an old, drunken, poverty-stricken coachman who thrashed her without mercy, should adopt her, and that she should take his name. In the end, this was the course agreed upon. May left the comfortable home of Mr. Naylor, and lived instead in a two-roomed tenement with Mr. Lomax in a slum. A little further treatment made it possible to break down the barricade between her two contending personalities, and, by putting each, as it were, into communication with the other, to reunite and synthesize them in a single and harmonious whole. When this was done, May Lomax ceased to be quite as prim and proper as she had previously seemed; but May Naylor, the jealous and vindictive letter-writer, vanished like a ghost at daybreak: and the scurrilous correspondence came at last to an end.[31]

We have seen that emotional disturbances and misbehavior are frequently connected with sex themes, but our study of the records does not tend to confirm the Freudian standpoint that behavior difficulties have their origin predominantly in suppressed sexual interests and are compensatory reactions, with fixations on the mother in the case of the boy and on the father in the case of the girl — the Œdipus complex and the Electra complex. According to this theory cases of stealing and running away, etc., would have this source. The Freudians "look for the mother" in case the boy is backward in school or plays truant. In the case of the California boy with the obsession for trains (No. 9) an attempt was made to trace this behavior back to a sexual experience, and one was found, but the running away began before the experience. On the other hand, as Healy has shown in great detail and as we have illustrated above, obscene talk, sex talk, forbidden talk, does frequently lead to delinquencies which are not sexual. Any profound impropriety, dirty talk, sexual or excremental, the knowledge that the mother was a thief, etc., is able to cause a mental conflict, and since the sex region is felt to contain the profoundest improprieties the conflict will more frequently appear in this connection.

But while these conflicts may lead to delinquencies their main bearing seems to be in the direction of the development of psychoneuroses. We quote a single case, involving the suppression of sexual information at home and a form of obsession related to certain early experiences:

23. The patient, Sally M., a girl of seven, was first seen in May, 1913; for four years she kept in touch with the dispensary. It was only after four years that in an interview she spontaneously gave the key to her behavior. . . . The father, an extremely earnest man, took his religious beliefs so seriously that he would not ride on a trolley car on Sundays; he had been brought up in a Methodist community where the sexes at church were seated apart. He

[31] Burt, Cyril: *The Young Delinquent* (University of London Press, 1925), 381–91.

had been much distressed by the patient, when at the age of four she refused to say her prayers. He had conscientious objections to the patient being taught dancing. The mother was strictly conventional, she reproached herself on one occasion for not having whipped her two year old boy who had gleefully referred to hearing his sister in the toilet. In such an atmosphere a child can not easily ask questions about many topics in which interest is extreme, and the curiosity which is balked with regard to tabooed subjects frequently manifests itself in a less direct manner. Thus one of the most striking characteristics of the child was her insistent questioning, which was often without rhyme or reason. She would ask her mother about self-evident affairs, e.g., " Am I still sitting at the table? " and in her visits to the hospital she was a peripatetic point of interrogation. . . .

In the second interview (June 4, 1913) the patient showed the same general characteristics as in the first interview. She was fidgety and inattentive, answered questions as if she were very stupid; she pretended that she did not know the nature of the building, nor the occupation of the physician. She referred to a relative, Cousin Ned, and said " Cousin Ned is 100." In this attitude of pretended stupidity we may perhaps see a sort of game, the patient amusing herself at the physician's expense, teasing him or coquetting with him. . . .

In the . . . interview of January 17, 1914, the patient showed distinctly coquettish behavior; some of her utterances were difficult to explain. She harped on getting fat; " Sam (brother) is fat; " she asked the physician to make her " fat by telephone; doctors make girls fat." It was impossible to mistake the coquetry in her behavior; she sent the others (the social service worker and a physician) out of the room and shut the door, then asked her own physician to attend to her. Later when the physician talked to a colleague who came in, the patient ran out, only came back under protest and then ran out again. She wanted the physician to find how heavy she was, asking him to lift her up; " Martha has been made fat — by telephone." This proposal to the physician is an early indication of the same trend which later becomes much clearer when she asks the physician to examine her down below. . . . During the interviews of the following three years this topic recurs again and again; she wishes the physician to make a physical examination, she does not wish his rôle to be confined to questioning. Some of her rather impatient sparring with the physician's questions may indicate her dissatisfaction with his failure to play the rôle she wants him to play. It is interesting to note that this is her conception of the physician's rôle; she conceives his relation with his patients to be very intimate. . . .

The child seemed to be fascinated by water. . . . That this was a topic of enormous interest to her, and apparently a problem over which she ruminated continuously, was shown in an interview on June 19, 1915. She had come to the dispensary after an absence of several months; after coming into the consulting room she shut the door (a point she had insisted on in previous interviews), and then abruptly pounced upon the physician with the question: "Where does the water come from into the kidneys? ("The blood.") I've never seen any water in the blood. ("You've seen blood.") I've never seen my bladder; my bladder isn't liquid, is it? Can you tell me all about that? Can I lay on the couch while I talk? (In previous interviews she had occasionally lain on the couch and had shown a tendency to expose herself). Are we going to have a talk? (A somewhat coquettish remark, and perhaps with a reference to the fact that the physician's examination consisted merely in talking, while later interviews show that she would prefer a physical examination). What is the screen for? ("For undressing.") Somebody might undress that somebody might see the bladder? (In this remark it becomes quite clear that in her mind the medical situation is associated with sexual possibilities, and that the sexual is represented by the urinary system). Will you answer all the questions I ask? What is that pipe for (pointing to waste pipe of washstand basin)? ("It is to remove waste water.") When I drink, I don't feel water going into my blood. How do things go down by nature? (Is she comparing the water pipe of the basin with human anatomy?) ("Where?") In your blood."

She fingered her wrist and said: "Is this a wall like this? (tapping wall of room). What are the walls of your body? (She says that her father had referred to the body walls.) If I get sick right here, will you do something to cure me?" This suggestion recurs in the interview: She asks what would happen if the elevator fell; if she broke her arm, would the doctor have to care for her? She stands on the couch reaching over as if about to fall, and thus necessitates the attention referred to. If something happen to her in the hospital, the physician will have to make a physical examination. This is the early foreshadowing of the trend which becomes so explicit later in her crude sexual proposals. . . . Later, when in the room, she runs at once to shut the door (this she had frequently done before; cf. January 17, 1914). ("How are you at school and at home?") "I don't know — you don't want to know how well I am sleeping — sometimes something keeps me awake — you don't want to know now, do you? (These remarks would suggest an effort to pique the curiosity of the physician and as if her being awake had some special significance for her; cf. her obscure spontaneous remark, January 15, 1915, about being sleepless and playing with her fingers to make horses out of them.) On the 31st of December the whistles kept me awake — you don't want to know if I'm best at school — listen — is there a whole lot of ink — the ink that comes down when you need it? How does it know when you need it? " This interest in the pen, a tube containing ink, may have the same origin as her interest in all water works, in the waste pipe of the washstand basin, in the flush of the toilet, an interest apparently derived from her intense interest in her own urinary system the meaning of which will later become quite explicit. . . . The mother (March, 1914) said, " The child is crazy about running water. She turns the tap a dozen times a day and would keep it going for hours if I let her."

On one occasion (1913) the teacher had been called on to rescue the patient who was trying to get down the sewer; Sally's explanation was that she wanted to see what was in the sewer. A long time after this incident, one rainy day when torrents were pouring along the gutters and down the sewers, she remarked " water can go down the sewers, but little girls can't." One day at the dispensary (March, 1914), when using the toilet, she said to the social worker, " Cannot anyone tell me where the water goes? Does it go 999 miles into the earth? " . . .

During the next month the report from school was one of odd behavior; she would gallop around the class, laugh raucously, throw down her books, play with saliva in her hands. When in a store she asked the woman innumerable questions, e.g., whether she had children, why she didn't get some. The patient had previously not expressed any overt curiosity as to the origin of children. Questions as to the origin of children had indeed been strikingly absent from the patient's repertoire; her mother remembered that Sally had recently asked where her little brother Sam was before he was born. . . .

During the three years of contact with the hospital, and notwithstanding the fact that Sally was on familiar terms with the social service worker and the physician, she had given few direct intimations as to the underlying conflicts in her nature. Her symptoms seemed to be the disguised expression of important instinctive forces under the influence of an unusually repressive home atmosphere. At the hospital the endeavor was made to give the child a freer atmosphere, in which she could discuss any personal difficulties. Her obsessive questioning on every possible subject seemed to be the expression of an insatiable curiosity, which did not have a direct outlet; the questions about the urinary apparatus and her fascination with all analogous waterworks seemed to cover some more fundamental interest, probably interest in sex matters. Her exhibitionism, her somewhat coquettish behavior, her verbal sparring, were all in line with this interpretation. . . . This was the situation when after a year's absence the patient was again seen at the dispensary. In this interview (June 9, 1917) the patient spontaneously revealed all the underlying factors and threw a flood of light on the mechanism of the disorder . . . quite abruptly and irrelevantly, she says: " If I were to ask about the bladder and kidneys would you tell me? . . . What happens when you have cold in the kidneys and the water comes so much, every three seconds? Why are you taking notes? You're not going to send that home to mother? " (" Have you to go to the toilet very often? ") " Sometimes I have to go every one second (jesting). . . . (" Do you drink much at night? ") Yes, that's one thing that makes me go to the bathroom — I drink eight gallons of water at night — don't you? — how much are you supposed to drink? One night last summer I had water-melon, I wet the bed that night." The fact that the patient drinks much at night would suggest the encouragement of a full bladder and bed-wetting rather than the opposite. . . .

Returning to the topic of urination, she says: " I have taken five cups and then was full to the neck . . . every time I take water I do it. My mother says I'll be sorry when I get older. I do it just for fun (her first frank admission of pleasure gained from the urinary system). (" Why? ") It's fun — it makes so much come out of the toilet (an evasive explanation, which perhaps she does not mean to be taken too seriously). You say the water comes from the blood (information given to Sally in the interview of June 19, 1915), and goes into the kidney and into the bladder — where does it go then? " She is now approaching the real center of her intense interest in the whole urinary system, and is indirectly, perhaps coquettishly, leading the physician to discuss the sexual apparatus. (" It goes into the toilet.") " And where then? (" To the sea.") And where then? (" To the clouds.") And then? (" It comes down in rain.") What! My toilet water? (" You drink to have the fun of water coming out? ") Yes — in order to have more water in the sea so that bigger boats can float." She darts out this somewhat sarcastic response very rapidly, and it is a good measure of her alertness; she thus for the second time gives an evasive answer to the question of what pleasure she derives from urination. . . . She asks whether if she were sick, the doctor would examine her; the sexual context of this question throws light on all her queries of the past three years as to whether the physician would examine her. The underlying sexual motive of these questions, although suspected at the time, has not been beyond doubt. She says she would like to (i.e., to be examined). If something were wrong what would he do down there? . . .

Nothing requires to be added to the clinical history, which gives a striking example of the complicated drama which may be staged in the child's mind. The conflicts which this child of poor nervous endowment found such difficulty in managing are due to instinctive forces which play a rôle in the development of everyone; and this experiment of nature may sensitize us to minor manifestations of similar conflicts in the life of the ordinary child.

In the light of this case it may be easier to understand other examples of aimless and obsessive questioning, of precocious intellectual research, of one-sided interests and fascinations, of indulgence in special games, of special attitudes to the physician, of toying with danger and with chances of injury, of eccentric behavior, and of anomalies of urination and defecation; and the basis of similar symptoms in adult patients may sometimes be traced to an early period, to the complexity of which conventional psychology has failed to do justice.[33]

In the records we find a certain percentage of children who are explosive, violent, inconsequential, cruel, insensitive to pain and punishment, incorrigible. These seem incapable of giving a consistent moral pattern to their behavior, in contrast to those just mentioned where the life has been morally organized and the trouble (mental conflict) is introduced by some factor disturbing this organization. These have been called the born criminal type, especially in England and on the continent,[34] and Dostoevsky has given some striking examples in *The House of the Dead* — the record of his prison experience. Maudsley first called this type the "moral imbecile." Foster and Anderson have given some examples among very young children:

24. When Charles [2 yrs., 10 mos. old] becomes angry he "takes it out" on another child or on the particular toy which has exasperated him. If he bumps his head on the table he is apt to say "I break the table" and kick it again and again. One day when riding a kiddie-kar around the house his foot got caught in the wheel and he upset. He hopped up with an angry expression and started kicking the kiddie-kar. At the first kick he began to cry and as he hurt himself more with each kick he cried harder. After he had kicked the vehicle eight times he sought his mother saying "bad kiddie-kar hurt me." He is an exceedingly active child in an awkward way, gives great leaps and jumps and strides, and often bumps into furniture. He is not in general a leader, but younger children are somewhat fascinated and try to imitate him when he knocks things down with a smash. He is easily excited and varies from a nervous talkativeness to a sad, crying state. He plays poorly with other children, but after grabbing all their toys, if his mother explains that the others need something to play with, he is just as active in forcing playthings upon them whether they want them or not.[35]

---

[33] Campbell, C. Macfie: "A Case of Childhood Conflicts with Prominent Reference to the Urinary System; with Some General Considerations on Urinary Symptoms in the Psychoneuroses and Psychoses," *Studies in Psychiatry*, 2:94–109, *passim*.

[34] Ellis, Havelock: *The Criminal;* Bleuler, E.: *Der geborene Verbrecher.*

[35] Foster, J. C., and Anderson, J. E.: *The Young Child and His Parents; A Study of One Hundred Cases.* Institute of Child Welfare, University of Minnesota, Monograph Series No. 1:51 (1927).

25. Whenever David [4 yrs., 11 mos.] goes into a crowd of boys, there is a fight; he is apt to be rough with the younger children and he is known as the " neighborhood pest." For the past year he has been bringing home things that do not belong to him, wagons, kiddie-kars, and the like. When asked where he got them he says he doesn't know, but he takes them to their owner when his mother insists. He is so destructive that Mrs. Zinmann is always afraid he will smash the toy before he gets it returned. David swears fluently though his father never does. His mother is somewhat amused at this but usually corrects him and talks to him at length about it. David teases his little sister unmercifully and is delighted when she reacts violently. He shows considerable cruelty and tortures neighborhood cats. No matter how seriously he is punished, he acts the same way next day. He puts the blame on other children. Mrs. Zinmann says the boy is totally irresponsible and cannot be trusted to do anything. He is hyperkinetic, likes to show off and blusters around before other children. Many of his reactions are infantile and emotional instability is marked. When he threw a temper tantrum in the clinic, his mother gave evidence of total inability to cope with the situation. . . .

Four months later his mother reports that David's improvement has been remarkable. She sees now that she was wrong in being impatient. He now plays well with his sister, is learning to dress himself, eats more vegetables, and has not destroyed anything since his father gave him a severe scolding for breaking a kitchen window. Two months later his kindergarten teacher was interviewed. She said that in David's first two weeks with her, his behavior was so extraordinary that she put forth considerable effort on him. He is now her " pride and joy, contented, interested and playing well with other children." The teacher also said that the boy showed " more marked anxiety and more marked lack of faith in the word of adults than any child she had ever seen." After another seven months, the report is that David's disagreeable conduct is now directed solely at his mother who persists in her nagging.[36]

Of this type Cyril Burt says:

Affection and anger, assertiveness and fear, curiosity and disgust, submissiveness and sex — all the human emotions, and all the animal instincts, are inherited by them to a degree unusually intense, and remain, throughout their earlier years, almost wholly unsubdued by loftier purposes or interests. First one impulse, then another, then a third, each contradictory to the last, and each successively excited by the changing situations of the moment, explodes forthwith into action. And the life of the unstable child becomes a series of discontinuous fulminations, like the pops of a Chinese cracker. . . . Here . . . compiled from a long study and condensed from numerous re-

---

[36] Foster and Anderson: *The Young Child and His Parents,* 119-20.

ports, is a concrete picture of the inconsistent type of temperament which so many young delinquents display. " Everything by starts, and nothing long." [37]

The most extreme examples — the one and a half per cent. who of the whole population are most emotional — I regard as " temperamentally defective," and the next most emotional 10 per cent. as " temperamentally unstable," using these phrases in a restricted and technical sense, and taking the percentages as no more than round approximations. The temperamentally defective I should define as persons, who, without being intellectually defective, exhibit from birth or from an early age a permanent emotional instability, so pronounced that they require care, supervision, and control for their own protection or for the protection of others. Broadly speaking, if we endeavour to make an age-scale for temperamental development, parallel to the age-scales measuring the growth of intelligence, the temperamentally defective child is one who shows less emotional control than would be manifested by an average child of half his chronological age; and the temperamentally defective adult, one who shows less emotional control than an average child of seven.

With this criterion, about 9 per cent. of my delinquent cases would be classifiable as temperamentally defective, and 34 per cent. as temperamentally unstable. In addition, there is a small but important group of cases in which the child's emotionality — demonstrably intense from infancy onwards — only rises to the pitch of excess about the time of puberty: these form the difficult yet hopeful cases of adolescent instability. They constitute 2 per cent. of the total group of delinquents, no insignificant proportion when it is remembered that three-fifths of the total group were still below the school-leaving age. If all three groups be added to make one, it will be seen that nearly half the juvenile offenders are distinguished by a profound and widespread instability of the emotions. . . . Thus, *among all the innate psychological characteristics of the delinquent, a marked emotionality is one of the most frequent, as it is one of the most influential.*[38]

26. No clearer instance of the unstable child could be found than Jerry Jones, the little murderer of seven, with whose story these chapters opened. The reports that I still receive upon his progress month by month demonstrate most plainly with what exceptional strength each one of his animal instincts is developed. From every home, from every school, from every institution to which he has been sent, the comments are the same.

He is, to begin with, desperately hot-tempered and pugnacious. It is a

---

[37] Dryden's paraphrase of Horace: Nil unquam sic impar sibi (*Satires,* III.i.18–19).

[38] Burt: *op. cit.,* 512–14.

trait his mother has noticed from the first weeks of his infant life. " On the least provocation," says one report, " he kicks, punches, and hits out at the other tiny children " — " fighting," as another report observes, " like one possessed." " Time after time he is the first to cause a quarrel." Each teacher who has charge of him quickly finds that " it is really unsafe to leave him alone with other children." He is destructive; and that to a degree often amounting to callous cruelty. He is perpetually smashing his play-fellows' toys; has tried to roast a kitten on the stove; and has battered a live duck's head upon the ground. Taking a silk-worm moth in his hand one day, he smiled mischievously, and saying, " Oh, the dear little thing," suddenly closed his small fist tightly upon it, to the horror of the children round him.

Many of his antics spring from sheer self-assertiveness and a love of self-display, a madcap desire to shock and show off, and generally to create a sensation. He has won many young hearts by his daring feats in climbing trees and by his dexterity in turning somersaults — always, of course, in public. But his love of domination leads to every sort of wild extravaganza. At one residential school the climax came when he climbed on to the roof of the wood-shed with the chopper in his hand, and, for a quarter of an hour, terrorized all below, boys, girls, and teachers alike, threatening to " do in " any who approached him. After that an urgent telegram was received in London begging for his speedy removal. . . .

Like so many young delinquents, he has shown, even at this early age, the instincts of sex. When he was but six years old, his first head mistress had remarked his indecent habits with little girls; and at his first residential school the superintendent again wrote that " on one occasion at least " he was found repeating his improper practices. At his present home, I notice, it is a girl who is his favourite playmate.

Nor has he much power of control over his simpler physiological impulses. There have been frequent protests because of his incontinence, which has shown itself in each of the usual forms. He is always hungry; and will pick up a rotten apple and munch it ravenously, or grab a cake or bun from the next child's plate.

Yet, amid all these unpleasant and aggressive traits, he also exhibits, with the queerest mutability, all the gentler emotions — fear and affection, submissiveness and grief — each developed in the same exorbitant degree.

His inborn timidity, so out of keeping in a would-be devil-may-care desperado, crops up in quaint and unexpected ways. On the farm he was greatly scared by the cow. " 'Twouldn't bite, would it? " he asked. — " No." — " Not if you called it names? " Much of his outward aggressiveness, indeed, is at bottom traceable not to pure temper, but to a strong admixture of nervy alarm. His vindictive outbursts come most easily when he is frightened at impending punishment, or when he is afraid lest another child should complain about his thefts, or seek to reclaim some toy that Jerry himself has taken.

Although, since my first investigation, little or no reference has been made to the original tragedy, nevertheless it is always near the surface of his mind. A year afterwards, when the doctor in attendance asked genially why he had been sent to the home, he at once responded: " For shovin' another chap into the cut." On his timorous little soul the menaces of his London neighbours seem to have stamped a mild obsessional anxiety. The victim's father and friends had threatened to drown Jerry, as he had drowned his tiny comrade; and were forever trying to decoy him in the direction of the canal. He now invariably inquires if there is water in the places he is going to; and seeing, one day, a well that supplied the local pump (for long a source of eager interest), asked tremulously: " What would happen if I fell in? " At first he refused to go to Brighton " because it was seaside," and he " would get drowned; " and, wherever he is taken, he always wants to know if " they " (the relatives of his victim) will find him " down there." The obsession reappears, though with diminishing frequency, in night-terrors; when roused from bed one night at ten o'clock, he shouted — " Garn, I'll ' do ' you; " and then subsided, as he wakened more thoroughly, into a meek and childish whisper: " Yes, please; I want to get out."

His affection appears in odd, impulsive outbursts. Even at his first school, which he so cordially detested, he showed the deepest devotion to his teacher; at another school his fondness for the mistress flared up in a burning jealousy of other children. When a walk was arranged he would ask: " It's just me and you, isn't it? No one else? " or blurt out angrily, " Wot d'yer want to let the others come for? " With his playthings, his cakes, and his sweets, he is often surprisingly liberal. And, as a rule, he is kind almost to chivalry towards whatever little girl may win his fancy at the moment. With animals he is as capricious as he is with his own companions. He will pelt the cat with stones; then cuddle it, muttering compassionately, " Poor kitty, did'ums, poor kitty." Being sent to a country house where there were no young people at all, he soon made chums with all the stray dogs in the vicinity; and now, at the age of nearly nine, he can be trusted to feed and clean the puppies and the rabbits without reminder — a praiseworthy feat for a boy of his type and years, with but the scantiest notion of cleanliness for himself.

Yet he loves a crowd; and it is in the midst of a knot of other little children that he becomes most violently excited. With older boys and girls, who for the most part soberly ignore him, he is comparatively still; and at times he can be as submissive and suggestible as on other occasions he is headstrong and assertive. Alone, with a calm but understanding adult, he proves docile, tractable, and obedient. Indeed, like a restive pony, he plainly prefers a firm hand on the rein.

Most of his feelings are but transient flutters. Yet, in his simple way, he is capable of an affection that is something more than a fleeting emotion, a primitive dog-like sentiment for an individual person, a regard and an attachment that will for a while endure. And, quite recently, he has approached the level of abstract hero-worship. At the moment, he is the fervent worshipper of one who to him can be little more than a pale pictorial figure and a name — Robin Hood. Jerry now walks out with a huge bow and arrow he has made, acting in fancy the part of the outlaw. He has given a precious shilling to a tattered organ-grinder, " because Robin was so good to the poor; " and one morning he asked: " Did Robin Hood have a cold sponge? . . . Then I will."

He is liable to moments of reckless merriment, and of misery no less abandoned. Ordinarily, he is a happy little ragamuffin, especially when away from other children, free and unopposed. He has a sharp sense of humour, a ready smile, and a mischievous grin; and often becomes convulsed with seemingly causeless laughter. Taken one evening to the pantomime, he entered noisily into the fun of the piece, beating time with the conductor, and calling out, " Good old Puss in Boots! " " Shake hands, Puss." On the way home in the bus, he tried a few practical jokes of his own, pulling the bell, poking fun at the conductor, and knocking off another boy's hat, saying at once: " 'Twasn't me. That little girl in front done it."

But he is equally susceptible to depression and grief. Many a time I have seen this heartless little homicide sobbing and screaming like a child of two. On the last occasion that he was brought to my office to be tested — being then nearly nine years old — he broke off, after twenty minutes' talking with my assistant, and, feeling a little tired and apprehensive, began to whine, " I want to go home." Soon he worked himself up into a hysterical tempest of tears. But in two minutes the squall was over; and, with a penny in his fist, he was answering as gaily as before.

Like most emotional children, he has a bright imagination. On his return from the South Coast by train, he peopled all the woods of Surrey with " little white men what rides on white 'osses." Fairies he takes earnestly to heart; and is full of half-original romances about their ways. His inventiveness is shown by the quick cunning with which he devises his impish pranks, and by the untruths he fabricates to glorify himself, or to elude detection and punishment.

About a year ago, in a couple of evening papers, there appeared a paragraph to this effect: " A little boy named Jerry Jones was found by a railway guard, asleep in an empty train at Brighton. He told the police that his mother had beaten him, and that he had travelled that day from King's Cross, escaping observation by hiding under the seat." As a matter of fact, Jerry was then staying at Brighton with a foster-mother; he had soiled his bed, and, in dread of a thrashing, had run off and hidden in a railway-carriage not many yards from his home. His story, which was garnished with much petty detail, was nothing but a circumstantial lie.[39]

There are also cases where through an impairment of the nervous system by encephalitis or head injury the behavior is so changed as to resemble closely that in the cases just cited:

In the fall of 1924 there were many children in and about Philadelphia whose behavior had been badly influenced by epidemic encephalitis. They were sick and could get no treatment: general hospitals could not take them because they interfered with the care of other patients; state mental hospitals would not take them because of their youth; classes for the feebleminded would not take them because they were too intelligent; expelled from school, they were thrown back upon their homes where they became a moral danger to their brothers and sisters and to the neighborhood. And finally if they were in desperation sent to a reform school, they were too unruly to be dealt with and came home after a time to continue their bad conduct. . . . [Under these circumstances the Pennsylvania Hospital undertook] the complete care and study of a selected group for a long time. . . .

Whether the behavior picture of post-encephalitis is to be regarded as really specific to that disease, is not yet clear. We have found evidence that nothing quite matches it except possibly the traumatic disorders. Such statements as that of Beverly and Sherman, who are tempted to make the diagnosis from the behavior picture alone, are found in the literature, and it seems to be true that no disease produces with any regularity conduct disorders of *any kind*, even disease which on *a priori* grounds we might think would be likely to do so. It is stated, for example, that no single case of behavior reaction has been reported in Birmingham in three years as occurring following epidemic meningitis. If we except syphilis with its exceedingly varied manifestations, chorea seems to produce most often a behavior picture. Auden sees much similarity between the psychic manifestations of chorea and encephalitis, and speaks of chorea as showing faulty emotional control, irritability, outbursts, reduction of powers of concentration, departure from correct conduct, muscular incoördination, weakness. At the same time one wonders, in the light of recent experience, whether "chorea" in these cases is not sometimes encephalitis.

Wimmer gives a very good account of the behavior case of the

---

[39] Burt: *op. cit.*, 507–12.

postencephalitic type. He sees uniformity in the picture, finds that the delinquencies are of an *impulsive* nature, displaying little planning, and says that the fully developed case reminds one of the erethic imbecile, as one may observe by considering the list of symptoms he records as characteristic, which follows:

" Restlessness, garrulousness, meddlesomeness, wideawake but erratic attention, curiosity, moods of foolish mirthfulness, irritability, queer manners, desire to tease, querulousness, marked emotional instability with outbursts of anger, etc., destructiveness, biting nails, auto-mutilations, wilful spitting on others, violence, fire-setting, cruelty, truancy, vagrancy, begging, dishonesty, mendacity, pilfering, shirking, precocious eroticism." . . .

The victims are distinguished by the severity of their symptoms, their great restlessness, the display of strong instinctive reactions, especially fighting, their propensity for interfering, and the presence of specific compulsive acts. Intelligence remains intact, and they do not lose their moral ideas.[40]

27. Edward [IQ, 93 in 1923; 90 in 1926]: The patient was born, according to the official certificate, March 5, 1914, which made him 11 years, 1 month when he was admitted to the hospital class. . . .

When he was six years old in the early part of 1920 he had a severe illness which is described only by his mother. She says that the illness began suddenly as Edward woke up in the morning saying that the room was full of animals and of people chopping wood. A day or two later he complained of pain in his head and had convulsions which lasted ten minutes; he was unconscious, his eyes were turned back in his head and his eyes have been crossed ever since. After this attack the patient was in a stupor for a week, unable to take nourishment and constantly twisting and turning his body and limbs; his feet and hands were never still. . . .

In the second year of school, at the age of seven, his work was unusually good and here he began to take books, pencils, victrola records, slip them under his blouse and take them home. He took any money that was lying around. In the second term he was transferred to another room and here he made his grade easily and neither his stealing nor his sleeping was in evidence. During the next summer vacation, he slept soundly all during the summer mornings and had to be awakened as late as one or two o'clock in the afternoon.

In the third year of school at the age of eight he began to steal again. He

[40] Bond, E. D., and Partridge, G. E.: " Post-Encephalitic Behavior Disorders in Boys and Their Management in a Hospital," *American Journal of Psychiatry,* 6:26–38 (1926).

was promoted in the hope that harder work would take up his attention but unfortunately quarantines made him lose time and he failed and was sent to a special school at the age of nine in the fourth grade where he was so much brighter than the rest of the children that his influence was bad. His school work continued to be very good but he was all over the room. " He collected everything from money to nails and paper. If these things were found upon him he had a line of defenses to prove that he was innocent. If anything he took was taken away from him he showed a tenacity of a bull dog in getting it back, scratching, biting, screaming as long as his strength would hold out, when he would either seem to faint or sink down from exhaustion." The teacher reports, " After I showed him where he scratched me he was profuse in his apologies and begged me to forgive him. I did, and he panted like a bird spent from beating its wings against the cage. He gave me presents which I afterwards learned he had taken from a store. I had them returned. He went to the store and demanded them to return the things to him; on refusal, he screamed and tried to get them. They finally put him out and he threatened to throw stones at the windows. They had to call the police. He is affectionate, courteous, always pleasant and shows designing worthy of a general but cannot be trusted." . . .

[When he entered the hospital] he had a solemn face with an unscrutable expression, " poker face." When he lies he does it with so much frankness and sincerity, not defiantly, but accusingly, that one feels brutal to suspect him. His expression is sometimes one of cranky obstinacy and at other times very sad; he smiles wanly but when he hears the music of his favorite " Nearer My God to Thee," his expression is as rapturously happy as that of an " angel child." He was interested during the mental examination and his attention was good. He showed unstable mood, changing from sadness to gaiety in a moment and from anger and fear to affection; he wanted to have a fuss made over him and to kiss the visitors that came on the ward. He has told the most absurd stories with the appearance of innocence. . . .

Much interest was centered in his eating habits. . . . He continually objected to eating his meals, hid food as often as possible, put his finger down his throat so as to regurgitate. In talking over his difficulty in eating, he said that he couldn't stand the yellow of eggs, that he just hated some food, that it seemed as if he would vomit; he didn't like brown cake and used to dislike ice cream; he thought that if he could be left alone a day or two and eat what he pleased he would eat enough; but he said people wouldn't give him enough time to get his stomach settled; he didn't like cauliflower, the sight or the taste of it; he also disliked cereals and buns, the latter were too doughy; some of the boys at the table who made noises made him sick in his stomach. He also disliked codfish and herring and he said he had all these dislikes for a long time; he said that he thought of some boys that are bad who killed things; he said Leo, a boy at home, killed a cat and cut the legs off. At breakfast he would stop to whine and cry and eat less and less and say that his food was coming up on him; he cried before finishing many meals. One time he asked not to have to eat dinner, tippled over a chair, threw food on the floor, blew soup over the table, shouted and whistled. When he was found with bread in his pocket he said he didn't know the bread was in his pocket; he guessed Robert put it there when he wasn't looking. He said he liked fruit best, almost any kind of fruit, but didn't like grapefruit or apricots, or fruit all mixed together. . . . He complained about the school, thought it wasn't a " right " school, the desks were not regular school desks, they didn't use ink, there was no big blackboard, the teacher didn't have the right books.

Edward has a fertile dream life, which has not been much explored. He dreamed of snakes; there was a snake that had bluish stuff all over its back like fancy stuff. There was a long snake that had three leaves on its back, and the dreamer cut the snake into three pieces, and another snake took the three leaves, put the snake together, put the leaves on its back, and then the snake came to life again. There were more snakes in dreams, a whole lot of snakes, and the dreamer killed them and chopped them up. There was a dream that he and his sister were in the cellar and a light globe broke. He was in the water, ships were there, and some man squirted water in his face. He dreamed that he was at home, was going to market, and two big negroes came out and got his sister. He went after them but couldn't find his sister, and then he went on a piece of paper to the end of a bridge. He dreamed that a boy caught a big whale, and made a house of it, and he and the boy got inside. There were other dreams also in which the mood appeared to be one of fear. So there is a strong fear trend in the dream life of this child just as there is in his waking life.[41]

Strecker and Ebaugh have studied the results of head injury on the behavior of thirty children:

In these children there was often a history of explosive outbreaks in school or at home, frequently of such severity as to make the child a menace to its associates. Several children made threats to kill. One boy (case 7) threatened to kill his mother and frequently struck her. In case 14, there was a total change in behavior reactions. The boy was uncontrollable, destructive, and at times had wild temper tantrums during which he destroyed furniture. He enjoyed pinching and scratching his schoolmates, and tortured animals. The overactivity in these cases was definitely related to an impure affect (tension

---

[41] *Ibid.*, 78–84.

state). In some patients, as in case 2, the mental reaction simulated a manic state with great psychomotor drive. This boy, aged 7, was also sexually precocious. The entire group of patients were unmanageable in school, and many had had extensive court experiences. . . .

The behavior disorders described bear a marked similarity to those common after acute epidemic encephalitis in children. One of us,[42] in writing of the sequelae of encephalitis, stressed particularly the total change in general character and disposition, with hyperkinesis and affective disorders such as we have here noted. Since both conditions are really organic reactions, we might expect this similarity. As in encephalitis, we also find in the post-traumatic group that the mental reaction may often represent an accentuation of the previous personality make-up. This point has been adequately emphasized by Adolf Meyer.[43] . . .

These disorders have a definite connection with delinquency, and indicate the need for detailed neuropsychiatric study of all children of this type. As the majority of our patients were referred from the schools, the importance of giving educational authorities data concerning the traumatic group is obvious. The effect of explosive behavior disorders in the school room naturally adds to the teacher's difficulties as do the fatigability and attention defects; all of them indicate the need of different educational requirements.[44]

Commenting on their data up to the present point of their investigation, Bond and Partridge say:

To try at the present time to draw very fine lines of distinction in the function of the basal mechanisms is obviously futile. What is important for us to consider is the fact that in encephalitis there is an organic basis, and that whatever the lesion may be there is a deep disturbance of functions which have a psychic correlate or issue in conscious behavior. Reactions at the lower levels are intensified: we have increased instinctive and emotional responses, hyperkinesis, automatisms, disturbances of tonicity, and the like. The gravity of the lesions must vary much in different cases, probably also the location. The main result, providing a general background for the whole class of cases, is an unbalance of functions of such a nature that there is over-activity at these levels. Responses to environmental conditions are to an

[42] Ebaugh, Franklin G.: "Neuropsychiatric Sequelae of Acute Epidemic Encephalitis in Children," *American Journal of Diseases of Children,* 25:89–97 (1923).

[43] Meyer, Adolf: "The Anatomical Facts and Clinical Varieties of Traumatic Insanity," *Proceedings of American Medico-Psychological Association* (May, 1903).

[44] Strecker, E. A., and Ebaugh, F. G.: "Neuropsychiatric Sequelae of Cerebral Trauma in Children," *Archives of Neurology and Psychiatry,* 12:443–53, *passim* (1924).

abnormal extent uninhibited, but whether this effect is to be attributed to the disturbances of the mechanisms directly involved in producing the activities or to interference with inhibiting mechanisms cannot usually be determined.

The pathology forms the *background* for the picture. It is not safe to conclude that it provides a necessary or a sufficient basis for the whole sum of the behavior reactions in encephalitis. It is not at all improbable that real pathological effects may be very slight at the most, while the behavior reactions are very pronounced and persistent. The brain functions more or less as a whole. Its integrity as a whole is the basis of a balance of functions which in certain periods of development is apparently a delicate one. It is an interesting fact that the character changes following encephalitis occur in the great number of cases in the middle period of childhood. It is hard to believe that the localization of lesions shifts definitely with age. What is much more probable is that this is a period in which the relations between lower and upper organs in the brain are not well established. On the mental side it is a time in which habits conforming to the demands of society are fairly well fixed, but are dependent upon the continued presence of authority. A brain disturbance which affects the lower levels may throw the whole balance out of adjustment, producing highly deviated behavior for which quite certainly one should not expect to find localized lesional correlates. The child is involved in a problem of reëducation of controls, it may be with some permanent handicap on the physical side; but there is seldom anything to suggest that there is lacking any essential brain mechanism. There is regression to a more infantile form of activity, not reproducing any stage of development as a whole, but showing the features of an earlier period in the uninhibited response to stimuli and the disregard of the external controls. The demands are immensely increased in some cases, and the capacity for satisfying them, or being satisfied with deprivations is lessened. There is then a fertile ground for the development of reactions having anger, fear, erotic feelings behind them, reactions which represent impracticable and socially undesirable forms of activity. These developments refer to the lesions, but are no direct correlate of them. In many cases there are both subjective and objective contributors to a sense of inferiority or general insecurity. The child *feels* weak, and is ready to over-react to any existing inferiority which previously he may even have been unaware of. He becomes over-sensitive to his small stature, his intellectual inferiority, his inability to compete in games. He has lost time from school, lost social contacts, and particularly he is suspected by his mates of being mentally affected. This last is a severe strain upon the already disordered emotions.[45]

---

45 Bond and Partridge: *op. cit.*, 98–100.

. The questions involved here require not only a further clinical but a psychological and sociological study. A considerable number of the children " spoiled " by their mothers behave like the post-encephalitic cases. Apparently there are constitutions with a chemically determined basis of excitability (see chapter XI). They are relatively numerous but training is usually adequate to exert a control giving socially tolerable behavior. Otherwise they become one of the several varieties of the spoiled child. It is reported that encephalitis results in the accentuation of the behavior traits shown by the child before the sickness, and at the same time it renders the control through training more difficult. Assuming that Burt's boy is an example of an explosive and imperfectly integrated constitutional type, he is nevertheless also an example of lack of supervision, so that he in fact resembles the post-encephalitic cases. Lack of supervision frequently produces in rulers, heads of families and others above authority socially unschematized behavior comparable with that of the post-encephalitic cases and of Burt's boy. Sociability and heartlessness, courage and cowardice, fidelity and treachery — an integration at the level of the spoiled child — are found frequently among the Italian condottieri, e.g., Caesar Borgia and Sigismondo Malatesta. Democracy was, in its origins, in part a determination to be rid of the post-encephalitic parallels.

If we may speak at all in terms of constitutional types, Agnes, in the following case, may serve as an example of the hyperexcitable constitution struggling with the attempt of society to regulate her behavior. She is domineering without cruelty. It can hardly be doubted that her hyperkinetic and dominant behavior is related to the at present mysterious chemistry of the glandular system. Doubtless the particular behavior manifestations recorded here, and at great length in the original record, are dependent also, as Dr. Woolley suggests, on the home situation, but however much she may be regulated and reconditioned she will always remain a terrible person to contemplate as adult:

28. Agnes was among the first registrants for the school. We first saw her before the school opened, in December, 1921, when she was three years and two months old. She was a chubby tot, with black curls, a somewhat Oriental type of face, and an eager, raucous little voice. She captivated every one by running about fearlessly, asking endless eager questions and conversing with

any one who would take the time. Agnes entered the school in January, 1922, and remained with us until the end of March, 1923, when she was four and a half. . . . She was the only child of middle-aged parents. . . .

Everyone who met Agnes recognized the executive in embryo. The problem was that of whether her intense egoism and selfishness could be subdued sufficiently so that the rest of the world would allow her to use her executive ability. The management of affairs seemed to be constantly on her mind. She often looked as though the weight of responsibility she felt were really too great for her. She soon learned the daily régime of the school and felt that it was up to her to see it carried out. " Isn't it time for our lunch now, Miss Henton? "she would say — and it would be! Time and again she anticipated the next move. Indeed we often said that the most maddening thing about Agnes was that she was usually right. Her desire to manage was not by any means entirely selfish. There was in it an element of wishing to be helpful to the teachers, and of desiring to do things for the other children. At times she launched forth into independent plans for the children. Agnes herself frequently wet her clothes during her nap. To save her this embarrassment, which she felt keenly, we had formed the habit of waking her up once during her nap and sending her downstairs to the toilet. One day the sleeping room was left without adult supervision for a few moments. The children all seemed to be asleep, and the teacher in charge stepped out. When she came back she found that Agnes had wakened several of the youngest children. She had them lined up at the head of the stairs and was saying to them, " Now you go down to the toilet, and when you come back I will have some more ready to go down! " . . .

By June, at the end of five months in the school, we felt that we had made real progress with Agnes. She had learned to take her turn and play her part as one, but only one, member of a group to such an extent that her personality report of June optimistically stated that her egoism had almost entirely disappeared. She had even learned to moderate her loud, rough voice. When she forgot, and spoke very loudly, she would say, " Miss Henton says I must talk softly." She was no longer a constantly disturbing element with her demands for attention, and seemed to understand that one person cannot monopolize the center of the stage. . . .

During the long summer vacation of three months, Agnes was once more under the exclusive management of her parents. Her mother was fully alive to her extreme selfishness and had tried to overcome it by insisting upon Agnes' sharing with other children when they were about. Neither parent, I think, had seen the importance of insisting upon Agnes' being considerate and unselfish with her parents. Like so many devoted parents, they felt that all the unselfishness should be on their side, without fully appreciating the bad effect upon the child. They admired her inordinately, and her father could not resist the temptation of showing her off — which was only too easy to do. She was allowed to be a little tyrant, and get her own way by whining and stamping her foot. Sometimes the mother, and sometimes the father brought her to school, and the scenes of parting were instructive. Agnes would frequently make a row about allowing them to go. She would stamp her foot — even stamp on her father's feet at times — whine, scold and command. Her parents, instead of departing promptly, would remain to argue and cajole. In the end they had to leave her still rowing — which she did lustily until she was sure they were out of earshot, when she instantly stopped, and devoted herself to the affairs of the school in perfect content.

When Agnes returned to the school in the fall of 1922, at the age of three years, ten months, we felt that all our work was to be done over again. She was once more the dominant and determined boss of the school. The room rang with her cries of, " I want to carry the tray — I want to play Polly Perkins. — Let me say it now, Miss Harley, I can. — Let me be Fair Rosey. — I don't drop my plate of food on the floor, do I, Miss Henton? " etc., etc. We had to begin again almost as though we had done nothing the year before. . . .

Her desire to dominate, and her ability to manage affairs were even more striking than the year before. She could never resist the desire to exercise authority. " He shouldn't do that, should he? " " Baby Billy can't have any beets today." " Did Miss Skinner say so? " she was asked. " No," replied Agnes, " but he mustn't have any today. They are not good for him." One morning when the telephone in the hall rang, Agnes told the children they must keep quiet because no one could hear over the telephone if they made a noise. When it was time for the children to sit down in a circle for a story-telling treat, Agnes would frequently anticipate the teacher. She would successfully get all the children seated, and then say, " Miss Henton — when you are not busy will you tell us a story? " . . .

Agnes' interest in sex had evidently become more definite. Several times she was found peeping behind the curtain when one of the little boys was using the toilet. When told she ought not to look behind the other children's curtains, she laughed disdainfully and went away. Later in the year — at four years, three months — she had evidently acquired at least the fundamental information as to where babies come from. She was being very obstreperous, and talking very loudly at the lunch table one day. The assistant at the table said, " Mercy, Agnes, where did you grow that you must talk so loudly and yell so much." She replied promptly, " I grew in my mother's stomach." . . . One day . . . one of the twins was sent up to bed as a punishment for having told a lie. The twins were so much alike that most

of us could not tell the difference between them. Shortly after this, one of
the twins was sent down from the brief morning rest to set tables. It was
considered something of an honor to be chosen to set tables. On this morning,
Agnes was one of those first sent down. When the twin appeared, Agnes ran
up to Miss Henton and said, " Well, you made a mistake this time, Miss
Henton! " " Did I, Agnes? " said Miss Henton. " What mistake did I make? "
" You chose the bad twin instead of the good one to set tables," said Agnes.
She was doubtless right, though it was hard to prove. . . .

Agnes' command of language and ability to interpret the spoken word
remained outstanding. Her crowning achievement consisted in learning to
read with very little aid. One day when a group of children were left alone
in the playroom for a time, Miss Henton thought they were suspiciously
quiet, and looked in to see what they were doing. Agnes, who was just four,
had collected them in a little circle about her, and was reading them a story
out of a book. Miss Henton, who knew her marvelous verbal memory, thought
she was " reading " by selecting the story from the picture, and then repeating it from memory, but when she tested Agnes, using a variety of books
with simple stories in them, she found that Agnes could read any of them
with ease. Indeed she amazed us with her facility in pronouncing quite difficult words from their appearance. We made no attempt to teach her reading
at school. Her mother reported that she had made no systematic effort to do
so at home, though she had answered questions about words when Agnes
asked them. As nearly as we could analyze it, her method of reading was to
make the sounds by syllables. She did not know the names of the letters,
but would give the sound if asked what the letter was. Her attack on a new
word was to divide it into syllables and sound each one separately. Words as
difficult as " grandfather " she got with little hesitation.

Characteristically enough, Agnes never wished to read without an appreciative audience. There were plenty of books in the school, to which she
had free access. She could usually find at least one student ready to help her.
Nevertheless she complained to her mother that she was not allowed to read
at school. What she meant by " reading " was being allowed to gather a
large and submissive circle of children who would then be required to sit still
and listen to her. The grade of her reading can be roughly indicated by the
fact that at the age of four years, three months, she read aloud to one of the
students the entire poem " The Night Before Christmas " with very little
aid. Her memory for words is shown by the fact that she learned the names
of each new set of students as they came along, and was soon calling each
by name instead of contenting herself with calling them all " teacher," as so
many of the children did. When Miss Henton read stories aloud which the
children had heard a few times, Agnes could usually tell what was coming

next. Even words as difficult as " irrelevant " she would remember and be ready to quote in the correct place. Before she left the school, she had not only learned to count but had learned to make the digits up to ten. . . . Agnes' mother felt that the necessity for humoring her in her young infancy because of her precarious health, was the thing which had determined her domineering habit. She said that by the time Agnes was seven months old, she was firmly convinced that she was the center of the universe, and the rest of it revolved about her as it had up to that time. Certainly none of us is wise enough to tell how much of the outcome is due to heredity, and how much to environment. Having beheld the complete subservience of Agnes' parents, one is inclined to feel that their attitude alone is adequate to account for the outcome. Her naughtiness was usually condoned on the ground that the child must be ill. Every command was obeyed and every desire granted if it was possible for her parents to do so.[46]

In anthropology, psychology, psychiatry, sociology, there has been a convergence of attention on the rôle of experience, or, as Dr. Esther Richards, whom we shall presently quote, has expressed it, the " rôle of situation," in the characterization of races and nationalities, social and professional classes, and types of normal and abnormal personality. The anthropologist is skeptical on the point of peculiar racial mental and emotional endowments; he thinks, rather, that racial and national traits and customs are like fashions of dress, not indeed changing seasonally but modifiable through decades and centuries of time, in connection with a changing world and changing experiences. The psychologist is going to extremes in his claims as to the influence of "situation." Since the work of Pavlov and Watson on the conditioned response the working idea of the behaviorists is that the whole personality patterning of the child is formed by social influences in the early months and years. The psychiatrist recognizes a neurotic constitutional basis of the behavior difficulties which confront him, but points out that the neurotic behavior manifestation can be obviated by the provision of certain types of situation. And on every hand the home is coming in for criticism as the point at which the child is spoiled.

Dr. Richards reports:

From September, 1920, to September, 1922, 623 children were examined in the Phipps Psychiatric Dispensary of the Johns Hopkins Hospital. Of this

[46] Woolley, Helen T.: " Agnes: A Dominant Personality in the Making," *Pedagogical Seminary*, 32:569–97 (1925).

number 167, or 26 per cent, seemed to be pure cultures of neurotic traits uncontaminated by mental retardation, delinquency, or somatic deficit of any kind. . . . Of the 167 children referred to above as showing pure cultures of neurotic traits uncontaminated by mental retardation, delinquency, or grave somatic deficit, 13 per cent exhibited a definite tendency towards hypochondriacal complaints. . . . The ages of these children ranged from three to fifteen years, and the duration of their complaints at the time they came to the psychiatric dispensary varied from three weeks to nine years. Their symptom-pictures of distress are strangely similar to those of the adult-invalid types — palpitation; shaking in stomach; headaches; pain in chest, abdomen, and legs; weakness; giddy spells; fullness in the epigastrium; " I feel all played out; " " Sometimes I vomit a lot, too." Behind these cries there was comparatively little background of somatic facts as discovered by pediatrician, laryngologist, ophthalmologist, or laboratory diagnostician. Fifteen cases were physically negative; four showed some eye strain; and two had a tonsil-and-adenoid condition for which operation was advised. From an etiological standpoint the most significant part of the chart record is found in the columns entitled *Reaction patterns* and *Situational data*. Here in all but one of these 22 cases, we see children who expressed complaints that they had absorbed from an atmosphere charged with hypochondriacal utterance and fear of disease, objectively reinforced by numerous prescriptions, patent medicines, and the medical folklore of neighborhood gossip. With the pattern of these reactions well established through the daily contacts of actual behavior, it needed but the catalyzing agent of some unusual circumstance or emotional strain to produce a symptom-picture quite baffling to the ordinary approaches of clinical procedure. The disease problem here embraces not only the complaining child, but the whole family of which he is so often an insignificant part. . . . Of the 22 cases described, 18 showed a complete elimination of complaints within a period of from one to two months after the first visit to the dispensary. One of the remaining four we were unable to follow because of the family's removal to another city. The three other children are as bad, if not worse, than before their first examination by reason of our utter inability to elicit the coöperation of the parents. One of these three victims of environmental malady is a county ward of one of the child-placing organizations of this state, and hence beyond the jurisdiction of our psychiatric social research. But the passing of somatic complaints has not been interpreted as arrival at a satisfactory adjustment goal.[47]

29. No. 4 was a Jewish boy of fifteen who was brought to us by his father in January, 1921. Belying his well nourished body and good color was a

---

[47] Richards, Esther Loring: " The Significance and Management of Hypochondriacal Trends in Children," *Mental Hygiene*, 7:44–49 (1923).

youth who slouched in his chair, grasped his head with both hands, and moaned aloud. " My head hurts awful. I have pains in my chest and stomach. My legs are so weak they are no good." The father, sitting helplessly by, volunteered that the boy " was never so strong always." As he enlarged upon the ills of this branch of the family tree, the dispensary record of the patient's mother was brought to the examining room. Upon it were these descriptive words written nine years previously: " Patient sits in chair pressing top of her head and moaning ' ouo '." During the passage of years this woman has acquired lengthy records in six different departments of our out-patient service, where she has complained, without discoverable physical basis, of " headache, dizziness, anorexia, heartburn, night sweats, flatulence, bloody stools, swelling of legs, palpitation, pain over heart, weakness." Her two oldest children (daughters) have dispensary records of the same general coloring.

The patient made the seventh grade at fourteen years in spite of very irregular attendance. He was " disgusted " with school and left it, to become in a year's time equally " disgusted " with innumerable jobs, which he held from two to three weeks at a time till unendurable somatic distress forced him to quit.

A complete physical examination found him in excellent condition. A report of this fact neither comforted nor convinced the patient or his family.

The social background was that of the Russian-Jewish immigrant. The parents came to this country shortly after their early marriage, and were immediately swamped by crowded living conditions, a stern economic struggle, and a rapidly increasing family. The father had aspirations to establish himself as a tailor, but the family demands for livelihood have kept him at his original job of presser. The mother has apparently never had the time or the urge to develop any interests outside the household and her own bodily sensations. With the coming of the children and their problems of development, the strain of domestic relationship became acute. Under a régime of petting, nagging, scolding, and utter lack of training in habits of living or behavior, the children grew up into a band of individualists who were constantly at odds with the school. Any attempt on the part of father or teacher to insist on simple discipline sent them howling to their mother, who immediately defended them by loud arguments delivered in their presence. At what point the adaptive mechanisms of the patient and his siblings began to take the form of hypochondriacal complainings it is hard to say. That such a pattern did crystallize, and did so by reason of certain determining factors of environment, are facts that it does not require a great stretch of the imagination to accept.

From the standpoint of therapeutic adjustment, this case has been a failure, and will probably continue to be so in view of the facts outlined above.

To be sure, the patient has worked six months on the same outside job, partly, one suspects, because his father insists on the boy's contributing something toward the family budget. At the close of the day's work, he falls heavily upon the parlor sofa, where he is not infrequently found with hat and boots on, describing his symptoms to an anxious audience. So far it has been impossible to get him to say that he enjoys a single moment of his life.[48]

30. No. 12 is a happier case. At the time of his first visit to our dispensary, he was a boy of almost nine years who was brought by his mother because of " weakness," " tendency to heart trouble," and " insomnia." Since birth he had been " under the doctor's care." As a baby he vomited much. . . . He attended school very irregularly up to eighteen months previous to his visit to the dispensary, when he was removed on a physician's advice because of sleeplessness. At the time of his examination he was still taking capsules at night for insomnia. . . .

Physical examination in our children's dispensary revealed a normal body in every respect. From a social standpoint, one found a boy who for seven years had been the only child in a home of comfort and indulgence. The father earned a good salary, but stated that in the last nine years he had spent over five thousand dollars in doctor's bills on mother and patient. The mother was always ailing, with symptoms referable to every organ in her body. In seeing and talking with her, one could almost reproduce in fancy her anxious watching for the appearance of her own weakness in the person of her only child. She carried him in her arms to kindergarten for a year, and subsequently warned his teachers to report at once any phenomena of behavior that might point to overstrain. . . . As a result, the patient at eight and a half years was bathed and dressed by his mother. He cried for what he wanted and was openly disobedient. When pressed in matters of discipline, he complained of feeling badly, and talked freely of his heart and stomach and nerves being out of order. The father's attitude was one of silent acquiescence and patience.

The first point in a reconstructive program was the elimination of drugs, insistence on regular school attendance, and avoidance of spoiling on the part of the parents. With such a background as that described above, it seemed unreasonable to expect that parents and child could quickly revolutionize their habits of thinking and acting, even though the former accepted the principle on which the physician's advice was based. Accordingly it was suggested that the patient board in a county home to which we sometimes send children in need of habit training. The patient was installed in this

[48] Richards, Esther Loring: "The Significance and Management of Hypochondriacal Trends in Children," *Mental Hygiene*, 7:50–51 (1923).

home, where a week later he was found by the worker, overalled and sun-burned, eating, without capriciousness and sleeping without medicine. . . .

The family's monthly visits to the farm were unannounced, and surprised the patient in embarrassing activities of vigor. As the time for their leaving drew near, he cried, begged to be taken home, and on several occasions even hinted darkly at headache and unwholesome food.[49]

These two cases were selected for detailed presentation because their material embraces facts typical of all the 22 children described in this report. The contrast in their adjustment possibilities and the difficulties actually con-fronted in this process are strikingly similar to the problems that occurred in the entire group. Here are two boys who have in common a history of long-standing hypochondriacal complaints in a setting of parental spoiling. In both, the utilization of symptoms for the purpose of dominating the home situation is self-evident. How much of this utilization was deliberate, and how much was the by-product of habitual action and thinking, it is impossible to estimate. The interesting feature of these cases is the remarkable likeness between the complaining reactions of the mother and those of the child. The very somatic discomfort can almost be localized area for area. Are we to put these two adult-child experiments of nature side by side and dismiss their occurrence as the phenomena of inherited nervous instability? . . . We speak of a focus of infection in anomalies of joint and gland behavior, even though the eye cannot follow the processes of transition, and yet we hesitate to speak of the infectious material of daily example, even though the conduct disorder of the mother can be recovered in almost pure culture in the com-plaints and behavior of the child. If play activities can be used as inter-pretative of the psychobiology of childhood, it would seem that imitation exerts no mean force in determining the stream of childish conduct. The simple start in *playing* this or that may go over into autistic flights into the world of make-believe so delightfully perfected in detail that they become habitual refuges from the drab and concrete. And if imitation and fancy grow into more or less conscious alliance in healthy play reactions, how much more easily can their unwholesome combinations of distress come into being in the presence of suggestive daily environment! Moreover, the longer the exposure to such environment, the more indelible the reaction patterns. For this reason the ideal adjustment in the case of No. 4 and No. 12 was their im-mediate removal to an atmosphere of better conduct examples until the independent reëducation of mother and child reached a stage where they would be safe for each other's society.[50]

---

[49] *Ibid.*, 51–52.　　　　[50] *Ibid.*, 52–53.

Comparing these data with those we have been considering on constitutional factors, we can appreciate the lengths to which social influence is able to go in the regulation of constitutional factors, and we learn to use caution in the recognition of the constitutional factors.

The following passage gives a striking illustration of different behavior in different situations. The two children behave, in fact, as different personalities in the home and in the nursery school:

31. December, 1925: Lisa [age 3 yrs., 6 mo.] is very small. . . . It is evident that she has traded on her size by playing baby at home and so getting something otherwise denied. She attracts the attention of everyone by her tiny form, her quaint expression and her purposeful activity. She is fully aware of this and is used to taking advantage of adults' interest and amusement.

When she cannot have her own way she cries, kicks and sulks. Being a bright child she realizes that this does not get anything for her at school but isolation and no spotlight, and comes out of her temper quickly. It continues at home, however, where she realizes that it annoys her mother — gets her attention and usually gets the desired result. . . .

When she came to us she had a band across the back of her head where she had pulled out her hair and her mother claims, eaten it. This is covered with new hair and we see nothing of the habit here. She continues to be very destructive at home. It shows here in her marking over tables, books, papers, etc., and in pulling the pictures off the cloth books. She kept her Christmas toys, however, longer than Florence [sister], really making an effort to be careful. . . .

March, 1926: Has begun again to pull out her hair. Has a spot as large as a half dollar near the top of her head where the hair is getting thinner. We never see her pulling at her hair during school time but each morning when she comes the spot is thinner.

The report from home is that her behavior with her mother is as saucy and defiant as before, that she is destructively active as ever, sucks her thumb and wets herself. Physically she seemed improved and her constant vigorous play with no evidence of overfatigue would seem to indicate that this is true. Whether with her increased vitality we will get a temporary increase in all forms of misbehavior which will later tone down, may be a probability. She is certainly trying us out with a saucy naughtiness in spite of many keen normal interests and normal activity. She has made a pattern of certain forms of misbehavior which get her attention at once at home and she gets real enjoyment from the anger and punishment which she can evoke from her mother. She can usually avoid this punishment with her quick motions, diving under the bed shrieking with laughter and darting about to avoid the stick her mother tries to reach her with. We turn the spotlight off misbehavior here as far as we can in justice to the other children and I feel that many times her misbehavior with us is an effort to get increased attention. Isolation and ignoring usually gets her back to normal in a short time for she cannot make a game of punishment with us. . . .

June, 1926: Her cheeks have rounded out and have some color. There is no evidence of hair pulling as the hair is an even length over her head. Every good quality of keen interest, motivated activity and leadership seems doubled. She shows no more aggressiveness or quarrelsomeness than the normal child. We have had a few sulks, good rest periods, careful toilet habits and no crying. . . .

September, 1926: Lisa has returned to us [after six weeks' summer vacation] very smiling and happy. Just as merry, active and coöperative as ever. Her stunts on the jungle gym are hair-raising but she seems as sure-footed as a cat. She has good color and her cheeks are well rounded.

The home report is thoroughly disheartening. The mother reports that she fusses about her food, that she sucks her thumb constantly and when punished by having it cut on the end by her mother laughed in her face and said " I don't care — do it again." . . .

She has begun to pull out and eat her hair. We sent her home at the end of July with her head evenly covered. She has returned to us with a bare spot as large as a silver dollar. . . .

We see no hair pulling at school and although fingers are often near her mouth at rest period there is no sucking. We are putting a gold star on the habit sheet each day when she keeps her hands down and she is making a determined effort."

Nancy [child from another home] shows none of the rough destructiveness her mother reports at home. She handles things carefully and is orderly in returning them to their places. She seems to enjoy plastercine so much that she was given some by the clinic visitor. Although she uses it carefully and legitimately here in the school the mother reports that she stuffed it into keyholes, openings in the gas range, etc., until the mother in a rage threw it away.[51]

At this point we begin to have a feeling of guilt on account of the multiplication and at the same time the mutilation of the cases we are citing, but we must add some further data illustrating the influence of home situations and infantile experiences in giving a psychopathological

---

[51] Caldwell, Grace M.: Records of the Boston North End Habit Clinic. Manuscript.

set to the personality of the child. This set may then become the dominant feature in the adult configuration of the personality. Both in a normal way, as in professional occupations, and in an abnormal way, in the psychoneuroses, there is a tendency toward specialization of interest going back sometimes to a critical experience, and this becomes the determinant either of a specialized efficiency or of mental conflict and maladjustment. We have already cited an excellent case of this kind (case 9) where an early experience gave the child an obsessive set which manifested itself in trains and travel, and we referred to the point again in our treatment of mental conflicts.

The following cases are related to conflict situations between parents and children, fear conditionings, the mystification of children, particularly with reference to questions of sex and the age-old question as to where babies come from, and an overdetermined solicitude, affection and regimentation. They are connected with negativism, undue dependence on parents, power devices, and habits of domination or of helplessness. It is not, of course, to be assumed that the home is always responsible for the pathological slants of the child. The child of nervous disposition may make any particular experience the occasion of the establishment of a peculiar behavior trend:

32. Negativism constitutes a very frequent stage of development in very young children. It seems to be a natural step in the development of personality. When a child begins to get a feeling of himself as an independent agency, he enjoys trying out his powers. Many mothers feel that this stage is a budding insurrection against authority which must be downed. Since training for the toilet constitutes a necessary field of discipline at this age, it is not surprising that the battle often takes place on this ground. . . . An independent, strong-willed child may become so absorbed in the battle that it is extremely difficult to stop it. Either he must be fought to a finish — and probably injured in the process — or his attitude must be peaceably changed from one of determination to wet himself to one of determination not to do so. An attempt to dominate unduly and unreasonableness and inconsistency of management are the parental attitudes most apt to call forth this pathologically negative reaction.

The point can be illustrated by the behavior of little Margaret, whose mother brought her to the Consultation Center very largely because she was still wetting her clothes in the day-time, wetting her bed during her nap, and wetting her bed at night, when she was almost four years old. . . . Her mother was an intense, high-strung little person, none too strong physically, who found it very hard to meet all the obligations of life. A younger child had arrived in the family at about the time Margaret should have been trained for the toilet. The mother felt physically unable to cope with the situation adequately at the time. She was impatient and inconsistent in her methods, and she attempted to make up by spasmodic severity what she lacked in systematic training. The effect was to arouse Margaret's antagonism. The child was one of the most negative that I have ever seen. One could be perfectly confident that any suggestion would be met with a negation. The satisfaction she got from thwarting her mother about the bed-wetting and her joy in the rows that resulted from it were one of the chief interests of her life. Her superior intelligence (her quotient was 133) made her no mean antagonist.

Margaret was accepted temporarily for observation in the nursery school. The first day she arrived accompanied by a bag containing a rubber blanket, a bed pad, and a change of clothing. After consultation with Miss Henton, the head-mistress of the nursery school, we decided to ignore this paraphernalia and say nothing whatever to Margaret about her bed-wetting proclivity. So far as she knew, no one in the school was aware of it. She loved the school from the first moment, and spent the morning intently watching the children and joining in their projects whenever she could. When it was time for Margaret to go up for her nap after lunch, she trotted up with the other children, keeping an eye out watchfully to see what they did. She was shown where her cot was, and promptly sat down upon it and began to take off her shoes as the other children did. When the others lay down to go to sleep, Margaret did the same. She went to sleep on the very first day and woke up, to our joy, perfectly dry. It was the first dry nap she had ever had. Occasionally, by taking her up two or three times, her mother had gotten her through a dry night, but never once had she had a dry nap. Not a word was said to her on the subject. She was simply taken for granted as a satisfactory member of the school.

She was in the school for three weeks and never once during that time did she wet her cot during nap time. However, during the same period, when she had her nap at home on Saturdays and Sundays, she reverted to her old habit. It seemed to us a complete demonstration that the cause of the enuresis was certainly to be found in the child's attitude toward the whole problem. At school she wished to do as the others did and to be approved of; at home she wished to thwart her mother and have exciting and interesting rows with her. She was later taken for several weeks by a member of the staff, and reached the point where she could be reliably dry in the daytime and have a series of dry nights, eight or nine in succession. She has not yet succeeded in eliminating the bed-wetting completely. As soon as she went home and returned to her mother's management and the home atmosphere, she relapsed somewhat, though not to her old level. We did our best to explain to the mother the source of the trouble, and to help her change her method, but the difficulty of transforming the atmosphere of a home and changing the emotional set between mother and child is great.[52]

Dr. Campbell and others have reported many cases showing the child's utilization of neurotic symptoms as power devices and the development of ambivalent attitudes — the mingling of love and hate toward the parent (Nos. 33 to 37):

33. A girl of five refused to go to sleep unless her mother was with her; she would not sleep if she knew that her mother intended to go out. If the mother sat down to read the paper, the child would sit up in bed and keep awake to make sure that the mother did not go out. As the mother could neither go out, read, nor continue her work under the decree of this dictator, she solved the problem by going to bed about the same time as the child.

In many cases the mother of a nervous child tells how she had to rock the child in infancy for hours, had to sit beside the child, had to accept many conditions imposed by the child. But in the majority of these cases she had to do it because she could not stand the displeasure and protests of the child and preferred to gain peace at the moment rather than to establish the child's sleeping habits on a good hygienic basis at the price of a transitory period of friction.

The five-year-old dictator mentioned above objected to nearly all food except sweets; if crossed, she pulled her hair and stamped her foot. She teased her little brother and objected to her mother's paying attention to other children.[53]

34. A boy of nine was still sleeping with his mother because he was afraid to sleep elsewhere; when he was transferred to his sister's house, he at first refused to go to sleep if his mother were not in the house. Any sickness of the mother caused him great solicitude; he was afraid that she would die, and said that in that case he would die the same minute. He dominated his mother; at his bath he would create an uproar if she did not arrange his clothes in just the order in which they were to be put on. The mother would not accept the suggestions which the physician made for a better régime;

---

[52] Woolley, Helen T.: "Enuresis as a Psychological Problem," *Mental Hygiene*, 10:42–44 (1926).

[53] Campbell, C. Macfie: "The Experiences of the Child: How They Affect Character and Behavior," *Mental Hygiene*, 4:314–15 (1920).

she said that it made the boy sick if she insisted upon his doing something that he did not want. One may add in regard to this boy that for breakfast his milk had to be flavored with coffee, that he had tantrums when crossed, and that his mother had taken very seriously complaints of pains in his legs, which disappeared after a single visit to the clinic.[54]

35. Among the gastric symptoms presented by neurotic children vomiting is not uncommon, and in some cases this symptom forms a very serviceable help to the child for the attainment of his ends. In both the following cases the neurotic symptoms of the child were fostered by the neurotic mother; what is laid at the door of heredity may often with more justice be attributed to the influence of the neurotic atmosphere supplied by the mother.

R. N., a boy of 17, was hardly able to read and write, but showed a surprisingly good reaction to the standard intelligence tests. His apparent backwardness was due to the almost complete neglect of school education, which was only partly justified by earlier sickness. His parents had tried on several occasions to send him to school; he then complained of headache and vomited when he was only a few yards from the house. The father one day insisted on the boy going to school, but the boy fell on the road as if in a faint, and was immediately rescued by the solicitous mother; from that date no further attempt at education was made and the boy remained in an exaggerated dependence on his mother, which pleased her very much. At 17 he used to climb on his mother's lap, and to say that he wanted to remain "mama's baby," and that he did not want to grow up. The mother had fostered in the child an attitude which was extremely strong in herself. She felt that a thread connected indissolubly the life of her mother, of herself, and of her child so that if one died the others would necessarily die. She said that evidently the child inherited his love for her; she herself had loved her parents so much that she cried for two years after she was married, until her parents came to live with her. . . .

In another case where the situation was very similar, the vomiting had a more direct reference to dietary matters. The patient, an only son of 9, was very capricious as to his diet, he would take only what he liked, and no more than he liked; he would accept milk only if flavored with coffee; as a rule he demanded steak for dinner. If his mother urged him to take more of some dish he would say, "I will vomit if you make me take another spoonful," and he kept his word.[55]

---

[54] *Ibid.*, 315.

[55] Campbell, C. Macfie: "The Neurotic Child: Some Familiar Symptoms and Their Problems," *American Journal of Diseases of Children*, 12:425–44, *passim* (1916).

36. The utilization of symptoms in a neurotic manner can not be more clearly exemplified than in the contrast between the two following cases, in which the symptoms consisted of involuntary movements. In one case we see the way in which a symptom, casually occurring in a child of good constitution, and correctly treated by the environment, passes without leaving a trace; while in the other case a similar symptom, perhaps of equally casual origin, is made use of by the neurotic individual and elaborated into a rather striking clinical phenomenon.

In the first case we have an experience, described by Scholz, which happened to himself when he was 10 years old. One day just before the writing lesson his right hand began to tremble, he could only make illegible scrawls, and with a certain pride he demonstrated the symptom to the teacher. The latter paid no attention to it, a little to the boy's chagrin, and his father, a physician, treated the matter as of no interest. The tremor never reappeared.

Contrast this with the following case of a school girl reported by Jung: In the second year of school in the writing class, which she disliked, her right hand began to twitch; soon she was unable to write, and had to give up the class. The involuntary movements spread and became general, a " hysterical chorea; " owing to these symptoms and to morbid fears her attendance at school was very irregular and at 12 was completely discontinued. On the onset of menstruation at the age of 15 the involuntary movements abruptly ceased, and were now replaced by a variety of other hysterical symptoms.

Here we see how a girl of poor nervous balance, which showed itself later in a variety of hysterical symptoms, had at an early age utilized apparently involuntary movements for a definite end. When the patient looked back on this period she realized that she had cultivated the disorder; she admitted that she could have controlled the movements if she had exerted herself and that it suited her to be sick.[56]

37. Out of her complete clinical history only one group of symptoms will be referred to, namely, those relating to her mother; these symptoms had made their first appearance at the age of 5 or 6. At that age, when she first went to school, she was accustomed to go half a block and then go back to ask her mother if she felt all right, if she felt she would die before the patient returned from school, if she were pleased, if she thought anything would happen, etc.; she sometimes repeated this performance two or three times before she arrived at the school.

In view of these symptoms we might be inclined to postulate merely a rather exaggerated emotional dependence of the child on her mother. The possibility of another interpretation is brought up by the following facts:

[56] Campbell, C. Macfie: *American Journal of Diseases of Children*, 12:425–44.

This girl, with the great solicitude for her mother's welfare, from the age of 16 had tantrums in which she bit and scratched her mother, and called her " fool " and " devil." She had of recent years asked her mother somewhat perplexing questions, as, for example, " Mama, do I wish you were dead? Would I rather have someone else for my mama? Would I rather have you dead or living? Mama, I don't mean that, do I? Is it just a bad thought? " The patient thought sometimes it was the devil that made her think those things.

Even before the age of 6 (the patient's statement) she often asked her mother if she were her mother's own child, or if she were an adopted child. Where do these elements come from that seem to contrast so strikingly with her official devotion to her mother? . . . The neurotic devotion to the mother in the present case may be a defense against the recognition of a latent antagonism, which the personality feels itself unable to deal with. Such an antagonism may seem to some to be a rather rare perversion of the normal emotional life; on the contrary, it is an inevitable result of the situation. The child seeks to assert itself, to dominate the environment, to live out its own natural trends, and in adapting itself to the necessary restrictions of an ethical environment it inevitably feels a restriction of its personality, and has some antagonism to the restricting forces. It is largely through the mother that the cultural environment brings its restrictions to bear on the child. So beneath the instinctive dependence and love of the child it is natural that we should find certain feelings of restriction and antagonism; and in the neurotic child both the opposing forces may have unusual strength, with symptoms such as those of the present case.[57]

The records of the clinics and of the hospitals for the insane are heavily weighted with cases of this kind. The other side of the picture is the utilization of children by parents as source of emotional gratification. The most painful of the records are those representing the attempts of parents to live in and through their children:

38. Frances, aged two, was brought to the clinic by her mother because she was making vicious attacks upon her little sister Ruth, aged four. The day before her visit to the clinic, she had bitten her sister on the abdomen and scratched her face rather severely. Investigation of this particular situation revealed the fact that the father had noticed, when Frances was but eighteen months old, that she showed rather unusual and amusing reactions whenever he petted her older sister. It soon became his pastime, when he came home from work, to make a great deal of Ruth in order to arouse jealousy in Frances. He did not realize the danger of this particular form of amusement.

---

[57] *Ibid.*

Here we have a good example of jealousy being developed in pure culture, an emotional reaction that we are all quite aware not infrequently leads to serious difficulties.[58]

39. Thomas, aged two and one-half, sits solemnly by the stove, smoking a pipe constructed out of two clothespins and reading a newspaper. The others amiably keep telling him that the new baby now has his place, and do all in their power to make him jealous and irritable and at outs with his universe. They threateningly say that the visiting lady will take him away in her bag. He looks eagerly in the bag, hoping that the nurse may have secreted the unwelcome new baby in there preparatory to kidnaping it.[59]

40. I know a sixty-year-old father who went to bed and stayed four years because his thirty-year-old son moved to a neighboring town in order to carry on his business to greater advantage. A clever and brilliant teacher of forty-two wrote me not long ago, " I should like to come down and visit you, but mother makes such a fuss when I leave her, and always does something to make herself sick." This woman has been separated from her mother only during her four years at college, and even then that devoted parent hounded her with daily letters saturated with accusations of neglect and selfishness. A telephone employee, superintendent of a city exchange, told me that at thirty-two years of age she had never bought a pair of shoes for herself. She didn't have the courage to select her own clothes because of the storm of ridicule and abuse she would receive from her mother. To meet the conflict of this family situation, she became a headache invalid. I have struggled in vain for six years to persuade two intelligent and genteel parents to allow their two daughters of thirty-odd years to have checking accounts. These dear old souls still follow their children to the front door with rubbers and measure out their cascara at night.

In attempting to salvage this adult wreckage, the physician is again confronted with facts of selfishness, jealousy, self-pity, and spite reactions complacently rationalized in the phrase " parental love." In common acceptance the love of parent for child is considered the highest form of affection in human relationships. And so it is in many an instance, rising to all the heights of sacrifice and self-forgetfulness portrayed in the poetry and prose of centuries. It is the very fineness of these qualities as they can express themselves in the parent-child relation that makes it so important for parents to cultivate the habit of being honest with themselves, to temper mercy with judgment,

---

[58] Thom, Douglas A.: " The Nervous Child and the Habit Clinics," *A Mental Health Primer* (1926), 24–25.

[59] Taylor, Marianna: " The Child and the Home," *Mental Hygiene*, 6:749–50 (1922).

to differentiate between guidance and tyranny, to avoid making childhood the butt of grown-up emotional immaturity.[60]

41. The mother of Jean was professionally, not socially, ambitious. Mrs. McRae had been a teacher before her marriage. Unfortunately she married before the days of careers for married women, and gave up teaching, which she loved, for domesticity, which she hated. She had four daughters, and she determined that through her girls she would have her frustrated career. They should all be teachers. The two older girls went into business. The next one became a laboratory technician. There was only Jean. Jean *must* be a teacher. Jean's I. Q. is 73. Jean's grade advisor calls her " a charming little girl." Miss Riley found her pretty and sensible and well bred.

" She seemed so terribly worth helping," Miss Riley says. " She has no capacity for academic work, but she obviously has other ability."

Jean failed in her courses at Ridge High School and kept failing. Her mother constantly accused the girl of laziness. Jean worked hard, but as her I. Q. of 73 clearly indicated, she was not equipped to cope successfully with an academic high school course. Miss Riley tried to explain the situation to Mrs. McRae.

" You know nothing about it," Mrs. McRae stormed, " I can decide what my children are fit for. I've made up my mind that Jean is to be a teacher and a teacher she shall be."

Jean stood it for five terms. Then the humiliation and discouragement of repeated failure were more than she could bear. She had entered high school late. She was seventeen and a " conditioned sophomore " in rating. Her mother said as long as Jean lived under *her* roof Jean would go to Ridge High School. Jean left her mother's roof. With Miss Riley's help she secured a clerical position with a life insurance company. That was two years ago.

Jean is doing very well. She has had several promotions. Her mother has " disowned " her. Jean has made no effort to see her mother. She says she has no desire to see her. The break is complete.[61]

The recent work in the child guidance clinics and the nursery schools has disclosed the fact that behavior troubles in small children, bad habits and emotional instability, are widely prevalent in the whole population. Foster and Anderson have made a study of the behavior of 118 children between the ages of 2 and 7, the attempt being to take children from families representing the general run of the population

[60] Richards, Esther Loring: " Practical Aspects of Parental Love," *Mental Hygiene*, 10:238–39 (1926).

[61] Ratliff, Beulah Amidon: " Those Problem Parents," *The Survey*, 55:671 (March 15, 1926).

and " normal " children, that is, those in whom there are no extreme personality or behavior deviations:

42. Realizing that the unusual and striking case is far easier to locate than the usual or ordinary case, an attempt has been made to counteract this tendency and to secure as representative a group of histories as was possible. To this end, we have interviewed the parents of many children whose behavior has never been discussed with a physician or welfare worker and who have not been in contact with any clinic or social agency. On the other hand, we have purposely eliminated cases which were so abnormal and unusual as to fall outside ordinary experience. [One hundred case histories are printed in this volume, but 118 were studied and the following table is based on this number]:

CLASSIFICATION OF ALL CASES BY PROBLEM AND SEX

Problem	Number of cases			Percentage of cases		
	Boys	Girls	Total	Boys	Girls	Total
Fears	13	14	27	19.7	26.9	22.9
Temper tantrums	12	6	18	18.2	11.5	15.3
Other emotions	23	21	44	34.8	40.4	37.3
Nervous habits	21	13	34	31.8	25.0	28.8
Over-dependent	5	2	7	7.6	3.8	5.9
Hyper-active	9	7	16	13.6	13.5	13.6
Fatigue	10	2	12	15.2	3.8	10.2
Sleeping	7	10	17	10.6	19.2	14.4
Handling genitals	2	4	6	3.0	7.7	5.1
Toilet Habits	7	5	12	10.6	9.6	10.2
Feeding	18	18	36	27.3	34.6	30.5
Over-imaginative	3	4	7	4.5	7.7	5.9
Improper language	4	1	5	6.1	1.9	4.2
Speech	13	8	21	19.7	15.4	17.8
Playmates	12	7	19	18.2	13.5	16.1
Authority	21	14	35	31.8	26.9	29.7
School	11	0	11	16.7	0.0	9.4
Miscellaneous	11	8	19	16.7	15.4	16.1
Total number of problems shown	202	144	346			
Number of cases	66	52	118			
Average number of problems per case	3.1	2.8	2.9			

The percentage figures are obtained by dividing the frequency of the given problem by the total number of boys, girls, or both combined as the case may be. In studying these percentages the reader should remember that one child may present several different types of problem.

In spite of the difficulties inherent in a classification by problem we have attempted to group our cases sufficiently to bring out salient features. " Fears " includes also timidity and night terrors. " Temper tantrums " includes all kinds from major tantrums in which the child throws himself about on the floor to minor ones in which he stands still and screams in an uncontrolled manner. " Other emotional problems " includes types of behavior described as antagonism, day-dreaming, destructiveness, excitability, feeling of inferiority, indifference, impulsiveness, extreme inhibition, irritability, jealousy, repression, self-consciousness, selfishness, sensitiveness, shyness, showing off, " spoiled," unhappiness, emotional instability, instability of attention, and vindictiveness. The various items under " nervous habits " have already been listed [thumb-sucking, finger-sucking, nail-biting, twitches, fidgety, etc.]. . . . " Over-dependent " means over-dependence on one or both parents. " Sleeping " includes problems connected with naps as well as the night sleep. " Over-imaginative " includes lying. " Improper language " includes swearing and language said to be " shocking." " Speech " includes baby-talk, lisping, stuttering, and so on. " Playmates " includes such things as annoying other children, bullying, cruelty to others, quarrelsomeness and teasing. " Authority " signifies a poor attitude toward authority and includes disobedience, impudence, obstinacy, negativism, and a stoical attitude in punishment. " Miscellaneous " [includes periodic vomiting, screaming when touched, feminine characteristics in a boy, objects to having hair brushed, eats mud, runs away, slow in dressing, unusual pains, chews hair, slow in learning certain habits, starts fire, poor motor control, listless, meticulous, petty stealing].[62]

This study makes it plain also that the attitudes of the parents are largely responsible for the bad habit formation of the children. Illustrations are given of parents who give in to temper tantrums for the sake of temporary peace; parents who force always immediate and implicit obedience, thereby stunting originality and initiative; parents who refuse to recognize that their favorite method of control does not control; parents who by punishment or disapproval succeed only in fixating the attention of children upon their bad habits; parents who show partiality in the family situation;

---

[62] Foster and Anderson: *op. cit.*, 6–20, *passim*.

parents who disagree as to procedure in dealing with the child; parents who themselves indulge in emotional outbursts; nervous mothers.

Dr. Jessie Taft says of the child just entering school:

Under the label " average or normal " we can find in our schools children who are unhappy, timid, self-conscious, jealous, ill-tempered, solitary, given to day-dreaming, moody, domineering, antagonistic, cruel — children in every possible state of unfortunate adjustment, but still tolerable to the group.[63]

Referring now to the foregoing narratives of cases taken as a whole, they do not present an adequate picture of maladjustment and delinquency. The enumeration of cases of mental disability, emotional instability, mental conflict, post-encephalitic disorders, specifications of stealing, truancy, adolescent flare-ups, family spoilings, etc., give the impression that we have located the sources of misbehavior — that it is like a sickness, that " something is the matter " with the child physiologically, mentally or emotionally, or that it is spoiled. But there is in addition a prevalent state of mind in the young — a determination to repudiate the way of life of the older generation and the conventional standards. Conformity, moral code, approved behavior, mean that there have been established general and usual behavior reactions through definitions of situations. The " don't " of the family and the " shalt not " of the commandments, and the legal code represent such definitions. The family, the school, the church, the court, are representatives of these definitions, of the social, moral, and legal codes. But the codes and definitions are themselves at present evolving, vague and unstable. There are rival definitions of situations. Literature and the moving pictures and the show girls may define the situation quite differently from the parent, minister or teacher. The difference in ideals and ways of life between the generations is consequently now very striking. Children may differ from their parents, or at least from their grandparents, in this respect as greatly as races and nationalities differ among themselves. There is thus a disharmony as to ideals and values, connected with the unstabilizing of society to which we referred in the introduction. We add, therefore, some cases of this disharmony between

---

[63] Taft, Jessie: " The Relation of the School to the Mental Health of the Average Child," *Mental Hygiene*, 7:674 (1923).

the generations and of the non-conforming state of mind of the young, beginning with children and ending with hardened offenders:

43. Children were overheard boasting to one another of their ability to get a teacher, or parent, or older person " going." Children would suffer a great deal just to find out how far they could go. They would stand a lot of scolding and even a whipping if they could gain a point over a parent. One mother reported a special problem in this respect. Her nine-year-old lad showed absolutely no regret when reprimanded for disobedience. He always had an excuse ready, and took cheerfully whatever punishment was given. If he was punished by being sent to bed early, he would say that he was tired and glad to go to bed. If he was kept from playing with other boys, he settled down to make the best of it. His mother would spank him, but even then he was master of his feelings and showed no sign of defeat. . . .

Some of the children were only idly curious, and were easily satisfied by an answer; but others were intensely serious and troubled over their problems, at least every now and again. Often they did some careful thinking and asked logical questions. Mocking or skeptical criticism often raised doubts in their minds. A little girl came in from Sunday school and was telling her mother the story of creation and of Adam and Eve as she had just been taught. Her eleven-year-old brother broke in by saying: " Don't believe all that bunk." This boy had developed a spirit of contempt for everything called religious, and had influenced the attitude of a whole class. They would have nothing to do with Bible study, and seemed to enjoy the reactions they got from parents and teachers when they assumed the irreligious and indifferent attitude.

This particular situation was an aggravated example of what the writer found in several classes. Boys displayed the rebellious spirit a little more plainly than girls. They would say: " We know all about that; we are tired of listening to that kind of a story about the Bible and Jesus." A group of girls of the same age would not say the same but they would pay no attention to the teaching that did not interest them. Groups of ten- and eleven-year-old girls did not care for meaningless platitudes, nor for poor stories.

Most children found it difficult to fit prayer and the unseen God into the mechanics of their world. Some had been taught to say formal prayers, but in different cases it was found that prayer had no real meaning to the children. Two cases show their reactions:

A mother of an eleven-year-old boy was sick. She suggested that he pray to God to make her well. He replied: " Thought Dr. A. was attending to that." The mother wisely replied, " All help comes from God, even the doctor's skill."

A nine-year-old girl who had whooping cough asked her mother if God would make her better if she asked him. The mother told the child to try and see. She confessed that she was not sure what to tell the child. The child did not get better very quickly, and was not very enthusiastic over the experiment.[64]

44. Four girls, fourteen, sixteen, fifteen and seventeen years of age are next on the calendar. They are high school students, healthy young Americans of good families. They are involved in a " school scandal." One was discovered by her teacher to possess a notebook of dull obscenities, sex jokes and drawings, together with improper parodies of popular songs, and what would have been, if true, a casual, supposedly witty account of rape on a school girl. These she had obtained from another girl, the delicate daughter of a minister, who in turn had received them from a taxicab driver. This young fellow, on being brought to court, was discovered by psychological examination to be feeble-minded. The notebook had circulated among students, brilliant, dull, rich and poor.

The four girls now before the court were the popular, well-dressed daughters of good families. They smoked, drank (when they could get it), rode home from dances in taxicabs with young men, took all night joy-rides, used a great deal of paint and powder, swore at their parents. Each had a " daddy," although the tenure of office and length of service of these young lovers were precarious. The girls were sophisticated, tired, any exertion, besides dancing, wore them out. They detested athletics, books and housework. They stood about average in high school work.

Three boys were also before the court, as witnesses, aged fifteen, seventeen and twenty. They were prominent students in scholarship and activities. They were not, it seems, " daddies " of these girls, but there was some imperative, diplomatic reason why they should help the girls who were in the scrape or the impending unpleasantness at home. So, the youngest boy obtained the parental automobile, the three boys and four girls eloped, that is to say, went to the neighboring county-seat to procure marriage licenses. En route gasolene gave out. Thereupon the parental car was abandoned, and a strange one commandeered. In talking it over at leisure it was decided not to marry, the parents would probably " fuss; " if one thing more than another was to be avoided it was a fuss. Now these girls were pretty and delicate, daintily reared, and the boys were " manly," " regular fellows " in good society, yet

---

[64] Chave, Ernest J.: *The Junior: Life-Situations of Children Nine to Eleven Years of Age* (1925), 68–79, *passim*.

in court they admit not only sexual familiarity, but promiscuity and disregard of simplest requirements of decency and affection which would arouse honest contempt in the mind of a longshoreman. Early in the morning they had arrived at a road house, and being without funds or gasolene, one of the boys telephoned to his parents. Now, charged with theft and immorality, they are before the court.

They presented an amazing contrast to their parents. One would have thought it was the parents who were laboring under the burden of guilt, while the children were calm and rather disinterested. Clearly the parents behaved as if the pillars of their family esteem had suddenly collapsed; dazed with surprise and humiliation they sat with bowed heads, utterly pitiable. On the other hand the young people were courteous, frank, submissive to questions of court, but there were frequent smiles and impatience at the futility of it all. . . . Sex is not sacred to them or terrifying; it is merely fun. . . .

Surprising as it appears after hearing evidence, the largest proportion of these boys and girls from high schools and good neighborhoods, if taken to court early for first delinquencies, if there they are wisely handled, under adequate probation officers, if home, school, church and court coöperate, make good. They do not repeat delinquencies, they look on their former conduct as a fad they have dropped; they become rather sober-minded, critical young American citizens.[65]

45. We are confronted in this country for some time past and at present by an army of outlaws, young fellows, mostly between the ages of sixteen and twenty-six. They are the gunmen and those who commit crimes of violence, aided by pistols, which are as common in the United States as lead pencils, and the speedy motor cars as the mechanisms of prevalent crimes. The large majority of these fellows are lacking in the normal emotions of love, sympathy, kindness, gratitude, friendship and a sense of civic obligation, but on the contrary they are cruel, cowardly, heartless, selfish, ungrateful and I may add godless and dangerous, and above all they are determined that they will never do any honest, continuous work. Living in the richest country in the world, in which the sum of a million dollars is talked about as ten thousand dollars would have been some years ago, their idea is to get what they call " easy money " by criminal methods so that they may not have to work, and have it to spend on their appetites, lusts, passions and vanities, for they are immensely vain and proud of their criminal records. The money they get by stealing and robbing goes mostly to gamblers and women of their own type, and the balance

---

[65] Van Waters, Miriam (Judge of the Los Angeles Juvenile Court): *Youth in Conflict* (1925), 43–47.

is spent recklessly in a style of living to which they ordinarily would not be accustomed.[66]

46. Her attitude toward prostitution was interesting to the psychiatrist. She said she found it " very hard to get along with decent people." She likes a sporting life because then she is her own boss. She can get along better with men than with women. She does not like women. She gets angry at them, but she never gets angry at a man. She says it seems like a gift, " it comes so natural to get along with men." She explains her drinking by saying that without it she would be " too bashful! " " I am so quiet and so cold I would not charm the party I am with without booze." She has no desire to be married. " If I live with a man and am not married to him, I love him so much better." When asked what she will do when too old to prostitute, she says she will go to an old ladies' home, " you have only to pay about three hundred dollars." She would rather do that than " have an old man living aside of me when I get old." She has never cared to have any children. "They are too hard to bring into the world and they wake you up at night." [67]

The study of behavior reactions and of their control thus involves causative factors lying in two general fields — the organic peculiarities of the individual (physical, mental, emotional endowments and deficiencies) and the learning process, the acquisition of habits and attitudes. In the following chapters we shall examine the approaches and programs of investigators and agencies working on these problems.

[66] McAdoo, William: " Crime and Punishment: Causes and Mechanisms of Prevalent Crimes," *The Scientific Monthly*, 24:415 (1927).

[67] Davis, Katherine B.: " Some Institutional Problems in Dealing with Psychopathic Delinquents," *11th Annual Meeting of the American Institute of Criminal Law and Criminology, Report for 1919*, 395.

CHAPTER II
The Treatment of Delinquency

WHEN the family, the kinship group, the traditional community influences are not able to regulate the behavior of the child and it becomes necessary to resort to other agencies and " correctional " measures, it is possible to leave him in his home with a warning, under the supervision of a probation officer, place him in another home (perhaps on a farm) or in an institution of some kind. Or, after the arrest and appearance in court the child may be held in a detention home, or in a boarding home, for mental examination and observation. A " parental school," a " twenty-four-hour school," a " reformatory," or " house of correction," and finally the penitentiary, may then be the " institutions " employed.

It is well known that until the latter part of the last century the legal pattern of procedure was followed in the case of the child as in that of the adult — punishment to suit the offense, which might, even in the case of the child, be as severe as the death penalty. The Chicago movement resulting in a juvenile court was, as we shall notice later, not the first attempt to modify the treatment of the child. And in Chicago the movement for a juvenile court was not an isolated conception but was connected with the work of the Hull House Social Settlement, the participation of women in factory inspection and child labor legislation, with the consequent direction of the attention of a group of women toward the whole problem of the disadvantaged child. The particular situation arousing indignation and the demand for legislation was the practice of confining small children in the county jail where they were subject to contamination by the hardened criminals. The leading principle of this new organization was that the state should still treat the offending child as a child, that the court should assume toward him the relation of a parent, and it seemed natural that one of the first steps in a practical program would be the preparation of a clean and proper home where the delinquent child could be detained, examined, taught and corrected, among those of his own age level, and eventually restored to society. What was thought to be an ideal " detention home " was therefore established.

One of the main sources of the defeat of any plan where a situation is prepared containing good influences, and where desirable habits are for a time established, is that the child will usually be returned in the end to the same situation (bad home, bad neighborhood) from which he came, and the old influences will reinstate the old habits. This is, however, a central problem in all the programs of reform, and not particular to the juvenile court. But the conception of a juvenile detention home contained a fundamental misapprehension as to the effect of the congregation of young boys who had shown bad behavior tendencies. As adults we have a naïve way of thinking of influence as transmitted from the older generation to the younger, and we appreciate the point that it is a horrible practice to place young children with old criminals, while influences seem to spread more rapidly laterally, as between members of a younger generation, than vertically, as between members of different generations. The congregation, therefore, of bad boys in juvenile homes and reformatories has had unexpectedly bad consequences. A preadaptation to influence, a somewhat correspondent stage of maturation and of situation have to be present or the influence is not transmitted. Thus, the influence of the example of a hardened and coarse woman might be revolting to the young girl, while the wild behavior of another young girl might serve as a stimulus and example. Similarly, young boys seem to be influenced toward bad behavior more positively by the tough boys under sixteen in the detention homes than by the old criminals in the jails.

The following passages, from one of a series of important behavior documents prepared in the Illinois Institute for Juvenile Research, will illustrate the influence of " detention " in its various forms in a given case. It will be noticed that the boy becomes progressively adapted to the influence of companions of the same or slightly higher age levels in the various institutions through which he passes. (The spelling of the original is corrected):

One day after a quarrel with my stepmother I ran away. . . . I begged and stole food for four days and was picked up by a policeman. I told him I was away from home because I didn't like it there. He called the patrol wagon and took me to the station. They took me to the Detention Home.

The Detention Home at first seemed like a palace to me. It was clean and in order. The very first night I took a nice bath (the first one I ever had), had a change of clothes, and a good meal. I felt like I'd never want to go back to that " old hole " (home) with my stepmother. I went to bed in a clean white bed, and I thought, " Well, is this jail? Who ever thought it was so nice? " But alas! my childish impressions were soon to be rudely shattered.

Inside the Detention Home I found a motley crowd of aspiring young crooks — young aspirants to the " hall of fame of crookdom." In their own minds they had already achieved fame in the world of crime, and proceeded to impress that fact upon the other boys. The whole thing seemed to be a lively contest, among young crooks, to see who was the biggest and bravest crook. They loiter about the place, congregating in small groups, talking about their achievements and ambitions in their common vocation, crime. The older crooks are gods, and stand around telling about their exploits. Much of it is bunk, but they succeed in making the other boys, especially the younger ones of more tender feelings and not so wise to the world, believe it. I listened eagerly to the stories, and fell into the web myself. I was really awed by the bravery and wisdom of the older crooks. Their stories of adventures fascinated my childish imagination, and I felt drawn to them. My timid spirit (you remember I was only nine) wanted to go out and achieve some of the glories for myself.

[In the Detention Home] I remember how Pattie A. impressed my childish mind. He was [sixteen] seven years my senior, a big, husky Irish lad, and a " master bandit." He was in for stealing automobiles, burglary, and " bumming " from home and school. To him the last mentioned offenses were only a minor infraction of the law. The young guys, me included, looked up to him. He paraded among us like a king on dress parade. My feelings of pride swelled to the breaking point when he picked me out and took a liking to me. He must have pitied me, for I was little and frail and timid. I listened eagerly to his stories of how he ran away from home because of his stepfather (like myself), and how he learned to open locks and break into houses and stores, and how he used to go to the White Sox ball park to watch cars for people, and then pick out a good one and drive it away. He was a wise crook, but he had a kind and tender heart. He sympathized with me and said he " knowed why I couldn't live at home with my stepmother, and that I didn't need to, because it wouldn't be hard to make a go of it on my own hook when

I got a little wiser and knowed a little more about stealing." He said, " Fellows like us, who didn't have no home, had to steal to make a go of it." He was a good pal of mine, and I felt real sorry when he was taken to court and sentenced to St. Charles. He didn't whimper when the sentence of two years was imposed, and I respected him for his courage and grit. It made me feel shame because I cried often about my predicament, but he simply smiled and showed a determined face.

During the two months while I was in the Home I met crooks of every creed and color. They were there for every crime, running away from home, bumming from school, taking automobiles, stealing from parents, shoplifting, breaking in houses and stores, petty stealing, and sex perversions. It was a novelty to learn that there were so many crimes and ways of stealing that I had never heard about. I was green at first, and the boys pitied and petted me, but I was well on the way to crookdom at the end of my second month in that place. . . .

[In the Detention Home eleven times for running away]. The judge asked my stepmother if she wanted me back home. She refused to take me, and told the interpreter that I was incorrigible and leading her children astray, and that a few years in the reform school would do me some good. The judge accepted her suggestion and committed me to the Chicago Parental School for three months. That was on December 3, 1915, and I was nine years and two months old.

My first night at the Parental School was the first time I experienced real sorrow and homesickness. The institution was surrounded by acres of tilled soil. To a common observer it was a beautiful scene to gaze upon, but to me, a timid boy of nine years, it was something new and lonely. I had never been out of the city before, and the quiet and peaceful surroundings made me very lonesome and sad. It all seemed like a foreign town to me, and it took me several weeks to get used to it. I couldn't sleep the first night, and the first day seemed like an age. The first thing in their procedure was to clip off the hair close to the scalp. We were then given the rules of the institution, which we had to adhere to strictly. If not — punishment was the sure result.

The institution had too much discipline. I was very scared and frightened, and put into submission from the first till I was released. Physically I was a slave, but mentally I was free, and I took advantage of this freedom and dreamed. I dreamed boyish dreams of the outside world, of my home and friends in the city. Many times I would be rudely awakened from my dreams during the day, and would realize that I was in a realistic world that was full of sorrow for me. Other boys had mothers to visit them and take candy and cookies to them, but I had none, only a selfish stepmother. She visited me once and tried to kiss me, but my soul could not take the caress, even though I tried. That angered her, and she didn't come down any more. Indeed, I did not miss her, for the less I saw of her the better I felt.

During the five months' imprisonment I worked as an errand boy part-time, and went to school. Discipline was so strict throughout the institution that a boy could not even talk, and there wasn't any interesting recreation or diversion. The boys all hated the place, and guards were hard boiled, and severe punishment was inflicted for the least infraction of the rules. For each misdemeanor a boy received a mark against his conduct, and it is removed by strenuous exercise, and if you were slack you would be anointed with cowhide, and they wasn't any too gentle about laying it on. The most common kinds of punishment were muscle grinders, squats, benders, standing in corner, whipping, confinement in "the cage," chewing soap, being deprived of food and sleep, strenuous labor, and making the sentence longer. Many times I experienced these forms of torture. Being just a child without friends, I cringed in fear and developed a childish revenge against the cruel institution. Why was I in such a place, and why was I punished, just because fate was against me. I was just a mere child, too weak to strike back or defend myself. My only pleasure was in my childish dreams, which carried me away into the free world outside. I dreamed boyish dreams of my chums, our stealing and roaming in the city, of my pals at the Detention Home, especially Pattie A., whose stories of adventure I could not get out of my mind. Some day I'd be big and brave like him, and then I wouldn't worry and have fear of these cruel officials. Other boys had nice mothers and friends to bring boxes of "goodies" to them, and stood by them in this cold old world, but I had only a disgusting stepmother. I got lonely and sullen and full of fear, but my dreams kept me alive, and I dreamed every day. There I started to be a dreamer of dreams. That is one of life's cynical jokes — how I could dream such beautiful dreams in such a hole of strict discipline and drabness. So I dreamed and existed five months, and on May 8, 1916, I was paroled to live at home. . . . I left home after a quarrel the third day, and met another kid and we sallied out to forage for ourselves. . . . That night we looked for a place to sleep, and found a spacious front porch that we could hide under and sleep. During the night I was awakened by a tug at my leg. Looking up I saw my old friend, a policeman, standing there, and he bade us go with him. We were taken to the Detention Home, this being the thirteenth time I had entered its pearly gates. I was an "old timer" there at the early age of ten, and being a kid, felt it was an honor to be so well known. Besides, I was a "habitual or professional runaway" and considered a "bad actor." In the home the kids all knew I'd "done time" and sort'a looked up to me for my wide experience in the world.

After a month I was summoned to court. The policeman said, "Your honor, this is a professional runaway. He will not stay at home and will not attend school. Also, he has a record in the Parental School." Looking at me, the judge said, " Young man, what is the trouble with you? Why don't you stay at home? Don't you remember what I told you when you were here before? " I was too scared to reply. He asked the stepmother if she wanted me, and she said she did not, so the judge said, " I'll enter a St. Charles order; he'll have to stay there." I was elated. I was going out on a train ride, and it would be the first one in my life. My companion was let free because it was his first offense, and his mother cried to take him back home. I thought I was better off than him, then. But I soon got down to earth when I was entered in the St. Charles School for Boys. . . .

I was awed by the sight of the St. Charles School for Boys, for it is a beautiful landscape to gaze upon from the outside. But it is quite a different place on the inside, as I learned during fifty-six months of incarceration there. . . .

The institution is built or designed a la military style, so that strict observance of the rules was necessary or punishment was due as sure as rain. Of course I knew I was in a reform school, and expected discipline, having been in the Chicago Parental School. But this wasn't discipline by any means; it was plain tyranny, and inwardly I harbored rebellion.

For making even a little noise or even talking out loud you would get a beating. The first night I thought I could never stand it. I got so lonesome for the city and my old pals that I couldn't sleep, and cried most of the night. Everything was under pressure and forbidden.

The boys were not allowed to talk in the cottage, either at the table, in the reading room or at work. So they slipped around in their soft house-slippers, quietly and weirdly, like ghosts in a haunted house. They reminded me of dumb mutes. This everlasting quietness, without any talking from my fellow prisoners, gave me a creepy, clammy feeling and almost drove me crazy for a few weeks. . . .

In each cottage is a house father and a Captain. The father is a man and lives in the Cottage. Most of the fathers that I had were pretty good, but the Captains were terrible. They are boys and selected by the house father. Usually they are " bullies," conceited and domineering and like to " lord it over," showing their authority. They also are " squawkers," and deceitful and favor some boys and " take out " their grudge on others. In many cases they are the worst boys in the Cottage, but they " get by " because of their position and they " stand in " with the father. In our disputes between the Captain and other boys, the father will always favor the Captain, even if he is in the wrong. So there grows up under the surface a lot of revenge and hate among the boys who feel they are not getting a " fair break." . . .

The institution has too much discipline. Every time you turn around you break a rule. So you are always in fear of doing something wrong, of breaking a rule and then getting a " bawling out " or some form of punishment. I was punished many times, often for trivial things, and many times because I wouldn't squawk, and there grew up in me a hatred against these enemies; a hatred that still burns. I still remember the times that I was kicked and cuffed, and these memories shall always live with me.

The different forms of punishment were beatings, bawling out, being deprived of food and sleep, muscle grinders, squats, haunches, benders, etc. In muscle grinders the victim gets down, stretches out on his toes and hands, and then goes up and down for an hour. It soon tires one out. In squats you put your hands behind the neck, then raise and lower yourself, bending the knees. An hour of this will leave anyone exhausted. In haunches, you stand on tip toes, arms outstretched, and raise and lower the body. Ten minutes of this and you'll do anything to be relieved. In benders you touch the floor thirty-one times with tips of fingers, without bending knees. One hour of this will cure any disease. Polishing the floor for hours while you are resting the weight of the body on the tips of the toes is another form of punishment. All of these are often accompanied with clouts and general razzing.

The strict discipline, hard punishment, no recreation, fear, and " unfair breaks " made life miserable. Besides, life was monotonous. While I yearned for freedom, I never received a letter of consolation or a visit from a friend or relative to brighten me. I became lonely, alone, never liked to be near people. Life held not a single charm for me. I learned to read books and to dream, and these took me out of my miserable surroundings into a new world full of novelty. I read all of Alger's books, some of them many times, and other books of adventure, and dreamed of becoming a success in the business world, like Alger's heroes. I wanted a chance to make good, for I had the ambition, but who would monkey with a little mite like me? I was cast by the wayside and forgotten, kept in St. Charles because that was the easiest way to get rid of me. After years of incarceration (five in all in St. Charles) I lost my ambition and became indolent, carefree and " drifty." I whiled and dreamed my life away without any concern for the future. My only interest was to get along any easy way, and the easiest way I knew was to beg and steal. . . .

There was lots of sex perversions in the form of masturbation and sodomy committed in Cottage " D." The bullies would attack the younger boys in the dormitories and force them to have relations. Some of the boys caught venereal diseases and had to be treated. That was very easy in a place like that, where there were a lot of boys living together in close quarters. Especially where the older boys mingle with the younger ones. The younger ones get all the bad habits of the older boys, and sex habits are very common in every institution where boys or men are confined. I've seen lots of it. I protected many little boys at St. Charles from older bullies, but that was only a drop in the bucket. I knew little boys who had sex relations with four or five older boys every night. It was easy in the dormitory to slip into another boy's bunk. They separate the boys by their weight, and that puts young fellows in with the old-timers, who are little, but well educated in crime. The old timer stands as a hero and impresses his superiority on the younger boys who are always ready to admire a brave crook. As a child in St. Charles I looked up to the fellows who had done deeds of daring in a criminal line. I wanted to go out and do something worthy of commendation too. While in Cottage " D " I met young crooks and old crooks, and began to think I was a pretty wise crook and began to tell lies about my exploits, to make a good impression on my fellow prisoners. . . .

[Paroled. Returned to St. Charles after twenty-four days. Paroled to a farmer, treated well, but bored and ran away. Sent to Holy Cross Mission. Protected by a prostitute. Returned to St. Charles]. The day of my parole came around eventually, and, dressed up in a suit the stepmother sent to me, I sallied out to seek my fortune, so to speak. With eight dollars in my pocket, which I had coming from the school, I thought I had a fair start, compared with some of Horatio Alger's heroes, whose stories of adventure I had read every one and was surely thrilled with every page, too. By this time I had a confident feeling that I could steal and make a success at it. I knew dozens of other boys who were making a go of it, and felt sure that I could do it also. Also, I made up my mind that I wouldn't take any more insults from anybody — I'd stand my ground against the world. I might die doing it, but I wouldn't die a coward. . . .

[Joined three other boys who had been in St. Charles]. These lads had been " jack-rolling " bums on West Madison street, and burglarizing homes on the North Side of the city. . . . We formed " The United Quartet Corporation " and started to " strong arm live ones " (drunks with money) and to burglarize homes.

My fellow workers were fast guys and good pals. We were like brothers and would stick by each other through thick and thin. We cheered each other in our troubles and loaned each other " dough." A mutual understanding developed, and nothing could break our confidence in each other. " Patsy " was a short, sawed-off Irish lad — big, strong, and heavy. He had served two terms in St. Charles. " Maloney " was another Irish lad, big and strong, with a sunny disposition and a happy outlook on life. He had done one term in St. Charles, and had already been in the County Jail. Tony was an Italian lad, fine looking and daring. He had been arrested several times, served one term in St.

Charles, and was now away from home because of a hardboiled stepfather. We might have been young, but we sure did " pull-off " our game in a slick way. So we plied our trade with a howling success for two months. . . .

[Wore the pants taken from the victim of one of these robberies and was identified by them]. My trial came up in the Boys' Court in front of Judge Charles McKinley. He refused to try me because I was so little, and referred me to the Juvenile Court. But they referred me back to the Boys' Court and said I was a nuisance and a hopeless case and a bad criminal type. I was glad to be referred back to the Boys' Court because I thought if I was to go back to " the bandhouse " I'd rather have some new scenery.

I went before Judge McKinley again [who] . . . then uttered the condemning words which branded me as a convict. My " rap " was one year in the Illinois State Reformatory and a fine of one dollar. . . .

I was handcuffed to another prisoner, thrown in line with a lot of other prisoners and under heavy guard led out to the patrol wagon — amid the stares of curious spectators along the street. Then to the County Jail. Speaking in plain words, it's the dirtiest hovel in Cook County — barring the Bridewell.

On entering the jail we were searched for articles not allowed there, took a bath and were assigned to a cell. On entering my cell I was greeted by two prisoners who were to be my cell buddies. Stanley was a first offender, charged with being a " holdup " man. " Bill," the other buddie, was an old offender, going through the machinery of becoming a habitual criminal, in and out of jail. Stanley was seventeen, and Bill was twenty-one. The first thing they asked me was, " What are you in for? " I said, " Jackrolling." The hardened one (Bill) looked at me with a superior air and said, " A hoodlum, eh? An ordinary sneak thief. Not willin' to leave ' jackrollin'' to the niggers, eh? That's all they're good for. Kid, ' jackrollin'' 's not a white man's job." I could see that he was disgusted with me, and I was too scared to say anything. He was a braggart, and conceited and hardboiled, and related his experience in the Bridewell and Pontiac. He described himself as a hero, and I believed him and was impressed and found myself putting on airs. Stanley, the other cell buddie, was timid and quiet, not hardened yet. He worried and complained against everything. Circumstance had simply pulled him down into the mire, and here he was struggling — a pitiful sight to behold. He was weak and cried, and was given the " razz " by Bill.

I stayed in the jail a week and enjoyed myself with Bill. I let Bill run over me and show his superiority, and then he didn't " razz " me like he did Stanley, " the kid," as Bill called him. Bill, being an " old timer " and a notorious character, was prominent in our block, so I thought I was traveling in fast society. I and he played cards together in our cell, and I listened to his startling stories of exploits. He showed me the plans for stealing he had worked out while in jail, and was going to use as soon as he'd get out again. He was a " wise head " and well educated in the criminal line.

Finally one morning I was awakened early and loaded into a patrol wagon with seven other prisoners, and conveyed to the Chicago and Alton Railway Station. We were on our way to Pontiac. At the station the people stared at us, and I felt ashamed of myself for the first time in ages. . . .

We reached Pontiac and were herded into a waiting truck like so much livestock going to the market. As we turned into a main street the front of the institution glared out before me, and on its top floated an American flag, as if to give an air of respectability to the sordid hole. . . .

I found Pontiac to be a very clean and sanitary prison compared to the County Jail. . . . We lounged around for fifteen days without working. During that time I learned all about the place from the older criminals, getting onto the " ropes " and learning what was proper and what was improper, and how to get by. . . . At the end of the fifteen days we were assigned to work. I was asked what kind of work I was best fitted for; I said that I was an experienced laundryman, having worked in the laundry at St. Charles. I passed the test for school work, and the school board decided that I had enough education, so I was assigned to work in the laundry, running a machine in the work room. . . .

The prisoner in charge of the mangle that I worked on was " Billie," a hardened criminal from Canaryville in Chicago. He was eight years my senior, and was in on a five to life sentence as a burglar and " stick-up " man. (He was since killed in Chicago in an encounter with the police). " Billie " took a great liking to me, mostly out of pity, and gave me instructions on how to " get on " in Pontiac, and how to " get by " with the police outside. He indelibly impressed two things upon my mind. First, never to trust anybody with your affairs in crime. You never know when a partner will " rat " you if he gets into a close pinch and finds it an advantage to " sell his soul " to the police. " Billie " would ask me questions about my " rap " and my past experiences, but he would not talk about himself. He was old and experienced, and was different from most of the " glib-tongued " young crooks that I had known in St. Charles. There everybody wanted to impress you with their exploits; out here things were different. The older crooks were confident and set in their ways, " more at home " with crime, and had gotten over the glib-tongue stage of callow youth. I studied " Billie " every day and saw how different he was from the youthful crooks that I had known before. I finally learned that most of the older crooks there were like " Billie," hardfaced, and with self assurance and took crime as a matter of business. Well did I know that " Billie " could tell me many deeds of daring in a criminal line, but he was too clever a crook to talk about his exploits to other persons, especially to a young crook like me. From the few stories he told me about himself I knew he was a criminal of rare cunning and ability. He was a fine example of young manhood — tall, agile, brave, keen, and full of nerve. I could vision him " sticking-up " a man without flinching. I could see him in the midst of a robbery, with the police closing in on him, and with his pals frantic and unnerved, yet " Billie " would be cool and self-possessed. In fact, I thought he could face death without a quiver or qualm. I longed for some thrilling stories from his past experience, but confessions never passed between his steel jaws, and I came to respect and admire him for it. After all, he was a real crook and somewhat of a novelty to me, until I got used to him.

Second, " Billie " chided me for petty stealing. His idea was to " do a big job or none at all." Of course, he considered that I was just a kid and wasn't old enough to " do a job " like him. He figured that the dangers and penalty were about the same whether you did a little job or big one, so you might just as well choose the best. Besides, he said that there was some satisfaction in doing a real man's job, and that it was easier to pay the penalty for a " big haul." That sounded reasonable to me, so I thought if I ever pulled another job it would be a big one or none. . . .

At work or at play out in the yard, the prisoners would form into small groups and talk about the " outside." The " outside " that was so near, just over the wall, and yet so far away in time. They would talk about what they were going to do on release. Most of them planned vengeance and crime. They would pull off a big deal and then retire in luxury. Even while in prison, which they hated, they did not think about being arrested again. Consequences didn't concern them much. They thought only of getting-by, and they were too egotistical to think that they would ever get caught again. It was only a " bum rap " that landed them in jail this time, and they would know better next time, so they thought. A few would talk about home and mother and " going straight," but these were the younger crooks, and they usually got the " razz " from the older ones. The ones with tender feelings didn't chirp much when the hard guys were in the group, and they usually were there. . . .

So I listened with open ears to what was said in these groups of prisoners. Often I stood awe-struck as tales of adventure in crime were related, and I took it in with interest. Somehow I wanted to go out and do the same thing myself. To myself I thought I was " somebody " to be doing a year in Pontiac, but in these groups of older prisoners I felt ashamed because I couldn't tell tales of daring exploits about my crimes. . . . So I kept quiet, happy enough to listen to the thrilling stories of adventure. " Mikie " O'Brien was " one-big-hero " in the place. He had done a lot of time and was in for

" big stuff," and besides, everybody had read about his brother, Smiling Jack O'Brien, being hung for " picking off a copper." He was certainly looked up to for that. I admired him. I used to watch him all the time in the yard and in the mess hall. I couldn't help it. Something about him caught my eye every time I got close to him. That wasn't only true in my case, but for everybody it was true, especially the younger crooks.

[Released from the Chicago Bridewell, or Home of Correction, which he calls the " House of Corruption," August 23, 1925, at the age of seventeen, the boy is preparing this narrative, which will later be printed].[1]

When the movements of the new-born child are hampered (as Watson has shown clearly in his experiments) there is a reaction of anger and resistance. When the young person is deprived of liberty and incarcerated the situation assumes the form of a fight. It is evident that a fight is not a socializing procedure, not favorable to the transmission of good influence. Furthermore, in order to carry on this fight it is necessary to have a prison personnel, guards and wardens who are able to take the situation as a fight. The attendants will therefore tend to be or become hardened persons. There is even a considerable unconscious recruiting of sadists for these positions in the prisons. Upon this point some of the criminologists have the most positive views, claiming that the institution can never be a suitable place for the reform of behavior:

Now, I would not do what Judge Cabot does — happily, rarely. I would not send a child to the ideal institution to which he commits the children, for the ideal institution does not exist except in his mind; and he commits the child really to the actual institution, which is not ideal. But the point of view which I am coming to is, that if we could have an ideal institution, it would still be a rotten place to send a growing child to.

Let us look at what the ideal institution could hope to do. It would cease the practice, which is almost universal, of demoralizing and brutalizing the children through the vicious character of those who are administering the institution and of the attendants. Even people of common intelligence and feeling are rare in those institutions. We are not going to get people of the type that is needed. But let me assume that we will get them, people of sensibility and intelligence and tenderness and wisdom, backed by the resources of science, which they have sense enough to utilize. I find it hard to assume it, and go on from that point, but I am going to assume it — what

---

[1] Life-Record, secured by Clifford W. Shaw (Illinois Institute for Juvenile Research). Manuscript. To appear as a volume, *The Delinquent Boy's Own Story*. (University of Chicago Press).

will we have then? Why, we will have an institution in which nobody, from the superintendent down to the " kid " last admitted, will be leading a normal life that bears a slightest resemblance to the life that we are going to expose him to after we let him out.[2]

From these items it might appear that the institution is something we ought to get away from as completely as possible. On the other hand, it is not certain that the institution is not capable of becoming the best device for the treatment of misbehavior. There is always a discrepancy between the institution and the ideas and sentiments of society; social structure changes more slowly than social feeling. This is the so-called " cultural lag " which Ogburn has so well described.[3] Bailey has given us an outline of the evolution of legal institutions as they relate to the child down to the beginning of the present century. In comparison with these historical situations even the institutions to which we have just referred seem very advanced:

In December, 1642, the [Connecticut] court laid down several " capital laws," which in 1650 were compiled into a code. This code was revised in 1672 and printed in the next year. The revision contained the two following provisions from the original code:

" If any Child or Children above sixteen years old, and of sufficient under-standing, shall Curse or Smite their natural Father or Mother, he or they shall be put to death, unless it can be sufficiently testified, that the Parents have been very unchristianly negligent in the education of such Children, or so provoked them by extreme and cruel correction that they have been forced thereunto to preserve themselves from death or maiming." (*Exod.* 21:17; *Levit.* 20:9; *Exod.* 21:15).

" If any man have a stubborn or rebellious Son of sufficient understanding and years, *viz. 16 years of age,* which will not obey the voice of his Father, or the voice of Mother, and that when they have chastened him he will not hearken unto them; then may his Father or Mother, being his natural Parents, lay hold on him and bring him to the magistrates assembled in court, and testify unto them, that their Son is Stubborn and Rebellious and will not obey their voice and chastisement, but lives in sundry notorious Crimes, such Son shall be put to death." (*Deut.* 21:20–21).

It was further provided in this same section that a girl over 14 convicted of incest or a boy over 15 found guilty of sodomy should be put to death.

[2] Kirchwey, George W.: " Institutions for Juvenile Delinquents," *The Child, the Clinic and the Court* (1925), 334–35.

[3] Ogburn, William: *Social Change* (1922).

Other capital crimes for which children over 14 years old were equally liable with adults were rape, bestiality, blasphemy, witchcraft, murder, false witness, treason, arson, idolatry, and man stealing. It must be remembered that these laws were not passed to meet possible exigencies, but that the penalties were actually enforced.

By the time of the compilation of the session laws in 1750 the rigors of these " Blue Laws " had somewhat abated. While the death penalty was still preserved against minors who committed felonies for which adults were also punishable by death, it had been abolished against " children who shall curse or smite their natural father or mother " and " stubborn and rebellious children." Penalties for other crimes were also mitigated. For instance, in 1672 the punishment for an incestuous marriage or cohabitation within certain limits was death, while in 1750 the penalties inflicted on both parties were: (1) That they stand on the gallows with a halter about the neck for one hour; (2) that " on the way thence to the county jail they shall be severely whipped, not exceeding 40 stripes each; " (3) that they suffer imprisonment; and (4) wear the letter I — of different color from their clothing and at least 2 inches long — on the arm or back of their outside coats. . . .

The Connecticut Legislature of 1816 was evidently in an iconoclastic frame of mind. The venerated idols of the penal system of " the good old days " were ruthlessly shattered. The stocks, the pillory, and the branding iron were relegated to the museum of penological atrocities. For instance, the crime of blasphemy was, under the code of 1672, punishable by death. The Revised Statutes of 1808 had reduced the penalty to " whipping on the naked body, not exceeding forty stripes, and sitting in the pillory one hour; " but the statute of 1816 swept away these time-honored methods of correction, and in their stead decreed that the blasphemer should be punished by " a fine not exceeding one hundred dollars, and by imprisonment, in a common gaol, for a term not exceeding one year." In the same way, the penalty for adultery in 1650 was death; this punishment was commuted to flogging, branding with the letter A on the forehead, and wearing a halter around the neck, in the revision of 1672; but the legislature of 1816 abolished these barbarous penalties and instituted instead punishment by imprisonment — for a man, in Newgate; for a woman, in a common jail — not more than five nor less than two years.

Something was also done for those already behind the bars. The act making mandatory upon masters and overseers of jails the provision of fuel and bedding for prisoners awakens us to a partial realization of what their lot must previously have been. Prior to the act of 1816 the juvenile prisoner slept on the bare ground of the prison floor, or at best in a hard board bunk, unless he were fortunate enough to have parents able to provide him with blankets.

Up to that time no prison had any provision for heating during the cold of winter, or for ventilation during the heat of summer. What wonder that men, as well as boys, often died of " malignant diseases " before even a short prison term could be served! . . .

The new era in the treatment of juvenile offenders in Connecticut was inaugurated by the State Reform School act of 1851:

" There shall be established, on land conveyed to this State for that purpose, a school for the instruction, employment, and reformation of juvenile offenders, to be called the ' State Reform School.' " . . .

Those who might be committed to this school were:

" Any boy under the age of sixteen years . . . convicted of any offense known to the laws of this State, and punishable by imprisonment, other than such as may be punishable by imprisonment for life. . . . And such sentence shall be in the alternative, to the State Reform School or to such punishment as would have been awarded if this act had not been passed." . . .

Until 1901 any boy under 16 years of age who could distinguish right from wrong was subject to commitment to this reform school. It was then provided that —

" No boy under 10 years of age shall hereafter be committed to the Connecticut School for Boys except upon conviction of an offense for which the punishment is imprisonment in the State Prison."

In 1902 the rule was made absolute that no boy under 16 should be committed to any jail, almshouse, workhouse, or State prison, except for an offense penalized by life imprisonment. Minor alterations in the provisions for this institution will not be enumerated here, since they are easily accessible in current statutes.[4]

In the present century, and since the establishment of the juvenile court, the conception of institutions as a means of improving the offender has had a rapid development. It would be possible to enumerate barbarities in certain reformatories as shocking as those of past centuries, but certain of them have progressed in their methods as rapidly as the best schools; they have manual training, the project method, organized sports, dramatic performances, etc. It has been found easier, in fact, to give a modern type of organization to a reformatory than to a public school. The superintendent has very pressing and critical problems to meet, and may assume a wide latitude in the formation of policy. Dr. Miriam van Waters, Referee of the Los Angeles Juvenile

---

[4] Bailey, William B.: "Children Before the Courts in Connecticut," *United States Department of Labor, Children's Bureau,* Publication No. 43:10–24 (1918).

Court, has made a study of thirty reformatories and training schools for girl delinquents, and the following extracts from her report reveal the rapid evolution of the institution of this type. At the same time her report reveals a very unequal rate of evolution of the various institutions:

In the institutions visited the average girl population was approximately 160. At the time of the survey there were about 4,900 girls and young women enrolled. The average age of girls in the state training schools was fifteen years. Those in the reformatories were all over sixteen. . . .

It is significant that the best institutions are sometimes found lodged in buildings designed for another purpose. Samarcand Manor, housed in the pines of North Carolina, was four years ago a fashionable experimental private school for boys. . . . El Retiro, the school for girls of Los Angeles County, was built originally as a sanitarium for rich convalescing tuberculous patients, and, hidden in an olive grove near the mountains, gives physical expression to the idea of adjustment, and of the restoration of the girl to confidence in normal life. . . .

The daily program for these 4,900 girls varies enormously. In one school at 5.30 A.M. a bell tolls, three hundred girls start to work scrubbing, or report to laundry, dairy and bakery. At 6.30 a breakfast is eaten in silence, while a matron stands on watch. At 7.00 some classes of instruction start, the teachers being matrons who have been on duty the night before. Work hours go on from 8.00 to 12.00 and 1.00 to 5.00 P.M. with no recess except dinner. There is no talking among the girls. After supper the girls are locked in their rooms. Occasionally there is an evening entertainment. Three times a year details are changed; that is to say a girl who has been working in the kitchen now goes to the laundry or sewing room. Chapel services and an occasional riot are the only breaks in the monotony.

In the majority of schools and reformatories the program is a wholesome interchange of work, study, play and expression. In the best schools the daily life is a model for young people anywhere. The daily shower bath; wholesome, joyous exercise; assignment to brief, useful tasks, performed under ideal conditions of light, sanitation and skilled supervision; the stimulating small class groups for study; merry conversations at meal time with good food, well cooked and beautifully served; hours of spontaneous free play, hours of restful sleep, frequent change in program, stimulating surprises, plenty of noise, books, pictures, music, pets and company — all these aids to life are provided in our best correctional schools.

"A minimum of scrubbing and a maximum of schooling," is the theory I go on, said one superintendent. I had heard of her before I reached her institution from a superintendent who disapproved; "She is trying to let these girls be natural and normal, and give them a high school education. You can't treat them that way." However, she was wrong; the trend is all in favor of "treating them that way." . . .

Dr. Carrie Weaver Smith of the Texas State School at Gainesville has probably gone further than anyone else in stressing the school side of the program. Nothing is allowed to interfere with education. If the work of the school cannot be made educational, then the girls should not do it; let the work be "hired out" is the idea apparently. So in this school men are hired to do the farm work and a large part of the laundry work while the girls engage in a scientifically balanced diet of study, work and play. . . .

The school department of Sleighton Farms has a splendid building and a highly trained staff. If a girl is taken out of school for work, the fact is listed on a card entitled: "School sacrifice," recorded against the record, not of the girl, but of the cottage matron. In addition to the regular academic work there are study clubs for nature-study, local geography, astronomy, bird and animal life and so forth. Record is kept of original observations by the students and incentives given. . . .

The school at Sauk Center is a vast community building, erected largely by the labor of the girls. There is a central auditorium with a fireplace and low book-shelves along the walls, covered with maps, pictures and specimens. The small schoolrooms open into the main room.

Chosen girls from certain of the institutions visited attend the local schools in the community. Idaho and Utah have started the experiment of placing the entire management of the state schools under the state board of education. Results of this experiment are awaited with interest. . . . Many experts believe that the goal of academic education in correctional schools should be chiefly stimulation and correct diagnosis. According to this view as soon as a girl has been correctly placed in school and has been awakened to the thousand interests of education she is ready to be placed under supervision in the regular schools of the community. . . .

Sleighton Farms is credited with originating the idea of carrying out self-government in correctional institutions for girls. The plan is modelled on a commission form of government. They have a limited responsibility for the conduct of affairs within the institution and fix certain minor disciplinary penalties for the infraction of rules. The plan works and there is little disorder. . . . Perhaps the most conspicuous example of genuine student government is found at Clinton Farms. Here each department has a commissioner with definite responsibility — the complex work of this farm, the high class dairy, bakery, maternity hospital, machine shops, stock raising and agriculture, being managed very largely by the girls and women committed. . . . Other institutions which practise some form of student government are: the State School of New Jersey, at Trenton, Sauk Center, Clinton Farms, the Connecticut State School, the National Training School, Washington, D. C., the State School of North Carolina, Samarcand, the Virginia State School for Colored Girls and El Retiro. . . .

Fannie Morse of Sauk Center, Minnesota, runs a farm of nearly two thousand acres, scattered over ten miles of the community. Girl teamsters, farmers, plumbers, carpenters, painters, electricians and landscape gardeners go all over these acres, busily productive. " Is this vocational? What can this sort of thing possibly profit a *girl?* " Mrs. Morse smiles. The typewritten records of her paroled girls speak for themselves: two of the girl plumbers work in hardware stores in the city, others teach in technical schools or agricultural colleges, scores of farms dotted all over the vast Minnesota fields show modern machinery, silos, model dairies, stock farms and truck gardening. And they are presided over by a new kind of farmer's wife, the girl graduate of Sauk Center. It is life like this that keeps a girl from the streets, stretches her imagination and enlarges her powers. There are failures, of course — life itself fails sometimes. . . .

Does this sort of thing coarsen the girls? A woman thought it did and said so within the hearing of a group of girl teamsters. They decided to give a party and a fashion show. Because they had money from their farm work they could afford even the extravagance of long white gloves. They designed and made their dresses themselves of dainty material. Then they invited the townspeople of Sauk Center and posed in front of the superintendent's blue velvet curtains in order to show the beauty of their gowns — a typical reaction to the Main Street community. . . .

No one who has not seen it can believe how complete is the miracle wrought by freeing the energies of the girl delinquent into the channels of creative work. Eve had spent seven years in state institutions. For several months she was in a school for the feeble-minded and was often confined in a straight-jacket. By merely rolling her eyes she could strike terror into the hearts of matrons. A new superintendent came to the state school. Eve is now in a city telegraph office in charge of an important division. The mystery? String beans. The new superintendent found the girl getting ready for a tantrum. She led her to the cellar where hundreds of rows of monotonous canned string beans were waiting the winter, and said, " Eve, I am dissatisfied with these vegetables; they are so ordinary, so poorly done; almost any canning factory could do as well," and the superintendent sketched her view of a state school as a vast center full of new industrial ideas and even beauty. Eve warmed to the project. Under her leadership glass jars replaced the cans, strips of red peppers alternated with the jade and ivory colors of the vegetables; there is undoubtedly poetry in vegetables and Eve realized it.

Helen, aged fifteen, had run away from three institutions, had bobbed her hair, wore boy's clothes, smoked, drank and beat her way on freight cars. She had an irresistible sense of the comic and she had gifted hands. In the Kansas State School she was set to making original dolls. She made them of cloth, of wood, and of paper. Their faces resembled those of the people she had met; porters, policemen, waiters, tramps, Japs, jugglers and matrons. She made rabbit dolls with human faces. Gradually as she sat day after day in her discipline room, for her language made segregation necessary, her dolls began to have a commercial value. She "found herself" and later when she was put in charge of a kitchen department her only gesture of independence was to hang a sign, which I am glad to state remained unmolested:

"NO SLANG HERE: BY HECK." [5]

The El Retiro school for girls mentioned in the report of Dr. van Waters, was, in fact, organized by Dr. van Waters and her associates, and has been very successful in adjusting girls through the formation of projects suitable to them:

The El Retiro school for girls uses the Juvenile Detention Home as a clearing house and holds a conference before admission. After prolonged observation, physician, psychologist, referee of the court, probation officer, superintendent, principal of the school, field worker and the recreation director meet and pool the results of their study. A program of treatment is then made for the girl before entrance, a tentative diagnosis and the probable outlook stated. A few weeks afterward a second conference is held at which the girl attends with a girl chosen from the student body to represent student body opinion (a mine of information hardly as yet touched by the social worker) and at this conference a definite project is reached. The new girl embarks upon an undertaking. The project may be defined as a student body activity undertaken by the girl during her life in the institution, a tangible something for which she is responsible, and in doing which she receives satisfaction and recognition.[6]

After residence at the El Retiro school [7] the girl is transferred, if this seems desirable, to the Girls' Business Club in Los Angeles:

---

[5] Van Waters, Miriam: "Where Girls Go Right," *The Survey*, 48:361-76, *passim* (May 27, 1922).

[6] *Ibid.*

[7] The El Retiro school is now reported as discontinued, owing to local politics.

The Los Angeles Business Girls' Club came into existence July fourth, 1921. At that time the need for an organization which could help girls handicapped by broken homes and other untoward circumstances to obtain a successful independent foothold in the community was increasingly pressing. Agencies well adapted to handle the initial stages of social recovery from the effects of severely disturbing conditions were at hand, but no means were available for effecting the final steps in the return of the girls to normal community life. . . . [The Club was organized and in 1923 was taken under the auspices of] the Los Angeles Business and Professional Women's Club. . . . Through the generosity of the club women and the subsequently available aid of the Community Chest, the girls now have a splendidly planned, large and viewy club house, with attractive parlors, cozy sleeping quarters, basement work-rooms and studios where they may carry on a wide variety of operations, from batik to dramatics.

The Club receives only girls who have no home resources and whose industrial status is that of the minimum wage earner or apprentice. It is non-sectarian. Girls come to the club through their own volition or from [various local agencies]. . . .

The number in residence is from sixteen to twenty. The club is self-governing; the girls hold regular weekly meetings in which they discuss club matters. The staff consists in an executive secretary, an assistant, a field secretary and a housekeeper.

Since the club opened, over two hundred and thirty girls have been in residence. Except for one girl received for emergency care, all have been under twenty-one years of age. . . .

Girls who prove to possess the qualifications for club life and industrial progress remain at the Club until they are wholly self-supporting and have formed habits of punctuality, industry, trustworthiness, and desirable companionship. They are then urged to leave so as to make room for those more ignorant and lacking in skill. The following indicates the activities of the girls subsequent to their club life: marriage, 20%; return to home, 25%; placement in private homes, 11%; other social agencies, 4%; at work in community under friendly supervision, 38%.

The Club aims to keep in touch with the careers of its girls, and by means of friendly supervision to aid them with their later problems. And, as the above indicates, the goal of a successful permanent community adjustment appears to have been reached in the cases of a substantial majority of the members.[8]

[8] Fisher, S. C.: "The Los Angeles Business Girls' Club," *Journal of Delinquency,* 9:238-41 (1925).

The Berkshire Industrial Farm, under the direction of Mr. Andrew G. Johnson, may be taken as representative of the best type of institution developed for delinquent boys in America. It is an old and privately supported institution and gives the impression of a boarding school rather than an institution for delinquents. There is a large farm, the physical surroundings are fine, including about two miles of waterfront, and there are opportunities for all kinds of winter and summer sports.

Beginning with boys from New York and the New England states, the Farm received in 1926 problem boys from fifteen states, sent largely by the bureaus of child guidance and city and county judges. There is, however, a definite and practical policy of selection. The routine work on the Farm is rather strenuous and the boys selected tend to be " normal," husky physical specimens. The other bases of selection are that the boys shall have an intelligence above " borderline," that they shall be white, between the ages of twelve and fifteen when admitted, and that the school shall become their legal guardian. There is also a strong selection of boys who are " promising." The school emphasizes good habit training, and the type of boy most often referred is the environmentally handicapped, the child who has been brought up in very poor surroundings, where the delinquency seems to have arisen directly from the home or neighborhood conditions. The Farm may thus be looked upon as somewhat the equivalent of the foster home. When the removal of the child from his environment becomes necessary he may be sent to a foster home or to an institution of this kind. The advantage of the Farm over the ordinary foster home is that the boy is given a much wider range of possibilities in discovering and using his abilities and is subject to the rather healthy competition of boys of his own age. There is a strong group morale and the enforcing of a certain sort of conformity by the group itself.

Many of the boys who come to the Farm seem to make an adjustment very simply. They enjoy the outdoor life and physical activities and find through them an outlet for their energy and desire for adventure. A good many of these give no trouble whatsoever, and when they leave the Farm are given jobs that approximate the conditions on the Farm as nearly as possible. There is a very good agricultural and horticultural department at the School, so that they are really skilled in these lines by the time they leave the Farm.

There is a resident psychologist at the Farm who gives the boys a variety of aptitude tests, and is in close touch with them to give vocational advice and bring about adjustments of that sort. Those few boys who tend towards the " intellectual " are given opportunity to attend a near-by high school, and efforts are made to get scholarships for them in other preparatory schools or in colleges when they leave the Farm. Seven of the 130 boys are now in high school. But most of the boys are not fitted for higher education and are taught trades. There is excellent trade training provided in auto-mechanics, house-building, agriculture, horticulture, printing and plumbing. No boy leaves the Farm until a job is actually found for him, and if he is unhappy or unfitted for the first job efforts are continued to find a more suitable one. This follow-up work is undoubtedly one of the reasons for the large percentage of successes. There is a psychiatric department, with a visiting psychiatrist and a resident psychiatric social worker. Although most of the boys adjust well to the group situation, there are some who are unable to adjust to it and are made very unhappy by the conformity which the group requires. It is with these that the psychiatric department has its greatest problems.

The general atmosphere of the place is happy. The boys are noisy and dirty and happy during most of the day. There are certain crudities and repressions which are, however, the things one associates with the traditional " good home." For instance, the matrons make the boys take off their shoes before they come into the cottages, lest they get the floors dirty. In the evenings the boys wash up and go to chapel. They seem to enjoy singing the hymns, and probably the long prayers and moralistic sermons are not a very serious burden. Until the arrival of Dr. Jewett, the psychiatrist, corporal punishment was inflicted in public, after chapel, and any boy who wanted to add a blow to the culprit was allowed to do so.

There are a good many runaways. It was estimated that there was probably one almost every week. There is no patrolling, and no attempt to bring the boy back forcibly if he runs away. They say that about three-fourths of these runaway boys go a very short distance and then telephone saying they want to come back. If they do not show up within a few days the police are notified, since the Farm is responsible for the boys. The first time a boy runs away he is not punished, but is punished after the second offense. Sometimes the running away does not mean that the boy wants to leave the Farm at all — he merely wants a little extra adventure. One boy, who had been gone three days, was found in a coal bin in one of the cellars. He had connected an electric light by arranging a complicated outside wiring, had stolen books from the various office rooms, food from the kitchen, and a blanket, and was having a three days' orgy of reading.

The whole policy of the Farm is, however, to provide as many legitimate outlets for adventure as possible — competitive football teams, camping, hiking, fishing, life-saving, etc.

It is stated by the authorities that there is 83% of success, but this statement evidently contains an error. What was done was to add up the boys who had left during the past five years and get the relation of the total successes during these five years to this total. Now the very close follow-up for the first year or so precludes the chance of much failure or delinquency. It is admitted that there is much more delinquency among boys who have been out five years than among those who have been out only a few months or a year. So this 83% is too high, as it lumps together the high percentages of successes of those who have been out a short time with the lower percentages of those who have been out a long time. It is undoubtedly true, however, that they do have a large percentage of successes, which would indeed be expected when one considers the whole basis of their selection.

The Children's Village at Dobbs Ferry, New York (Managing Director, Mr. Leon Faulkner), is another semi-private institution receiving delinquent and problem children from the courts or their parents. The Village comprises some thirty cottages and about four hundred acres of land. There is no farming but there is a large truck garden and much work to be done on the grounds. The life is largely out of doors. The children play football, baseball, etc., and have games with outside teams.

Originally all children were accepted whom the courts chose to send. But it was found very difficult to carry out programs with such a heterogeneous group as resulted. During the last two years there has been a selection. Negroes are no longer accepted, nor the definitely feebleminded, nor children from families where it is thought an adjustment can be made outside an institution. All the children are serious problems in one way or another. There are only about thirty girls, this

(1927) being the first year girls have been admitted. None of the girls is a serious sex problem; sex offenders, as we understand it, are not accepted unless the offense has been of a rather incidental sort, growing out of bad environmental conditions, etc. Some children are accepted who have not actually been delinquent but who are in danger of becoming delinquent, the so-called " pre-delinquents." The children range in age from seven to seventeen years.

There is much about the Village of the regular orthodox institution. There are no walls or uniforms, but very restricted freedom of movement. There is " detail " four times a day. The children are not allowed to go around without guards or monitors, except in the case of certain honor boys for certain specific purposes.

The most unfortunate aspect seems to be the " grading " system. The regular period of commitment is two years (there are a few short time cases taken for examination and remand to the judges) but in order to get out the boy must pass through certain conduct grades, and this passing depends on freedom from a certain number of demerits. Demerits may be given by any of the staff, the house-parents, etc. With good behavior and absence of demerits the term may be shortened by a few months. Similarly, an excess of demerits lengthens the term of commitment. Not only is this psychologically a bad system, through carrying a completely negative suggestion, but it makes the school a place in which " time " is served, puts a premium on being good merely in order to get out.

An exceptionally good aspect is the system of classification. When a boy enters the first few days or weeks are given up to getting adjusted, having a psychological, psychiatric, medical, educational examination, etc. Then, after each of the staff concerned has made a separate estimate of the child, the child is seen by the staff, given a sort of informal group interview, and then the staff on the basis of all the individual tests given, and this group interview, comes to a decision as to the classification of this boy, what groups he shall be placed with, etc. If things work smoothly he is let pretty much alone but seen again at the beginning of the next term, results checked up, and changes made if necessary. If there is trouble and he does not adjust to the arrangement made, the staff has another meeting, considers all the facts and tries some other adjustment. This empirical placing in the groups seems to bring very good results.

The school work seems to be up to the standard of an ordinary good public school, and fulfils Regents' requirements. Some of the boys attend the public high schools, as their full academic work at the Village does not extend beyond the grades. In the psychological examinations at entrance a variety of tests is given, to select out those not only of the predominately verbalist type but also those showing marked special abilities in any line, the perceptual-motor type, etc., and all this is used as a basis for classification. The older boys all take pre-vocational work in addition to academic work. This pre-vocational work, preparing printers, electricians, plumbers, carpenters, etc., is rather limited in scope. In addition there is a manual class for the younger children who are markedly of the non-verbal type, those having quite low intelligence quotients but who are not feebleminded in any other sense. Here the whole idea is individualization. An extraordinary variety of work is offered, and many things are tried out by each child until something in which his interest can be enlisted and for which he has an ability is found. Then, with these children, there is a real correlation of the academic work with this manual preoccupation, with, it is claimed, very marked success. Certainly the æsthetic qualities of many of the things done are of a high order, and the children seemed alert and happy.

The training school (Superintendent, at the time of our visit, Mr. Calvin Derrick) is an important feature of the Village. Workers are trained here for executive and other positions in children's institutions. At the time of our first visit to the Village an interesting experiment was going on, introduced by a Mr. Frederick Ambuhl, a Swiss, who was a pupil of Mr. Derrick in the training school and had ideas derived from his experience with a clinic for children in Germany. It was arranged to turn over to him a cottage and the seventeen worst boys in the Village, those for whom no adjustment seemed possible, all of them nervously unstable, unhappy in any situation, and dreadful centers of trouble wherever they were. The cottage was furnished with scarcely more than beds, the grounds a perfect jungle, and everything in disorder. The boys became interested in making the place their own. They collected old chairs, re-upholstered them, painted everything, made curtains, cleared the grounds, built a chicken coop, a guinea pig house, a rabbit hutch, an outdoor fireplace, in the basement a theatre, with a real and very excellent stage, scenery and back-drop, a chapel, with an altar, many candles, and what not. They were interested all the time in what they were doing. Special talents had been discovered, so that every boy was distinguished in some way. One was a good dramatist, another a good actor, another an expert at carpenter work, etc. They staged amateur plays and had always some project in which they were tremendously involved. They had the teacher come to their own cottage, and boys who had never been able to sit still five minutes, never able to learn, were found studying quietly and intensely, writing letters home, etc. They were out of doors every possible minute, had built a rustic arbor and table and benches and ate out of doors all spring and summer. They had certainly made a good adjustment under the circumstances. On a recent visit to the Village we found this project suspended, at least temporarily, owing to the withdrawal of Mr. Ambuhl.

It is worth recording that Mr. Ambuhl thinks the only way to manage psychopathic boys of this kind, or indeed any problem boys, is to deal with them in small groups, and to have persons with certain qualifications managing them, or rather drawing them out. He does not think that the usual type of person who goes in for this work can possibly become successful, that is, the social worker type, wishing to do good, academically inclined, usually emotionally maladjusted. He said that in Germany he went about the country and found old women, " comfortable " people, who were tremendous successes in dealing with the children. With regard to these boys, he feels that the most important thing is to get them adjusted to some situation for a period sufficiently long to give them some stability. They are ordinarily passed from one person to another because they are so troublesome. He realizes, of course, that with some of the serious cases of nervous instability there is little guarantee of permanent adjustment to modern life situations. That is, they will probably adjust as long as things go smoothly, but undue strain is likely to cause a break. He feels, also, that if there is to be any transfer of adjustment from that obtained in the institution to the ordinary home life, the institution must be de-institutionalized to a greater degree than is the case at the Village. Groups should be much smaller, with more care in the selection of house-parents.

Mr. Derrick felt also that the selection of house-parents was on a wrong basis. The pre-vocational instructors and their wives are the house-parents, which means that a person is selected because he is primarily a good carpenter or a good plumber, not primarily because of his personal qualifications, and his wife is just taken along with him. The boys are therefore not sure of getting the understanding and type of training from the house-parents which is most desirable.

The psychiatric clinic was organized in 1927 and the work is consequently not far advanced. Dr. Williams, who is in charge, has an interesting view on the function of the institution in the treatment of the problem child. He thinks that the dull-normal child is the one benefiting most from institutional life. Children of superior intelligence, he says, should almost never be sent to institutions. They can do much better among the various resources of the outside environment under appropriate direction. The limitations of the institutional environment are not favorable to these cases, but suitable to the dull-normal where drill in habit formation is the essential procedure. Certainly some of the children in these institutions are better situated than they would ever have been under other conditions. The institution is taking the form of a school and camp instead of a penitentiary — a school of the experimental type, one in which more attention is given to problems of behavior than problems of learning, and this is probably the form which will eventually be taken by all schools for children. In the case of the delinquent sent to an institution there always remains the stigma of the experience, but certainly also this tends to have less and less significance.

We believe the George Junior Republic is usually thought of, especially by Europeans, as embodying some sort of idealism from the beginning — a conception of the original purity of human nature, or of the principles now exemplified, or designed to be exemplified, in Soviet Russia. But it was far from any form of idealism in the beginning. Mr. George came to New York City from the neighborhood of Freeville, interested himself in boy life, was molested by an east side gang (the Graveyard Gang, with an inner circle calling itself The Sons of Arrest), conquered the leader in a boxing bout and took charge of the gang. Later he established a fresh-air camp at Freeville for children too tough for the other camps. The farmers of the vicinity generously contributed food to the campers, but these robbed their benefactors, undertook no duties, complained of the food, inquired what they were to have to take home, why they came there anyway if not for presents, and were so generally pestiferous that Mr. George was in despair. He was a believer in labor, law and order, and used a barrel stave continuously.

At one time a barrel arrived from New York containing clothing. The boys appeared, several of them having slashed their clothing to tatters in order to secure better. At that time Mr. George formulated a policy. He offered a desirable suit, estimated by the boys as worth five dollars, to the boy who would work at ditch-digging for five days. There was a general hooting, but after a day or two a boy offered to work for the suit. Afterwards no child received any delicacies or anything he wanted without working for it. One element in the evolution of the Republic was the discovery that the boys would fight for what they had earned by work. Another was an inspiration of Mr. George. Instead of whipping two boys who had robbed the farmers he turned them over to the group for judgment. The ability to pass judgments on others is one of the things dearest to the human heart. A court was formed and all the departments of government. Later the movement was rationalized and idealized, as a device for giving children practice in citizenship. Eventually there were 36 buildings in Freeville and various industries, including the publication of a monthly periodical, *The Citizen* (now suspended).

The Republic receives problem children (of both sexes) from various sources, much as in the case of Berkshire and the Children's Village. Mr. George announced he preferred children " *generally* bad ":

Life at the Republic for its young citizens is much the same as it is for grown people in any city of the United States. Citizens live according to their ability and industry. The law is that they must pay for everything they get — the food they eat, the bed they sleep in, and the amusements they enjoy. Time spent in the classroom is counted as labor. They have a Grammar School and a High School, and citizens are prepared for the New York Regents' Examination, which entitles them to enter many of the leading colleges.

No one is compelled to work; but if he doesn't work, he loses standing in the community and is unable to secure the comforts of life. There is plenty of opportunity for everyone to work. The Republic maintains a number of industries: farming, dairying, carpentering, printing, baking, laundrying, banking, storekeeping, etc. Citizens are paid in Republic currency for everything they do. They are employed and dismissed just as grown people are anywhere in the world. If a citizen is lazy or indifferent, he will gradually descend the scale until he reaches the bottom; then, through necessity, he will have to climb up. Often a citizen will go so low that he will have to appeal to the Republic police for help; when this happens he is given a rough bed in the Republic jail, and a bowl of soup with a piece of dry bread.

Having worked for everything they get the citizens learn to value property and take interest in laws for the protection of property and the comforts of life. Thus they assume civic responsibility as a natural sequence to having had economic responsibility placed upon them.

A rigid rule [was established] in the early days of the Republic . . . that under no circumstances shall the citizens be interfered with by the Board of Trustees or any grown up person in the making or enforcing of their laws. The laws of the Republic are the laws of the United States, and the State of New York, and in addition those made by the citizens themselves. Once a month there is a meeting of the Town Council. At this meeting any citizen may propose an amendment to existing laws, or propose new laws. Proposed laws and amendments are discussed at length, and finally voted upon by the citizens' body.

The Republic police enforce laws with greater strictness than do the police of most cities. When a culprit is brought into the Republic court he realizes that he is facing a serious situation. If an offender desires to employ counsel to defend him, he may do so, for the Republic not only has lawyers but boasts also a Bar Association, which gives examinations to those wishing to practice law within the Republic. If a citizen, through the cleverness of his lawyer, escapes punishment after trial, his case is settled, even though the heads of the Republic know that he is really guilty of wrong-doing.[9]

There have been several reproductions of the plan and the most active of these at present is the George Junior Republic of Western Pennsylvania, at Grove City (Earle D. Bruner, Superintendent).[10] Other branches are located at Litchfield, Connecticut, and Chino, California.

The self-government is a successful and picturesque feature. There is no doubt that children are able to enforce discipline themselves where adults fail. They can prevent deviation from any norm they have set up, but they tend to be very hard on each other and to reproduce the worst forms of adult disciplinarianism. Self-government solves the problem of the adults in charge and is a very convenient device, but as

[9] From the literature of the George Junior Republic.
[10] See George, W. R., and Stowe, L. B.: *Citizens Made and Remade* (1912); Bruner, Earle D.: *A Laboratory Study in Democracy* (1927).

a method of treating delinquency it is questionable how lasting the influences will become since the children have depended on a form of group approval which may have little extra-institutional force.

Owing to vicissitudes, including the war, the whole movement was interrupted and has been rather inactive, but the parent Republic at Freeville (J. B. Kirkland, Executive Director) is at present introducing a research plan in connection with the work. It is proposed to receive a relatively small number of children whose behavior is bad but who are neither mentally deficient nor psychopathic, with a view to determining how far this system, applied to a limited group, will prove efficient in the correction of bad habit formation. It is proposed also to work in some plan of coöperation with members of the neighboring Cornell University and other academic centers.

Opposed to the institutional plan of providing a situation where the behavior of the delinquent child may be improved is that of substituting another home, a " foster home," with better influences and better control. The motives leading families to undertake an arrangement of this kind have varied as widely as possible. Under the system of indenture, which was so largely used in this country in early times, the primary object was to make some disposition of the child in the absence of prison facilities, and the labor of the child was accepted as compensation. At present these motives exist also but there are powerful sentiments connected with family life behind the willingness to accept a strange child in the family. The large number of childless people and the survival of the feeling that a family is not a family and the parties are not personalities without a child, has brought about a situation where the demand is so great that not enough desirable children can be provided by the hospitals for adoption. There are complaints from childless mothers of favoritism in this respect in the institutions which have children to distribute, and we have the phenomenon of one class of woman bearing children to be reared by another. This sentiment operates also in connection with the dependent and delinquent child which may be accepted with the idea of adoption in case it proves satisfactory. There is also, especially in certain localities, a positive feeling of obligation to service in such cases.

Massachusetts has been most closely identified with the concept of keeping the family intact, restoring the family if possible, or eventually placing the child in a substitute home. This state has, indeed, formed institutions for the orphaned, pauper, crippled, vicious, epileptic, insane, feebleminded and delinquent, taken all together, and then worked toward the separation and dissemination of these elements through the community and into homes as far as possible. It is recognized that all the features of the after-procedure of the juvenile court were derived from or foreshadowed in Massachusetts — probation, placing in families, the visiting teacher, the cottage system, the " training school " instead of the " almshouse " or " reformatory." Samuel Gridley Howe, who first developed language in a deaf and blind person (Laura Bridgeman) in the Perkins Institute, commanded great respect in public affairs and was very insistent on the point that the family and not the institution should be emphasized in training and correction:

His cardinal maxim was that the family, and not the overgrown asylum or school, was the best place for the child to be trained, the patients to be nursed, and the harmless lunatic to be cared for — in case these subjects of care were suitable for family life. On this point Dr. Howe held that more could be received into households than was then the practice, and that nothing but trying the experiment would prove how many were suitable.[11]

As the result of historical influences of which the above are items, Massachusetts has a constellation of formal and informal welfare agencies which can hardly be paralleled. One thousand and forty-nine organizations of this character made returns to the Department of Public Welfare during 1925.[12] Of these 129 were child-helping agencies — 46 of them located in Boston — and the activities of these child-helping agencies have left very little special work for the probation officers. There are, in fact, only five of these connected with the Boston juvenile court, as against about 150 in Chicago. As a result also of a peculiar history and tradition of righteousness a large number of individuals and families are prepared to devote themselves in an almost consecrated way to any good cause. It is consequently a fact that the juvenile court of Boston has never had a detention home. It has used a number of selected " boarding homes " instead, thus avoiding at the

[11] Sanborn, F. B.: "The First State Boards of Charities," *The Survey*, 13:117 (November 5, 1904).
[12] *Annual Report of the Department of Public Welfare of the Commonwealth of Massachusetts for the Year ending November 30, 1925*, 60–78.

outset any institutional experience, and has placed the largest possible number of cases in foster homes.

The whole attitude is one of faith in the normal family grouping, and the aim is never to place a child in an institution if a good family situation can be made available for him. The distrust of institutions is widespread. Most of them are used as temporary homes for children until they can be placed. There are probably fewer institutions in Massachusetts than in any other state, certainly any state of its size. Such institutions as there are are chiefly for defectives, the markedly abnormal or persistently delinquent. The combinations of probation plus placement in foster homes, and parole plus placement in foster homes are very frequent. The social attitude towards placing of children is very interesting. Extraordinarily able types of women, college graduates, etc., are willing to take children into their homes. The amounts paid for board are very small and the supervision by the agencies is quite strict, yet some 12,000 adequate homes are made available each year. This does not mean that it is not necessary in many cases to resort to the institution but that this is avoided as often and as long as possible.

The numerous agencies interested in the child coöperate with the court and the Judge Baker Foundation, referring difficult cases to the Foundation and assisting in treatment after the child has appeared in court and been examined by the clinic of the Foundation. The procedure is somewhat as follows:

When a case is referred by the agency the representatives of that agency place all the facts and background of the child before the Judge Baker Foundation. The child is interviewed by the workers of the Foundation, the family situation looked into, the Confidential Exchange is consulted for further clues, and the child is given psychological and psychiatric examinations. There is then a summary of the case at a staff conference at which the representatives of the agency referring the child are present. The situation is discussed with the various workers, all the facts are brought together, treatment is outlined and a tentative prognosis is made. Then the Foundation turns the case over to the agency for treatment, but continues its contacts in most cases, with psychotherapeutic treatments, and has the agency report the progress of the case so that a complete follow-up record is available. Every six months there is a conference of the whole staff of the Foundation and each agency with which they have dealt, and the agencies are called to account for each case in which the Foundation has been involved. There is a general discussion of methods and of the probable causes of success or failure in the given case, and a decision as to future treatment. These conferences are considered the best type of education in mental hygiene for the agencies. There are so few established principles that abstract lectures are somewhat out of place. The workers get a much clearer idea of the principles involved through the actual observation of the methods used in their own cases and through the practical working out of the methods prescribed. They are brought face to face with the complexities of behavior problems, with the empirical nature of most of the remedial measures and with the many uncertainties of prediction of human behavior situations.[13]

It is recognized that placing children in families is always associated with certain disadvantages. Young married people secure girls in this way, girls from 8 to 12 years old, give them the care of the children, the nursing, dressing, feeding, and the mother leaves the house to go to teas and bridge parties. Farmers exploit the labor of young boys, and astonishment is expressed that the child does not do well in " a perfectly good home." Very frequently when trouble arises the persons in charge assert their " authority," and a struggle follows and an attempt to " break " the child. We have noticed this especially in the cases placed directly by the children's aid societies, perhaps without the advice of one of the more enlightened clinics. In spite, therefore, of the favorable conditions for child-placing in Boston, Healy and Bronner have felt that their successes were limited and that they did not really know what was going on — whether the successes when they did have them were due to the treatment. Recently, however, they have made a significant contribution based on their later and better controlled work with foster homes. Working in association with Boston agencies, they placed 501 delinquent children in selected foster homes and observed them from two to ten years. But in the final tabulation of results only 355 cases were used because the work of the public agencies was done under certain disadvantages and proved incomparable. The 355 cases contained, however, some of the most difficult problems:

We soon found that the main lines of cleavage in results was along the lines of diagnoses made from a psychiatric standpoint. It seems to make little

---

[13] Conversation with Dr. Bronner.

difference how delinquent the individual is, or what his heredity is, or what his early environment is, economically considered, or the sex of the individual, or whether he had been in court or not, or the age at which placed — all these are of minor importance apparently as far as outcome is concerned.

If, however, the individual showed abnormal mentality or personality characteristics, his chance of success was vastly less than if of normal mentality. The mental defectives did not do nearly so poorly as the other abnormal group. It is to be noted that of ten, those of abnormal personality had more time and money spent on them than did the regular run of the normal group. Of 217 individuals of normal mentality 90% made good on placing — and by that we mean that they for the most part ceased their troubling, as it were. Of repeated offenders (who were in the majority) 81% were successes. Of 40 non-repeaters 92%, and of those merely presenting personality and habit problems (62 cases) 95% were successes. On the other hand, of repeated offenders (70) who were of abnormal mentality or personality, only 36% were successes in placing. Of the total abnormal group (102) 45% were successes. It is to be understood that diagnosis of psychopathic personality or constitutional inferiority, etc., was not made on the basis of the individual's delinquent behavior.[14]

In the volume covering these experiments (now in press) [15] Healy and Bronner and their associates have summarized their results in the following table and have given particular attention to the question of the psychopathic personality. Their general conclusion that these cases can be better handled in institutions may be compared with the experience of the Children's Village, mentioned above:

---

[14] Communication from Dr. Healy.

[15] Healy, W., Bronner, A. F., Baylor, E. H. M., and Murphy, J. P.: *Reconstructing Youthful Behavior: Problem Children in Foster Homes* (Knopf).

SUCCESS AND FAILURE CORRELATED WITH MENTALITY CLASSIFICATIONS

339 CASES PLACED BY PRIVATE AGENCIES (16 INDETERMINATE OUTCOMES OMITTED)

	Normal Mentality		*Defective*		*Abnormal Mentality or Personality*	
	Success	Failure	Success	Failure	Success	Failure
Delinquents Repeated Offenders	94(81%)	21(19%)	4	2	25(36%)	45(64%)
Non-repeaters	37(92%)	3(8%)	4	1	9	7
	131(85%)	24(15%)	8	3	34(40%)	52(60%)
Personality & Habit Problems	59(95%)	3(5%)	6	3	12(75%)	4(25%)
	190(90%)	27(10%)	14(70%)	6(30%)	46(45%)	56(55%)[16]

Whereas it was possible to succeed with normal individuals, even those engaged in polydelinquency, to the extent of about 80 per cent, only about 40 per cent of all offenders of abnormal mentality or personality were successes. Thus the older notion that the fact itself of delinquency stands almost irrevocably as an obstacle to the development of a normal social career must go by the board. There is no truth in the old saying, " Once a thief, always a thief," or in any analogous proverbial utterance. Delinquents as such show remarkably good promise for moral therapy. It is only when delinquency appears in an individual who shows pathological mental or personality characteristics that the outlook is desperately poor. . . . In the tables giving single and polydelinquency as related to success and failure and to mentality, it will be seen that mentality affects the results much more than does the number of types of delinquency committed. But there is a decrease of success for both the normal and abnormal as the number of types of delinquency increases — for the normal, however, the decrease is slight; for the abnormal it is very marked.[17] . . .

What is included under the category of " personality problems " is somewhat difficult to state, because it is largely the degree of the tendency or trait that causes the individual to be considered a problem. We use a rather

---

[16] *Ibid.*, chap. 24.   [17] *Ibid.*, chap. 24.

common-sense gauge — when the child has in his own home or elsewhere been
very difficult to manage on account of troublesome behavior, he has been
considered a " personality problem." Although much that he does might be
denominated " misconduct," yet it is hardly delinquency in the ordinary
acceptance of the term. We include severe temper spells, excessive irritability,
stubbornness, sullenness, extreme jealousy, selfishness, great cowardice, reck-
lessness, or much lying in the form of fabrications or in self-defense. Personality problems total 14 per cent of the entire group of placed cases.

Habit problems, only 6 per cent of the series, include enuresis, masturbation, and other sex habits. Habits of less importance, such as smoking, nail-
biting, over-eating, etc., of course, are found in members of our group, but
on the basis of these alone, no case has been included among this group of
problem children. . . .

What we have used as a standard for estimating success and failure requires
a specific statement and should be kept clearly in mind. Success, most con-
servatively stated, means in all cases, whether representing behavior, personality, or habit problems, that the individual has made a steady gain in
ability to master his difficulties and maintain a position as a desirable member of a family and of a community.[18]

It is very necessary to determine quickly when habits of delinquency have
become too firmly set for foster home care. In that case the institution can do
more for the child and can keep him from becoming a menace to others.
There occasionally comes a time when group care is the only hope as the
child is entirely controlled by his impulses and proves unmanageable even in
a good environment.[19] . . . Psychiatrists and social workers have made
little headway; it may be that the only remedy is colonization under the
guidance of educational and psychiatric experts. We are convinced that some
such measure is necessary, because in the community, whether in their own
or foster homes, such individuals are very costly by virtue of their erratic
behavior and misconduct and the bad influence they have on others. This
group, together with other abnormal types of children, requires much more
discussion of definitions, diagnoses, characteristics, social problems involved,
and possible treatment. We hope to offer this in a future monograph.[20]

We are impressed with the program of the juvenile courts, with the
evolution of the institutions and agencies associated with it and with
the research which has accompanied the court procedure, as illustrated
by the foster home experiment just mentioned. But the juvenile court
system is not strongly developed except in the large cities, and while
great numbers of successes can be cited from the records a large com-

---

[18] *Ibid.*, chap. 22.   [19] *Ibid.*, chap. 22.   [20] *Ibid.*, chap. 24.

parison indicates that the system as a whole is not successful as a means of preventing or treating delinquency:

Although every State but two has legislation authorizing the establishment of special juvenile courts or juvenile sessions, the juvenile court movement is still in a relatively primitive stage. In the 22 years since the first juvenile courts were established the idea has taken root in every large city, but its extension into rural communities and small towns is largely a question for the future.

Three years ago, in a survey covering the whole of the United States, information was secured from 2,034 courts authorized to hear children's cases; only 321 of these courts approached even the minimum of special equipment for children's cases, that is, separate hearings, regular probation service, and provision for recording social as well as legal information. In half the States, less than one-fourth of the population were within reach of courts with these special facilities. Several of them reported no special equipment in any court.

Only 25 per cent of the population of this country live in cities of 100,000 or more inhabitants; 55 per cent live in rural areas. Yet, while juvenile courts or juvenile sessions were found in all the cities with populations of 100,000 or over, and in 70 per cent of the total population living in cities of from 25,000 to 100,000, courts with special equipment for dealing with children were available to only 15 per cent of the population of rural communities and to 28 per cent of the total in cities of 5,000 to 25,000. . . .

In most courts the probation staff is deplorably inadequate, as to numbers at least. The court must depend on the public treasury for its equipment, and economy usually governs appropriations of this kind. Probation, including investigation and supervision, can be effective only when the worker has a fair chance to deal with each case as well as he knows how. . . . The probation officer with one to two hundred children under his supervision might be able to do an effective piece of work with from half to a third of this number. . . . In one large court — and it is one of the most respected — we are frankly told: " Our staff can hardly make a beginning in probation work, they have so many other duties." [21]

With reference to the success of the best juvenile court work taken as a whole, Dr. Healy who was the first court psychologist, and Dr. Bronner who has been associated with him from the beginning, have recently issued a volume [22] comparing and estimating their work in Chicago and Boston during a period of twenty years:

[21] Lundberg, Emma O.: " Juvenile Courts — Present and Future," *Proceedings, American Prison Association* (1921), 48–50.

[22] Healy, W., and Bronner, A. F.: *Delinquents and Criminals* (1926).

Our present research is based on material gathered by us in the form of case studies of juvenile repeated offenders in Chicago and in Boston, and on follow-up work, a study of after-careers, all done as a part of our regular routine or under our direction. . . .

By juvenile repeated offenders we mean young people who have continued in delinquency after very definite efforts on the part of some one in authority to check their misconduct. By far the most of our cases had been in the juvenile court at least twice. (There is little practical value in taking first offenders for scientific comparisons, because their delinquencies sometimes are accidental or so slight that the offender in essence or by intent is non-delinquent, and the treatment given may properly have been merely nominal or little more than that.)

Utilized for this study are: (1) three groups of juvenile repeated offenders with later careers traced: (a) a series of 920 studied by us in Chicago between 1909 and 1914 and followed up as a special research in 1921–1923, (b) a series of 400 young male offenders who appeared in the Boston Juvenile Court in 1909–1914, whose careers were studied in 1923 in relation to further delinquency, (c) a series of 400 boys, also repeated offenders, originally studied by us in Boston, 1918–1919, and very well known to us in their after-careers through our regular following of cases.

(2) For statistical analysis we used 4000 cases consisting of 2000 offenders studied by us in Chicago between 1909 and 1915, and 2000 studied in Boston from 1917 to 1923. These larger series, used in groups of 1000 each, represent no selection whatever, except as they were repeated offenders of juvenile age.[23]

In this study one of the objects is to view successes and failures comparatively in two cities differing not only in general character but in the methods followed. A comparison becomes, therefore, extremely difficult. The extraordinary differences between the whole juvenile court make-up in the two cities is seen in the fact that for a corresponding five-year period, in Boston 9.5% of the total juvenile court cases were committed, in Chicago, 40%. However, in proportion to the population, Boston had four times as many cases brought before the juvenile court as Chicago, a very significant fact, since in Chicago a vast number of delinquents were dealt with by police officers specially assigned to deal with juvenile offenders. On the other hand, the Massachusetts laws are very particularistic; there are many minor offenses listed in the statutes, such as spitting on the sidewalk, climbing fences

---

[23] *Delinquents and Criminals*, 12–13.

of railroad yards, swimming without a bathing suit, etc., etc. There is nothing strange about this part of the situation; many cities and states have quite as particularistic ordinances; but the real difference comes in the administrative policy backed up by the social attitudes. The policy here is strict enforcement of laws regarding all offenses, including these petty ones. As a result, the chance of a " delinquent " appearing before the court at his first actual offense is much greater here than in other places.

To give a fair comparison of the two cities Healy and Bronner used comparable series of repeated offenders and found that 74% of the Chicago young repeated offenders were committed, 29.5% of the Boston series for the same years, and 40% of the more recent series.

In dealing, however, with the selected series, i.e., of young repeated male offenders, as above, all kinds of variables are introduced which really make the two series incomparable. It is admitted, for instance, that this contrast in policy may be due to differences in the types of offenses; the statistics show that the Chicago boys committed more serious offenses than the Boston boys. There is also a very great difference in the treatment of the individual under parole from the juvenile correctional institutions in the two states. In Illinois parole is only nominal; in Massachusetts it extends to the age of 21. Furthermore, the placing out in foster homes of paroled juveniles, with follow-up of foster homes, is utilized very largely in Massachusetts, scarcely at all in Illinois. Of the 577 boys on parole from Lyman at the time of the writing of this book only 241 were returned directly to their own homes, and 336 were placed in carefully selected foster homes. It is, therefore, not possible to make a fair comparison of crude numbers or percentages of commitments.

Nevertheless, it is of interest to compare the relative success and failure among the committed and non-committed, and we find, in the Chicago series, of 256 male failures, 86% had been committed as juveniles, and of 156 successes, 56% had been committed. " Or, putting it another way, of the 311 boys committed, 219 (70%) were failures, while of the 109 not committed only 37 (34%) were failures." But " presumably the committed represent the most difficult offenders." This being so, it appears that we are attempting to compare the incomparable. About all that these figures show is that the more serious the offense and the more difficult the offender, the more likely he is to be sent to an institution, and the more likely he is to repeat his offense after he comes out of the institution. But whether this all depends on the difficult nature of the offender, the serious nature of the offense, or the treatment at the institution, certainly cannot be answered by a comparison of this sort. The only way it could be answered would be to select a number of cases showing the same outstanding differences in mentality, environmental surroundings, etc., who had committed the same offense, and compare the results in the cases of those who had been committed to institutions and those who had not. The large proportion of failures among those committed to institutions would certainly seem to show that the institutions do not markedly check delinquency. " In either city the number finally sent to an adult correctional institution is, doubtless, the fairest gauge of the extent of serious crime (6% Boston, 37% Chicago)." But we have as yet no adequate test of the relative success of institutional and non-institutional treatment for *the same type of offender.*

Admitting that a different type of research must be undertaken before we can make these particular comparisons, the main interest of this volume is the general success of the juvenile court as method of treatment, and on this point the authors make the following statement:

Tracing the lives of several hundred youthful repeated offenders studied long ago by us and treated by ordinary so-called correctional methods reveals much repetition of offense. This is represented by the astonishing figures of 61% failure for males (15% being professional criminals and 5% having committed homicide), and 46% failure for girls (19% being prostitutes). Thus in over one-half the cases in this particular series juvenile delinquency has continued into careers of vice and crime. . . . Continuing as offenders there appeared in adult courts no less than 209 of the 420 boys whom we knew when they appeared in the Chicago juvenile court. And of these 157 had charged against them offenses so severe that they received commitment 272 times to adult correctional institutions, a considerable number for long terms. Taking criminal statistics by and large this is an immense proportion to be coming from any series of consecutive cases studied merely because they were repeated offenders in a juvenile court. It represents a most disconcerting measure of failure.[24]

The juvenile division of the court of domestic relations of Cincinnati is attracting attention at present, especially from the officials of other

[24] *Delinquents and Criminals,* 201–2.

courts, because it is thought to have the greatest success by the most informal procedure, with a minimum of commitments to institutions and no systematic use of foster homes. This is a very interesting claim, especially in view of the preceding statement of Healy and Bronner, who represent the most scrupulous and organized work, and calls for a somewhat detailed examination.

This court, presided over by Judge Charles W. Hoffman, serves the whole of Hamilton County which had a population in 1925 of 508,000, distributed over 698 square miles. The juvenile division has jurisdiction over delinquent, dependent and neglected children, truants, mothers' pensions, and the prosecution of adults who contribute to the delinquency of children. Twenty-one hundred complaints of delinquency are handled yearly. Nearly 500 dependent children pass through the division and over 500 mothers' pensions are handled. This load is far too heavy for the facilities of the division.

Arrests are for comparatively minor offenses, and in this respect the situation resembles that in Boston and differs from that in Chicago. " Loitering," " suspicion," " pre-delinquency," are found among the charges. The great majority of the cases are dealt with unofficially by referees of the court. Fully 95% of the cases are not docketed, no petitions are filed, no lawyers are involved, there is nothing resembling trial or sentence. No complaints are adjusted by the police, in contrast with the system in Chicago where 18,000 are so adjusted annually. In 1924, 1,359 offenses of boys were handled unofficially, 48 officially. However the complaint may have been filed, the child goes first to the referee. All hearings are private. In the boys' department first and minor second offenses are handled as " desk jobs," heard in fifteen minutes to half an hour of very informal conference. Probably one-third of all cases are disposed of without any investigation of any sort.

Between 15% and 20% of the cases get psychological examinations (10% of the boys), which means that only this percentage ever gets a somewhat serious social investigation. Some cases go to the Central Clinic, which, however, accepts only two cases a week from the court. This means that only 5% to 7% of the cases ever have psychiatric diagnosis of an adequate sort.

The procedure in the girls' department is about the same, but every girl who has not been tested in the public schools or elsewhere is given a psychometric examination, and some effort is made at a social investigation of each case. This social investigation is of a meagre sort, largely by means of office interviews.

The referees have the unofficial right to make all dispositions save commitments. Cases go to the judge only when the referees request conference. He is rarely, if ever, consulted on girls' cases. He is consulted on perhaps 15% of the boys' cases. There is no appeal from the decision of the court in official cases. If the family resists the case is handled officially, but the threat is almost always sufficient to get compliance.

In 1926, 47% of the boys' cases were dismissed, that is, the difficulty was adjusted in conference with the parents and the boy returned home without supervision; 31% of the boys were put on probation, remaining in their families; 1.3% were committed to Glenview School for problem children; 2.3% were placed in institutional homes for children; .5% were placed in foster homes and .5% were placed with relatives. Three boys were returned to reformatory institutions in other states; none were put in reformatory institutions in Ohio.

Of the girls' cases in 1926 (the girls' department used a different classification of dispositions in its report, which has been reduced as nearly as possible to the terminology of the boys' department), 40% were dismissed (the difficulty being adjusted after conference with parents and the girl returned home without supervision); 22% were placed on probation, remaining in their families; 5% were committed to Hilcrest School for problem children (the girls' equivalent of Glenview) or the Oakcrest Home maintained by the Big Sisters; 2.3% were placed with relatives or in foster homes. No girls were committed to correctional institutions, though three were " returned " to such institutions for violations of parole.

From these items it is quite evident that the practice, as well as the avowed policy of the court, is not to place children in correctional institutions as in Chicago, not to place them in foster homes as in Boston, but to place them on probation in their own families where supervision seems necessary. We have seen that there is among social agencies a determined policy to keep children out of the court, and Judge Hoffman has shown an equal determination to keep them out of institutions.[25]

---

[25] " The instruments of social control, especially in respect to criminal behavior, unquestionably have broken down. The present system of imprisoning law-

The resources of the Cincinnati court, institutional and other, for special diagnosis and treatment are limited, peculiar and not fully utilized. We have noted that the court itself is not organized for thorough and general psychiatric examinations. The Central Clinic, financed as an experiment by the Council of Social Agencies, accepts cases from the court, but, as we have seen, only two a week, which greatly handicaps the work of the court. The Juvenile Psychopathic Institute of the Jewish Hospital is unsurpassed in its facilities for examination and treatment. It is perhaps the outstanding example of an efficient institute of this kind in the country. But it accepts cases from all agencies and from private families; the capacity of its residential home, where children are kept under observation for an average period of three weeks, is only twelve children at a time. In consequence of these limitations only a small number of court cases reaches this institute.

There are in Cincinnati two schools for problem children which may be utilized by the court, Glenview, for boys, and Hilcrest for girls. These were formerly opportunity farms administered by the city but

---

breakers, irrespective of their physical and mental makeup, and releasing them after a certain term of months or years has not protected the public or rehabilitated the offender. The doctrine of absolute rather than relative responsibility persists in the criminal procedure and sustains the practice of attempting to suppress criminal instincts and prevent crime by the application of external force, usually in the form of punishment. . . . In the communities in which [crime commissions] have functioned there has been no reduction of crime, greater than that in communities having no crime commission.

" There are 2,000 or more children coming every year into the juvenile court of this county. Of these we have found it necessary this year to commit no more than 12 to the Industrial School at Lancaster. We have committed no girls to the Industrial School at Delaware within the last three or four years. We have invariably stated at the time of commitment that because of their incurable tendency to commit unlawful acts they would become on their release a menace to the community. Our predictions have been fulfilled. . . . We hope finally with the aid of the social organizations and the Council of Social Agencies to so provide for the care and treatment of every delinquent child that it may never enter a criminal career. We trust that the time may come when the sphere of the juvenile court as an institution for diagnosis and treatment of children with conduct disorders will be exceedingly limited and hospitals substituted for the care of children of this character." — (Hoffman, C. W.: "Psychiatric Symposium," *The Cincinnati Journal of Medicine*, 1926. Read at a meeting of the Academy of Medicine of Cincinnati, November 16, 1925).

within two years have been turned over to the Board of Education. Of these Glenview had reached a low ebb and had for a number of years served as a catch-all for those who could not be placed elsewhere — feebleminded awaiting commitment, the psychopathic boy for whom there is no provision in Ohio, vicious older delinquents of the recidivist type, perverts who were a menace to the community, and a few truants. It was the cesspool of the juvenile court, practically unsupervised and totally unclassified, and had been allowed to run down physically, the city refusing to appropriate sufficient funds for its upkeep.

Hilcrest was in somewhat better condition, but had a heavy proportion of defectives, and a few years ago a good many of the " old rounders " who walked Cincinnati streets were committed to it along with girls who had committed their first sex delinquency. It has always had almost entirely sex delinquents. There was no classification.

The institutions were turned over to the Board of Education as a result of a long concerted agitation on the part of the social agencies of the city. There is still a sprinkling of the population that came at the time, though it has been pretty well cleaned out. Glenview now admits boys between 8 and 15 only. There is classification by age and color. There are two cottages for white boys, one an 8 to 12 group, the other a 13 to 15 group. There is only one colored cottage; the colored boys are admitted between 11 and 15 only. The school has been completely reorganized by the director, Mr. Wiseman, formerly of the Berkshire Industrial Farm. Hilcrest admits girls between 12 and 16. Practically all the girls have had sex experiences or have displayed abnormal sex interests and behavior. No colored girls are admitted. The number of older girls makes it difficult to handle younger girls and few are committed. Both schools admit only children whose intelligence quotient is above 75 (dull-normal group up), who are clearly not psychopathic, who are difficult behavior problems, and whose behavior seems clearly due to environmental factors which it has been found impossible to control. All cases are given psychometric tests at the court or the Board of Education and are sent through the Central Clinic before admission. Dr. North, of the Central Clinic, spends a day a week at the schools and keeps in touch with the progress of the cases. The instruction is by teachers of the public school system.

Children come to the schools both from the juvenile court and from the public schools. In either case written consent of the parents to the child's remaining for a period not less than one year is secured before admission. In case parents object, or it is feared they will go back on their bargain, the cases are officially committed through the court.

The capacity of each school is about 75. Both are full, with waiting lists. During the year the Board of Education sent 35 boys to Glenview, the court 12, and the rest were carried over; the Board sent 16 to Hilcrest, the court 25, and the rest were carried over. These schools provide, then, a place for the treatment of considerable numbers of normal but very difficult court cases. Still, when we consider the number passing through the court, they are not greatly utilized.

As we have noted, there are at present no institutions in Ohio to which psychopathic juveniles (those whom Judge Hoffman terms the "scientifically proven incurables") can properly be committed. The court hesitates to commit such cases to Lancaster and Delaware and is working for a new institution. There is, therefore, in many cases a failure to meet the practical demands of the situation.

We have seen that in Boston child-placement is utilized extensively, that the homes are selected with great care and that the child is minutely supervised. In Ohio all child-placing is through agencies licensed by the State Department of Public Welfare. The court cannot place children directly but only through these agencies. The placement is in so-called "boarding homes" which may take as many as four children at a time. The boarding home situation is most unsatisfactory, the selection being made without regard to the desirable qualities of the foster mother, and the resources of these homes are inadequate. Moreover, by a peculiar provision of the Ohio law, the court forfeits all right to further supervision of the child when it is committed to one of these boarding homes. There are also a number of private institutional homes for children, some of them very good, and two state industrial schools for children of juvenile court age, Lancaster, for boys, and Delaware, for girls. But, as the dispositions show, these homes and institutions are infrequently utilized by the Hamilton County Court.

As noted in discussing court procedure and dispositions, of 2,100 cases handled in 1926, only 100 were referred to the Central Clinic, 7 to the Juvenile Psychopathic Institute, only 37 cases were sent to Glenview and Hilcrest, only 29 were placed with relatives, or in boarding homes, only 27 were placed in institutional homes, and none was placed in a correctional institution. Partly due to limitations of the capacity of available agencies, partly due to its policy, the court utilizes outside agencies very little, either for diagnosis or treatment, and, as we have seen, its own facilities are inadequate for either.

On account of the policy of placing few children in correctional institutions parole is not an important factor in the Cincinnati situation, but probation, returning the child to the family under nominal supervision, plays so important a rôle in the court policy and practices that it merits detailed consideration.

Of the 2,069 cases that passed through the court in 1926 only 705 were retained under the jurisdiction of the court. Of these, 594, or 84.3%, were placed on probation. Of the 132 girls placed on probation, only 34 were under the supervision of court officers. These court officers are trained case workers and do good work. But they report that while there have been some outstanding successes these have been very few. The personnel is not adequate for careful probation work (the load of the girls' division has tripled in the past two years — from an average of 30 to 40 new cases per month in 1925 to an average of over 100 new cases per month in 1927) and nothing like case work with particularly difficult girls is attempted. The remaining 88 cases were probated to private individuals or agencies.

Of the 462 boys probated during 1926, less than a dozen were under the supervision of the court officer. Police do not serve as probation officers, as in Chicago, on either boys' or girls' cases. The rest of the boys were probated to the " Big Brothers " through the Juvenile Protective League. The monthly average of boys on probation in 1926 was 335. Of these the court officer averaged 7, the Catholic Big Brothers League 70, the Big Brothers Association (Jewish) 20, the Big Brothers Club (white) 75, and the Big Brothers Club (colored) 170. The law requires that where boys are probated to private organizations or individuals, the organization or individual shall be of the religious faith of the boy probated. No reports have been required of or given by the " Big Brothers " and " Big Sisters " on the cases probated to them. No records have been kept. The boys are probated to the organizations as such. The Catholic and the Jewish Big Brother Leagues enlist business and professional men as actual big brothers and are doing notably good work, but not in close coöperation with the juvenile court.

A new factor was introduced into the situation September 1, 1927, with the formation of the Juvenile Protective League, a central administrative agency for the Juvenile court, Ohio Humane Society, Catholic Big Sisters League, Catholic Big Brothers League, Protestant Big Sisters Club, Protestant Big Brothers Club, Jewish Big Sisters Association, Jewish Big Brothers Association, Newsboys Protective Association. The first step under the new organization was an attempted survey of probation. The records of the court were found to be in terrible shape. Many cases were on probation of which the court had no record whatever. The court recorded other cases as probated to given agencies when the agency had no notification and had never had contact with the boy. The court did not know how many boys were on probation. Some cases on probation had not been looked up within 18 months. Many had been lost track of. Active and closed cases were hopelessly mixed. When a study was undertaken of 29 Lancaster paroled cases, records of some 18 were missing, etc.

The work of the Big Brothers and Big Sisters was equally confused, and the efforts to raise the standards and have records kept have as yet been unsuccessful. The Big Brothers have frankly said they do not want to bother with all "these 'scientific' recommendations of the court and the clinics." The Big Sisters are even less effective than the Big Brothers.

The officials of the Cincinnati court are very frank and objective in their comments on every aspect of the situation. With reference to probation, we found general agreement that there is practically no probation work worthy of the name being done. One of the workers has failed to find one case of constructive probation among the boys, another says there is negligible supervision outside her own officers, and that many of the Big Sister contacts have been positively disastrous — worse than no probation.

The claims of success made for the Cincinnati court are based on three supposed facts: (1) the low rate of juvenile delinquency in Hamilton County, (2) the small ratio of recidivism, and (3) the fact that without the use of correctional institutions the rate of commitment to reformatories and the penitentiary has not increased.

There are figures presented by the court and the Bureau of Municipal Research tending to confirm these claims, but we do not take them up because of the very incomplete state of the records and because no studies of delinquency have ever been made anywhere which make it possible to compare the delinquency rate of cities, either with reference

to causative factors or superiority of court procedure. Boston, as
we have seen, brings children in for trivial offenses, and adjudicates no
cases outside the court. Chicago brings children in for relatively serious offenses, but adjudicates (through police officers) 18,000 cases or
more outside the court to about 1,600 that pass through the court.
Cincinnati brings children in for relatively slight offenses and adjudicates no cases outside the court. Cincinnati's rate (2,100 to 493,000)
looks very high when compared with Chicago (population, 3,000,000),
but when we consider the 18,000 cases adjudicated outside the court
in Chicago the comparison means nothing. Again, we have no data to
determine whether Cincinnati brings children in for as trivial offenses
as does Boston. The complaints vary also according to the attitudes
and rulings of the officials, as when in 1925 a Cincinnati statute against
" watching autos," long on the books but never before enforced, was
enforced for one year, thus accounting for 100 of the boys' cases.

If the work of the Cincinnati juvenile court is superior, this is not
affecting the adult crime rate favorably. Frederick L. Hoffman has
computed the homicide rate of 28 American cities with about 21,000,-
000 of population for 1924 as 10.3 per 100,000, but the rate for Cincinnati is 15.3. For Toledo the rate is 8.3, for Columbus 8.8, for Cleveland 10.7, for Boston 5.1, for New York 6.4, for Philadelphia 7.6, for
Baltimore 9.5, for Chicago 17.5, for New Orleans 32.5.[26] In other respects also — burglaries, robberies, etc., — the crime rate of Cincinnati
is unusually high.

But we point out that it is idle to speculate at present on the crime
and delinquency rates and on other behavior expressions of different
localities because no one has been able to bring any solution to these
questions. Taking homicide as an example:

There are in the United States an average of about 30 homicides every day,
probably 10 times as many in proportion to population as in England. It is
common, however, to find wide variation in localities. It often puzzles us to
determine the cause of these variations. Difference in methods of administration of justice does not explain, for often there is no substantial difference.
For example, it is hard to explain why there should have been 2 homicides in
Jersey City and 26 in Newark in the same year — less in Jersey City in
proportion to population than in London; or why there should be 1 in Grand
Rapids and 26 in smaller Youngstown; or why there should be 20 among the

---

[26] " Homicide Record for 1924," *The Spectator*, 114:3-4 ff. (May 21, 1925).

combined populations of Fall River, Grand Rapids, New Bedford, Lowell, Yonkers, Springfield, Mass., and Worcester, and 208 in Detroit with about the same population; or 11 in Milwaukee and 73 in smaller Cincinnati; or 13 in Seattle, 30 in Minneapolis, 34 in Omaha, 131 in Kansas City; or 50 in Wisconsin, 223 in Indiana, 445 in Tennessee and 553 in Georgia; or 21 in Maine, New Hampshire and Vermont, with a combined population of one and a half million, and 355 in Florida with a population of about a million.[27]

There are, therefore, evidently obscure and undetermined causal factors operating in Cincinnati and in other cities making it impossible to explain their delinquency rate either separately or comparatively at present. It seems quite plain, however, that the Cincinnati court has no elaborate procedure and no efficient coöperation. Psychological and psychiatric technique is little used, institutional facilities are meagre and little employed, probation is nominal. The typical procedure is to bring the child into court, talk to him seriously and turn him back into his family and community without supervision. And yet this procedure seems relatively successful, comparable, Dr. Healy thinks, with the successes he and his associates are having in Boston with precisely the opposite policy — the most thorough study of the case and the most consistent use of the rich social resources of the community. If, then, the Cincinnati court by either a wise or an opinionated neglect of the careful study and supervision usual in the better type of juvenile court secures results comparable with those of the more systematic procedures, it suggests that we have idealized the juvenile court as an institution and that its successes, where it has successes, are not closely correlated with the procedure but due to unknown causes.

---

[27] Hallam, Oscar: "The Essentials — Minnesota's Experiment," *Journal of Criminal Law and Criminology*, 18:338 (1927).

CHAPTER III

Psychiatric Child Guidance Clinics

FOLLOWING the establishment of child clinics in a few of the juvenile courts the idea was developed of organizing clinics to serve whole communities. These received problem cases from the courts, the schools, the social agencies and directly from homes. And in addition to clinics located in cities, demonstration and traveling clinics were organized in order to encourage local interest and extend the service to the general population as widely as possible. This work was first undertaken and promoted on a large scale through the field demonstrations carried on under the Commonwealth Fund Program for the Prevention of Delinquency:

Division II [Child Guidance Clinics] of the Commonwealth Fund Program is administered by the National Committee for Mental Hygiene through its Division on the Prevention of Delinquency and the Division staff has been primarily engaged in supervising demonstration child guidance clinics in cities which desire subsequently to establish under local auspices permanent child guidance clinics to serve the schools, the social agencies, the juvenile court, and parents in dealing with children presenting problems of adjustment to home, school or community. . . .

At first the work . . . was concerned mainly with the study and treatment of children already under supervision of the juvenile courts. By properly directed methods of treatment it was believed that the social rehabilitation of such children and the consequent reduction of delinquency in the community could be definitely advanced. In practice, however, it soon became evident that work with children who present behavior problems would be more effective if the problem were recognized and dealt with before the behavior had become so serious as to necessitate some form of court action. This meant that it became increasingly necessary for the demonstration clinics to establish direct contacts with the public schools, with social agencies, and with homes.

In the light of experience, then, the objectives of this part of the Program have been broadened to cover a more general type of clinical service to the children of the community. This new emphasis on the constructive aspects of the mental hygiene of childhood implies no abandonment of the specific aim of preventing delinquency, but rather the recognition that the best preventive technique is a broad and positive effort to redirect the energies of maladjusted children before they become problems in the community.[1]

Locally supported child guidance clinics were established following demonstrations in St. Louis, Dallas, Los Angeles, Minneapolis, St. Paul, Cleveland, and Philadelphia. One failure — Norfolk, Virginia. . . . Consultant service was established to provide assistance to communities in organizing child guidance service, advice as to methods of clinical work, securing and training personnel, etc. Communities served include Pasadena, Richmond, Memphis, Macon, Milwaukee, and Baltimore. All of these cities established clinics, two, Richmond and Baltimore, with temporary financial assistance from the Fund. Those in Memphis and Macon were later discontinued.[2]

Those responsible for this experiment have repeatedly expressed the conviction that it is impossible to establish clinical service in a community with the expectation of immediate success in the prevention of delinquency and that the degree of success depends largely on the number, quality and coöperation of existing local agencies:

It has become increasingly apparent that the degree of success obtainable is in close correlation to the amount of coöperation the demonstration clinics are able to obtain from communities. Demonstrations cannot depend for success upon themselves alone. It is a slow and painstaking job to fit the clinic whose work is at first little understood, into the network of social, medical, recreational, and educational agencies already established in the community, so that clinic activities will be effectively and smoothly coördinated with theirs. For this reason, the demonstration periods have been increased from six months to a year [and later to two years]. The results of the demonstrations conducted in accordance with this new plan indicate the wisdom of the change.[3]

---

[1] *Commonwealth Fund Program for the Prevention of Delinquency. Progress Report* (1926), 15–16.

[2] *Commonwealth Fund. Annual Report* (1924), 27.

[3] *Ibid.*

A special feature of this program was the formation in New York City of a Bureau of Children's Guidance designed not only to give treatment to selected children but to train a staff of psychiatric social workers, test the possibilities of the clinical line of procedure and prepare case materials for study and publication:

From the beginning the intake has been carefully limited. Cases chosen for study and treatment must fulfil three definite purposes. First, they must illustrate a wide range of childhood problems in order to give students broad training for their responsibilities in the field of case work after the training period is over. Second, they must contribute to the assembling of material for teaching and must therefore involve a need for prolonged social treatment rather than for brief contact with the psychiatrists. Third, they must throw light on the background of current psychiatric issues since they are to furnish data for the publication of new scientific material in the mental hygiene field.[4]

It was planned that this experiment should continue for a period of five years. This time has now elapsed and Porter Lee, Director of the New York School of Social Work, with which the Bureau was associated, has made an interesting attempt to evaluate the work of the Bureau of Children's Guidance in a study based on the results of the five years' accumulation of cases. The evaluation was in terms of the proportion of " successful " adjustments brought about in cases under guidance during this period:

During the five-year period, 822 children were accepted at the Bureau. Twenty-three proved to be cases requiring so slight a service that they were not counted among the cases treated, 116 were withdrawn by parents or other responsible persons before the end of treatment, 92 were dropped by the Bureau before treatment began. There were various reasons for dropping this group, including the removal of the family to a distance too great to make effective contact possible, the discovery by the Bureau before treatment began that there was no possibility of securing parental coöperation and, in some instances, the discovery that the children were of such low grade mentality as to be unsuitable for treatment at this type of clinic. This left 591 who were carried through a period long enough to permit reasonably adequate treatment, in so far as adequacy of treatment is a matter of time.[5]

It should be noted that the evaluation is based on a " selected "

---

[4] *Commonwealth Fund Program for the Prevention of Delinquency. Progress Report* (1926), 13.

[5] Lee, Porter R.: "An Experiment in the Evaluation of Social Case Work," *Journal of the American Statistical Association*, 23:168–69 (1928).

group rather than on one representative of the general run of behavior problems in a community. The cases withdrawn by the parents and dropped by the Bureau are evidently of the sort that would be most difficult to handle. While, of course, the Bureau has had no chance to carry out a complete treatment program in these cases, it is questionable whether many of them should not be considered " failures " from the general point of view of a program of this character (excluding, of course, the cases of " removal of the family to a distance too great to make effective contact possible "). The cases included, then, undoubtedly represent those in which the type of treatment is given the fullest possibilities of effective results.

The methods of evaluation and the results are described as follows:

The objectives of the Bureau in each of the 591 cases carried through the treatment period could be stated as emotional adjustment of the child through better understanding of his problem. The attainment of this objective implied a change in his own attitude and changes in the attitudes of his parents and his teachers, with resulting changes in the active relationships between the child on the one hand and his parents and teachers on the other.

Our effort in evaluation took the form of classifying cases which had been under treatment as having resulted in successful adjustment, partially successful adjustment or in complete failure in adjustment. The statistical difficulties presented by such a project are at once apparent. What do we mean by adjustment? It is a matter of judgment and there are no perceptible gradations between complete adjustment, however defined, and partial adjustment and so on down the line to complete failure in adjustment. We, therefore, abandoned any idea of a precise measure of the success of the Bureau and confined ourselves to an effort to study the cases under treatment in such a way as to give us the most substantial basis possible for a judgment by the staff regarding the Bureau's success.

This project was carried out through a special study by the whole staff of all of the cases numbered from 200–299 in the Bureau's files, representing its work during the earlier stages, and all of the cases numbered from 500–699, representing the work of the Bureau in its later stages. In this group of 300 cases, there were 196 which had been carried through the treatment period. The Bureau's data on these cases were compiled in three separate forms of record, all of which were considered both in treatment and in the staff evaluation. The first compilations were the case records themselves, which were unusually complete. The second compilations were certain diagnostic and progress sheets which were kept currently in the treatment of the cases and recorded briefly the problems defined by the staff, the treatment undertaken and the progress or lack of progress noted. The third was a special analysis in which all of the data regarding the patient and his environment were classified so as to indicate whether each item in his history as we had become aware of it seemed to have either a favorable or unfavorable significance in the problem of his adjustment. Each of the 196 cases was reviewed by the staff in the light of these compilations of data and in the light, also, of their acquaintance with the case and, as a result of the review, each case was classified as successful, partially successful, or failure.

We next gave consideration to possible ways of checking this judgment of the staff. . . . We made an effort to secure from the parents of the children in the group of cases numbered 600–699 an estimate of the progress their children had made during the period of treatment. In this group there were 71 cases which had been carried through the treatment period, all of which had been included in the staff appraisal. In 10 of these it was not possible to interview the parents. . . . There remained 61 children in this group whose parents were interviewed by one person, a competent social worker trained in mental hygiene but not a member of the staff and, therefore, not a party to the staff appraisal of these cases. The data resulting from these interviews were considered by this worker in consultation with some other persons, not including members of the staff, and interpreted by her as indicating the judgment of the parents regarding the successful or unsuccessful adjustment of their children. These interviews varied in length, but they were all long enough to give a careful worker a sense of the parents' point of view. This point of view was then translated by the worker into terms of success, partial success or failure with respect to the child's adjustment.

The result of the staff appraisal of the 196 cases carried through the treatment period was as follows:

Success	93	48 per cent
Partial Success	61	31 per cent
Failure	42	21 per cent
Total	196	100 per cent

The results of the two appraisals, by the staff and by the families, in the 61 cases involved in both studies were as follows:

		Family Appraisal		
Staff Appraisal	Success	Partial Success	Failure	Total
Success	23	7	3	33
Partial Success	11	9		20
Failure		5	3	8
Total	34	21	6	61

These two studies seem significant to the staff for two reasons. First, we think they carry us a step beyond faith in our program and illustrative cases as a basis for faith in our results. I should be willing to suggest that the Bureau was successful in approximately 48 per cent of its cases, partially successful in about 31 per cent and failed in about 21 per cent with rather more confidence than I could have felt regarding any estimate in terms of percentages without these two studies. Second, the check furnished by the study of the point of view of the parents seems enlightening.[6]

These data are indeed illuminating. We mentioned the selective process whereby the cases actually evaluated were those in which a greater proportion of successes would be expected than in the general run of cases coming to a clinic. In addition, the evaluation was made, as Lee points out, " By the group which did the work and the group which had the greatest stake in the results of the whole experiment." [7] Under these circumstances, the degree of " success " obtained must be considered surprisingly small. Less than half of these selected cases are considered by the workers themselves to be unqualified successes, and almost a quarter are considered unqualified failures.

This is further evidence of the complexity of the " adjustment " process, and of the difficulty of interpreting the value of any particular approach. Certainly the psychiatric approach, in its present form, is far from being the panacea that its more ardent and less objective advocates have claimed.

One further point should be noticed, that the proportion of " successes " shown in a study of this kind is not necessarily attributable to the agency under consideration. No " control group " was studied, i.e., no attempt was made to discover how great a proportion of children having the same difficulties as the children in this group and subject to approximately the same influences, with the sole exception of psychiatric treatment, would make " successful " adjustments. Until such a study with a control group is made the most that can be said for such an evaluation as this is that it shows the proportion of successes occurring coincidently with, but not necessarily attributable to, certain specific sorts of treatment.

Lee attributes the successes largely to the Bureau, although admitting the lack of finality of the evidence:

---

[6] *Journal of the American Statistical Association*, 23:169–71.   [7] *Ibid.*, 173.

Taking them at their face value, whose success or failure do they indicate? . . . We can say with some confidence that 591 children when they first appeared at the Bureau presented serious conduct problems, traceable largely to emotional factors, and that at the end of the period of treatment in 48 per cent of these cases there had been a successful adjustment on the part of child, parents and teachers, in 31 per cent of the cases there had been a partially successful adjustment, and in 21 per cent of the cases there had been a complete failure to adjust. Within the experience of every member of the staff of the Bureau and, very likely, within the experience of every member of this audience, children quite as disturbed emotionally as those who came to the Bureau have achieved what the Bureau staff would regard as successful adjustment without the aid of a child guidance clinic and, indeed, possibly without the deliberate aid of any other person. How many of these Bureau children would have achieved successful or partially successful adjustment had they never been brought to the Bureau? We do not know. How many of the failures would have achieved successful adjustment except for the effort of the Bureau in their behalf? We do not know. If we concede, nevertheless, a large amount of credit to the Bureau for its work, as we do, it still remains true that in practically all of the successful or partially successful cases these adjustments were obtained largely through the coöperation of the parents and teachers. In some cases this coöperation has been so intelligent and faithful as to make the parent seem to be the most important factor in the outcome. Whatever success or failure these figures indicate must be regarded as success or failure on the part of children to adjust, with the Bureau as one factor and, as we believe, the leading factor in the result. We find significance in the fact that in most cases the Bureau was the only new factor in the situation after the appearance of the child at the clinic and that practically every other agency and person who continued an interest in the child during the period of treatment had previously made an unsuccessful effort of some kind to deal with him and his problem.[8]

In July, 1927, the original five-year program of the Commonwealth Fund on methods of preventing delinquency terminated. The Bureau of Children's Guidance and the clinical demonstrations were discontinued and an Institute for Child Guidance was established in New York City as a teaching, coöperating, coördinating and advisory organization " to make possible further study and research in the field of mental hygiene for children; to provide clinical facilities for the training of psychiatrists, psychologists and psychiatric social workers

---

[8] *Journal of the American Statistical Association*, 23:172–73.

in practical child guidance work; and to offer additional clinical facilities for the thorough study and treatment of children presenting problems in behavior. The Institute will be administered by a specially organized board and will be affiliated with the National Committee for Mental Hygiene, the New York School of Social Work, and the Smith College School for Social Work." [9]

This Institute is recently organized but the Director, Dr. Lawson G. Lowrey, has made a statement representing the policy of the project from which the following are extracts:

The central feature of organization for mental-hygiene work, as I see it, is clinical work with the groups of [problem] children. . . . There are several conceivable ways in which this could be done. The most satisfactory method, in my opinion, is that of the central independent clinic group whose services are available to social agencies, schools, courts, physicians and hospitals, and parents. This method of organization is preferable to the method of organizing a series of clinics to serve these agencies individually. Such a central clinic should be staffed with psychiatrists, psychologists, psychiatric social workers, and the needed clerical group, in order to make effective its clinical service and in order to develop that degree of community coöperation which is absolutely essential in work with maladjusted children. In individual instances, communities have set up such clinics in relationship to some specific agency dealing with children, as, for example, the clinic in the public schools in Minneapolis, the various court clinics, and so forth. From a practical point of view, however, if one accepts, as I do, the central principle that the clinic is a coördinating, coöperating center and that it must establish broad lines of coöperation with all the institutions, including the home, that enter into and affect the life of the child, the desirability of an independent organization and position seems quite clear. . . .

It is, in my opinion, a mistake for such a clinical group to attempt to carry under treatment any considerable proportion of the cases it studies. To do so would not only reduce its opportunities to deal with the constantly increasing stream of cases that the community sends to it, but would prevent the development in other agencies of their own treatment attack and of their use and understanding of mental-hygiene principles in their own work. Wherever possible, it is clearly desirable to carry on treatment measures coöperatively, the agency of primary responsibility for the child carrying out the social-manipulative measures, the clinic carrying on the more technical psychotherapeutic measures. The bulk of the clinic's cases should always be, it seems to me, those which we call consultation cases, meaning thereby that

---

[9] *The Commonwealth Fund. Annual Report* (1926), 47.

after the study a report and recommendations are given to the agency of primary responsibility and further contacts are made by the clinic to follow up and see what the outcome of the situation has been, or on request of the agency as new situations arise. To make this consultation service effective, it is necessary to have a very clear understanding between the agency and the clinic, and there must be constantly developing a greater and greater realization of each other's problems, points of view, technique, attitudes, and vocabulary, so that the report to the agency will have meaning in terms of functional effectiveness. . . . As the plan stands at present, there would be, for all children coming into the hands of social agencies for a long-time placement, a routine mental-health study with a report to the agency, but with no assumption of responsibility for the final plan on the part of the clinic. It would give to the educational system, agencies, and court a problem service concerned with the study of children who present known problems in adjustment and the development of the treatment of such defects. We hope to provide for the court a special sort of routine mental-health survey through which cases would be chosen for more intensive study and treatment in coöperation with the probation staff.

We have come to the conclusion that there is a definite technique in the setting up of adequate coöperative relationships with another agency. This technique, in our opinion, involves three steps. The first step consists of lectures or group discussion through which the mental-hygiene principles involved in work with children may be presented to the entire staff of the agencies with whom one wishes to work. If this is a very large staff, this preliminary work should be done with the supervisory group, since through them all of the case-workers in that agency may be effectively reached. It will be necessary also to develop in the agency one or more workers who, through some six months of assisting at the clinic, become completely familiar with it and acquire a great deal of information concerning mental-hygiene principles as applied to their own field. . . .

It is clear that in the clinical services, as outlined so far, there is constantly being carried forward a mutual education between agencies and clinic which in the long run increases the effectiveness of clinic work and adds to its caseload capacity. It is, perhaps, not possible in any community, and has not been possible here, to develop these coöperative services with all the agencies that might use them. It has recently been pointed out that we have done far too little work with the settlement houses, with the recreation workers, and with the orphanages, yet until satisfactory coöperative work with case-working agencies, the court, and the special divisions of the schools has been established, it is impossible to do very much with the other groups, and in a community plan I would not advise trying to reach all of the groups at once, but, instead, attempting to reach first those groups with which satisfactory working relationships are the most important.[10]

Partly as the result of the operation of the juvenile courts and of the Commonwealth Fund demonstration clinics, the clinical service given by states and institutions is being modified and extended to include conduct problems as well as problems of health and mental deficiency. And in view of the fact that the cities are provided with many hospitals and clinics the present movement is toward an extension of clinical service to the rural population. This movement is particularly noticeable in about nine states. Pennsylvania, for example, had 38 traveling clinics in 1924; in Ohio 67 clinics were held in 23 counties during 18 months in the years 1920–1922; in New York, in addition to 44 mental clinics held under the State Hospital Commission (1924) and 51 regular clinics (monthly) under the State Commission for Mental Defectives, traveling clinics were held in 30 localities during 1923–1924.[11] The character of this work in its most recent form is illustrated in a report of a representative of the Mobile Clinic of the Iowa State Hospital:

A number of states, usually with the assistance of some outside group such as The National Committee for Mental Hygiene, have undertaken mental-hygiene surveys as a basis for a legislative or building program for the adequate care of their insane, epileptic, and feebleminded. State societies for mental hygiene have carried on educational work in many smaller communities and have established clinics to be taken over later by local agencies. Private foundations have supported county-wide demonstrations in mental hygiene in connection with general health programs for children. State departments of public welfare have employed psychiatrists to give mental examinations in the state wherever requested, and some colleges and universities have offered a limited psychological service to the public schools in connection with their extension work.

Adequate psychiatric-clinic service is also gradually becoming available to communities at a distance from the larger centers of population. Connecticut, the seat of the first state society for mental hygiene, has made

[10] Lowrey, Lawson G.: " Program for Meeting Psychiatric Needs in the City," *Mental Hygiene*, 10:471–76 (1926); reprinted in *The Child Guidance Clinic and the Community*. Commonwealth Fund: Division of Publications (1928), 31–38.

[11] *Directory of Psychiatric Clinics for Children in the United States*, prepared by the Joint Committee on Methods of Preventing Delinquency (1925).

notable progress in the establishment of local clinics in several of its smaller cities. In other states various types of traveling clinics are being developed. A number of the state hospitals now hold regular clinics in different parts of their districts to which not only paroled patients, but also children and border-line cases in the communities visited come for consultation. In Massachusetts, the state hospitals have undertaken to carry out the provisions of the law for the compulsory examination of all children in the state who are three years or more retarded in school, and clinics for such children are conducted on a state-wide basis. In Illinois, the Institute for Juvenile Research at Chicago, functioning under the state department of public welfare, detaches members of its staff from time to time to make mental-hygiene surveys or to hold clinics in certain of the smaller cities of the state. The Colorado Psychopathic Hospital has been working closely with the state health bureau in its travel-ing child-welfare clinics and has given psychiatric examinations in from 10 to 12 per cent of all the cases surveyed. Minnesota maintained a psychiatric unit in the field for a year as a step toward the establishment of a state psychopathic hospital, but was obliged to discontinue it because of lack of further appropriations.

The Iowa experiment with a mobile mental-hygiene clinic differs from these others in several respects. It was undertaken by the State Psychopathic Hospital in January, 1926, for a period of two years with a twofold aim: first, to determine the need and the feasibility of providing such a psychiatric service for the state in addition to the hospital and out-patient services offered at Iowa City; and, second, to supplement the research program of the hospital through field studies of problem material, particularly as en-countered in the schools. In support of the latter project, funds were secured from the Division of Studies of the Rockefeller Foundation which enabled the hospital to organize a special research unit of workers and also a field unit, the latter consisting of a psychiatrist, a psychologist, two psychiatric social workers, and a secretary, who have been assisted from time to time by graduate students in psychology and in sociology from the university. The director of the psychopathic hospital and an executive assistant have super-vised the administration of the program, and the latter has acted as field organizer for the mobile clinic. The mobile-clinic staff have devoted their full time to the clinics in the field and have offered consultations both to adults and to children, with no restrictions upon the type of mental problems that might be presented to them. This field unit is at the same time an organic part of the psychopathic hospital, intimately sharing its resources and facilities and taking an active part in its research program. The Extension Division of the State University of Iowa has paid the traveling expenses and has provided the supplies for the field unit, and the communities visited have contributed toward the maintenance of the staff while in their district.

It was decided at the outset that the field unit would visit only those communities in which invitations were forthcoming from enough representative groups to insure a wide selection of cases and adequate coöperation in carrying out recommendations. During the past year and a half, inquiries have been received from twenty or more places and nine invitations for clinic visits have been accepted. Four of these clinics have been held in counties in which the largest towns had populations of from 3,600 to 9,000 and two in cities of 36,000 each. One clinic was held in connection with the ungraded classes in a larger city, and two at the state orphanages at Toledo and Davenport. In the community clinics, the initiative in securing the clinic was taken by the local social worker in four instances, by the school nurse in one, and by the school director of child study in the other. . . . The clinic staff have been called upon to address various clubs during their visit, but have not undertaken a program of general mental-hygiene education through formal series of lectures or study groups. They have rather concentrated upon demonstrating the application of psychiatry to individual problems and have developed the educational side of their work through contacts with the referring agencies, teachers, and parents in the individual cases examined and through informal discussions of general problems with the committee members and others who manifest special interest in the clinic's work. In three communities visited, classes in child study for parents and teachers conducted by parent-education workers from the state teachers' college helped to prepare the way for the clinic and nicely supplemented its diagnostic service. . . .

The clinic has adhered to the hospital's policy of intensive study of the individual case from as many angles as possible and has not attempted any surveys or group studies for statistical purposes. The staff has remained from five to ten weeks in each county visited and has been able to examine about twenty cases a week. A period of six weeks in the field, followed by two weeks at the hospital to write reports, has proved a satisfactory distribution of time, with one month during the summer at headquarters for work with the research unit on methods of examination and retraining, and one month for vacations.

Up to the beginning of the present clinic, 1,106 cases had been examined by the mobile unit, including those seen during the initial experiment in Greene County. Of these, approximately one-third were girls or women and two-thirds were boys or men. In age, they ranged from one and a half to seventy-six years, but almost 95 per cent were of school age — i. e., between five and eighteen years. The sources from which these cases were referred were as follows: schools, 707; state orphanages, 198; relatives, 74; social agencies, 57; doctors, 26; courts, 10; school nurse, 6; self, 11; at the clinic's request, 17. Excluding the institutional cases, over three-fourths of the cases referred were received directly from the schools. The problems for which the school cases were referred fell chiefly into five groups, namely: poor school work in all subjects, poor school work in one particular subject, undesirable behavior, undesirable personality traits, and very superior ability. Relatives referring cases came with requests for advice in medical, behavior, and child-guidance problems. The courts were interested in questions of responsibility and in recommendations as to the best disposition of their cases from the psychiatric point of view. The social agencies referred problems of mental disease, mental defect, antisocial behavior, unemployment, vocational guidance, child training, and the like. In the clinic's examinations, however, social, educational, intellectual, physical, and psychiatric problems were found indiscriminately in all groups with little reference to the source from which the cases came, and the primary factor in the situation appeared to lie sometimes in one and sometimes in another of the fields studied.[12]

The Illinois Institute for Juvenile Research is beginning a systematic program of state-wide service in addition to the local activities and research projects at headquarters in Chicago. Dr. Herman M. Adler, the Director and also the state criminologist, has outlined the program of the Institute as follows:

The plan for the state of Illinois, as at present outlined, includes two main divisions of service. The first consists of the institution service, which concerns itself with the study and treatment of individual cases in the state penal and correctional institutions. According to the organization of the department of public welfare, there are also certain institutions which utilize the services of the mental-health organization under the division of criminology without being officially assigned to that division. These are the two institutions for the feebleminded and the schools for the deaf and the blind, as well as the soldiers' orphans' home. The other division of the work is designed to be preventive and extramural. This part of the work consists of the service given at the headquarters and its out-patient clinic, the branch at the Juvenile Detention Home of Cook County, the pre-school and nursery-school work at Hull House, and the work at the La Salle-Peru Township High School and the Glenwood Manual Training School. In addition to this there are traveling clinics which visit periodically the various cities of the state.

This plan calls for a permanent unit at each of the institutions, two traveling clinics on permanent duty, two units at headquarters, and one unit at the

---

[12] Lyday, June F.: "The Place of the Mobile Clinic in a Rural Community," *Mental Hygiene*, 12:77–82 (1928).

juvenile court. At present this plan is by no means complete in its operation because of the scarcity of personnel — particularly because of the difficulty of obtaining clinical psychologists and psychiatrists not only competent to do the work, but willing to go out into the field and be stationed at the penal and correctional institutions — but it is gradually being put into effect. We have now an almost complete unit at the penitentiary at Joliet, where we have a psychiatrist, a part-time psychologist, and a clerk, and are about to add a psychiatric social worker. The reformatory for boys at Pontiac and the Southern Illinois Penitentiary at Menard are covered by visiting clinics at monthly intervals. We are about to put in a permanent staff at the reformatory. A clerk is assigned to each institution, and at present there is a psychologist at the training school for boys at St. Charles and at the school for girls at Geneva. . . . At the headquarters, that is, the Institute for Juvenile Research itself . . . there is a chief psychiatrist, a chief psychologist, and a chief psychiatric social worker, each of whom is responsible for the entire service of his division of the work. In addition to this service staff, there will be attached to headquarters a body of research workers of various grades, from graduate students to recognized authorities in the lines of work undertaken.[13]

There is also the beginning of a movement to introduce mental clinics into the high schools and colleges, not merely as a method of handling behavior problems as they arise but as a systematic exploration of the personality of the students as a body, with a view to discovering and correcting latent and secret maladjustments:

At Yale the mental-hygiene department is a part of the student-health department of the university and is closely allied to the medical school. This situation has proved to be ideal; coöperation could not be better. . . . [But] how does one reach the students who have problems? At West Point, mental hygiene was an outgrowth of the medical department. For many years such things as depressions, phobias, and anxiety states were treated by cathartic pills and iodine. These measures having proved ineffective, it was finally decided to try a mental approach. I do not say this deprecatingly, for, after all, West Point was one of the first schools in the country to employ a full-time psychiatrist, and its former method of handling mental problems was not unlike that practiced, and still practiced, in the best general hospitals. The hospital at the Military Academy had always been a sort of escape for the cadets. They had used it on every possible occasion because it afforded

[13] Adler, Herman M.: "Program for Meeting Psychiatric Needs in the State," *Mental Hygiene*, 10:718–19 (1926).

relief from the monotony of discipline, drill, and classroom. It was not difficult, then, to reach the boys with mental problems.

At Yale, during the past winter (1926–27), the members of the mental-hygiene staff have met a small group of freshmen every night in the week. These conferences were held in a comfortable room furnished with easy chairs and an open fire. A short talk was given on the general purpose of the department and the principles of mental hygiene, and then discussion was encouraged. The questions asked might well be the excuse for a separate paper. The following are only a few of them:

What causes lack of confidence?
Why does a boy change his girl about once a month?
What is the soul?
What causes a nervous breakdown?
How do you cure an inferiority complex?
What are vocational-guidance tests?
Why does a man go to sleep while studying?
How do emotions motivate conduct?
What would you do for a man who is failing in studies due to being in love? Would you tell him to get rid of the girl?
Can you tell by our questions and general reactions at this conference what our problems are and what our attitude is to your talk?
What is a complex?
Are mental disorders inherited?
In choosing a vocation or profession should one be guided by his natural inclinations?
Is present civilization increasing nervous disorders?
Do you ever cure any of these problems?
Don't you find students very reluctant to consult you about their problems by talking them over?
Does fear of disease cause the disease?
Will you cite some specific examples of life failures that might have been prevented by proper mental hygiene in college?
Is there any sexual basis for friendships between people of the same sex?
Does a restrained sex life offer greater chance of success and achievement?
What has this got to do with psychoanalysis?
Will there be any talks on sex?

A number of students have come to the department for help with their problems after almost every conference. It should be emphasized that attendance at these conferences was entirely voluntary. A letter was sent to each man, inviting him to come. The figures on attendance are rather interesting. There were three series of talks to each group. At the first series, 30 per cent of those invited attended. At the second series, the attendance dropped off markedly, but of the number who came, 54 per cent had attended the first talk. In the third series, there was another drop in attendance, but 70 per cent of those who came had attended other conferences. This would appear to indicate that we were reaching a group who were interested, and perhaps the problem group. In addition to the men who come for help with their mental problems as a result of these conferences, students are referred by the department of university health and by the deans and professors for scholastic or behavior difficulties, and some from all classes seek out the department, frankly requesting help for mental difficulties.

One would like to have all patients come voluntarily. Unfortunately, that ideal situation has not yet been reached. It was a source of some gratification, however, to receive recently, from the headmaster of a nearby preparatory school who has been sending us his problem boys, the following statement: " Bill Jones has asked to come in and see you. He is coming voluntarily just as Tom Smith did. You see it is working out just as I had hoped — the boys are asking to come to you now; they are not being sent."

The problems that we see fall rather naturally into four groups: there are the students with frank mental disorders; those who have scholastic difficulties; those who come in with frank sex problems; and finally, those with personality or behavior problems. As to the relative frequency of these types, our records for the present school year are as follows:

Frank mental disorders ....45 per cent
Scholastic difficulties ....25 per cent
Sex problems ....15 per cent
Personality problems ....15 per cent

It was a bit surprising to us that 20 per cent of all the problems that we have seen this year have been essentially depressions. I do not wish to discuss student suicides, but this figure may throw some light on a situation that has already received too much publicity. In using this classification, I am simply recording the presenting symptom, the reason why the student consults the doctor. One must not lose sight of the fact that most of these problems are mixed. The boy who has a scholastic difficulty undoubtedly has an emotional problem, the boy who has a mental illness may have in addition a sex problem, and the personality problem is apt to include all four. . . .

Since October, 1926, the mental-hygiene department has seen problem students from six colleges and fourteen preparatory schools. It seems very questionable whether these consultations have any great value without some means of follow up. One sees a student sent in from some distance for an hour or two; one speculates on the situation; one is inclined to classify, to prognosticate, and then to make certain recommendations; and after all one is very likely to be wrong. . . .

What are the results of our treatment? I do not think we are in a position to know at the present time. Most of you probably remember the first article on mental hygiene and the college student by Dr. Frankwood E. Williams, which appeared in 1921. Perhaps you also remember that following this an article appeared anonymously entitled *Mental Hygiene and the College Student Twenty Years After*. In this article the writer mentioned a study he had made of 75 per cent of his classmates twenty years after graduation, and he made the remarkable statement that 40 per cent of them were neurotic, psychoneurotic, or psychotic. I hope we will not have to wait twenty years in order to learn our results. Sometimes we feel that we have solved a problem in an hour, sometimes in six hours; occasionally a man has to be followed throughout a college year. It is now and then recommended that a student leave school for a year and adopt a health program.

At Yale we have been paying especial attention to the freshman class, and for this reason: Often, I think, we feel that we have patched up a problem in a few hours or a few weeks and we are proud of a poor job. We lose sight of the student — he graduates or is lost track of — and we have no way of checking up whether or not the readjustment is permanent.

With the freshman class we will have an opportunity to follow the individual for a period of at least four years. After that — well, after that, I hope a method will be found of checking up for another four or eight years. Our knowledge will not be complete until this is done. Here the psychiatric social worker may be of help. At Yale, she has been extremely useful in investigating the home conditions of the problem student. Perhaps she can also learn for us how well we have succeeded with our patients after graduation, how well our mental hygiene has panned out. It is of the utmost importance that we should know this.

I hope you will take what I have said about the Yale plan for mental hygiene in the nature of a very preliminary report, because we have no way of knowing yet how many mistakes we have made.[14]

The most thoroughgoing and emphatic experiment with the application of a psychiatric procedure to a body of students which has come to our attention is under way in La Salle, Illinois, and the associated

---

[14] Kerns, Harry N.: "Experiences of a Mental Hygienist in a University," *Mental Hygiene*, 11:489–95 (1927).

townships of Peru and Oglesby. This is one of the enterprises in coöperation with the Illinois Institute for Juvenile Research:

The Bureau of Educational Counsel is a personnel service in the High School and Junior College, at La Salle, Illinois. Although there have been extensions and new ramifications since the Bureau was established in September, 1923, the main objective — the careful study of the individual student — remains the same. General emphasis falls on the study of behavior, the development of personality, and the adjustment — or better, the foreseeing and preventing — of emotional conflicts common to adolescent life. . . . Although the work is essentially educational and ethical in scope, advanced mental hygiene is the chief instrument of research and psychiatric social work is the technique employed.

Established in a school and bearing the educational stamp, the Bureau sought to avoid all connotation of abnormality or pathology commonly associated with social case work and psychiatry. Accordingly the department was named the Bureau of Educational Counsel, and the director, a psychiatric social worker, became known in school circles as a counselor. ., . . The Bureau is not a psychiatric bureau; it is not a psychopathic institution; it is concerned with disease or abnormality only as it is discovered in supposedly normal groups. . . .

As to the procedures to be adopted . . . invaluable assistance [was found] in the psychology of the confessional, which is the original psychiatric interview, and in the psychology of confidence which lies at the basis of all the historical expressions of this great human truth. The law of evidence, the fruit of centuries of legal thought, gave important suggestions for the right human approaches in ethical interviews and examinations. But the therapeutic ideals were found in the history of religion. . . .

In order that there should be in the mind of the student no idea of possible stigma attached to a contact with the Bureau, as might be the case were the inadequate and the difficult ones first to receive attention, the majority of students first referred were those of average, superior, and special abilities. To emphasize further this point several prominent seniors were referred the first year for special study. Each of these represented superior endowment, high general scholarship, and a special ability; and in each case a thorough study including intelligence tests, special ability tests, personality studies, and social history, was made preparatory to the psychiatric interview. With the Bureau's interest centered in this type of student, it was not long before contact was voluntarily sought by other students and a few of those who had not been seen early in the program expressed regret that their interviews had been delayed. . . .

Group talks on aspects of mental health are given to the students during the school year by the director of the Bureau. The approach is made through the subjects of personality and behavior. The freshmen and sophomores, who are reached in small informal groups of about thirty, are first given personality blanks which furnish material for general discussion. Occasionally an entire class-period is devoted to the discussion of one trait, as excuse-forming or day-dreaming, when the mechanisms involved are simply explained. The groups of upper classmen are larger and the talks are presented more formally but the subject-matter is much the same. Regardless of size of group or of its age-level the main aim of the talks is to cause the students to think in terms of personality and behavior — to make them personality-conscious. The psychiatric aspects of the subject are given by the psychiatrists from the mental health service of the school who address student groups from time to time. . . .

The intensity of the case work varies. One case may require only interviews with students, parents, or teachers; another may demand not only such interviews but also repeated home visits, visits to physician or employer, and other interviews and visits necessary to the carefully investigated and treated case. For instance, the summary card of one student shows eleven interviews, three other interviews (interviews with others relative to student), thirteen home visits, nineteen telephone calls, eight letters sent out, and thirteen letters received. There is also the psychiatric contact, transfer to a special academy after counselor's consultation with officials of that school, and later a transfer to another high school where the student was graduated from the college preparatory course with high standing. Case work in this instance covered a period of two years. . . .

Conformably with the general policy of the program of the Bureau, the mental health service favors the superior student. It is not the problem case or the difficult student that is most frequently listed. Since the number must be more or less limited, an attempt is made to choose those students who will be able to gain most from such attention. Usually it is the superior student who is appreciative of its value and ready to coöperate. He may be one of high native capacity whose achievement is not correlative; or he may be one who maintains his superior achievement but whose general adjustment invites improvement. More and more, requests are received from such students for psychiatric attention; and, though a few of these may have been first prompted more from curiosity than from any other motive, their response has been serious and coöperative. Although the mental health clinic devotes the major part of its time and attention to superior students, it does not limit itself to them. The average student is also represented, as is an occasional handicapped student who is studied from a vocational guidance point of view.

The average IQ of students referred to the clinic is 112. . . . In cases where there are psychiatric examinations, the notes are kept separately from the social notes but are recorded in the same chronological form and kept in the same record folder.[15]

It will be noticed that this carefully guarded and mystically expressed psychiatric approach favors the exploration of emotional life, confessions, interviews, soul-moulding, regeneration, and is, in part, a program designed to develop "personality-consciousness." A consciousness of self, an awareness of one's status and social relationships, is very important, but it is questionable whether a systematic mass inquisition into psychopathic traits, the direction of the attention of the total school population inward and toward the discovery of possible abnormalities and anomalies, has not mischievous implications. Self-analysis and indwelling, beyond the point where this contributes to the development and regulation of activity projects, is in itself a pathological tendency. There is evidence that dwelling on disturbing mental conflicts is favorable to their continuance and that activity projects, removing the attention from them, is the device favorable to recuperation. This is apparent in many children showing behavior difficulties. We have cited the experience of Dr. Richards with hysteria by imitation (p. 74), and the following case may be taken as illustrating the point:

A young boy of 11 years, normal physically and mentally, was placed with a middle-aged couple in a country home after unusually careful consideration of the boy's needs and the foster father's qualifications. The agency and the directors of the Judge Baker Foundation frequently conferred before and after placing in regard to this case and, indeed, the foster father himself came to report and talk over the situation in conference. The boy was recognized to be a difficult sex case on account of some early experiences and development of masturbatory practices. (He showed no homosexual proclivities). The foster father was high-minded, warm-hearted, wholesomely religious, with a fund of information about nature and much appreciation of a young boy's needs. The surroundings were quite desirable. But the little fellow was a bad failure in this good home. Why?

---

[15] "The Bureau of Educational Counsel: A Student Personnel Department of the La Salle-Peru Township High School and La Salle-Peru-Oglesby Junior College, History and Description of a Personnel Program," *Report for 1923–1926*, 1–27, *passim*.

The man interested the boy in nature, the stars, the woods, he taught him many things through games and work. There was no trouble with bad companions. But the boy continued to engage in sex practices. The good man prayed with him that he might have a clean heart and a clean body, he talked with him about fine subjects at bedtime, he kept him active during the day, he put mittens on the boy's hands at night so that he should not touch his body. He utilized these and other methods to enforce " clean behavior." Then it happened that the boy several times ran out and stayed in the woods, even in the most inclement weather, and indulged in veritable orgies of masturbation. This was plainly a reaction to strivings and repressions.

This most estimable foster father made the fatal mistake of keeping the subject alive in the boy's mind. In spite of all warnings, the man himself had the sex problem constantly before him as a worry. He was bound to save the boy. His many efforts must have indicated his concern. His inquiries, prayings, admonitions, and devices, all gentle and thoughtful, failed because he would not recognize the cardinal psychological feature of such treatment — the trouble must have a chance to get out of mind in order that substitutive interests can have sway. He overemphasized the sex behavior, especially from the emotional standpoint. He called attention to it by his solicitude as well as by his restrictions. The boy never had a long enough opportunity to forget.

The subsequent history of the boy who had much conflict about it all and who wanted to help himself is interesting. In the next foster placing there were no such ideals of fine interests for him, but he did better, although with some recurrences of his orgies. After a time he was returned home and there for long his behavior represents a complete moral recovery. And it is very instructive that in retrospect the boy says that the first foster father did a great deal for him, he remembers now much of it. He desires to go up into the country and visit the man and tell him how he thinks of the different things he was taught there.[16]

The Yale experience, where the attendance at the discussions fell off at the successive meetings but the proportion of those coming repeatedly increased, probably means, as interpreted in the report, that there was a selection of those having personality difficulties, but it is also possible that these mass conferences were facilitating the formation of a group of introverts. It is known that young people and people in general have little resistance to suggestion, that fashions of thought and fashions of dress spread rapidly through conversation and imita-

[16] Healy, Bronner, Baylor and Murphy: *Reconstructing Youthful Behavior: Problem Children in Foster Homes* (in press, Knopf), chap. 7.

tion, and that any form of behavior may be normalized through conversation and participation of numbers. The current conversations about psychoanalysis and the vocabulary of this cult are working in this way on the population. Young people are beginning to normalize their pathological traits or to claim them if they do not possess them. " I am," they say, " an unstable personality and the ordinary reactions are not to be anticipated from me." In this way the method of psychoanalysis has possibilities of unstabilizing as well as stabilizing.

The whole question of what factors in a treatment process of this sort lead to successful adjustment is an important one. Does the analysis itself, the process of becoming " personality-conscious," produce the adjustment? To what extent must changes in situations and activities be associated with the analysis? Finally, in what proportions do adjustments take place concomitantly with changing situations and activities and without the process of analysis?

The lack of a standardized approach makes answers to these questions impossible at the present time. Treatment plans which deal with behavior by working from the psychic processes outward must always face a certain indefiniteness (see chap. XIII).

CHAPTER IV

Community Organizations

A N IMPRESSIVE number of organizations are carrying on programs which are either the modern expression of the neighborliness and mutual aid which characterized societies in earlier times or a
form of idealism which has originated and spread spontaneously among
a group of socially minded people.

The aim of some of these organizations is to meet the crises which
arise in the lives of individuals. The Salvation Army and the charity
organizations represent the most immediate aid in distress, the settlements represent the improvement of conditions in bad localities, the
Children's Aid Societies have still another function. The main relation
of this work to research programs is much the same as that between
medical practice on the one hand and physiological investigation on the
other, or between legal procedure and the study of society. Disorders
and disasters arise and medicine and the law cannot wait but must act
with or without regard to the past and the future. At the same time the
experiences and records of the workers of some of the social agencies
are among the most important data for the study of social processes,
and in connection with these relief organizations there may be developed
definite research features and remedial policies.

The number of relief and emergency organizations is very great.
In Boston alone the total number of " private charitable corporations "
for all ages, including institutions, societies, nurseries, dispensaries,
etc., is 430, and more than 40 of these have to do with children. Philadelphia is equally notable for its organizations of good-will and service.
Many of these organizations are historical, religious and pietistic in
their origin, and many of them are not functioning very efficiently.

The history of the Women's Protective Association of Cleveland affords a good illustration of the work of an emergency organization and of the steps by which a constructive policy with research features may be developed:

The organization whose problems are set forth in the following pages, had its beginnings in a very definite emergency in the city of Cleveland. This city had at one time a segregated district of houses of prostitution, which in 1915 was, with one ordinance, abolished. Inside of 24 hours, therefore, the houses were closed, and crowds of young women and girls were on the streets, or sitting on their suitcases in the railroad station, irresponsibly waiting for whatever might happen to them next. It was obvious to the most callous observer that something had got to be done to protect them from the public and to protect the public from them, and for that immediate purpose the Women's Protective Association was started, with one field worker and an office at the Police Station.

From these beginnings the association has expanded so that in six years there are nine field workers, a liaison worker who divides her time between the police court and the association, a psychologist, and an executive secretary in charge of all. The offices are in the center of the city, with seven consultation rooms and there are two houses in which the girls under investigation may be placed until some further disposition can be made of them. The first is Sterling House, a well built attractive dwelling house, accommodating thirty girls. Although the problem of the prostitute is constant and influences every situation, there are also in Sterling House runaways and shoplifters, deserted wives and homeless strays, who find shelter within its walls. Here our young women must stay until they have a hospital examination, until their stories are verified, and their difficulties thoroughly sifted. After Sterling House they are sent home, placed at work, or committed to an institution as the case may be. If they obtain work in the city, they are still under the supervision of their particular field workers no matter where they live. If they desire, however, they may live at the second association House, Prospect Club, which is run by a Matron and by the girls themselves and where they may live for $6.00 a week. The association is supported by private contributions and by the City Community Chest. Its object is to handle cases out of court so far as possible, to save the overworked court on the one hand, and if possible, to save the girl from a court record on the other. Although the association has no legal right to arrest any one, or to force penniless girls or women of questionable character to accept its ministrations, it has the good will of the authorities who have this right, and they make it possible to give the individual in question the choice of being handled through the association, or of being arrested in the usual manner, and handled through the court. Most of them choose the association and prefer Sterling House to the Police Court or the Jail.

Every girl is given a mental examination upon her arrival. If her case must go to court the examination goes with the report to the judge. If she is sent home, returned to her work, or recommended to an institution, the record is passed on to whomever it may concern. The Psychological clinic has only been a regular part of the association for a few months, so this report can only be made of the 178 cases, which comprise three months' entries. The Stanford-Binet test was given as a preliminary with every case and the average mental age was found to be 11 yrs. 8 mos., although the average chronological age of the girls was 19 years. The charges against them, or the difficulties for which they asked assistance, were as follows:

Immorality — commercial and otherwise 89
Vagrancy and out of work 28
Runaways from home 22
Stealing — mainly shoplifting 20
Forging 6
Suspicious characters 5
Rape 3
Family difficulties 3
Murder 2

Of the 178, three had sixteen year intelligence, and twenty-seven had between fourteen and sixteen year intelligence. If we grant that sixteen years intelligence is too high a standard for the average adult, there were still only 16% of our women of normal adult intelligence, according to the fourteen year old standard. Moreover, there were 15 adults with a mental age of 9 yrs., or an I. Q. of .56 or below, some ranging as low as .37 and .32. Despite the fact that individuals as low as this are a public menace and that every one agrees that they belong in an institution, the State Institutions are over-crowded, and the new ones, though promised, are not built. No matter how much we all agree that an institution is where such adults belong, such an opinion puts no roof over their heads. In not only these cases, but in others almost as bad, it has been necessary to find positions where women of such low grade mentality can make at least a feeble effort to earn their livings. For such women there seem to be the following choices in wage earning: a low type of unskilled factory work, and housework of a simple nature where the employer is willing to put up with incompetency for the sake of getting low-priced help. The factory work is usually of the nature of wrapping goods, like chocolate bars, boxes and other merchandise; sewing buttons; punching holes in leather straps; cutting paper into standard sizes, and similar operations. One factory has frankly assumed it as a civic duty to take its share of morons for simple work. Several girls have made good in this factory, one at sewing and another at turning the trousers of suits right side out when they are finished. In such cases, the feebleminded girl usually likes the work for a time. As one girl said " I have a lovely job. I cut corners off the pieces of paper all day long." However, even this girl with a " lovely job " soon tired of it, and had to be supplied with another task equally simple. In our experience, this class of labor is as easily tired as children and must constantly change to new work. Because promotions never come to them, they demand frequent lateral moves to atone for a lack of vertical progress. . . .

To summarize the report of the activities of our organization, we are spending the time of 12 trained workers, an office staff, and a large and influential set of Board members in working with unfortunate women and girls and their relatives and friends. Out of a random sample of 178, there is a saving remnant of 18% who will make good by earning their own livings, maintaining decent family standards and keeping permanently out of trouble. But these figures do not quite tell the whole story. Although such a discouraging percentage of the whole number are permanent successes, even the work with the others serves a purpose. While they are in our charge, the public is being protected from irresponsible women and the trouble which they make. And even those who are not permanently successful are likely at least to be less complete failures than they were before. They may not ever look out for themselves altogether, but they learn to do so to a greater extent than if they had not been with us. The medical attention, the domestic training, and the friendly treatment which they receive, is for many the only personal attention they have ever had. The treatments for venereal infection alone relieve a vast amount of suffering, which would otherwise be absolutely unchecked. Moreover, the Association offices are for many of them a kind of Club where they may drop in on their holidays and be certain of a welcome. Here they may ask for help in their money difficulties, for advice about their work, and for sympathy in their many love affairs which often run anything but smoothly. Even the weaker sisters who have back-slidden many times, appreciate this semblance of family life which they find in the association offices and houses, and if they do not profit by it as much as we wish they did, at least they are better off than they were before.

If the public could ever be aroused to insist upon adequate institutional care for the hopeless 30% on whom our efforts are wasted except for temporary relief, our constructive activities might be indefinitely extended to other and especially to younger girls. If the average age of our cases might be 14 or 15 instead of 19 years, we are sure that our percentage of permanent cures might be much increased. Our workers, if relieved from the hopeless cases, might be put upon patrol work, to pick up the younger girls at the dance halls, theatres, railroad stations and eating houses, where their troubles usually begin. If we knew them before their bad habits were too well established, the later tragedies of ruined health and lost self respect might be averted. Our workers could spend more time with the schools from whose lower grades our charges are recruited and could branch out into many lines of preventive work in collaboration with the Travelers' Aid, with policewomen, with truant officers and with religious bodies — work which is now impossible because the older incorrigibles necessarily demand first aid and attention.

When we are tempted to discouragement, however, the memory of the girls who six years ago were sitting on their valises in the station, waiting for chance escorts to unknown destinations, encourages us to feel that at least some things have now, through the efforts of the Association, become impossible.[1]

Other types of voluntary organization represent varieties of idealism and some of them claim that their programs are adequate for the solution of social problems if only they have a universal application.

Representing religion and a moral way of life on the one hand and physical manhood and participation in sports on the other, the Young Men's Christian Association has been in a favorable position to become one of the characteristic American institutions. Without being a charitable organization it has been able to place a club, with recreations, companionship, shelter, helpful influence, a degree of " ease with dignity," within the reach of a large number of young men and men of middle age to whom these advantages would have been otherwise inaccessible. It is, in fact, a low-priced men's club, representing at the same time lofty ideals. On account of its character it has been able to make a wide appeal for public support and to command the time and interest of large numbers of able and solid men of affairs in organizing and financing its enterprises. It is now in operation in over 8,000 places in North America and throughout the world. The following statement is from the literature of the Chicago office of the Y.M.C.A.:

It is a high-grade, low-cost young men's club — Christian but nonsectarian.

---

[1] Wembridge, Eleanor R.: " Work with Socially Maladjusted Girls," *Journal of Abnormal and Social Psychology*, 17:79–87 (1922).

It is an athletic organization that does not use men and boys to promote athletics, but uses athletics to develop men.

It is a night school for young men who work by day.

It is a home for young men away from home.

It helps young men not only to help themselves, but to help the other fellow.

It is a place for a young man to find friends and to make himself a friend to the man that needs friends.

Its fellowship, clubrooms, gymnasium, baths, classes and all other practical advantages are open to young men of all faiths.

Over 39,000 different young men and boys were related to each other as members of the Y.M.C.A. of Chicago during the year 1925. While experienced business men serve to direct the policies and handle the business affairs of the Association, as members of the managing boards, the actual working committees — the service groups which carry the work and the message of the Association to the young men and boys in the 21 organized departments and the committees which they serve — are young men and boys. Four thousand seven hundred and thirty seven different members served on the committee forces during 1925.

The business of this movement is to aid in growing character. The effectiveness of The Young Men's Christian Association is well known in directing boys and young men to attain this greatest of life's possessions thru fields of service in which the Association works, namely in religious and moral education, in physical education, thru its social opportunities, and thru its great variety of educational classes, clubs and lectures, all of which is designed to fit boys and young men for the work of life in the home, in business and profession, and for citizenship. " It is of the utmost importance and often particularly difficult to keep the good boys good." [Number of members during 1925, 43,951, of which 33,188 were men and 10,763 were boys. Net assets for 1923, $11,047,991.48].

The Boy and Girl Scouts are character education organizations making use of the child's interest in nature, adventure, pioneer life, Indian lore, woodcraft and the acquisition of skill and distinction:

The aim of the Scout movement is to inculcate character, which, though essential to success in life, is not taught within the school, and being largely a matter of environment is too generally left to chance, often with deplorable results. The Scout movement endeavors to supply the required environment and ambition through games and outdoor activities, which lead a boy to become a better man, a good citizen. . . . Every step in the scouting program is but a means to this end. The variety and interest of, as well as the practical knowledge insured by the tenderfoot, second-class and first-class tests, are, after all, but a means for holding the interest of the boy, pledged to the Scout Oath and Law, under such leadership as will bring about character development. Likewise the whole scheme of merit badges is primarily for this same purpose. The form of troop organization, the scoutmaster and his assistants, the local council, and indeed the National Council and all of its officers, are also but a means to this end. The character development manifests itself in health, efficiency, chivalry, loyalty, patriotism and good citizenship.[2]

Scouts are met in 57 civilized countries, which countries represent 91% of the world's population. In the first sixteen years of scouting (beginning 1910), over 3,000,000 boys became members. [In 1927 the membership was reported as 346,000]. To join, a boy must be 12 years of age. The annual dues are 50 cents. Of the 110,000 adult scout workers in the U. S. less than 500 are paid workers and these only to help the volunteers better serve the boys.[3]

[The Scout Oath]: On my honor I will do my best:
1. To do my duty to God and my country, and to obey the Scout Law.
2. To help other people at all times. 3. To keep myself physically strong, mentally awake, and morally straight.
[The Scout Law]:
1. A Scout is trustworthy. 2. A Scout is loyal. 3. A Scout is helpful. 4. A Scout is friendly. 5. A Scout is courteous. 6. A Scout is kind. 7. A Scout is obedient. 8. A Scout is cheerful. 9. A Scout is thrifty. 10. A Scout is brave. 11. A Scout is clean. 12. A Scout is reverent.
[First Class Scout requirements]:
(1) At least two months' service as a Second Class Scout.
(2) Swim fifty yards.
(3) Earn and deposit at least $2 in a public bank (Premiums paid on life insurance, if earned, are accepted), or plant, raise and market a farm crop.
(4) Send and receive a message by Semaphore, including conventional signs, 30 letters per minute, or by the General Service Code (International Morse), 16 letters per minute, including conventional signs; or by the Indian Sign Language code, thirty signs per minute.
(5) Make a round trip alone (or with another Scout) to a point at least 7 miles away (14 miles in all), going on foot, or rowing boat, and write a satisfactory account of the trip, and things observed.
(6) (i) Review Second Class First Aid requirements. (ii) Describe methods of panic prevention, what to do in case of (iii) fire, (iv) ice, (v)

---

2 Statement of James E. West, Chief Executive, Boy Scouts.
3 *Boy Scouts of America: Handbook for Boys.*

electric and (vi) gas accidents; (vii) what to do in case of a mad dog bite, or snake bite. Demonstrate the treatment, including dressing where necessary, (viii) for a fracture, (ix) poisoning, (x) apoplexy, (xi) heat exhaustion, (xii) sunstroke, (xiii) frost bite and freezing; also demonstrate the treatment for (xiv) sunburn, (xv) ivy poisoning, (xvi) bee stings, (xvii) nosebleed, (xviii) ear-ache, (xix) grit or cinder in the eye, (xx) stomach-ache; (xxi) demonstrate transportation of the injured; (xxii) demonstrate the triangular bandage on the head, eye, jaw, arm (sling), chest, fractured rib, hand, hip, knee, ankle and foot. (Roller bandages may be substituted on arm and ankle.) (xxiii) Demonstrate how to make and apply a tourniquet.

(7) Prepare and cook satisfactorily, in the open, using camp utensils, two of the following articles as may be directed: Eggs, bacon, hunter's stew, fish, fowl, game, pan-cakes, hoe-cake, biscuit, hardtack or a " twist " baked on a stick, and give an exact statement of the cost of materials used; explain to another boy the method followed.

(8) Read a map correctly, and draw, from field notes made on the spot, an intelligible rough sketch map, indicating by their proper marks important buildings, roads, trolley lines, main landmarks, principal elevations, etc. Point out a compass direction without the help of the compass.

(9) Use properly an axe for felling or trimming light timber; or produce an article of carpentry, cabinet-making, or metal work made by himself; or demonstrate repair of a decaying or damaged tree. Explain the method followed.

(10) Judge size, number, height, and weight within 25 per cent.

(11) Describe fully from observation ten species of trees or plants, including poison ivy, by their bark, leaves, flowers, fruit, and scent; or six species of wild birds, by their plumage, notes, tracks, and habits; or six species of native wild animals, by their form, color, call, tracks, and habits; find the North Star, and name and describe at least three constellations of stars.

(12) Furnish satisfactory evidence that he has put into practice in his daily life the principles of the Scout Oath and Law.

[There are 76 merit badges representing fields of skill and knowledge, for example, first aid, electricity, insect life, reptile life, civics, music, etc. These 76 fields are arranged in 12 classes relating to as many possible professions and the boys are advised to seek merit badges in the fields related to their proposed life-work. A First Class Scout may become a Star Scout, a Life Scout, an Eagle Scout when he has gained ten, fifteen and twenty-one merit badges, some of them in designated fields, and fulfilled certain other requirements].

[Examples of " good turns "]: Helped put out a burning field. Got a ball out of a tree for a boy. Picked up nails and glass out of the street. Cut wood for another boy who was sick. Went to town to get husband for sick woman. Assisted a Russian boy with English grammar. Put light over a dangerous place to prevent accidents.

[Examples of Scout activity]: East Burke, Vt., Troupe No. 1: Papered and painted schoolrooms. Improved school furniture. Put a winter's supply of wood in a widow's woodshed. Gathered inscriptions from the gravestones in a number of cemeteries for a local historian. Papered the Methodist parsonage. Gave first aid in a bicycle accident. St. Louis, Mo.: Painted all fences at Wesley House. Kept playground at above Settlement in good shape. Painted apparatus and rolled tennis courts at Settlement. Helped to distribute milk to poor from clinics. Assisted in maintaining discipline, Wesley House, playground, during last year. Also assisted in maintaining Settlement House.[4]

The average duration of the boy scout's life is not above three years. The percentage of membership of those in the twelfth, thirteenth and fourteenth years is approximately the same, and these years represent about 75% of the membership. The 19-year age class contains only fifty-eight one-hundredths of one per cent of the membership. The turnover of scouts and of scout masters is large. It appears that about 20% of the troops and 35% of the scout masters are lost annually.

No criticism of this situation is to be made, however, since youth is a transitional period. A criticism of the interests represented in the program, in comparison with other possible interests, is also out of place, since great liberty should be recognized in the choice of leisure-time activities. We do not take up the question of the effect on character and integrity of a program where the competition for honors is so systematized and overemphasized. There is reason to conclude that the effect is bad.[5] But in general we seem to have here a good influence with bizarre features. The most serious limitation of the program is that it is not adapted to the under-privileged boy, does not appeal to or receive the boy who is a behavior problem, and practically does not touch the great mass of gang life which we have described and from which delinquents and criminals are largely recruited. This is a limitation also of the Y.M.C.A. and other programs which we shall presently consider.

---

[4] From the official literature of the Boy Scouts.

[5] See May and Hartshorne: "Experimental Studies in Moral Education," *Religious Education*, 22:712–15 (1927).

It is a repetition of the situation we shall see in the chapter on character education in the schools, where the good children were amenable and the bad ones inaccessible.

The Girl Scouts is a rapidly growing, admirably conducted organization, modeled on the Boy Scout program, with appropriate modifications. For example:

During the past two years there has been a steadily growing demand for the festival and pageant. Local groups finding it necessary to demonstrate Girl Scout activities in ways other than a literal translation of the program have turned to the festival for a solution.

This form of celebration is most suitable because it is an occasion of joy. Be it a sixteenth century revel with games and masque and athletic stunts, or just a series of dances on the village green, the festival is for all people. There is no discrimination, it is community drama pure and simple.

Several cities in the middle west that still maintain a green in the center of the town have decided this spring to bring back the custom of the town crier. He will call the town folk to the green where the Boy and Girl Scouts bring on the Maypole. Stillwater, Minnesota, is doing such a festival.

The largest performance of the year was the St. Louis festival given last April with 2,400 Girl Scouts participating. Every Girl Scout in the city and county took part provided her dues were paid.

There are two forces in America today which catch the imagination and influence the character of hero-worshipping youth, not only in America but the whole world over. One is our courageous, adventurous, forward-going pioneer; the other our picturesque, colorful American Indian. Both lived in the open and followed the trail. We are restoring our pioneer heritage through our Girl Scout camping, insofar as pioneering, trailing and trips into the open find expression in our camp programs. Trip equipment and trained leadership for such small group expeditions from camp as a woods base represent the next development for our established camps. Minneapolis reported two successful covered wagon trips last summer. Greater use of picturesque, historically accurate Indian material is noticeable, not only in our dramatics and story telling, but in our handicrafts and equipment. A whole Indian village is part of the Springfield, Mass., camp, and the tepees at Camp Tecumseh (Cincinnati) and the Dismals (Alabama) bear witness to a spreading influence.

During 1926, 58 courses have been given by our national instructors in 52 institutions with a total enrollment of 2,099 students. 23 of these courses received full or partial academic credit. June, 1927, will end this particular exploration in Girl Scout training which began in October, 1922. From 1922 to January, 1927, the total number of students enrolled has been 8,769 — 259 courses, given in 143 different institutions, in 41 states.

Ten full nature courses have been given throughout the country. In turn Leaders, who have gone out from these courses, have shared their broadened outlook with the Girl Scouts themselves, and more camps have been dedicated to nature activities and more week-end cabins have been fostered. Leaders' Associations everywhere have had special evenings devoted to nature aims and methods and many Councils have reported nature courses for those leaders who have expressed themselves as especially anxious to gain an understanding of their girls through this phase of the educational program.

This growth in interest during the second year of the Nature Trail program may be demonstrated by numbers of nature badges distributed which surpassed the increase of 1925 over 1924 by 1,516; 2,883 more group and proficiency badges were distributed in 1926 than in 1925. Camp Directors everywhere report the Observer as being the " most popular " nature activity in camp. The Tree Finder presents its popularity as a proficiency badge with the greatest single increase of 438 as an argument for its existence and has proved the value of separating this study from the more general Flower Finder of old. With 4,724 full sets of the Nature Trail Guides already in the field there can be no doubt as to their having met an urgent need, and after an extended time the revised nature program will be carried out everywhere in a satisfactory way. This year there are 250 nature councillors as compared with 208 in 1925. In 1925 the total active paid membership was 138,174 as compared with 162,009 in 1926, or an increase of 18.7%. [Membership, November 30, 1927, 163,234]. And yet only one-quarter of all our Girl Scout Councils are reaching more than 7 girls in every hundred of Girl Scout age, while only 24 are reaching more than 14 in every hundred.

The average time a girl remains in Scouting is three years. When under Local Council, it is found that the girls remain one or two years longer. This may be due to the giving of training courses for leaders which brings them greater enthusiasm for the program, or the inspiration received through conferences and leaders' meetings. On the other hand, only a comparatively few Girl Scouts reach the rank of first class.[6]

As a form of recreation and a means of spending leisure time this activity has the same advantage as that of the Boy Scouts, in that it provides a variety of interesting activities, and the same disadvantage, in that it reaches relatively small numbers and probably those who need it least:

---

[6] Report of the National Director, Jane Deeter Rippin, for 1926.

The Federal Census of 1920 shows over ten million girls between the ages of ten and nineteen; five or six million between ten and fifteen. Roughly, one in every ten people is a human being approaching or leaving girlhood; one in twenty is a girl under fifteen and over ten. Subject to correction from my fellow speaker, Mr. Scott of the Camp Fire Girls, and from the representatives of other organizations working with girls of these ages, I am ready to hazard an estimate that all of us together do not touch more than ten per cent of the total number. In fact, I believe that this estimate is generous. Two years ago, the Education Department of the Girl Scouts made a survey of our troops in the state of New York with special reference to the size of the communities in which they were to be found. We were gratified to discover that we had 21,000 Girl Scouts in the state, but our complacency was short-lived when we realized that this number represented a little under two per cent of the New York State girls of Scout age.[7]

We point out also in the following description that projects having recreational and interest features certainly equal to those of programs of the type we have described, may develop in a favorable public school situation, and will have the added advantages of greater spontaneity and the involvement of all the children in a community:

[A description of one of the group activities in the Winnetka public schools]: A number of eight-year-old children have been reading and talking about the Vikings. The facts necessary for the intelligent understanding of references to Vikings in current literature, or for any other similar purpose, are few. Some reading, some map work, some pictures, suffice in a short time to teach children who the Vikings were, what sort of people they were, where they lived, how the geography of their country affected their character and their activities, how they in turn affected the history of northern Europe. Detailed knowledge in this field is not necessary or important for the average school child. The few things he will really need to know about the Vikings and their country can be readily and happily learned in a fairly rich setting in two or three weeks' time. But the teaching of these facts, the discussion of the lives and habits of Vikings, have aroused the interest of this particular eight-year-old Winnetka group. The Viking feast-hall and feast catch their imagination. Someone suggests that they make a feast-hall. Another suggests that instead of building such a hall they transform their whole schoolroom

---

[7] Elizabeth K. Adams (Educational Secretary, Girl Scouts): Paper read at the 11th Recreation Congress, Atlantic City (October 18, 1924), before the Section Meeting on "Recreation Life for Girls," and printed in *The Playground* (February, 1925).

into one. Suggestions fly thick and fast. There are vigorous discussions. Each child's mind begins working independently toward the common purpose of making the classroom into a Viking feast-hall. One suggests a throne for the king and queen. Another says they should have feasting tables. Another remembers the shields and swords that Vikings would be carrying — another the costumes they would be wearing — another the need for a Viking boat.

The teacher enters into the discussion and the activities. She reads extensively herself to be able to answer the questions poured out by the children. She makes suggestions but is careful to stimulate rather than dominate the group. Here is a group enterprise of the children's own choosing. For weeks their minds and hands are busy with the problem of transforming their classroom into a feast-hall of the Vikings. Some go down to the lumber yards and succeed in borrowing lumber to construct the feast tables. They can get it by agreeing not to drive nails in it. Each child makes himself a shield, with his own original design. The art supervisor comes in here, and discusses with the children the kinds of designs the Vikings used and how they can get Viking effects. The supervisor of music utilizes the interest in Vikings to teach the children some old Norse folk songs. The playground director teaches them Norse folk dances and Viking games.

When the feast-hall is completed there is a feast. Everyone has to be dressed for it. Costumes are made. The meal is planned, the children reading wherever they can find information. Guests are invited — the principal, the music, art and playground directors, the superintendent of schools and one or two parents who have been helping with the costumes and will help with the food. Therefore there must be a little program, some Viking stories, a song and a dance.

It is the day of the feast. All desks have been cleared out of the room. In their place are the long feasting tables and crude benches. At each end of the room is a throne covered with a canopy backed and flanked with tapestries — original productions of the eight-year-old children, but with the Viking feeling. Against the side of the wall lies the Viking boat. There is straw on the floor, and several dogs lie about. Each Viking comes in his costume, bearing his shield which he hangs on a hook. The guests, too, are arrayed in Viking costumes. Mutton stewed with mint is passed around in large wooden bowls from which each Viking helps himself with his fingers. The bones are thrown to the dogs on the floor. Coarse bread and fresh strawberries are parts of the feast. Then comes the mead. One of the children has a father who works in the stockyards in Chicago. The child has persuaded him to bring home three or four dozen steer horns. The children have painted designs on these horns and lined each with a paper cup. The mead is a grape juice punch, and as the children fill their horns and quaff the mead they sing old Norse songs and tell tales of adventure.

Such a project may take as much as three months from its inception to completion — an amount of time totally disproportionate to the factual knowledge the children may gain. But factual knowledge has not been its primary purpose.

Through those three months every child's imagination has been stimulated. Every child has had an opportunity to develop his own particular abilities, to carry out his own particular desires. Every child has varied from the rest. Every child has created, but all the children have worked together toward a common end. Each has seen how the success of his own labors depends upon the successful work of his fellows. Each has seen how the progress of the group as a whole depends upon each individual's doing his full part, making his own contribution.[8]

The Columbian Squires is a religious-ethical-cultural society of older Catholic boys sponsored by the Knights of Columbus:

The object aimed at in the foundation of the Columbian Squires is to prepare Catholic young men to become worthy members of the Knights of Columbus. This ideal will be reached through the development of the youth religiously, intellectually, socially and physically according to his Model, the youth Christ, " Who grew in stature, and age and grace before God and man."

Each unit of Squires in a council is called a circle, which is composed of a variable number of sectors. Each sector comprises a maximum number of sixteen Squires under the direction and guidance of a Knight, called the counselor. The circle elects its own officers from its membership. The whole program of activities is directed by the counselors under the supervision of the Father Prior, who is a priest. The several counselors form an advisory board under the chairmanship of the Grand Knight.

The Columbian Squires is distinctly an older boy program. It is planned for this purpose, limited to boys who have attained their fifteenth birthday, and having for its specific purpose the promoting of the ultimate aim of Christian education as described above, " the transforming of the child of the flesh into a child of God," particularly as this can be done by a Program of Activities with major emphasis on the social-civic objective. It is first and foremost a school of citizenship. The qualities of citizenship it would inculcate are those preserved and developed in the Christian Catholic culture of

[8] Washburne, C., and Stearns, M. M.: *Better Schools: A Survey of Progressive Education in American Public Schools* (1928), 173–77.

the ages, interpreted in the light of American ideals of freedom and democracy. It may make its first appeal to the heart of the boy through organized athletics, but its primary aim, worthy home membership and worthy citizenship, must be kept constantly in mind to prevent its degeneration into an organization purely athletic in purpose. Character building is always first, not muscle making.[9]

The predominance of the religious element in this program is indicated by the following tests:

Church Worship Test: Use of prayer-book at Sunday Mass; Know the Life of Our Lord; Systematic and proportionate giving of some definite amount every Sunday of the year; Reading the life of some heroic Catholic leader (400 marks).

Church Relationships: Reading a Catholic journal every week; Attendance in the sanctuary or choir or as ushers sixty times; Rendering service in church work on ten occasions; Membership in some parochial society (400 marks).

Christian Doctrine Test (Obligatory): Usual Prayers; Catechism; answers to be obtained from the Papal Catechism (800 marks).

Religious Help Test: How to serve Mass; How to serve Vespers and Benediction; Knowledge of symbolism of Church ceremonies and ornaments; Preparation of person and room for administration of the Last Sacraments; How to administer baptism in case of necessity (400 marks).

Religious Habit Test: Habit of daily devotions; Habit of daily reading of Lives of the Saints; Habit of daily visit to the Blessed Sacrament; Habit of constant carrying of beads and scapular (400 marks).

Mission Study Test: The reading of three of the following, or similar works: Life of St. Francis Xavier, Cardinal Lavigerie and White Fathers, Jesuit Missionaries in America, Campbell's Reductions of Paraguay, Life of Father De Smet, St. Peter Claver; Membership in Catholic Students Mission Crusade; Reading of missionary magazine for one year; Twenty hours' service in missionary cause (400 marks).

There has also been established a Boy Life Bureau to supervise and direct the activities . . . in this field and to coöperate with the major organizations supplying boy leadership such as the Boys' Club Federation, Boy Scouts of America, Big Brothers, Playground and Recreation Association, and the American Red Cross.

As a boy masters his work during the season, he will be allowed to present himself for examination; in some cases, before the Counselor, in other cases,

---

[9] From the literature of the Columbian Squires and the Boy Life Bureau of the Knights of Columbus.

before a Board of Judges composed of Knights. The test will be held very seriously and the marks given only according to real merit. Of course, no member is expected to undergo all of the tests in one year, nor should such a course be encouraged. Certain tests should be held before as large a gathering as possible of the Knights; this would stimulate the boys to greater efforts to excel in the tests, both as regards number and marks. The tests must not necessarily be held during the regular meetings but can be held at the convenience of the Counselor and the candidates.

At Christmas and May, in the presence of the conclave and friends of the Squires, the results obtained by the Squires will be solemnly proclaimed.

When a Squire has passed tests entitling him to an aggregate of 4,000 merit marks, he will be awarded a bronze emblem of the Order; when he has earned a total of 6,000 merit marks, he will be awarded a silver emblem, and when he attains 10,000 merit marks, he will be awarded a gold emblem.

These emblems will be awarded in solemn manner and may be worn by the winner only, under penalty of deprivation of membership.

For graduation a minimum of 8,000 merit marks shall be required.[10]

This organization is of recent origin, dating from 1922, and is not highly developed in practice. An extensive program of activities for younger Catholic boys has not been developed.

The Big Brother and Big Sister organizations are a movement to enlist the personal interest of men and women of good-will in behalf of individual boys and girls, particularly those who have come before a juvenile court. Organizations and institutions are utilized, but the main emphasis is placed on personal influence. Protestants, Catholics and Jews are alike participating. The recruiting of the Big Brothers and Big Sisters is done largely through lectures before clubs and churches. The condition and character of those volunteering to act as Big Brothers and Big Sisters are carefully investigated before they are accepted.

The following suggestions are made to the Big Brothers and differ only slightly from those made to the Big Sisters:

Call on the boy in his home as soon as possible. Now is the time he needs you most. By knowing the life he leads and the home conditions, a better understanding of his difficulties may be gained.

Get acquainted with his father and mother. They have been told that a Big Brother would call and try to help the boy to keep out of trouble. They may

---

[10] *Ibid.*

be suspicious of your good intentions, but your own personality will probably give them confidence.

See what can be done to improve home conditions. The lack of real home life is generally the cause of trouble. Few parents really understand adolescence and you can very often enlighten them.

Do not give any money except in extreme cases, but notify us of the need.

If he is not regularly attending school or employed, the first thing to do is to get the boy back in school. A great deal may be accomplished by arousing his ambition.

If the family actually needs his support, try to get the boy employment where he can learn a good trade. Perhaps your own office, where he could have your supervision, would be good temporarily. Our office can sometimes help, but the results are better if you personally can secure it.

Try to devise occupations for his evenings — a gymnasium, night school or social club. We may be able to help you find convenient ones.

See that he gives attention to his teeth and have your physician, dentist or oculist examine the boy, if you think that adenoids, malnutrition, defective teeth or sight is the cause of retardation or perversity.

Invite him to your own home and make him feel that he is welcome. It will probably be a revelation of " home " to him. Please do not take him to night entertainments or allow him to be away from home over night.

Invite him to visit you at your office or place of business. He may have no conception of the possibilities of a business or professional life.

Take him to a ball game with you. It is a good way to get acquainted and make him realize that you too are human and but a little older; a concert or a good, clean drama might awaken new interests.

Take him to church with you occasionally and see that he attends regularly — either at church or Sunday school. It is essential that every boy receive some moral education.

Lend him books or magazines and try to encourage a habit of reading. Secure a card for him at a convenient Public Library and show him how to use the privileges.

Try to find out his particular abilities, and endeavor to mould his choice of a vocation.

Get him to assume some responsibility, and to realize his duty to cheerfully help others.

Get him to write to you once in a while, and always answer him promptly.

Keep your promises. Remember the force of example.

Please report to us frequently in regard to his progress, change of address, or employment. . . . Unless we hear to the contrary, we will have to assume that you are doing nothing for him, and will make a reassignment.

[Examples of activity]: The Big Sisters Council [of Rochester, N. Y.] has coöperated with 37 agencies in aiding 320 Little Sisters to solve problems involving home conditions, recreation, employment and environment according to the report of the secretary, Miss Elizabeth R. Mertz. Fifty of the Little Sisters now being served by the Council are girls more than 16 years of age, the Council being the only agency doing case work with problem girls of more than 16. A trained worker has been added to the staff to help provide such girls with proper environment, recreation and employment. There are 192 Big Sisters now affiliated with the Council. They have made during the past year 2,982 visits. The office staff has had 2,387 conferences with girls and made 2,200 home visits. The second series of instruction meeting for prospective Big Sisters has been concluded.

Particularly significant is the scholarship work of the Jewish Big Brothers [of Cincinnati, O.] which supports nine boys in colleges and universities; one, a little brother of exceptional capacity, is now a junior at Yale. The Big Brothers number 725. As a result of their work there are now few Jewish boys in correctional institutions from Hamilton County.

The high point of the work of the Catholic Big Sisters [of Brooklyn, N. Y.] for 1926 . . . was the establishment of a sinking fund of $30,000 to make the Big Sisters a permanent part of the social welfare work of the Borough. This sinking fund invested in first mortgage guaranteed bonds was part of the $38,365 proceeds netted from the Big Brothers and Big Sisters Boxing Carnival directed by Edward J. Kenny. After donating $1,600 for a Big Sister to the Holy Family Hospital and $1,000 for the Big Sister Free Milk Fund, the balance was deposited in savings banks to be withdrawn as required for current expenses.

The report for 1926 stresses prevention. Of 1,400 cases, 1,200 were preventive. They included finding employment for 367 people, locating 157 girls and women in suitable homes and establishing a student relief fund which has enabled 50 Brooklyn boys and girls to complete their school courses. During August and September 2,670 quarts of milk were distributed by the Free Milk Fund. More than 4,300 articles of clothing and 100 pieces of furniture were given to the destitute.[11]

The Big Brother and Big Sister Federation (Rowland C. Sheldon, Executive Secretary) reports the number of the Federation's local Big Brother organizations as 502 (39 member organizations plus 463 non-member); the number of communities served as 460 (43 by member and 417 by non-member organizations). There are no boy members.

[11] *The Ounce* (August, 1927).

The paid men workers in member organizations number 135, and the volunteer Big Brothers 4,233.

The misbehavior of boys, especially as it takes the form of delinquency, tends to be groupwise and predatory. We have noticed that in 90% of the cases of stealing by boys brought before the Chicago juvenile court during a certain period two or more boys were involved. Thrasher's volume, *The Gang*, discloses the great importance and extent of this spontaneous association of boys among themselves and makes it plain that the route to professional crime is usually through the gang. Partly in recognition of this situation and partly as an element in more general social programs, there has been an extensive development of clubs organized for the benefit of boys. One of the older of these organizations, the Hull House Boys' Club, may be taken as an example. It will be noticed that this program, while providing for the individual boy who has no gang relations, also receives and provides for gangs as a whole, not attempting to dissolve them immediately:

The Hull-House Boys' Club occupies a five story building devoted entirely to men and boys club work. In addition there is a well equipped gymnasium with running track, shower baths, etc., in another building.

The policy of the Club has been to meet the needs of the boys in the neighborhood. No boy is excluded for reasons of race, mental capacity or economic standing.

There is a combination of the mass and small club organization. Any group of boys may come to the Club as a group and retain their own organization. They are given a room in which to meet and a leader is furnished to help them with their program, they are also given a special period on the gym. as a group for team practice. This is the method used to influence the gang activities so vital in our neighborhood. . . .

Within a radius of four blocks of the Club there are scores of boy groups, or gangs, as they are usually called, of all ages. These are the natural groupings of the boys themselves and common to all boydom; but in the densely populated sections of our cities, especially those known as " foreign communities," these groups take on a somewhat more intense form of organization. They are made up of boys living in well-defined areas, such as both sides of the same street between two intersecting car lines. Here they play together, from toddling infants, always within sound of the shrill voice and under the watchful eye of their parents, who after the day's work gather in front of their houses to discuss the latest gossip, and to talk about the good times they had when they were children in the " old country."

When the boys become old enough to attend school or the movies, they do so in groups, and as soon as school is over or " The End " flashed upon the moving picture screen, back they go to play in the home street. They feel strange and out of place in other parts of the neighborhood. If they visit near-by parks or playgrounds for special games or swimming, it is always as gangs and never as individuals.

As the years pass this feeling of solidarity becomes more intense, and if one of the families moves away to another street, or even to a distant part of the city, the boys return to spend their leisure time with the old crowd. If one should be unfortunate enough to get into some difficulty with one of the gang, the entire group are his enemies. A fight with one means a fight with all.

It is with these natural groupings (misdirected or utilized by unscrupulous leaders, they become the gangs of newspaper and criminal notoriety) that the Hull-House Boys' Club does its intensive work. The boys are received as a group and encouraged to formally organize into a club under a leader, a room is given them in which to conduct their meetings, and a period in the gymnasium set aside for their team practice and the playing of matched games. Tournaments and leagues are arranged in which the different clubs take part, competing against each other under trained leadership.

The wishes of the boys determine the type of club they will have, and the membership in it is limited to those of their own choosing. They elect their officers, collect their dues, and are free in carrying out their ideas as they would be were they to have a club room on their own street. . . . [Enumeration of eleven clubs holding weekly meetings during the past year].[12]

The Boys' Club Federation is an organization to promote the formation of clubs, to study their operation, and to provide information and advice to communities organizing and operating clubs. The Federation undertakes through a technical staff to make regional surveys in order to determine favorable locations for the erection of clubs, to provide architectural plans, etc. This organization reports for 1927 a total membership of 227,201 boys in 276 boys' clubs:

The United States, Canada and six foreign countries are represented. The United States Clubs are located in 122 cities in 32 states, the District of Columbia and Hawaii; the Canadian Clubs in six cities and five provinces; the English Clubs in nine different cities, making a total of 145 cities where units of the Federation are now reported.

[12] Communicated by Wallace W. Kirkland, Director of the Hull House Boys' Club.

An increase of 25,030 in the past two years is recorded in total membership, 17,284 being the increase in American boys between January, 1926, and January, 1928, and 7,746 the increase in membership in England, Canada, Holland, Australia, New Zealand and India.

Sixty-three Clubs now report a membership of more than a thousand, ranging from 1,000 to more than 9,000 members. Headed by the Boys' Club of Boston, which is now the largest Boys' Club in the world, with a membership of 9,405, the first twelve Clubs in the Federation are as follows: Boys' Club of Boston, Mass., 9,405; Boys' Club of New York, New York City, 8,036; Germantown Boys' Club, Philadelphia, 6,038; Jewish People's Institute Boys' Department, Chicago, 5,192; Worcester Boys' Club, Worcester, Mass., 5,129; Newsboys' Republic, Milwaukee, Wis., 4,500; Salem Fraternity, Salem, Mass., 4,000; Chicago Boys' Club, Chicago, 3,439; Pawtucket Boys' Club, Pawtucket, R. I., 3,257; Lawrence Boys' Club, Lawrence, Mass., 3,143; Providence Boys' Club, Providence, R. I., 2,958; Union League Boys' Club, Chicago, 2,955.

More than $12,264,793 represents the value of buildings owned by 108 Clubs. . . . The largest and most modern Boys' Club building in the membership of the Federation, the new Jefferson Park Building of the Boys' Club of New York at 321 East 111th Street, opened on December 18th, 1927, represents an investment of $750,000, and is planned to care for a membership of 6,500 boys from the district immediately surrounding the Club.

A review of 1927 shows that during the year 31,699 boys attended camp. One hundred forty-nine Clubs are now conducting vocational and hobby classes, a total of 686 classes having been held in 64 different subjects, ranging from woodwork to barbering and from jewelry making to bricklaying. Woodwork and cabinet making is the most popular subject, with an annual increase of 10 per cent in number of classes operating in the last four years, a total of 101 such classes now being conducted. Art classes are second in popularity, printing third and radio fourth. Classes in radio show a decrease of 25 per cent in 1927. There is a notable increase in the number of paid and volunteer workers, boards of directors and especially the membership of ladies' auxiliaries, which has increased from 3,430 in 1926 to 8,635 in 1927. Adding the 4,176 paid and volunteer workers and the 2,446 members of boards of directors, this gives a total of 15,257 workers and directors, or an average of 55 workers per Club.

Dramatics, debating, dancing, moving pictures, shows — every phase of wholesome and instructive amusement is a part of the Boys' Club general scheme for development.

One of the strongest claims of the Boys' Club is that it does the maximum work with the minimum outlay. The expenditures reported by 72 representative Boys' Clubs in the United States with a membership of 91,712 showed an annual per capita cost of $9.25.[13]

In the studies it is now making of the boy situation and in its regional surveys the Boys' Club Federation has confirmed what has been emphasized by Thrasher and is mentioned in the report of Kirkland, quoted above, that the gang organization of boys, especially in the larger cities, is very solidary and that their behavior is so different from boy behavior as we know it as to constitute a different type of personality and, so to speak, a different civilization. The situation is a repetition of the one met in the problem of the contact of races and cultures where each group brings its separate body of habits, prepossessions and prejudices. The ecologists and ethnologists have determined that there are in the world greater and smaller regions which they term " areas of characterization" profoundly marking the individual and group traits of these regions. In the cities the slum regions in particular are areas of characterization profoundly marking the habit systems of the boys.

It is also a misapprehension to suppose that there are no play opportunities in these regions. There is not the recreational, supervised and athletic play of the parks, the Y.M.C.A. and the boys' clubs, but there is the unsupervised play of vacant lots and pool rooms, and for the older boys the life and death adventure of gang warfare and criminal enterprise, with money, dress, freedom from work, and girls. Their life does not lack stimulation. It is reminiscent of the Borgias, Sforzas and Malatestas:

The Valley Gang on Fifteenth Street, Chicago, has had an active life of over thirty years. . . . Its members have boasted that they have worn silk shirts and have ridden in Rolls-Royce automobiles since the war. Their great opportunity for wealth came with prohibition and their entrance into the rum-running business. Eventually they controlled a string of breweries both in and out of Chicago, and their leaders are said to have made millions in these enterprises. One of them occupies an exclusive North Shore estate purchased for $150,000. Their money has stood them in good stead, for they have been able to employ the most expensive lawyers to defend them and when serving sentences in certain penal institutions they have been permitted

---

[13] *Annual Report of the Boys' Club Federation for 1927*, and information from Robert K. Atkinson, Secretary.

to come and go almost as freely as though they were living at a hotel. At present they dress in the height of fashion, ride in large automobiles with sleek chauffeurs, and live on the fat of the land. . . . [When playing indoor ball in a park a member of another gang remarked, in the presence of the athletic director, " I don't see how in hell a fellow can get his mind on this game "].[14]

Realizing that bad boys are usually associated in gangs and that it is very difficult to convert a boy so long as he remains in his gang surroundings, boy workers have attempted to win over the gang as a whole. Under this influence the Union League Club of Chicago developed the notable plan of forming a club with advantages which would outrival those of gang life:

Included in their plan was the notion of making the boys, many of whom were at that time wasted economic material, valuable workers. In pursuance of this purpose the Union League Boys' Club was established in a large well-equipped building at Nineteenth and Leavitt Streets, a district known for its high rate of delinquency, and a director of unusual ability was engaged. Within three years the membership was built up to more than seventeen hundred boys and young men, and the director found places in industry and business for more than eight hundred of them. The situation with regard to juvenile delinquency in the area was changed; whereas formerly it had been the rule for a boy from this district to be brought into the courts, it now became the exception. Juvenile delinquency in this police precinct actually decreased 81 per cent. (The decrease for the city as a whole during the same period was relatively small). The judge of the Juvenile Court is reported to have said that twenty clubs like this in Chicago would put him out of business, and the Chief of Police, " If there was a boys' club in every precinct, juvenile delinquency could be reduced to the minimum."

The general policy used by the club in dealing with gangs is to break up the natural groups and build supervised clubs in their places. One of the first steps is to enlist the interest of the gang leader. There is danger in inviting the whole gang to come in at one time. The leader in such cases may take the attitude of expecting to run the building. Backed by his gang, any slight objection which he may raise to the procedure of the club may result in his telling the boys' worker to " go to h—— " and in a rapid get-away by the whole gang. For this reason it is not the custom of the club to take in the gang as a group, but to enrol its members as individuals and offer them something better than the gang can give. The leader is first interested and put on

---

[14] Thrasher, Frederic M.: *The Gang* (1927), 433–35.

a team; ultimately the rank and file of the gang follow and are interested in special activities.

One feature of the club which facilitates the method described above is the " flytrap." This is a room (close to the vestibule and adjacent to the offices) in which there are five pool tables. Here boys from the street, especially the younger fellows, can play. Two or three men work quietly among these boys, getting acquainted with them, and learning their personal histories and aptitudes. When there is a vacancy in the band or on a team, these men furnish the names of boys with whom they have become acquainted in the " flytrap." In this way these boys are drawn into the club and interested in some regulated activity.

The success of the club has been due to a large extent to the dynamic personality of the director, Robert D. Klees. The characteristic twinkle in his eye betokens a more than ordinary understanding of human nature. He analyzes leadership in a very simple way: it consists, first, in knowing people, understanding them; and secondly, in being a little ahead of them. He is greatly admired by the members of his club, who frequently consult him as to their vocational possibilities. Those who prove themselves to be worthy know that they are sure of his assistance in getting a position with some public utility or large business in the city. It is not difficult to enlist the interest of the most capable members of the gangs in this way and consequently to develop an intense loyalty to the club, to which they are under considerable obligation for their advancement. The director differs from some boys' workers in that he is not a weak apologist for the present economic order, but a partner in it. He shows the boys that it pays to play the game as he teaches it and to play it honestly.

The object of the director is to win the confidence of the boys and to enjoy the friendship of the whole neighborhood. His method is strictly non-sectarian and his hall is open to any religious or other group for a large social meeting.

The policy of the club is not to permit self-government to the limit, not to let the gang come in and run the building. Supervision is regarded as necessary, although the boys may govern themselves if they play fair. The method of securing their coöperation, however, is not compulsion, but indirect inducement.

The interests and activities which serve as substitutes for those formerly promoted by the gangs are many and varied. A band of fifty pieces has been fitted up at a cost of $3,500; an orchestra and a bugle and drum corps are also maintained. Each player, with whose parents the club has a written agreement, is intrusted with his own instrument. The club also maintains classes in wood-working, basket-making, and mechanical drawing. An average of one hundred boys visit the club library each day. The dramatic class presents a number of plays during the year, having recently given " As You Like It." The club camp is attended by four or five hundred boys each summer. A scholarship fund is maintained to encourage attendance at college. There are two home visitors, and plans have been made for a dental clinic.

The athletic program of the club is designed gradually to replace the unsupervised type of " athletic club," of which there are still a number in the district. The very best athletic equipment is furnished for the gymnasium. On Saturday mornings the gymnasium is open and free to everybody. Any gang can come in and whistle and sing to its heart's content. During this period occur boxing bouts, which are supervised so as to give the bully an opponent who can lick him if possible. Strong teams are developed in the various sports, especially football, basket-ball, and baseball, for which excellent coaches are provided. Regular series of games are listed on printed schedules. The club does not permit its team to play for money, as is the custom with the unsupervised clubs. In spite of the lack of monetary incentive, however, the club baseball team played twenty-eight games with the best amateurs in one season and won every game.

By putting the most capable gang athletes on a team, the whole gang is captured. This was accomplished in one case with a rowdy baseball team which always played for money or a keg of beer. The pitcher, a boy of eighteen years, heard of the club baseball team and asked if he could pitch. He agreed to be sportsmanlike and was given a place. This broke up the gang team and led eventually to five of its members becoming regulars on the club squad.

The director's understanding of human nature is indicated in the case of the " dethroning " of an arrogant gang leader known as " the king." A boy was finally found who considered himself sufficiently skilled in the pugilistic art to whip " the king." The occasion soon presented itself and even though it was Sunday, the boys went out of the club and, in the midst of a group of spectators who guaranteed fair play, had their fight. The result was such a drubbing for " the king " as to completely dethrone him and win his gang to membership in the club. In another case some boys wanted to be thrown out, so that they could brag about it to their gang across the street. Instead, the director had them brought to his private office and told them that they could not return to the club until they brought their fathers with them; they could not brag about this.

The result of these methods of dealing with boys has been that ultimately the members come to possess something of their director's enthusiasm and self-confidence and take real pride in their loyalty to their club.[15]

---

[15] Thrasher: *op. cit.*, 520–23.

The membership of boys' clubs and similar organizations has not usually been extensive enough to reach a large percentage of the total boy population, and the leaders of the work confess that they have not been very successful in reaching the gang boy and the bad boy in general in their neighborhoods. The Boys' Club Federation has prepared a statement on delinquency in Chicago and the number of boys reached by the combined efforts of boy organizations:

In 1926, of the [19,566] complaints against juveniles investigated by the Police Probation Officers, about 18,000 were Boys. The number of complaints requiring official investigation was equal to one in every 10 boys of juvenile age in the City. Of this group, one in every 12 committed some offense, serious enough to be brought into the Juvenile Court. So serious, in fact, were these cases that all but 40 were committed to institutions or placed on probation. . . .

In 1926, 682 juvenile delinquents were committed to institutions for correction. . . . The number of complaints recorded by the Juvenile Court does not adequately measure the dangerous situation that is developing in early boyhood, to be discovered in the young men of 17, 18, 19, 20 years. In 1926, there were 12,711 arrests of boys 17 to 21. The arrests are equal to one in every seven young men of that age in the City. Not only is the number of arrests greater in proportion to population than the juvenile record, but the offender is no longer a child. This is the age in which crimes of the greatest severity are committed. No doubt the record includes some duplications and many minor offenses as well as excluding some unapprehended cases and many for serious offenses. . . .

Within the City of Chicago, there are approximately 282,690 boys between 8 and 18 years of age. [An estimate based on the records of all clubs having a membership of over 50 boys, the Young Men's Christian Association and the Boys Scouts of America, shows that] at least 221,979, or 79%, are unreached by existing boys' work facilities.[16]

It has also been determined by the surveys of the Boys' Club Federation and by those of the Chicago sociologists that only boys from a relatively restricted area frequent the boy organizations. The New York office of the Federation has prepared spot maps of membership in a large number of boys' clubs and worked out the effective radius of a club, and makes the following statement:

---

[16] Statement of the Boy Conditions in Chicago. Prepared by the Boys' Club Federation. Manuscript.

Approximately 60 per cent of the boys who attend the club will come from within a half-mile radius, and 85 to 90 per cent from within a three-quarter mile radius. These figures will vary in different localities and are affected by local features, such as railroad tracks, busy streets, etc.[17]

In commenting on their work, therefore, the officials of the boys' clubs and similar organizations emphasize the necessity of multiplying the clubs sufficiently to reach all the boys in all the desirable regions. And this is evidently very important, but even so, the main difficulty remains untouched. The good boys tend to frequent the clubs and the bad ones tend to remain away. In the report of Mr. Kirkland we noticed that the gang boys were encouraged to use the club as gangs and did this freely, but there remained a large element untouched by the club influences. He reports further:

For the past few years I have been attempting a study of the solution of the so-called " boy problem." My observations so far show that our present methods do not, and cannot be expected to, reach nearly 100% of the boys. We are also aware that a large percentage of the official delinquents are from the group of boys who are outside the membership of the present agencies. Our Boys' Clubs, Y.M.C.A.'s, Scouts, etc., by their very natures tend to act as sieves, eliminating a certain percentage of the boys they are trying to reach. I find that were it possible to increase the number of the present agencies to their " ideal " limit, there would still be a " boy problem." For instance, if we were to increase the number of Boys' Clubs in Chicago to 500, there would be a decrease in the number of official delinquents, but there would still be a great number, and the decrease would not be in proportion to the increase in the number of Boys' Clubs. This would be true of all other present agencies. This conclusion is arrived at by the fact that in the immediate area, within a four block radius of our Boys' Clubs, we find many boys not connected with the Club, nor directly influenced by the Club's activities, and among this group will be found the largest number of delinquents. These boys are delinquent not because they are not members of the Club, but in spite of the Club. And they will continue to be delinquent, were the number of Clubs in their area increased.

My opinion is that there are 70% of the boys in our neighborhood not being directly reached by existing social organizations. These boys are all aware of Hull House, and are possibly influenced by it in an indirect way, but when I use " directly reached " I am thinking of something definite, such as the regular attendance at classes or some other activity. This opinion is based

---

[17] Communication from Robert K. Atkinson, Secretary.

on observation only, so could not be quoted as though it were based upon fact.

I have been connected with the work here for the past six years and have had opportunity of seeing many boys grow up into young men. As I look over this group, I find that the ones who seem to have been helped are those who have been definitely connected up with some personality over a period of years.[18]

It could be made to appear from statements of juvenile court judges and boy organization officials that this movement is highly successful, at least in certain places, and that it is the solution of the problem of delinquency and crime; all that is needed is an extension of the work. We do not wish to take up these statements in detail. General statements and testimonials are like epitaphs. But we refer to a statement of Judge Arnold of the Chicago juvenile court which has been much discussed because it implies that a boys' club is rapidly cleaning up one of the worst police precincts in the city:

During the twelve months following the establishment of the Union League Boys' Club, the juvenile cases reported to the police of the 18th Precinct show a decrease of 73%. There was a time when delinquent Boys' cases from this district was the rule, now a case from this district is an exception.[19]

This is the club mentioned by Thrasher in the document quoted above, and we do not at all question that a very successful experiment is going on there, but what happened in this case seems to have been not so much a reduction of delinquency as a change in policy on the part of the police. Of approximately 18,000 boys whose delinquencies came to the attention of the police in 1926, only 1,430 were taken before the juvenile court. That is, the police use discretion and release or parole to their families a large proportion of the cases. It would therefore be very natural that the police of this precinct should use their discretion at this point and parole or virtually parole a larger number of the boys to the club, and we are informed that something of this kind is in fact done. It is known that the policy of the police can make the crime rate appear to be almost anything. If the patrolmen are instructed to go easy in a certain district and make fewer arrests, the

[18] Communication from Mr. Kirkland.

[19] Judge Victor P. Arnold, from unpublished data in the New York office of the Boys' Club Federation.

crime rate seems to diminish. If another commissioner instructs them to clean up the district the rate seems to rise. If in 1926 the police of Chicago had adopted the Boston plan of taking practically every case to court it might have appeared that boy delinquency had increased more than 1,000 per cent.

A similar claim is made for the boys' club of Worcester, Massachusetts:

We have in the Boys' Club five thousand boy members, not a hand-picked lot because we have no membership limitations whatever, either of minimum age, character, religion, color or money. These boys are a considerable proportion of all the boys in Worcester likely to get into trouble.

During the year June 1, 1925, to June 1, 1926, over nine hundred names of boys under twenty-one years of age appeared on the police blotters for delinquency and crime. Of this number only thirty-four were members of the Boys' Club. Those outside the Club produced practically all the delinquents and criminals. . . . At fourteen years of age, we have exactly half of all the boys in Worcester in the Boys' Club. There were eighty-six boys of this age whose names appeared upon the police blotters during the year mentioned in the circular. Of this eighty-six, only seven were members of the Club. In other words, with 50% of boys of that age in the Boys' Club only 8% of the delinquents were members of the Club.[20]

But the literature of this club shows also that about the time this claim was made the club was making a drive for an auxiliary club in a bad " north end section," and that much of the delinquency comes from this section. It is conceivable that the present club, situated in a good residential district and unpenetrated by the boys from the bad districts, is constituted almost entirely of good boys. We might even, by an exaggeration, reproach the management for allowing 34 of its members to go wrong. We do not imagine this is precisely the situation, but this is a case where a general statement, which is in fact a partial statement, means nothing at all.

We are at present skeptical of any claim that a boy organization has gone into a bad region and reduced juvenile delinquency by anything like so heavy a percentage. All such statements have to be checked up against possible administrative and other factors which might have produced part of the change.

---

[20] From the literature of the Worcester Boys' Club.

Assuming that the claims of certain of these clubs are correct, it would be very important to know as fully as possible the conditions which have produced this relative success. The Boys' Club Federation, which is a research as well as a planning body, has now undertaken to study this situation in regard to the district served by the Boys' Club of New York where, it is claimed, juvenile delinquency is 60% less year after year than in contiguous districts.

We may distinguish between keeping the person good and reforming him after he has become bad. The boys' organizations have drawn mainly those who have remained good and have been relatively successful in keeping them good, if indeed they would not have remained good under any circumstances. In one of its pieces of literature the Chicago Y.M.C.A. says: " It is of the utmost importance and often particularly difficult to keep the good boys good." Up to the present the bad boy has proven as difficult a problem as the bad man. Nevertheless, the organization of boys among themselves, in spite of its incomplete success, may be regarded as a most promising field for further experimentation. We have found that the responsible and thoughtful leaders in the boy organizations do not claim that their particular programs are sufficient when taken alone. They do claim that they have a powerful instrument for the control of boy behavior, capable of much further development.

The organized movement for recreation and playgrounds which began in the late nineties has also become one of the distinguishing features of American life. This attractive feature of life appeals to everybody, without reference to political parties, and interest in children and in sport, civic pride, the idea of " the city beautiful," make it possible to secure large public and private support.

In 1926, 790 cities maintaining community recreation programs under leadership reported to the periodical *Playground* (32 cities having such programs did not report):

This is the greatest number of cities which have ever reported and is an increase of 288 over the number for 1921. Most encouraging is the increase in the number of paid leaders from 11,079 in 1921 to 17,090 in 1926. The number of volunteer leaders has increased to 8,625. Other significant indications of growth are found in the total of 10,123 separate play areas under leadership and in the number of city governments appropriating funds for the support of community recreation activities. The training of leaders again achieved a perceptible growth, as shown in the reports from 145 cities having training institutes. In 125 of these cities the total enrollment of workers was 5,073. The enrollment of volunteer workers in the training institutes in 65 of the 77 cities reporting was 3,094. . . . The total expenditure for public recreation in 1926, as reported by 665 cities, is $19,202,123.25.

[Of the 758 cities sending complete reports the managing municipal authority was a Playground and Recreation Commission in 197 cities; a Board of Education in 124 cities; a Park Board in 127 cities; a City Council in 10 cities, etc. In 17 cities municipal departments combined in the management of playgrounds and community centers, e.g., Park Commissioners and Boards of Education].[21]

The magnitude and rate of acceleration of this movement are very impressive, and also the tendency to associate the direction of leisure time with the schools. Recently also the directors of this work have realized that along with the healthful and recreational activities there is a unique opportunity to work on the behavior of the boy. The situation is congenial, the children participate in large numbers, all of them desire to excel in some line and are responsive to the suggestions of the instructors. In some localities, therefore, the directors of the play programs are making studies to determine the interest trends and aptitudes of the children, with a view to vocational direction and the development of well-balanced personalities.

In the following report it will be seen that in the organization of work two general principles are followed — the children collaborate with the director in the selection of the sports which are emphasized, and inter-playground competitions are arranged on a basis which is designed to give distinction to the participant both personally and as member of a group:

It seems to us that, craving distinction as all of us do, one of the motivations behind our recreational pursuits is the desire to achieve recognition and enjoy applause, developing personality and placement not only in one's own self-respect, but also in the eyes of one's fellows, by doing a thing which appeals to some answering capacity more or less latent in us, and doing it well enough to become a recognized performer. As a result of this reasoning, we present, cafeteria style, a varied recreational menu, attempting to attract youth into

---

[21] *The Playground: Yearbook Number* (April, 1927).

undertakings for which he has natural inclination, and dignifying the results of his participation by scoring toward an all around inter-park supremacy, the achievement of every park representative throughout the year, in all of our competitive events, which are programed to include a wide range, (1) of physical undertakings, (2) a comprehensive sampling at least, of constructive activity, such as the model aeroplane tournament, kite and sail-boat tournaments, etc., (3) some representative things in the field of æsthetic enterprises, where the thing done or created verges on the field of art undertakings, (4) a few items appealing to use of one's mentality rather than muscle in combat, such as checkers, chess, puzzle solution, and so on, (5) certain things which are motivated largely by the altruistic urge. Scoring the points won to the credit of each institution, we announce monthly the relative standing of the eighteen parks in aggregate accomplishment. The person whose ability lies in mechanical lines or inventive capacity is as much a contributor to the community rating by this means as is the star athlete, and this device alone has been of material help to us in preventing the athlete, in his lordly sense of superiority, from laughing out of court certain " sissy " things, which he holds in contempt, but which are very real interests to certain elements in our juvenile community life.

To check roughly on our own arbitrary selection of these activities, we have several times issued a questionnaire, calling it a recreational preference ballot, and organizing with the machinery of an election the collection of the filled-in sheets. Of course, this device is subject to all the objections inherent in a questionnaire method of assembling information. We provide, however, for a signature on each ballot, and with all due allowance for the inaccuracies of a questionnaire procedure, I think the results have been somewhat helpful to us, and we have plotted curves of the indicated popularity of various types of recreational undertaking, according to the age of the respondent. Some of the curves resulting have been rather interesting, for instance, the crest of the wave of interest in hiking coincides with the years in which the runaway tendency is most prevalent, and we get certain indications as to when more elaborate undertakings emerge or subside. . . .

Some years ago we began observing some of the implications running along with physical activity. Instances came to our attention with some frequency indicating that under the surface in this whole field of dealing with people's sport interests, we were dealing with things of apparently high voltage. It requires some power to re-route an entire life, and break a boy out of all of his existing habits, but we saw it done very frequently under the mere inspiration of an athletic enthusiasm. If we could subject this enthusiasm to control, and direction, it appeared that we might experiment in a new laboratory of human behavior. For instance, one of my prize athletes who is now a successful contractor here in the city, told me his own history — membership in a boys' gang, whose chief object was thievery to get the means for a drunken debauch from their barn basement hangout, was his first entry into social contacts outside the family circle. He was so frail he had been taken out of school at fourteen, and was unable to go to work, was a cigarette addict, and practically all of his energies went into the gang exploits. With the opening of the park, he spent his spare time all summer throwing a base ball in the park games, and at the end of summer, stepping out of the shower room before a mirror, he noticed for the first time some muscle showing in his right arm, as he reached up to scratch his head. He rushed into the Instructor's office to exhibit this muscle, and the Instructor told him if he would cut out the booze, and lay off the cigarettes, they would make a man of him. He resigned immediately from his gang, burned up his cigarettes, refused the beer served at supper table that night, and was waiting at the gate for the Instructor next morning.

This was in 1905. He told me the story in 1910, because he was reminiscing on the way home from the national tournament, holding in his hand the diamond medal for the amateur national heavyweight wrestling championship of the United States. He went on to state that coming up as fast as he did, after getting under way, he developed an overwhelming temper. His first athletic skill was in the game of Basket Ball, in which he became a well known star. Going into the final game for the city championship one night, the opposing team, fearful of his ability, were playing him very closely, constantly fouling him when the referee's attention was distracted. He became angrier as the game progressed, and finally, on being put out of a critical play when the score was very close and the game was nearing its climax, he lost his head, slugged the man who had fouled him, was caught at it, and thrown out of competition for a year. This proved to him that if he was ever to get anywhere in athletics, he must learn to control his temper. He did not feel able to talk it over with anyone, but began watching himself to sense the exact nature of the thing he had to fight. He observed that when his temper began rising, he first muttered silent curses under his breath, at the opponent. He resolved to stop this by quitting his habit of profanity. Later he discovered that he was substituting slang, and stopped that. Fighting himself in this fashion, he gradually came to the ability to hold himself fairly well on his home floor, but was still doubtful as to what might occur in the city championship crisis, and one day he talked with one of the older athletes who was a wrestler, asking how this friend could stand the punishment of that sport without getting sore. Old Max Lutbeg, the man he inquired of, told him to take up the sport, if that was his difficulty, explaining that anger only resulted in more severe punishment, and assuring him that if he could learn to control himself on the wrestling mat, he never need have any fear as to losing his self-control on the basket-ball floor. He plunged into wrestling, as a result, and came to be an ardent devotee of the game.

Partly as the result of experiences of this type, we recast our system of grading athletic successes, and we evolved a new process of scoring athletic achievement, giving conduct, as evidenced in a contest, an even greater weight in determining the winner than the successful scoring of points, usually considered as winning the game. After some rearrangements and experiment, we now score Victory as a 30% factor, Sportsmanship a 50% factor, and what we term Reliability, a 20% factor — Reliability meaning the time element in keeping one's appointment with team-mates and spectators at the scheduled time, promptly at the blowing of the whistle, or other official signals. . . .

We have also expanded our program of competition to take in representative activities other than athletic. Our present outstanding individual is one Johnny Rappold, whose only interest a few years ago was in baseball, which he played indifferently, with the result that whenever a good player arrived he was thrown off the team to make way for a more skilled performer. He gradually drifted out under this humiliation, to a place on the sidelines. There was one activity, however, in which he stood equal chance, and that was in shooting craps, and he became a confirmed participant in that game. We finally brought before the park audience in his neighborhood some boys who were skilled in making and flying model aeroplanes, and Johnny was instantly captivated by the sight of the model planes, and set to work to master the extremely fine technique in the making of these craft. He is now undoubtedly the foremost boy expert in the nation. All of his leisure time is taken up with this sport. He went back to school to study some of the engineering principles involved, graduated from one of the technical high schools, and is now saving his earnings to send himself through an engineering course at one of the universities, and has dropped out completely from the crap shooting avocation.[22]

In Chicago also a plan has been worked out for the benefit of handicapped children:

The child who is persistently undervalued, whose opinions, remarks and queries are always laughed at, whose efforts are invariably criticised for shortcomings, rather than praised for what they accomplish — all these are robbed

[22] Communication from V. K. Brown, Superintendent of Playgrounds and Sports, South Park, Chicago.

of any basis for self-confidence, of any feeling of self-respect. They are deprived of the sense of joy of accomplishment and of success. The " cripples " and the " awkward " have a hard road to travel. The other children are cruel to them. They are forced to a recognition of their inability to meet the more favored individual on common ground. . . .

The problem on the playground is to give these types of children an opportunity for participation in activities; so that they may feel a part of the whole group. The impetus and initiative must come from within the child. It should be the function of the playground teacher to attempt to find out what it is that is seeking expression, and to help the child in the unfolding and development.

This calls for individual treatment and special classification. The playground teacher has greater opportunities to deal with each case separately than the schoolroom teacher. His contacts are more intimate. It remains for the playground worker to carefully classify interests into groups and to program activities appealing to each group, and graded degrees of difficulty, and progressive opportunity for achievement. Development begins with the sense of accomplishment.

Care must be taken in organizing this special group that they do not feel that they are in need of separate treatment. Their efforts must be treated with respect and consideration, they must see that they are considered to be as important as any other group.

A plan has been formulated to meet just this problem. Achievement Clubs are being organized on each playground. Any boy or girl may join the club, but the membership button (the visual sign of achievement) is withheld until a certain number of points have been acquired by the individual representing his accomplishments.[23]

The highly organized gang life in Chicago presents a serious problem to the playground authorities and the following procedure has been tentatively formulated:

Due to excessive publicity given gang activity in the city, we determined to find out in just what manner the entire corps of playground instructors were meeting the problem, and to what extent gang membership interfered with the playground program. . . .

The records of the playground instructors show that there are 226 gangs in the playground areas, 205 of which are boy gangs, and 21 girl gangs. Of the total number of gangs, the average ages are given as follows:

[23] English, C. H. (formerly Supervisor, Bureau of Recreation, Department of Education, Chicago): *Annual Report for the Year Ending December 31, 1924.*

4 gangs 9 years of age		32 gangs 15 years of age
2 gangs 10 years of age		20 gangs 16 years of age
2 gangs 11 years of age		44 gangs 17 years of age
7 gangs 12 years of age		22 gangs 18 years of age
12 gangs 13 years of age		10 gangs 19 years of age
62 gangs 14 years of age		5 gangs 20 years of age
		12 gangs 21 years of age

It is noted that the ages 14 and 17 are in the majority. The first group is in the beginning of adolescence, and the second post adolescence. The younger group is more mischievous, while the latter is more frequently vicious.

Names of gangs often indicate the type of activity and locations. Some typical names are herein given: Rangaboos, Carmen A. C., Pearls, Cocky's gang, Irish Aces, Panthers, Swamp Angels, Hell Towners, Alley Cats, Roamers, Erie Sparrows, Black Jackets, Speed Boys, Bucktown, Revali Blues, Kerfoots, and Sticky Fingers.

Of the total number of gangs (226) 109 are classified as mischievous, while 46 are vicious. It is found that 120 are good material to work on. 112 out of the total number of gangs or 50% have been incorporated in the playground programs. Only 25 have thus far refused to be friendly and take some part in playground activity.

It is encouraging to observe that 50 per cent of the gangs are actually a part of the playground groups. The fact that only 25 gangs are still un-approachable speaks well for the ability of the instructors to interest and incorporate these units into their program. In all other groups at least a part of the gang is taking active part in the activities. [Report of instructors on their experiences with gangs].[24]

The policy of all extensive parks and playgrounds is to provide forms of recreation for all age levels and in the majority of them some of the projects are designed to involve all the members of the locality and thus restore or promote community unity and good feeling. The buildings may be used as community clubs or centers, and most frequently mass activities, folk dances, pageants, etc., are organized for and by the children, with the parents as spectators. Pageants have been organized in Oakland, California, for example, in which from two to three thousand persons participated.[25]

It appears, in fact, that the main divergence of policy in the public

[24] *Ibid.*
[25] Nash, Jay B.: *The Organization and Administration of Playgrounds and Recreation* (1927), 398.

playgrounds is between those in which the programs are heavily weighted with the æsthetic and mass interests and those placing the emphasis on personality development and the schematization of individual life.

The Rotarians, Kiwanis and Lions are organizations of business and professional men for the promotion of relationships among themselves, and their programs include also the promotion of the welfare and efficiency of their communities and cities. They represent civic pride and are to some extent a socialized expression of the spirit of the lodges which formerly strongly characterized American life. These organizations form their social programs from point to point in their several communities, they promote the work of other social organizations, organizing drives and providing funds. They form projects of their own, supplementing the programs of other organizations, employ other organizations in the operation of their own projects, take over the techniques of the other organizations, but in a coöperative way and without rivalry. They may, for example, act as Big Brothers individually, at the same time promoting the work of the Big Brother organization, and in their separate work with boys they may use the Boy Scout organization as a part of their programs:

Rotary International . . . is an organization now established in 44 countries, having some 2,700 clubs, possessing some 133,000 members. In the United States alone, there are some 800 Rotary clubs promoting programs in Crippled Children work; some 700 clubs operating Student Loan Funds. Approximately 600 Rotary clubs are promoting Back-to-School campaigns; 2,100 Rotary clubs in the United States have Boys' Work committees.[20]

The back-to-school campaigns are for the continuance in school of the greatest possible number of children:

[Because of the dropping out of large proportions of pupils immediately before and during high school] it would seem especially desirable to put on a School Continuation campaign, particularly during the summer vacation, with the definite purpose of acquainting the boys and girls, and their parents, with the facts concerning the great practical value of a thorough education, and encouraging the attendance of the children at school.

Also, steps may well be taken in conjunction with the school authorities to

---

[26] Communication from Chesley R. Perry, Secretary (January, 1928).

give throughout the school year a series of inspirational and informative talks to the school children by qualified Rotarians and others to encourage the taking of the fullest advantage of all educational opportunities.

A Back-to-School campaign should be planned for the follow-up of boys who do not report for the opening session of the new school year.

If this plan is properly carried out it will result in heading many a boy toward a thorough education and thereby help him to make much more of his life and opportunity than otherwise would be the case.[27]

The problem of juvenile delinquency is approached in the program of the Rotarians by the promotion of recreational facilities, by strengthening the work of the existing boys' work organizations, through sex hygiene instruction by special lectures, etc.:

The Rotary Club of Toledo, Ohio, has a specialist in boy psychology who gives his time exclusively to work with boys referred to him by the Judge of the Juvenile Court. . . . This plan works out most satisfactorily and has resulted in a marked decrease in the numbers of " repeaters " and adult offenders who were first booked as juvenile delinquents.

The Rotary Club of Chattanooga, Tennessee, has made an application of the Big Brother idea in a novel way and one that has great possibilities.

A number of high grade boys equal to the club membership were invited to attend a club meeting. Each boy was paired off with a Rotarian with the intention that the acquaintance thus started should continue throughout the entire year. In the idea there is no thought of charity; the purpose being that each Rotarian give to at least one boy enough of himself and his time so that the personality and character of the Rotarian may contribute in a definite and lasting manner to the well-being and right development of the boy.

The plan provides that these boys are not to be boys from the Juvenile Courts, but fine youngsters who because of the death or absence of their fathers, or for other reasons, lack the influence that Rotarians may bring them. It is proposed that each Rotarian arrange with " his " boy for regular meetings, alternating between his place of business and his home and the boy's home, and that the Rotarian visit the boy's school from time to time. [Surveys of boy life are promoted and regional maps are used showing influences affecting boy life]. . . . Maps will show by color work, pins and other means the conditions, favorable or otherwise, to character building. Such maps placed in the public library will serve all organizations working for the boys.[28]

---

[27] From the literature of the Rotary International.   [28] *Ibid.*

Vocational guidance is carried on in part by bringing the boy into relations with a Rotarian member whose profession may interest him:

Every Rotary club is a logical vocational guidance bureau. The Boys' Work program should give Rotarians the opportunity of relating themselves to vocational guidance within their individual classifications.[29]

The Kiwanis International (1,670 clubs) has given attention to " underprivileged children," and to " vocational guidance and placement." Their methods resemble very closely those of the Big Brothers, but they do not usually handle serious problem cases:

The object is to bring to a selected group of under-privileged children in the immediate vicinity, greater opportunities for moral, mental, spiritual and physical development. To provide for each child, through the assignment of a properly qualified member of the club, the personal interest that means so much in the early formative years of a child's life. The assistance of Kiwanis ladies should be enlisted wherever possible, especially in connection with girls' work. . . . As other organizations are better qualified than a Kiwanis club to care for the child who is of chronic unsoundness in health and morals, this program does not provide for these classes. . . . The average " bad " child who has run afoul of the law is ordinarily too much of a problem for a Kiwanian. He needs the attention of one especially qualified. We suggest that you confine your work largely to children of broken homes, the class from which " bad " children are largely recruited.[30]

Nevertheless, the members of a number of Kiwanian clubs have acted as probation officers of juvenile courts and for boys released from reformatories.

The record of Kiwanian activities for 1926 enumerates nearly 36,000 separate enterprises of which the following are samples:

Altoona, Pa. Operated the largest theatre in the city for one week with a total attendance of almost 13,000 people and made a net profit of over $2,500 for the under-privileged child fund.

Boston, Mass. Sent ten under-privileged girls to Camp Kiwanis each week. Built an addition to the main camp building. Raised $2,500 for children's work.

Chillicothe, Ohio. First local club to pass resolution for the continuance of present placement system of county child welfare work in opposition to contemplated change to institutional plan by board of county commissioners.

---

[29] From the literature of the Rotary International.
[30] From the literature of Kiwanis International.

Columbus, Ind. Ten members of the club were selected by Judge Julian Sharpnack of the Juvenile court to act as sponsors for ten boys who were brought into court. Each boy must report to his sponsor once each week.

Jersey City, N. J. Handled from twenty to 30 needy cases during each month of the year. Supplied food, employment, hospitalization and medical treatment for children. Secured homes for orphans, aided family in which the mother was dangerously ill, and returned a father to the United States after he had abandoned his family and fled to Europe. Raised $5,000.00 by a Kiwanis show.

Kansas City, Kan. Participated in Kiwanis day at the Boys Industrial School in Topeka. Our regular work of aiding boys leaving the state reformatory to find new environment and employment is meeting with success.

Monmouth, Ill. A group of Kiwanians have financed the Fine Arts theatre which is owned by a Kiwanian. Monmouth needed a theatre where good, clean pictures and vaudeville would be shown and this is now being done at the Fine Arts. The financing of the theatre was a matter of some $13,000.00 The Kiwanis shelter house in the city park has been completed at a cost of $1,100.00.

Ottawa, Ont. Secured positions for 50 boys. Held the second annual hobby show of the Boys' club, displaying woodwork, toys, stamp collections, sign painting, and pet animals; financed the Hallowe'en masquerade dance and the proceeds were used to further our boys' welfare work. Since our Boys' club was organized, 47,016 youths have held memberships and received attention and aid.

Pontiac, Mich. Kiwanians volunteered to become responsible for interesting seventeen boys assigned to them by the juvenile judge, in scouting and to see that they progressed sufficiently to attend camp. Each boy attended camp two weeks. In one case, an operation was performed which resulted in a great improvement in the boy.

Quebec City, Que. Remitted $2,100.00, the proceeds of the Kiwanis Frolics, to the board of directors of the Hospital de L'Enfant Jesus, this institution taking care of children.

Shamokin, Pa. The club has started the custom of having one boy from each of the three high schools of the city attend Kiwanis meetings for a period of two months. At the end of that time each boy is allowed five minutes on the club's program to speak on his observations of Kiwanis and its worth to the community.

Somerville, Mass. Completed fund of $2,500.00, to build a Somerville Dormitory at the Salvation Army Fresh Air Camp at Sharon, Massachusetts, to accommodate 400 Somerville under-privileged children in groups for periods of ten days each.

Riverdale, Toronto, Ont. The Boys' Work Committee is erecting an advertising sign poster at the eastern entrance to the city. This sign will also carry thirteen advertisements of members which will give a revenue of $900.00 per annum to carry on the boys' work program.

Riverside, Calif. Riverside Kiwanis started a fund for a widow with five children by donating a check for $100.00. Aided by our newspaper members, this fund has grown to a trifle over $2,000.00, the goal being $2,500.00 so that a small chicken ranch may be started for her so she may in a measure be self-supporting. The summer camp in the mountains provided entertainment for 65 children.[31]

Lions International (1,187 clubs) has sponsored especially health programs (undernourished children, milk funds, dental clinics), tubercular camps, summer camps and orphanages.

It is not strange that the idea should not have presented itself until a late date of constituting the police as an organization for the oversight of problem children. One of the chief means of combatting antisocial behavior is to hold the offender in contempt, to shun him socially and to terrify him, in addition to pursuing and punishing him. The evildoer has been treated as the enemy of society and the officer of the law has been the delegated enemy of the evildoer, and it has been difficult to think of this relation in any other way. It was only in 1899 that an exception was made in favor of the very young offender and the juvenile court was organized to treat the delinquent child as a member of society who was in need of guidance and retraining.

During the years 1914–1917 Arthur Woods, as Police Commissioner of New York City, put into operation a vigorous and comprehensive program for the prevention of crime through the socialization of the police which has excited a wide interest in America and Europe:

The preventive policeman is the policeman of the future. However faithfully he does it he can no longer fully justify himself by simply " pounding the beat." . . . Police forces must try to keep crime from claiming its victims as Boards of Health try to keep plague and pestilence away.[32]

The general plan necessarily involved adults and families as well as juveniles and had a number of features. Eleven thousand policemen,

---

[31] From the literature of Kiwanis International.
[32] Woods, Arthur: *Crime Prevention* (1918), 123.

a body of socially minded men, coming from the people and close to the people, were utilized.

The first step was concerned with the condition of the population living on the economic, social and moral fringe, whose situation often brought them near calamity and desperation. During a crisis of unemployment in the winter of 1914–1915 a Police Relief Fund was raised, largely among the policemen themselves. Sixty-one welfare organizations were stimulated and integrated among themselves. The police provided relief until the cases could be investigated and assigned to the suitable permanent organizations. Nine hundred families or approximately 5,000 persons were assisted from the police fund. Four thousand bundles of clothing were sorted and distributed by the police department to 6,390 persons. The members of the police department secured 2,811 positions for men and women.[33]

The next step was an arrangement with the parole commission to parole prisoners to the police department, which undertook to find employment for them. " I have seen many a prisoner," said Colonel Woods, " who had been inexorably, it almost seemed with deliberate purpose, driven step by step straight into an eddy of fate where there seemed nothing else to do but steal. And one could not help wondering whether ' the rest of us,' caught in the same swirling current, would have done any better ": [34]

Policemen have always regarded as suspicious the young men and boys who graduate from our city reform and penal institutions. Experience has shown that these boys are very likely to turn to crime for the greater part of their livelihood, their associations in the institutions seeming often to have the effect of turning them toward a criminal life instead of against it.

If this is true, it is certainly our duty to give special attention to this group, since they are especially likely to commit crime. From the beginning of the administration we tried to impress it upon the inmates of such institutions that the police would help them if they wanted to lead an honest life. We sent sergeants to talk in the institutions and tried to convince the inmates of our sincerity of purpose. . . . The experiment was tried of having policemen act as parole officers for these boys. At first we designated only sergeants, but

---

[33] Unpublished Report on Unemployment and Destitution, by Leroy Peterson and other members of the Police Department (1915). Also *The Survey*, 35:166 (November 13, 1915).

[34] Woods: *op. cit.*, 37.

later as the work grew, a certain number of selected patrolmen were assigned to the work under the sergeants.

The sergeants selected suitable places to meet the prisoners, always away from the station house. In the first interview the sergeant is expected to show the paroled prisoner that he wants to be his friend, that he and the Police Department as a whole stand ready to assist him in his start toward earning an honest living. If the boy cannot find a job the policeman is to try to help him to do so. The fact that he has been a prisoner is to be concealed, except that it is told to the boy's employer in order to avoid misunderstandings and blackmail. The big job of the sergeant is to try to influence the life of the person who is in his charge so that he will form habits that will make him a self-supporting and self-respecting member of society. He must remember that the purpose of parole is to help and reform; exactly how to do this must be left largely to his judgment and intelligence, since individual cases differ so widely.

From July 16, 1916, to date, the Parole Commission has placed 1,558 prisoners under the charge of parole policemen. Of that number 750 have earned their release, some conditionally, others in full. At present there are 508 prisoners under the supervision of policemen. Of this number 480 have jobs which they seem likely to succeed in; and of these 150 were unable to get employment without the assistance of the policeman. Of the total number, less than 5 per cent. have been arrested for other crimes while on parole, and less than 10 per cent. have been returned for violation of parole.

We believe the results have shown that policemen make excellent parole officers. Their experience has been such that they know human nature pretty well, and they know particularly the kind of life and the kind of temptation that these boys are subject to. The province of the policeman is to keep down crime; he realizes, therefore, that if through his efforts he can change these boys from lawbreakers to self-supporting and worthy citizens he is thereby accomplishing exactly what is the object of his profession, and that he is accomplishing it far better by these preventive methods than he would be if he waited and arrested the same boys after they had committed crime. Employers also seem ready to take a chance with boys who have been committed, if a policeman has an active interest in these boys and is using his influence to keep them straight.

This helps to solve one of the most hopeless problems in connection with all work with prisoners: the difficulty of getting them a chance to earn an honest living. And the former prisoner, too, seems to feel a sense of relief and security under this system which he never felt before. He apparently realizes that the forces of law and order, instead of trying to waylay him, are trying to help him, and he gradually concludes that he has nothing to fear if he does his part, that his old life can be lived down and that he is being not merely given a chance, but helped along. He finds that the police supervision is not persecution, but just simple, kindly help.[35]

In order to promote better relations between the child and "his enemy the cop," Christmas trees were arranged in the station houses. In 1916, $57,000 was collected in cash, over $15,000 in merchandise and 40,439 children were entertained. Another method of promoting friendly relations between the police and the children was talks in schools by police officials:

The men giving these talks were usually sergeants of considerable experience and fathers of growing children. The sergeant spoke to the young audiences as he would to his own youngsters, instructing them on how to cross streets on their way to and from school and generally how to conduct themselves in city traffic. He impressed on them the friendliness of the policeman and his accessibility to everyone in trouble. "Make a friend of your friend the policeman" was the gist of his message. More than half a million children benefited by this direct contact with an officer of the law within the sheltered walls of the schoolroom.[36]

We have noted above the failure of boys' organizations to appeal to or receive the boy lowest down in the social scale and the most inclined to delinquency. In this experiment a Junior Police force was organized to care for the boys not influenced by the Y.M.C.A., the Boy Scouts and the boys' clubs:

Boys between the ages of eleven and sixteen years were eligible to membership in the Junior Police force. For the purpose of organization the police precincts were divided into zones of from four to eight blocks each. There was a company of Junior Police for each zone, which was made up as far as possible of boys living within the zone. The police captain in each precinct assigned a regular police officer to direct his Junior Police and to instruct them in drill. This police officer named the officers of the companies in his precinct, took in new members, made promotions, arranged the program of company meetings, and generally directed activities. . . .

Each company of Junior Police was instructed by the police officer assigned to it in athletics, personal hygiene, cleanliness, swimming, first aid and safety

---

[35] Woods, Arthur: *Report of the Police Department of New York City, 1914–17*, 73–74.

[36] Peterson, Leroy: "The Police and Boys' Work," *Welfare Magazine*, 19:50 (1928).

and rules of the road, as well as drill and discipline. Exercises in calisthenics were given to build up the boys' bodies and to satisfy their interest in sports, baseball games and track meets were held between companies of the different precincts. In the summer months the policemen assigned to Junior Police work would take their companies on boat rides or to the country for hikes or to the beach for swims. Sometimes the boys would be invited to the Big League baseball games as guests of the management.

[The movement] grew until it had thirteen thousand members in the greater city. When Captain Sweeney took charge of the precinct in which he organized the first company of Junior Police, an average of twenty-five boys a day were being arrested for minor offenses. He gave orders that such arrests were to cease and set about to devise ways of keeping the boys out of trouble.

After he had his Junior Police force going, the number of complaints against boys in his precinct rapidly dwindled. Where formerly hundreds of dollars were spent in this precinct replacing windows broken by boys, broken windows became a rare occurrence during the four years the Junior Police flourished. Bonfires in the streets, complaints of all kinds against gangs of young boys rapidly diminished.[37]

Perhaps the most important feature of this program was a system of Crime Prevention Patrolmen whose function was to study the behavior tendencies of the different city localities and to anticipate and prevent forms of delinquency and crime. These patrolmen were the field-workers of a larger group of Welfare Officers, some of whom adjusted complaints in the stations and homes somewhat as we have seen this practice in operation in Chicago:

The experiment was tried . . . of assigning Crime Prevention Patrolmen to some of the more busy precincts for the purpose of having them ferret out conditions in the precinct which seemed to be having the tendency of leading boys and girls astray, so that vigorous measures could be taken to combat these influences. A great deal of good has been accomplished by these men.

Many temptations to petty stealing were discovered. The kind of stealing that this gave boys a chance to do was regarded by them purely as play, but led soon to the genuine article, and the thoughtless playful boy found himself, often before he at all realized it, a law-breaker. Conditions in many parts of the city seemed made to order to lead boys into crime. In fact, it has often seemed to me that in some parts of the city it is practically im-

---

[37] Peterson, Leroy: " The Police and Boy's Work," *Welfare Magazine*, 19:50–52 (1928).

possible for a growing, healthy boy to play at all without doing something against the law. The boys, most of them, are as good boys, and if given a chance would grow up into as good citizens, as any other boys, but they are, by no fault of their own and none of their parents, required to grow up under conditions where they haven't half a chance.[38]

The Welfare Officers found plenty of work waiting for them. Boys were playing truant, were smoking cigarettes when eight or ten years old, were taking drugs, were practising unnatural habits, were stealing fruit, candy, coal, were spending their time in pool parlors, were trying to make friends with young men of questionable character. Or they were just running wild, like healthy young animals, and the wildness was bringing them into conflict with the ordered tameness of city life. The Welfare Officer was to get acquainted with the boys, treating each one as a separate problem, and trying to hit upon what might be needed to swing the boy away from his bad habits or associates. Sometimes the mere friendship of the big brother policeman was enough, sometimes father or mother or friend, when spoken to, was able to do what was necessary, having had no idea of what the boy had been doing. Often boys were taken to settlements, or clubs of various kinds, were given work, if old enough, were introduced to other boys of better character than those they had fallen in with. The policeman didn't preach, he didn't threaten; he made friends with the boy, appealed to his pride, and tried to find a wholesome outlet for his natural activity. It was extraordinarily satisfactory work. Thousands of boys were helped, and we would not admit one failure, the nearest approach to failure being cases where we had *not yet* succeeded. And results were already showing, in improved order in neighborhoods where boy-population was large, and in the reduction of juvenile offenders.

The same work was done, to a less extent, for girls. It was not so extensive as the work with boys, for the two reasons that girls didn't seem to get into such bad ways as boys, and that policemen were more successful with boys. Women police officers, working among girls along these lines, could produce splendid results.[39]

Previous to the inauguration of Welfare Work [some of] these conditions would not be noted by any City Department. For instance, the Police Department would not take action until a crime had been threatened, attempted, or committed. The Probation Officer did not make an investigation until a person had been arrested and brought before the Court. The Parole Officer's

---

[38] Woods, Arthur: *Report of the Police Department of New York City, 1914–17,* 78–79.

[39] Woods, Arthur: *Crime Prevention,* 116–18.

work was not undertaken until the prisoner had served his term or a portion of his term and had been placed on parole.[40]

Welfare police work cannot be carried on in a haphazard manner. To achieve its purpose of constructive crime prevention welfare officers must devote their entire time to it.... There should be a special squad of welfare policemen, just as there is a special squad of traffic policemen, in every city police department. Welfare officers should not be burdened with conventional police duties that interfere with the proper handling of their welfare duties. Efficient traffic regulation would be out of the question if the police department, instead of having a regular staff of traffic men, should assign members of the regular patrol to traffic duty from day to day. It would be just as impossible to have effective welfare police work if the administration kept shifting the personnel of the welfare staff. . . .

In cities of the United States where police heads and police policies are apt to change with each shift of the party in power, welfare work, just as traffic, should be established by law as a distinct division within the police department. In no other way can its permanence be insured under the present system which permits politics to affect police administration.[41]

Unfortunately this convincing experiment, carried on with so much energy, was terminated at the end of three years, owing to the changing character of American politics.

August Vollmer, chief of police of Berkeley, California, has identified himself more than any one in America with the problem of improving the character of the police force, but he has emphasized their intellectual equipment, relying rather excessively on their preparation to pass certain mental tests and also on the development of a police school for training in the refined methods of crime detection, etc.[42] But the procedure we have seen in New York, involving the participation of the police in the problems of the community, has even greater importance for the improvement of society and of the police system itself.

[40] Woods, Arthur: *Report of the Police Department of New York City, 1914–17*, 78.

[41] Peterson, Leroy: "The Police and Boys' Work," *Welfare Magazine*, 19:59 (1928).

[42] Vollmer, August: "The School for Police as Planned at Berkeley," *Journal of Criminal Law and Criminology*, 7:877–98 (1917); "Aims and Ideals of the Police," *Ibid.*, 13:251–57 (1922); "A Practical Method for Selecting Policemen." *Ibid.*, 11:571–81 (1921).

Some European cities are now introducing a system of Children's Police which combines somewhat the functions of the New York Welfare Police, the probation officer, the juvenile court and the clinic:

Commissary C. E. G. Hogendyk, in the course of an article on " Children's Police in Amsterdam," gives some interesting facts concerning this novel feature of Dutch civic life.

In 1920 the organisation of . . . children's police came into existence as a subdivision of the Amsterdam municipal police force. So successful has the venture proved that in three years the staff has been trebled, and now includes one commissary, two inspectors, three inspectresses, four women officers, eighteen men officers and three clerks. These form the centre of all police intervention in civil and social questions so far as minors (i.e., those under eighteen years of age) are concerned.

The duties and powers of the children's police are distinguished from those of the regular police, though the distinction does not appear to be clearly defined yet. The new force — all plainclothes officers — has a triple viewpoint, viz. the protection of the child where necessary against himself, against his guardians and against the dangers he may meet in social life.

Day and night officers supervise minors in the streets, railway stations, markets, cinemas, dancing saloons, public-houses, etc., for the prevention of mendicity, truancy, vagrancy, and for maintenance of those prohibitive regulations especially established in the interests of the child. Their work is preventive, corrective and, where necessary, repressive; their prime object is to be counsellor, helper and protector to the minor brought before the court of first instance. General police who come into touch with a juvenile offender give notice to the children's police.

The headquarters of this service is as unlike a police-station as it is possible to make it. Here the harassed mother brings her obstreperous son for guidance as to his management. Here the pre-trial investigations are prepared for the children's judge, and the arrangement for placing in an institution or under other guardianship carried out. The collection of data for research work is filed together with information concerning offenders.

The English Children Act and others of a similar nature enjoin the separation of juveniles from contact with adult offenders, and the Dutch scheme seems to carry out this principle to its logical conclusion.[43]

It is plain that the permanent and general socialization of the police will involve a considerable participation of women. Until recently the function of the police was so largely one of pursuit and capture that

---

[43] Trought, T. W.: *Probation in Europe* (1927), 123–24.

the presence of women in this connection was not conceivable. The opening wedge was the employment of women as matrons for women accused of crime and held in jails:

The earliest employment of women in this field in the United States was as a result of special circumstances or of special activities of women's organizations, as for example, in 1845, when the American Female Reform Society secured the appointment of six women matrons in New York City to serve at the Tombs and on Blackwell's Island in order that women convicted of crime might be cared for by members of their own sex.

So far as is discoverable, however, it was not until 1905, during the Lewis and Clark Exposition in Portland, Oregon, that a woman was put in charge of a competent force of social workers and given police power in order to deal effectively and directly with social conditions threatening the moral safety of young girls and women.[44]

The first policewoman in the United States was appointed to superintend skating rinks and movies in order to enforce the ordinance prohibiting children under fourteen years of age from attending these places. A similar law regarding dance halls brought them also under her supervision where, in addition to patrolling, she made it her business to watch out for very young girls. A policewoman in another city aided in the enforcement of the curfew law and the law forbidding the use of tobacco in any form by persons under twenty-one. The duties of the policewomen first appointed in two other cities were defined as " protective rather than punitive," and consisted in patrolling parks, movies, dance halls and skating rinks.[45]

At present there is an International Association of Policewomen and women are on the police force of 218 cities in the United States:

As nearly as we can estimate the total number, there are 590 policewomen in the country today. There are 100 in New York City, 45 on the Detroit force, 23 in Washington, 18 in St. Louis and 15 in Cleveland.[46]

When women began to be regularly added to the police departments there was a good deal of confusion as to their functions and in some cases the heads of departments disposed of them by confining their

---

[44] Davis, Katharine B.: " The Police Woman," *The Woman Citizen* (May 30, 1925).

[45] Additon, Henrietta: " The Policewoman," *Proceedings of the 10th Annual Conference of the International Association of Policewomen* (1924), 51–52.

[46] Communication from Helen D. Pigeon, Executive Secretary (April, 1928).

activities to the station house as matrons. The experiment was also tried, sometimes ironically, of assigning them to regular patrol duty as in the case of men. Eventually the plan having the most general approval was the creation of women bureaus as separate police units and responsible to the Police Commissioner. Among the items endorsed by the International Association of Police Chiefs held in San Francisco in 1922 were the following:

The Policewoman is a necessity to organized police departments.

Policewomen attached to the department shall be under the direct supervision of the Chief of Police as a unit in the department, and, where there is a sufficient number, one of them shall be a ranking officer in the department. . . .

The primary function of policewomen is to deal with all cases in which women and children are involved either as offenders or victims of offenses. Crimes by or against females, irrespective of age, and boys up to the age of twelve, should be the special responsibility of the Policewomen. They should discover, investigate, and correct anti-social circumstances and conditions in individual cases, and, in the community, deal socially and legally with all delinquent women and children, give or secure social treatment calculated to result in reform, and supplement the work of policemen in securing evidence and convictions in special cases that will aid in correcting evil conditions.

This is in essential agreement with the wishes of the organization of policewomen:

In a report given before the National Probation Association in Milwaukee [in 1921] we considered the duties and responsibilities of the policewoman in those communities well equipped with other social agencies. There was general agreement that policewomen's work might cover the following activities: (1) detective work on special cases involving women and children; (2) locating missing women and children; (3) maintaining a bureau of information for women desiring information or help from the police; (4) patrol work: patrol work includes general supervision and inspection of amusement parks, dance halls, cafés, cabarets, motion picture theaters, skating rinks and other public amusement places; scouting and patrol work on the streets, in public parks and around railroad stations. The preventive work as it concerns women and children will constitute one of the main features of the women's work. Just as the patrolman is responsible for nuisances on the sidewalks of his district, the policewoman should be responsible for such moral nuisances as indecent movies and their lurid posters, and unlighted places frequented by young people at night. Police-women should have definite instruction regarding the bad conditions they are to look for, report on and correct; (5) attendance at police court; (6) supervision of conditions in local jails or places of detention where women and children are held when such institutions are under the control of the police department.[47]

Details of the activities of the women police in a large city may be illustrated from Detroit:

The Women's Division completed its seventh year of operation in 1927. Employment of women officers has come to be considered an important activity of Departmental work.

The women officers do protective and preventive police work which has to do with women and children. When the Women's Division was organized 75 per cent of the girls brought before the Juvenile Court charged with immorality were prostituting and their offenses were with older men. By 1927 this figure had been reduced to 5 per cent. The Judge of the Juvenile Court feels that the work of the women patrol officers in supervising commercial recreation and in investigating conditions which lead to delinquency is largely responsible for this improvement.

During the year 14,375 women were admitted to the Women's Detention Home. Investigation brought out the fact that among this number were many young girls just beginning a life of wrong-doing. Efforts were made in every case to bring these girls back to a right way of living. In many instances they were returned to their families in other cities.

A total of 3,420 complaints pertaining to women and girls was made to the Division. All of these were investigated and the needed assistance given. Of these cases, 1,003 involved women 21 years or older, 780 more than 17 years and up to 21, and 1,637 who were 17 or under.

All cases involving those 17 years or younger always have been taken into Juvenile Court, as prescribed by law, but it was necessary to take girls above that age and up to 21 into Recorder's Court where trial must be founded on alleged criminal acts. These cases, however, were not really in the same class as those involving women 21 years or older, who were of legal age.

There was really no legal machinery to carry on protective work among the girls from 17 to 21 years, though the need of it had long been apparent. The 1927 records, for instance, concerned girls above the Juvenile Court age but not of legal age. It was therefore that those close to this work sought to obtain legal means of protecting the hundreds of girls of these ages who annually fell into the clutches of unscrupulous persons.

---

[47] Additon: *op. cit.*, 52.

A bill known as the Wayward Minor Act was drafted and submitted to members of the Legislature who introduced the same and had it enacted into law. This statute, after becoming operative, was first used in December, 1927, the Juvenile Court having refrained a short time from applying it until the necessary legal machinery could be set up.

With the Wayward Minor Law it is expected that in the future much can be done for girls between the ages over 17 and up to 21 years by presenting their cases before the Juvenile Court where the necessary protective action may be taken. Not only is the law applicable to those who become involved in acts pertaining to violation of the moral code, but as well to those who are incorrigible or who may otherwise need legal supervision.

Reports of missing girls and women during 1927 totalled 1,167. Of the Detroit cases, 94 per cent of the missing persons were found, while 62 per cent of those reported from other cities were located. Of all those listed as missing, 80 per cent were under the age of 21 years.

Officers who are doing patrol duty dealt with 2,046 persons, 1,769 women and 277 men. Division members handling court cases investigated 1,388 complaints, recommended 711 warrants, 449 on immorality charges, 197 for dishonesty and 65 miscellaneous. A total of 1,578 visits was made to dance halls. Complaints against 730 reported undesirable places were investigated.[48]

It is recognized that police organization tends to be semi-military and inflexible and that policemen tend to be " hard-boiled." Police practices and attitudes are, however, the result of the limitation of their functions to definite lines, as in the case of military organizations and other forms of regimentation. On the other hand, we have seen in the New York experiment how readily policemen are converted to social enterprises. If governmental agencies are to be socialized they must be given social functions. There is no question that the police should be associated with social work, that women should be a part of the police and that the entrance of women into the activities of the police will facilitate the socialization of police work. The main problem relates to the division of function between the police and the other agencies doing social work. The visiting teacher work, the social aspects of the child clinics and child guidance institutes, the study and management of cases under investigation and on probation, are now largely in the hands of women. The case workers are themselves dependent on the psychologists, psychiatrists and sociologists, and their work is becoming progressively a study of behavior in connection with the treatment of the case. Bad behavior trends are often set up in infancy, mental

[48] *Detroit (Mich.) Police Department, 62nd Annual Report* (1927), 9.

deviations, disabilities and conflicts are involved, the case worker has always a problem of retraining, and under the best handling and during long years the result is frequently disappointing. The participation of the police will be a benefit to the whole situation and what the limitations of their functions are will be determined by experience, but " prevention and protection " as used in their programs is not a simple matter. It involves coöperation and integration of work between persons specialized in different ways.

From one standpoint all the programs which we have reviewed in this chapter are to be regarded as contributions to our civilization, to the level of general culture. They should also probably be regarded as an expression of the assumption by various community interests of responsibility for the child's adjustment. There is a growing recognition — reflected in programs of this sort — that conditions favorable to the control of behavior are not developed in the urban family. There is also a recognition of the inadequacy of the punitive and reformative attempts of the community in dealing with delinquency.

The variety of origins of the programs throws interesting light on the diffusion of these attempts. These originated from as diverse sources as religious sects, business men's organizations, private philanthropic organizations and police departments. All of them are based on an attempt to provide situations for the development of social or moral behavior. All of them proceed through the use of activities intrinsically interesting to the children. Some of them use these activities frankly as a bait for getting the children's attention in order that particular religious or moral ideas may be implanted. Most of them, however, — particularly the boys' clubs and recreation schemes — rely on the development of a code through experience in favorable situations where aptitude and performance may lead to success, and where this success will be accomplished in a social setting.

The disadvantage under which these programs are working is that they reach children at the age levels where their behavior trends have already become pretty definitely structuralized, and also that they reach the better adjusted and least delinquent of those at these age levels. In the next chapter we shall examine the school as an organization which has an opportunity to handle all the children, young and old, good and bad.

CHAPTER V

The Treatment of Maladjustment in the Schools

THE SCHOOLS have tended, on the whole, to be markedly conservative. Democratic systems of education are a phenomenon of modern times and they have taken a long time to shake off their aristocratic predispositions and adapt themselves to changing needs.

Until comparatively recent times schooling was definitely for scholars and those preparing for the learned professions, government and the priesthood. " Book learning " was confined to the few, and education in its broader aspects of learning techniques and the elements of culture necessary for an adaptation to the life of the times was carried on primarily in the home. The adequacy of such a system of education depended largely upon the stability of the family and the relative simplicity of the material culture. It is generally recognized that the tremendous growth and increasing complexity of the objects of material culture since the industrial revolution have brought about great changes in the organization of social life, not the least important of which has been the decrease in the economic functions performed by the family, and its consequent general lessening stability. As one after another of the arts and the crafts has been taken away from it, its educational functions, depending as they did on the intimate connections of the family with the prevalent material culture, have tended to become ineffectual. Along with the passing of the family as an effective educational agency has come the expansion of the school. The functions evacuated by the family, however, have not passed directly or immediately to the expanding school system, but have fallen, quite planlessly, to agencies variously adapted to perform them. For many years the democratizing of education meant merely making available to more people the sort of formal education that had been available to the few, i.e., " book learning," irrespective of individual differences in aptitudes or of the proportions assumed by this phase of education as a means of adaptation to the total cultural situation, and only quite lately have the schools tended to take account of other aspects of culture. Their curricula are now broadening to include those neglected elements in education which were once adequately fulfilled by the family. The more important changes have been those which recognize the need of developing many types of proficiencies, manual, mechanical, artistic, as well as the narrowly defined " intellectual," and which are preparing for vocations and a more complete adaptation to modern life.

With the broadening in the functions and the curricula of the school have come problems of handling maladjustment on the part of the children. When the school took as its province merely the narrowly defined " intellectual life " of the pupils, it held itself responsible for a very small share in the handling of behavior problems. If the crude disciplinary measures used within the school failed, the child was thrust back upon the family either by suspension (until, in theory, the family should have brought about a change in attitude and behavior and the chastened child could once more be accepted in the school group) or, in cases where conformity could not be achieved, expulsion from that particular school. Problems of truancy were handled by officers of the school who had police powers and whose function it was to bring the truant back, and see that punishment was meted out to parents and the truants, if they were recalcitrant. This punishment took the form, in the last instance, of sending the child away to a " parental " or truant's school for a period of time. Children who did not learn the required subjects at the prescribed rate of speed were " left back " and this form of treatment was also meted out as a disciplinary measure for misdemeanants.

Unfortunately, this statement of the school's methods of handling behavior problems is not entirely obsolete, for it represents prevalent practices. But there is observable a new and very important trend. The assumption of new functions in education is forcing the school to take account of other aspects of behavior than the purely intellectual. The school is now taking over from the court, the clinic, and other social agencies a large share of that responsibility which the increasing helplessness of the family had thrust upon them.

The first expressions along these lines were in the direction of substituting the school for the juvenile court as the agency for handling delinquency and pre-delinquency. This position was taken by Thomas D. Eliot as early as 1914,[1] and again formulated rather definitely by Additon and Deardorff in 1919, and the same view has been repeatedly expressed:

Each city, probably each county would require an extension or a reorganization of its personnel to include a department of adjustment, to which teachers, policemen and others could refer all children who seemed to present problems of health, of mental development, of behavior or of social adjustment. For good work, this would require the services of doctors, nurses, psychiatrists, field investigators, recreational specialists. . . .

The ideal would be to have the school act as a reserve parent, an unusually intelligent, responsible and resourceful parent, using whatever the community had to offer, making up what the community lacked. . . .

All neglected, dependent and delinquent children, whether of school age or not, would fall within the province of [the department of adjustment]. For these children, we would have the authority of the school extend from infancy to adult life. . . . We should [thus] get entirely away from the concept of penalizing children for their offenses and from the stigma of courts and reform schools. . . . We should establish our thinking firmly on an education basis. The fatal gradation of reform school, workhouse, county jail, and state prison would be broken. . . . Wherever possible, we would have [dependent children] sent to the public schools. Homes for " friendless " or " destitute " children belong with scarlet letters, stocks and debtors' prisons. . . .

With the clearing away of old names and associations should come better opportunity to meet the needs of girls before they reach an advanced stage of incorrigibility. . . .

[Arrangements should be made for] pooling the juvenile court's probation officers, the truancy department's numerous officers, the school nurses, the medical inspectors, the special schools and reformatories and all the rest of the specialists on the physical, mental and social troubles of school children, into one department of adjustment. . . . Only the most determined blindness could prevent [the school board member] from seeing how the truant officer and the probation officer overlap. . . . He could surely see the waste in having the schools, on the one hand, building up a staff of doctors and nurses, and the juvenile court, on the other, trying to duplicate this machinery — both sets to serve the same group of children.[2]

---

[1] *The Juvenile Court and the Community* (1914).
[2] Additon, H. S., and Deardorff, N. R.: " That Child," *The Survey*, 42:186–88 (May 3, 1919).

The educational system is broader than the brick and mortar equipment of the compulsory education period. Public opinion should demand that it expand its special services for children outside of school hours and ages, whenever they need such services.

Police and public should then be gradually trained to bring children first to the schools for correction, not to the police station or court. Educational authorities would then take the child to court if it proved necessary. It would not so often prove necessary, because children would be brought to the adjustment office of a school at an earlier stage of malbehavior more easily corrected by persuasion.[3]

The influence and opportunities of the school period cannot be over-emphasized. The school has now come to be recognized as the logical place from which to work for the prevention of delinquency and other social problems. . . . The school has signal opportunity to detect symptoms of child maladjustments as they appear in school dissatisfactions, poor school work, indifference, in persistently troublesome or erratic behavior, in rumors of undesirable companions or unwholesome interests, in apparent neglect, in environment or home conditions that are dangerous or predisposing to delinquency.[4]

The longer I study the needs of children requiring special care the greater appears the importance of the public schools as the first relay-station where potential defectives of all descriptions, physical, mental, educational and social may be recognized and where treatment may be begun. Yet we go on nonchalantly expecting problems of individual maladaptation to be suddenly solved by our police, the courts and public institutions after the potential deficiency has blossomed forth into either a definite social menace or a distinct social liability.[5]

At present this sentiment has taken the form of a demand that the school shall take over the responsibility for the " whole child," not merely his delinquent phases and not alone his reading, writing, figuring capacities, but the development of his whole personality. The school would thus become a behavior training organization rather than an institution for learning. This, at any rate, is the tendency, although not so explicitly expressed.

---

[3] Eliot, Thomas D.: " Welfare Agencies, Special Education, and the Courts," *American Journal of Sociology,* 31:73–74 (1925).

[4] Culbert, Jane F.: " The Visiting Teacher," *Annals of the American Academy of Political and Social Science,* 98:82–83 (1921).

[5] Kohs, Samuel C.: " The School as an Agency in Preventing Social Liabilities," *School and Society,* 12:325 (October 16, 1920).

But the question arises as to what forces the school can command in meeting this demand. The greatest handicap, perhaps, has been the teaching personnel. The whole tradition of education has emphasized intellectuality, or, more specifically, the reading and writing processes. (Arithmetic has never been allowed to assume the primary place that the literary talents have taken in the "hierarchy of intelligences"). Hence, the teaching staff has undoubtedly been unduly selected from among those who have facility in the reading and writing processes, and who, themselves, will be inclined to place undue emphasis upon these elements in their attitudes towards their pupils. That is, their interest in the child will be in direct proportion to its demonstrated abilities to learn in the traditional manner. It has been found necessary, therefore, to train a staff of special teachers to deal with the pupils who have been found to need other sorts of training — the manual-minded types particularly. The inability of the regular teachers, under present conditions, to cope with even the problems of intellectual maladjustment without the aid of experts is shown when one examines the ramifications of procedure of the type described by Irwin and Marks. They describe a four-year experiment carried on in a New York public school to determine the requirements of the different types of children found there, and to work out adequate means of fulfilling these requirements:

One notable feature of Public School 64 was the growth of special classes. This was the result of the experimental policy adopted. As the school recognized its problems, special classes of various types were created in the effort to meet them directly. The easy solution of elimination had been abandoned at the outset. During the four years of the experiment, no boy was sent to disciplinary school nor to any other place of last resort. On the contrary, many children were sent to Public School 64 by other schools, both public and private, and were frankly offered and accepted as extreme problems. Furthermore, it was our practice to seek out bright children in the neighborhood and enroll them in our school. Thus it came about that, in the development of the plan, the number of special classes grew to be larger than the number of regular classes in the school.

The special class is the most direct aid possible in the individualization of the child. The regular classes are the carriers of the traditional methods and must wait for their improvement upon the indirect influence of methods learned from the teaching of admittedly exceptional children. In Public School 64, the number of special classes was an indispensable part of the experiment, since it provided within the school itself a recognized field for a special kind of educational enterprise. . . . We undertook, by the application of scientific standards, to learn certain strategic facts about every incoming child. He was given primarily a psychological test and received a psychological rating. This was set down tentatively to be revised by a retest at the end of a year. He was given an eye examination and, when glasses were needed, they were with a few exceptions provided and worn. This was achieved with the assistance of a competent social worker. The child was weighed and measured and his percentage of underweight or overweight computed by standard tables. The children who had a normal psychological rating, who had no eye defects, and who were within a small percentage of the proper weight, we considered good risks from the school's point of view. They represented at a rough estimate between 60 per cent and 75 per cent of each class. Care of the other 25 per cent became the task of the visiting teacher and the health worker and their volunteer aids. On the basis of these physical and mental examinations were developed . . . various types of special classes. . . .

The intention of our plan was to allow each child to proceed at his own rate along one of a series of vertical tow-paths which provided for all speeds from hare to tortoise. We assumed, on the basis of the results of the psychological tests, that this speed was something stable within the child's own personality, and did not depend to any very great extent on whether he had a headache or a cold or was a truant or a " Smart Aleck." Now and then a teacher will tell you that this child or that does not deserve to be promoted because he is a truant. If you suggest that he will become a worse truant if " left back," she will propose the truant school. As the psychological test is used more and more in the school, it becomes the child's best defense against being " left back " or even demoted for extraneous reasons. The treatment of truancy by this crude and irrelevant punishment becomes less possible when the child has a psychological test to back up his claim to an established place in the group.

In our school, the practice was to make amendments gradually as new light was shed on the children's ability. So long as a teacher has three or four very backward children, a slightly maladjusted child is not noticed. When, however, the cruder differences are removed by homogeneous grouping, the individual differences in other respects begin to appear. . . . No child is kept back because of his psychological rating, if his work proves him able to keep up with a higher group. The test is merely a tentative guide by which to find certain actual differences early. In fact, it proved distinctly easier to shift children from one place to another for a tryout under the new classification, than it had been under the former grading method. The simple explanation was that all of us knew the children better than we had known them before.[6]

Many private schools throughout the country have been assuming an experimental attitude towards education and have developed methods of meeting individual needs. But one of the most interesting projects of this sort has come through the reorganization of a public school in one of the suburbs of Chicago. Under such a system the chance of maladjustments such as we have indicated in cases 16, 17 and 18 (pp. 35-43) is negligible:

Winnetka . . . has developed the Individual Technique and demonstrated that individual progress is possible under public school conditions without additional expense, or, after it is once launched, any harder work for the teachers or administrators. Children can be promoted as individuals, yet their activities in groups are more encouraged than hampered. . . .

Spelling was the first subject to undergo rejuvenation at Winnetka. It was easily done. All the children were examined at the beginning of the semester on all words they were expected to learn during the semester. Some of them already knew all but a dozen or so of the entire list. The average child was able to spell about two-thirds, and even the poorest spellers could spell some of the words. Then why, since most of the pupils already knew so many of the words that represented their year's work, must all the children study all the words in a daily lesson each day, as had been done before?

The teachers checked in each child's own speller the words he had missed. These were the words he knew he must master before the end of the term, but he was turned free to learn them at his own natural speed. The result was, as has been said, that some of the students finished their year's spelling the first day. And knew it thoroughly, too. Even the slowest of the children didn't have to study as many words throughout the year as would have been the case under the old plan.

Reading was next. The reading ability of children the country over varies widely. In the fifth grade alone, an examination showed that some children had third grade reading ability, some fourth, some fifth, some sixth, and some up to seventh, eighth and even above. A child who has only third grade reading ability will learn to read most rapidly, and digest what he is reading most easily, if he is given plenty of third grade reading work, and allowed to run along in it unforced. That is much better than being made to plow through a Fifth Reader. But the child who can read books like *Treasure*

---

[6] Irwin, E. A., and Marks, L. A.: *Fitting the School to the Child: An Experiment in Public Education* (1924), 24-104, *passim*.

Island with ease and enjoyment, has nothing to learn from a Fifth Reader. He has already progressed further than that, and Fifth Reader work will only hold him back and form bad mental habits.

This time, as before, all the children were tested at the beginning of the year. One of the reading tests that are now familiar to most teachers was used. When it was shown what a wide variety existed in the reading ability in each grade, books were bought that supplied the needs of each individual child. Why not? It was a simple and obvious solution — and it didn't cost a cent more than to buy thirty books all exactly alike. The children were delighted, and the results, as before, were excellent.

Recitations were discarded. The children did not read aloud to the class — they read to the teacher one at a time, while the rest of the class studied. It took the teacher no longer to hear them read one at a time to her alone than to hear them read one at a time to the entire class. It was less nerve-racking, too, for everyone concerned. The good readers were no longer forced to sit, itching with eagerness to correct, or completely bored, while the slow readers struggled through a difficult paragraph. They went ahead, reading to the teacher only occasionally while she was able to give more time and help to the slow ones. . . .

The Winnetka schools — and others working along the same general line — are made to fit widely differing individuals, therefore, in two ways: In giving all children mastery of the commonly needed knowledges and skills, individual differences are allowed for by making it possible for each child to progress at his own rate, sticking to each job until it is completed — 100 per cent — then going on to the next. And in the group and creative activities encouragement and scope are given to individual variations, originality and initiative being developed, but developed under social conditions that will make the child aware of his oneness with the group. . . .

A deliberate effort is being made in Winnetka to develop social consciousness in children. Half of each morning and half of each afternoon are given over to group and creative activities. These activities are not marked, they are not for the purpose of teaching knowledges and skills — those are handled by the Individual Technique in the other parts of the day — they do not affect the pupil's progress. Their sole purposes are the development of individuality and training in social consciousness.[7]

There are various efforts of this kind to bring about adjustments in the intellectual spheres — the " platoon school," whereby the day is organized in " shifts " representing study, work (manual), and play; the " Dalton plan," whereby, instead of studying different subjects, an

---

[7] Washburne, C., and Stearns, M. M.: *Better Schools: A Survey of Progressive Education in American Public Schools* (1928), 173–287, *passim*.

individual assignment (project) is made, and the requisite "tools" acquired in connection with the working out of the assignment — and other similar plans. Later in this chapter we give details of how a whole city school system (Rochester) has become modified to meet individual needs. These procedures represent, however, a relatively small part of the American public school system. The prevalent practices are still generally conservative.

The helplessness of the teachers in dealing with problems other than those of primary mental adjustments has been marked. Here again the processes working for the selection of teachers are important factors in the situation. A large part of the teaching force is made up of inexperienced young women, who are passing the time until they are married. And it is probable that a large part of the "professionals" is quite inferior, except in reading-writing-figuring capacities, to most of those entering certain other professions. Assuming the possibility of more mobility than actually exists, the most energetic persons might be supposed to go into the business world, the most sympathetic into social work, the most inquiring into research. There are no data at hand to show whether this is true, but the reading of a large number of records of maladjusted school children shows that a great many teachers have failed completely in handling even the simplest problems that require sympathy, an open mind and energetic procedure, and suggests that there is an unduly large number of psychopathic or badly adjusted personalities among the teachers themselves.

It is interesting to note, therefore, that the actual impetus to the movement for handling the behavior problems of school children has come usually from social service organizations and often through them has permeated the school system. In the first stage experts were drawn into the schools to handle the behavior problems, then, in some places, persons from the regular teaching staff were assigned work of this type, and recently there has been a tendency to involve all of the teachers, from the very beginnings of their careers, by incorporating work of this sort in teacher training courses. It must not be thought that these "stages" represent any necessary evolution; all three processes are functioning at the present time.

Probably the most important, and certainly the most widespread and vigorous of the movements designed to meet the needs of the school in handling problem children is the visiting teacher movement.

The visiting teacher is generally a person with professional experience both in teaching and social work who works from the school to the home. Problems of maladjustment are referred to her by the teachers. She makes a study of the home and neighborhood influences that are bearing upon the child, and, in attempting a plan of treatment, she brings to bear the resources of school, home and neighborhood. She tries to interpret the school to the home and the home to the school. Regarding the origin and general set of the movement the following statements may be quoted:

The work of the visiting teacher had a triple origin. In the school year 1906–1907 New York, Boston, and Hartford, Connecticut, developed simultaneously, but independently, a similar type of work to meet a common need. For a long time thoughtful educators had realized that even with the extension of the work of the attendance officer, the school nurse and the special classes there were still children, neither truants, delinquents nor those physically handicapped, for whom the school was not functioning effectively. Even in a school system representing the most advanced educational thought there was still the child who failed to make the prescribed progress or who failed to measure up to the expected standard of behavior. These children were frequently referred to as " difficult " or " problem " children.

Each failure was evidence of a maladjustment somewhere along the line. To find the cause of this maladjustment, whether it lay in the school, in the home, in the neighborhood or in the child himself, to find the cause and then to seek its adjustment, this was the preventive and constructive purpose for which the visiting teacher was added to the school system. It was evident that someone representing the school was needed to get acquainted with the individual child and to bring about a closer co-operation of home and school.

To make the most out of the five school hours the teacher must understand something of the child's life during the other nineteen hours of the day; and in order not to undo the work of the five hours the home must be in close touch with the school and must understand its aim and demands. Otherwise home and school may work, quite unconsciously, at cross purposes. Home, school, and neighborhood, each is familiar with a different child, and unless there be someone to see the *whole* child, the many-sided individual, and to help the teacher and parents to understand him and to work out together a plan to meet his individual needs, there is danger that the educative agencies at work upon his plastic nature may leave warped or undeveloped some essential element of his character. . . .

As has frequently happened in other educational experiments, the visiting teacher movement was initiated in some cities by private organizations, and, after the value of the work had been demonstrated, was taken over by the Department of Education. In New York, the work originated in two settlements in which workers with the children felt that they needed to get in closer touch with the teachers of the settlement children. They found that besides securing help from the school they could be of assistance to the teachers, both in obtaining better co-operation of the parents and in understanding certain children who had been enigmas. As a result, one resident in each settlement assumed the special work of calling on the families of those children who presented serious social or educational problems, and this worker came to be known as the school visitor or visiting teacher. A committee to extend and develop this work was shortly afterwards formed by the Public Education Association which maintained the work until the Board of Education was convinced of its value and established it as part of the school system. In Boston the work was started by a group of public-spirited citizens, whose example was followed by women's clubs and settlements. In Hartford, the third pioneer, the work was undertaken upon the suggestion of the director of the Psychological Laboratory, who realized the need of it in connection with his work with problematic school children. . . .

It is interesting to note that while the same fundamental need has been recognized, yet in different cities the work has been approached from different standpoints. In some cities it was introduced by those interested in the up-building of community life; in others by those working with unadjusted school children; psychologists, women's clubs and parents' associations which especially recognized the need of closer co-operation with the school; by others who were interested in the causes that lie back of irregular attendance and poor scholarship; and by child welfare workers who saw children in danger of falling between the two seats of authority — the home and the school. The roots of this work are widespread and its ramifications many.[8]

The visiting teacher movement is related both to education and to the child welfare movement. Historically . . . the impetus for its establishment came in many instances from those interested in social work. (The Public Education Association of New York City should not be included in this statement, since the educational emphasis has always been of first importance). Even in those places, however, where, in the beginning, the relief aspect of child care was stressed, it has gradually incorporated educational purposes and methods. It thus marks an integration of the two movements, education and child welfare. Other innovations in the school, such as medical inspection, manual training, domestic science, and mental tests, were introduced in many cases

[8] *The Visiting Teacher in the United States*, published by Public Education Association of the City of New York (2d ed., 1923), 11–13.

by outside influences to meet the needs of the defective or exceptional children. Like these, visiting teacher service is gradually adapting itself to meet the needs of all school children.[9]

The function of the visiting teacher is the " adjustment of conditions in the lives of individual children to the end that they may make more normal or more profitable school progress." This adjustment of conditions makes the visiting teacher a link between the home and many independent agencies. She first goes to the school, then to the home, and lastly enlists the cooperating agency necessary in solving her specific problem; thus she gathers up the loose threads, focusing them upon the school and the home as centers.[10]

We shall describe in some detail how the visiting teacher situation has been worked out in three totally different types of organizations — the first, an organization which was planned purely for social service, the second, a public school system, and the third, a private association whose aims have been largely educational.

The White-Williams Foundation in Philadelphia represents the most interesting and one of the most important developments in the visiting teacher movement. Organized on a pietistic, salvationist basis in 1800 and called the Magdalen Society, its purpose was to afford relief to " that class of females who had been unhappily seduced from the path of innocence and virtue and at times feel desirous of a return thereto." Its early procedure, as outlined in its reports, was to place the " distressed females " in " respectable and religious families as a temporary asylum." But within a few years the Society had acquired a house, hired a matron, employed a " moral instructress " and become thoroughly institutionalized. As early as 1849, however, it was recognized that the institutional treatment was not meeting with marked success. In the report for that year it was deplored that, up to that time, nearly half of the inmates had been discharged for insubordination. It was further recognized at that time that energy might better be spent on preventing delinquency than on bringing about repentance after the fact. George Williams, one of the founders, in this same annual report, expressed the hope that " the time will come when some

---

[9] Oppenheimer, J. J.: *The Visiting Teacher Movement*, published by Public Education Association of the City of New York (1924), 20.

[10] Gleim, Sophia C.: " The Visiting Teacher," *United States Bureau of Education, Bulletin* No. 10:8 (1921).

liberal provision will be made for girls who do not come within the class for which our houses of refuge are designed. They need proper attention to their physical development and judicious direction towards some appropriate employment for a livelihood." Nevertheless, the institution functioned as an institution until 1914, when the property came into the hands of the city, and the house was torn down. Shortly after that the control of the board was radically changed and considerable conflict arose as to the future function of the Magdalen Society. An extraordinarily able, tactful, and far-sighted woman, Miss Anna B. Pratt, was given charge of an investigation (December, 1916) into the work being done for girls in Philadelphia, New York, Boston and Chicago, and her investigations left her in no doubt that the proper handling of the problems of delinquency among girls was to begin preventive work with them before the habits of delinquency had been formed. She suggested that the Society institute a program of work with girls who were leaving school for industry. In accordance with these suggestions the name of the Society was changed to the White-Williams Foundation for Girls, and vocational counseling was started in connection with the Junior Employment Office of the Bureau of Compulsory Education. The experience of these counselors showed that by the time the girls were ready to enter industry their behavior trends were pretty firmly established. It became apparent to Miss Pratt and her associates that these girls must be reached earlier in their school careers, and the board was persuaded to put counselors in the schools. As her report expresses it: " Within four months, the society was working directly in the schools. That brief period had been sufficient to show that when girls came for their working papers it was very often already too late to give them the help they needed." At this time the first concern of the Society was vocational counseling and the administration of a scholarship fund to enable girls to stay in school who would otherwise have had to take out employment certificates. The problems raised brought the counselors in close touch both with the teachers and the parents, and their functions were continually widened to handle maladjustments of all sorts. It became apparent that the problems they were dealing with were by no means confined to girls but were problems common to children, and in February, 1920, the charter and constitution were " revised on the most liberal lines to allow the Foundation ' to aid in all ways possible in the progressive

solution of social, economic, and civic problems, especially such as
may affect the immediate or ultimate interest of children of school
age '." Since that time the school counseling ("school counselor" is
synonymous with "visiting teacher" as used by other organizations)
has proceeded, with many ramifications. The White-Williams Foundation, indeed, has done more than any other organization in testing out
the value of visiting teacher work in all conceivable types of school
situations. Its aim has been to demonstrate to the school and to the
community the need and value of this type of treatment of problem
children. Counselors have been placed in schools in upper class districts,
in the most congested tenements, in foreign neighborhoods, negro neighborhoods, schools for physical and mental defectives and in parochial
schools, as well as public schools. The policy has been to place a counselor in a selected school for a long enough period to demonstrate to
the community and the school board the possibilities of such work. At
this time the school board usually places a counselor in the school,
leaving the White-Williams Foundation free to withdraw and begin
another demonstration in some other type of situation. In this way it
has been possible on very limited funds to permeate practically the
whole school system in Philadelphia. At the same time that the Foundation was trying to give the movement as wide a spread as possible
among the different types of schools and neighborhoods it was pushing
the work further and further back in the grades. The counselors had
begun with girls who were getting working certificates, and discovered
that the behavior difficulties had their origins long before this time.
After they got into the schools their first efforts were made in
the higher grammar school grades, but they soon found that they
were missing large numbers of children who left school before these
higher grades, and that of those found in these grades their behavior trends had often become firmly established. On pushing the
work further back the greatest proportion of behavior difficulties (including truancy and retardation) had been found in the fifth grade,
which suggested that the origins were to be found further back still,
and led the Foundation to place counselors as far back as the kindergarten and to emphasize the importance of dealing with the
younger children.

As the Foundation defines the work of school counseling, it seems to
have two purposes. On the one hand, the school, through its counselors,

must actually meet the problems of the serious misdemeanants, the juvenile delinquents, and the seriously maladjusted who are now in their grades. This means the development of empirical methods of reconditioning, bringing to bear all the influences of the school, the home, and the neighborhood. On the other hand, the school must seek, again through its counselors, to get at these behavior difficulties at their very beginnings. This, too, must be by empirical methods since so little is known of " causes " of maladjustment. It will be worth while to examine, through its own reports, how this work has been carried on by the White-Williams Foundation. Regarding vocational counseling, and what it finally led to, this summary appears in an official review of the Foundation's work for a five-year period:

Visiting the Bureau of Compulsory Education which issues the working certificates to children between the ages of 14 and 16, the new director found a condition among children applying for working certificates, not unique to Philadelphia, but one that suggested that here were the outlying islands of a great continent of work to be done. It was obvious that in a large proportion of instances the parents, or, too often, the children themselves were making an important decision about the child's future without regard to opportunities, health, fitness, necessity for going to work, aptitudes, talents, or much of anything else that might be thought pertinent except the few dollars which the child might earn at the start. Here was evidently a great strategic point from which to give many of these drifting little barks a friendly shove toward a better harbor, and to take in tow some of those gravely in need of study and careful guidance. . . .

As the counselors interviewed child after child, heard their stories, saw what jobs were open to them, sounded their minds about school and work and family, it became clear that, although much could be done to help these children as they were leaving school, the great opportunity lay further inland in the school system. Every school principal's office is, for eyes that see, a coign of vantage for discovering the social problems of the people whose lives touch it — and whose life is not related to this pervading institution? The child's school attendance, itself, is often a sensitive barometer of the child's home conditions. Sickness, widowhood, unemployment, insufficient income, ignorance, mental defect and other handicaps all operate in the direction of irregular attendance and premature withdrawal from school. The child's behavior is often an index to less conspicuous causes of difficulty. Parents who fail to understand, parents who have an atrophied sense of responsibility, unhappy parents, foolish parents, parents harassed and oppressed

— all of these are registering, as the camera man says, on the mind of the child. Sometimes the results are not immediately perceptible; sometimes they are spectacularly disastrous. Some children fail to "pass" at the end of the year, some children are inattentive, some make trouble for the teacher, some "take it out" on their schoolmates; they all strive to meet their mental, physical and spiritual needs in the only ways that occur to child minds, often without knowing the meaning and consequences of their acts. Some have the good fortune to find wholesome outlets. Others are not so situated.

By the time the children come to the Bureau of Compulsory Education to get working certificates, for a large percentage of them the die for further school attendance has been cast. Many have jobs already promised them, to others who have been waiting impatiently for their fourteenth birthday, getting out of school and into a job has an irresistible glamour. The necessity of wage earning has been so firmly impressed upon some that readjustment at the last moment to another plan is very difficult.

The counselors saw the need of a firm foundation of educational guidance upon which vocational guidance could be based. Accordingly, the White-Williams Foundation staff of school counselors was organized. At first it was thought sufficient to begin with children in the fifth and sixth grades. But it was not long before it was seen that the place to start is at the real beginning of the child's school life. Even then some children do not get a fair start. They enter school with defects of eyes, ears, teeth, tonsils, adenoids, nutrition — to mention a few of the more common physical handicaps. For the first time in their lives they are brought into sharp and rigid comparison with other children. If their handicaps are such that they cannot keep up with the majority of the children in their groups, they thus add to their troubles by having the habit or attitude of failure impressed upon them.

In this connection it should be recalled that under our system of compulsory education we force into schools many, many children who would otherwise have been kept, or at least allowed to stay, at home — the "delicate" child, the excessively shy child, the child with some obvious defect, the child who does not care especially for books or activities that appeal only to the intellect. Now we make all of these children attend school, but we have not yet adapted our educational system to their needs. Our schools are still very largely the kind that were developed for the selected group of children who came because they had a real bent for bookish learning. The very rigid application of old rules to the new population of the schools has possibilities of doing irreparable harm. Among those children with whom the White-Williams Foundation school counselors have come in contact, have been many who were desperately discouraged and unhappy — one so abjectly miserable that she talked of suicide if she were forced to continue. With our compulsory system of education it has become acutely necessary to make the school fit the child.[11]

A great deal of the energy of the counselors has been taken up by the maladjustments connected with problems of health. Although it is specifically stated in the Manual of the White-Williams Foundation that "health problems [should be accepted] only when they appear to the counselor to be the cause of one of the other difficulties, or when referred by doctor or nurse for special social attention," it has often been found impossible to treat many problems of unadjusted behavior without first, or at the same time, remedying the physical difficulties. Perhaps this is partly due to the greater tangibility and apparently more immediate urgency of the physical as against the emotional problems. Furthermore, the helplessness of the families in knowing how to use the medical resources of the community, their indifference, or actual inability to give up the necessary time, has tended to thrust problems back upon the school for solution:

The outstanding facts in our work with the little tots in the Shippen School are the amount of physical defects and the per cent of school retardation among these very young children. The question arises: Is the home accepting its share of the responsibility when it passes on, to the school, children in poor physical condition? Furthermore, what is the relation between school retardation and physical deficiency? As the work at the Shippen School progresses, some light should be thrown upon these problems.

In October, 1919, one of our Counselors began visiting the homes of the kindergarten children to win the co-operation of the parents and to have them remedy all the defects in the children of pre-school age in their families and she will follow these boys and girls as far as possible through the grades in order to see what the removal of defects will do for them.

The school physician made an early physical examination of each child. Of the twenty-eight examined, only three were without some physical defect, decayed teeth and undernourishment being the most common.[12]

As we analyzed our records this summer, in the preparation of the statistical report, one problem fairly clamored for attention — " Too many of our children are physically defective." " Most of my cases are health problems."

[11] *White-Williams Foundation: Five Years' Review for the Period Ending December 31, 1921, 4–8.*

[12] *White-Williams Foundation: One Hundred and Twentieth Annual Report for the Period Ending August 31, 1920, 14.*

" I have spent most of my time urging parents to correct their children's physical defects," wrote one Counselor after the other. In one class of sixty-two kindergarten and first-grade children we found only ten who had no physical deficiency. The percentage of failures in this first grade was 57 per cent. Examinations in another school showed physical defects in twenty-one out of twenty-two children who were over age for their grade. In still another school, where practically every child is retarded, only ten out of sixty-five were in good condition. In still another school eighty-five retarded children out of eighty-eight known to have been examined were found to be physically defective. While some of these boys and girls would undoubtedly have been retarded in school even had they had the best of medical attention, there were evidently a large number whose progress was definitely delayed by septic tonsils, adenoids, decayed teeth, defective vision and hearing.

It especially interested us to discover that there was so large an amount of physical defect in the first grade, showing that the home was not doing its part.[13]

The visiting teacher is often handicapped by the lack of resources offered by the community for treatment of its misfits. The White-Williams Foundation has occasionally been forced to supply the materials which its school counselors could utilize in bringing about adjustments. The following is an example:

There are over 7,000 children in the Philadelphia schools who are more than three years retarded. Many of these are girls fourteen and fifteen years old, who, for one reason or another, are still in the fifth and sixth grades. We have been forced to consider especially the needs of these little women — for one after another, as misfits in the schools, or chronic truants, they are brought to us by attendance officers and harassed principals. A psychological examination frequently reveals no serious mental deficiency. The causes of retardation are numerous, but there appears to be, in most cases, a mental inability to absorb, which the prescribed work of the fifth and sixth grades does not relieve.

Boston has discovered that nearly 50 per cent of her retarded boys are only temporarily in need of receiving instruction through " action." Reports from her prevocational centres indicate that probably one-half can be helped over this period and sent on through academic courses if the right sort of hand work is provided at the right moment. For some time we have been experimenting with our backward girls in the Trade School, and have discovered that not more than one-half of those we have sent there have been able to profit by the definite trade training which the school offers.

[13] *White-Williams Foundation: One Hundred and Twentieth Annual Report for the Period Ending August 31, 1920*, 41.

We therefore made plans for organizing in the Stevens Annex of the Lincoln School a special home-making class for backward girls who have been under our care. The emphasis was to be on household arts — cooking and sewing — but a certain amount of related academic work was also to be given. In order to make the interest vivid and the work as practical as possible the rooms used were to be furnished as a flat by the girls themselves, under the direction of the teacher, who is to be supplied, and has been promised, by the Board of Education. We assigned to the group a Counselor to do the home visiting and to make the social diagnoses.[14]

The general purposes and policies are summarized in the following quotation:

It is toward this general direction of introducing flexibility, of studying each child as a personality, as a unique combination of possibilities, and of giving him individual attention that school counseling is pointed.

How does the School Counselor translate these general purposes into living realities? What does the counselor really do for the child? First, it is necessary to find out what sort of person this youngster really is; what is his physical condition, what kind of mind has he, what have been and are his surroundings — his home, his neighborhood, his companions. What are the ideas of goodness, of badness, of social recognition, of stigma, of the purposes of life, of those among whom he has lived and from whom he has acquired his standards and ideals? Where serious hardships and handicaps are revealed the School Counselor puts the child and his family in touch with the many resources of the city for helping them solve all sorts of problems. The facilities of hospitals, sanatoria, visiting nurses, mothers' assistance fund, the family welfare societies, clubs, churches, settlements, and the host of other organized sources of help are brought into play. The teacher is shown just what lies back of much that would otherwise be inexplicable in the child's behavior. In some situations and with some children a person not hampered by the conventional responsibilities of parent or teacher can exert a powerful influence.

For the children who should remain in school but whose financial condition will not permit their further attendance, there are scholarships. Like a good many other things in education, this matter of scholarships is much bigger at the top than at the base. . . . Surely if the college graduate needs help to go on, the child who has had only an elementary education has a much greater need. Scholarships and fellowships for older students can be awarded most advantageously only when all who have real capacity and ability are put in the way of competing for them. This means the exercise of some solicitude in seeing that exceptionally well endowed students are enabled to get through the

---

[14] *Ibid.*, 29.

preliminary stages and up to the places where they can enter the lists for the bigger prizes.[15]

The extent of the service to " problem children " may be gathered from the fact that during their first ten years, from June, 1917, to June, 1927, 9,367 children were given personal guidance and service and 298 of these were also given financial assistance to remain in school from one to six years each.

The necessity of educating the teachers in an appreciation of the behavior difficulties of the children has been found as important as the necessity of educating the parents. This the White-Williams Foundation has done in two ways: first, giving special training through a system of scholarships to teachers now in the public schools; and second, working directly with the girls in the normal schools:

A . . . project which promises to make a marked difference in the attitude of teachers toward their pupils and toward the whole program of individualizing education, was inaugurated in the fall of 1921. Twenty-five scholarships were offered to teachers in the public schools for a special course in " Social Work in the Schools " given at the Pennsylvania School for Social Service. Credit of 1 1-2 units toward a bachelor's degree is given by the University of Pennsylvania and by Temple University to those successfully completing it. Nearly ninety teachers and principals applied for scholarships and so many inquiries came from others that two other courses have been organized for the second semester, one at the request of the special class teachers.

The course requires attendance at one lecture a week, and at least two hours a week spent on a special child or group selected by each teacher from his own class. Home visits are made, the child's progress in school watched, a closer personal relationship between teacher and pupil established. Where it has seemed wise, arrangements have been made for the teacher to take the children to clinics for mental and physical examination. The effort has been consistently to arouse these teachers to the social side of their work, to encourage them to do what they can, and to show them where to turn for help to do what they themselves lack the time and specialized knowledge to undertake. This is a significant effort toward getting into the regular training courses for teachers this point of view in education and a method and technique for putting these new ideas into operation.[16]

15 *White-Williams Foundation: Five Years' Review for the Period Ending December 31, 1921*, 8–9.
16 *Ibid.*, 11–12.

The contact in the normal schools has been obtained in three ways: first, through the sociology department which requires the students to get first-hand knowledge of the various social service agencies in the city; second, through the counselors who have been placed in the schools of practice by the White-Williams Foundation; and third, through field-work in counseling by a group of senior sociology students under the leadership of a White-Williams Foundation counselor. This work is described as follows in a recent publication:

One of the latest and most inspiring projects has been carried on in co-operation with the Sociology Department of the Philadelphia Normal School, whose staff have planned a new course in social service, required for all students, to acquaint them with the aims of social work and the various social resources of the city. In response to their request a White-Williams counselor has been working for the past year in one School of Practice and in September, 1927, one was placed in still another such school. Not only does this give to many of the pupil-teachers an opportunity to discuss individual children with the counselor and to learn the value of personality studies, but in addition it permits a selected group of senior students to substitute for the required course one under the leadership of the counselor, involving one class period a week for the consideration of various types of personality problems, and two afternoons of field work. The response of these young teachers has been most encouraging. Since 1922 the Foundation has been carrying on a similar plan in connection with the Department of Education at Swarthmore College.[17]

In Rochester, New York, also, the whole school system has been permeated by the visiting teacher movement, but its origins and development have been quite different from those of Philadelphia. Here is a city which has prided itself on the excellence of its schools and developed them to such a standard that " to-day, in the opinion of educational authorities, the Rochester public school system stands among the very best in the country. According to Professor George D. Strayer of Columbia University, it may safely be ranked among the highest five per cent." [18] This school system is not only providing some of the best possible educational opportunities for the natural " book-learners," but it early recognized and provided for those children who

[17] *White-Williams Foundation: School Children as Social Workers See Them, June, 1917 to June, 1927,* 5.
[18] Ellis, Mabel Brown: *The Visiting Teacher in Rochester* (1925), 23.

must learn in other ways and who have other types of proficiencies and abilities to be developed. The elementary education is attempted in such a way that it should be possible for all the children going through the Rochester schools to attain it as a common foundation. But there has been a great deal of study and intelligent direction in order to make this ideal approach reality. Psychological tests are given the children leaving kindergarten. If they are found to have special disabilities in learning to read they are placed in a pre-primary grade and given special types of instruction in reading. Up to the fourth grade there are special classes for the slightly retarded, in which the ordinary two-term grade is given in three terms. The school conceives it to be its duty to give every child the body of knowledge and experience comprised in the curriculum of the first six grades.[19]

It has recognized, however, that all children cannot get this body of experience and knowledge in the same way or at the same rate. There have been organized, therefore, in addition to these classes for the slightly retarded, ungraded classes for the seriously retarded, speech correction classes, lip-reading classes, special classes in English for foreign children, sight-saving classes, orthopedic classes, open air classes for the undernourished and anæmic, etc. The aim is, wherever and whenever possible, to work these children out of these special classes into the normal groups by giving them instruction in techniques to be used to minimize their handicaps.

When the sixth grade is reached, another set of mental tests is given and pre-vocational work is arranged in the junior high school. Before taking the pre-vocational work, each boy is given time in the " try-out shop," where his aptitudes and interests are tested by all sorts of practical situations, and each girl is given similar try-outs in household sciences and arts. Special classes are available, too, for children particularly gifted, who are able to progress faster than the normal group or who can be given an enriched curriculum.

The city which has developed a school system of this sort has tended quite naturally to be preoccupied with the problems of retardation.

---

[19] Incidentally, it is a very broad curriculum — as Superintendent Weet expresses it: " Comprehensive enough to include the tools of language and number," but with courses designed also to emphasize physical health, social intelligence, the æsthetic life, and to gratify " the universal craving for the use of the human hand." — (*Rochester Democrat-Chronicle*, March 15, 1926).

Having devised a curriculum which seems to meet the needs of the individual in modern life, its aim has been to make this curriculum effective for each child passing through the elementary school, adapting methods to individuals as far as possible by forming small special classes and attempting to make these small classes so homogeneous that retardation within the group, and failure, would be relatively infrequent.

In spite of the excellence of its internal structure the school was forced to a recognition of the fact that other forces were playing upon the child, of which it had little understanding and over which it could, therefore, exercise little control. It was undoubtedly this situation which brought about the appointment of the first visiting teacher in Rochester in 1913. Superintendent Weet, at that time, made the following statement:

The appointment of Miss Emma G. Case as visiting teacher is the first step in an attempt to meet a need of which the school system has been conscious for some time. It is an undisputed fact that in the environment of the child outside the school are to be found forces which will oftentimes thwart the school in its endeavors. While this has long been recognized, yet the endeavor to remedy such counteracting conditions, as far as possible, has not come to be regarded as an established function of the public school. The appointment of a visiting teacher is an attempt on the part of the school to meet its responsibility for the whole welfare of the child. There are few of the children in our schools who are suffering through the wilful neglect and abuse of parents. Whatever suffering comes for which the home is responsible, comes largely through ignorance and necessity. It will be the function of the visiting teacher to enlighten and aid its relieving. Her aim will be to secure maximum coöperation between the home and the school.[20]

For seven years Miss Case was the only visiting teacher in Rochester, and it is interesting to note that when the expansion of the visiting teacher department was brought about in 1920 it was again because the school system was being " thwarted in its endeavors," — this time by the fact that, with all the force of the law behind it, the school was finding itself unable to maintain proper attendance on the part of the children without the parents' coöperation, and was very much in need

---

[20] Quoted by Ellis: *op. cit.*, 39–40, from the Fifty-Sixth Report of the Rochester Board of Education.

of a personnel, with training in social work, who could get back of the causes of absence and bring about parental coöperation with the school:

No sooner had knowledge of the kind of service which the visiting teacher was giving begun to permeate the schools than requests began to come in for an extension of such activities. It was, of course, a physical impossibility for any one person to do all that obviously needed to be done, and as results were achieved in this case or that, people's eyes were opened to other needs not so obvious and hitherto unsuspected. Teachers began to see as children who might be helped certain boys formerly passed over in despair as hopeless incorrigibles. They began to worry about certain inoffensive children who were abnormally seclusive or who did not seem to make friends or who did not work as well as their ability warranted, and as they saw these new needs they became increasingly insistent in their demand for help.

It happened that the pressure upon the Board of Education for the appointment of more visiting teachers culminated at about the time the bureau of efficiency was completing an intensive study of causes of absence throughout the city schools. . . . In the final tabulation, causes of absence were classified under six headings: Sickness, Family, Weather, Church, Miscellaneous, and Inexcusable. . . . This classification revealed the surprising fact that of all whole-day absences the heading " Miscellaneous " absorbed 27.6 per cent and the heading " Inexcusable " 3.4 per cent, while in the half-days under consideration " Miscellaneous " leaped to 42.3 per cent and " Inexcusable " went up to 10.2 per cent.

It was evident that non-attendance for reasons not reported as connected with health, family conditions, weather, or church, and yet not considered by teachers as " Inexcusable " and distinctly not reported as truancy, presented a very serious problem. In the minds of those who studied these figures the conviction grew that probably a good many cases could be transferred from the " Miscellaneous " to the " Inexcusable " column if the real truth were known, and that undoubtedly both totals could be largely reduced if someone equipped with both understanding and authority could go from the school to the homes to explain the whole situation to parents and to enlist their coöperation. At the same time it was realized that such a person would encounter many family situations where help as well as explanation must be given, and where familiarity with social service agencies and methods would be a great asset.[21]

As a result of this situation the Board increased the visiting teacher staff by three. Each of them was assigned to a single school, in order to make intensive effort possible:

---

[21] Ellis: *op. cit.*, 44–45.

Within these schools, they were expected to study the causes of truancy and non-attendance and work towards their removal. . . . The visiting teacher department functioned according to this arrangement from approximately the time of its organization in September, 1920, through June, 1924, a period of four school years. During that time, the professional staff was increased from four to sixteen and the number of schools to which teachers were assigned rose from three to thirteen.[22]

The experience of these years showed that the visiting teachers were being disproportionately drawn into attendance problems as such, just as in Philadelphia the counselors were, by force of circumstances, drawn disproportionately into health problems as such. In September, 1924, the whole attendance department was reorganized in such a way that it relieved the visiting teachers of the cases which depended merely on non-attendance, and the Superintendent sent out the following memorandum:

Hereafter principals of those schools in which visiting teachers have been placed are not expected to use the visiting teacher for cases of truancy, as such. . . . The function of the visiting teacher is to get into the home where the school has reason to suppose that the failure of a given child to make normal school progress, or normal school adjustment, is due to faulty conditions in the environment of the child outside of school. Irregular attendance may or may not be a factor in this problem.[23]

By the end of 1927, there were 16 visiting teachers functioning in the Rochester schools and four others doing specialized work. Here we have, then, a public school system in which a visiting teacher department grew up largely because the schools were unable to solve the problems of retardation and attendance without taking the home situation into consideration, although these schools had developed internally an excellence that placed them in the top rank of American school systems. We see the visiting teacher developing from an agent of the school whose purpose was to bring about such corrections in environment, etc., as would allow for the smooth working of what the school considered its primary functions to a factor increasing extensively the actual functions of the school, which is now assuming responsibility for the child in his social relationships and adjustments as well as in his intellectual or vocational relationships and adjustments.

---

[22] Ellis: *op. cit.*, 46–48.   [23] Ellis: *op. cit.*, 50.

The general excellence of the school system, the development of high standards of work, the freedom of the whole system from political influences, has meant a gradual improvement of the teaching personnel, and there is evidence that Rochester has an unusually high-grade teaching personnel. It is not surprising, therefore, that the tendency has been to carry over certain of the visiting teacher functions to the regular teaching staff. And this has brought about one of the most interesting and significant developments in the whole visiting teacher movement, i.e., the generalization of the visiting teacher function.[24] This does not mean that there is or will be no place for the specialist, for the training of the ordinary teachers has not been such as adequately to fit them to handle many of the behavior problems of the children, and, furthermore, the present organization of the school system does not permit of small enough classes to make it possible for the ordinary teacher, even if trained to do so, to carry this added burden. Nevertheless, two important features of the Rochester system suggest that there is quite definitely a trend in this direction to which the school system will probably ultimately adapt itself.

From the very beginning of their work in Rochester the visiting teachers found not only that it was necessary to interpret the school and its aims to the family of the child but that the child's teachers in the school were often completely ignorant of the complications in the family life. In part this arose from the fact that Rochester has had a rapidly changing population, due to the changing industrial situation. It had formerly been a city dominated by the optical and kodak industries which drew a highly skilled, stable and fairly homogeneous type of labor. But as it became a center of some importance in the clothing industry large numbers of newly arrived immigrants came there with their varying customs and standards. In one school, for instance, the racial composition is 31% Russian, 18% Italian, 15% American, 9% Ukranian, 7% Turks and 5% Poles.[25] The school

---

[24] We have seen this tendency also in the work of the White-Williams Foundation.

[25] The following short descriptions of the various neighborhood conditions surrounding the schools where visiting teachers are installed give an indication of this change and the variety of problems it has brought: " Old residential section rapidly changing because old houses are either being remodeled into cheap apartment houses or giving place to new apartment houses. The American population is decreasing because of this. . . . Downtown foreign tenement district with all the

teacher often had no conception of the implications, or indeed the existence, of this multiplicity of standards. She turned a case over to the visiting teacher with the expectation that the visiting teacher would be able to bring about a modification of parental attitudes and thereby of the child's behavior. The adjustment was expected to be brought about all on one side. The impossibility of achieving results, unless the teachers could be brought to a clearer understanding of the forces involved, led one visiting teacher to organize an interesting experiment

---

problems involved in the lack of comprehension on the part of foreign parents, the indifference and low standards of shoddy American families, by run-down tenements, low wages, cheap shows and large factories. . . . Old residential section gradually being taken over by Italians buying homes. This neighborhood presents a sharp contrast in homes and economic status. . . . Homes of the middle class with majority of American families owning small modern houses on the outskirts of the city. . . . Cheap rooming house district with a shifting population and a turn-over of 50% during the year. . . . Includes a part of the city's main business section and is rapidly turning into a cheap rooming house section with a large percentage of transients. . . . One half of this neighborhood consists of an inferior business section where a shifty class of Americans live in blocks or rooming houses. The other half is a residence section which for the most part has been abandoned by Americans and is now occupied by Italians ranging from a very poor and ignorant group to some who have comfortable or creditable homes. . . . Originally a German settlement, this neighborhood of small homes has now become almost entirely Italian. . . . Crowded Italian section which is about to have one school playground. . . . Families are large and live either in small cottage houses formerly owned by German immigrants or in large frame houses converted into four or five family tenements. Into the resulting congested living conditions, the school is trying to inject American standards of cleanliness and sanitation. . . . Semi-rural gradually becoming Italian. . . . This is a ' 100% ' American district — a district of families who have been more prosperous than their forebears and have moved from small nearby towns to gain the advantages of city life. They yearn for material prosperity. The mothers in the community know each other well and have a common desire for raising home standards and educating their children. Consequently there is often some feeling of rivalry over school progress. . . . A rural district at the edge of city limits with no unifying community forces. . . . Housing many nationalities this neighborhood is one of the best equipped from the standpoint of organized social resources. . . . A neighborhood of varied nationalities the majority of whom are buying the cottage-type homes in which they live. . . . Southwest section of the city formerly known as 'Dutch town,' now a conglomerate neighborhood of fifteen nationalities over 53% of which is Italians." — (" Individual Differences," Visiting Teacher Department, Rochester, *Staff Bulletin* No. 4, *passim,* 1927).

in her school — one of the largest and best in the city. She had each of the teachers select several children who were special problems, visit the homes, talk to the parents, observe the child's activities, etc. The visiting teacher then had conferences with the teachers, discussing the significance of their findings and explaining techniques which had been found successful in dealing with similar cases. Thus there was built up an appreciation of the part the teacher could play in getting at problem children in the early stages of the problem. This acted as a stimulus to the teachers to be on the lookout for symptoms of maladjustment, to settle many of the problems without recourse to the visiting teacher and to use the visiting teacher purely as an adviser.

For several years, too, the visiting teacher technique has been included as a part of the training course for all students in the city Normal School, from which all the teachers are drawn. This has been looked upon, not as preliminary training for those who intend to become visiting teachers, but as a part of the necessary equipment of all those who intend becoming ordinary teachers:

Since the aim of the visiting teacher is to work with the class room teacher to develop a better understanding of the child, it has seemed advisable for Normal School students to be given not only a careful explanation of the work but a bit of actual child study work with the visiting teacher. Thus they see for themselves the value of a more comprehensive contact with the child and his governing influences.

During the past two years the senior class of the Rochester City Normal School has been doing some required work along this line in connection with their student teaching. The class has been divided into three groups corresponding to the six-week practice assignments so that each group begins its work with the visiting teacher at the beginning of one of these periods. During the first week, the student selects some child who gives evidence of a deviation from the normal calibre of the grade: — it may be conduct, scholarship or some personality trait which is keeping him from making normal progress. During the six weeks that follow there is an opportunity to observe the child in the school background and at the same time become acquainted with his home and neighborhood life. The group meets the visiting teacher once each week for conference.

The first meeting is given over to a general outlining of social and economic conditions affecting the child, the complexity of the school system which makes close contact between the home and school more difficult, and the place that the visiting teacher is trying to fill in the light of these conditions. The remaining meetings take the form of reports on information gained about the child from school permanent record and health cards, child study reports, observation of reactions and attitudes in the class room and from home visits with visiting teacher at which times, home conditions, attitudes, and influences are observed. The student teacher also makes an effort to get acquainted with the child during free periods and learn from him how his spare time is spent and what his chief interests are. In the light of all the information gathered from these different sources, a diagnosis is attempted and suggestions made as to how the school and coöperating agencies may make adjustments or supply some needs in the child's life.

This brief insight into the allround life of the child has proven very interesting and enlightening to the prospective teachers and created a desire on their part to know more completely the influences and environment of the pupils who may be under their instruction in the future.[26]

This course has now been in force for some time and a number of the girls who have taken it are teaching in the city schools. No comparison is available of the actual handling of behavior problems by these teachers with the methods and results obtained by other teachers, but it is claimed that the new teachers are alert in detecting behavior difficulties, discriminating in referring them to the visiting teacher, and are able to settle many of the minor problems without reference to the visiting teacher.

The coöperation existing between the various parts of the school system in dealing with difficult problems is shown in the following instance, which is typical of others:

A change in the district lines made at the beginning of this school year brought to the Wilson School many additional problem children, including a gang of over-age boys. These together with a number already in the school presented quite a difficult situation both in discipline and organization. The Visiting Teacher felt that one of her most important tasks was to do all she could to get hold of these boys by securing their coöperation and meeting their needs, not only for their own good but for the good of the school spirit in general. At the opening of school a few of the leaders among them were asked by the Visiting Teacher to help in locating the non-entrants from their neighborhoods, and in this way a friendly contact was made. Through the coöperation of the Child Study Examiner a survey was made of the over-age

---

[26] Visiting Teacher Department, Rochester, *Staff Bulletin* No. 2:21–22 (1925).

boys and a plea made for an ungraded class. For this class a man instructor was to be secured if possible and an especially arranged schedule including a generous amount of Manual Training and Gymnasium.

Such a group was formed having for its teacher a young man — a graduate of the University with an interest in athletics. This latter fact in itself was enough to secure the respect and interest of the boys simply from a physical standpoint, and made up for his lack of methods, since we felt the important training for this type of boy so soon to leave school was that of citizenship rather than book learning.

However, through the coöperation of Child Study Department, Class teacher, and Visiting Teacher both work and class morale has gradually improved. The first four boys who were truant were sent to the Visiting Teacher office and after a talk with them the Visiting Teacher suggested that they have a banner for attendance and promptness to be brought to the Visiting Teacher office each day when they were 100%, to be used as example to other children who came in the office for these failings. They agreed to this and made up their time for truancy constructing such a banner. Since then there has been practically no real truancy among them. They have not done so well regarding tardiness but are improving. After several talks with them after school about recreation they asked Visiting Teacher to arrange for a Boy Scout troop, so the Visiting Teacher took sixteen of them over one evening to a neighborhood center for the organization meeting. They have been very enthusiastic about it ever since.

Several boys who belong to the gang were not placed in the ungraded group because of their ability to do the work of a regular grade. Two of these were leaders and separated from the others and seem to have got interests in their grades which have made different boys of them. Those on probation to the Children's Court have made good during the term. The boys in the ungraded group are 13 or 14 years of age and have I.Q's varying from 63 to 86. Three of them have been transferred to Shop School this month and the others have been promoted within the group. Those left in regular grades have been either full or trial promotions.[27]

Another interesting aspect of the Rochester situation is the relation of the school department to the court. In making itself responsible for the behavior adjustments of the children the policy of the school has been to resort to the court only after using all of its own resources but, in the necessary cases, to establish a basis of coöperation with the court. Thus, in regard to absences, the classroom teacher refers to the prin-

[27] " Snapshots from the Visiting Teacher Field, Rochester," *Staff Bulletin* No. 3:7–8 (1926).

cipal only those cases where she cannot herself bring about an adjustment; in cases where bad home conditions are thought to be basic the visiting teacher takes over the case. In cases of definite truancy the attendance officer handles the situation. Where the pressure of greater authority is thought advisable the parents are haled before a " school court," and only as a last resort are parents and children turned over to the City Court. Thus we see the following proportions in regard to the treatment of truancy, as reported in the *Rochester Democrat-Chronicle* for July 1, 1926:

During the year 1924–25, the [attendance] department handled fourteen thousand cases of absence, 1,414 cases were heard in School Court, and 408 cases adjusted in City Court, with 398 convictions, forfeitures and commitments.

With regard to offense other than truancy an informal connection with the juvenile court has been brought about whereby every case of a child of school age coming before the court is referred back to a special visiting teacher (known as the " court representative ") before trial, and this visiting teacher sends the court a report of this child, giving particulars about the school adjustment. At present the school authorities are looking forward to an adjustment with the court whereby cases in which the school is carrying on an investigation and treatment shall be turned over to the school without court action, and eventually, perhaps, the school will handle most of the cases of school children without regard to where the misbehavior originated.

We are not making any attempt to present a picture of the visiting teacher movement as a whole. It has not as yet attained any great proportions in the school system. We have chosen to present at length a picture of the movement in the two places where it has been most vigorous and where it seems to be most deeply rooted. Another reason for presenting the Philadelphia and Rochester situations in so great detail is the significant point that the movement has attained its deepest roots by such different means in two such different communities.

The interest of the Public Education Association in the visiting teacher movement has been quite different from that of the organizations which we have just described. In Philadelphia and Rochester the movement grew up within the community in response to locally recognized needs, sponsored in the one case by a social service organization which had a traditional hold upon the community through a period of actual service extending over more than a century, and, in the other case, growing up in direct response to the changing needs of an extraordinarily mobile and progressive school system. In both cases, then, the development was indigenous. The Public Education Association is a national organization (affiliated with the Commonwealth Fund) interested primarily in educational problems. Its policy has been to bring about the development of the visiting teacher movement by setting up demonstrations in various communities. Thirty communities were selected from among the 270 applying for this service, on the basis of their facilities for carrying on the visiting teacher work at the end of the three years' demonstration and their willingness to pay one-third of the visiting teacher's salary during the demonstration.

The work of the Association has been of particular interest in that it has attempted to implant visiting teachers in communities where the demand may have been more often stimulated by the Association's offer than an outgrowth of consciously recognized needs. It will be impossible to know just how successful such a demonstration has been until several years have passed. The demonstrations are all drawing to a close now, and of 28 actually closed [28] 24 communities have continued the work on their own initiative, in 19 cases employing the same visiting teacher sent out by the Association. The taking over by so many of the communities of responsibility for the visiting teacher work indicates that the demonstrations have aroused an effective interest in the movement. How far this interest will be sustained, how far the movement will develop under this stimulation, is an important problem to which the next few years should give some answer.

These demonstrations of the Public Education Association have covered a very wide area, representing, indeed, a national undertaking.[29]

---

[28] Two were extended for another two-year period.

[29] An enumeration of the localities where visiting teachers have been placed gives an idea of the wide geographical distribution of the work. The thirty communities include three rural counties: Boone County, Missouri; Huron County, Ohio; Monmouth County, New Jersey; and the following twenty-seven cities: Berkeley, California; Birmingham, Alabama; Bluefield, West Virginia; Burlington,

A report written by Miss Jane Culbert tells of the type of problems met with in the beginning of the demonstrations:

While the selection of cities and suitable candidates for each represents a considerable task in itself, and an important phase of the Committee's work, yet the supervision of the visiting teachers in the field has been the main work of the central staff this year. All but four of the visiting teachers were new to the work and all but one, strangers to their supervisors. Our main objective therefore has been the building up of a staff organization. We have tried to develop a spirit of mutual confidence and to achieve high standards without limiting initiative, or freedom to adapt that work to the needs of the various communities. . . . All but two of the visiting teachers were visited by each of the three supervisors. . . . The plan was made deliberately in order that all the supervisory staff might have a view of the whole field and be in a position subsequently to discuss problems and policies in the light of first-hand acquaintance with both visiting teachers and communities.

The time of the supervisors on these visits has been spent in visiting schools, meeting the people in schools, social agencies, or the community, with whom the visiting teachers were coöperating, going over records, both for content and form, advising on problem cases or difficult situations, clarifying policies and frequently speaking to groups of teachers or social workers.

Two Regional Conferences, in Richmond (February) and Omaha (January) relieved the visiting teachers from a sense of isolation and gave them the feeling of working shoulder to shoulder with colleagues who also had difficulties to meet. . . .

The staff is not without limitations. The quality of work can be improved, of course, and will be. But the amazing thing is, that with the necessity of appointing candidates without experience in this special field, we have secured so high an average of work. Work with individual children has been good, and principals have been pleased with the results. The coöperation received from the schools has for the most part been gratifying. The coöperation of social workers has been secured. So far the visiting teachers have fitted into their communities and have won the approval of the superintendents and gained

---

Vermont; Butte, Montana; Charlotte, North Carolina; Chisholm, Minnesota; Coatesville, Pennsylvania; Columbus, Georgia; Detroit, Michigan; Durham, North Carolina; Eugene, Oregon; Hutchinson, Kansas; Kalamazoo, Michigan; Lincoln, Nebraska; Omaha, Nebraska; Pocatello, Idaho; Racine, Wisconsin; Richmond, Virginia; Rochester, Pennsylvania; Rock Springs, Wyoming; San Diego, California; Sioux City, Iowa; Sioux Falls, South Dakota; Tucson, Arizona; Tulsa, Oklahoma; and Warren, Ohio.

the support of civic groups. It sounds easy, but the difficulties of starting new work in a new place, single-handed, and isolated, have been greater than was anticipated. Repeatedly the supervisors have been impressed with the skill with which the teachers have worked into their communities and with their ability to keep up work with the children while meeting the many demands made upon them to speak, serve on committees, and the like.[30]

One very interesting part of these demonstrations has been the placing of visiting teachers in rural districts, where the problems met with are different from those met in city schools and where the functions of the visiting teacher will therefore tend to develop somewhat differently. For instance, the visiting teacher [31] placed in Monmouth County, New Jersey, found very different problems and very different attacks upon them necessary from those ordinarily found by the urban visiting teacher. Much of Monmouth county is open country, with social patterns markedly contrasting with its urban portions (such as Red Bank). It is very difficult for the visiting teacher to make contacts and obtain information from the family or the neighbors in such country districts. The city family has few social contacts depending primarily on location, i.e., with neighbors, as such, but to the country family, in its relative isolation, social contacts will often depend primarily on location. The immediate neighbors have a unique social importance. Furthermore, the country person often owns his land, and almost always regards his residence as more or less permanent, which tends to make the immediate neighbors also a somewhat permanent part of the environment. It, therefore, becomes very difficult for the visiting teacher to get any sizing-up of the general family and social situation through contacts with the neighbors, since the neighbors will be reluctant, under these circumstances, to discuss each other with strangers. The family, too, is likely to resent inquiry and is not conditioned to the methods of social and health workers as is the city family. Furthermore, the attitude towards the school tends to be very circumscribed. Country families have been known to resent strongly, for instance, the introduction of any form of physical training. The children are sent to school to learn from books, and other activities are thought of as wasting time which really belongs to the family. (The

---

[30] *Annual Report of the Commonwealth Fund for 1923,* 44–46.
[31] Communication from Miss Rhea Kay Boardman.

children are, of course, often an economic asset and are used extensively after school hours on the farm, etc.).

When the visiting teacher actually becomes accepted in a social situation of this sort, she is likely to have a great paucity of agencies with which to carry on her treatments. Although it has been the policy of the Public Education Association to insist that the function of the visiting teacher is to deal with children who do not get along, or are definitely maladjusted in school, and that her function does not extend to health problems or charity problems as such, the visiting teachers in these rural districts have often found themselves forced to take up all the functions of a general social worker, since the community has not provided these other facilities. Hence the development of the visiting teacher movement in the rural districts is probably more along lines of general social service than along the more specialized lines developed in the more highly organized urban communities.

Contrasting interestingly with the work in rural counties is the intensive work this Association has done in providing five visiting teachers in the New York City schools. This is a more permanent charge of the Public Education Association than its work in the thirty demonstration centers (to a further description of which we shall return) and is described in the Commonwealth Fund Program for the Prevention of Delinquency as follows:

[The program has] included provision for the placing of a visiting teacher in each of five public schools from which children are referred to the Bureau of Children's Guidance [a psychiatric clinic, see chap. 3]. These teachers were engaged and at work early in 1922. A part of their task is to bring to the attention of the clinic those children needing its service, to assist in the special treatment recommended, and to aid in the field training of students from the School of Social Work.[32]

The Public Education Association has attempted to free these five New York City visiting teachers from the ordinary social work routine and to develop what it considers the functions that belong exclusively to the visiting teacher. The work of these visiting teachers has been interesting in that they have aimed to reach the various sections and strata of the New York population. One of the schools, for instance, is in a distinctly upper class neighborhood, others are in the slums. One of the

---

[32] *Progress Report* (1926), 33.

visiting teachers [33] reports that in her school, where there were children from contrasting economic strata, she found no disproportionate number of cases of maladjustment in any particular stratum. The types of maladjustment tended, however, to differ markedly. Among the " lower classes " there were the more overt forms of misbehavior, forms which were verging on actual " delinquency." Among the " upper classes " the maladjustment more often took introverted forms — general instability, severe nervousness, etc.

Much of the work of these visiting teachers has been concerned with the adjustment of the " dull-normal " children. The schools have provided special classes and types of work to which the extreme deviates can often be adjusted, but has little to offer this unhappy intermediate group, and it is with this group that the visiting teacher in New York City is often facing her hardest problems.

The experience of these visiting teachers is the same as those of the White-Williams Foundation with respect to the point at which behavior problems originate. The tendency is for the visiting teacher to devote as much time as possible to the children just entering school. One visiting teacher,[34] who is making this a special aim, pointed out that entering school may be the first important social adjustment that many of these children have been called on to make — that it is often a period when the types of behavior patterns which they have developed in the home or on the street are utterly inadequate to meet this new situation. She emphasized the point that many of the visiting teacher's future problems, particularly in the way of attitudes towards teachers, anger reactions, grudges, etc., may have originated in these first contacts with the school.

The present policy of the Public Education Association is quite definitely in the same direction as that observed in the Rochester situation, i.e., towards the extension of the visiting teacher viewpoint and the encouragement of the ordinary grade teachers to take over some of these functions. During the summer of 1927 the Commonwealth Fund financed a course to be given by visiting teachers in six normal schools, in the following centers: Western Reserve University, George Peabody College for Teachers, University of Kansas, Michigan State Normal College, University of North Carolina and the University of

---

[33] Communication from Miss Lois A. Meredith.
[34] Miss Meredith.

Washington. These courses appear to have been very successful, as requests for further work have been received. Courses will be given in all of these centers except the University of Kansas during the summer of 1928, and, in addition, at the Universities of Alabama, California, Minnesota, Missouri, Wyoming, and New York University.

In addition, under the influence of the demonstrations, more or less adequate courses of study in visiting teacher work are already in operation in Detroit, Michigan; Lincoln, Nebraska; Warren, Ohio; Burlington, Vermont; Richmond, Virginia; Winona, Minnesota; Rock Springs, Wyoming; and Portland, Oregon. In some of these places, the situation is very interesting as showing the trend of attitudes. In Richmond the younger teachers are said to besiege the visiting teacher for explanations of the problems they are meeting in their children and for knowledge of the techniques to be used in handling these problems. In Rock Springs, a mining town, girls go out directly from the senior year in high school to teach in the district schools, and a course is given them in the last year in high school by the visiting teacher. There seems to have developed among the teachers a tendency to handle as many of the behavior problems of the children as they can by adjusting the child in the school rather than turning him over to the principal as " incorrigible," " beyond control," etc. It would be interesting if records could be made available showing the possible effect of this tendency upon the proportions of suspensions and expulsions.

Although the visiting teacher movement has not yet attained any large proportions in the school system as a whole, the growth and spread of the movement during recent years suggests that it is probably meeting a pretty universal need. Already in 1921 it was said that

the movement has grown gradually and steadily until at the present there are visiting teachers in at least 28 cities in 15 states in all parts of the country, differing widely in size and character.[35]

The spread and growth of the movement is indicated by the following table, showing the geographical distribution of visiting teachers in January, 1928, as compared with July, 1921:

---

[35] *The Visiting Teacher in the United States,* published by Public Education Association of the City of New York (2d ed., 1923), 12.

	July, 1921	January, 1928
Alabama	0	1
Arizona	0	4
Arkansas	0	0
California	0	3
Colorado	0	1
Connecticut	3	4
Delaware	0	4
Florida	0	3
Georgia	1	1
Idaho	0	0
Illinois	3	8
Indiana	0	1
Iowa	2	2
Kansas	0	5
Kentucky	1	1
Louisiana	0	1
Maine	0	0
Maryland	0	0
Massachusetts	18	19
Michigan	0	4
Minnesota	14	25
Mississippi	0	1
Missouri	1	5
Montana	0	0
Nebraska	0	2
Nevada	0	0
New Hampshire	0	0
New Jersey	7	9
New Mexico	0	0
New York	26	47
North Carolina	1	1
North Dakota	2	0
Ohio	5	21
Oklahoma	0	1
Oregon	0	3
Pennsylvania	6	11
Rhode Island	0	5
South Carolina	0	0
South Dakota	0	1

	July, 1921	January, 1928
Tennessee	0	0
Texas	0	1
Utah	0	0
Vermont	0	1
Virginia	1	4
Washington	0	1
West Virginia	0	0
Wisconsin	0	3
Wyoming	0	0
Hawaiian Islands	0	2
Porto Rico	0	1

Whereas there were 91 visiting teachers in 28 communities in 15 states in July, 1921, this had increased to 205 visiting teachers in 78 communities in 34 states by July, 1927.[36]

That the movement has been tremendously stimulated by the Public Education Association's demonstrations seems unquestionable, but it also probably often represents an independent growth within the separate schools in the direction of the general social extension of the educational functions. The Annual Report of the Commonwealth Fund for 1926 states the matter thus:

At the time of the adoption of the Program, visiting teachers had been established in only twenty cities in the United States. Since that time, thirty-seven cities, in addition to the twenty demonstration centers, have adopted the work, and at least twenty-four others have developed an active interest which in many cases will undoubtedly result in the appointment of visiting teachers. The increase in four years' time from twenty to seventy-seven cities definitely committed to an attempt to understand the problems of the individual school child is extremely significant from the educational as well as the social point of view. It is impossible to state, of course, that this is the direct result of the Program but undoubtedly much of the initial interest has been aroused through the activities of this Division either by letters, pamphlets, addresses and visits or by the knowledge of the practical work carried on in the demonstration centers.

[36] Communication from Miss Ethel B. Allen, of the National Committee on Visiting Teachers, affiliated with the Public Education Association.

Concerning the whole visiting teacher movement there are some data showing the proportions of the different types of problems handled by the visiting teacher, the different types of treatment used and the different social agencies used in bringing about adjustments.

In a study made by the Public Education Association data were obtained from 57 visiting teachers regarding the problems for which children were referred to them, and the frequencies of reference. The following table shows the relative frequencies of the general reasons for reference. It is interesting to note the differences in the order of frequency of the various problems as among the different visiting teachers, reflecting probably the differences in the needs of different communities and the different background out of which the visiting teacher movement originated:

GENERAL REASONS GIVEN FOR REFERRING CHILDREN TO THE VISITING TEACHER

Reason for Referring Children	Total Number of Visiting Teachers naming this reason as occurring among their cases	Number of Visiting Teachers naming this reason as occurring first, second, third, etc., in order of frequency among their cases					
		1st	2d	3d	4th	5th	6th
1. Maladjustments in Scholarship .	57	25	10	8	7	4	3
2. Adverse Home Conditions	57	16	11	11	10	6	3
3. Irregular Attendance	56	15	13	10	8	6	4
4. Misconduct	53	3	15	7	8	15	5
5. Lateness	49	1	4	9	10	8	17
6. Physical Condition	45	3	4	7	12	12	7 [37]

Thus, of the causes enumerated, each one had first place in at least one community, but first place was most often given to maladjustments in scholarship, adverse home conditions and irregular attendance ranking next in importance. It will be noted also that the first two of these causes were of universal occurrence, and some of the visiting teachers never had cases referred for the other causes. This is, of course, what would be expected, since the primary functions of the visiting teacher are generally conceded to be the interpretation of the home background

[37] *The Visiting Teacher in the United States*, published by Public Education Association of the City of New York (2d ed., 1923), 23.

to the school in cases of maladjustment to school conditions, and of the school's aims to the home in order to secure the coöperation of the home in furthering these aims. In cases where lateness and physical condition are prominent in the visiting teacher's work, it is probable that she is being drawn into these because of the inadequate resources of the school and the community.

In addition to these general reasons for reference the same visiting teachers enumerated specific reasons, which are summarized as follows:

A study of the general trend of the frequency with which the several reasons . . . occur shows that:

1. Under "maladjustment in scholarship," the order of frequency is: "deficiency in lessons," "retardation," "subnormality," "precocity."

2. Under "adverse home conditions," the order of frequency is: "poverty" and "neglect" — the two most easily recognized by the class teacher — "improper guardianship," "cruelty," "immorality in the home."

3. Under "misconduct," the order of frequency is: "conduct in school," "conduct out of school," "conduct involving morality."

4. Under "irregular attendance," the order of frequency is: "suspicious absence," "home conditions," "half-day's absence." [38]

Regarding the types of treatment used, this same inquiry obtained data from 60 visiting teachers. It is significant that, of the two measures noted as used by all, the loosely defined "personal influence" is one. This probably means that because of the paucity of scientific knowledge in the field of behavior and its control, and the empirical nature of all the methods commonly used, the visiting teachers often actually do not know the steps they have taken in the treatment of their cases, or where the steps are definitely known they may find it quite impossible to classify them objectively:

SUMMARY OF MEASURES USED

Measures Used	Affirmative Answers
1. Personal Influence	60
2. Information Brought Back to the Teacher	60
3. Co-operation of Outside Agencies	56
4. Physical Examination	56
5. Mental Examination	50

[38] *Ibid.*, 25–26.

SUMMARY OF MEASURES USED (*continued*)

Measures Used	Affirmative Answers
6. Financial Relief	50
7. Recreation	45
8. Change of School Recommended	44
9. Change of Interest	42
10. Change of Class Recommended	41
11. Change of Environment	41
12. Referring to Society for Prevention of Cruelty to Children	40
13. Change to a Special Class Recommended	37
14. Promotion Recommended	36
15. Demotion Recommended	30 [39]

In various detailed reports by the Rochester visiting teacher department there is found to be a disproportionately large number of cases referred for home conditions, as compared with other cities, and a relatively small number of cases referred primarily for scholarship, doubtless due to the excellence of the school system and to the other agencies included in this system which deal with these problems. These reports give a much more intelligible and specific analysis of the methods of treatment, yet here, too, such indefinite categories as " Changing Attitude " and " Improving Emotional Atmosphere " loom large.

The following table shows the situation as reported for the year 1926–27:

Major Cases	Total
I. Number of children worked with	1193
II. Major reason for Visiting Teacher interest	1193
Scholarship	123
Home conditions	410
Behavior	515
Miscellaneous	145
III. Treatment:	
A. Child — total	2679

[39] *The Visiting Teacher in the United States,* published by Public Education Association of the City of New York (2d ed., 1923), 49.

Major Cases   *Total*

   1. Changing attitude toward study 274
   2. Changing attitude toward school 397
   3. Changing attitude toward conduct 744
   4. Improving habits of regularity 311
   5. Improving health habits 232
   6. Improving social relationships 140
   7. Changing attitude toward family 117
   8. Better use of leisure time 164
   9. Arrangement for home study 44
  10. Building up self-respect 256

B. School 1577
   1. Changing attitude toward child 196
   2. Better understanding of home condition 701
   3. Program adjustment 86
   4. School clinics 57
   5. School Nurse 249
   6. School Doctor 74
   7. Child Study 153
   8. Changing of school 61

C. Home 1985
   1. Urging medical treatment 317
   2. Changing of attitude toward child 257
   3. Changing of attitude toward school 311
   4. Improving emotional atmosphere 77
   5. Improving supervision 422
   6. Arranging opportunity for play 99
   7. Arranging opportunity for sleep 48
   8. Arranging opportunity for study 44
   9. Arranging opportunity for diet 42
  10. Improving discipline 209
  11. Family adjustment 108
  12. Improving moral conduct 51

D. Community 824
   1. Recreation 237
   2. Relief 155
   3. Health 187
   4. Correction 117
   5. Family Welfare .... 128 [40]

[40] *Annual Report of Visiting Teacher Department, September, 1926, to June, 1927.*

Of course, here, as in similar tables in other studies, expressing indefinite materials in statistical form does not give them any greater definiteness, and may, indeed, merely cloud the issues. These " categories " cannot be taken too seriously, except the ones in which some perfectly objective procedure occurred, e.g., program adjustment. And it is obvious from this table that the great majority of the cases can be referred to no such perfectly objective method of treatment.

The table quoted from the Rochester report above lists a number of social agencies which are used by the visiting teacher. In the study of the Public Education Association 57 visiting teachers reported themselves as coöperating with social agencies, with the following frequencies:

Agencies	Number of Visiting Teachers
1. Relief Societies	57
2. Children's Courts or a Substitute	51
3. Girls' Clubs	51
4. Society for Prevention of Cruelty to Children	50
5. Probation Officers for Children	50
6. Recreation Centers	50
7. Church Societies	47
8. Boys' Clubs	47
9. Psychiatric Clinics	45
10. Nurseries	44
11. Parents' Associations	35
12. Employment Bureaus	32
13. Probation Officers for Adults	23 [41]

These data show that the principle of the visiting teacher movement is gaining a foothold in the schools, but one cannot predict in just what form the schools will actually take it over. Up to the present the visiting teacher has been performing a variety of functions, depending on local needs. These functions have often been of such a nature as to seem quite definitely to belong to other organizations, as, for example, the assumption of responsibility for health needs of school children

[41] *The Visiting Teacher in the United States,* published by Public Education Association of the City of New York (2d ed., 1923), 19.

because of inadequate health facilities in the community. Gradually, however, the visiting teacher's functions seem to be defining themselves as the correction of cases of maladjustment (intellectual and emotional) to the school situation. The treatment that has been found necessary has included following the child into all the ramifications of his activities, calling upon all the resources of home and community, and, at the same time, modifying the situation in the school. The trend seems to be in the direction of having the actual grade teachers take over as much of this work as possible, developing in them a responsibility to the child that does not end in caring for his intellectual needs but gives a more inclusive definition to " education." It is possible that there will always be a place for the visiting teacher as a specialist and that, as the school becomes more socialized in its approach, the functions of this specialist will become more rigidly defined.

There have been other developments, however, where the schools have taken over responsibility for behavior problems without the introduction of a visiting teacher. The stimulus for the handling of behavior problems has come from the ordinary grade teachers, who have met together to consider means of handling the non-intellectual problems of the classroom. The need for a specialist has usually been felt, and has been met either by calling in an outsider or by relieving certain of their own body of some of the ordinary duties and making it possible for them to get the specialized training and to have the leisure to study these problems intensively. Probably the most interesting of these developments is the plan that has been worked out in Erasmus Hall High School in Brooklyn.

This high school is one of the largest college preparatory high schools in greater New York. It has high standards, and because of its function as a college preparatory institution its curriculum emphasizes the intellectual aspects of education. In 1921 certain members of its mathematical department became interested in mental testing, took special training in group testing, gave tests to all of the students and instructed the teachers in the grading of the tests. These teachers were very much puzzled by the great discrepancies between intelligence scores and achievement in school. " Problem students " were thought of as those whose achievement did not correspond to the prognosis given by their intelligence quotients. It was thought that personality factors, or factors in the home background, might be at the basis of these discrepancies, and in response to the expressed needs of the faculty for assistance in getting at these factors one of the teachers was relieved of some of her classes in order that she might interview students and their parents and conduct home investigations. Within two years this had become a full-time position, contacts with clinics and public agencies had been established and there had been an extension of the concept " problem student " to include other types of maladjustment than the intellectual. Miss Agnes Conklin, who holds the position at present, has brought with her an intimate knowledge of the workings of the school and an excellent training in psychology and sociology. Regarding the present status of this work, she says:

There has been emerging in the growth of this work an embryo psychological clinic which is, of course, destined to go much further than anyone can at present predict. It may be interesting to recount at this point the salient features of this history:

1. The growth of this work in the school from no time allowance at all to full time allowance, with a separate office and equipment and a recognized administrative department.

2. A history of viewpoints all moving toward a steady conception of the width of the problem, the variety of knowledge necessary to carry forward the work, and the necessity of keeping abreast of what is going on in the field as a whole.

3. The discovery on the part of all who had a part in directing this work that the first fundamental was *training*.

4. A continued evolution from the interest in a few spectacular individuals to interest in the many; the progressive change of attitude from an original dealing with subnormal pupils to the idea that any student, of whatever I. Q. or social status, may need counsel.

5. The systematic organization of the mechanics of handling problem records, investigations, and the like.

6. Continuous expansion of the contacts with outside agencies which may be of help.[42]

From the beginning this was not considered as work which should be turned over to clinicians and which would, therefore, relieve the ordinary teachers of all responsibility except that of reporting troublesome cases. The emphasis has been laid on the participation of all the teachers in the work of dealing with these problem students. The

---

[42] Communication from Miss Conklin.

specialist has been selected from within the school partly because of her intimate knowledge of the school organization and has been used for those contacts which the heavy programs of the ordinary teachers made it impossible for them to make. No " demonstration " can have the influence that a person of this sort is able to exert, both because of the closeness of her contacts with the teachers and because she knows exactly how flexible the school organization is — exactly what wires may be pulled, and when, in order to bring about a particular adjustment.

The main work of dealing with the problem students is carried on through the Student Welfare Committee, with the specialist as chairman of the committee. Regarding its organization and technique, Miss Conklin says:

The committee has been called a Student Welfare Committee and . . . at present has eighteen teacher members. Every teacher in the school has to choose to carry on one outside activity and these teachers prefer to work in this field. All members of the committee can administer the group tests and at the time of the entrance of the freshman class, all correct test papers. Four members of the committee are volunteer home visitors who are not trained to take the family history in the familiar manner of the social worker but, when a family history is needed, it is secured from the parent in the office of the Student Welfare Committee and a supplementary home visit often enhances our knowledge of the problem. Others on the committee take difficult students under the wing and by personal contact and counsel, they help a great deal with behavior problems. Three members of the committee are taking the Master's degree with courses in this field because of their interest in the work. In addition to the teacher members of the committee, there are fifteen student office workers who do the alphabetizing, filing, etc., necessary to carry on the clerical end of the job. The work is by no means confined to the members of the committee since it is very common for teachers who are not so-called members of the Student Welfare group to handle problems under advice of the committee chairman exactly as committee members do.

The work permeates the whole school organization and can best be understood in the perspective in which it operates. The organization of the school starts with the principal and two administrative assistants one of whom handles ordinary discipline and one of whom is the school program maker. The three executives co-operate very closely with the Student Welfare Committee. Cases reported by the principal are likely to concern appeals made by parents about the discharge of their students from school. The disciplinary officer reports habitual offenders against the school rules, truants, and cases in which her dealing with disciplinary problems has revealed unfortunate home conditions. The administrative assistant in charge of program will make any program to order and we have all kinds of special provisions for cardiacs, the lame, and so on, as well as shortened days and irregular arrangements of the study program in individual cases. A " grade " in high school is considered to be an entering class which remains a unit until graduation eight terms after entrance. Each of the eight grades is under the leadership and advice of a grade adviser chosen from the school faculty. There are always nine grade advisers; the adviser who receives the entering class is a kind of fixed post who guides the class through its first term in school at the same time that he trains his new grade adviser in the task of taking over the grade and carrying it to graduation. The grade adviser has anywhere from 500 to 1,000 students in charge. He is responsible for planning the programs so that each student can reach the college of his choice; he interviews parents and students constantly about the status of scholarship; he gives advice to students and their parents in any matters affecting their school progress. The grade advisers each have their own offices. They teach three classes in the first three periods in the morning and the rest of the day they may be found in their offices for interviewing. These officers work constantly with the Student Welfare Committee asking for advice, reporting cases for investigation and so on. They are the most likely to report cases which show a good score and poor achievement, or vice versa, as well as to seek advice on students of low I. Q. who are failing in the course. It is the policy of the school to train a great number of the teachers in this work of the grade adviser so that over a period of years, many have had the experience and have had insight into the problems. In addition to these sources for the report of cases, any teacher may at any time report a student who seems to need help. At the end of each term, teachers are specifically notified that this is the time to report new cases to the Student Welfare Committee for investigation. The committee also co-operates with other school officers.[43]

In its methods of treatment, also, the Student Welfare Committee secures the maximum of coöperation and utilizes to the fullest all the resources of the school:

All speech defect work is in charge of a trained person who consults with the chairman of the committee in the cases she is handling, especially in cases where physical examinations are necessary or where clinic treatment is needed. The employment placer in the school co-operates with the committee in secur-

---

[43] Communication from Miss Conklin.

ing after-school employment and in placing students who, for one reason or another, have to leave school. The physical training departments both have physical examinations for all students at the beginning of each term. This health record is accessible to the Student Welfare Committee and additional examination of sight, hearing and the like can be made right in our own gymnasium department. The committee co-operates with all teachers in charge of outside activities such as athletics, dramatics, choral clubs, art clubs, orchestra societies, and so on since frequently adjustment is helped by studying a student's interests and making use of them in some pleasant way in the school. At the beginning of the term, the Student Welfare Committee notifies all official teachers of the problems in their classes and where it is practicable, the teachers are advised as to how they may be personally helpful in handling the problem. In some cases, as in the cases of epileptics, all teachers who have a contact with the student are notified of the physical condition, of the nature and duration of the seizure and what to do when it occurs. After cases have been reported and investigated, word is sent back to the teachers as to what the findings are and what, in general, we are planning to do with the problem. . . . It will be clear from this description of the work that it interlocks in the organization as a whole, that a great many members of the faculty know about the work and are interested in it and actually doing it, and that it depends for its success on the utmost co-operation of the teaching group.[44]

The technique of handling a case is described as follows:

[The case] may be reported from any of the sources described. . . . A form for report on the student is sent out to each subject teacher. It takes about a week to get all these records returned and, meanwhile, the student is sent for to take the Stanford Binet test. At that time, his school adjustment is discussed with him and inquiry is made into his aims, his interests, his feelings about himself, etc. The family history is taken from his point of view and record is made of this picture of himself before there is a record from teachers or parents about him. Next, attention is directed to the physical condition of the student. The developmental history as given by himself is accessible, the school health record is secured, and sometimes search is made into his record of absences and the reasons for them. The mother is then sent for and a family history, including the student's personal history, is secured from her. The apparent problem is discussed with her and her point of view is recorded. The chairman of committee decides whether or not more expert advice from a clinic or psychiatrist is necessary and undertakes the necessary steps to make the adjustment. All of this carries along with it the co-operation of the teachers

---

[44] *Ibid.*

and the family after the problem has been explained to them, and it includes, of course, the willing co-operation of the student himself. Students once reported to the committee are kept on the records until graduation or until they leave school for other reasons; if they have been in our charge, we do not allow them to leave school unless we know, and usually assist in, the next step they are taking.[45]

The interesting part of this situation is that it seems to have reversed the process which we have come to regard as typical in developments of this sort. Instead of implanting or bringing in a specialist who gradually develops in the teachers an appreciation of behavior difficulties in the students, after which the teachers take over certain of the functions of this specialist, we have here a situation in which the appreciation of behavior difficulties developed first among the teachers. They set about solving them as best they could and then developed a specialist who would take over aspects of the work for which they had no time or insufficient training and who would bring to them such specialized knowledge in psychology and psychiatry as applied to the problems.

A development, resembling the Erasmus situation in that certain teachers in the school take over behavior adjustment functions, is found in the New Trier Township High School (Winnetka, Illinois) under the principalship of Frederick Clerk:

Pupils entering New Trier — which is a township high school of some 1,500 students — are carefully classified by tests and elementary school records. Twenty to thirty of them are assigned to each advisor. They remain with the same advisor through the entire four years of their high school career.

The advisor must visit the home of every pupil — supposedly during the first year. Clerk sends out a broad hint to the homes to invite the advisor to dinner as early as possible. It is with the advisor that the parent confers on all matters pertaining to the child's school life. The child, too, goes to the advisor for help and counsel and for the planning of courses.

There is one " advisory period " every morning, when the advisor meets all members of his or her advisory group — the whole twenty or thirty of them. This period is the time when, under the chairmanship of the group president, announcements are made, questions of school policy are discussed, social events are planned, or when children may confer individually with the advisor. Twice a week the advisor uses this period for

---

[45] Communication from Miss Conklin.

discussing problems of how to study, ethical standards, social behavior, and educational guidance generally. Every afternoon from 3:00 to 3:30 the advisor is available for personal interviews with individual children. The advisory group becomes a small, compact, intimate unit, moving through school together, however divergent the academic programs or extra-curricular activities of the children.

The advisor *never* disciplines. Disciplining is done by the dean of boys or dean of girls. The advisor, if anything, acts as a defender of the advisee, or at least as an interpreter of him or her to the dean. And the advisor never violates the confidence of a child, or uses a confidence against him.[46]

There are various other developments in which the schools are assuming social responsibility, building up methods of studying the " whole child," and taking definite steps towards the prevention of delinquency. In Milwaukee the responsibility for all misdemeanants is assumed by the attendance department, which establishes contact between the school and the home:

The " School Welfare " department refers to the juvenile court only cases in which the parents cannot or will not co-operate in remedying the condition which leads up to delinquency. A child who has committed some misdemeanor is brought with the parents to the office of the supervisor of attendance. There the case is thoroughly discussed with the child and the parents. When they feel that the parents are able and willing to correct the child they turn the child back to them and thus avoid a court record against the child. Minor delinquency cases settled in this office average about 200 per year. Mr. Pestalozzi, the supervisor of the attendance department, says that the school should guide the child through the school years and protect it against a court record. This can be done, he says, by referring all minor child delinquencies to the school authorities instead of to the juvenile court. In the year 1920–1921 the attendance department made 33,205 investigations. There were only 57 cases that appeared before the juvenile court. Of these 57, 41 were cases of children who neglected to attend the continuation school which all working children must attend one-half day each week.[47]

In Milwaukee there has been for some years a " tough boy " school that has taken over the training of " discipline cases " from the regular classrooms all over the city. Here, it was found, was a field for manual training that threw new light on the subject. Boys who had been rated almost incorrigible

---

[46] Washburne and Stearns: *op. cit.,* 301–3.

[47] Eliot, Thomas D.: " The Juvenile Court and the Educational System," *Journal of Criminal Law and Criminology,* 14:39 (1923).

in the schoolrooms of the old type would come over to the institution for unduly retarded or unruly cases and, under skilful guidance in courses that gave abundant opportunity for various phases of manual development, would improve splendidly.[48]

In Cincinnati, under the direction of Dr. Helen T. Woolley, a Vocational Bureau was set up by the Board of Education. For many years the emphasis was on preparing children who must leave school for industry in such a way that they would make satisfactory adjustments in their work life. Physical and mental tests were given, the curriculum modified for special cases and the children supervised after they left school. The Bureau has since developed many other interesting aspects. In the psychological laboratory all sorts of problems are referred from throughout the system: truants from the attendance department, " incorrigibles," children suspected of needing to be placed in special classes, under-age children applying for admission, applicants for scholarships, etc.:

The present organization of the Vocation Bureau includes the following departments in addition to the Psychological laboratory: *The Individual Adjustments Division,* which is concerned with the making of school, home and social adjustments of individual children. This department is very active both in bringing individual cases to the attention of the Psychological laboratory for study and in following up individual cases and carrying out recommendations regarding treatment. *The Child Accounting Division,* which includes the attendance department, the Employment Certificate office and the school census department. *The Occupational Research Division,* which conducts research in the fields of occupation and gives vocational counselling. *The Scholarship Committee,* which administers funds for scholarships which are furnished by the Community Chest and other private sources.[49]

Arrangements are also made with the Psychopathic Institute for psychiatric examinations of children referred from the Psychological Laboratory. Regarding the types of problems with which the school deals, Dr. Fernald says:

One of the main reasons for referring children for examination is failure to do the work of the schools satisfactorily. This failure may be due to general

---

[48] Washburne and Stearns: *op. cit.,* 185.

[49] Fernald, Mabel R.: " Psychological Service to School Children," *The School Index,* 13:298 (May 27, 1927).

mental limitation and may call for placement in a special type of class such as that provided at the Seguin school or, in the case of a lesser degree of limitation, in a class of the opportunity type.

Again, children are referred for quite the reverse reason, because they show superior ability.

Children are referred for all types of behavior difficulties. Many of the children suffering from epilepsy, who appear in the schools, are referred for examination.

All children who are leaving school to go to work at the minimum age at which this is permitted, are given psychological examinations provided they have not met the grade standards which the law requires. The vocational counsellors make use of both group and individual examinations in their advising of children.

Within the school system there are certain schools which are given very intensive service by the Psychological laboratory. All children placed in special classes for mentally defective or borderline children are given individual psychological examinations. All boys referred to the Boys' Special school, a disciplinary day school, are given psychological examinations either before or after their admission. The school system now maintains the two schools formerly known as the Girls' Opportunity farm and the Boys' Opportunity farm. Changes have been made in accordance with this plan and they are now recognized as definite parts of the public school system, under the names of Hilcrest school and Glenview school. Responsibility is placed with the Psychological laboratory for passing on all cases considered for admission to these schools. This is done in co-operation with the Central clinic.

The services of the laboratory are called for extensively in connection with the various classes for children with marked physical handicaps; the blind and those children with lesser visual defects but still in need of the work of sight-saving classes; the deaf and semi-deaf; the crippled and those so handicapped through heart disease that they are admitted to the School for Crippled Children.

In addition there are also many cases which come by direct reference from the various agencies doing social work. The Psychological laboratory stands in particularly close relationship with the Juvenile Court since the Psychological clinic there is under the supervision of the director of the Psychological laboratory and since there is much overlapping of problems. The other social agencies of the city refer children for examinations for many different reasons. Of special importance among these are the problems of adoption or home placement and problems of institutional placement.[50]

---

[50] *Ibid.,* 298.

The more recent developments in the individual adjustment division seem to be towards the establishment of a visiting teacher system, somewhat as was done in Rochester. And a most interesting tie-up with industry has been brought about, whereby children in the trade schools alternate two weeks in school and two weeks in trade or industry, a policy that undoubtedly makes for the better adjustment of the young workers.

It seems obvious, when we consider movements such as the visiting teacher movement and the behavior clinics developing in certain schools, along with the development of special classes and special forms of education, that the schools are broadening their functions to a marked degree. They are no longer merely for the scholars, they no longer emphasize merely the intellectual aspects of education. They have been faced with the problem of universal education and have recognized that the existence of vast individual differences in learning must make them unbend and devise different methods of meeting these different individuals, if the problem of universal education is to have any solution.

There has also grown up an appreciation of the fact that the schools must take over many of the functions which have previously been left to the family but which the family is finding itself increasingly unable to perform. These functions have often fallen to the clinic, the court and the institutions, but they, too, are looking to the schools as the logical place for the study and control of behavior problems.

CHAPTER VI
Character Education in the Schools

IN the preceding chapter we outlined some of the changes in the schools, particularly with regard to their growing tendency to take over responsibility for the child's behavior. We were concerned there with the attempts to prevent maladjustment by modifying and changing the school situations, bringing the whole curriculum in closer touch with the needs of modern life, and with the programs for dealing with maladjustment on this same basis of " making the school fit the child." In this chapter we are dealing with another extensive movement in the schools which may also be interpreted as an effort to take over responsibility for the child's behavior, but with an emphasis on " character building," towards which programs of moral instruction have been directed.

This movement, too, is relatively modern, most of these programs having been formulated during the last ten years, and as in the case of the other behavior programs they must be interpreted partly in terms of the changing family and community organizations. A generation ago the rôle of moral precepts was regarded as an important one in the proper up-bringing of a child, and influences of this sort were brought to bear on him largely in the home and later in the church. The undoubted breakdown of the church as an institution for the control of the younger generation has probably been one of the reasons underlying this development in the school. It can indeed scarcely be understood except in terms, on the one hand, of the " good thoughts — good deeds " precepts of the Sunday school and church and, on the other hand, of the general movement which we have described elsewhere, whereby the school is tending constantly to assume more functions in social control.

In some of the schedules direct preceptual instruction is favored. In this case the base of the procedure is usually a " moral code " enumerating the virtues of honesty, responsibility, obedience, gratitude, courtesy, fair play, clean living, economy, patriotism, etc. The most celebrated of these preceptual codes is *The Children's Morality Code for Elementary Schools,* by William J. Hutchins, selected by the Character Education Institution of Washington as the result of a competition. The first " law " of this code is that of " self-control ":

1. I will control my tongue, and will not allow it to speak mean, vulgar or profane words. I will think before I speak. I will tell the truth and nothing but the truth.
2. I will control my temper, and will not get angry when people or things displease me. Even when indignant against wrong and contradicting falsehood, I will keep my self-control.
3. I will control my thoughts, and will not allow a foolish wish to spoil a wise purpose.
4. I will control my actions. I will be careful and thrifty, and insist on doing right.
5. I will not ridicule nor defile the character of another; I will keep my self-respect, and help others to keep theirs.

Eleven other laws follow, with about the same amount of expansion. This code has been largely utilized in the school programs and some of them reprint it entire. The direct teaching programs usually begin with a code of virtues in some form which is developed by the addition of materials in the way of bits of poetry, slogans, proverbs, designated reading, etc., and indications to the teachers of the concrete procedure by which the same moral precepts and social virtues may be exemplified and made attractive in connection with the various subjects of instruction in the successive grades. The attempt is to give a social and moral meaning to all the subjects of the curriculum. The extent to which this is done, and the ramifications of this type of program whereby no part of the curriculum is given without driving home its moral implications, is seen in the following items from the *Utah Character Education Outline,* a 60-page program prepared by a committee [1] for the use of elementary and high schools:

[1] The chairman, Dean Milton Bennion, has been also for six years chairman of the Character Education Committee of the National Education Association.

Cultivation of ideals and habits of honesty, reliability, trustworthiness and personal responsibility: Developed by being honest in face of temptation, by telling the truth when a falsehood would be a protection. Aim to secure frank statements from pupils in all instances that arise where they have violated rules, cheated, committed offenses. Discuss effects of lying, unreliability, or betrayal of trust when instances arise, setting forth or picturing the situation to them as clearly as possible. Set up strong incentives for being honest, reliable, or trustworthy by picturing outstanding examples. Show relation of these virtues to courage and bravery.

Lead pupils to adopt suitable slogans to stimulate enthusiasm in favor of ideals, such as: " A good pupil is truthful," " To win confidence one must be reliable," " An honest man is the noblest work of God." These may be followed by rules of conduct in the form of declaration of purpose; such as " I will speak the truth at all times. I will be honest, in word and in act. I will not lie, sneak, or pretend, nor will I keep the truth from those who have a right to it."

Work out slogans and rules of conduct, as for honesty: " Wicked men obey from fear; but the good, for love," " An acre of performance is worth a whole world of promise." In the adoption of these slogans and rules, the skilful teacher will manage the situation so that the impulse comes from the pupils as a result of a felt need. Also use suitable selections from literature to illustrate the value of this principle. . . .

[Concerning the cultivation of thrift and economy]: As a sample of what may be done in school with pupils of the intermediate grades and to make the matter very definite and concrete the following suggestions are offered concerning the care of school books:

In training pupils in the proper care of books the important thing to keep in mind is that success depends almost entirely upon habit formation. Habits are formed by repetition, by the right kind of practice. Aim to establish the following habits in your pupils in connection with the use of books: 1. The Habit of Clean Hands: Strive without ceasing to fix the habit of seeing whether one's hands are clean before handling a book. 2. The Opening of New Books: Whenever new books are given out be sure to have pupils open them properly. Take time to have them do it carefully so as not to break or strain the back. Don't attempt to show a roomful at a time, but take a small group and after they are proceeding nicely, start another group. If you are not acquainted with the correct method of " breaking in a book," have your principal show you. 3. The Turning of Leaves: See to it that pupils form the habit of turning the leaves carefully and correctly. In most instances it should be done by lifting the upper corner of the leaf with the forefinger, avoiding pinching or crumpling the leaf between the thumb and forefinger. Do not tolerate the practice of wetting the thumb and pushing the leaves over from the lower half of the page. Frequent drills should be given the entire class in the proper method of turning the leaves. Be on your guard constantly to correct the nervous habit of crumpling leaves, fussing with the covers, playing with the book in an idle manner. 4. Holding the Book: Train pupils to avoid placing the thumb in the center at the bottom of the book when holding it to read. The book should always be held in a way that will not injure it. 5. Marking Books: Check carefully on the matter of pupils marking up or writing in books. Have them erase all marks you detect in them. 6. Carrying Pencils, Notebooks and Papers in Books: Use all diligence in breaking up the habit of carrying pencils, notebooks or bundles of paper in books. Guard against this tendency in yourself. Have pupils provide themselves with suitable book markers made of heavy paper. 7. Covering Books: Books in constant use should be covered. See that covers are put on neatly.

In all the above suggested practice in habit formation be sure that pupils understand the reasons for this procedure; and, in so far as possible, cultivate a sense of obligation to practice thrift in the use and care of books. . . .

Have pupils take an active part in keeping their room in order. Show by examples in arithmetic the waste or loss from broken window glass, broken benches, torn shades, etc. In other words, make them sense the responsibility of helping to take care of the school plant.

Care of clothing: Cultivate the ideal in pupils of keeping their clothing clean and in good repair. Use instances of carelessness for problems in arithmetic to show how much is wasted. Stimulate pride in wholesome neatness, but discourage vanity or excessive costliness in dress. [Similar instructions follow for the cultivation of nine other major virtues]. . . .

The student should be lead: 1. To love good literature and to admire the ideals, sentiments and heroic struggles that it portrays because we tend to become like that which we admire. 2. To receive inspiration and renewed faith from the friendship, beauty, sublimity and vision embodied in literary masterpieces. 3. To appreciate the heroic struggle of a soul in adversity, as often portrayed in literature, and to develop as a result, increased courage to face one's own difficulties. Example: The life of Stevenson with his cheerful struggle against illness. Read his requiem:

> " Glad did I live and gladly die,
> And I laid me down with a will." . . .

7. To discriminate between that which is good, because it results in human betterment, and that which is bad, because it results in human misery; and to stimulate enthusiasm for the good. 8. To realize that " information, inspiration and recreation are available in books." . . .

[Concerning Ivanhoe]: To appreciate and to cultivate: The beautiful dignity of Rowena; the unflinching courage and sacrifice of Rebecca; the generosity of Richard toward his enemies; the modesty and heroism of Ivanhoe; Cedric's firmness and his loyalty to his race; the lowly Gurth's faithful service and happy content in doing his duty; Wamba's saving sense of humor and his happy solution of perplexing situations; the good sportsmanship practiced by the outlaws.

To recognize and to avoid: The weakness, the superficiality, the selfishness, the love of display, the dishonesty and the false ideals of value held by John; Brian's braggadocio, brutality and absence of the finer elements; the hypocrisy of Prior Aymer; DeBracy's unreliability and mercenary tendencies; Athelstane's disgusting intemperance and amusing self-satisfaction.

[Concerning Silas Marner]: In undertaking the study . . . it should be the task of the teacher to lead the students more fully to appreciate the following underlying principles of character growth and real success in life:

To sense the fact that there is no defeat except from within, no really insurmountable barrier save our own inherent weakness of purpose. External forces influence but do not absolutely determine character. Men are under the dominion of law; transgression of laws must inevitably bring its penalty: obedience brings freedom.

Try as he may, man cannot live independent of his fellows. We are " part and particle " of one another. We cannot even bear alone the punishment of our own misdeeds. So intricately are our lives woven with others' that a weakness in us must color and mar more than our own existence. We succeed only by working with other men and for other men.

As supplementary to the two foregoing aims the following might be suggestive: 1. In human service there is no high or low degree. 2. The love that we give away is the only love we keep. 3. We do not realize happiness through material wealth. 4. It is dangerous to play with temptation. 5. Sowing wild oats always brings pain and sorrow. 6. There is in the world a real need of neighborliness. 7. The importance of a happy home needs to be realized. 8. An individual act may have far-reaching effects upon society. . . .

[Objectives in the study of mathematics]: 1. To develop self-reliance, resourcefulness, persistency, honesty, truthfulness and integrity. 2. To make more real to the student the human significance of such terms as budgets, taxes and expenditures. . . . 4. To help the student to realize " how indispensable a contribution this subject has made and is still making to science and invention;" " it has supplied kindred interests of thought with a standard of clarity, rigor and certitude." 5. To instill a sense of gratitude to those who have untiringly studied the subject in order to use it for human advancement. . . .

[General standpoint for the teaching of the social sciences (history, civics, sociology, economics)]: The social studies, through emphasizing group relationships and social responsibilities, add an indispensable factor to character education.

Students should be led to appreciate the fact that the isolated individual cannot function in ethical-social situations; that good acts of good people, from the individualistic viewpoint, do not necessarily make a good family, good church, or good state, since it is only when individual behavior is related to and co-ordinated with the group interests that social-ethical values are realized. It must be understood, however, that individuals are always the responsible moral agents because the group as such has no power of initiative apart from the members who compose it. It is the function of the group to stimulate and direct activity, to take over, utilize and conserve the contributions of the individuals, and so give meaning and purpose to their activities. . . .

[Objectives in the teaching of history and civics]: To develop appreciation of human interdependence, and hence of the need of coöperation born of sympathetic understanding and good will; to impress the fact that progress depends upon energy directed toward human betterment . . . to recognize the fact that worthy citizenship is not conditioned upon race, color, or creed, but rather upon high personal service. . . .

[Objectives in the teaching of science]: To lay the foundation for " that close, accurate, and sympathetic investigation of the ways of nature by which man better enables himself to make right use of her abundant gifts," as applied to " his health, his home-making, his industries, and his intercourse with his fellow beings; " to recognize that given causes under the same conditions always produce the same effects and that man should so regulate his conduct that the operation of causes in nature will contribute to his benefit rather than to his injury; to realize that valid conclusions can be derived with certainty only from adequate data. This should lead to the development of open-mindedness, love of truth, fairness, and exactness; to foster appreciation for the contributions of science to human progress and gratitude toward men of science who have made these contributions.

[Objectives in the teaching of geography]: To teach the facts of human interdependence in matters of industry and health; of art and science; of philosophy and religion. To show that " each country has something unique to give to every other." To stress " the fact that the world's raw materials are limited in quantity and that some lands are more favored than others; " moreover, that the chief occasion of wars has been the clash of desires to move the supply of material wealth, " or to bar competitors from trade routes or fields of investment.". . .

[Objectives in the teaching of agriculture]: To cultivate investigating habits — close observation and interpretation of nature's ways and the discovery of methods of control whereby these ways may be made to contribute to human welfare. To develop ability to initiate plans and faith to proceed with their execution; ingenuity to meet adverse conditions successfully, in so far as it is humanly possible. To cultivate sympathetic interest in growing things — domestic plants and animals — and through this a greater appreciation of life in general with its many complex problems. To develop a sense of wonder and humility in the presence of creation; of gratitude for man's ability to exercise a measure of regulative control; and through all a spirit of reverence for the power that is expressed in nature. . . .

[Objectives in the teaching of foreign languages]: To develop a sympathetic appreciation of the habits, customs, and ideals of other people through the medium of their own tongue; to break down the spirit of provincialism and exclusiveness and to develop thereby a cosmopolitan attitude which reveals itself in a genuine respect for those who are different from us. . . .

[Objectives in the teaching of art]: To cultivate a growing appreciation of the beauty found in form, color, and design and so to develop an abiding interest in art which will help to enrich life. To show " that education in beauty " does not " come entirely through the attempt to create," but that appreciation of beauty can be learned, for all can be taught to enjoy. To appreciate " the fact that there are values in life which cannot be measured in terms of material standards." To realize the fact that " to see beauty and to love it is to possess large securities toward living a happy and a worthy life." To associate the beauty and harmony of fine art with the beauty and harmony of the moral life rather than with the sensuous life. To see that vice is ugly, that virtue is beauty expressed in the conduct of life. . . .

[Objectives in the teaching of music]: To give a sympathetic insight into the national life of peoples through their folk songs, national airs and ballads. To create a common bond between peoples through music as a universal medium of understanding. To develop musical expression and appreciation as a unifying influence in home, school, church and state. To strengthen school spirit through whole-hearted contributions to school singing; through part-singing and glee clubs to develop the feeling of comradeship. To take advantage of the fact that good music is inspiring and elevating, and that loyalty, courage, truth, friendship, sympathy and patriotism may be taught by means of musical selections portraying such qualities. . . .

[Objectives in the teaching of the household arts]: To study the basal " functions of the home in the progress of mankind." To introduce " sound ideals of marriage by emphasizing the fact that the joint care of their children " is a natural means for parents " to develop their own personalities." To impress the fact that " the paramount concern of a good home is the personality which it is to develop in each of its members; " i.e., that " physical well-being, comfort, refinement and beauty should all be valued in the light of their contribution to growth of character in both parents and children." To " consider how home life is affected for better or worse by urbanization, commercialized recreation " and other phases of modern society.[2]

We give this program in this detail (and it should be noted that it is but a portion of the complete program) because it illustrates so well the attempt to evolve the whole curriculum into a means of moral instruction: working from slogans and rules for conduct, utilizing homely situations such as the manual treatment of books as exemplifications of great moral " principles "; determining in detail what is to be set up for admiration and emulation and what is to be deprecated in literature, describing in detail the moral standpoint from which mathematics, history, civics, sociology, economics, science, geography, agriculture, foreign languages, art, music and household arts should be taught.

A number of cities, notably Boston, Milwaukee, Detroit, Los Angeles, are employing similar programs, with different distributions of emphasis. One of the best considered of these is that of Milwaukee, where the concentration is on " citizenship." The Boston program is weighted with quotations from literature.

The Pathfinders of America, founded by Mr. J. F. Wright, may be also mentioned here because they are an organization for moral instruction in the schools. The method is one of picturesque talks by a speaker who is able to arouse the attention of the children and is reminiscent of the procedure of the religious revivalists. It is possible to secure invitations to operate in the schools on the ground that the teaching is moral but not religious:

Once a month the Pathfinder instructor goes into each room (during school hours) and delivers a lecture on some prescribed subject; two weeks later, without the Pathfinder instructor but under the supervision of the room teacher, presided over by their class president, the class devotes one period to the discussion of that month's lesson, after which they write a letter to the Pathfinders, telling them what part of that month's lesson appealed to them most, and how they could make the best use of it in their daily lives. Thus two periods and time for writing one letter each month are assigned to the study of " Human Engineering." This constitutes the method in the public

---

[2] *Character Educational Supplement to the Utah State Course of Study for Elementary and High Schools.* Department of Public Instruction, Salt Lake City (1925).

schools. . . . We organize the classes into what we call a Junior Council, after which they elect their own officers, and meetings are conducted and Path-finder Lessons discussed in a manner prescribed by Parliamentary Procedure. They realize that it is their own club, or Council.

In January, 1926, the Pathfinders of America were conducting over 400 classes in the public schools of Detroit, 50 classes in New York City and Brooklyn, as well as classes in Connecticut, Ohio, Indiana, Georgia, Canada, England, India, and Turkey, reaching children from the 5th grade up through high school. [The organization operates in prisons also].[3]

The character of the lessons on "human engineering" may be gathered from the following letter by a young girl who evidently faith-fully reflects the contents of the lectures:

I gave [another girl] my Pathfinder sheets and we read them over and over. The lesson that impressed her the most was a lesson that you gave quite a while ago, "Human Engineering." Your lessons have helped me a great deal. . . . I am sure that from all those most helpful lessons that you gave, I will develop a fine character. . . . I was thrilled to the smallest fibre of my heart when you spoke of us playing Columbus to ourselves. Pauline and I now have become explorers, and we are exploring the greatest continent there is — "ourselves" — and happy will be the moment and blessed the day when we'll discover our true nature. . . . After thinking over this lesson I find that you yourself are the motor of your body. Your eyes the headlights which shine out to show you the way ahead. Your ears are the gasoline tanks to fill with fuel for the journey of life. Your mind is the brakes and other controls with which to run yourself. Your conscience is the chauffeur who steers you into the right path unless the steering gear, your mind, fails to work with your conscience and throws you into the deep thorny ditch of wrong-doing. Only you yourself can do that.[4]

The Knighthood of Youth is a character training program organized for boys and girls between the ages of 6 and 12, before they are old enough for such organizations as the Boy and Girl Scouts. It is as if the young person impersonated a knight and kept a diary and graded himself on his behavior. "Young children see no incongruity in letting girls assume such titles as herald, esquire, knight." The plan assumes the coöperation of the teachers of the children. The movement is planned for schools and is directed by the National Child Welfare

---

[3] From the literature issued by the Pathfinders.   [4] *Ibid.*

Association. It is also used in settlements, clubs and private homes. At present its influence is not widespread:

The basic equipment of the knighthood is a series of five charts, each containing a set of character-training exercises. These have to do with such practical, everyday duties as " I put away my books and toys when I was through with them," " I said only what I believed to be true," " I kept my shouting and rough-housing for the playground, or where they would not annoy others," and " I tried my best to do things for myself before asking help." *

The charts are graded according to the age and progress of the user, but on every chart the exercises embody 12 fundamentals of character: Obedience, carefulness, reliability, self-reliance, neatness, politeness, honesty, self-control, good temper, kindness, helpfulness at home, and thrift. Each chart is sufficient for keeping the record during 16 weeks.

In addition to the regular exercises, each chart contains a blank space for special exercises which may be written in by the parent, teacher, or child. One little fellow asked his father to write in, " I did not suck my thumb." An older girl inserted, " I spoke in a low, sweet voice." Some parents will wish to include a record of doing home tasks, while others may write in a record of religious duties.

Every night the child checks up his chart at home, with his parents' help, for one aim of the knighthood idea is to enlist the coöperation of the parents.

At frequent intervals, preferably every week, the would-be " knight " presents his exercise chart, checked up by himself and signed by his father or mother, for the teacher's inspection and encouragement and in order that his record may be entered on the knighthood register of his class or " circle." It is a proud moment when, by having performed 70 per cent of his exercises in a given week, he is credited with a " knightly feat." And still happier are the moments when, by a succession of " feats," he earns the titles of esquire, knight, knight banneret and knight constant, with their accompanying badges.

The knighthood course in character training is intended for use about 24 weeks in the year as an integral part of the school life — not as an added burden on the already weary shoulders of the teacher, but as a means of making the school a better place for teacher and children to live in.

While the work of marking the charts is all done in the homes, the knighthood thought will help to enliven and motivate the whole curriculum. All of history and literature are, of course, full of chivalric material. The art class will enjoy designing heraldic emblems, etc., the English class will become enthusiastic over the project of writing a knighthood play or pageant, and the class in sewing will gladly make costumes, insignia, and banners.

Although the knighthood idea may and should thus permeate the whole life of the school, the actual time devoted exclusively to knighthood affairs by the teacher need be very little — less than an hour for the entire week. In many schools, the ceremonies for granting titles, the knighthood playlets, and talks by the principal or visitors concerning the knighthood are made a part of the morning assembly of the school. It is a stirring sight to see the boys and girls, foreign born and native, many of them from very poor homes, many of them from prosperous ones, but every face shining with the joy of worth-while achievement as they step forward to present their records and receive recognition for their effort.[5]

It is quite certain that under these conditions children reporting on their own behavior will often be dishonest, and often their parents as well. The results will confirm a remark of the psychiatrist Adolf Meyer: " Parents and teachers may quiz, but it is often useless to ask a child a direct or especially a plainly jeopardizing question about things of importance to himself." [6] May and Hartshorne [7] have made an experimental investigation of the behavior known as " deception or deceptive tendencies, or the kind of conduct that is ordinarily called cheating, lying and stealing," and reached the conclusions, among others, that (1) " When dishonesty is rewarded dishonesty will be practiced; (2) mere verbal promises to be honest and verbal formulations of the ideal of honesty do not produce general honest habits."

A second general type of character education is largely indirect, employing the project method. The students are formed into a group, with duties, objectives, problems and goals. They are, as far as possible, a society, making decisions, forming judgments and carrying on activities. Moral precepts are neglected and the main purpose is adaptation to group life:

The moral curriculum must busy itself with problems, projects, and actual situations, rather than with " virtues." The virtues will take care of

---

[5] Haviland, Mary S. (Research Secretary, National Child Welfare Association): "Knighthood of Youth," *School Life*, 12:36 (1926).

[6] " Normal and Abnormal Repression," *Progressive Education Association Bulletin* No. 13.

[7] " Experimental Studies in Moral Education," *Religious Education*, 22:712–15 (1927).

themselves if children learn to live well together, meeting situations as they arise in the midst of vitalizing occupations. It will have to be acknowledged that definite, conscious attempts at nurturing the virtues become more or less artificial. . . . The normal impulses must be implanted in the muscles of children rather than pass smoothly across the lips. When mouthed, the virtues become trite; when constantly reiterated they lose their freshness; when rubbed into the surface of consciousness they cause irritation.[8]

The following program represents the organization of about 250 children among themselves in the junior high school of the State Teachers College, Kirksville, Missouri:

The children are in 10 groups with some 20 to 30 in a group. All the teachers share in the responsibilities for character education, though they do not participate noticeably in any dogmatic instruction for character education. Indeed, it is agreed among the teachers that they will not evince any manifest desire for superimposed moral instruction.

At the outset social science, as a subject participated in by all the children, was used as a basis for organization. From various points of view there were discussions, reports, and findings as to what comprises a good citizen and how good citizenship accomplishes desirable results in a community.

Many responsibilities shared in by good citizens were made clear. The children were led to see that organization is essential in order that group activities may coöperatively accomplish what is found to be desirable. The children easily come to understand that law is discovered and not created.

There were discussions of historical events, among them the Conference of Arms in Washington. The idea of conferences of many varieties came into mind. These children are accustomed to freedom and self-activity. Each one thinks his way into new knowledge through habitual use of his own apperceiving knowledge. The members of each group bring into the conference a pretty stimulating variety of views and proposals.

Each of the 10 existing social science groups elected one boy and one girl to meet in a common conference with the director of the school. The children were led to think of themselves as comprising a conference of young representative citizens, all sharing in responsibilities and proceedings.

In each conference various problems were announced for consideration. In one of the conferences three major problems were proposed for the several groups to carry into operation. They were:

First. The problem of traffic in corridors at the passing of classes and individuals before and after class periods.

---

[8] *Character Education Methods: The Iowa Plan.* Character Education Institution, Washington, D. C.

Second. The problem of conduct in the corridors and in all rooms at all hours of every day.

Third. The problem of conduct during assemblies of the entire school and during the various periods for the voluntary activities. . . .

Some of the outstanding features and results may be observed from the following outline of departments:

1. Department of Safety: Traffic rules and traffic officers; vigilance committees in assemblies and classrooms; informal courts organized every two weeks in social science classes to consider conduct of offenders, if there be any.

2. Department of Welfare: Looking after absent pupils; visiting the sick; providing flowers for the sick; providing programs for assembly periods; organization of service groups recognizing commendable acts of service in students of the school as well as in the service groups.

3. Department of Sanitation: Looking after sanitary conditions of corridors and all rooms by appointed inspectors; issuing room permits to pupils who eat in the building.

4. The Department of Property: Directing a " lost and found " bureau for the return of lost articles. After a two-year trial of the simple plan above described it is the judgment of the director and teachers that self-directed conduct leads to character and that character is the only assurance of permanently right conduct. It is not the intention of the director and the teachers to materially enlarge the branches of their simple concrete plan but rather to understand it better and adjust themselves more effectively and more happily to its operations.[9]

In the " case-conference method " problems arising in the school concerning " Property rights, social adjustment, school loyalty, sense of duty, classroom deportment, moral attitudes, courtesy, good taste, community spirit, health, home membership, promptness, self-reliance, self-control, vocational choice, scholarship," [10] are referred to the pupils. During a " free hour," perhaps once a week, the teacher presents some moral problem, preferably one involved in a situation which has arisen in the school. She indicates the issues involved but does not participate in the discussion. It may be that a decision is not reached at once but at a later meeting, after discussion by the children outside the class and consultation with parents. Toledo, Des Moines and

[9] Kirk, John R.: " Exemplification of Character Education," Appendix to *Character Education, Bureau of Education Bulletin* No. 7 (1926).

[10] Reading, Paul M. (Supervisor, Edward Drummond High School, Toledo): *Case-Conference Method* (1927), 6.

Providence are among the schools using the discussion method with various details:

First, we must select typical cases in which each member will, to some extent, see himself; in which every child will recognize some features which have been items of his own experience.

Second, we must relieve the situation of all special features which make it an individual or a typical case, and which might lead to embarrassment or to prejudice for or against any one decision.

Third, we must have social decisions and social attitudes. Lack of social results has been one of the troubles in our practice of trial by jury, honor courts, student self-government, and other devices. . . .

" Harvey takes a ring that he finds in the wash-room of our school. John, his chum, sees him take it, without Harvey's knowing that John sees. The loss is not advertised until three days later. Then Harvey is both ashamed and afraid to return the ring, since he has made no effort to find its owner."

[The teacher throws open the discussion by asking the question]: " Should John tell what he knows about his friend Harvey? "

[The Conference]. Pupil: No, I don't think he should tell. But if he knew Harvey meant to steal, he should tell. However, he might speak to his friend Harvey.

Pupil: Why?

Pupil: Because he wants to find out whether he had just forgotten about it, or really meant to steal it.

Pupil: I believe John didn't want to tell for fear he would lose his chum.

Pupil: If I were John, I would tell the principal right off.

Pupil: I would tell my parents, and see what they say.

Pupil: John ought to go to Harvey and ask him if he was going to give it back, and if Harvey refused, John should go to his parents and do what they say.

Pupil: I don't think the parents ought to be brought into this thing. John and Harvey should settle it themselves. Isn't that right, sir?

Conference Leader: I'd rather not answer. What do the rest of you think?

Pupil: I don't think John ought to tell the principal, as he is liable to lose all his friends, and they would call him a " tattle-tale."

Pupil: Probably the owner of the ring is always bragging about what he owns, and Harvey might have meant to steal the ring.

Pupil: Maybe the ring isn't valuable. Maybe it's a ten-cent ring.

Pupil: Value has nothing to do with it; besides, how can you tell what a ring is worth by just looking at it?

Conference Leader: Is Harvey's act stealing?

Pupil: No — not in a way.

Pupil: Well, it isn't deliberate stealing.

Conference Leader: What is deliberate stealing?

Pupil: Why, taking it with a purpose of keeping it.

Pupil: If this is the second time Harvey took something, we know that it is stealing.

Pupil: No one knows whether it is his first offense or not.

Pupil: I think if it was his first offense, I would let him off easy, but I think he should be punished for what he has done. But, if it was his second, I should punish him more severely.

Pupil: If it was a habit of his, he could be accused of stealing other things around the school.

Conference Leader: Is stealing a habit with some people?

Pupils (in chorus): Yes!

Conference Leader: Is *not stealing* a habit?

Pupil: No.

Pupil: That's control over your will power.

Pupil: If you do that, it's a habit.

Conference Leader: Do what?

Pupil: Control your will power, and let other people's things alone.

Conference Leader: How many agree that this act is stealing, and that Harvey is a thief?

Pupil: That does not seem a fair way to say it. [Continuation of discussion; adjournment; pupils consult parents, reassemble on a later day and reach a decision. The conference leader has expressed no opinion during the whole discussion].[11]

As another example the following formulation of a problem is presented to the pupils:

To the principal of a school Mr. Hargrove wrote a letter in which he said: "I am taking my son, Harold, and my daughter, Janet, out of your school because the students there tell dirty stories and smutty jokes. I cannot submit my children to the influence of such habits nor to the companionship of young people who do such things. The whole community knows about these stories in the school."

1. Does Mr. Hargrove take dirty stories too seriously? Reasons?
2. Is the father's charge true about our school?
3. Do many children here tell such jokes and stories?
4. Is Mr. Hargrove too careful? Should he put Harold and Janet " on

[11] Reading, Paul M. (Supervisor, Edward Drummond High School, Toledo): *Case-Conference Method* (1927), 7-11.

their own " — allow them to depend on themselves and make the best of the school as it is?

5. Is there any value to these stories?

6. What are the effects of telling them? Of listening to them?

7. Is the telling or repeating of these stories unavoidable in a school?

8. Would Mr. Hargrove listen to our defense if we claim that our school is no worse in this matter than other schools?

9. Should the school be " cleaned up "? Is " cleaned " the right word, or is it a " prejudiced " word?

10. Mr. Hargrove as a taxpayer expects some action — he says so. Is it the principal's job? A problem for teachers? For the student body?

11. If some pupils write dirty stories or smutty notes, does that change matters? Why, or why not?

12. Is it any worse for girls to tell these stories to each other than for boys to tell them to other boys?

13. Do pupils attach the name of our school to such things when they repeat them outside, rather than the names of those who told them?

14. Is the one who listens and laughs, but who never tells any stories himself, to be blamed?

15. What if young people get some of these dirty jokes from magazines or sometimes hear them in public places?

16. Is it all right for older students to tell such stories, but not right for younger children? What are your reasons?

17. What is your answer to Mr. Hargrove? [12]

In the mention of these programs we have attempted to select the better examples. A number of the programs have features which are evidently trying to the patience of the pupils. Thus, in the program of one of the large cities there is a " character test," of the multiple choice type, called " The Things I Do." Eighty items are included, of which the following are representative:

Crossing the street
  1. I never look first   2. I always look first   3. I look if told to ( )

Slamming doors
  1. I sometimes slam them   2. I never slam them   3. I like to slam them (·)

---

[12] Reading, Paul M. (Supervisor, Edward Drummond High School, Toledo): *Case-Conference Method* (1927), 38-39.

In talking
   1. I always talk too loud
   2. I often talk too loud
   3. I talk nicely ( )

At home
   1. I always help
   2. I never help
   3. I help, if asked to ( )

After school
   1. I always play alone
   2. I play with just one
   3. I want a crowd ( )

When with small children
   1. I pick on them
   2. I let them alone
   3. I am nice to them ( )

In doing work
   1. I do it pretty well
   2. I do the best I can
   3. I don't care how I do it ( )

In getting my lessons
   1. I never copy from any one
   2. I copy, if I can
   3. I often copy ( )

With my money
   1. I am careful what I buy
   2. I buy useless things
   3. I am careful sometimes ( )

For the blind
   1. I feel sorry
   2. I try to help them
   3. I make fun of them ( )

[The examiner says] : " Please do not look at any paper but your own, for we want to find out just what you do. Be sure to tell what you do.

" If the words are too hard, raise your hand and we will tell you what the words mean. You will know most of them.

" Each question has three answers. You are to draw a line under the one answer in each set that tells what you do, then put the number of that answer within the parentheses at the end of the line " [and explains the eighty items seriatim as the pupils make the marks].[13]

In giving the results of this test and explaining the action of certain pupils who " rated themselves low and did so correctly," the report

[13] *Character Education in Detroit, First Report of the Detroit Committee on Character Education* (1927).

adds: " It might even be suspected that their badness was expressed in seeing how poorly they could rate themselves on the character test."

The question of the effectiveness of programs such as those we have described is an interesting one. Unfortunately there has been no check-up of the results. Certain considerations suggest themselves, however, in regard to these programs.

There were three general types of programs from which we presented selections: those depending largely on a code, those in which the curriculum is used as a basis for moral teaching, and those emphasizing activities or projects.

The process of character education by means of a code calls for the repetition of certain principles of conduct and their exemplification, with commendation or rewards (as in the Knighthood of Youth) for virtuous acts. It depends on the assumption that it is possible to super-impose a code — an assumption on which behavior materials would throw some doubt. The child's code tends to be developed in connection with his activities and wants, and in a social setting, i.e., in connection with the standards and behavior of his group. The superimposition of a code of moral phrases, slogans and rules of conduct will probably be effective to the degree that the child's own conception of what is ad-mirable is utilized.

It has been observed in experiments on corrigibility and incorrigibil-ity that there is in the schools " undoubtedly a graded order, from those children who do not seem able to adjust themselves to the social and mandatory requirements of the school to those who are promoters of the one and cheerful acceptors of the other." [14] This statement defines very well the limitations of the direct teaching character education programs and all programs in which situations are prepared or pre-sented to a body of young people. Some will respond positively and some negatively. That is to say, there are already among pupils, so to speak, as in congregations, saints and sinners, and the precepts do not reach precisely those they are designed to reach, and those whom they do reach do not need them.

The children in the school who are " corrigible," who conform gen-erally to the rules and get their satisfactions through the school activ-ities, are probably appealed to by codes of the sort that the teachers develop. But those children who get their satisfactions largely, or even partly, in connection with their own groups, who find a rival definition of the situation in these groups, seem to be not greatly affected by these codes or positively repelled. An interesting example of how a code may be defined in a child in complete contrast with the direct teaching to which he has been subjected is given by Watson. Richard, a child of five years, had been talked to freely about questions of sex and reproduction. There had never been any embarrassment or treatment of these matters as different from any other interesting facts:

About a month after this he " *blocked* " all questions about babies. This was something new. I said to him, " Richard, what do you know about where babies come from? "

" I don't know anything."

" But don't you want to talk about it any more? "

" No."

" Why not? "

" Anna [friend of own age level] says it isn't nice to talk about babies." [15]

In many of the programs there is an overanxiety to associate a moral lesson with all the subjects taught, as if the materials of study were designed to substantiate the virtues of the moral code. In reading some of these programs we were reminded of the admonition of an old church father: " Press not the breasts of Holy Writ too hard lest they yield blood instead of milk."

There appears also in some of the programs a gross failure in the distribution of emphasis on the values enumerated. It is assumed that all subjects contain character values alike for all persons and that all persons should extract all the values from all the subjects. For example:

1. He should be offered opportunities through music classes in our junior high schools and high schools for vocational study, by entering the field as a performer and artist, either instrumentally or vocally.

2. He should be given choice of study in piano or major instruments of the symphonic orchestra or band, through ensemble playing.

3. He should be given opportunity to enter the field of voice and have the advantage of careful voice training.

4. He should have the opportunity to study Harmony and prepare himself to give the world original work.

---

[15] Watson, J. B.: *Psychological Care of Infant and Child* (1928), 170–71.

5. He should be taught various instruments of orchestra and music knowledge which eventually may lead him into industrial life as follows: Manufacturing of instruments, publishing music, repairing, and tuning instruments.

6. He should learn all branches of music. This early musical training often provides the foundation for the teaching of music.[16]

A program of this kind ignores the point that character formation does not take place through the assimilation of all possible values but by the organization of certain values among themselves, and that rejection is quite as important as selection. In fact, selection comes through rejection.

In the history of teaching and in the organization of schools the preceptor has not been in a very intimate and influential relation with the pupil, and the question may be raised of the relative influence of the teacher as compared with other associates of the child. May and Hartshorne have made experiments on the question, " Does the child's knowledge of right and wrong tend to be more like his Sunday-school teacher's, his parents', his adult club leader's, or his child friends'? " Their results, which are presented statistically in some detail, show practically " no relationship between the knowledge of right and wrong which Sunday-school teachers have and which their pupils have . . . a negligible influence of day-school teachers on the moral knowledge of their children . . . [the] possibility of a slight influence by club leaders," [17] a decided influence of friends, and the greatest influence of parents:

Though not extremely high, the home reveals by far the highest relationship between children's knowledge of right and wrong and that of major influence groups, viz., parents, friends, club leaders, public school teachers and Sunday-school teachers, the degree of relationship ranging from an r of .545 between children and parents to an r of .002 between children and Sunday-school teachers. [School teachers .028; club leaders .137; friends .353]. . . . The

---

[16] " Character and Conduct," *Los Angeles City School District, School Publication* No. 60:35 (1923).

[17] Hartshorne, H., May, M. A., and others: " Testing the Knowledge of Right and Wrong," *Religious Education Association, Monograph* No. 1:47–48 (1927). The writers point out that the value of Sunday-schools and clubs would be shown better by comparison of scores of those who are regular or old attendants and those who are irregular or new. Also that the failure of this study to show that Sunday-schools are contributing " does not mean that they are not so contributing. A universal negative is not established in one study."

two more natural groups of home and friends are the most significant though neither is high enough to warrant being called the predominant influence. . . .

The evidence from this study seems to suggest that in the field of moral knowledge greater results will be obtained by emphasis on education in the home and amongst friends than in the other groups. Undoubtedly other factors exist that influence children in this regard which need to be discovered before we can determine what the most significant influences really are. The lack of relationship between leader and led in the formal groups where moral teaching is attempted directly, especially in the club and Sunday-school, indicates that the leader's ideas at least are not getting across to the children. . . .

The wide differences in means and the relatively low correlations between the scores of the same children in the different situations indicate quite clearly that a child does not have a uniform generalized code of morals but varies according to the situations in which he finds himself. In other words, he has a Home code, a School code, a Sunday-school code, etc., or else adapts a code fundamentally his own to meet the more insistent demands of the occasion. Knowledge of right and wrong is a specific matter to be applied to specific situations which the child encounters in his daily living. Perchance this lack of a fixed general code is due to the secularized life with which we surround our children. We may have to get more of a moral unity in the individual child. Suffice it to say, the task of the moral and religious educator is concerned with the complete life of the child and not with a portion set aside for so-called religious instruction.[18]

This work of May and Hartshorne throws interesting light on the points we have been raising, i.e., as to where codes are developed and their probable failure to be effective when they are too remotely related to the child's goals. We have indicated that preceptual teaching seems to be possible when certain activities of the preceptor are in line with the child's goal. This has been the experience of many of the visiting teachers who are successful in bringing about a change of conduct in a young girl where the teacher has failed, but a clue to some of this success is got from the detailed records of the visiting teachers where it is evident that they share or understand many of the young girl's interests and values: matinées, nice clothes, lunches in restaurants, with palms and music, figure in the records. The particular code which it is desirable to instil will have a greater chance of success on a basis of this sort than where all the precepts, from discouragement of

---

[18] *Ibid.*, 50–51.

" excessive vanity " to the care of books, are superimposed with no regard for the wants and admirations which the child has already formed.

With regard to the project method, its superiority over the preceptual is obvious. Virtues are in part evolved unconsciously, and if exposure is made to situations which develop desirable behavior patterns the plan is to that extent good. The difficulty with much of the project work in these character education programs, however, is the triviality of the projects themselves: the concern is often with problems of traffic in the corridors, regulation of sanitary ordinances, fire prevention, etc. The emphasis is largely on the development of civic virtues.

The superiority of the visiting teacher work and of such programs as that of the Rochester school system over programs of the type described in this chapter is apparent. The former emphasizes the production of adjustment, the latter the development of virtues. The visiting teacher deals directly with situations and the development of activities, which become the basis for whatever preceptual teaching is necessary. The amount of moralizing is kept at a minimum. As a system of character education the preceptual method is inadequate in the school as it has proved itself inadequate in the family and the church. The mere multiplication of precepts is like the creation of more laws when the old ones have failed to work.

CHAPTER VII
Parent Education

THE EFFECTS of the concentration of " education " in the schools and their lagging response in taking over those functions which cannot be defined as narrowly intellectual have been considered with relation to the child. We have seen the confusion that resulted from the failure of the schools to assume responsibility in these matters, and the multiplicity of agencies that arose to fill the gap. We have further seen new developments in the schools within the last decade or so, whereby they are tending more and more to supplant these other agencies and to assume responsibility for vocational and social adjustments — to become "behavior institutions." But what of that great mass of adults who were turned out upon the world as children half-educated with regard to the adjustments demanded of them, ill-prepared vocationally and bound by traditions which the changing economic and social order made entirely obsolete? Our interest in these adults lies chiefly in their functioning as parents and teachers and in their ability to handle the behavior problems of children. We have seen abundant evidence of their limitations in the handling of specific situations. We shall now consider what agencies are open to them to fill the gaps left in their education and how far these agencies are adequate in meeting the problems with which they are faced. The field of parent education is one that has developed, self-consciously, very recently. Its significance can perhaps best be brought out in its relation to the whole background of adult education.

The first thing impressing us is the tremendous number of persons involved in one or another of the adult education schemes. As Keppel expresses it: " Adult education has now become one of our major industries." It is, indeed, in its present form, very recent, and its growth has been tremendous. " There are at least five times as many adults, men and women, pursuing some form of educational study as are registered as candidates for degrees in all the colleges and universities in the country." [1] Keppel cites the following statistics. There are at least a million and a half students registered each year in the three hundred and fifty correspondence schools; a million in the public evening schools, the part-time and continuation schools; one hundred and fifty thousand in university extension classes; one hundred thousand in Y.M.C.A. courses, and an equal number in other similar courses; thirty thousand in workers' education classes; hundreds of thousands reached through the state and federal agencies in agriculture; and hundreds of thousands at art and natural history museums. " To these we must add the attendants of the Chautauquas and the lyceums, and the men and women who are following a serious course of study with the help of the local library. We must reckon also with the inaudible spectators of visual education and the invisible auditors who take their nourishment by radio." Keppel further points out that, except for education with a propaganda aspect, most of these forms of adult education are paying propositions. Even the extension courses at universities are made to pay their way and rarely use any part of the endowments which other courses may draw upon. They represent, then, to quite a large degree, things for which there is considerable popular demand (spontaneous or created), things for which adults feel a need and are willing to pay.

Just what are these things that adults are getting from these various educational schemes? By far the greatest part seems to be concerned with vocational advancement. For instance, about 80% of students by correspondence take vocational courses. Noffsinger lists over two hundred courses given by correspondence schools, and says:

This list is instructive. It should be examined closely. For in it is illustrated the whole nature of correspondence education. Consider the courses: Auctioneering, Brokerage, Butter Making, Cartooning, Chalk Talks, Railway Conductor, Detective, Nursing, Foot Culture, Horsemanship, Hypnotism, Life Planning, Inventive Science, Speech Correction, Playwriting, Ventriloquism, Piano Tuning, Theology, Chemistry and Dancing. There are good

---

[1] Keppel, F. P.: " Education for Adults," *Yale Review*, 15:419 (1926).

schools and bad schools, as we have seen. There are some branches of learning or technical training that can be taught by correspondence provided the school is honestly administered, gives such courses only to those who are prepared to master them and has teachers of the first rank in conscientiousness, pedagogic training and ability. There are other courses that can never be taught by correspondence, no matter what the school or who the teacher. A student who takes some of these courses from a reputable school may be reimbursed for his money and effort; a student who takes any of the courses from a fake " university " is defrauded, no matter what the course; a student who takes certain of these courses from even the most reputable school has wasted his time and money, for they cannot be taken by correspondence. A school must be weighed not only by its permanency and its maintenance of standards but by the nature of its curriculum. If it offers certain courses, it misleads the student, however honest its intentions. The questions involved in consideration of correspondence schools are not only moral. As most correspondence schools go now, moral questions are uppermost, for an appallingly large proportion of the schools are little better than frauds. But pedagogic questions are also involved. And even a school which is moral may be attempting what is, from the point of view of educational science, unjustifiable. And though its motives may be honest, it is earning an illegitimate profit.[2]

A large part of the remaining 20% taking courses by correspondence is also — though somewhat less directly — concerned with the vocational aspects of the courses. For instance, there are the self-styled " universities " and " colleges " which are really diploma mills, granting anything up to or beyond the degree of Doctor of Philosophy. They are patronized largely by " clergymen and school teachers who find it a vocational asset to have a scholastic degree." There is another class of schools which teaches the " professions " of naturopathy, electrotherapeutics, and other healing cults. There is still another offering courses " neither cultural nor vocational: Applied Psychology, Personal Efficiency, Memory, Diet, Physical Development, etc." And regarding the significance of the movement, Noffsinger concludes:

For better or worse the correspondence school is the channel of education followed by more American adults than any other. What education these adults get if any, how much and what kind, depends on how education by correspondence is administered and by whom.

In the first place, it is incontestable that there is a need for such an agency.

---

[2] Noffsinger, John S.: *Correspondence Schools, Lyceums, Chautauquas* (1926), 32–34.

No matter how alluring the advertising and resourceful the salesmanship, the correspondence school could not get 1,500,000 new students every year unless some demand for such instruction existed. The correspondence school may meet the need badly; but it meets it and no other agency does. The fact is that vast numbers of the American people are unprepared to earn their livelihood. They find themselves with the responsibilities of maturity and at the same time lacking the necessary training to better themselves materially. They cannot go back to school; they must seek training elsewhere. The public educational system does not provide it except in certain larger centers; they must look elsewhere. The correspondence school goes out to them.[3]

A good part of the university extension work, though on a somewhat higher plane, is comparable with the correspondence schools. A number of the universities have "home study" courses, which are conducted by correspondence, a large part being directly vocational. Hall-Quest made an intensive study of the subject and found well-defined extension service in forty-one universities and colleges, this service being of several distinct types. There is found systematic group instruction either on the campus or other centers. In addition to the more usual activities there are included in this service foreign tours, schools for scout masters, athletic coaches, the deaf and dumb, social workers, "citizenship schools," and citizen military extension. There is the systematic individual instruction, carried on by correspondence. There are several sorts of service in the field of disseminating "general and technical information," e.g., a municipal reference bureau gives information concerning elections, ordinances, etc.; certain members of faculties will give personal attention to inquiries from citizens; news letters and bulletins are sent out; library service is usual, including the sending out of packets of books to clubs or individuals, supplying bibliographies, etc. There is the type of service called by Hall-Quest "informal individual culture and employment" which includes guidance in individual reading, in reading-circle courses, employment service for specialists. There is "community culture and utility service," including agricultural projects, boys' and girls' club work (considered indirect parental education), home demonstration work, organization of community centers, community drama, music and institutes, community business surveys, campaigns for civic improvement, lecture and

---

[3] Noffsinger, John S.: *Correspondence Schools, Lyceums, Chautauquas* (1926) 86–87.

lyceum work, radio service, engineering and forestry extension, general welfare, research by request of organizations, and reports on investigations. There is public school service, including inspection of the schools, sponsoring debating leagues, physical education contests, coöperation with parent-teacher associations, school surveys, museum and library service, etc.:

> Summarizing . . . brings into somewhat clearer light what is meant by university extension at present. It is a form of adult education that offers sustained instruction principally in English, education, engineering, commercial subjects, romance languages, history and mathematics, there being also a considerable number of courses in philosophy, psychology, sociology and ancient languages, all of these offerings being determined by the availability of the course to extramural teaching, the size of a university department, and public demand, the latter being largely vocational but the courses, in the main, of a broadening content, most of them being credited toward degrees. The university meets public demand by means consistent with its own standards of what constitutes education and within limits that have been set for the university by circumstances which often the university cannot control.[4]

Noffsinger presents interesting data on two other forms of " educational agencies " which reach large numbers of people, i.e., the lyceums and chautauquas. The lyceum is described as " a bureau which sends out popular lecturers or musical teams to small towns several times a year for a fee which yields a profit." The fourteen bureaus for which he was able to obtain statistics gave programs to 3,000,000 persons in the following proportions of " subject matter ": 9.2% dramatic performances, 19.6% lectures, 50% musical offerings, and 21.2% miscellaneous entertainment. " Since the fourteen bureaus whose figures are given constitute only half the field, a conservative estimate of the total lyceum audience every year is 5,000,000 ":

> These figures are eloquent of the change in the character of the lyceum. The old lyceum was given to solid discourse and serious debate, to concern with matters of science and politics. Now one lyceum offering in five is a lecture, the rest is entertainment. And what are these lectures? The platform that once was occupied by Emerson, Thoreau, Lowell, Agassiz and Holmes now sounds to what the lyceum profession itself calls the " mother-home-heaven "

---

[4] Hall-Quest, A. L.: *The University Afield* (1926), 104.

message. A check of 3,000 lecture titles taken at random showed 53%
to be of the category designated as inspirational. One quarter might with
charity be called informational and the rest were of a civic or educational nature, also using those adjectives broadly. A small, a very, very small,
proportion indicated substance; the rest, even of those called informational
or civic, were patently thinned out and sweetened; direct examination of
lyceum evenings bears out the indications. . . . The lecturers, in the overwhelming majority, are professional speaking troupers, those who can moralize
heavily without touching real moral issues, who can philosophize entertain-
ingly, be very deep and yet amusing, who can sound the broad note and
always end optimistically. Here are found the political hack, the lame duck
office-holder and the misfit clergyman. They " glad-hand " oratorically and
collectively. Now and again there is an exception, a celebrity in the public
eye who is a drawing card; he is sincere, but his managers see that he elim-
inates all but the human interest.[5]

The Chautauqua Institution originated as a summer school and a
literary and scientific circle, which are still in existence and reach
relatively few people, but the " chautauqua as most Americans know
it . . . is a travelling or circuit chautauqua operating in the summer
months as a circus " and reaches great numbers of people:

There are a score or more of bureaus operating such chautauquas or circuits
and they serve at least 6,000 communities. As in the case of lyceums, these
communities are villages. A check of 1,430 places having chautauquas showed
that 25% were villages of 750 population or less, 50% were villages of 1,750
or less, 75% were towns and villages of 6,000 or less. . . . Figures obtained
from twelve of the biggest chautauqua bureaus . . . represent something
like half the total number of bureaus of any importance and . . . show an
aggregate attendance of 13,650,000 for a summer. They estimate the number
of different individuals attending at 2,400,000. It may be said, then, that
5,000,000 persons attend chautauquas every year. . . .

In general, what was said of the lyceum programs applies equally to the
travelling chautauquas. They consist of music, lectures, and " entertainments " — superior vaudeville, calculated to amuse in conventional ways.
The lectures are of the lyceum type — mother-home-heaven. The chautauqua
gives the public what it thinks the public wants, and the public takes it,
which makes money for the chautauqua and thus spares the chautauqua any
need of conceiving and carrying out a program with more specific gravity. But
it is also possible that the public would also be found to want — that is, be

---

[5] Noffsinger: op. cit., 115–16.

willing to pay for — something better. Nobody knows, and certainly the chautauqua makes no effort to find out. Nevertheless, 5,000,000 persons in the United States depend on the chautauqua for mental and imaginative recreation and exercise during the summer, as they do on the lyceum during the winter. Neither can be ignored, no matter what one think of it.[6]

And Noffsinger further points out that although " the educational content may be described as a trace . . . in most of the communities which resort to the lyceum and chautauqua the choice is between them and nothing at all." [7]

This represents the bulk of adult education, as it now exists. There is, of course, a better sort of education for some adults in the larger cities. On the academic side there is a possibility of obtaining high-grade instruction at the universities and colleges; there are superior sorts of public lectures and libraries. The " cultural " facilities, e.g., music, art, and drama, are greater. But though it may be better in quality in the larger cities, it is not, for the great majority of adults, very different in kind.

What of the adult education schemes that are directed towards parents as parents? Parent education should probably be thought of as partly vocational, partly " welfare " and partly " individual-cultural." The need for it cannot be separated from the need for adult education generally. Like these other schemes, its needs have been consciously formulated only recently and its growth has been tremendous. It has taken many forms and had many origins. We cannot present it as a unified approach; we can merely indicate its trend. We have indicated that a good part of adult education can be considered as a result of the lagging response of the schools in adapting themselves to a changing social order. But even if the schools expand their functions to include responsibility for vocational and behavior adjustments — as many of them are now doing — their effective functioning is impossible without the coöperation of the parents. The child is still in the home for a longer period each day than he is in the school. And some parents are becoming more and more conscious of their inability to handle the problems that arise, just as some schools have faced the impossibility of bringing about their ends unless they can either obtain complete control of the child or draw the families into their program of

---

[6] Noffsinger: *op. cit.*, 126–30.   [7] Noffsinger: *op. cit.*, 141–42.

" education." Hence come two of the origins of the parent education movement — the growing consciousness of parents that they are in need of " guidance " and the growing inability of the schools to carry on the new functions which have been thrust upon them.

From the point of view of long-time functioning and numbers of parents involved, the Parent-Teacher Association should be considered first, although its functions as an educative organization are much slighter than those of other parents' organizations. It is quite definitely political, diplomatic and reformist in many of its aims; its policies are largely directed towards bringing about " ends " — whether the end be the establishment of a juvenile court or serving a midday lunch in public schools or the production of " better understanding." Most of the problems dealt with are such that the best results can be obtained through the coöperation of school and home, since they affect the functioning of the child in many aspects.

" The National Congress of Mothers and Parent-Teacher Associations was organized February 17, 1897. It is a National organization with State branches. . . . It is the originator and promoter of the movement to establish a Parent-Teacher Association in every public school. . . . A Parent-Teacher Association is an organization of parents, teachers, and others interested, for the purpose of studying reciprocal problems of the child, the home and the school and the relation of each to the community and the state in order that the whole national life may be strengthened by the making of better, healthier, more contented and more intelligent citizens." [8] Indirectly, of course, such an organization is an important adult educational influence. And it has shown the same tremendous growth (quite out of proportion with general population growth) that we have seen in every other form of adult education. The membership was 1,000 in 1897 (at the time of its establishment), grew steadily past the 100,000 mark by 1917, and reached an estimated 700,000 by 1924.

The function and organization of a parent-teacher association depend largely on the local situation. In an analysis of parent-teacher organizations, Ila Delbert Weeks [9] discusses these functions in detail. The greatest interest of the organizations seems usually to center

---

[8] " Parent-Teacher Associations," *University of Iowa, Extension Bulletin* No. 142 (February 15, 1926).

[9] *Ibid.*

around problems of public welfare. " The Parent-Teacher Association as an organization has always been primarily interested in the welfare of the child. This interest has led the organization to be more or less active in improving the environment of boys and girls through a variety of methods." Among these methods are the formation of committees to promote " better films." These committees either preview the films, write to the producers " to commend or disapprove," or post conspicuously their rating of films. Another method is aimed at the general improvement of rural communities. With regard to influencing legislation, the general method is " by writing courteous letters to congressmen telling the measures in favor of which their organization has gone on record and asking them to vote for the measures." The measures generally favored are spoken of as the " Six P's " and are those affecting Peace, Prohibition, Protection of children, Physical education, Protection of the home, Public school. Special emphasis is made locally with regard to the protection of children, e.g., regulations regarding truancy, dependency, probation, recreation, etc. In many states the Parent-Teacher Association is actively involved in charity, and in many others in promoting " Americanization " activities.

Its directly educational functions include attention to " humane education " (described by Weeks as " an important phase of character education "). Emphasis is being increasingly placed on pre-schools. " Twenty states are already organized for the purpose of furthering this movement." Mothers' study circles, and other groups, are formed under the auspices of the Parent-Teacher Association, and are devoted to a discussion of the problems specific to this age level. Progressive education is fostered by many groups. Demonstrations of modern educational procedure are sometimes given before these groups. The greater emphasis, however, is usually placed on the need for up-to-date physical equipment. Leaders are now being trained in many universities and normal schools in the scope and methods of organization. The other educational activities noted by Weeks may be briefly summarized as kindergarten extension, beautifying school grounds, better music and more art, the decrease of illiteracy, promotion of scholarships and general improvement of moral education.

Plans aiming more directly at parent education are carried on through the Home Service Department of the national organization and local committees. The emphasis tends to be very largely from the point of view of home management. Efficiency and thrift are emphasized. Attention is also paid to recreation and social standards and children's reading.

Finally, a large part of the energy of most parent-teacher organizations is directed towards specific health problems, with emphasis on methods of preventing and curing " malnutrition, disease, poor posture, adenoids, enlarged tonsils, defective vision, decayed teeth and ear trouble." The methods include coöperation with existing health organizations, promoting clinics, providing hot lunches at the schools, etc.

Summarizing, then, the general background of adult education, as represented by these and similar projects, we find that their sphere of influence is very great. We find, too, that taken together their emphasis is three-fold: vocational (as represented largely by the correspondence schools and university extension); narrowly " cultural " (as represented by the more idealistic schemes, as certain forms of workers' education, and commercial ventures of the lyceum-chautauqua type); or physical-material (as represented by a large part of the Parent-Teacher Association activities, the health organizations, etc.). A very small part indeed is consciously and intelligently either sociological or psychological. As represented by these activities adult education has not become " behavior-conscious," as has much of education generally. We must now, however, consider an increasingly important group of activities comprising the specifically parental-educational, and corresponding in the adult field to the visiting teacher and other school behavior approaches for children.

It must not be thought that we are unduly minimizing the value of all the kinds of education which we have just discussed. Even if we look at it entirely from the viewpoint of the child, it is probable that he will have more satisfactory parents if they are vocationally adjusted, have a control over the material aspects of their environment and have enriched their minds and emotions with literature, music and art. Granting, however, that these schemes may bring about such adjustments (and there must be very serious doubts as to how far they do this) there seems to be a very small part of them that could be considered a preparation for the handling of either the slight or the grave maladjustments of children. For every student of behavior has had brought to his attention that behavior difficulties, even delinquencies, occur with considerable frequency in what are technically known as " good " homes, i.e., the well-managed homes of the economically and vocationally superior and the " cultured."

The projects aiming specifically at the education of parents in the problems of parenthood had very diverse origins, with great differences in emphasis and in methods. The more important of these have been recently joined together under a central committee known as the National Council of Parental Education, which acts largely as a clearing-house for making available methods and materials and for formulating general policies. A great deal of information has been collected through this Council on the various sorts of parental education that are in progress throughout the country. Let us consider some of these projects in some detail.

A large part of the impetus of the parent education movement must be credited to the Child Study Association of America. Indeed it was this association that sponsored the conference in 1925 which resulted in the formation of the National Council of Parental Education. The forerunner of the present association began as a single group in 1888 and functioned continuously until the formation of the Federation for Child Study in 1909, which in turn gave way to the present organization in 1924. This is a private organization, and it does its most effective work in New York and one or two other large cities. Leaders are trained and sent out to groups of parents, and the aim has been defined in such a way that varied groups rather than a great number of groups will be reached. In many ways the Association should be considered a propaganda organization. There are over 2,000 persons enrolled in study groups, and about half that number are in or around New York. At the New York headquarters the aim is to develop as many different kinds of groups as possible, both with regard to subject matter of the courses and with regard to the economic and social strata reached:

We always have a group studying the pre-school child; one studying the pre-adolescent; a group working on adolescent problems and post-adolescent problems; a mental hygiene group; an elementary group in sex education; and an advanced group in sex education. We have mixed groups of fathers and mothers studying sex education and the biological foundations of child-hood. We also have advanced groups . . . in which graduates of study groups discussed . . . rather technical aspects of behavior problems and set themselves the task of translating into everyday language some of the things that they had learned through all the years of study group work. . . .

One study group . . . serves the purpose of training lay readers of study groups. . . . Each meeting is prepared by a committee and is led by a different person. In that way a greater number have practice in leadership. This group has been in existence for twelve years, and all our speakers and all our present leaders in New York City have received training and practice in it.[10]

As regards the type of parents reached by the study groups, Mrs. Gruenberg prepared a statement for us in April, 1927, showing the composition of the groups from the point of view of the education of the mothers in 58 chapters sending in their reports for the year previous. This statement is as follows:

College trained .... 23 chapters
College trained, and " middle class " ...... 5 chapters
Middle class .... 13 chapters
Very wealthy finishing school .... 1 chapter
Working mothers .... 5 chapters
No record .... 11 chapters

It is obvious that they are reaching a very limited and very well-educated portion of the community — fully half of their chapters reaching college-trained women.

The most of the groups deal with what is known as " general child study " (24 of the 58 reporting). There are seven chapters dealing with the pre-school period specifically, three each dealing with infancy and early childhood, pre-school to adolescence, early adolescence, adolescence, and mental hygiene, two dealing with pre-school and adolescence, and one each dealing with infancy, childhood, childhood and early adolescence, sex education for mothers, later adolescence, case study, vocational education, behaviorism, development of child's personality, home situations.

These fifty-eight groups sending in reports represent only one-half to one-third of the total groups in existence, but it is probable that

---

[10] Gruenberg, S. M.: " The Child Study Association of America: Its Organization and Methods," *Conference on Parental Education* (Bronxville, October, 1925), 169–70.

they are pretty representative. Mrs. Gruenberg, in the report cited above, mentions groups of " colored mothers, immigrant mothers of various nationalities, foster-mothers in connection with orphan asylums, workers in child-caring institutions."

In contrast with most of the organizations which we have studied, the program of the Child Study Association quite definitely emphasizes behavior study and the discussion of behavior problems. Three methods are generally followed. In the first the group is organized as a sort of reading circle, where the mothers have assignments from the various theoretical discussions of the problems, and the leader directs the discussion. After deciding on the general subject for study the procedure is described as follows:

The chairman calls the meeting to order and asks for a reading of the minutes of the last meeting. . . . After the reading of the minutes those members who have had assignments are asked to read their abstracts, which then become the basis for discussion by the group. . . . Every member tries to read at least one of the assignments before each meeting and as much other material on the subject as possible.[11]

The rather formalistic and dogmatic nature of these groups is further shown by the " objectives of the meeting " which are listed as follows:

1. To formulate clearly the *basic principles* of the subject under consideration;

2. To relate these, wherever possible, to other topics previously studied;
3. To stimulate interest in further study and discussion;
4. To encourage an open-minded, searching attitude;
5. To train each member to observe her own children in the light of *accepted principles;*
6. To pool experiences and ideas which may be mutually helpful.[12] [Italics ours.]

Of the second method it is said:

Some groups — especially those whose members are accustomed to academic procedure — base their work upon a text book presenting a particular psychological point of view.[13]

---

[11] Pilpel, Cecile: *Child Study Groups. A Manual for Leaders.* Child Study Association of America (1926).

[12] *Ibid.,* 15.

[13] *Ibid.,* 17.

The third technique " is based upon the actual immediate problems of the members of the group." The Association, although encouraging the latter method in special cases, seems to favor the more academic methods. They have prepared a " source book " containing excerpts from " authorities " on the different phases of child study, and have also prepared a series of pamphlets on the subjects more commonly presented. " These pamphlets deal with various subjects connected with the development and education of children and furnish a definite outline for study, and practical suggestions for child training in the home and in the community. . . . An effort is made to keep the material abreast of the best current thought." The titles of the pamphlets are Obedience, Rewards and Punishment, Truth and Falsehood, Curiosity, Use of Money, Habit, Imagination, Health Training of the Pre-School Child, Answering Children's Questions, Sex Education. Much of the detail of this work is frankly dogmatic, much of it is good sound common sense. One feels that it is an extension into this particular field of the ordinary woman's reading and discussion club. There is no particular way of judging of the effectiveness of such a procedure. That it is good in its emphasis on behavior problems as problems for parents to face and try to solve is unquestionable. And it is of undoubted importance in getting women to think in these terms. Some of it is bound to be carried over into practice. At any rate, it is undoubtedly better for them to think in terms of child behavior than in terms of Shakespeare's Women or Contract Bridge.

The central office of the Child Study Association extends its activities beyond these groups. They have a speakers' bureau " composed of graduates of our study groups who have made themselves proficient in one or two topics. They are booked to give simple talks to mothers' clubs and other groups. The speaker first chooses her topic, writes out her outline and presents her talk to a group of our leaders. They criticize it very severely, and she resubmits it before she goes out to give it in public." [14] About two hundred such talks were given in or near New York during 1925.

Courses have been given for others than parents, e.g., a course was given to camp directors (at their own request). At the request of the Ethical Culture School a course was given to governesses and mothers' helpers. Work has been done with girls taking the home-making course

---

[14] Gruenberg: *op. cit.,* 171.

in New York continuation schools. An orphan asylum arranged for a course of lectures for their social workers who go into foster homes. Another interesting feature, in that it approaches more nearly the project method and links up so closely with the schools, is a group known as " visiting mothers ":

The visiting mothers are a group of women who worked in the child study groups for a period of years and who coöperate with the visiting teachers of the public school system. The visiting teacher chooses one or two of these visiting mothers to work with her with one particular family, and the mother then is a liaison officer between the visiting teacher, the school, the home and any other organization that may have to be drawn in to help in the case of the particular child in question. The problem of the child is brought back to one of our groups in which an expert psychiatric social worker discusses this particular case with the visiting teacher and the group of these visiting mothers and some of our leaders and decides what the next steps are to be. Thus the material collected by the visiting mothers also forms a basis for study group work.[15]

The Association has also a series of general lectures, open to the public, and arranged conferences, open to members of the Association only. It maintains a correspondence service in which questions of mothers regarding their problems are answered personally. At the time of Mrs. Gruenberg's report they were receiving from forty to fifty letters a month. They hope to get some light on what parents consider to be their problems through correspondence of this sort. There is a parents' library service, with a service for non-local members. Annotated bibliographies are put out on various subjects and a magazine is published.

Another important private organization, which reaches very much the same class of parents as the Child Study Association, is the American Association of University Women, of which Dr. Lois Hayden Meek is educational secretary. The origin of this branch of the work of this association is described by Dr. Meek as follows:

The American Association of University Women, at its national meeting in July, 1923, accepted as part of its educational program the recommendation of the educational secretary, " that the branches study the problem of the pre-school age." This inaugurated a new educational interest which is

---

[15] Gruenberg: *op. cit.*, 172.

primarily a project in adult education, a project which aims to bring university and college women into more intelligent understanding of young children and the agencies established for their education.[16]

As to the reasons for the development of this field of study among University women:

In the first place, we find in the United States a large group of university graduates who are married women with families. In fact, of the 25,000 members in our association the greatest number are homemakers. Such women are necessarily concerned with the education and training of their children. But very few of them have had anything in their university education which prepared them for this responsibility. . . . Besides mothers, there are other groups of university women who are interested in this project. Many of the women who are in professional work have chosen vocations which are concerned with children — nursing, medicine, social service, education, and clinical work. When these women took their training, very little emphasis was placed upon a study of child life and since that time much information has been developed.

There is another group of university graduates in the United States — women of leisure who give a great deal of time to civic affairs and philanthropic endeavors. Such women are active in political campaigns where there is usually some educational issue, such as voting of bond issues for school purposes and election of school officers, or members of boards of education. They are serving on local school boards of education, they are often chairmen of community committees and thus have a vital part in determining policies and practice in schools. They are organizing and directing agencies for child welfare such as health clinics, day nurseries and recreation houses. . . .

For the large group of college trained women who are dealing with adults, in business, in homes, in teaching, in medicine, in social work, it is essential that they understand something of child life as a basis for understanding adult life.[17]

Each branch of the American Association of University Women was asked to have a meeting on pre-school education, and study groups were formed locally, under the general guidance and with the advice

---

[16] Meek, Lois H.: " A Pre-School Project for University Women," *Progressive Education,* 2:38 (1925).

[17] Meek, Lois H.: " New Ventures in Education for University Women," *Journal of the American Association of University Women,* 20:17 (1926).

of the educational secretary. These groups increased in numbers from 23 in 1923–1924 to 293 in 1926–1927.

Guidance materials and outlines are sent out from the central office. The procedure in the groups tends to be of the academic sort. There are either lectures by specialists, followed by discussions, or book reviews on assigned subjects by the members of the group, followed by discussion. In the outline sent out and the books assigned the aim is to give the members of a group a common background of knowledge to which their questions and discussion can be related. A text-book is advised for " groups who are just starting and need a simple procedure. . . . The use of several books is more difficult. Each member of the group reads the text-book and several read parallel references. . . . The most advanced work can be done by the use of a reference library guided by outlines or questions." [18] Suggestions are given to the mothers for observing the behavior of the children in an attempt to " guide that garrulous talking about experiences with children."

In addition to the organizing and supervising of study groups the central office has a traveling library, which is available to groups and individuals, maintains a service for answering the questions of individuals and dealing with them directly, and distributes generally a large number of pamphlets, reprints, etc.

We see, then, that these two large private organizations are reaching an increasingly large portion of the better educated middle and upper class women, are presenting them with the behavior viewpoint, arousing in them an interest in these subjects and making the ground receptive for the application of methods discovered empirically or scientifically.

And these two organizations represent but a small part of the parent education movement as a whole. It is in the middle west that the movement has reached its fullest development. The programs of several of these middle western states deserve somewhat detailed consideration.

One of the best developed state programs is that in Iowa. Here the movement has had its center in the activities of the Child Welfare Research Station at the State University of Iowa. This station was

---

[18] Meek, Lois H.: " The Educational Program of the American Association of University Women," *Child Study Association of America, Conference on Parental Education* (Bronxville, October, 1925).

established in 1917, concerned itself at first largely with problems of physical welfare, and did not develop its adult educational functions until 1924, when the Parental Education Division was organized. By this time there were many organizations in the state which had developed some sort of parental education program, and there was already a widespread popular interest in child study. Through the Kindergarten and Elementary Division of the State Teachers College a nursery school had been established a number of years before this and courses were given in child care. The emphasis was almost wholly on the physical side, and not until 1926 was a psychologist added to their staff. At this time, also, their extension service added a field-worker in parent education. At the Iowa State College of Agriculture a nursery school was introduced by the home economics division and functions in their parent education program. The approach through the Child Welfare Research Station has been through answering inquiries sent to the station, personal interviews, talks at conventions (State Conventions of the Woman's Christian Temperance Union, Nurses' Associations, the State Fair, Parent-Teacher Association, American Association of University Women, etc.). Study groups are organized throughout the state, with the emphasis on the study discussion methods rather than on lecture courses:

We send out a small travelling library from the University. Assignments are made, outlines and questions furnished on topics which are related to the needs of the individual groups. Very early in the work a woman said to me, " There are twenty women in this group (farm women who had had an organization for three years) of whom five or six, if you asked them, would read a book and make a report. The others will not. Won't you make out some questions on the assignment? " We have followed the plan all year of making out questions in addition to giving assignments for each lesson. Very often we find women getting interested in the questions and reading because they want to know the answers. Very few formal papers are written. We have had very informal organization because most towns and communities have all the organizations they can carry. We have made study, not organization, the important thing, having only a chairman, a secretary, and someone in charge of publicity.[19]

---

[19] Youtz, May P.: " Iowa State Program of Parental Education," *Child Study Association of America, Conference on Parental Education* (Bronxville, October, 1925), 93.

The programs at present have centered chiefly around the State University and the State College, the emphasis in the former being on behavior and in the latter on child care. At the Child Welfare Station (with a home laboratory and several nursery school groups) there are study groups, a correspondence course and observation and laboratory work. In the summer parents who come to the University to take the course in " Child Life " leave their children in the nursery school, and are thus able to combine in a very striking manner the theoretical with the practical observation.

As to the extent of the movement, the following statement was issued by the University in April, 1927:

One hundred twenty-nine groups of parents engaged in study prove that Iowa is interested in Parental Education through the study of the child. Many organizations are coöperating in the program and are so vitally interested in it that duplication of effort is possible. In order to avoid this duplication and coördinate activities, representatives from all organizations interested met with representatives from the three state educational institutions in Des Moines September 24, 1926. The group there assembled voted to form a State Council for Parental Education, inviting to its membership any organization interested and giving to the organization the right to send to the Council meetings as many representatives as it wished.

The aim of the Council is to focus the activities of the organizations composing the Council on a definite program of Child Study and Parent Education in Iowa and to develop a concept of Parent Education through Child Study as a community undertaking, greater than any one organization's capacity, but dependent upon the efforts of each.[20]

The organizations listed as willing to aid in furthering the program of parental education in Iowa include public health nurses, school nurses, tuberculosis nurses, dental clinics, oral hygienists (all these being under the county, city or school nursing service); Sheppard-Towner clinic for infant and maternity welfare; local public clinics, including the permanent infant welfare clinics, psychological clinics, psychiatric clinics, and the Children's Hospital in Iowa City; tuberculosis, heart and venereal disease clinics; State wide clinics, including a mobile mental hygiene clinic sent out by the Psychopathic Hospital

[20] Mimeographed pamphlet issued by State University of Iowa, on Parent Education in Iowa (April 15, 1927).

of the University; general consultant and clinic service at the various hospitals; extension service courses through the three state institutions (State University, Agricultural College and Teachers College), including lectures and study courses on principles of nutrition, health care, psychology, particular behavior problems. Other agencies which are prepared to give specific service are the American Association of University Women, American Legion Auxiliary, Iowa Congress of Parents and Teachers, Iowa Farm Bureau Federation, Federation of Women's Clubs, Red Cross, State Teachers Association, Women's Bureau of the Federation of Labor, Woman's Christian Temperance Union, State Council of Religious Education. They list also a number of national organizations which will give service.

It is obvious that the movement has developed to a considerable degree when these various organizations have been brought under a unified state council. Its ramifications extend among both the rural and the urban population, and through some of these ramifications it must reach a very large part of the parent population of the state — how effectively, it is impossible to say. At any rate, many parents and teachers are thinking about the child and his problems in objective terms.

Other of the mid-western states have developed programs comparable in scope and organization with the Iowa program. In Minnesota the program has formed itself around the Institute of Child Welfare at the University, where the extension program is particularly emphasized. This takes three forms: (1) There are two courses under the regular extension program, given for college credit in St. Paul, Minneapolis and Duluth. These courses are in Child Development and Training, and Educational Methods for Young Children. (2) These same courses are given by correspondence, also for college credit. (3) A correspondence course " designed to meet the needs of the average mother in dealing with everyday problems in the home, in gaining a better understanding of the child, and in acquiring more satisfactory methods of management and control . . . is given without credit and without fee." [21]

The demand on the University people to give lectures, etc., on the

[21] Dixon, Edith D.: " University of Minnesota Program in Parental Education," *Report of the 2nd Annual Conference, Council of Parental Education* (Merrill-Palmer School, Detroit, October 25–28, 1926).

subject of child development has been very great, but an intensive rather than an extensive program has been emphasized:

We are constantly besieged with requests for talks and lectures before conventions and public gatherings of various sorts. Last year we gave eighty-two such talks. We also put on a course of six lectures on The Growth and Development of the Young Child. Each lecture was given by a member of the University faculty — a specialist in the field. But we are coming more and more to feel that, unless the talk is followed by the organization of some type of study group, we are not justified in giving the time. We are therefore placing our emphasis more and more upon organization of study groups for longer periods, more frequent meetings, and, as far as possible, more preparation on the part of the group. We believe that the parent should be taught how to observe his own children and how to solve his own problems.[22]

Anderson has made an interesting analysis of the clientele of this parental education program at Minnesota. Certain data were obtained regarding both the registrants in the free correspondence course (which had been widely advertised through circulars distributed at state and county fairs, by parents of the nursery school children, etc.) and the study groups organized in the three cities of Minnesota:

This study is based on the registration cards of 540 persons enrolled in study groups and of 750 persons, residents of Minnesota, enrolled in the correspondence course between October 1, 1926 and April 15, 1927. All enrolled, with one exception, are women. There is some overlapping between the study group enrollment and the correspondence course enrollment, 18% of those in the study group having registered for the correspondence course.

The entire enrollment of the study groups is confined to the large cities and their suburbs. The enrollment in the correspondence course is state-wide, the 750 persons being distributed in 173 communities, some of which are cities and some of which are merely post offices at which mail is received. Of the 86 counties in Minnesota, 71 are represented. It is evident that the correspondence course reaches many communities and places which would not be reached by our other extension methods such as study groups demonstrations and county projects.[23]

Of the 750 registrants in the correspondence course, 59% are found in the large cities which contain only 30% of the population. Thus it is

[22] *Ibid.*, 63.

[23] Anderson, John E.: " The Clientele of a Parental Education Program," *School and Society*, 26:179 (August 6, 1927).

evident that the city population is more interested and accessible to such a program than the country. A wide age range is reached in both the correspondence course and study groups, i.e., from 15 to 64 years. The mean age for the correspondence course is 32.5, and 59% of the registrants are between 25 and 35. For the study groups, 53% are between 25 and 35. Only about 7% of the correspondence registrants were unmarried, and 2% of the study group. The majority in both groups had been married less than ten years.

As regards the social and educational status of these registrants, they are classified according to their husbands' occupations and compared with similar occupational class percentages found in Minneapolis:

We see that the correspondence course draws four times as many from the professional group, three times as many from the semi-professional and managerial group, and over one and one-fourth times as many from the highly skilled trade and clerical groups as is to be expected. From the less highly skilled trades and minor clerical, it draws one-third, from the semi-skilled class, one-fourth, and from the unskilled labor class one-twentieth as many as is to be expected. Study groups draw four times as many from the professional group, three times as many from the semi-professional and managerial group, the same percentage from the highly skilled and clerical group, three-fifths as many from the less highly skilled trades and minor clerical, two-fifths as many from the semi-skilled class and only one-eighth as many from the unskilled classes as is to be expected.[24]

The average number of children per family for the correspondence course registrants is 1.90 and for the study groups 2.08. 62% of the correspondence group children and 48% of the study group children are at the pre-school age.

Data are also given with regard to the education of the registrants:

[Of the correspondence group registrants] 13.7% or approximately one-seventh have had four or more years of college work, 48.2% have had some work of college level, 69.2% have had four years' high school or more, 85.9% have had some high school education or more, and only 14.1% have had eighth grade education or less. Of the study group registrants, 15% have had four or more years of college work, 43.5% have had some work of college level, 61.6% have had four years' high school education or more, and only 22.1% have had eighth grade education or less. The median educational attainment

[24] Anderson, John E.: "The Clientele of a Parental Education Program," *School and Society*, 26:181 (August 6, 1927).

for all groups falls in the fourth year of high school. It is apparent then from this data that both the correspondence course and the study groups in the state of Minnesota draw their clientele from individuals who have had at least some high school education, and that almost half of the individuals have had at least some education beyond the high school level.[25]

Regarding the effectiveness of the course, some indication may be gained through the number of sets of answers sent in to the questions appended to the correspondence lessons. Only 16% for the city group and 25% of the rural group had sent in one or more sets of answers when this article was written:

These figures are obviously inadequate because of the fact that some of the people covered by the study are just beginning the course, whereas others of the people covered by the study are virtually through with it. There is a somewhat greater tendency for the persons in the town and rural groups to send in answers to the questions. The general fact may be stated that for a correspondence course of this sort without any particular pressure brought to bear for answering questions, approximately one-fifth of the individuals sent in one or more sets of answers.[26]

This is the only careful analysis that has been made of the clientele of the parent education groups. It has a bearing on the questions raised by a consideration of the Child Study Association and the American Association of University Women, i.e., whether those who need it most are getting any of this education, whether it is not in many cases a substitute activity for general women's club interests and whether the span of attention to the subject matter is very great.

Other aspects of the work in various localities should be considered. In Oklahoma, for instance, in addition to the mother-craft work done through the University, the fathers (at their own request) were given a course in home economics. The outline of this course is interesting — the topics presented extending from Family Relationships through Nutrition to Correct Dress and Table Practice!

Dr. Van Waters has parent education groups in connection with the juvenile court in Los Angeles. Regarding the parents whose children actually get into court, she says:

Our parental education consists, first, in explaining to the parents the true nature of the court. Usually in filing a petition, parents want the child to

---

[25] *Ibid.*, 183–84.   [26] *Ibid.*, 184.

have a lesson or to be punished in ways which their squeamishness or concrete imagination do not permit them to do. It is made clear that the procedure is not one of punishment but involves understanding and the use of all the scientific knowledge available. . . . We try to let the parents think that they should use the court with no more hesitation than they would use a clinic. We try to explain to them that the court is really simply a superparent. . . . We always have both parents and the step-parents, if any, in court. The child first tells his or her story alone, and then the parents tell their problems. The child is not always present during parental disagreement, though later they are all brought together. The situation is gone over and over, until each one has had a chance to explain his point of view, and then all meet together in a sort of mutual consultation.

At first the court always places the responsibility for a solution on the parents. . . . The question is " What would you like the court to do for your child? What do you think is the best thing to do now that you have heard all the facts? " And similarly to the child: " If you could make a plan for your-self, what would you do? " . . . When children report in court, they must always bring their parents if the parents can be found and for that purpose we have hearings late in the evening or at any hour convenient to the parents. . . . The report is like a clinical consultation and a record is kept of it. If parents cannot come for good reason, we require written reports from them, even if they are almost illiterate — just some expression of what they think has been accomplished and what the problems are. . . . In every case, there is presented to the court a written summary of the scientific work. Where it is at all possible for parents to make use of it (and I think this is true in more cases than we imagine until we try it) this summary is given to the parents. . . . The court is also used as a factor in the education of parents in the community who do not think they have problem or abnormal children but realize they have children they cannot get along with. All sorts of people consult us. . . . Another phase of the work consists of lectures to groups of parents who have asked for class organization. This is done by the referee through the use of university extension.[27]

In Denver, under Judge Lindsey, widowed mothers receiving pensions were organized into a class to discuss the problems of their children. In Detroit, also, a parent education program is carried out with the mothers' pension women. This is largely individual work by the pension officers who see the mothers frequently, both in the home

---

[27] Van Waters, Miriam: " The Juvenile Court as an Agency in Parental Education," *Child Study Association of America, Conference on Parental Education* (Bronxville, October, 1925).

and at the office. The group work, which is confined entirely to the foreign-born, emphasizes largely the physical, or problems of general "Americanization," e.g., one group had as its aim the teaching of the use of milk to Italian women:

When the first class in teaching the use of milk was completed, a prize was given to the mother who had introduced the use of milk most extensively into her own family. The program was extended to a class in citizenship interpreting to the mothers the meaning of our legal holidays and our national heroes, and gradually they developed into English classes. . . . The subjects which have been most popular in the group work are citizenship, nutrition, and home nursing.[28]

It is interesting to note the wide variation in origins of the various approaches, in technique, in subject-matter and in the groups reached. There are various programs in addition to the ones we have mentioned — each reflecting a slightly different emphasis. The movement may get its impetus from a private organization, a research institute, a state university. It may emphasize the physical (e.g., nutrition), the material (e.g., home management), the "cultural," or the psychological, in many different phases. It may have leaders with varied backgrounds, and part of its program may be devoted to training leaders.[29] The programs which we have considered thus far tend to be built around the ordinary academic procedure and to be largely in the nature of "study groups." We will now consider a well-developed phase of parent education where the working out of a project empirically is emphasized rather than the study of principles and where observation of actual procedure looms more important than study from books. This phase of the work has developed in the centers where nursery schools, particularly the more experimental nursery schools, have been organized. The nursery school has been a recent development in America. The movement in England preceded its developments here by a number of years, and arose largely as an attempt to correct remediable physical defects in young children before they were entered in the regular schools. In America the nursery school has emphasized the idea of habit training.

---

[28] Sanders, Clare: "Parental Education in the Mothers' Pension Department of Detroit," *Report of the 2nd Annual Conference, Council of Parental Education* (Merrill-Palmer School, Detroit, October 25–28, 1926).

[29] A special course of study, directed towards training leaders, is a feature of the parent education program at the Teachers College Institute in New York.

The general opinion has been that the pre-school level is particularly fertile both for the study of the origins of behavior trends and for training in habit formation. We have seen, indeed, that the various treatment plans for behavior problems have emphasized the need of getting at children at the earlier age levels. And, indeed, most of the parent education emphasis has been on the younger age groups, except for the special studies of the adolescent.

Nursery schools, which have been established at the several child welfare research centers (Minnesota, Iowa, New York, etc.) have become intimately connected with the parent education movement, both for the actual training of mothers in the observation of their own children and the carrying over of methods of approach learned there, with an even greater emphasis on the training of potential parents. The latter is achieving a greater proportion of the emphasis because with actual mothers, who have had several years of practice in inadequate procedures of their own or traditional devising, the process of effective reëducation becomes very difficult, whereas with " pre-parental " education the process is greatly simplified. The emphasis upon the actual training of parents of nursery school children has come through the hampering of the nursery school procedure by the practices of the parents. The nursery school, whether it has had as its chief emphasis habit training or providing suitable conditions for the development and growth of the young child, has found that parental understanding of its aims and active coöperation with the parents is necessary. In practically all places where nursery schools have been established parental education, although perhaps of a most informal sort, has become a part of the program. The situation is stated as follows in the Proceedings of the Second Conference on Nursery Schools held in New York April 22–23, 1927 (National Committee on Nursery Schools):

The nursery school's chance of success with the children is greatly increased when the mother has [an] intimate understanding of its aims and methods. . . . There seemed to be general agreement that an essential part of the work of a nursery school is the education of the parents of its children; an opportunity which we cannot afford to miss. This belief was so general that someone asked, " Is the nursery school for the benefit of the parents or for the benefit of the child? " The answer was, " Primarily for the benefit of the child." Whatever is done for the benefit of the parents is done because it benefits the child.[30]

---

[30] P. 15.

This education of the parents may take several forms. In most places the parents are encouraged to bring and call for the children themselves. In that way they have constant contacts with the nursery school teachers and behavior problems are discussed as they occur both in the home and in the school. Parents will bring their problems to the teacher. In connection with the parent education work in places such as the Teachers College Institute for Child Welfare Research there are lectures by staff members, by outsiders of prominence, and there is a parents' study group, led by the director of parental education. Perhaps, however, the most valuable work of the nursery school in educating parents comes through their observation of, or actual practice in, the school. In one of the smaller private nursery schools, for example, the Cambridge nursery school,

the requirement . . . is made . . . that every mother shall give half a day a week to helping in the nursery school, shall attend mothers' meetings, and shall coöperate with the school in every way. . . . The plan of having the mothers help has been very successful. The mothers are eager to come for their half day of work and are eager to learn all they can from being with the children and from watching the director and conferring frequently with her. The mothers report at mothers' meetings on special topics in regard to which they have made careful observation while at the school.[31]

The mothers do not usually have this actual practice in the nursery school but in most places they are specifically encouraged to spend time in observation. At Cornell, because of a very long waiting-list, they are able to make certain requirements with regard to the coöperation of the parents. In addition to observation in the nursery school, this coöperation

involves the attendance at group meetings, and these meetings include not only the parents, but also the maiden aunts, grandmothers, maids, housekeepers — in other words, the other adults in the family. Mothers of children in the nursery school are met once a month in the general group, and they also have individual interviews once a month.[32]

---

[31] *Proceedings of the Second Conference on Nursery Schools* (National Committee on Nursery Schools, New York, 1927), 15.

[32] Perkins, Nellie L.: "The New Child Training Laboratories at Cornell University," *Child Study Association of America, Conference on Parental Education* (Bronxville, October, 1925).

At the Merrill-Palmer School in Detroit they have recently made a plan whereby each mother will be required to spend one day in the nursery school, under supervision, because of their conviction that the nursery school should act as a laboratory for parents. They have emphasized largely pre-parental education, which we shall consider later, but have also a well-developed program of education for the parents of their nursery school children:

When the child is admitted to the school, a conference with the parents as to our purposes and methods is arranged, and no child is admitted without an agreement on the part of the parents to coöperate. Following this, the various specialists who examine the child arrange conferences with the parents so that the point of view of each may be presented. Frequently, the fathers are called in at these conferences, even when they have not volunteered in the beginning.

We wish, whenever possible, to have the children brought in every day by one parent or the other, because we feel that the casual daily contacts with the nursery school staff should have great educative value. . . . We feel that the most important agency through which to educate nursery school parents is the child himself. As the child develops, the parents, observing his reactions, are better able to understand the methods used. We are able to check up on our own accomplishments with the parents through our daily observations of the child. From the child's attitude we can judge if the methods used at home vary widely from those of the school. . . . When we find, from observation of an individual child, that parents are failing to understand our point of view and our methods, our staff makes an effort to establish a closer contact.

We ask parents to fill out for us various types of blanks, some of them daily. Other blanks are filled out by the specialists through conferences with the parents. Still other records are kept by the parents themselves. . . . Much of the information we get is indefinite and not of great value but the blank itself has great educational value for both the parents and the students who later see it. . . .

We now have regular monthly meetings for the parents. The topics discussed are suggested by the school experiences, and we get, for the most part, excellent response. . . . [The meetings] consist almost entirely of discussion, the main topic being presented by some member of the staff. Out of these discussions we feel that we get the parents' point of view, and they have been of great assistance to us in every way.[33]

[33] White, Edna Noble: "The Merrill-Palmer School: Its Program of Parental Education," *Child Study Association of America, Conference on Parental Education* (Bronxville, October, 1925).

These plans are fairly typical of the parental education centering around the nursery schools. The nursery schools are used as laboratories in which the parent sees or participates in the solution of problems in the school which she has been unable to cope with in the home. In her continual contacts with the staff of these schools problems that have occurred are brought up for informal discussion. This discussion will usually be of benefit both to the teacher and the parent: the child may make an adjustment with regard to some behavior problem in the one situation and fail of adjustment in the other. By continual checking up of procedure in the two situations by those actually involved good empirical solutions of the problems may often be reached. The parent is then in a much more receptive state for the " general principles " of the group meetings than if she had not had this approximation to laboratory experience.

An interesting variant of this laboratory procedure is that used by Dr. Arnold Gesell in his Psycho-Educational Clinic at Yale University. Here there is no nursery school, but a consultation center, to which parents with behavior problem children can come. The clinic is fitted up as a very interesting play-room — as are the play-rooms of the nursery schools. One end of the room is ingeniously screened and lighted in such a way that it appears from the inside to be a solid wall. On the other side are arranged chairs, and a perfectly clear view of the nursery is possible. The clinician deals with the children in groups. The parents sit behind the screen. The procedure is very like that of a good nursery school. Specific problems are dealt with, easily and without undue emphasis, in the group. The parent notes the clinician's technique, and, after a period, is given a chance to take the clinician's place as director in the nursery, while being observed from behind the screen. Thus the parent gets a very objective idea of how to deal with her child's problems, and by repeated visits to the clinic is often able to bring about the solution of serious difficulties.

The plans that we have considered have concerned themselves either with actual parents or with those who are in some way at present connected with children, e.g., nurses, teachers, etc. The emphasis, however, is being more and more placed on the training of persons who are likely to have contact with children, either as parents, teachers, etc., before they have a chance to establish their habits, i.e., before they actually become teachers or parents. We noted this development quite definitely with regard to the visiting teacher movement. Similarly, we find parent education making its approach through " pre-parents." And here we find exactly the same procedures noted in the general parent education movement, i.e., the acedemic procedure in groups, the informal group procedure, the laboratory observation and the laboratory practice.

A study has recently been made of the extent to which the public schools give education which might be considered pre-parental. The development of child care courses in the public schools is very recent, although training in home economics has become almost universal. This study was confined to the courses given in 1926 specifically in the field of child care. A questionnaire was sent out to all the states, and only five reported no courses at all given in child care. As to the extent of these courses, and the source, the following data are presented:

The reports received in this investigation show that approximately 76,500 school pupils received instruction in child care in the United States during a period of one year. . . . Twenty-eight State courses of study, 29 local courses of study and the Mothercraft and Red Cross manuals were received. Eight, or 29%, of the State courses of study were from vocational home economics departments; 9, or 32%, were from the child hygiene departments of State boards of health; and 11, or 39%, were from general home economics departments of education. One, or 3%, of the local courses of study was from a science department; 3, or 10%, were special courses, and 25, or 86%, were from home economics departments. The largest percentage of both State and local outlines were received from home economics departments of education. These outlines and courses of study have been published only recently. Most of them are dated 1924, 1925 or 1926; one is dated 1922–23.[34]

These courses, then, largely reach the home economics students, and it is not surprising that the behavior content is small:

The replies from school officials concerning the subject-matter of the courses presented in their schools show the following phases of child care most frequently presented:

Physical care and clothing in 94% of the places.

Habit formation in 88% of the places.

Physical development in 87% of the places.

Mental and social development in 55% of the places.

---

[34] Crabbs, L. M., and Miller, M. L.: *A Survey of Public School Courses in Child Care for Girls* (Merrill-Palmer School, Detroit, May, 1927), 45.

Prenatal care in 49% of the places.

Heredity and reproduction of life in 43% of the places.

Analysis of those outlines and courses of study that were received shows the following phases of child care most frequently included:

Clothing in 92% of the outlines and courses of study.

Infant feeding in 83% of the outlines and courses of study.

Bathing the baby in 70% of the outlines and courses of study.

Needs of the baby in 61% of the outlines and courses of study.

Physical habits in 51% of the outlines and courses of study.

Child feeding in 44% of the outlines and courses of study.[35]

It is obvious, then, that although the subject is receiving increasing emphasis, as shown by the recency of development of any courses at all in child care, we must look to the more specialized branches of pre-parental educational effort to find any adequate study of behavior.

The most outstanding of the institutions emphasizing pre-parental training is the Merrill-Palmer School in Detroit. The idea upon which this school was established is expressed in the will of the founder, that " girls and young women of the age of ten years or more shall be educated, trained, developed and disciplined with special reference to fitting them mentally, morally, physically and religiously for the discharge of the functions and service of wifehood and motherhood, and the management, supervision, direction and inspiration of homes." A good deal of discretion was left to the administrators as to the exact form this instruction should take. The result has been a most interesting experiment in the field of pre-parental education. The main part of this program has concerned a resident group of young women, sent by various colleges and universities, usually with a home economics background:

The school offers courses in child care to senior and graduate students in a number of colleges and universities of recognized standing. Coöperative arrangements have been made whereby they receive full credit from their home institutions for work done at the Merrill-Palmer school. At present, students to the number of forty-five, representing twelve institutions, are studying at the school. The students come for periods varying from a term to a year, living at the school in four groups under a coöperative plan.[36]

[35] *Ibid.*, 51.

[36] *The Program of the Merrill-Palmer School,* (October, 1927).

The main idea of the school is training through participation in, and observation of, definite situations as well as courses in the " principles " of mental and physical development of the child, household arts, etc. Each of the four groups has a separate residence, and each girl in the group takes a turn at functioning in the various rôles of the " home-maker," e.g., hostess, planning the meals, purchasing the food, supervising the preparation and serving of meals, etc. There are two nursery schools and each student spends a number of hours each week, first observing, then functioning, in the school. Each student is assigned two or three of the children for special study, is given an opportunity to have contacts with the parents of these children, and frequently to observe them in their home situations as well as in the nursery school. A particularly interesting arrangement has been made with one of the nursery school families (parents and four children) considered a " normal " or well-adjusted family, whereby a room is rented in this family continuously during the school year. Each student is allowed to occupy this room, take meals with the family, be there continuously over the week-end, for a period of ten days or two weeks. During this period they follow the children in the nursery school, and thus have an opportunity to observe the functioning of the children in the two situations, to get a pretty clear idea of how the problems may be carried over from one situation to another, what compromises have to be made, how difficulties are met, etc.

In addition to the actual experience of the students in the various phases of child care, group instruction is given in the Mental Growth and Development of Character in Young Childhood, Educational Methods for Young Children, Physical Growth and Development of Young Children, and Social Factors of Child Life. These courses are all linked up with actual laboratory experience.

Other places have developed specialized work in pre-parental training. Cornell University also emphasizes the laboratory aspects of the training. In a four-year program started in 1925, the plan for the students was stated as follows:

Since we are convinced that the best way to present this subject is through first-hand information and contacts, instruction is largely through clinical methods. For this, special facilities for meeting parents and children had to be developed and five forms of contact have been provided.

(1) The nursery school offers all students an opportunity to study and observe modern methods of handling the normal pre-school child under environmental conditions especially planned to meet the needs of this period.

(2) A consultation center associated with the nursery school serves parents who wish to refer problem children for examination and advice.

(3) Over-night care is offered where the cause of the trouble (misconduct, faulty food habits, etc.) cannot be located without prolonged observation or where treatment in the home is impossible.

(4) A second consultation center associated with the family and child welfare organizations of Tompkins County serves as a laboratory for students who wish social service experience, and an opportunity to deal directly with the more complicated behavior problems.

(5) A survey of one hundred families including social, economic, medical and psychological aspects of human relations with careful follow-up work for one year is planned as a research problem in methods of presentation and treatment. Only advanced students are eligible for this service, but the survey as planned offers excellent first-hand experience in meeting normal family situations and is to serve as a kind of internship before placing students in positions of responsibility.

In these five centers of contact, students will see and hear practical problems discussed and analyzed, treatment outlined and follow-up contacts made. Lectures and discussions are centered about these situations and there is ample opportunity for first-hand experience under supervision. Classes in household management, interior decorating, child feeding, child clothing and child training each get laboratory experience in the nursery school and the over-night care of children. The problems do not come singly and there is generally something of interest to every group of students. Child training is taught from many angles wherever it is presented.[37]

The unique feature of this program was the over-night care of children presenting behavior problems, and the consequent experience the students got in the control of the total situation. It is interesting to note how this program has been modified:

Miss Margaret Wylie representing the nursery school of Cornell University reported a full day program including luncheon and nap. In addition, Miss Wylie reported that 24-hour service has been given in five cases (never more than two at one time) the period of service ranging from 10 days to 8 weeks. . . . Children with typical difficulties, such as thumb-sucking, overstimulation and non-feeding, were selected for overnight care. Miss Wylie reported that

---

[37] Perkins: *op. cit.*

satisfactory results were obtained in several or all cases while children remained at the nursery school 24 hours a day but when they returned to their former environment, the erstwhile difficulties recurred. During the past year, no 24-hour service was attempted. Instead, workers have gone into the homes. Six home studies were made. These were not satisfactory as the parents were self-conscious about food, etc., and so normal conditions did not prevail. Workers now go into the homes for observations from 3–6 p.m.[38]

" The Vassar Institute of Euthenics," whose expressed aim is to " bring together into one division of instruction the contributions of the social, economic and natural sciences to the improvement of living conditions, with special emphasis on the study of the child and the family group, for the definite purpose of training leaders in this field and of incorporating in the consciousness of every college woman a sense of the values which science may contribute here," [39] is another recent development in pre-parental education. This project is notable because of its sound academic basis, as well as the emphasis it is placing on laboratory experience through the recent establishment of a nursery school.

Other similar projects are springing up, and we may look for further development along these lines. The general trend seems to be in the direction of training for parenthood in the earlier years. The limitations to the education of existing parents are admitted, just as any sort of adult education must be limited in its accomplishments. Adult education is necessary to care for those who are caught in the conditions caused by the lagging response of the school to the demands of changing society. It will probably always be necessary, for perfect institutional adjustment is a thing unheard of, but the more important developments are to be looked for in changes in institutional policy. Parent education faces all the difficulties — and in more intense forms — inherent in adult education generally. It is vitally necessary now to take care of the existing maladjustments, but the greater emphasis is being placed on the prevention of these maladjustments for the next generation of parents. This is well expressed by Dr. Woolley as follows:

---

[38] *Proceedings of the Second Conference on Nursery Schools* (National Committee on Nursery Schools, New York, 1927), 9.

[39] Macleod, Annie L.: " Euthenics in the Curriculum," *Vassar Quarterly,* 10:22 (1924).

Because the problem is so immediate and pressing for parents, one is often tempted to feel that the education of the public in the realm of child nurture should begin with the parents of young children. An added reason for making them the chief objective is that they are immediately faced with the problem and have accordingly the strongest reason of any one for being interested. Instruction gains all the vitality of a live issue. The desirability of providing such instruction for parents is undoubted, but there are very good reasons for believing that the problem can never be fully met in this way. In the first place, compulsory education for parents is utterly impracticable, and the parents who need it most are usually those who would fail to present themselves for any instruction offered on a voluntary basis. In the second place, the practical obstacles to going to school are too great to be overcome by most parents. The daily routine of earning a living and of caring for babies and doing housework is too exacting.

Knowledge which it is important to impart to all of the children of all the people must take the channel of the public school, and must be introduced into the curriculum some time before the end of the compulsory education period. The project before us, then, in furthering general information on the subject of child nurture, physical or mental, is to find a way of instructing the youth in its fundamental principles some time before they leave school. The great and obvious difficulty of introducing instruction about child rearing at this level, is that school children are not as yet faced with the problem, and it may be difficult to get their interest.[40]

---

[40] Woolley, Helen T.: "Vassar's Adventure as a Psychologist Sees It," *Vassar Quarterly*, 10:27 (1924).

CHAPTER VIII

The Psychometric Approach

THE SCIENTIFIC approaches to the study of the child have been, from the physical side, studies of growth and nutrition, and from the mental side, studies of growth and capacity. Both approaches have considered behavior as a correlate or function. The physical approach has tended toward an emphasis on environment and health. Improve living conditions and thereby do away with rickets. Remove diseased tonsils and teeth and improve behavior. A well child is a good child or an adequately adjusted child. The mental approach has tended much more to emphasize hereditary limitations, and, until more recent years, to consider segregation of the mentally unfit as the solution of behavior difficulties.

Because of their great claims, and because of the very interesting developments in certain of their theories and of the vast amount of data which they have accumulated, the approach of the mental testers deserves a somewhat extended consideration. Although our primary interest is in the data which the mental testers have collected regarding the relationship between intelligence and behavior — the implications of these data, and the claims that have grown out of them — it is necessary first to sketch briefly the status of mental measurement in general.

In studies of physical capacity the problem is to make a series of measurements of the organ and calculate capacity, within definitely known limits of error. The result is expressed in readily defined quantitative terms. In measuring physical growth, two methods have been used. In the first, the same individuals are measured at successive periods of time. Working with animals in the laboratory it is possible to control the environmental conditions and hence obtain a picture of growth relatively uncomplicated by inequalities in the stimuli from one period to the other, but in the measurements of humans it is possible to control the environment only within limits that are so wide as to have little meaning; innumerable factors enter in to complicate the picture of growth. Nor can most of these factors even be allowed for or measured. Growth, therefore, is measured in terms of a large number of unknown variables, and norms can be only approximate at best. Rather than carry through measurements on the same individuals over a period of time, therefore, a more common method is to get large numbers of individuals at successive age levels — keeping environmental conditions as nearly equal as possible — on the assumption that the large number involved will tend to equalize the error from one period of growth to another.

It is obvious that there are great difficulties involved in both of these methods, that neither of them separates the environmental influences from the innate predisposition to growth and that unless a very careful study is made of the nature and extent of these environmental influences the results will have a limited applicability. The precision of measurements, the expression of results to the nearest millimetre, means very little when we have so inexact a notion of just what it is that is being measured so precisely.

So, with regard to physical measurements, the situation resolves itself as follows: at any given moment capacity or present status can be measured with great precision, but the parts contributed to this present status by innate predisposition and environmental influences cannot be separated, and the studies of growth have thrown little light on the problem because of the impossibility of controlling the various environmental factors and the present lack of exact knowledge about them.

Passing now to mental growth and capacity, the difficulties are increased a thousandfold. The anatomist cannot separate out the environmental influences from what he is measuring, but the sum total of his measurements gives him something tangible. When he applies the callipers in a certain position, for instance, there is no question as to what specific thing he has been measuring. The etiological factors may be obscure, but the organ or part measured is expressible in quantitative terms and has an objective reality about which there is no controversy. Mental capacity and growth, on the other hand, can be measured only indirectly, and the meaning of the results obtained becomes a matter of great controversy. There is no general agreement as to the nature of intelligence and there is no scientific way of checking whether the empirically determined tests measure what their sponsors claim. The quantitative expression of the results obtained on the tests — far from giving them greater precision — tends often merely to confuse the issues and add to the controversy.

Rigid definition must precede exact measurement. And before examining the nature of the mental measurements it will be necessary to consider how rigid the definition of mental functions may be — how narrow and how objective the limits. It is scarcely necessary to go into the detail of the controversy which has arisen regarding the nature of intelligence, although the kinds of tests developed have undoubtedly been affected by the view held by the investigator, i.e., whether intelligence is a unitary character and can be measured as such, or whether it represents a group of variously correlated functions which can be measured only separately, but any one of which gives some indication of the status of the individual with regard to others. The tests were devised originally, of course, with some assumption made as to what they were measuring, but their empirical nature and the difficulty of checking up on them has led to much disagreement as to just what function or functions they measure. The controversy seems to have come to a deadlock, with some psychologists claiming that intelligence is what the mental tests test and others claiming that general intelligence is far more complicated than any of the tests have yet indicated, and that its more significant aspects have not yet been touched.

Indications of these general attitudes may be seen in quotations from a symposium on general intelligence and its measurement which appeared in the *Journal of Educational Psychology:* [1]

E. L. Thorndike:

In measuring a person's general status in intelligence and in inferring therefrom what his rank in native intellectual capacity in general is, what we do is to test him with a fair sampling of data and operations. . . . This sampling should be wide enough and its various components should be easily enough

---

[1] " Intelligence and Its Measurement: A Symposium," 12:123–47, 195–216 (1921).

weighted, so that the resulting judgment should be about his *general* status and *general* capacity — if we are to claim that it is general.[2]

F. N. Freeman:

I conceive intelligence to be a somewhat more inclusive capacity than is implied when it is used as a name for our present tests. For this reason, it seems to me that it would be better to use a term of somewhat narrower connotation to designate these tests. The mental capacity designated by the term intelligence seems to me to include, besides the elements which are usually measured by our tests, certain other types of capacity which they measure scarcely at all.

The capacities measured by our tests may be described from the structural point of view as involving chiefly: sensory capacity; capacity for perceptual recognition; quickness, range or flexibility of association; facility in imagination; span or steadiness of attention; quickness or alertness in response. Excellence in capacities of this sort is well designated by the term brightness. We recognize, however, that a person's achievement, or even his intellectual capacity, does not seem to correspond perfectly with his capacity in any of these various specific traits or with all of them put together. We sometimes say that a person is very bright but not very intelligent. We mean that he does not use his mental powers in such a way as to be most productive. The characteristic which I am referring to is sometimes called temperament or moral character, but it seems to me it can be shown that there are certain intellectual traits which are left out of our present scheme of tests and which should be included in a total conception of intelligence.

These additional characteristics may be described as: mental balance; co-ordination of the mental processes; the judicious management of the processes of learning or reflection; mental control; mental adjustment; the direction of the attention toward the significant aspects of experience; a due degree of non-suggestibility; the adoption of intellectual purposes and the adaptation of means to their satisfaction; sensitiveness to significant combinations between experiences which illuminate one another or which are effective in building up systems of thought; balanced and sane reaction to the entire world of things, ideas and persons.[3]

S. S. Colvin:

An individual possesses intelligence in so far as he has learned, or can learn to adjust himself to his environment. . . . . An inspection of intelligence examinations clearly shows that those who framed them have not confined their

---

[2] *Ibid.,* 125.   [3] *Ibid.,* 133–34.

tests to problem solving, even in its rudimentary forms. These tests measure an individual's intelligence largely in terms of what he has learned, thus obtaining indirectly a measure of his learning ability. . . . If the individual has the requisite skill and knowledge he can satisfactorily perform these tests. They are appropriate tests for intelligence only on the theory that they test ability to learn by discovering what has already been learned.[4]

L. M. Terman:

Many criticisms of the current methods of testing intelligence rest plainly on a psychology which fails to distinguish the levels of intellectual functioning or to assign to conceptual thinking the place that belongs to it in the hierarchy of intelligences. . . . If intelligence is the ability to think in terms of abstract ideas, we should expect the most successful intelligence tests to be just those which involve the use of language or other symbols.[5]

R. Pintner:

Because we are dealing with something which we hardly know how to define, because we are groping for means to measure reactions to extremely complex and different situations, we must be very careful not to limit in any way the type of material we use. Intelligence is shown in dealing with things as well as with words, in dealing with living men and women as well as with symbols, in handling a paint brush or chisel as well as a pencil, in carving stone or laying brick as well as in making verbal responses. We, therefore, need intelligence tests of all types. And by intelligence tests I mean tests of the general ability to do all sorts of things as opposed to educational and trade tests which are specifically made to measure the knowledge which an individual has been directly taught.[6]

V. A. C. Henmon emphasizes the need of " a scale for intellect, not a scale for intelligence," and says:

Any test which requires mental processes, be they either on the sensory-motor level or on higher levels, which measures the sensitiveness, responsiveness, and retentiveness of the nervous system, is a test of intellectual capacity. . . . It is not a matter of the kind of mental process involved primarily. A properly constituted test of intellect ought, therefore, to take a wide sampling of so-called lower as well as higher processes and the relative weights to be assigned to each element determined. . . . The so-called general intelligence tests are not general intelligence tests at all but tests of the special intelligence upon which the school puts a premium.[7]

---

[4] " Intelligence and Its Measurement: A Symposium," 12:136–37.
[5] *Ibid.*, 129.   [6] *Ibid.*, 140–41.   [7] *Ibid.*, 196–97.

Others in the symposium emphasize the fact that " intelligence is only one of the elements in mentality," and that the volitional and emotional characteristics are important and have scarcely been touched upon.

And so we find that the whole problem of mental capacity is complicated by the fact that the psychologists are not agreed as to the functions included and the tests which have been devised to measure mental capacity cannot be checked back to the functions which it is claimed they measure. The result is a kind of reasoning in circles: tests are devised to measure intelligence whose exact nature is unknown, and then intelligence is defined in terms of performance on the tests.

With the study of mental capacity in such an inexact state, it is, of course, useless to expect that the studies of mental growth will be any more exact. And yet the concept of mental age arising from these studies has been extremely valuable. Binet, who was the first to formulate this concept clearly and to experiment along these lines, assumed that the functions of the mind behaved, with regard to growth, very much the same as other physical functions, i.e., approached a limit at maturity. He devised a set of tests of varying degrees of complexity and gave them to children of different age levels. He found, as he had expected, that the more difficult the test seemed to be, *a priori,* the older the child generally had to be to solve it, and that the chronological age of the child was an indicator of the sorts of tests that could be solved. He experimented with a number of these tests and found that certain of them could be grouped at each chronological age because they could be solved by two-thirds to three-fourths of the children tested at that chronological age. Thus, tests indicative of a mental age of twelve years were tests which it had been proved could be solved by, say, 75% of an unselected group of children whose chronological age was twelve years, by practically all children at older chronological ages and by very few at younger chronological ages.

Following out this assumption Terman and others devised the " intelligence quotient," or IQ, i.e., the ratio of the mental age to the chronological age, on the assumption that " normal intelligence " would be represented by the large mass of persons who would test at age and therefore have an IQ of approximately 100. It was therefore further assumed that the intelligence quotient would be constant over a period of time, since mental growth was defined as a function of chronological age. The limit of mental growth was further defined by the tests as being, on the average, sixteen years. Mental growth, then, was defined in terms of the increasing ability manifested, over a period of time, in the performance of certain tests which were assumed to measure mental capacity.

The original set of Binet tests has been revised, " standardized," "validated," and the "reliability" determined. The process of standardization meant that the tests were given to large numbers of children at each age level and norms for performance computed. The reliability was determined by the consistency of the results with similar tests and by the internal consistency of the tests. The validity was determined by taking independent estimates of intelligence — the teachers' opinions, scholastic performances, or a combination of several of these estimates — and correlating them with the results obtained on the tests. It is not our object to criticize in any detail these methods of devising, standardizing and validating the tests. It is sufficiently clear that the results obtained on the tests are open to many interpretations because of the very fact that they measure indirectly qualities, psychological in nature, which are necessarily ill-defined. And the numerical expression of these results cannot give to them a precision or definiteness that the original data lack.

Let us examine the results obtained in these mental tests, and consider their implications from the standpoint of their correlation with behavior.

In the first place, how good are mental tests as a diagnostic agent? When they were first standardized they were given to large groups of school children, presumably unselected, at the various chronological age levels, from 6 years to maturity. The results showed that the ability to pass the tests was distributed among these groups in a continuous frequency curve, with most of the children passing all of the tests set for their chronological age (as, of course, was a necessary result of the way the tests were devised) and hence with the modal group falling at 100 IQ, the curve tapering off gradually towards each end, i.e., a few children could pass scarcely any of the tests at or below their age levels and a few could pass practically all the tests that had been devised. These were supposed to represent the extremes of mental superiority and mental defect.

It soon became obvious that this particular frequency distribution obscured some very important facts about the distribution of these mental abilities. Different modes were found to exist for different races, for city and rural children, for children of different social classes. The tests were given to inmates of feebleminded institutions, and none of them tested over twelve years mental age. This was then assumed to be the dividing line, for adults, for mental defect. Sixteen years mental age had been assumed to be the average limit of mental growth, on the basis of standards established when the tests were given to a small group of high school students and business men. The tests were held to be diagnostic of mental ability, and mental ability was assumed, quite specifically, to be highly correlated with behavior, with ability to adjust to the conditions set down by society. As mentioned above, it had been found that practically no inmate of an institution for mental defectives tested over twelve years mental age, and when the tests were given to inmates of prisons and other adult or juvenile delinquents (the juvenile delinquents were, of course, in the higher chronological age levels for which mental tests were available) it was found that many of them tested below twelve years, and that relatively few of them approached or exceeded the norms set up by the tests standardized for school children. It was therefore assumed that in diagnosing mental defect the tests at the same time gave an explanation of delinquency. Terman's statement that " all feebleminded are at least potential criminals "[8] is fairly typical of the claims that were made.

The diagnostic value of the tests, as picking out the mental defectives from the general population and, as a corollary, designating the nation's potential criminals, was brought seriously into question when the tests were given to the draft army. By using the assumed standard of 12 years as the dividing line between mental defect and normal intelligence, some 47% of the adult white inhabitants and 89% of the negroes of the country would be diagnosed as feebleminded. Thus, the old standards were called into serious question, for obviously it is absurd to assume that we have a proper diagnostic agent in tests that diagnose almost half the adult population as defective, and as being " at least potential criminals." These results have, indeed, called into question very seriously the value of applying such tests at all to adults. They showed that large numbers of the drafted army and, therefore,

---

[8] Terman, Lewis M.: *The Measurement of Intelligence* (1916), 11.

presumably of the whole adult population, had IQ's as low as those of many of the inmates of institutions for mental defectives. The tests were, therefore, not diagnosing the type of " feeblemindedness " that incapacitated individuals for the ordinary demands of society. This was the first real test that had been made with a sufficiently large group of unselected adults, the adult norms having been established from the results obtained on a few high school children and a few business men — only 62 persons altogether. The only other adult applications had been with groups of criminals, where it was assumed that the low standards resulted from the connection between the mental defect, thus diagnosed, and the anti-social behavior. When these new " norms," obtained from the army draft, were applied to the results obtained with criminal groups, it was immediately apparent that mental defect thus defined was not the differentiating factor between the criminals and the drafted men — since the distribution of IQ's, and the average intelligence so diagnosed, was found to be practically the same (see discussion of Murchison, below, p. 365).

It should be immediately acknowledged that the invalidating of the mental tests as a diagnostic agent with regard to the mental ability of adults did not necessarily invalidate them with regard to the mental ability of school children, and, indeed, as we shall later show, they have been a fairly successful agent in diagnosing those children who do not get along in the ordinary course of school instruction — those children who should be put in special or " opportunity " classes and who should be given types of training other than that standardized by custom. These results, however, certainly indicate that the tests are not testing innate abilities, for the relative superiority of school children over adults could scarcely be accounted for on the basis of differences in their innate abilities but must probably be looked for in differences in the immediate environments. There is evidence at hand to show that instead of diagnosing differences in innate ability the IQ tends to diagnose, or to reflect strongly in its diagnosis, differences in environment. Terman has given a different interpretation. He found marked differences in the IQ according to the social class of the children, but attributes this to other causes:

Of the 1000 children, 492 were classified by their teachers according to social class into the following five groups: *very inferior, inferior, average, superior,* and *very superior.* A comparative study was then made of the distribution of I Q's for these different groups. The data may be summarized as follows:

1. The median I Q for children of the superior social class is about 7 points above, and that of the inferior social class about 7 points below, the median I Q of the average social group. This means that by the age of 14 inferior class children are about one year below, and superior class children one year above, the median mental age for all classes taken together.

2. That the children of the superior classes make a better showing in the test is probably due, for the most part, to a superiority in original endowment.[9]

Thus he accounts for the differences in IQ among the different social classes largely on the basis of differences in innate abilities. Indeed, in a later study under his supervision, a study of the early mental traits of geniuses, where the aim was to measure the degree of innate ability for each of these geniuses on the basis of historical data and assign IQ's, this connection is assumed to be so close that the IQ (the measure of " innate " ability) is diagnosed from the social status, or occupational class, of the parents of the genius, in the absence of other data.[10]

But other studies have shown the close correlation between IQ and various environmental factors. Isserlis, working with Burt's tests on English school children, found

a distinct correlation between the intelligence of school children and their environment, whether measured by the economic position of the parents, by the care taken of the home, or by the clothing of the children. The partial correlations for constant age are uniform in sign, of order .3 to .4 and five to six times greater than their probable errors.[11]

The relation of intelligence scores to the occupation held was brought out very clearly in the results of the tests given to the drafted men. The median Alpha scores ranged as follows:

---

[9] Terman, Lewis M.: *The Measurement of Intelligence* (1916), 72.

[10] Cox, Catherine: *The Early Mental Traits of Three Hundred Geniuses.* Vol. II of *Genetic Studies in Genius,* edited by L. M. Terman (1926), 47 ff.

[11] Isserlis, L.: " The Relation Between Home Conditions and the Intelligence of School Children," *Great Britain, Medical Research Council, Special Report Series* No. 74 (1923), 17–18.

THE MEDIAN SCORES IN ARMY ALPHA OF MEN CLASSIFIED AS BELONGING
IN CERTAIN OCCUPATIONS

Occupation	No. of Cases	Median Score
Farmer	6886	48.3
General machinist	1251	62.8
Railroad clerk	308	91.4
Bookkeeper	458	100.9
Accountant	202	117.9
Stenographer or typist	402	115.0
Mechanical engineer	45	109.7
Civil engineer	53	116.8 [12]

Other studies have been made showing the relation of the intelligence of children to the occupations of their fathers. The results obtained by Pressey and Ralston are typical of these studies. They tested 548 unselected children 10 to 14 years of age and found:

1. Of the children of professional men, 85% made scores above the median for the total group; of the children of executives (independent business men, foremen) 68% rated above the median for the total group; of the children of artisans (unskilled workers) 41% rated above the median, and of the children of laborers only 39% rated above the median.

2. The groups overlapped largely, though not completely. Both extremes of the distribution contained some members from each occupational group: however, the artisan and laborer groups predominate at the lower end of the distributions while the professional and executive groups show a majority of the high scores.

3. Analysis by test shows these findings to be constant for all four tests. It is argued from this that the findings have some general reliability.[13]

Terman found, in his study of gifted children, the following proportions for the fathers' occupations as compared with the proportion in the population of Los Angeles and San Francisco:

[12] Freeman, Frank N.: *Mental Tests* (1926), 452.

[13] Pressey, S. L., and Ralston, R.: " The Relation of the General Intelligence of School Children to the Occupation of Their Fathers," *Journal of Applied Psychology*, 3:373 (1919).

	Fathers of Gifted Children	General Population
Professional	29.1%	2.9%
Public Service	4.5	3.3
Commercial	46.2	36.1
Industrial	20.2	57.7 [14]

These studies have shown conclusively that there is a marked correlation between intelligence, as measured by the tests, and such environmental factors as social status and occupational class. But it is possible to make two completely opposing interpretations of these data — and the data, as they stand in these studies, give us no solution to the opposition. Terman claims that his results mean that " the children of successful and cultured parents test higher than children from wretched and ignorant homes for the simple reason that their heredity is better." [15] Colvin, discussing the results of tests given to children of Brookline and Cincinnati, in which the Brookline children made consistently higher scores than the Cincinnati children, says:

An average Brookline child of twelve would have, according to the results of these tests, a mental age about two years in advance of the average Cincinnati child. Are we to conclude, then, that the Cincinnati children are really inferior in innate intelligence to the Brookline children? I am inclined to think not. The great difference in the scores I attribute to differences in opportunities to learn words and their meanings. Examinations of the Otis tests, and other similar tests, will show that success in passing these tests is conditioned largely on extent and accuracy of vocabulary and on verbal ingenuity. In no single element entering into school attainment do children vary so much as in the knowledge of words and the ability to use words. Much of this knowledge and skill is determined by the home environment. Brookline is, on the whole, a center of culture where the children acquire at home an ability to use English in a superior degree. The same is not so conspicuously true in Cincinnati. . . . Clearly, the differences were differences in verbal ability, not in innate intelligence.[16]

[14] Terman, L. M.: *Mental and Physical Traits of a Thousand Gifted Children.* Vol. I of *Genetic Studies in Genius* (1926), 63.

[15] *Measurement of Intelligence*, 115.

[16] Colvin, Stephen S.: "Principles Underlying the Construction and Use of Intelligence Tests," *Yearbook of the National Society for the Study of Education,* 21:21–22 (1922).

Isserlis claims that from his data " we are entitled to conclude that progressive improvement in home conditions may be expected to react favourably . . . on the intelligence of school children." [17]

Now, of course, data of this sort show nothing as to whether the poor environment or poor occupational status caused the low intelligence quotients, or whether people of low intelligence quotients drifted into or were born into and unable, congenitally, to climb out of inferior environments and inferior occupations. Indeed Terman, although extremely dogmatic in the interpretation of his data, as cited above, admits later in his book that the data are not conclusive, and throws out the following challenge: " A crucial experiment would be to take a large number of very young children of the lower classes and, after placing them in the most favorable environment obtainable, to compare their later mental development with that of children born into the best homes." [18]

The nearest approach we have yet had to such a " crucial experiment " has just been completed and published by Frank N. Freeman, Karl J. Holzinger and Blythe Clayton Mitchell.[19] So superior is the methodology of this study and so significant the results that we shall quote from it at considerable length. Their aim was to measure the influence of environment on intelligence. They realized that experiments of the sort described above did not solve the problem as to whether heredity or environment was the variable involved, or whether, indeed, both heredity and environment were varying at the same time:

In order to overcome this difficulty it is necessary to compare persons who are alike in heredity but who have been subjected to different environment or, on the other hand, those who are of diverse heredity but who have been under the influence of the same or similar environment. By the application of intelligence tests, the extent to which one or the other of these factors affect the score could then be determined.

The most completely satisfactory method of bringing about such variations of one factor independently of the other is the experimental method. The experimental method might be used if a group of individuals with similar heredity could be divided into two groups and then subjected to widely

---

[17] *Op. cit.*, 18.

[18] *Measurement of Intelligence*, 116.

[19] " The Influence of Environment on the Intelligence, School Achievement, and Conduct of Foster Children," *Yearbook of the National Society for the Study of Education,* 27:103–217 (1928).

different environmental influences. Such a procedure is obviously difficult to follow in dealing with human beings. It occurred to the writers, however, that the adoption of children might give conditions which resemble the main features of such an experiment. It may be assumed that foster children taken from a society for the care of dependent children will have a heredity which is somewhat below the average. The evidence in our study goes to show that this assumption is justified. There is also reason to believe that when such children are adopted they are introduced into an environment which is superior to that of their own family. This assumption also has evidence to support it.[20]

The children studied included only dependent children who had been committed to the Illinois Children's Home and Aid Society, and placed out for adoption in foster homes. Significant comparisons were made between results on intelligence tests which had been given before adoption, in the case of one group, and results after they had been in the foster home a number of years. Another significant comparison was between children of the same family who had been placed in different foster homes, the homes being rated on a scale which took into consideration the material environment, evidence of culture, occupation of foster father, education of foster parents, and social activity of foster parents. Both these comparisons had held heredity constant, letting environment vary — and the third significant comparison held environment constant, letting heredity vary, i.e., concerned itself with a comparison of the intelligence of the own children of foster parents with the foster children. These comparisons deserve detailed consideration. With regard to the first, that is, the comparison of the intelligence of children before and after being in the foster homes, the authors say:

If the intelligence of a group of children were measured before and after they had been under the influence of a certain environment it would be possible to measure the effects of that environment independent of heredity.

Such conditions are met by a group of 134 children who were given mental tests several years previous to the present study, in the majority of cases just before their placement in foster homes. These tests were made by the Institute for Juvenile Research with the use of the Stanford Revision of the Binet Scale. Since they were administered by the trained psychologists of the Institute they may be regarded as reliable. The results of the tests may, therefore, be directly compared with those found in the present study.

---

[20] *Ibid.*, 105–6.

The first tests on these children were made for various reasons, the chief being a suspicion of low mentality. In case a child showed signs of dulness tests were usually given to the other children in the family also. Other children were tested because their parents were known to be defective. In some cases a prospective foster parent asked that the child be given a test in order to be assured that he had normal mentality. Occasionally a child exhibiting abnormal behavior was given a mental test.

In order to trace separately the effect of different types of environment the 134 cases were divided into three groups.

1. In 74 cases the child was placed in a foster home shortly after his first mental test and spent the entire intervening time in that home.

2. The second group is made up of 38 children who spent the interval between the tests in more than one foster home or institution.

3. The remaining 22 were children who were given their first test some time after their placement in a foster home.

It will be noted that these groups represent three different environmental situations. In Group 1 the environment changed, probably for the better, just after the first test and remained the same after that time. Since the children in Group 2 spent the interval between the tests in several environments no complete measure of the influence could be obtained. In Group 3 the children lived in the same environment before and after the first test, hence it was impossible to determine the entire influence of the foster home by the change in intelligence during the interval.[21]

An appreciable gain in IQ was found for Group 1. It was found, however, that these children had entered the foster homes at a fairly late age, averaging eight years, and that the foster homes averaged lower in status than those for the whole study:

In order to throw further light on the effect of these factors, type of home and age of placement, the data were divided in two ways. As noted before, the mean home rating index of this group was 16.7. The children were put into two groups for which the home ratings fell above and below this value. . . .

These figures indicate that the children in the better homes made a gain of 5.3 points in intelligence. Since this value is four times its P.E. it may be regarded as significant. In the case of the poorer homes a very insignificant gain was found (.1). Owing to the faulty standardization of the test, however, the gain of 5.3 would probably mean an actual gain of about 10.4 points, while the slight gain in the case of the poorer homes group would mean a

---

[21] "The Influence of Environment on the Intelligence, School Achievement, and Conduct of Foster Children," *Yearbook of the National Society for the Study of Education*, 27:115–16 (1928).

gain of about 5 points. . . . These facts show that improvement in intelligence is directly related to the type of foster home. . . .

The second division of the group [was] made on the basis of age. . . . The two groups consisted of children who were above and below the mean age of the entire group. The children of the older group spent the years from 10 to 14 in the foster home, while the interval for the younger children was from 6 to 10.

The observed gain for the younger group was 5.2 points while for the older group there was a slight loss in I.Q. It might also be noted that both groups actually made significant gains since about 5 points would need to be added in both cases to correct for the test. The difference of 5.6 points between the two gains is significant, which would indicate that improvement in intelligence is appreciably greater in the case of younger children.[22]

The children in Group 2, who had been shifted about during the interval between the tests, made gains that were scarcely significant, and those of Group 3, who had been in the foster homes for some time before the test was given, likewise showed insignificant gains:

The large gain made by the children of Group 1 appears even more significant in the light of the smaller gains made by the other groups. The children in this group were those who were placed in foster homes just after their first test and have remained in those homes since that time. This constitutes the chief difference between this group and the other two. It would seem, therefore, that their greater gain was due, at least in part, to their more favorable environment. It should be noted that the children of Group 3 may have at some time made a gain as great as that of Group 1, but such could not be determined in the present comparisons because there was no record of their intelligence before they entered the foster home.

The results on these Pre-Test groups ["Pre-Test groups" are those who had had tests before being taken into foster homes] have shown that children placed at eight years of age in relatively poor homes show a significant gain in intelligence. A much greater gain might be expected had they been placed at an earlier age in higher grade homes.[23]

The second important comparison made by these investigators also represented an attempt to hold heredity constant by comparing children of the same family who had been placed in different homes. A group of 159 children (forming 130 sibling pairs), consisting of pairs who had in every case been separated at least four years, gave the necessary data:

---

[22] *Ibid.*, 118.   [23] *Ibid.*, 122.

The correlation between the intelligence of these 159 children and their foster home rating was .40±.04, indicating a tendency for the children raised in better homes to be brighter. A point to be considered is the extent to which selection might affect this relationship. If the better parents had adopted brighter children, that is, made their selection on the basis of intelligence, the observed correlation might have been due to this fact alone and could not be attributed to subsequent environmental influence. While it is impossible to determine the amount of actual selection for this group, a consideration of the matter from several angles has lead to the conclusion that it probably exists but not in sufficient amount to account entirely for the strong correspondence found between the child's intelligence and his foster home. . . .

The siblings were paired in two ways. According to the first method the score for the older of a pair was always tabulated in the same direction on the table, while in the second scheme every pair of scores was entered twice. . . .

The average age of separation of these pairs was 5 years 4 months. The mean age at the time of the test was 12 years 8 months indicating an average separation period of over 7 years.

One of the most important correlations found in the study was that between the present intelligence of these siblings. This coefficient was .34 ± .05 by the method based on age and .25±.06 by the double entry scheme. Both of these results are considerably lower than the correlations usually found for siblings reared together. The " coefficient of heredity," as it is called, is approximately .50. It thus appears that residence in different homes tends to make siblings differ from one another in intelligence.

A factor which affects the above relationship is the age at which the siblings were separated. For the siblings of this group who were separated after both were five years of age the correlation between their intelligence was found to be .49±.08 on the age basis (N=38) and .43±.09 by double entry. These results are similar to the usual coefficients of fraternal resemblance. The corresponding correlations found in the case of siblings separated before either was six years old (46 cases) were .32±.09 and .25±.09 respectively. Separation in foster homes at the early formative years of life thus appears to account in a large measure for the lowered heredity coefficient. . . .

In order to study the differential effect of the homes upon the resemblance of the siblings the 125 pairs were divided into two groups according to whether the difference in the home ratings of the pair was more or less than 4 points. The correlation between the intelligence of the siblings raised in the more similar homes (62 pairs) was .39 ± .07 by the age and .30 ± .08 by the double entry method. For the pairs in widely different homes (N = 63) the correlations were .28±.08 and .19±.08 respectively. These results furnish some evidence that siblings raised in distinctly different environments are less alike in their mental ability than are those raised in the same or in similar environments.[24]

The third important comparison of this study represents an attempt to control the environment, letting the heredity vary. The comparisons are between two unrelated children who have been raised in the same home. There were forty pairings of a foster child with an own child raised in the same home, and seventy-two pairings of two unrelated foster children raised in the same home. The foster children were found to be inferior in general intelligence to the own children, the mean intelligence quotient for the two groups being 95.1 and 112.1. The authors emphasize, however, that, although the environment was the same, the period of residence in this environment had been from birth for the own children and for less than two-thirds of their lives for the foster children:

From the data for this group it is apparent that adopted children are considerably lower in intelligence than own children in the same homes. It is probable that the difference is due partly to heredity and partly to early environment. The intelligence of the foster children would quite probably have been greater had they been adopted earlier in life. Comparisons made later show that the earlier children are adopted the higher is their intelligence.

Significant correlations [of the order of .4] were found when the intelligence of the foster children was compared with that of own children or with the rating of the foster home.[25]

The data on the foster children raised in the same home gave a correlation of .37 between the intelligence of these foster children — showing again the equalizing effect of similar environment on the intelligence quotient:

In conclusion, it should be noted that there was probably some tendency for two children of similar mental ability to be placed in the same foster home. If such selection did not exist the expected correlation between the intelligence of the two children at the time of their adoption would be zero. It would still be zero after several years of residence in the same home unless the intelligence of the children was modified by the new environment. Since all

---

[24] " The Influence of Environment on the Intelligence, School Achievement, and Conduct of Foster Children," *Yearbook of the National Society for the Study of Education,* 27:126–29 (1928).

[25] *Ibid.,* 138.

of the observed correlation of .40 could hardly be due to selection, it is highly probable that such modification actually took place. The influence of environment, therefore, is shown by the fact that when two unrelated children are raised in the same home, differences in their intelligence tend to decrease.[26]

Now, all this evidence regarding the environmental concomitants of " intelligence " has very important bearings upon the diagnostic value of the intelligence quotient. The IQ has been shown to vary with social class and with occupational status. This study of Freeman and his associates shows the very important fact that it varies for people of the same heredity, depending on the social environment in which they have been placed and on the length of time they have been exposed to any particular environment, and that it tends to become equalized for people of different heredity placed in the same environment, again depending on the period of exposure to the environment. This dependence is far from being absolute, but it is sufficient to show that in considering the IQ as a diagnostic agent the influence of social status and occupational class as well as of innate mental ability should be taken into consideration.

Another important study that has recently been made on foster children contributes interesting evidence as to the influence of environment on the IQ. This is the study published by Barbara Stoddard Burks on " The Relative Influence of Nature and Nurture upon Mental Development; a Comparative Study of Foster Parent-Foster Child Resemblance and True Parent-True Child Resemblance." [27] This study was made at Stanford University under Terman's direction. The methodology is quite different from that used by Freeman. The problem here was to work out the exact proportions contributed to IQ by " nature " and by " nurture." The study " seeks to evaluate the effects of nature and of home nurture through a study of two kinds of familial resemblance, one of which is dependent upon nurture influence alone and the other upon a combination of both nature and nurture influences." [28] The familial group where the resemblance was dependent on nurture alone was com-

[26] " The Influence of Environment on the Intelligence, School Achievement, and Conduct of Foster Children," *Yearbook of the National Society for the Study of Education*, 27:139–40 (1928).

[27] *Yearbook of the National Society for the Study of Education*, 27:219–316, (1928).

[28] *Ibid.*, 221.

posed of 204 foster children and their foster parents. The bases of selection were as follows:

1. Children were placed in their foster homes before the age of 12 months. (The average age of placement of our group proved to be 3 months, 2 days.)
2. Children were legally adopted — not merely cared for in free or boarding homes.
3. Children were between 5 and 14 years, inclusive, at the time of the investigation.
4. Foster parents were white, non-Jewish, English-speaking, and American, British, or north-European-born.
5. True parents (so far as was definitely known) were white, non-Jewish, Americans, British, or north-Europeans.
6. Children were placed in the home of a married couple, both members of which were alive and living together at the time of the investigation.
7. Cases must be accessible to the three centers — San Francisco Bay region, Los Angeles, and San Diego.[29]

The group where the resemblance might be considered due both to nature and to nurture consisted of 105 children and their own parents. These served as a control group and were matched with the foster group as follows:

1. Children of the Control Group were matched with those of the Foster Group for age, sex, and number of five-year-olds who had had no kindergarten attendance.
2. Control families were matched with foster families for locality, type of neighborhood, and occupational field of the father.
3. Non-Jewish, white American, British, or north-European families who spoke English were taken.
4. Both parents were alive and living together at the time of the investigation.
5. Only one child per family was tested (though families were not selected with respect to size).[30]

Children and parents were given the Stanford-Binet test, homes were rated according to the Whittier Scale, which is supposed to be an index of environment. This scale is a composite of ratings on necessities, neatness, size, " parental conditions," and parental supervision. The parents were also rated on a " culture scale " and data were collected as to their education, interests, books in their library, " artistic taste," etc. The correlation coefficients between the child's IQ and his own parents'

[29] *Ibid.*, 236. [30] *Ibid.*, 242.

IQ are of the order $+.5$, whereas those between the foster child's IQ and his foster parents' IQ are of the order $+.2$. Some of the correlation coefficients used are very difficult to interpret, but the inference is probable that the child's IQ is more closely related to his own parents' mental age than to that of his foster parents. To find the proportion contributed by nature and nurture, multiple correlation coefficients were worked out between the child's IQ and the foster father's mental age, foster father's vocabulary, foster mother's vocabulary and family income in the one group and child's IQ with own father's mental age, own father's vocabulary, own mother's mental age and " Whittier index." The multiple correlation coefficients were respectively .35 and .53. These were corrected for " attenuation " (see Appendix for explanation) giving corrected coefficients of .42 and .61. This led to the author's conclusion that " the multiple correlation corrected for attenuation (.42) is a measure in the Foster Group of the effect of home environment upon differences in children's intelligence. More precisely, the *square* of this multiple (.17) represents the portion of the variance of children in ordinary communities that is due to home environment." [31] And " in the Control Group the square (.37) of the multiple correlation corrected for attenuation (.61) represents the *combined* effect of home environment and parental mental level upon the variance of children's intelligence." [32] It is further concluded that 34% represents the " unique contribution of parental intelligence," and that the major share of the remaining variance is " probably . . . due to congenital endowment since in known modes of hereditary transmission the influence of heredity is *always* far stronger than parental correlations alone would indicate." About 5% of the variance is allowed for " random somatic effects of environment " and the final conclusion is reached that " close to 75% or 80% of IQ variance [is due] to innate and heritable causes." [33]

These conclusions, of course, go far beyond the data. However, taking the results, rather than the conclusions, in conjunction with those found by Freeman, we are impressed with the inference that emerges from both of them, i.e., that the IQ is quite definitely a function of environment as well as of " heredity," although there is no conclusive evidence as to the relative influence of the two factors.

The studies which have recently been made on changes in the IQ of

[31] *Yearbook of the National Society for the Study of Education*, 27:298 (1928).
[32] *Ibid.*, 299.   [33] *Ibid.*, 304.

pre-school age children throw further light on the environmental factors in the intelligence quotient. The tests at the early age levels are generally admitted to be imperfectly standardized and more subject to variation because of emotional differences than at the later age levels. Nevertheless, there should be a certain comparability for groups, selected in various ways, at these age levels. Dr. Helen T. Woolley presents data on changes in the IQ of nursery school children from the Merrill-Palmer School, as compared with changes of children of the same age levels selected from similar environments in other ways who had not had nursery school experience and were at the time on the waiting list of the Merrill-Palmer School. There were forty-three cases in the nursery school group and thirty-six in the control group. The age range was from two years six months to five years two months, and the interval between tests from seven to fourteen months. Her results were as follows:

One third of the Merrill-Palmer children have increased 20 points or more in intelligence quotient whereas only 6 per cent. of those on the waiting list . . . have made increases of that amount. On the other hand, in terms of decreases, there were only 10 per cent. of the Merrill-Palmer group who decreased 20 points or more while there were 16 per cent. on the waiting list. . . . If one allows a range of change of 5 per cent. plus or minus, in which the result is called constant, then the figures come out as follows: In the Merrill-Palmer group there were 63 per cent. increases, 18.5 per cent. decreases, and 18.5 per cent. constant. The average increase for the group which did increase is 19.7 points, whereas the average decrease for the group which decreased is 10.8 points. The corresponding figures for the children on the waiting list are that 33 per cent. of them increased, 36 per cent. decreased and 31 per cent. remained constant.[34]

Her conclusion is:

It . . . seems to be true that a certain part of what we later call " level intelligence " may be due to the opportunities to learn given to young children. Very young children may show striking increases of intelligence quotient when placed in a very superior environment. We do not as yet know how permanent these increases are. What evidence we have shows that they tend to be maintained, though perhaps not at quite so high a level. Doubtless much will depend upon whether the superior environment can be maintained over

---

[34] Woolley, Helen T.: " The Validity of Standards of Mental Measurement in Young Childhood," *School and Society,* 21:479 (April 18, 1925).

a long enough period to consolidate the gains the child has made, and make them a really permanent part of his equipment.[35]

These data are interesting from the point of view of the studies made by both Freeman and Burks. They tend to support Freeman's conclusions about the greater effects of the environment on the intelligence of the children who are adopted at the younger age levels.

An investigation by Dr. Florence Goodenough at the Institute of Child Welfare of the University of Minnesota, however, brings forward results that conflict with those of Dr. Woolley. Unfortunately, the studies have not been made in comparable statistical units and cannot, therefore, be directly compared with each other. Dr. Goodenough's study

is based upon a comparison of the intelligence quotients earned by 28 children before and after a year's attendance at the nursery school conducted by the University of Minnesota Institute of Child Welfare with the corresponding mental ratings of an equal number of paired controls.[36]

This pairing with a control group was done very carefully, the children being matched in regard to sex, age, IQ on each of two tests with interval between the tests, paternal occupation, education of parents and nativity of parents. The nursery school group was divided into two age groups, ranging from 2 years to 2 years 6 months, and from 3 years 3 months to 4 years 2 months respectively:

The mean IQ earned on the first test by the younger group was 110.9, on the second test 114.1, on the third test 122.4. The mean ratings of the older group were 111.6 on the first test, 119.5 on the second test, and 128.1 on the third test.[37]

For the younger control group the mean change in IQ was practically the same as for the younger nursery school group, being 8.0 and 9.9 respectively. There was somewhat greater difference in the case of the older nursery group and older control group, the mean changes being 12.5 and 8.8 respectively. Although not in the same form as Dr. Woolley's data, it is obvious that the differences found are much less than those found on the Merrill-Palmer children. Actually, the older nur-

---

[35] Woolley, Helen T.: "The Validity of Standards of Mental Measurement in Young Childhood," *School and Society*, 21:482 (April 18, 1925).

[36] Goodenough, Florence L.: "A Preliminary Report on the Effect of Nursery School Training upon the Intelligence Test Scores of Young Children," *Yearbook of the National Society for the Study of Education*, 27:361 (1928).

[37] *Ibid.*, 364.

sery and control group is the only one comparable with Dr. Woolley's data, and this does show a greater amount of change than the younger. The results must, therefore, be considered somewhat inconclusive, although all these investigations confirm the opinion that the IQ is a function of environment. The only question is one of degree.

The value of the intelligence quotient depends ultimately upon its prognostic ability. If an IQ, within a specified range, picks out certain classes of people whose abilities and behavior trends are shown to be linked up with this intelligence quotient, then, given an IQ or a series of IQ's, we should be able to predict future performance and behavior. Within what limits has this predictive value of the IQ proved valid?

Before we can give an adequate answer to this question we must run through some of the evidence bearing on the relation of IQ to performance in school, for it is in this field that we have reason to expect the prognostic ability to be greatest.

The IQ obtained is very closely related to the amount of schooling obtained. There are many data at hand to show that, on the average, this generalization holds true. But the interpretation of these data is open to the same difficulties as were found in the interpretation of the correspondence between occupational status and environment, on the one hand, and intelligence on the other. Does the person with more schooling rank higher on the intelligence tests than the person with less schooling because of the dependence of intelligence tests on matter learned in school, or is the correspondence due to the fact that only those of high intelligence can progress far in school?

First, let us consider the nature of the evidence regarding the relation between intelligence quotient and amount of schooling. Cyril Burt's study of the intelligence of unselected London public school children took account of this relationship by computing each child's score on educational tests as well as on the Binet and other intelligence tests, thus getting comparable intelligence quotients and educational quotients. He found a correlation of .738 between the two for 689 children, ranging in age from seven to fourteen. Furthermore, by holding age and intelligence (as measured by a special reasoning ability test) constant, he found a correlation between the Binet intelligence quotients and educational quotients of .61. This gives evidence of a marked connection between the two.[38] More interesting still, he found that those school

---

[38] Burt's interpretation of the meaning of his partial coefficients, when he worked out the regression equation as indicating " the relative proportions in which the

children who were most retarded mentally were still more retarded educationally.

But Burt and the others who made similar investigations were still faced with the problem of explaining the basis of this connection between the amount of educational achievement and the intelligence quotient. The most nearly conclusive study made in this field was an attempt by Hugh Gordon [39] to get at the roots of this problem by studying and comparing the intelligence and educational quotients of children who had had varying degrees of schooling. Regarding the general bearing of this investigation he says:

In the course of some investigations among physically defective children it was found that not only in scholastic attainments were they much below the average — a fact that was well known — but also that their so-called " mental " attainments were equally low — a result that had not been generally suspected. At first it seemed reasonable to infer that the retardation in scholastic attainments was chiefly due to inferior native ability. On further investigation, however, it became clear that this lack of " intelligence," as measured by the " mental " tests used, could not be due to heredity or environment, but that it was probably due to their lack of schooling — a result in direct opposition to the opinion held by many authorities. For example, Terman, who carried out an extensive revision of the Binet-Simon tests (the Stanford scale), and whose tests were used throughout the following investigations, says: " That the lack of schooling does not prevent a subject from earning an average or superior score in the test is shown by the cases of S. S. and Gipsy Mary."

On the other hand, Cyril Burt, in his extensive researches among London children, came to a somewhat different conclusion. He says in reference to the Binet-Simon tests: " But to achieve distinction, at all events in a trial so academic as the Binet-Simon tests, experience must be heavily supplemented; it must be reinforced either by the artificial aids supplied by a civilised society or by the natural stimulus of an unusual native wit. Imagine two children,

three factors — age, intelligence and school attainments — together determine a child's achievements in the Binet-Simon tests " and claimed that this equation showed that " one-ninth is attributable to age, one-third to intellectual development, and over one-half to school attainment " (*Mental and Scholastic Tests*, 1922, 183) is grossly erroneous, as Holzinger and Freeman pointed out in " The Interpretation of Burt's Regression Equation," *Journal of Educational Psychology*, 16:577–82 (1925).

[39] " Mental and Scholastic Tests among Retarded Children," *Great Britain Board of Education, Educational Pamphlets*, No. 44 (1923).

aged seven and seventeen respectively, both possessing an intelligence equally normal, neither having passed a single hour in school. The younger, as a consideration of the several tests will show, might reach a mental age of six; the older, despite ten years seniority, barely that of nine. So barren is growth deprived of opportunity."

These quotations are of special interest, as during the series of investigations a number of gipsies were actually tested, and also nearly the same number of Canal Boat children, whose attendance at school had been negligible. Among the latter were found children who may be regarded as representing almost exactly the two cases suggested by Burt in the above quotation.

The conclusion as to the influence of attendance at school on the mental tests led to an investigation among Canal Boat children who had had little or no schooling, and a still further investigation among gipsy children whose attendance at school was well known to be very irregular and intermittent. Finally, a very different type of retardation was tested — that of "backwardness" in ordinary Elementary Schools, due apparently to natural dulness and not to lack of schooling.[40]

The findings with regard to the physically defective children were as follows:

There is a very close approximation between the average "mental" and "educational" ratios — 86.7 and 86.9 respectively. The correlation between these two ratios was for one school .785, P.E. .025; for the other, .707, P.E. .037. The mean of these two correlations (roughly .746) differs but little from that (.738) found by Burt after a most searching investigation among normal children. . . .

The low average "mental ratio" [IQ] did not appear to be due to: (a) Social environment and heredity, as these were of a character one would expect to find in an average or medium school; or to (b) The physical defects themselves, apart from the resulting loss of schooling, except in a few diseases such as hemiplegia and diplegia.

The low average ratios ("mental" and "educational") seem to be undoubtedly due to the loss of schooling brought about by the various physical defects. The attendances from 5 years of age of 84 of these children were accurately determined; the percentage of possible attendance was found to be 48, compared with the 88 per cent. average attendance of ordinary Elementary School children. The correlations between the "mental ratios" and these attendances, and between "educational ratios" and these attendances were found to be exactly the same, namely, .313, P. E. [probable error] .066. These correlations are high considering the various factors involved, e.g.,

---

[40] Ibid., 5–6.

possible education at home. The fact that the correlation between the " mental ratio " and attendance is exactly the same as that between the " educational ratio " and attendance definitely indicated that the lack of schooling has had the same effect on the " intelligence " (as found by the tests) as it has had on scholastic attainments.

These conclusions are still further strengthened by the results obtained when the " mental ratios " for various diseases are compared. Although at first it appears that some physical defects have a more marked effect on the " intelligence " than others, yet it is equally evident that the higher " mental ratio " for any given disease is nearly always associated with a better attendance, the exception being such diseases as hemiplegia and diplegia, both of which are due to some defect of the brain.[41]

In order to test further the conclusions obtained with the physically defective children Gordon made studies of two other groups of children who had had very little schooling, i.e., Canal Boat children and gipsy children. His findings were as follows:

Canal Boat population live an isolated life, almost patriarchal in character. In health, morals, etc., they compare favourably with town dwellers of the same class. The children are " scandalously undereducated; " their attendance at school averages about 4 to 5 per cent., compared with the 88 per cent. of children in ordinary Elementary Schools. . . .

The average mental ratio of the seventy-six children tested was 69.6 — a very low ratio when compared with those found in ordinary Elementary Schools. In a very superior (socially) school the ratio is 112; in a very poor school, 87; in schools for physically defective children, 85, and in schools for mentally defective children, 63. . . .

The educational ratio of the thirty-six children who could do the simple scholastic tests was only slightly lower than the mental ratio (70.4 and 71.5 respectively). . . . The correlation (a) between the mental and educational ratios was .715, P. E. .054 — a high correlation.

The correlation between " intelligence " (test) and age was (—) .755, P. E. ± .033 — a very high negative correlation, indicating unquestionably that with an increase of age there was a corresponding decrease in " intelligence." The same conclusion was to be drawn from a comparison of the mental ratios of the children in the same family. Here also it is evident that even in the same family the older the child the less " intelligence " he has. This result makes it almost certain that the low average " intelligence " of the children in this school is not due to heredity, seeing that the youngest children test more or less normally, i.e., are of average " intelligence."

---

[41] " Mental and Scholastic Tests among Retarded Children," *Great Britain Board of Education, Educational Pamphlets,* No. 44:31–32 (1923).

The tests found most difficult were those that might be expected to have been influenced by schooling, *e.g.*, the vocabulary and drawing tests, and the making of sentences; those found the easiest were tests that are generally judged to be more independent of schooling, such as the absurdities, counting thirteen pennies, and repeating numbers backward. . . .

In the case of gipsy children also there has been a serious lack of schooling, and many attempts have been made to provide them with more education, but the question is surrounded by many and great difficulties due to the nomad habits of their parents. It is not merely a school question, but a question involving the life and habits of the gipsy population. Gipsies seldom stay in one place for any considerable time, except perhaps during the winter months; at other times they are moving from place to place fruit-picking and hopping, etc., *e.g.*, attending race meetings. The attendance of the children at school is therefore very irregular and much broken up. On account of this irregularity and of the unconventional mode of life, it seemed likely that an investigation on gipsy children on similar lines to that on Canal Boat children might yield interesting results, more especially as their attendance at school might probably be considerably more than that of Canal Boat, but considerably less than that of physically defective children. . . . They [gipsies] live a nomadic life, but they have much more social intercourse than the Canal Boat population. Their standard of health and living is fully up to that of the agricultural population. Their attendance at school is very irregular, averaging about 35 per cent. instead of the 88 per cent. of the ordinary Elementary School child. . . .

The average mental ratio of the 82 gipsies was 74.5, a very low ratio, but higher than that of the Canal Boat children (69.6); 35 per cent had a mental ratio under 70. . . . The educational ratio of the 60 children who could do the simple scholastic tests was 2 per cent higher than the mental ratio (77.4 and 75.4). . . .

The correlations between the mental ratios and attendance (.368) and between the mental ratios and age (—.430) are both very high considering all the circumstances. The correlation between the mental ratios and educational ratios (.784) and between the mental ratios and the reading (.641), the adding (.645) and the subtracting ratios (.712) are all very high, especially that between the mental and educational ratios. . . .

These results seem fully to confirm the conclusions formed in the previous investigations on physically defective and on Canal Boat children, namely, that the mental tests used do not measure native ability apart from schooling except in the case of very young children, and, further, that for all practical school purposes simple standardised scholastic tests are of equal value.

The far more important question suggested by these results is whether there is any mental development apart from mental effort and such mental exercises as are generally associated with school life. The answer to this question probably depends on the social environment of the children. In a good social environment a child's development would not be so dependent on the effects of schooling as in a poor social environment in which there was little or no intellectual life. Further, it would seem that too long a delay in a beginning of school life has had a very injurious effect on such children as have been tested, that, in fact, it is almost impossible to make up for such delay. As to whether these children would do any better in " performance " and other tests is a question of much interest.[42]

Gordon's final comparison was with children who might, on other grounds than the tests, be considered dull, i.e., children in special classes, who had not been able to get along in the ordinary school classes. The results showed a somewhat lesser connection between mental ratio and educational ratio, the correlation coefficient being .668. The correlations between attendance and mental ratio and attendance and educational ratio were small when compared with those obtained for the gipsy children but the attendance-educational relationship was closer than the attendance-mental.

An investigation of this sort, quite naturally, leaves many questions unsolved, and does not give any final answer to the question of the dependence of intelligence quotient on the amount of schooling received. It does show quite definitely that there is a tendency for the IQ to vary directly with the amount of schooling received. Gordon's own conclusions from his data are stated as follows:

From the results obtained among children who get most of their education at school and very little at home it is very evident that the mental tests used do not measure their native ability apart from schooling, except in the case of children under 6 or 7 years of age. Whether this inability is due to the lack of development of mental powers or to the mental tests being mere tests of school attainments is a question of some interest. It seems probable that without the mental exercises (which are provided as a rule by schooling but among children in a higher social status by home influences) there is little mental development of an intellectual character. Whether there is among such children mental development in other directions is quite another question, which can only be answered by devising and standardising tests suitable for the special kind of environment of the children under investigation. . . .

[42] " Mental and Scholastic Tests among Retarded Children," *Great Britain Board of Education, Educational Pamphlets*, No. 44:43–60 (1923).

In conclusion, it is quite evident that, although the mental tests used do undoubtedly test some kind of ability or abilities, such abilities are not developed without schooling or its equivalent, and as a consequence the tests do not evaluate them apart from schooling except *perhaps* in the case of children under 6 or 7 years of age.[43]

Returning, then, to the question of the prognostic value of the intelligence quotient, the data which we have presented suggest that this prognostic value would be more limited than the psychometrists have usually claimed. Even assuming that innate mental qualities determine behavior, we have seen that these mental qualities (it seems almost anomalous to call them innate) are distinctly modified by the environment, and are quite definitely bound up with the amount of schooling received. It would seem probable, therefore, that the predictive value of the IQ would be limited to conditions of quite stable environment.

We should expect from the history of the preparation of the tests that the IQ would give a good prognosis of the ability of a child to get along in school. When, however, we examine the data that have been accumulated on the relation of IQ to success in school (as measured by school grades) they show clearly that the IQ taken by itself gives no more than a fair prognosis of school success. W. W. Charters says in this connection:

Correlation between intelligence rankings and school marks is not high enough to be considered more than prima facie evidence of its existence. The correlation runs from plus 0.40 to plus 0.60, and plus 0.50 is the accepted average. This means merely that there is a slight tendency for bright students to make high grades in class, and it means nothing more. In general, the brighter students make higher grades, but not often enough to give us much confidence in predicting more than that they *ought* to make higher grades.[44]

Just how little this must mean in considering individual cases is shown in a typical example, worked out on the basis of the intelligence tests at Brown University:

It may be said that with coefficients between intelligence and scholastic standing having a central tendency around .45, the following statements represent the facts as they have been found to exist at Brown University. (" High " and " low " refer to ranks on the psychological tests):

---

[43] *Ibid.*, 87.

[44] " Success, Personality, and Intelligence," *Journal of Educational Research,* 11:169–70 (1925).

1. " High " men have a good chance of graduating. " Low " men have a much smaller chance.

2. Roughly speaking, three-fourths of the " high " men do satisfactory scholastic work. Only one-third of the " low " men do so.

3. Among the men who receive " warnings " at mid-term (semester one) the " low " men out-number the " high " seven to one.

4. " Low " men are from five to seven times more likely to have poor academic records at the end of the first semester than are the " high " men.

5. As a group, the academic work of the " high " men is far ahead of the class achievement as a whole and the work of the " low " men is of a distinctly inferior quality.

6. Coupled with poor academic work at the end of the first semester a low psychological score is a reasonably just criterion for dismissing men from college at that time.

7. Four times out of five the scholastic honors awarded in college go to " high " men. The rest of the chances belong to the " medium " men since the " low " man is practically out of the running. He may have about one chance out of a hundred of getting one honor but almost without exception those who get more than one honor are " high " men.[45]

Considering the claims that have been made for them, it is amazing that the intelligence tests give no better prognosis of school success than that " roughly speaking, three-fourths of the ' high ' men do satisfactory scholastic work " and that the " ' high ' men have a good chance of graduating."

Breed found, indeed, in dealing with a large group of pupils that when " classified into three sections by the composite of three intelligence tests and the classification is later checked by carefully obtained objective measures of school achievement, the error of classification is found to run as high as 50 per cent., — half of all the pupils." [46]

If, then, no more than half the children progress in school in accordance with the prediction that their IQ would make, we must accept the fact that we have in the IQ a very inadequate prognostic agent of scholastic success. And there is no trustworthy evidence at hand to show that its prognostic qualities are anything like as good for the vocational

[45] Colvin, S. S., and MacPhail, A. H.: " The Value of Psychological Tests at Brown University," School and Society, 16:122 (July 29, 1922).

[46] Breed, F. S.: " Shall We Classify Pupils by Intelligence Tests," School and Society, 15:409 (April 15, 1922).

or extra-school activities as for success in school. Charters says in this connection:

If we turn from the school field to the vocational field and seek to predict success in business from intelligence scores, the case is strikingly hopeless. On numerous occasions it has been demonstrated that the correlation between intelligence scores and success in salesmanship drops below the school correlation of plus 0.50 and hovers around zero. The bright man is no more likely to make a good salesman than is one less bright. The methods of measuring success may be faulty, but it is a peculiar fact, as well as a significant one, that no matter what the method for measuring success may be — be it earning power or judgment of executives — there is no correlation.[47]

Let us consider further the evidence coming in regarding the successful adjustment of institutional cases of the feebleminded to the ordinary demands of community life. Bernstein's experience at Rome, New York, was that about 40% of the institution cases could be either put immediately on parole or cared for under the limited supervision of the colony scheme, and that, of those sent to colonies, one-third could thereafter be paroled.[48] Of 82 feebleminded girls under the supervision of the New York Probation and Protective Association, after a period of one to two years, " 4 were lost track of, so that their adjustment is an unknown quantity; 35 are considered to have done well, in that they have not been delinquent and have worked with fair regularity; and 43 were failures in community life." [49] Pintner and Reamer made a study of a group of 26 delinquent girls, wards of the Big Sisters Association:

The result of our study is negative, in the sense that so far as this group of girls is concerned, the mental tests were not prognostic of their success after leaving the Big Sisters Home. Considering the cases as divided into two groups, normal and backward, we find that the backward group is just as likely to make good as the normal. Our study lacks a sound objective criterion by which to measure success in the world. Owing to the circumstances the emphasis was laid upon the moral behavior. This is undoubtedly to a very great extent a condition dependent upon the environment, and it would seem

[47] Charters: op. cit., 170.

[48] Bernstein, C.: "Colony and Parole Care for Dependents and Defectives," Mental Hygiene, 7:449–71 (1923).

[49] Greene, E.: "Histories of 79 Feebleminded Girls Under Supervision in the Community," Mental Hygiene, 7:788 (1923).

that the type of girl studied, whether normal or backward in intelligence, has not the ability to protect herself against an unfavorable environment.[50]

These studies indicate that large proportions of diagnosed feeble-minded are able to take their place in the community, with apparently satisfactory economic and social adjustment, and that large proportions of those selected on the basis of high IQ do not adjust well in ordinary public schools and colleges.

Many investigators have called attention to this low prognostic value of the IQ. Some years back Stenquist made out " The Case for the Low IQ," and purported to show that the demands of modern civilization were often met most successfully by those who tested low on intelligence tests. " What shall we say," he asks, " for the lamented low intelligence of the New York boy who escaped from an institution for mental defectives, and who before the authorities recaptured him had obtained and was holding a job paying him $37 per week as a foreman in a blacksmith shop? " [51]

Of course, the citing of cases showing the low or high prognostic value of the IQ in this or that situation is futile. The problem is fundamentally a statistical one and, in the few fields where it has been attacked statistically, the prognostic value has not been found to be high. Children do not, on the average, progress in school in the way predicted by their IQ's, the feebleminded from institutions do not adjust in society in the ways predicted by their IQ's, and the success of business men, salesmen or executives seems to occur entirely irrespective of the IQ. All this should be said with limitations, the chief of which is that the IQ has been shown quite definitely to possess a fairly constant and reliable negative prognostic value in some fields. The limit may be roughly set below which a child may not pursue successfully a high school career, or a college course. In a study of successful business men, Bingham and Davis found that, although there was no correlation within the group between intelligence and success, their intelligence scores all fell within the upper half of the population (as determined by the scores of the draft army), " which suggests that at least this minimum of mental

---

[50] Pintner, R., and Reamer, J.: " Mental Ability and Future Success of Delinquent Girls," *Journal of Delinquency*, 3:78–79 (1918).

[51] Stenquist, John L.: " The Case for the Low I.Q.," *Journal of Educational Research*, 4:243 (1921).

alertness as measured by an intelligence test, is important for business success." [52]

Another limitation to the statement that the IQ does not predict is suggested by other evidence. Dean Johnston reported at the Hanover Conference in 1925 that college achievement, i.e., success or failure in the courses, could be predicted with an error ranging from 0% to 2% if intelligence scores were combined with high school performance, whereas either high school performance or intelligence tests taken alone gave an error of prediction amounting to about 9%. This suggests that qualities entering into performance, of a non-intellectual nature, are a partial determiner of success, but that their predictive value alone is no greater than that of intelligence tests alone. Combined, however, they are a useful prognostic agent.

The whole question of non-intellectual determinants of behavior will be considered at length in the next chapter. Here we shall confine ourselves to one further illustration, showing even more clearly than the one given above, that the prognostic ability of the IQ is increased tremendously when certain non-intellectual factors are taken into consideration. Quoting Charters again:

It may be that we could better predict success if we canvassed the traits of personality. Difficult as is this task with our present technique, it must be done and the findings must be used to supplement intelligence scores. Indeed a beginning has been made in these respects. May's recent study at once comes to mind. In this significant investigation he ranked 450 Freshman students in the University of Syracuse on the honor-point basis, where A carries three points; B, two points; C, one; and D, zero. Then he ranked the students on the basis of intelligence scores, and found that the correlation was plus 0.60, which is slightly higher than the correlation usually found. He then measured their industry by a somewhat crude but ingenious method, he computed the average number of hours spent in study by each student and used this as a measure of his industry. The data secured from the students had a high degree of reliability.

The correlation between the time spent in study and honor points was plus 0.32 and shows that industry alone measured thus is not as good an index of probable success as is brightness alone. Yet when he combined industry and brightness and correlated this factor with success as measured by honor points, the correlation rose to plus 0.80. Intelligence alone is plus 0.60; industry alone

---

[52] Bingham, W. V., and Davis, W. T.: "Intelligence Test Scores and Business Success," *Journal of Applied Psychology*, 8:1 (1924).

is plus 0.32; intelligence and industry combined is plus 0.80. Thus we see in this typical study what everybody expects — that if the student is both bright and industrious his chances for making high grades are appreciably increased.[53]

We cannot yet come to any definite conclusion as to the part played by mental abilities or disabilities in determining behavior. The data which have been collected on the subject have led to a modification of the claims of ten years ago — a modification which is tending more and more to minimize the part played by mental functions as over against temperamental or personality functions, which we shall discuss in our next chapter.

The case for the IQ as a determinant of behavior seems to us to rest now on the evidence which we have presented and other similar evidence which we shall briefly summarize. Soon after the mental tests were devised and the concept of the IQ evolved, the claim was made that low intelligence was the determining factor in misconduct and delinquency. This claim was based on statistical evidence, since it was assumed that the norms established by giving the tests to school children were generally applicable. These norms differentiated the feebleminded in institutions from school children, and when they also differentiated groups of adult criminals from the school children, in the same direction as the feebleminded in institutions, it was assumed that in feeblemindedness, as diagnosed by the tests, was to be found the determining factor in crime. And similarly in high intelligence was to be found the determining factor in good conduct and successful adjustment to life. Assuming that these norms were correct, it is easy to understand that the apparent separation of the criminals from the generally well-behaving population led to a belief that herein lay the explanation of crime, and that behavior was a correlate of intelligence. This led to claims of the type made by J. Harold Williams concerning the Whittier State School boys that " low intelligence, in many cases of delinquency, would alone account for the offenses committed." The only qualification he makes is that there are in any group of delinquents " a few children of normal and superior intelligence, whose delinquency must be accounted for in some other way." [54] And again: " On the whole, it may be said that high

---

[53] Charters: *op. cit.*, 171.

[54] Williams, J. Harold: "Delinquent Boys of Superior Intelligence," *Journal of Delinquency*, 1:33–34 (1916).

and low intelligence mean success and failure respectively, with reference to the ordinary requirements of society." [55]

On the other hand, the discovery of the inadequacy of the norms has led to a radical revision of the conception of the rôle played by inferior intelligence in delinquency. Murchison [56] compared the intelligence of the draft army, for certain selected states, with the intelligence of the criminals in those same states and found no significant differences in averages or distributions.[57] On the other hand, the most careful studies of juvenile delinquents do show a greater proportion of feeblemindedness and mental dulness than would be found among groups of unselected children. Healy and Bronner present data for 4,000 cases of young repeated offenders. Of these data they say:

On the one hand, these figures show clearly that the mentally abnormal among delinquents constitute a much greater proportion than is found among the general population. Yet, on the other hand, those who have so stressed the part played either by feeblemindedness or mental disease in the production of delinquency will obtain from these most carefully developed findings small support for their extreme statements.

Stated in total, 72.5% of our 4000 repeated juvenile offenders were found to be definitely mentally normal. . . . The feebleminded appear among serious delinquents from five to ten times more frequently than in the general population, but, even so, they form not more than one-fifth as many as the mentally normal. Our total is 13.5% clearly feebleminded.[58]

Slawson found about thirteen times as many deficients among delinquent boys in institutions as compared with groups of non-delinquent boys. His figures correspond almost exactly with those of Healy and Bronner:

We find among the total population of delinquents tested, which is 1543, that 13.4% are tested intelligence deficients. This figure is based upon a

[55] Williams, J. Harold: "The Intelligence of the Delinquent Boy," *Journal of Delinquency, Monograph* No. 1:51 (1919).

[56] Murchison, Carl: *Criminal Intelligence* (1926).

[57] The meaning of Murchison's data may very possibly be that these mental tests applied to adults, whether army or criminals, are not satisfactory — for the results of tests carefully applied to juveniles (here cited) show, beyond question, a disproportionate number of mental defectives among the delinquents. It is, therefore, extremely unlikely that there should not also be a disproportionate number of feebleminded among adult criminals.

[58] Healy, W., and Bronner, A. F.: *Delinquents and Criminals* (1926), 150–51.

comparison with a presumably unselected population, irrespective of social status or nationality. Of this delinquent population, 16.4% are of borderline grade intelligence, and 29.8% are, therefore, either deficient or borderline.[59]

Burt reports upon this point:

I find that, of the juvenile delinquents whom I have tested with the Binet-Simon tests, 8 per cent and no more are mentally defective. . . .

Placed beside the sensational statistics from America, my own percentage must seem low. In itself, however, it still reveals among the delinquent population a proportion of mental defectives five times as great as among the school population at large. Mental defect, beyond all controversy, therefore, is a notable factor in the production of crime.[60]

Fernald, Hayes and Dawley summarize their comparisons of the mentality of their 563 delinquent girls with various non-delinquent groups, as follows:

Summarizing, then, the results of such comparisons as we have been able to make of the mental capacity of delinquent women with that of non-delinquents, it appears: that the average mental capacity of the delinquent women whom we have examined is lower than that of any groups of non-delinquent adults with regard to whom we have data. That, however, the above statement does not imply a selection of individuals entirely from the lower end of the scale of intelligence for the delinquent group. . . . The range of the delinquent group was found to be practically coextensive with that of the army group, our most representative sampling of the general population . . . [and] the difference between the means of the delinquent and the non-delinquent groups, while affording adequate indication of a distinction between the two groups, is not extreme in amount.[61]

Assuming the validity of this statistical evidence, it is obvious that we have here no explanation of crime or misbehavior in general. It is not even permissible to claim that the inferior intelligence was the determining factor in the delinquencies of all the cases of feebleminded offenders, since so many feebleminded persons, with IQ's equally low, lead regular lives, and since there is so much overlapping in the intelligence distributions.

A study of case histories suggests the importance of low intelligence

---

[59] Slawson, John: *The Delinquent Boy* (1926), 160.

[60] Burt, Cyril: *The Young Delinquent* (1925), 300.

[61] Fernald, M. R., Hayes, M. H. S., and Dawley, A.: *A Study of Women Delinquents in New York State* (1920), 433.

as causing misbehavior in certain cases, as also the factors of dulness, special disabilities (causing school maladjustment and leading often to truancy, etc.), but also the importance of superior intelligence with no outlet for special abilities. In a study of behavior problems among school children, M. E. Haggerty found the occurrence of the most problems among the mentally inferior and the mentally superior:

A gradual increase in the behavior score is evident as the level of intelligence moves downward. Beginning with a score of 5 for the *very superior* group the score grows in magnitude successively for the *superior, normal, dull,* and *border-line* cases and reaches its maximum of 36 for *definite* feeble-mindedness. A striking exception to this order occurs at the other extreme of intelligence where the five pupils of intelligence quotients of 140 or more exhibit a higher behavior score than any group excepting the dull, border-line, and feeble-minded.

The obvious tendency for behavior problems to increase at both ends of the scale of intelligence is probably to some degree significant of the less satisfactory adaptation of the school to these extremes of ability.[62]

The intelligence quotient, as determined by the tests, then, has been shown to be a fair diagnostic agent in dealing with school children but a poor diagnostic agent in dealing with adults. It has been found to vary with social classes, occupational classes and racial groups. This variation has been shown to be functional in the case of environmental influences. The evidence points strongly to a similar direct dependence on the amount of schooling received. Its prognostic ability has been fair in picking school successes and poor in picking business successes, but when certain non-intellectual traits have been taken into consideration, the combined prognostic ability of IQ plus non-intellectual traits has become much higher. Its causal relationship with behavior has been shown to be variable. Behavior problems and delinquency occur with all degrees of intelligence, but the maladjustments of the feebleminded and the dull lead to delinquency in larger proportions than do those of the normal. Special disabilities and abilities and generally superior intelligence seem also to lead to behavior difficulties disproportionately. Our conclusion is that intelligence, as measured by the tests, is a factor to be considered in any study of behavior but that it is rarely, by itself, a causal explanation of any particular type of behavior.

---

[62] "The Incidence of Undesirable Behavior in Public-School Children," *Journal of Educational Research*, 12:113–14 (1925).

Methodologically considered, the tests we have reviewed have a real value for behavior study in that they have been applied to so widely differing groups. Terman's " standardization " of the tests was based on the performance of relatively large groups of school children and a few adults. Children were included from different social levels as indicated by the occupation of the parents, etc. Terman analyzed the results for these different groups, found different types of performance, and, assuming that the tests measured innate ability, drew conclusions as to the relative intelligence of various social classes. Other studies were made by other investigators in which similar differences were found between rural and urban populations, between inhabitants of different cities, between different racial groups, etc.

It is very important to know all these concomitants or correlatives of intelligence (as measured by these tests) in order to be able to allow for these in studies of behavior. If, for instance, low intelligence is associated with low social class, and delinquents are shown to have low intelligence, the connection in the latter case may be due to the fact that delinquents come from low social classes and in any adequate investigation, instead of comparing delinquents with an unselected population, they would be compared with a group from the same social class. Similarly with other correlatives. From this point of view, studies such as those of Terman, Pressey and Ralston on the occupational differences in intelligence, that of Colvin on the geographical differences, and many others, are important. These studies, however, have no importance as contributing any causal explanations. It is not possible to tell from studies of this type whether the low intelligence caused the individuals to take their places at a low occupational level, or whether the low occupational level in which they were placed by circumstances determined the low intelligence level. The conclusions that were drawn from studies of this sort were based on one or the other of the assumptions that intelligence as measured by the tests was innate intelligence and therefore largely unmodifiable by environment, or that intelligence as measured by the tests was a function of environment. And the same is true with the studies which showed a close connection between intelligence and the amount of schooling. The most important of these is that of Hugh Gordon, which showed a pretty definite connection between IQ and schooling for individuals of relatively the same social status, i.e., gipsies, canal boat population and children in the London special classes for physical defectives.

All studies of this type should, however, be regarded as the beginning of investigations, rather than as leading to any conclusions. Given results of the kind found in these studies, investigations must be framed in such a way as to put to a real test the assumptions mentioned above. The investigations of Freeman and his associates, of Goodenough and Woolley, represent definite tests of these assumptions. In the one case children of similar heredity, with known IQ's, were taken from one environment and placed in another, and after a period of time their IQ's were compared with those of children unrelated to them but brought up in the new environment, and with their own siblings who had been brought up in the old environment. In the other case, control groups were used by taking two groups of children of similar heredity, known IQ and (in many respects) similar environment, and subjecting one group to a special environmental influence. The changes in IQ were then compared for the two groups. In Burks' study, also, the comparison of IQ's of foster children with their own parents and with their foster parents contributes valuable evidence. These studies are very important when considered in connection with studies of the prognosis given by the IQ. This has, in fact, been found to be variable, as we have seen, and to have more value negatively than positively. But to the degree that any prognosis of success in various ways may be given by the IQ, then, the possibility of the IQ being functionally related to certain environmental situations has great significance from the standpoint of social procedure. From this point of view, also, the whole theoretical question of nature versus nurture in relation to intelligence is not important. The tests may be assumed to measure *effective* intelligence, in so far as they give a good prognosis, and if this effective intelligence is modifiable by certain situations the implications for procedure become obvious. The checking up of tests by various criteria of success and adjustment to determine their prognostic value thus becomes important, and, where it is possible, the derivation of other tests. This at-tempted with tests of special abilities and tests of the rather than the verbal type, and by the combination of the tests of other aspects of personality.

CHAPTER IX
The Personality Testing Approach

AT the time of the introduction of intelligence tests there was an inadequate realization of the fact that the emotions, the habits, the glands, the blood, the sympathetic and autonomic nervous systems and the whole organism participate in thinking and behavior. As more accurate studies were made of intelligence it was found that its correlation with general or specific performance, i.e., with " behavior," was never very high, and it was tentatively concluded that the dynamic factors in the individual make-up, those factors which are variously described as " personality," " temperament " and " character," should be studied in their interrelationships with intelligence and physique in the hope that a more reliable prognosis of behavior might be obtained.

There has been, during the past ten years, a flood of literature describing the various attempts to measure personality differences, to define the various components of character, and to measure the relationships between these various factors and behavior. The difficulties facing those who attempted to measure these factors have been even greater than those facing the mental testers.

The primary difficulty has been to make such definitions of the traits to be measured as to give any degree of reliability to the measurements. Abstr   elligence was, in itself, not difficult to define. And the variety of   developed in the traditional learning made the formation   simple. But with regard to personality traits it has often   t to establish the objective validity of the trait itself. Defi-   d tremendously and have been largely subjective.   eral agreement (even general agreement among the   an be obtained as to the test situations which will be valid indications of the trait in question. Great difficulties have further arisen with regard to the generality of any trait as determined by any test situation or paper and pencil test. Claims have been made that " honesty," for example, is an entity, which would be indicated by a specific test situation and that this would then carry over to other situations, but these claims have been controverted by evidence seeming to show that honesty is a different thing in different situations, e.g., " taking " things at home and stealing from a store.

An idea of the extensiveness of the field may be gained from the bibliography and classification of personality and character tests made up by May and Hartshorne,[1] which, " except for a few important articles . . . covers the period from 1920 to 1925 inclusive. The productivity of these years has been so great that it has been necessary to omit all reference to rating scales and techniques even where their use has been so guarded as to approach objectivity of measurement." [2] There are 197 titles in this bibliography, and the classification made by the authors is interesting as showing the claims that have been made. In addition to summaries and " batteries," these tests fall under three main headings, as follows:

Tests and Techniques Intended Primarily to Measure Objectively (and Mainly in Terms of Conduct) Certain Personality Traits and Types of Behavior

1. *Aggressiveness.* Measured by the difference in quality and quantity of certain types of mental work done under normal or standard conditions and the same or similar work done under . . . conditions involving certain social and mechanical distractions.

2. *Ascendence-Submission.* Measured by the strength of reaction to an imaginary situation containing a mild rebuke.

3. *Caution.* Measured by the relations between the items omitted, attempted, right and wrong in an intelligence test, especially by the ratio of the items attempted to the items wrong. Measured by reactions to situations requiring that subject " take a chance."

4. *Compliance.* Measured by length of time a child will try to open a box containing a cherished object.

---

[1] May, M. A., and Hartshorne, H.: " Personality and Character Tests," *Psychological Bulletin*, 23:395–411 (1926).

[2] *Ibid.*, 395.

5. *Confidence.* Experimental technique. Subjects judged length of lines, ethical situations, etc., and then rated the degree of confidence in the accuracy of their judgments.

6. *Conformity.* Measured by the number of conventional preferences in a multiple choice paper and pencil test.

7. *Conscientiousness.* Test of the conscientiousness of conscientious objectors to military service by a social and religious background questionnaire.

8. *Decision Speed.* Various kinds of test material used with this central point. Speed of decision is measured by the time it takes the subject to decide in such things as checking traits, comparing weights, lengths of lines, judging the letter of greatest frequency on a card, etc.

9. *Expansion-Reclusion.* Measured by the type of reply made to a standardized want advertisement.

10. *Deception.*

    (a) Detection (not measurement) by inspiration-expiration ratio before and after truth-telling or lying.

    (b) Detection by systolic blood pressure.

    (c) Detection by associative reaction times.

11. *Honesty.* Many tests and techniques used.

    (a) The overstatement test. Measured by differences between claimed and actual abilities.

    (b) The paraffin paper test. Duplicate test performance made on paraffin sheet removed before subject corrects his own paper.

    (c) The peeping technique. Peeping shown by degree of success in placing pencil point in scattered circles or in threading mazes when eyes are supposed to be shut.

    (d) Books read technique. Measured by number of fictitious titles pupils check as having read.

    (e) Identical errors technique. Measured by number of identical errors students sitting near each other will make on a short quiz.

    (f) Duplicating papers technique. Papers duplicated by examiner before being corrected by pupils. Changes shown by comparison with duplicates.

    (g) The overchange test. Will the subject keep overchange?

    (h) The missent letter technique. Will the subject keep money mailed him " by mistake."

    (i) Technique to check students faking laboratory experiments.

12. *Incorrigibility.* . . . A battery testing honesty, emotionality and moral judgment.

13. *Originality.* Twelve tests in which originality is supposed to be displayed.

14. *Perseveration.* A laboratory technique for measuring this phenomenon and showing its relation to persistency of will.

15. *Perseverance.* Measured by the length of time a subject can stand on his toes.

16. *Persistence.* Measured by length of time pupils will stick to a disagreeable task.

17. *Self-Assertion.* Measured by the length of time a child will play with a non-preferred toy without demanding the preferred one which he knows is available.

18. *Self-Assurance.* Measured by the differential between what the subject thinks he can do and what he actually does using (a) a string figures test and (b) a modification of the Binet paper folding test.

19. *Self-Estimation and Evaluation.* Measured by:
    (a) The differential between self-estimates and scores on an objective test.
    (b) The differential between ratings of self as is, as should be, and as others are on identical traits.

20. *Social Perception.* Measured by ability to judge the emotion, feeling, or mental state exhibited in facial expressions and recorded in photographs. Standardized photographs are used.

21. *Social Resistance.* Measured by the degree of resistance in social barriers which a child will overcome in getting acquainted with a stranger.

22. *Studiousness.* Measured by:
    (a) The differential between scores in an intelligence test and scores on an unannounced quiz in classroom work.
    (b) The number of hours per week spent in study.

23. *Suggestibility.* Measured by:
    (a) A wide variety of suggestion tests.
    (b) A specially prepared paper and pencil test of twenty elements.

24. *Trustworthiness.* Measured by a variety of performance tests.

*Tests and Testing Techniques Intended to Measure Primarily
the Affective Aspects of Personality*

I. *Instincts and Emotions.*

   (a) Laboratory Techniques for Measuring the Relative Strength of Emotions and Instincts.
       1. By association times to words intended to tap various emotional types of complexes.
       2. By the differential between routine mental work done

under normal or standard conditions and the same or identical work done under emotional distractions of various sorts.

3. By judgment of the varying degrees of persuasiveness of Hollingworth's standard advertisements.

4. By moving pictures of facial expressions and head movements made in response to a wide variety of emotional stimuli.

5. By measuring systolic blood pressure and inspiration-expiration ratio when the subject is exposed to emotional stimuli . . . and by the psychogalvanic reflex as well.

6. By recording bodily movements and expressions and verbal expressions under above conditions.

(b) Laboratory Techniques for Measuring General Emotional Instability.

1. Measured by the number of times the subject will withdraw his hand from an apparently very dangerous situation which he has been assured by the experimenter is perfectly harmless.

2. Measured by electrical changes in the body. The psychogalvanic reflexes.

3. Extrovertive and introvertive tendencies have been measured (described above).[3]

(c) Paper and Pencil Tests of Emotionality and Emotional Instability.

1. The Pressey XO tests [have been found by investigators] . . . to differentiate certain psychopathic types of personality and degrees of emotional maturity and predict academic success as well if not better than intelligence tests.

2. Emotional questionnaires.

(a) The Woodworth Personal Data Sheet was compiled . . . for use in the army. It consists of 120 questions intended to reveal psychopathic tendencies.

(b), (c), (d), (e) [Revisions of this questionnaire.]

(f) Other questionnaire studies in the field of emotions, instincts and other dynamic traits. . . .

---

[3] I.e., in the tests described as compliance, self-assertion, social-resistance, etc., and in the tests for ascendence-submission, expansion-reclusion, etc.

II. *Mood and Temperament.*

  (a) Laboratory Techniques.
  1. *Cheerfulness and Depression. Optimism and Pessimism* have been measured . . . by the use of the galvanic reflexes and the free association method.
  2. The effects of *Encouragement and Discouragement* on mental work have been tested. . . . And the effects of *Praise and Reproval* on increase in mental output have been measured.
  (b) Paper and Pencil Tests. The Downey *Will-Temperament* tests are the most outstanding of all efforts to measure the dynamic traits. . . .

III. *Attitudes, Interests, Preferences, Prejudices, etc.*

  (a) General Social and Religious Attitudes and Interests.
  1. A true-false test of religious and social opinions and attitudes. Applied to college students.
  2. Hart's Test of Social Attitudes and Interests and Personnel Assayer. By a special technique of recording likes and dislikes, favorable and opposed reactions, beliefs and disbeliefs, in respect to specific situations, he attempted a measure of a wide range of attitudes.
  3. A set of questions requiring scaled responses as to belief in, certainty of, and desirability of, the propositions involved in the questions.
  4. Four attitudes tests: character preferences, reading preferences, activity preferences, and an association test, all aimed at measuring the child's general attitudes on a variety of questions.
  5. Shuttleworth's University of Iowa Assayer. Based on the Hart technique.
  6. An attitudes test based on selected traits aimed at measuring likes and dislikes of various traits.
  7. Six tests designed to measure fair-mindedness by eliciting the expression of prejudices on various religious, economic, and political issues.
  (b) Tests of More Specific Attitudes.
  1. *Fair-mindedness.*
  2. *International-mindedness.* Measured by . . . a general information test.

3. *Money-mindedness.* Measured by . . . Hart's technique.
4. *Open-mindedness.* Measured by a questionnaire.
5. *Public-spiritedness.* Tested . . . with two forms of a free association test.
6. *Liberal* or *Progressive* attitudes in politics have been measured with a questionnaire scale. . . .
7. *On Prohibition.* Measured by a multiple choice test.
8. *On Race Relations.* Measured by a multiple choice test.
9. *Social Distance,* or attitudes toward various social groups. . . .
10. *Sociality,* or ability to " mix " well. . . .

(c) Tests of Specific Interests.

1. Measured by the number of irrelevant words crossed out in reading interesting and dry passages.
2. Measured by score in a " paired associates " memory test.
3. Measured by information tests:
    (a) Based on subject's supposed interest.
    (b) Interest in sports measured by information.
    (c) Recognition of pictures.
4. Measured by free association. . . .
5. Measured by recording behavior of children in a museum.
6. Measured by having schoolboys hand in each day an envelope containing the most interesting thing they could find or a description of it.
7. Interest analysis . . . interest analysis blanks designed to detect vocational interests.

Tests and Techniques Intended to Measure Primarily Social-Ethical Ideas and Judgment

I. *Tests Requiring the Ranking or Rating of Situations.*

1. The ranking of sixteen offenses based on the worst practices of university men.
2. Seven lists of words, seven words in a list. In each list the words are ranked according to shades of meaning, the two extreme words being given.
3. Moral Judgment Test, consisting of rating acts on a four-place scale according to degrees of blameworthiness.
4. Pupils' ideas of relative values [measured] by having them rank a list of reasons for (1) going to high school, (2) reading good literature, (3) saving money.

5. Tests of religious ideas consisting in ranking in their order a set of answers to seven questions.
6. Ethical Discrimination Tests. Requires the ranking of ten offenses, ten meritorious acts, and ten ambitions.
7. Ethical Discrimination Tests. Requires the ranking of children's acts.
8. Ethical Discrimination Tests . . . an offense rating test.
9. Scale for measuring moral and religious values, involving the ranking of twenty-five situations in three different ways.
10. An offense rating test.

II. *Tests Requiring Various Sorts of Responses to Imagined Situations.*
    (a) The Moral Dilemma type of test.
        1. Fernald's Ethical Perception Tests.
        2. Moral Knowledge Tests. Two tests of this type, Comprehensions, of the Binet Comprehension type, and Provocations, calling for a judgment of rightness or wrongness on a specific act.
        3. Ethical Discrimination Tests . . . of the Binet Comprehension type.
        4. Four tests of this general type.
    (b) Tests of Foresight of Consequences.
        1. The subject is required to indicate the desirable and undesirable consequences of various solutions to a moral problem contained in a story.
        2. Two such tests, a story completion test, and a word consequence test in which the subject underlines the word that is the best and the one that is the worst consequence of the stimulus word.
        3. The completion type of test in which various phrases are filled in to complete the story.
    (c) Tests of Ability to Recognize or Identify the Moral Element in a Situation.
        1. Parables interpretation test, multiple choice type, requiring the pupil to find the true meaning of the parable.
        2. A true-false test with twenty-five moral judgment questions.
        3. A Recognition test, requiring the pupil to indicate whether a given act is lying, stealing, cheating, etc.
        4. The Binet Fables.

5. Stories [used] and pupil [required] to state the lesson or moral of each . . . picture [used] and the child [required] to identify the moral element in the situation.
6. A moral judgment test . . . in which the worst word in a list is crossed out.
7. A social-ethical vocabulary test.
8. Historical incidents [used] and the subject [required] to judge the motive in each act.[4]

From the point of view of the claims made, this concise and excellent summary is startling. If these tests and techniques truly measured the things they were " intended " to measure there would be little more that we should need to know about the human being, his motives and his performance, and knowing so much, there would be little behavior that we could not predict, and predicting so much, we could surely control. It becomes very necessary, therefore, to examine the actual results obtained, in order that we may see how nearly they approach the picture of the measured and predicted behavior suggested by this outline. It is unnecessary, however, to concern ourselves with very many of the tests listed. Few of them have been widely enough applied to give results that will throw much light on behavior trends. Many of them have been so poorly defined and the situations were set up in such a way that the results have no vestige of reliability. Some of them have, however, been carefully set up, have developed valid techniques and brought out consistent and reliable results. A few of them have been in a form where wide application was possible, and it will be interesting to see what predictive value they have.

Let us first consider one or two of the many attempts that have been made to measure differences in personality in terms of changes in physical states as these physical states are represented by blood pressure, respiration, muscular reactivity, reaction time, fatigue index, etc.

One of the simplest and most clear-cut of these studies is the attempt by Moore and Gilliland to measure " aggressiveness." Ratings by faculty and students were obtained on the relative aggressiveness of a class of 89 students. The 13 rated " most aggressive " and the 13 rated

---

[4] In the original article by Hartshorne and May: *op. cit.*, the author of each of these tests, and the exact reference to the study in which the test appears, is given in each case. The above represents the classification used by Hartshorne and May (395–403) with all authors and references omitted.

" least aggressive " were then taken as the subjects of the experiment. The first technique developed was that of measuring the eye control of the subject during a personal interview:

Common sense has it that the shifty eye is generally a sure sign of personal weakness, if not of downright dishonesty. The first test was designed with a view to bringing this element of behavior into quantitative relation with the trait aggressiveness. Each of the twenty-six subjects was required to perform a somewhat difficult series of mental additions while constantly returning the fixed gaze of the instructor who sat facing him. The addition series were standardized as to difficulty . . . and the subject performed them with the knowledge that accuracy and speed were essential. But he was emphatically instructed that under no circumstances should he let his gaze wander from that of the man facing him, as all movements of the eyes were to affect his score seriously. . . .

It will be seen that a total of 72 movements are recorded against the least aggressive as compared with 6 against the most aggressive men. Not one of the aggressive group averted his gaze more than twice during the five series of additions, whereas ten of the thirteen least aggressive subjects shifted their eyes four times or more. If a steady eye does not positively guarantee the presence of aggressiveness, as may be judged by the fact that three of the least aggressive subjects were able to maintain practically constant fixation, a marked lack in this respect is almost invariably accompanied by a lack of aggressiveness. . . .

Whether we compare the average number of movements of the aggressive and the unaggressive subjects, or compare the number of subjects in the two groups who lost control to the extent of making two or more eye movements, we find evidence of at least ten times as much control in the upper group as in the lower. Thus the simple behavioristic fact of the ability to look another person in the eye seems to have such a high significance regarding the presence or absence of aggressiveness as to warrant giving it an extremely prominent place in any scoring method devised as a measure of this trait. The correspondence is in fact so close as to justify the generalization that a stop watch and a pair of fixed eyes are the only indispensable laboratory equipment necessary for estimating roughly the degree of aggressiveness in at least four-fifths of the subjects.[5]

These investigators found also a close correlation between the aggressiveness ratings and the ability to resist certain types of distraction while performing mental arithmetic problems.

[5] Moore, H. T., and Gilliland, A. R.: "The Measurement of Aggressiveness," *Journal of Applied Psychology*, 5:100–2 (1921).

Probably the most outstanding attempt to test out and evaluate the various approaches of this general type to the study of personality has been the series of researches by Carney Landis. He has set up most carefully controlled situations in order to test out the relation of various emotional experiences to the physical expression of these experiences. We shall give, in some detail, the methodology used in one of his studies because of the significance of this particular approach, and we shall then take up the results he has found in regard to the interrelationships of various criteria of emotionality and their significance from the standpoint of behavior.

In his study of " General Behavior and Facial Expression," [6] the problem is stated as follows:

A comparable description of the actual behavior of different individuals during situations of emotional nature is not to be found in the literature. It seemed desirable to arrive at some method by which real emotional disturbances could be engendered. This disturbance should consist not only of one type of emotion such as fear, but should involve as many distinct forms of reaction as possible working up in a cumulative manner so as to give a pronounced emotional upset. With such a technique it would be possible to observe and record objectively the reactions of a number of persons under the same conditions and hence arrive at a comparative description of emotional reactions. This description should, among other things, give answers to such questions as the following. What facial expression, if any, typifies an individual's reaction in a given situation? Is there a pattern of expression which is well correlated with the verbal characterization of a certain " feeling "? What criteria of emotionality are valid? Are there sex differences in emotional stability or expression? Do " centrally aroused emotions " give definite patterns of response? What factors enter into the emotionality of any individual? What situations are most provocative of emotional disturbance?

In general the purpose of this present study is to describe, analyze, and classify the general behavior of normal individuals, with especial reference to facial and head reactions, verbal reactions and sex differences during a controlled series of situations designed to arouse emotional response. [7]

Great care was taken to have an experimental set-up of such a sort that the reactions of the subjects would be to the situations rather than to the laboratory or to the experimenter. The subject's room was arranged as a studio, with little apparatus in view. A camera was focused

---

[6] *Journal of Comparative Psychology*, 4:447–501 (1924). [7] *Ibid.*, 453.

on the subject through a small opening in the wall, blood-pressure and respiration records were taken, and conversation, etc., recorded. The subject was then presented with 16 situations, designed to produce a cumulative emotional upset. There can be little doubt that emotional upset must have occurred as the aftermath of the situations presented in detail below:

1. *Popular music.* Three jazz dance records, " Bebe," " Love Tales," and " The Parade of the Wooden Soldiers " were played on a phonograph. This consumed about ten minutes and together with the next situation was conducive to a relaxation from the apprehension with which most subjects entered into the experiment.

2. *Technical music.* Two violin pieces, " Jota de Pablo " and " Perpetuum Mobile " played by Duci de Kerekjarto were played on the phonograph. Both of these records are marked by their virtuosity and technique, " Perpetuum Mobile " having almost no melody.

3. *The Bible.* The subject was given a Bible opened to a place and instructed to read St. Luke, 6:18–49.

4. *Truth and falsehood.* The method here used . . . consisted of presenting the subject with two sheets of paper, face down, marked respectively T and L. The following instructions were then read to the subject. " Here are two papers, one marked T, the other L. Choose either the T or the L and then place the paper you did not choose to one side. If you choose L you will find points of circumstantial evidence attaching you to some crime. You are to invent a lie which will clear you of these charges on a cross-examination which I will make. If you choose T you will find an alibi provided for this crime. All you have to do is to familiarize yourself with the story and tell the truth on examination. Try to deceive me on the L and to tell the truth in an unexcited way on the T. We shall do this twice. The second time choose to do the opposite thing from what you did the first time. I will leave the room for five minutes while you make up your lie or familiarize yourself with the alibi." On cross-examination, which was made from questions previously prepared, the experimenter stated his questions in a slow, clear, matter-of-fact way, pausing between each question so that the blood pressure and the inspiration-expiration ratios might be obtained.

5. *Ammonia.* The subject was given a tray containing a row of six bottles and instructed to uncork and smell each in turn. All except the fifth contained substances with a mildly pleasant odor. The fifth bottle was labelled " syrup of lemon " but contained strong aqua ammonia.

6. *Shot.* The experimenter stopped at this point and suggested that the subject had smeared some of the markings on his face (see below) and that it

would be necessary to burn a little cork and re-mark his face. He then stepped behind the screen and lighted a firecracker which he dropped beneath the subject's chair. He signalled for a blood pressure reading and took photographs immediately after the explosion.

7. *Faux pas.* The subject was given a sheet of paper and a pencil and told to write a full description of the meanest or most contemptible, or the most embarrassing thing he ever did. " Try to describe some event which still disturbs you even to think about." After he had written this description the experimenter took the paper and read aloud what the subject had just written.

8. *Laughter.* It was hoped that some sure stimulus for laughter, such as a joke, might be obtained but in this we were not successful and so this situation was omitted after the first two subjects.

9. *Skin diseases.* Ten illustrations in color, depicting especially morbid skin diseases, were taken from Neumann's " Atlas der Hautkrankheiten " (Vienna, 1896). These were presented to the subject with the instructions, " Look these over carefully imagining yourself similarly afflicted."

10. *Mental multiplication.* The subject was given a card with two numbers such as 79×67 printed upon it. He was told to fix the numbers firmly in mind and then to multiply the two while noise distraction was used. For this noise a piece of sheet brass was clamped rather loosely to the table in front of the subject. The experimenter then filed on the brass vigorously and in an irregular manner with a coarse file. The experimenter kept urging and talking to the subject during the noise so as to cause further distraction as well as to keep the subject trying. These problems were attempted by each subject. The subject was kept at each problem until he called out the right answer or until it became apparent to the experimenter that entirely too much time would be consumed in the process. This situation was very effective in arousing considerable disturbance on the part of most subjects.

11. *Pornographic pictures.* A set of French photographs of a pornographic nature was presented to the subject with the instructions, " Look these over carefully." The experimenter was careful not to laugh or appear self-conscious during this or the next two situations.

12. *Art studies.* A set of posed photographs of feminine artist's models was presented to the subject with the same instructions as in situation 11.

13. *Sex case histories.* Several of the most pornographic of the case histories from Ellis' " Psychology of Sex," as well as several other brief case histories, were given to the subject with the instructions, " Read over these case histories."

14. *Frogs.* A chair was placed on the right side of the subject. A covered pail which had been concealed behind the screen was set upon the chair. The sub-

ject was instructed, " Without looking into the pail, shove the cover to one side and then put your hand inside to the bottom of the pail and feel around." The pail contained several inches of water and 3 live frogs. After the subject had reacted to the frogs the experimenter said, " Yes, but you have not felt everything yet, feel around again." While the subject was doing so he received a strong make and break shock from an induction coil, attached to the pail by concealed wiring.

15. *Rat.* The table in front of the subject was covered with a cloth. A flat tray and a butcher's knife were placed on the cloth. A live white rat was then given to the subject. He was instructed, " Hold this rat with your left hand and then cut off its head with the knife." This situation was tried with 21 subjects. Fifteen subjects followed instructions after more or less urging. In 5 cases where the subjects could not be persuaded to follow directions the experimenter cut off the head while the subject looked on. In 2 cases the decapitation for various reasons was not performed.

16. *Shocks.* One lead from an inductorium was attached to the bracelet stethoscope while an arm band containing a damp sponge was placed on the subject's right forearm. This arm band was connected to the other pole of the inductorium. The subject was then given a card upon which was printed two numbers, such as 347×89, and told to multiply these mentally while he received electrical distraction. . . . The shocks were of the make and break variety and were varied from a just noticeable intensity to a strength which caused the subject to jump from the chair. This situation following the long " grind " of the other situations brought about a very real disturbance in most cases. The punishment was continued until either some very real emotional expression was given or it was apparent that the subject was not going to give way to any marked expression. In only 1 case was a subject able to complete the multiplication.

17. *Relief.* The experimenter stepped behind the screen and rattled the connections about a bit as though preparing for another situation. He then stepped out and said, " Well, that finishes it. Just as soon as we get the final blood pressure and respiration records you are through."

The entire series took a little over three hours.[8]

There were 25 subjects in the experiment: 12 men, 12 women, and 1 boy. Most of the situations produced very marked responses and, as Landis remarks: " The fact that most of the subjects were psychologists who had had more or less laboratory experience and yet gave way to emotional disturbance gives some indication of the effectiveness of the

[8] *Journal of Comparative Psychology,* 4:457–60.

series." Pictures were taken, during the experiment, of " every notice-able change of facial expression." The number of pictures per individ-ual varied from 16 to 42. The faces were marked with charcoal in such a way as to set off the functional muscle groups. The degree of involve-ment of each of the muscles was rated, from the pictures, as " absent," " slight involvement," " moderate involvement," " full or extreme in-volvement," and each of the pictures was ranked, subjectively, for " ex-pressiveness."

The results of the analysis of these photographs and of the verbal re-ports given by the subjects showed that there is " no expression or group of expressions which typifies any situation " and " no correspondence between the pattern of response and the name given by the subject to the emotion."

There were, however, interesting differences between individuals, which tended to be consistent:

Certain individuals habitually use certain muscle groups, certain expres-sions, and almost never use certain other groups. This is of the nature of a mannerism or habitual reaction. These particular expressions were given ir-respective of situation or of later verbal reactions. There was also a constancy in type of bodily reactions over and above that called out by the situation; certain subjects at all times used many hand movements, others reacted negatively to all stimulations, i.e., tried to resist or avoid the situations, while still other individuals reacted positively to the stimulation, facilitating the entire procedure. In certain situations a sex difference in the total reaction pattern was also rather marked. The clearest example of this occurred during electrical punishment. Here many of the women cried and begged the experi-menter to stop the situation, while several of the men became angry and pro-fane, snatching off the arm electrode, and refusing to allow the situation to proceed further.[9]

The question of the interrelationships existing between the various criteria of emotionality is taken up by Landis, Gullette and Jacobsen, with various data on these same 25 subjects. Before starting the situa-tions described above

reaction time was measured (15 subjects) for 100 choice reactions to two sound hammers of different intensity. Following this the subject tapped with a telegraph key as rapidly as possible for three periods of ten seconds each. Finally the subject worked for 10 minutes on half of the recognition vocabulary test which forms part of the University of Minnesota's entrance intelligence examination.[10]

In addition to the photographs, systolic blood-pressure, verbal reactions, and gross bodily movements were recorded during the experiment:

At the end of the situations the reaction time, tapping, and vocabulary tests were repeated.

Some days after the experiment each subject was asked to estimate the length of time elapsing between the end of the experiment and the recovery from the emotional upset. This, of course, furnished merely a rough subjective estimate but it served to give a ranking of the stability of the subjects. Its validity will be considered in more detail later.

The subjects were also given a Pressey . . . X–O test of emotionality and the Woodworth . . . questionnaire and their height and weight obtained.[11]

The subjects were then rated, by several persons, as to emotional stability and expressiveness. The following data on the individuals were in a form where correlations could be worked out:

1. Expressiveness, Experimental, Objectively measured (including head movements).

2. Expressiveness, Experimental, Objectively measured (omitting head movements).

3. Expressiveness, Experimental, Subjectively estimated.

4. Stability, Experimental, the subject's estimate of the time which it took him to recover from the emotional upset of the experiment.

5. Amount of laughter, Experimental. Since photographs were taken of each change of expression, it is possible to compute the percent of the subject's reactions which showed a smile, grin, or laugh and to rank these percentages.

6. Emotionality, Rating scale estimate. . . .

7. Stability, Rating scale estimate. . . .

8. Expressiveness, Rating scale estimate. . . .

9. Score on the Woodworth questionnaire.

10. Pressey X-O test of emotionality scored for affectivity.

11. Pressey X-O test of emotionality scored for idiosyncrasy.

12. Range of systolic blood pressure during the experiment.

---

[10] Landis, C., Gullette, R., and Jacobsen, C.: "Criteria of Emotionality," *Pedagogical Seminary*, 32:213 (1925).

[11] *Ibid.*, 214.

13. The variability of systolic blood pressure. The number of changes of direction of pressure corrected for number and frequency of readings.

14. Reaction time. Fifteen of the subjects did a series of 100 choice reactions before the experiment and 100 choice reactions after the experiment. The subjects were ranked from the one showing the greatest increase in reaction time to the one showing the largest decrease.

15. Tapping test. Fourteen of the subjects were tapped three ten-second periods before and three ten-second periods after the experiment. The individuals were then ranked as for reaction time.

16. Vocabulary test. Thirteen of the subjects were ranked according to their increase or decrease in score before and after the experiment on the two halves of the recognition vocabulary test.

17. Height-weight ratio. Subjects were ranked according to their height-weight ratio.

18. and 19. Fatigue coefficients. The difference between the number of taps the first ten seconds and the third ten seconds before the experiment was divided by the number of taps of the first ten-second interval. This gives the fatigue coefficient (Laird) before the experiment. The same process was gone through to derive the coefficient for the tapping after the experiment.[12]

It should be stated, parenthetically, that the Pressey X–O (Cross-Out) Tests are an attempt to place the individual with respect to the number of emotionally-toned responses he makes to words (affectivity) and with respect to idiosyncrasy, i.e., his disagreement with the " blames " and worries of people generally. For example, the subject is asked to cross out every word unpleasant to him in lists such as the following: disgust, fear, sex, suspicion, aunt; and to cross out everything about which he has worried in lists such as: injustice, noise, self-consciousness, discouragement, germs. There are similar lists for crossing out things considered wrong, and a list of controlled association-words.[13] The Woodworth Questionnaire is considered in detail below (p. 419 ff.).

Landis and his associates admit the unreliability of their correlation coefficients, taken individually, but claim " that they offer such indications of interrelationship as to be highly suggestive."

The inter-correlations of these various criteria are certainly highly

---

[12] Landis, C., Gullette, R., and Jacobsen, C.: " Criteria of Emotionality," *Pedagogical Seminary*, 32:217–18.

[13] Pressey, S. L.: " A Group Scale for Investigating the Emotions," *Journal of Abnormal Psychology*, 16:55–64 (1921).

suggestive. They show very clearly that the criteria are measuring " emotionality " in varying degrees and that they are undoubtedly not all measuring the same aspects. All of which, the investigators claim, " goes to show that there is no fixed standard, and in the absence of such a standard we must fall back upon the consistency of the results and the number of significant correlations which any suggested criterion will give with other commonly accepted criteria ":

What then are the best criteria of emotionality examined in this study? Before answering, we must ask another question: What use do we wish to make of the criteria? If the criterion is to be used as a check of tests of emotionality, then the rating scale offers a satisfactory criterion, while the height-weight ratio offers a check for the rating scale. For experimental purposes some such measure of muscular activity as we have used in our " Expressiveness, Including head movements " gives a valuable criterion since it offers a combined factor of " expressiveness " and the augmented motor activity of emotional disturbance. For practical purposes of vocational and personnel work, the rating scale is probably more valuable than the test here investigated. Reaction time before and after some emotional shock would seem to be a valid criterion, but more research is needed on this test. The tests of aggressiveness probably give as practical a combination as is available for vocational and personnel work at present. For practical every day purposes the amount of laughter is a valid criterion of expressiveness but not of stability.

To what extent is aggressiveness indicative of stability? The rating scale showed that these factors are closely allied in the minds of most individuals, since the correlation of ratings of stability and unexpressiveness are very high. That this is actually the case is not very certain. We find that the actual stability (a doubtful standard) gives no significant correlation with expressiveness, but that significant correlations are found with reaction time, tapping test, vocabulary test and variability of blood pressure, which all seem to be fairly good criteria of stability. On this basis, we must conclude that expressiveness (amount of facial muscular activity) is more indicative of stability than instability.

Is systolic blood pressure indicative of emotionality or a direct measure of the degree of emotionality? To the latter part of this question we can say with comparative certainty " No." Since our results are in direct contradiction to the commonly accepted belief that range and variability of blood pressure are legitimate criteria of emotionality, we rather hesitate to be dogmatic. We can only say for this group high range and variability of pressure tend to be associated with stability rather than instability.

Are simple motor tests, or tests of complex behavior such as a vocabulary test, indicative of emotionality? We offer evidence, based on a limited number of cases, that these tests are indicative. We find that reaction time tends to be increased by emotional disturbance rather than decreased, as has been implied by several writers.

Is physical make-up indicative of emotionality? We find some evidence that it is. The macrosplanchnic tends to be expressive and to show the motor disturbance and stable blood pressure which we found concomitant with emotional disturbance.[14]

June Downey's Will-Temperament tests are one of the best known and most widely applied of all personality tests. These tests are based on the theory that muscular movements and their inhibitions reveal temperament and that certain simple situations, most of them involving handwriting, are good indices of general muscular movements and inhibitions. The bases for the development of these tests are described by Downey as follows:

The author's approach to the will-temperament test involved considerable preliminary experimentation. Two lines of investigation were followed: (1) An attempt to determine whether muscle-reading could be developed into a scientific method for study of individuality; and (2) an investigation of the degree to which personality could be determined from exercises in handwriting.

A word is in order concerning both types of investigation.

One of the most interesting demonstrations of the motor consequences of an idea is found in the common vaudeville stunt known as mind-reading, but which is more correctly termed muscle-reading. In such performances the mind-reader attempts to discover the place where an object is hidden by touching the hand or shoulder or forehead of some one who knows where it is and who by his unconscious movements guides the mind-reader to it. The information the trained muscle-reader may get from the guide, through contact, is truly amazing. It is quite possible to guess the number of which a person is thinking, or to identify a particular ace in a deck of playing cards, or to locate one word in a volume of several hundred pages, or to find a pin in a big building. . . .

In the author's own laboratory a series of experiments is now under way, in which the mind-reader gets his signal for recognition of the number of which a companion is thinking from the delicate dilation of the pupil of the eye which is a reflex movement absolutely outside of conscious control. . . .

But muscle-reading, although extraordinarily suggestive in its outcome, is not adapted to general testing, for the following reason: It depends too much

---

[14] Landis, Gullette and Jacobsen: *op. cit.*, 230–31.

for its success upon the skill of the operator, or muscle-reader . . . [and] the use of delicate apparatus is not practicable in rapid and extensive testing. . . .

The author's next departure concerned itself with the use of handwriting exercises in revelation of temperamental differences. The transition from muscle-reading to investigation of handwriting was a natural one to make, since in connection with muscle-reading it had been discovered that a very easy way to select a particularly good guide was to have him write for a short period while counting aloud, doing mental arithmetic, or in some other way keeping his attention off the writing. If he carried on the double process easily, and if, in addition, he wrote more rapidly under distraction than he did usually and enlarged his writing in size, he was pretty sure to be an excellent guide in muscle-reading.

Writing under distraction of attention throws into the foreground, in fact, the same contrasting temperaments that muscle-reading does: (1) the explosive suggestible individual who easily lets go of muscular control and produces involuntary automatic movements; and (2) the highly controlled individual who surrenders conscious guidance with great reluctance and shows this in the writing experiment by producing either a greatly retarded hand or else one excessively reduced in size. For tapping this particular trait of degree of motor-impulsion handwriting under distraction suggested itself as an appropriate test, and one whose outcome could be graded in terms of increased speed and size of writing, as will be shown later.

It seemed possible that handwriting exercises might be used to test other temperamental traits. Many handwriting experts believe that from a person's writing they can tell much about his character. . . . The writer became interested in these attempts to interpret personality from the handwriting, and instituted a series of researches to determine whether they held any measure of correctness. . . . In the main the beliefs of the graphologists were not confirmed, but some of their ideas were in part found to be correct.

Such possibility as there exists of reading character from handwriting is due to the appearance in handwriting of the signs of the free release of the motor impulses that produce writing or the reverse. In other words, it is possible to identify in handwriting signs of motor explosiveness and motor inhibition.

These signs were identified by the author through two distinct lines of experimentation:

(1) The production of automatic writing; and

(2) The determination of the characteristics of handwriting that is deliberately disguised.

Samples of automatic writing were obtained for study by a long period of training in which the persons concerned learned how to write automatically a memorized verse while the attention was concentrated on reading a story aloud or silently. It was found that the automatic hand was a large, light, continuous hand slanted toward the right, with, frequently, superfluous strokes or random movements. It gave evidence of hyperkinetic tendencies.

When conditions were reversed and attention was definitely concentrated upon handwriting in the endeavor to produce a disguised hand or one completely unlike one's usual hand, very different characteristics appeared. A disguised hand shows evidences of excessive control and inhibition. It is a small, heavy, cramped, broken hand, with a tendency toward vertical or back-slant. It may also exhibit artificial ornamentation and bizarre curlicues.

In the ordinary writing it is possible to see manifestations of the free or obstructed release of writing movements such as are exaggerated in automatic and disguised writing, and on the basis of these signs it is possible for an expert to draw conservative conclusions concerning the penman's general characteristics.

The interesting thing in this connection was the confirmation of the author's previous conclusion that differences in constitutional motor make-up are mirrored in activity.

It appeared also that handwriting exercises would be an excellent way of recording the acts of individuals when confronted with certain situations, because writing is a muscular movement that leaves behind it a permanent record, and nearly everyone knows how to write.[15]

Having determined upon her method and its justification, Downey built up three groups of tests about the three phases of the dynamic pattern that seemed most essential to her: " (1) those of speed and fluidity of reaction; (2) those of forcefulness and decisiveness of reaction; (3) those of carefulness and persistence of reaction." Four tests were devised for each group. The first group included tests " intended " to measure speed of movement, freedom from load (ratio of natural speed to capacity speed), flexibility, speed of decision. The second group included tests " intended " to measure motor impulsion, reaction to contradiction, resistance to opposition, and finality of judgment. The third group " intended " to measure motor inhibition, interest in detail, coordination of impulses and volitional perseveration.

Let us consider first what these tests actually embody in order that we may come to some conclusion as to whether they really measure what Dr. Downey claims. The " traits " in the first group are measured respectively as follows: by the time taken to write the phrase " United States of America "; the ratio obtained by dividing the normal by the

---

[15] Downey, June: The Will-Temperament and Its Testing (1923), 49–58.

speeded time of writing; the capacity to disguise the handwriting and to imitate model hands; the time taken by the subject to check on a list of character traits those descriptive of himself. The traits in the second group are measured by the speed with which writing could be maintained under distraction and the magnification or decrease of writing under these conditions; the reactions of the subject to deliberate contradiction regarding an earlier choice of an envelope; the reactions of the subject to blocking the pencil-point when he is writing his name with his eyes closed; the amount of time spent in revising the checks made earlier on the list of character traits. The measurements in the third group are: the length of time the writing of the given phrase could be voluntarily retarded; the exactness with which a model is imitated, when instructions are given to copy it as exactly as possible, and when only general instructions are given, and the relative time consumed on a rapid and an exact imitation; the writing of the given phrase on a very short line at top-speed; the time spent in working out a disguised hand.

There is little independent evidence that the traits named are actually measured by the tests listed. This is, indeed, a difficulty faced by all tests of personality. Intelligence tests have usually been " validated " by having teachers, etc., rate the pupils with regard to intelligence. It turned out that this method gave fairly high correlations, but the reason was undoubtedly the great dependence of intelligence tests on the subjects learned in school, and the familiarity of the teachers with the performance of the children in just such situations as the tests involved. But rating in traits such as these claimed to be measured by the will-temperament tests presents no such simplicity, and the results that have been obtained from them are ambiguous. As May points out:

One difficulty seems to be that judges simply cannot identify the psychological traits supposedly measured by the Downey tests. . . . For example, take the first trait, Speed of Movement. The rater is asked to judge an individual on his general speed of movement. The judge naturally thinks about how quickly he moves, how fast he walks, how fast he talks, etc. But the test measures how fast he writes. If the judges were asked for an opinion of the subject's speed of handwriting, the correlations might be higher. If this is the case, then these results show that the Downey tests do not measure the traits named in the labels.[16]

---

[16] May, Mark A.: " The Present Status of the Will-Temperament Tests," *Journal of Applied Psychology*, 9:39–40 (1925).

It seems obvious that much more fundamental research will have to be done on the relation of various speeds of movements before speed of handwriting can be accepted as a valid test of the trait generally. And this limitation [17] applies not only to other of the traits listed here by Downey, but to practically all of the tests in the first section of the summary by May and Hartshorne.

What part has the will-temperament, as measured by these tests, been shown to play in determining behavior? A study made by Poffenberger and Carpenter is strongly suggestive as regards the part played by will-temperament in success in school. Ninety-seven school children in grades 6, 7 and 8 were ranked for school success by each of three teachers, and the average ranking obtained. The average ratings gave correlation coefficients around .70 with mental age and IQ. On the basis of the scatter diagrams, the subjects were divided into two groups — one in which the success was greater than the IQ indicated, and the other in which the success was less than the IQ indicated. These groups were designated the " Success " group, and the " Failure " group. They were then given will-temperament tests, with the following procedure and results:

Each one of the twelve parts of the test was plotted separately against each other part. . . . These were inspected to find critical combinations of scores, or those that were characteristics of " Success " or " Failure " in school accomplishment. Thirty-one of the pairs were found to give such combinations of scores and these were used in our computations described below. The records of each individual in our two groups were examined, and whenever he had score in any pair of traits which put him in the " Success " area of a scatter diagram, he was given a score of 1 for that combination of traits; whenever he had a

---

[17] The so-called validity given to tests of various sorts by correlations with ratings should be seriously called into question. Only by comparing actions with actions, and finding their intercorrelations can test situations be validated. Rating is, of course, accepted as a short-cut to behavior-observation, on the assumption that persons who know the subject well will be able to rate him in terms of a great number of previous behavior-observations, which in turn have taken their places in a comparative scale composed of similar behavior-observations on all other persons with whom the rater has come in contact. But the tricks that bias plays with regard to memory, the almost chance over-weighting of some specific act, the subjectivity of definitions of traits, the part played by varying traditions, etc., in these definitions, necessarily make ratings exceedingly unreliable and inconsistent, even by the most " honest " and careful raters.

score which put him in the " Failure " area of a diagram he was given a score of — 1 for that combination of traits. If the scores obtained in this way by each individual child for the whole thirty-one combinations are averaged separately for two groups the following figures are obtained:

	" Success " Group	" Failure " Group
Av. of plus scores	9.4	3.5
Av. of minus scores	3.6	9.9

The above figures do suggest that the group of " Success " children possesses certain combinations of scores in common, and that the " Failure " group possesses certain different combinations of scores in common.[18]

The combinations of will-temperament traits which were associated with failure and success were then worked out in detail, with the following results and inferences:

The five pairs of traits whose possession is most indicative of success and the five whose possession is most indicative of failure are given below:

" Success "	" Failure "
Swift coördination and swift decision on self.	Slow coördination and swift decision on self.
Motor impulsion and flexibility.	Lack of both motor impulsion and flexibility.
High speed of movement and freedom from load.	Low speed of movement and freedom from load.
Care for detail and lack of motor inhibition.	Lack of care for detail and motor inhibition.
Flexibility and high assurance.	Flexibility and low assurance.

This brief study suggests two conclusions, each of which should be further tested upon large groups of subjects and with more refined technique:

1. Certain so-called character traits do contribute to success or failure in school work. These are, on the whole, what common sense would lead us to expect. For instance, speed and flexibility of reaction, assurance, perseverance, and care for detail are traits indicative of success, while the failures tend to lack speed, and flexibility, to be careless and not persevering. Other traits take on significance when one goes back of the mere name and analyzes the actual task performed. All such important traits should be discovered and an attempt made to determine their relative weight.

2. These traits are such as can be measured by relatively simple test

[18] Poffenberger, A. T., and Carpenter, F. L.: " Character Traits in School Success," *Journal of Experimental Psychology*, 7:70–71 (1924).

methods, which might be incorporated into our present intelligence examinations with slight modifications. Care for detail, perseverance, freedom from load, and flexibility would seem to the writers to be most readily measured in this way.[19]

Other studies have not shown uniformly consistent results in the prognostic value of the will-temperament tests. For instance, Downey herself reports a distinct raising of correlation coefficients when grades in school are correlated with a combination of intelligence tests scores and will-temperament test scores over the correlation coefficients between intelligence scores alone and grades in school. But the will-temperament scores alone are found to give a lower prognosis (i.e., lower correlation) of grades than the intelligence tests. Summarizing the evidence, May says:

As supplements to intelligence tests the WT tests have great promise. But what behavior may be predicted by the WT tests alone has not been determined.[20]

As to the relation between the behavior called delinquency and will-temperament there is little evidence. Bryant obtained, however, suggestive results in a comparison of delinquent boys at the Whittier State School with a control group of high school boys comparable in age, intelligence, etc., with the delinquents. There were marked differences in the average of total scores obtained and the range of scores for the two groups. The range of the control group is from 40 to 81, of the delinquents from 22 to 75. The two medians are respectively 61 and 45.5. We have seen, in our discussion of the relation of intelligence test scores to delinquency how unreliable the conclusions are until the tests have been more carefully validated and until the various factors influencing the tests have been more carefully studied. The same limitations apply, of course, in dealing with tests of this sort. Bryant's own conclusions with regard to her data are as follows:

From our present data, the significance of total scores of delinquent and non-delinquent juveniles shows that the total score *per se* is somewhat an indication of delinquency. The range and median are both appreciably lower than in the control group. The close correspondence of the control group total

[19] Poffenberger, A. T., and Carpenter, F. L.: "Character Traits in School Success," *Journal of Experimental Psychology*, 7:73–74.

[20] May: *op. cit.*, 48.

scores to the norms for superior adults would seem to make this difference more one of delinquency than of intelligence or age.

Speed of decision brings out an appreciable difference between the two groups. This difference we felt to be more one of emotional maturity than speed of decision. A certain degree of self-understanding and insight into the individual problems is noticeably lacking in the majority of delinquent boys. Sometimes it is the ability and sometimes the habit of a normal amount of introspection, or both, that the delinquent boy lacks. As a whole, the delinquent group is far less able and ready to wrestle with the subjective problems brought on with adolescence.

Motor inhibition tends to bring out some difference between the two groups, but the difference is less marked than in speed of decision. *Coördination of impulses*, however, points out a striking difference. Adolescence and, to a small degree, intelligence are apparently factors here, but delinquency is also present. This deficiency in the delinquent boy is not a surprise. He lacks that ability to grasp a situation and bring to a focus all his resources in an effort to master it. One is frequently impressed with this sense of energy and latent ability, but absence of that trait which enables him to put this power to use.

This scale has evidently hit upon two or three of the more striking differences between delinquents and non-delinquents. The elements in speed of decision and coördination of impulses seem to bring out important differences. Whether or not these tests have been rightly labelled is a matter of less concern until a sufficient number of cases have borne out the indications of the findings with this small group.[21]

As to the relation between will-temperament and intelligence, the total scores on the will-temperament tests have been found to give uniformly significant correlation coefficients of the order of about .5 with intelligence test scores. The individual tests have been found, however, to have inconsistent relations with intelligence tests scores. Downey claims that the tests may be said to measure the quality rather than the level of intelligence, but there is little proof that this is so. May's deduction from the evidence is: " The only thing we can say is that they test something that does not appear to be intelligence but which correlates highly with scores on intelligence tests." [22] And his final conclusion regarding the value of these tests is expressed as follows:

---

[21] Bryant, Edythe K.: " Delinquents and Non-Delinquents on the Will-Temperament Test," *Journal of Delinquency*, 8:63 (1923).

[22] May: *op. cit.*, 49.

Can behavior be predicted by these tests? The results seem to show that academic success is in some instances better predicted by a combination of WT tests and intelligence tests than by intelligence alone. But when we consider the rather high correlation between some types of intelligence tests and the WT tests we wonder how much of the prophecy is due to intelligence and how much to temperament.

While it is true that the WT tests will not foretell what any person will do in a given situation, yet the general nature of his reactions may be predicted. For example, Downey would say that the will-profile will foretell whether or not an individual's responses will be strong or weak, deliberate or impulsive, aggressive or its opposite, and so on. This type of prediction is very desirable and it seems that the WT tests have definite value at this point.[23]

Closely related to the study of will-temperament are the studies of personality in terms of introversion and extroversion. These, however, are of several widely diverse types, and have neither been so widely applied as the will-temperament tests nor so widely checked against behavior. The most clear-cut of these studies is by Leslie R. Marston.[24] He describes his problem as follows:

Introversion and extroversion as emotionally determined character tendencies have been distinguished physiologically on the basis of the disposition of the energy aroused by emotional stimulation, extroversion being the ready issue of such energy in overt adjustments to the environment, introversion being the dissipation of such energy within the organism or its drainage through non-adaptive skeletal channels. The most effective stimulus to the inhibition of skeletal expression in the introvert . . . is social.

If this distinction between the introvert and extrovert is valid, then it should be possible to differentiate individuals of the two types by their reactions to situations that exaggerate the opposing tendencies in the respective types. Two general methods of making such behavior distinctions suggest themselves, (1) the rating method, according to which classifications are made on the basis of prolonged and intimate contacts with the individual to be classified, and (2) the behavioristic method, in which the individual's reactions to natural yet controlled situations are observed. These methods . . . are probably best adapted to the investigation of personality traits of young children.

The specific problem of the present investigation has been to determine, by

[23] May: *op. cit.*, 50–51.
[24] "The Emotions of Young Children, an Experimental Study in Introversion and Extroversion," *University of Iowa Studies in Child Welfare*, 3 (No. 3):1–94 (1925).

means of these methods, to what extent young children's reactions to their environment, particularly social, are conditioned by constant tendencies to introversion and extroversion.

The subjects of the investigation were 100 children between two and six years of age. Of this number fifty-six comprised the main experimental group, made up of children from the Pre-School Laboratory of the Iowa Child Welfare Research Station of the State University of Iowa. The remaining forty-four children comprised the control group. . . . The range in ages is from twenty-seven to sixty-nine months for the thirty-one boys, and from twenty-three to seventy-one months for the twenty-five girls [in the main experimental group] with average ages of 51.3 and 51.2 months respectively. The average mental age of the boys exceeds their average chronological age ten months, and the average mental age of the girls exceeds their average chronological age thirteen months. The intelligent quotient range is from 82 to 153 for the boys, and from 85 to 158 for the girls, with averages of 119 and 125 respectively. There are no significant sex differences of central tendency in height and weight. The outstanding fact is the intellectual superiority of these children who come largely from homes of the university community.[25]

His first step was to develop a rating scale consisting of twenty traits of introversion each paired against a corresponding trait of extroversion. There was, of necessity, a good deal of arbitrariness in the traits chosen to represent introversion and extroversion on this rating scale, and, although Marston claims that " the various traits included in the scale described manifestations of introversion and extroversion largely in terms of the organism's disposition of the energy aroused by emotional stimulation," yet it would be very difficult to prove that judgment of these traits depended on any such basis. It is, indeed, difficult to understand how many of these traits could be rated at all objectively, e.g., " does not pass quickly from elation to depression," " emotions not freely expressed," etc. The average of the ratings on the fifty-six children seems to differentiate three " types," the extrovert, the introvert and the ambivert. " Profiles " of the seven children rated as most introvert and those rated as most extrovert show that there is no overlapping on any of the ratings of the twenty traits. Marston takes this to mean that the rating scale is highly diagnostic of introversion and extroversion. A very just criticism may be made of any study of this character, however, i.e., that the statistical results show merely how the raters

---

[25] *Ibid.*, 16–19.

judged a group of children — were probably diagnostic to a large degree of the rater's mental qualities and did not necessarily show much about the children themselves. The definition of personality types which Marston makes on the basis of the children's reactions to experimental situations is very much more convincing:

Each of the fifty-six children . . . was placed in five distinct situations. . . . In general the children reacted to the experiments as to natural situations. Their school training was most favorable to the success of the methods employed. They were accustomed to " games " with adults in the examining rooms, and after the first or second " game " of this series were eager to accompany the experimenter in quest of new activities. Notwithstanding the fact that no artificial rewards or punishment were bestowed, strong motivation was the rule. . . . In a few instances, however, a child refused to play the " game," but inasmuch as the same child usually refused in more than one instance, refusal was a characteristic reaction of certain children and as significant of emotional traits as was coöperation in other children.[26]

In the first of these experiments the trait " intended " to be measured was the degree of social resistance on the part of the child to the approach of a stranger:

The occasion of this experiment was the child's first meeting with M (the experimenter). An assistant whom the child knew engaged him in an interesting activity in the examination room, a portion of which was so screened as to conceal M from the child's view. M made known his presence by noisily moving about to prevent serious fright in the child when later he should suddenly be left alone with M. . . . After a short time the assistant left the room, having first asked the child to await her return. In leaving the room she so adjusted the screen as to bring M into full view and at the same time provide the child a ready means of concealment. M, seated at a low table and manipulating an attractive toy, a teeter-tauter, busied himself with his notes and the toy, and entirely ignored the presence of the child unless the child overcame all social resistance, approached M, and began playing with the toy. This indifference was maintained for sixty seconds. If the child did not promptly break through the social resistance and approach M it is probable that the minute of indifference increased the resistance, which M then sought to overcome. At the close of the minute M looked up at the child for a moment but did not smile or make other overtures of friendliness. For another thirty seconds he busied himself with the toy and his notes and then again looked up, this time smiling at the child. After another thirty seconds he looked up and asked the

---

[26] " The Emotions of Young Children, an Experimental Study in Introversion and Extroversion," *University of Iowa Studies in Child Welfare*, 3 (No. 3):49 (1925).

child, " Do you like to teeter-tauter? " If the child's special resistance had not yet been overcome, after another thirty seconds M looked up and asked cordially, " Would you like to play with this teeter-tauter? " If the child failed to approach and play with the toy at this recognition, M said reassuringly " You may; come over and play with it." If the child still refused, M urged persistently.[27]

The reactions to this experiment were classified as showing six degrees of social resistance, which were assumed to range from complete introversion to complete extroversion. These were described as follows: (1) " Child refused unyieldingly to play with the toy or fled from the room; " (2) " Child refused at first, but played with the toy after considerable urging; " (3) " Child accepted the offer to play with the toy after receiving assurance from the experimenter or accepted with marked hesitancy of manner; " (4) " Child promptly accepted the offer to play with the toy without assurance or urging from the experimenter; " (5) " Child made advances to the experimenter, but did not approach at once or play with the toy before being recognized by the experimenter; " (6) " Child did not wait for recognition, but promptly approached and played with the toy." [28]

The second experiment was designed to measure the degree of compliance, which, Marston claims, " may safely be considered an introvert trait except in those extreme cases of introversion . . . in which negativism is pronounced ": [29]

As the child entered the examination room, M directed his attention to a toy celluloid duck floating in a shallow pan of water, and after securing his interest asked if he would like to play a game with a " lot of ducks." M then suggested that while he finished some work at the table, the child open the box containing the ducks, after which, M assured the child, they would play the game. The box was a Corona typewriter case with complicated fastenings. . . . Three minutes were allowed, during which time M recorded the child's reactions to the situation. If the child gave up, M stimulated to renewed effort by reminding him of the duck game. At the close of the three minutes M offered his assistance and opened the box.[30]

There were found to be five type reactions, ranging again from extreme introversion to extreme extroversion, and described in behavior terms, as in the first situation. The children who did not become interested in the game, and refused to have anything to do with it, were scored for extreme introversion.

---

[27] *Ibid.*, 50–51.   [28] *Ibid.*, 54–55.   [29] *Ibid.*, 57.   [30] *Ibid.*, 57–58.

The third experiment attempted to measure the caution factor, but " the technic failed to differentiate quantitatively definable degrees of caution as qualities of introversion and extroversion." [31]

The fourth experiment was designed to measure interest. " The direction of interest, inward towards one's own mental processes or outward towards objects, is probably the most generally recognized single criterion of introversion and extroversion ": [32]

The environment selected for the experiment was Mammal Hall of the University Museum, containing a wide variety of interesting animal exhibits. . . . At the entrance to the hall M gave the child the lead, assuring him that he might go anywhere he liked. M recorded by a line on tracing paper over a specially prepared plot of the hall the child's course from exhibit to exhibit. Stops were indicated by a cross, questions by question marks, and the child's position at the close of each minute by an encircled numeral. . . . M did not converse with the child except to answer questions. At the end of fifteen minutes the visit was concluded unless the child had previously indicated his desire to return to school, in which case M consented. If the child refused to move away from the entrance or away from M, the latter led the way to some of the exhibits, recording his own path with a dotted line.[33]

The children were scored from extreme introversion to extreme extroversion by the number of stops they made. The reaction types corresponding were: (1) " The non-coöperative; " (2) " The inhibited introvert refused to move spontaneously about the room and depended upon the experimenter for motive and direction; " (3) " The interested introvert traveled a short distance, manifested keen interest in the environment, to the degree of absorption, remained long before each exhibit, and therefore observed few different exhibits; " (4) " The disinterested introvert traveled a long distance, stopped infrequently before exhibits, showed a general lack of interest in the environment, and tended to resort to habituated reaction, such as walking; " (5) " The extrovert traveled a long distance, stopped frequently before exhibits, and generally manifested a keen but rapidly shifting interest in the environment." [34]

The fifth experiment was designed to measure the degree of self-assertion:

[31] " The Emotions of Young Children, an Experimental Study in Introversion and Extroversion," *University of Iowa Studies in Child Welfare*, 3 (No. 3):65 (1925).   [32] *Ibid.*, 65.   [33] *Ibid.*, 65.   [34] *Ibid.*, 68–69.

Three attractive mechanical toys were exhibited and the child was asked with which toy he wished to play. . . . Whatever his choice, M gave him one that he had not chosen, but promised him that he could play with the other toys after he had played with the one given him. When, during a three-minute period, the child asked for another toy or at the close of the three-minute period if he had not asked for another, M gave him the second non-preferred toy. He was given the preferred toy if during a second three-minute interval, he asked for it, or at the close of this interval, he had not asked for it. The child was permitted to play with the preferred toy for five minutes. The other toys were left within his reach so that he might return to them if he wished. The toys were a teeter-tauter, a swing, and a merry-go-round, similar in their circular movement, in being easily manipulated, and in carrying similar miniature toy children.[35]

Marston considers this a good measure of introversion and extroversion generally rather than of the trait he "intended" it to measure because of the fact that perseveration of interest (held to be an introvert trait) might invalidate it as a measure of self-assertion in the case of some children "whose failure to ask for another toy was clearly due to the interest they developed in the toy that had been substituted." Reactions were scored again from the extreme introvert (non-coöperative) who was given o, to the extreme extrovert, who promptly (within a minute) abandoned the non-preferred toy and demanded the preferred one, and was given a score of 5.

The importance of these results lies in the fact that behavior types are quite definitely differentiated [36] by the experiments used here, and that these experiments have probably some meaning in the terms of Marston's definitions of them. The scores obtained on each of the experiments correlate positively with the scores obtained on each of the other experiments to a degree that is usually significant. The total scores correlate with the ratings by about .50. All of which probably means that there is a general "extroversion-introversion" factor in a child's habitual reactions, which manifested itself in his reactions to specific experimental situations, and which raters who know his general behavior were able to identify fairly satisfactorily.

The significance of these results lies in the fact that these great

[35] *Ibid.*, 71-72.

[36] Irrespective of the method of scoring, which is, of course, quite arbitrary. The particular distribution given either by rating or by scoring on experiment is a function of the method of scoring.

differences in types of reactions are so clearly differentiated at so early
an age level. From the standpoint of their significance for behavior
study, little is known. How far these traits are correlated with " success " in various types of adjustments, how far they are modified by
training and experience, etc., is not brought out in a study of this kind.

Other studies of introversion and extroversion have dealt with adult
reaction-types. Allport and Allport make out a case for the qualitative
rather than the quantitative approach in these studies on rather loosely
defined *a priori* grounds. They say:

Individual differences are so great and personal traits so vaguely related to
the solution of problems that the notion of an age scale in personality has no
significance. Moreover, personalities of divers sorts succeed equally well in the
general adaptation to situations of practical life. It may be added that differences of personality are of a qualitative rather than a quantitative sort. These
difficulties stand in the way of the development of a personality measurement
based on the correlation between tests and familiar objective criteria such as
those of intelligence. We must strive toward a descriptive treatment rather
than quantitative. Our aim is personality study and description rather than
personality testing.[37]

They take the point of view that personality reactions occur in the
" field of social interaction," and that the description of personality, to
have any validity, " must be the description in quantified terms of that
personality by a group of persons with whom he is wont to come into
contact. It is with the average of the ratings of such a group of persons
that our instruments of analysis must be correlated." Without going into
any detail here as to the difficulties facing any such methodological
problem, let us consider what results the Allports get in their personality
analysis. Their aim is, after all, to get what might be considered a
clinical picture of the individual. This clinical picture is finally given in
terms of extroversion and introversion. They applied ratings in various
traits, and certain crude tests to fifty-five individuals, and plotted these
on graphs in " quantified terms."

The categories into which their analysis of personality falls are listed
as Intelligence, Emotional Breadth and Strength, Self-Expression, Extroversion-Introversion, Ascendance-Submission, Expansion-Reclusion,
Compensation, Insight and Self-Evaluation, Social Participation, Self-

---

[37] Allport, F. H., and Allport, G. W.: " Personality Traits: Their Classification
and Measurement," *Journal of Abnormal Psychology*, 16:6 (1921).

Seeking and Aggressive Self-Seeking, Susceptibility to Social Stimuli. It is unnecessary to go in any detail into the authors' treatment of most of these traits. The definitions are usually obscure and the treatment non-objective. Test situations which were set up and tried out for most of these traits seem to have given results unsatisfactory to the authors. They report, however, two or three test situations, which gave interesting results. These tests are described as follows:

Test of Ascendance-Submission. For the purpose of measuring this trait an Active-Passive Reaction Study was devised. This study consisted of the description of a number of typical situations in each of which the ascendant-submissive relation was involved. The subject was asked to react in a spontaneous, emotional manner to these situations, and to write down immediately the way in which he would conduct himself if faced with the conditions described. This type of test, to be sure, presupposes the co-operation of the subjects, and an interest on the part of each in actually analyzing and truthfully presenting his own type of behavior rather than in merely making a good impression.

Following are two of the typical situations presented in the Active-Passive Study. They will serve to give the reader a general idea of the test method as well as of the nature of the ascendant-submissive relation which we are now considering.

(1) Suppose you are 10 years of age now, but with the traits you actually had at that age. You are playing war with some boys the same age. (a) Are they likely to make you fight on the side of Germany? (b) If they do, what will you do about it?

(2) Upon leaving college you become a salesman and are trying to sell a life insurance policy to a middle-aged financier of great note. He says, " Young man, I don't know how long you have been in the game, but you will never succeed unless you acquire more experience and confidence in yourself." What will you say or do?

In the first situation (fighting on the side of Germany) an interesting series of scores was derived. It was found that the individuals who appeared on the basis of their answers in the Reaction Study as a whole to fall in the ascendant group reacted usually by recording an active struggle to keep from being made a German, or at least a refusal to play the game under such humiliating circumstances. The submissive individuals were, in three cases out of every four, those who simply acquiesced and played the rôle of the German. Another response indicating the trait of submission, though to a less degree, was the attitude of acceptance with the idea of making Germany win. . . .

It is significant that when all the situations had been scored there was usually a sufficient incidence of the ascendant and submissive answers in the case of any individual subject to allow for a fairly consistent and certain decision as to the type to which the individual belonged. When the subjects were all ranked from the most ascendant to the most submissive on the basis of these scores the correlation with the ranking by Personality Rating was found to be .40. Considering the tentative nature, both of the situations used and the method of scoring, as well as the inadequacy of the technique of rating, this correlation is high enough to justify further development of tests of this nature. . . .

Test of Expansion-Reclusion. We endeavored to get a measurement of this quality by asking the subjects each to write a letter answering an advertisement of a position, a letter in which one would be free to tell as much or as little about one's self as desired. The advertisement which was answered was worded as follows:

> Wanted: Young men for detective work; good government
> positions ahead. No experience required. Address, Ganor,
> St. Louis, Box 177.

The instruction was to answer this advertisement as seriously and with as natural a reaction as if actually seeking the position. The subject could say as much or as little as he chose.

The letters produced were read and scored by a group of twelve graduate students in psychology on the basis of the trait of expansion-reclusion. The score of 1 was given to a letter indicating the most expansive personality which they could imagine to occur in a group of 50; the score of 50 indicating the most reclusive. The following expressions of this trait were borne in mind in rating the letters: a considerable number of references to self, statement in detail of qualifications, particularly those of a rather personal sort, and the development of subjective ideas, feelings, and interests in relation to detective work. The absence of these characteristics combined with general meagerness or brevity, and the general impression of conveying little about the personality, were grounds for scoring the letter on the reclusive side of the scale.

Examples of the expansive and reclusive types of letter are given below:

Letter of D (Expansive):

Mr. Ganor, Box 177,
St. Louis,
Dear Sir: —

In replying to your ad, I should like to say that I am desirous of undertaking this work because I feel introspectively capable of doing the work. I think that this line of occupation is one that cannot fail to keep up my interest — is one

extremely variegated and opening up new channels of adventure at each succeeding step — of which, I must say, I am extremely fond. I do not hesitate to
say that I am positively certain of being able to do the work knowing as I do
that I am gifted for it and shall undertake it, if successful in obtaining the
position, in the full confidence that I will make good. I must acknowledge,
however, that I have had no practical experience whatever in this line, but I
think my lack in this respect will be compensated for by my enthusiasm for
undertaking this work.

Hoping to hear favorably from you,

Very sincerely yours,

Letter of R (Reclusive):

Mr. Ganor,
Box 177,
St. Louis, Mo.
Dear Sir: —

Having seen your advertisement for men for detective work, I am writing
you that you may consider me as one of the men desirous of entering that
work. At present I am a senior at Harvard University expecting to finish my
course about the last of June. Until that time I would not be able to consider
entering your service, but if you do not expect to enroll men immediately, I
would be glad if you would keep me in mind, knowing that you could count on
me surely by the end of June, 1921.

Sincerely,

The correlation between the average ratings of the letters made by the
twelve judges and the Personality Rating was .34, which again must be considered suggestive in the light of crude and tentative methods.[38]

The personality graphs, based on the ratings and tests, are analyzed
as follows:

Certain types seemed to fall out from our fifty-five graphs; viz., the strong
type of personality (extroverted) either social or a-social, and the weak type
of personality (introverted) either social or a-social. We find interesting relations between these major types of personality and temperament itself (emotionality), e.g., the tendency of the extroverted individual to have narrow and
strong emotions and of the introvert to have broad but superficial emotions.
In general the emotionality of the strong type is of greater breadth and
strength than the emotionality of the weak type.[39]

---

[38] Allport, F. H., and Allport, G. W.: "Personality Traits: Their Classification
and Measurement," *Journal of Abnormal Psychology,* 16:14–17 (1921).

[39] *Ibid.,* 36.

The Allports claim to have made no more than a tentative approach to the study of personality. Their personality graphs are interesting as showing differences in reactions in general terms of introversion and extroversion, but the non-objective nature of most of their work detracts from the value of these items (even though they are expressed in " quantified terms "). They, too, have made no attempt to trace out the prognostic value of tests and ratings of this character with regard to the individual's " success " in various types of situations. They content themselves with the entirely *a priori* statement that " personalities of divers sorts succeed equally well in the general adaptation to situations of practical life."

A third attempt to define and test personality reactions in general terms of introversion and extroversion should be mentioned. This is an approach from the point of view of abnormal psychology and presents what appears to be a successful method of differentiating the extremes of introversion and extroversion as represented by dementia praecox (schizophrenia) and hysteria (psychoneurosis) respectively. It is suggested that this method will also differentiate between " normal " extroverts and introverts, but the evidence is somewhat inconclusive.

Travis' study is based on the observation of the characteristics of the two types of abnormals:

The more one comes in contact with cases of schizophrenia and hysteria, the more one is convinced that they embrace two diametrically opposed sets of characteristics. The one abnormality is characterized by suggestibility, splitting of consciousness, and dissociation. The other is introversion, shattering of the personality, and negativism.[40]

He concluded that these characteristics would probably evidence themselves in the raising or lowering of the auditory threshold during reverie, and that this change in threshold might be an index of personality type. To test this out, he set up an experiment as follows:

The apparatus used in this experiment . . . consists of a tone generator, resistances to control the intensity of the tone, a receiver, by means of which the tone is heard by the subject, a key and buzzer circuit whereby the subject can respond when the tone is heard, a crystal to serve as an aid to the imagination of the subject, and a make-key for the experimenter. . . . The silent key

---

[40] Travis, Lee E.: " Suggestibility and Negativism as Measured by Auditory Threshold During Reverie," *Journal of Abnormal Psychology*, 18:354 (1924).

of the response circuit, the crystal, and the watchcase receiver are in the dark room, which is considerably removed from the laboratory, while the remainder of the apparatus is in the laboratory. . . .

The observer is seated comfortably in a rocking chair with the elbows resting on the arms. When the watchcase receiver has been firmly adjusted, the individual is placed snugly against a table of average writing height, on which is the crystal and the silent signal key. The mercury key is quite sensitive, but still some effort is necessary to make contact. Both the key and the crystal can be shifted so as to be most convenient, and the individual is always asked to make everything as agreeable as possible in order that distractions and annoyances might not interrupt the day-dreaming.

The threshold before the crystal-gazing is obtained with the lights on and the crystal removed from sight. The observer is told to attend strictly to the tones, taking special pains not to let the mind wander, and respond every time a tone is heard. He is told that the tones will become fainter and fainter, and is advised to concentrate fully on the task at hand. When this threshold is ascertained, the lights are turned off except the blue one under the crystal, the crystal is replaced, and the following instructions given. . . .

" Relax completely and forget all present surroundings, such as the receiver against your ear, the signal key beneath your finger, the chair in which you are sitting, and the table on which your arm is resting. Just day-dream and build air-castles, letting your mind wander wherever it will. Do not particularly listen for the tones which you have been hearing. Do not, however, resist them. Think that if they come your finger will press the key. Gaze steadfastly into the crystal, which will aid you to abstract. Do not permit your eyes to wander, but keep them fixed on the crystal. Suggest to yourself that you are drifting and floating away into a restful and relaxed condition of existence. Do not be afraid to lose yourself in reverie as you will not be disturbed for quite a long time."

It is difficult adequately to describe the appearance of the crystal illuminated by the blue light beneath. Briefly it gives the appearance of the heavens on a clear, star-lit night. The whole setting of course is suggestive, and has such an effect upon the hysterical type of individual. The data indicate the influence of such an environment upon the other type of personality.

After the observer is left in the dark room for five or ten minutes subliminal tones are given. If responses are elicited the intensity of the tones is decreased until no responses are forthcoming. On the other hand, if the subliminal tones are not responded to, the intensity is increased until the individual does respond. In the case of the observer whose threshold lowers during crystal gazing, the faintest tone to which he will respond is taken as his threshold during that period. In the instance of the individual whose threshold rises during crystal gazing, the tone needed to elicit a response is taken as the threshold for the period. . . . All tones are given in such a manner as to avoid any possible chance of the operation of a summation effect.

After the crystal gazing threshold is verified by being ascertained two or three times during the crystal gazing period, which generally lasts from thirty to sixty minutes, the observer is interrupted, the lights are turned on and the crystal removed. The instructions given and the method used for obtaining the threshold after the crystal gazing period are the same as those for obtaining the threshold before crystal gazing. Care should be taken to make sure that the observer, especially one of the hysterical type, is thoroughly aroused, or the lowered threshold may continue to function in the following period. Daydreaming is so pleasurable to some individuals that when it is once begun under such favorable circumstances as the crystal gazing situation affords, it may continue to operate in the post-crystal gazing period.[41]

The data which Travis obtains in this study, although based on a very inadequate number of cases, are highly suggestive. He first tried the experiment on 15 abnormal individuals, 14 of whom had been diagnosed by hospital psychiatrists. In all the seven cases diagnosed as belonging to the psychoneurotic group (five of them determined hysterias) the threshold lowered during crystal gazing. The threshold of the other seven, all of whom had been diagnosed as dementia praecox, rose during crystal gazing. He then applied the experiment to 10 " normal " individuals, and found that the thresholds of six of these were lowered and four raised during crystal gazing (in lesser degree than the abnormals). Judgments by from 3 to 5 persons who knew each observer " more or less intimately " — as to whether he was suggestible, accessible and sociable or negativistic, inaccessible and seclusive — were obtained on nine of these subjects. In all of the cases where the threshold was raised, the judges agreed that the subject was negativistic, inaccessible and seclusive. In four of the cases where the threshold was lowered, there was complete agreement that the subject was suggestible, accessible and sociable, but in two cases where the threshold was lowered the judges disagreed.

In a later study, Travis reports the results of applying the same test to 22 psychoneurotics and 24 dementia praecox patients. He found that all of the psychoneurotics experienced a lowering of the threshold during crystal gazing. All of the dementia praecox cases except three, about whom

---

[41] Travis, Lee E.: " Suggestibility and Negativism as Measured by Auditory Threshold During Reverie," *Journal of Abnormal Psychology,* 18:355–59 (1924).

there is considerable doubt as to the accuracy of the diagnoses, experienced a rise of the threshold during crystal gazing.[42]

Roland C. Travis [43] supplemented this technique by a technique for measuring the changes in the visual threshold as well. He tested 20 schizophrenes and 20 psychoneurotics, all of whom had been diagnosed at the Iowa State Psychopathic Hospital. He used a modification of Lee Edward Travis' method of obtaining auditory thresholds, and the following method for obtaining visual thresholds:

The subjects . . . were allowed at least 20 minutes dark adaptation before the experiment began. The threshold was accurately determined after complete dark adaptation, before, during and after the reverie period. . . .

When the subject was dark adapted he placed his head in the proper place in the headrest and looked steadily at the fixation light a few minutes before the experiment began. The instructions to the subject before the reverie period were as follows, " Keep your eyes fixed steadily on the small red light which will remain on continuously. A larger white light will appear periodically just below the red light, and when you see the white light, press on the key under your finger. This light will get dimmer and dimmer, but every time you see the light press on the key." . . .

The instructions for the reverie period in the visual test were as follows: " I will now turn on the phonograph and play some music (' Annie Laurie ' sung by McCormack). Relax completely and forget all present surroundings and just let your mind wander where it will as you listen to the music. Keep your gaze on the red light. When the large white light comes on, press on the key. Look steadily at the red light, listen to the music, and let your mind wander where it will." The threshold was determined after the phonograph had been running one minute.[44]

Of the 20 schizophrenes 13 showed both raised auditory and raised visual thresholds during reverie, but whereas 18 showed raised auditory only 14 showed raised visual thresholds. Of the 20 psychoneurotics, 16 showed both lowered auditory and lowered visual thresholds during reverie, but 19 showed lowered auditory and 17 lowered visual thresholds. These results suggest that change in auditory threshold is a better diagnostic agent than change in the visual threshold during reverie, but that both have a rather marked diagnostic value.

---

[42] Travis, Lee E.: " A Test for Distinguishing between Schizophrenoses and Psychoneuroses," *Journal of Abnormal Psychology*, 19:298 (1924).

[43] " The Diagnosis of Character Types by Visual and Auditory Thresholds," *Psychological Monographs*, 36:18-37 (1926).

[44] *Ibid.*, 22-23.

These studies of personality in terms of extroversion and introversion are methodologically significant. They have all been based on too few observations to warrant the conclusion that we have in them a means of predicting overt behavior, either specifically or generally, on the basis of the results obtained from these tests. It has been shown that the tests differentiate with regard to certain traits, just as intelligence tests differentiate with regard to certain traits, although in regard both to these and to intelligence tests there is no surety as to what these traits are. These tests have not been widely enough applied, however, to know to what degree the differentiation they make corresponds to other behavior differentiation, e.g., success in school, delinquency, etc., and, therefore, it is not known how far personality differences, as measured by these tests, determine conduct of any particular kind. We consider later these tests in relation to other personality tests from this general point of view and pass now to the consideration of a group of measurements that have been devised with the quite definite and explicitly expressed purpose of differentiating certain types of conduct in which personality differences have been assumed to exist because known conduct correlated with differential responses to types of situations.

One of the most complete attempts yet made to measure personality differences in terms of differential conduct is that by Vernon M. Cady.[45] He takes the point of view that the most important social problem is the relative adjustment of various individuals to the institutional units into which society is divided. He maintains that the measurement of the differential responses of individuals to any specific situation is possible, and that if enough situations representative of one particular institutional unit be set up the relative adjustment of individuals to this institution may be determined. His problem was to measure — in terms of " corrigibility " — the relative adjustment of children to the institutional unit represented by the school:

There is undoubtedly a graded order here, from those children who do not seem to be able to adjust themselves to the social and mandatory requirements of the school to those who are promoters of the one and cheerful acceptors of the other.

This classification of children in terms of their social adjustments does not attempt to explain the reasons or causes of such adjustment or non-adjust-

---

[45] " The Estimation of Juvenile Incorrigibility," *Journal of Delinquency, Monograph* No. 2 (1923).

ment. There are many factors involved here arising both from the school and from the individual nature of the children. It is of primary interest, however, to establish the fact that this order exists, and that the range of differences exist in not only one school but in every school, not only at one age of the child, but at every age.

The next important problem is to set up test situations the differences of response to which shall parallel, step by step, the school behavior record. Should it be possible to do this the foundation will be laid for further study of causative factors which in turn may be indicated with more or less success by test methods.[46]

The tests which Cady used represented little that was new. In trying to obtain a good " sampling " of situations, he took over and modified tests that had been tried out by other investigators. He finally evolved a " battery " of five tests which gave the desired differentiation in response — a differentiation that showed a correspondence with other evidence of degrees of adaptation to the life of the school.

The first test in the battery is of the performance test type:

The application of performance tests to the measurement of moral tendencies has naturally been considered by workers in this field. It has been found possible to modify the older performance tests by the introduction of some new factors and thus to make the task very easy from the point of view of an intelligence test and yet extremely difficult, if not impossible, to score a success and at the same time follow instructions. The performance test has an advantage in being free from opinion as to what constitutes a right or wrong response. The test becomes a document carrying its own obvious meaning. We have only to obtain the usual statistical information relative to the distribution of scores. . . .

[Performance tests used are]: On the circumference of the large circle are placed five small circles of varying size and distance from one another. The task is to close the eyes and place a cross in each of the small circles as the hand moves from the starting point around the large circle in the direction of the arrows. In order to prevent measurement, the fingers of the left hand are placed within the curve at the bottom of the sheet. There are five trials, the work being examined by the subject and the score recorded after each trial. . . .

Another form . . . is that of five nested squares. Beginning with the smallest square, No. 1, the task is to draw a line in the pathway marked by the arrows with the eyes closed. To cross the enclosing lines means a zero score

---

[46] *Ibid.*, 16–17.

for the subject. The second square is traced in the reverse direction. As before, the eyes are opened and the score written after each trial. The total possible score is five. Between each attempt the subject is urged to observe his previous work, and if he has crossed the lines to not do so again.[47]

Cady claims that, in addition to the factor of group influence, this test measures the degree to which individuals will take advantage of a situation, where this is made possible, in spite of specific instructions to the contrary. He recognizes, however, that a complicating factor is the inhibition of visual habit, which this test calls out, but claims that, even so, " the habit tendency is pitted against the general integrity of the individual."

The second test in the battery is also an adaptation of an intelligence test — of the " completion " type. Quoting Voelker, he says:

" This test is given on a prepared four-page folder, the sentences with the blanks being on page one, and the completed sentences being on page four. Page two is entirely blank. Page three has a coating of paraffin." . . .

On page one a number of Trabue Completion sentences are printed. . . The papers were distributed either singly or fastened to other tests. The group was cautioned at the outset against turning or opening the folder while the test was being described to them and the preliminary directions given. The subjects were told, in advance, that the answers were on the last page and that they would be asked to score their own papers. The answers, however, were not to be consulted until all were through with the test and ready to begin scoring. By announcing in advance that each person will have a chance to check his sentences and to enter his own score, opportunity is given to cheat, if the person is so disposed. The object in having the pupil score his own paper is to give him additional opportunity to take advantage of the situation. A time limit of four minutes was made for boys of 13 and 14 years of age in the upper grades and of five minutes for boys of the same age in the lower grades. This time was found sufficient for the purpose in hand, namely, to get a good start on the easier sentences. It is desirable that the last sentences on the form be sufficiently difficult to prevent more than a very few from correctly completing them so that all will have opportunity to alter or add to their work if they desire. At the same time they should not be made discouragingly difficult. Unless the group be kept under close observation during the exercise some of the members will steal a glance at the back page from time to time.[48]

---

[47] " The Estimation of Juvenile Incorrigibility," *Journal of Delinquency, Monograph* No. 2:50–52 (1923).

[48] *Ibid.,* 59–60.

Regarding the nature and purposes of the third test, which is of the variety known as an " overstatement " test, Cady says:

If we give the subject an opportunity to make statements about his abilities or the information he possesses on various subjects and then later give him an opportunity to prove his statements, we shall have the elements of an over-statement test. Let us suppose we have asked him if he knows about twenty or thirty different things such as: Who invented the wireless telegraph? Who invented movable type? Do you know how to read music from notes? When the " quiz test " is given to cover such a series one of three results may happen: he may actually know what he says he does know, he may know more than he claimed that he knew, or he may know less than he claimed that he did know. Since most people tend to overstate themselves this kind of test is commonly known by this name.

If we go further and give the subject a chance to score himself on how well he knows a subject or a bit of information, say by using " zero " to mean that he knows nothing about it, " one " that he knows something about it, " two " that he knows it fairly well, and " three " that he knows it very well, we shall have a means of adding up his assigned values and obtaining his score of claims. It is then a simple matter to contrast this score with the . . . score obtained in the " quiz test " and to give a minus, plus or zero score to the subject for his performance as a whole. If he understates himself he obtains a given number of positive units; in like manner overstatement gains a certain number of negative units. When the test is given to a group the obtained differences between claims and accomplishments is then arranged in serial order and placed in the correlation table.

The test as used in this series was given in three stages with as many forms. Ten questions were asked at first dealing with skill and interests adapted to thirteen- or fourteen-year-old boys; then followed ten questions which prepared the way for the final quiz test.[49]

The fourth and fifth parts of the battery were a questionnaire designed to detect psychoneurotic tendencies (a modification of the Woodworth questionnaire which is discussed below, p. 419) and a moral judgment test, designed to test the actual knowledge of social practices and of " right and wrong." The latter, Cady admits, is probably more an indication of general intelligence than of general corrigibility, except in so far as the two are related.

The selection of subjects was made in such a way that the pupils who were unable to adjust to school conditions to a degree that they were

---

[49] *Ibid.*, 66.

considered markedly incorrigible by their teachers could be contrasted with those whose adjustment was such that they were considered markedly corrigible by their teachers:

Typical schools for a given community were chosen. The principals were then asked to supply the names of the worst and of the best boys in the school. These two lists were then equalized in number (very few changes were necessary here, as the two groups usually balanced each other) and cut down arbitrarily to test unit and age requirements. The principals were then asked to supply a list of names equal in size to either of the extremes to be composed of boys who were neither bad nor good, but who were of the required ages. There were then three groups of equal size, representing three grades of moral character. These names were then mixed and made into test units. . . . In addition to this preliminary classification by the principal, all of the teachers who knew the boys were asked to rate them. . . . They were, of course, ignorant of the tripartite division.

In the second phase of the field-work an unselected population in a different locality was used . . . composed of thirteen- and fourteen-year-old boys. The city in which this work was done had a population of some 900 thirteen- and fourteen-year-old boys. This number was reduced to about 700 by the omission of a few schools which did not seem to introduce an element of selection, i.e., by the unusual type of the schools omitted. Acceptance only of ratings from teachers who were certain of their judgments . . . nullified the effort to secure an unselected population and reduced the population to a final 150 cases.[50]

By using the judgments of the teachers in these 150 cases as the criterion of incorrigibility, the five tests were " validated." They gave correlation coefficients with this criterion ranging from .414 to .188 — all indicative of low relationships. The multiple correlation of the battery with the criterion, however, is .578, which indicates that the tests, taken together, are diagnostic to an appreciable degree.

When these tests were given to 70 boys in the Whittier State School, all of whom were delinquents, " with one exception the median scores of the State School boys exceed the public school incorrigibles and both considerably exceed the scores of the public school corrigibles." [51]

It appears, then, that this battery of tests does differentiate between those boys who have been able to conform to the social demands of the school and those who are maladjusted. That this differentiation is

---

[50] " The Estimation of Juvenile Incorrigibility," *Journal of Delinquency, Monograph* No. 2:46 (1923).

[51] A high score is unfavorable, i.e., indicative of incorrigibility.

not by any means perfect is obvious from the results which Cady gives. How far " corrigibility " as regards the school situations and as indicated by these tests is correlated with " corrigibility " in regard to the demands of other institutional units is not known. The predictive value of these tests for adjustments outside the school is merely indicated in the differential response obtained when the tests are given to actual delinquents, i.e., those who have become seriously maladjusted to other institutional units than the schools. The results on these tests indicate that, for the ages studied (9 to 19), there is no growth in " corrigibility." If this result means " once corrigible, always corrigible," it might be assumed that the predictive value of these tests as regards the same, or substituted, situations would be quite high. But, on the other hand, it may mean merely that the coercive aspects of the institution have an approximately equal influence, but upon different individuals, for the several units of time. Obviously, the problem that arises is to follow through a group, whose " corrigibility indices " are known, into future school and extra-school adjustments.

A study quite similar to Cady's in purpose and in the techniques used is that recently published by Raubenheimer.[52] He explains his general purpose as follows:

[52] Raubenheimer, Albert S.: "An Experimental Study of Some Behavior Traits of the Potentially Delinquent Boy," *Psychological Monographs*, 34, No. 6 (1923).

Although both Cady and Raubenheimer have taken over certain of the tests originated by Voelker (Voelker, P. F.: *The Function of Ideals and Attitudes in Social Education*, 1921), we have not taken his study into consideration in this chapter because of the fact that it is very distinctly a study in education, or *treatment*, rather than an " approach " to the study of behavior. His aim was to test out whether an " ideal " could be taught, by a definite sort of training. " Trustworthiness " was the ideal he sought to teach. In order to test out the efficacy of the training, the subjects were placed in various situations designed to show trustworthiness, or lack of it, before and after the period of training. The tests were " validated " by the usual sort of judgments, and by the usual juggling with correlation coefficients (correction for attenuation) until they reached a " meaningful " size; but there was no attempt to validate them by their actual selective value in differentiating between known delinquents and non-delinquents, etc., as both Cady and Raubenheimer did. Besides the tests described by Cady and Raubenheimer (the circles and squares test, paraffine completion test, overstatement test, etc.) there were several other ingenious tests designed to test trustworthiness. The distinctive feature about these " tests " was that they presented " real " situations, in which often the subject did not know he was being tested, e.g., whether subject will accept a tip, return a borrowed article at the time promised, accept over-change, accept money sent " by mistake " through the mail, etc.

The purpose of this study was to attempt to devise a method of analysis whereby some of the delinquent tendencies in boys could be determined prior to the overt expression of such tendencies, or rather, before the crystallization of such tendencies and desires into permanent habits of thought and action.

Because of the baffling complexity of the many factors that influence the development of human behavior, and because of the almost total absence of reliable experimental methods for the study of personality (when intelligence testing is excluded), it must be stated at once that the development of a method that would yield a reliable and valid diagnosis and prognosis for the *individual* was beyond the aim and possibility of the present study. The immediate aim was rather the development of experimental methods of differentiation between groups that are known to be stable, healthy-minded, reliable, and truthful (according to the present standards of the school and of society in general), groups that are less stable, healthy-minded, reliable, and truthful, and those that have already become special charges to society, because of their social maladjustment. It is only after such a method of differentiation on a broad, though defined, basis has been established, that a more detailed experimental analysis of the factors that are prophetic of delinquency within the individual can be undertaken. Of course, it might not be overdaring to hope that even this method of differentiation on broad lines might reveal some of the detrimental factors at work with particular individuals. That, however, is of secondary concern in this study.[53]

Raubenheimer acknowledges the difficulty of setting up situations that will call for genuine behavior reactions: the most that can be done is to get an approximation of a situation " in response to which the subject would unfold his desires, preferences, interest in forms of activity, social likes and dislikes, respect or disrespect for the claims of the law and of society in general." [54]

The situations which he set up were based on the practices of delinquents as described in the literature, and as found in case records of the court, the State School, etc., and comprised such

problems as would throw light upon the following questions: (1) To what extent does the boy readily seize upon a chance to appear as having exceptional book knowledge, but falsely so? (2) To what extent will the boy seize upon an opportunity to appear as being well informed concerning a wide range of facts, and as having thoroughly mastered a variety of activities, when that is not the

---

[53] Raubenheimer, Albert S.: "An Experimental Study of Some Behavior Traits of the Potentially Delinquent Boy," *Psychological Monographs*, 34:1 (1923).

[54] *Ibid.*, 9.

case? (3) What is the persistent trend in the choice of his associates? To what extent is his choice characterized by an interest in questionable and harmful determinants? (4) What is the trend of his interests in various forms of activity? To what extent are they antisocial or questionable socially? (5) What is the habitual reaction to different social and educational institutions, like the school, the home, Boy Scouts, etc.? To what extent do they reveal questionable judgment? Questionable adjustment? (6) To what extent does the boy recognize the harmful results of antisocial practices? In how far does his judgment harmonize with accepted social standards? The emphasis in all these questions is on the nature and extent of an interest in and preference for matters questionable for the healthy development of the boy, and on his habitual reaction to his own abilities and range of information.[55]

It is unnecessary to go into any detail regarding the situations which he set up. They are similar to those devised by other investigators, and are quite as questionable in the meaning which can be given to their results. They consist of (1) a test to determine the number of fictitious titles of books a subject would check off as having read; (2) a test consisting of brief character descriptions (" in terms of interests and activities . . . [which] cover a wide range of actual conditions and experiences of boyhood . . . [forming] a graduated series of questionable or desirable influences "); (3) a test consisting of book titles " all specially created, each title suggesting some phase of boyhood activity, questionable and otherwise, as forming the theme of the book . . . [and] the subject was asked to indicate the order in which he would care to read the books; " (4) a test consisting of groups of three activities, one desirable and two " questionable," and the subject was asked to check the activity he preferred in each group; (5) a " controlled association " experiment, in which " various institutions that enter into the life of the subject, like the teacher, the scout movement, policemen, smoking, etc. [were taken]; then four statements, such as are frequently made about these matters, were developed in connection with each — three being questionable and one acceptable — and the subject was asked to mark the *one* that came nearest telling how he felt about the institution in point; (6) a test in which the subject was asked to rate the seriousness of certain offenses (" the offenses are those of actual boys now committed to reform schools "); (7) an overstatement test, of the same type as that used by Cady. Raubenheimer's selection

---

[55] *Ibid.*, 16.

of subjects for the test was similar to Cady's. Instead of taking judgments of general adjustment to an institutional unit as his criterion, however, he had teachers select " the 25 per cent most reliable, stable, healthy-minded, and the 25 per cent least reliable, stable and healthy-minded eleven-year-old and thirteen-year-old boys, from grades 4 to 8, in a socially and educationally privileged community in Los Angeles " and a similar group " in a socially and educationally *less* privileged community in Los Angeles." Further groups were selected from two Parental Schools and from the Whittier State School (for delinquents).

The results, which are given an elaborate statistical analysis, are ambiguous, if these tests are assumed to give valid evidence of " potential delinquency," for although the Parental School boys are usually shown by the tests to have more unfavorable scores than the " most stable " groups, and although there is often a similar differentiation between the " least stable " and the " most stable " groups, the Whittier School boys, who represent the only group of serious delinquents tested, often have more favorable scores than any of the other groups. Obviously it is ridiculous to claim that a test differentiates " potential delinquents " when *actual* delinquents show up so favorably. Nevertheless, Raubenheimer concludes: " The nature of the test responses demonstrates that the form and character of the tests served the purpose for which they were developed, viz., that of getting an expression of the questionable interests and tendencies of boys " and that " one of the main characteristics of the potentially delinquent is his lack of appreciation of moral and social values." [56] It is difficult to see what the tests differentiate, in view of this great discrepancy in the Whittier School results. Raubenheimer gets over the difficulty, to his own satisfaction, by assuming that the environment and training at the Whittier School have brought about these favorable scores, whereas without this training the boys would have had unfavorable scores. He neglects the implications of these results and bases his conclusions on the unfavorable scores of the Parental School boys on the assumption that " the Special School subjects were the most *natural* types of delinquents."

These tests of Cady, Raubenheimer and others, have attempted to measure behavior " objectively " either by pencil and paper techniques or by actual performance tests. Test situations were set up and the

---

[56] Raubenheimer, Albert S.: " An Experimental Study of Some Behavior Traits of the Potentially Delinquent Boy," *Psychological Monographs*, 34:105 (1923).

responses were taken as definite behavior indices, more or less closely related to general behavior trends.

Somewhat different are the approaches depending on the individual's sizing-up of his own past history in behavior or ideational terms. One of the most widely used of these techniques is a questionnaire designed to indicate emotional stability or instability. As first devised by Woodworth, this questionnaire was made up of an inventory of 116 questions, based on psychoneurotic symptoms. The answers would, it was thought, indicate whether or not the individual tended towards the instability characteristic of psychoneurotics. The purpose of this questionnaire was to segregate from the draft army those exhibiting psychoneurotic tendencies. It was later adapted to several studies of children and has given interesting results from the behavior standpoint. Its use with children has shown that it is a fairly good differentiating agent as among certain groups already differentiated with regard to physical stamina, "racial temperament," school accomplishment, and delinquent behavior. In the adaptation of Woodworth's original questionnaire to children some of the questions have been simplified, all those relating to the sex life of the subject having been eliminated and some questions added. Two modifications have been published, one in 1920 by Buford Johnson.[57] Her modified questionnaire contained sixty questions, of which the following (the first ten on her list) are typical:

1. Do you like to play by yourself better than to play with other children? .... Yes No
2. Do the other children let you play with them? .... Yes No
3. Did you ever run away from home? .... Yes No
4. Did you ever want to run away from home? .... Yes No
5. Do people find fault with you much? .... Yes No
6. Do you think people like you as much as they do other people? .... Yes No
7. Did you ever get lost? .... Yes No
8. Do you ever feel that people are staring at you? .... Yes No
9. Does it make you uneasy to cross a bridge over water? .. Yes No
10. Do you mind going into a tunnel or subway? .... Yes No [58]

Johnson's aim was to find whether there were any differences in emotional stability between children who were "normal" physically and

[57] "Emotional Instability in Children," *Ungraded*, 5:73–79 (1920).
[58] *Ibid.*, 75.

those who were markedly below par. She gave the questions to a group of 40 fifth-grade boys in a nutrition class " formed by selection of children who were undernourished according to the standard of age, height and weight index used by Burks and Boas," and to a control group of 35 fifth-grade boys " who were found to be nearly normal in accordance with the height-weight standards."

The *a priori* assumption with regard to these questions was that " normal " individuals would not give answers symptomatic of psychoneurotic tendencies. In all groups of " normals " to whom the questions have been given, however, many questions are answered " pathologically." Johnson assumed, on the basis of these known results, that 15 " pathological " answers indicated a tendency towards abnormality, and 25 or more warranted " grave suspicions." Giving each " pathological " answer a score of 1, she found that

the distribution of scores for the control group ranged from 0 to 34 with an average of 7.14. Six, or 17 per cent, had from 15 to 25 wrong answers and one 25 or more wrong answers.

The nutrition group has twice as many as the control group with significant tendencies. Each group contains one pupil of more serious abnormalities.[59]

These same boys were tested for strength of grip by the dynamometer and were also given the steadiness test (number of contacts required to punch holes). There seemed to be interesting tendencies observed in the varying relationships between emotional instability as indicated by the questionnaire, strength and steadiness. The numbers are too small for reliable generalization, but Johnson concludes:

There are at least two types of emotional instability that we should recognize in the consideration of the output of energy or capacity for muscular control. One is so stimulated for the moment as to get a temporary control, the other has not the ability to control and is made more uncoördinated in such tests by the realization of this. Measurements of fatigue might prove helpful in the differentiation of the first group.[60]

Mathews [61] made an extensive study of the Woodworth questionnaire, resulting in further revisions, and the final inclusion of seventy questions. She tested a large group of " unselected " school children,

---

[59] " Emotional Instability in Children," *Ungraded*, 5:77 (1920).

[60] *Ibid.*, 77–78.

[61] Mathews, Ellen: " A Study of Emotional Stability in Children," *Journal of Delinquency*, 8:1–40 (1923).

575 boys and 558 girls, with an age range of 9 to 19 years and a grade range of 4th grade to 4th year of high school. Her final revision of the questionnaire was made in the following way: A great many questions, based on the Woodworth inventory, were given to this unselected group. The revision was made to include only those questions which were not answered disproportionately by " normals " but which were answered disproportionately by " abnormals," i.e., small groups of children selected as probably emotionally unstable, including 8 diagnosed as " neurotics," 37 Protectory girls, and a group of 376 " orphans " from an institution. The questions are in the same form as Johnson's revision and the subject matter is classified under the following headings:

1. Fears, worries, perseveration, etc.
2. Physical symptoms, pains, weariness, incoördinations.
3. Unhappiness, unsocial and anti-social moods.
4. Dreams, phantasies, sleep disturbances.

[The one] about getting lost does not seem to belong in any of these classes.[62]

The results obtained are summarized as follows:

1. Children may respond to the questionnaire with as few as 2 or as many as 70 unfavorable answers.

2. Boys, as a group, give fewer such answers than do girls.

3. Young boys tend to give more unfavorable answers than older ones, whereas the opposite tendency is shown by girls.

4. There are definite race differences, the Italians leading in size of score, while the Jews have as a group slightly larger scores than do the north Europeans.

5. Children selected because they show nervous or temperamental difficulties respond, as a whole, with more unfavorable answers than do those who are not so selected.

6. Within every group there is a great variety of scores, so that the different groups overlap considerably.

7. The self correlation of the scores of a group of boys is $+.667$. These findings are not so convincing as we would like, but when we consider that human beings are prone to resist and deny their emotions, especially the more troublesome ones, the fact that our results point somewhat vaguely in the right direction encourages us to believe that such a questionnaire will be useful as a means of finding the children in a group who are laboring under special difficulties of this sort.

---

[62] *Ibid.*, 5.

Examination of the results of separate questions shows that some of these have more discriminative value than others, especially with boys. . . .

The sexes respond so differently that it seems impossible to make a list that is suitable for both.

The data at hand are better adapted for boys than for girls, perhaps because the original personal data sheet was devised for men.[63]

Mathews' study is valuable chiefly with regard to the data obtained for an unselected group of children. Her results on the groups of known conduct deviations are ambiguous, perhaps because based on such small numbers. It remained for Slawson[64] to get comparable data for a significantly large group of delinquents and to test the validity of the questionnaire as a differentiating agent. He gave the questionnaire to 834 delinquents in three New York institutions, covering the same age range (9–19 years) as that of Mathews' 516 unselected boys. Slawson presents these data in full, and they give evidence of significant differences between the unselected and delinquent groups. A low score on the questionnaire is " favorable " — i.e., supposedly indicative of emotional stability — therefore the percentages of delinquents at or below the median for unselected boys gives an indication of their emotional stability as compared with the unselected boys. Only 8% of the boys at the New York House of Refuge, 19% at the Hawthorne School, and 41% at the Berkshire Industrial Farm were at or below the median of the unselected group, and the percentage for all three delinquent groups combined was only 15.6% at or below the median of the unselected group. Except for the boys at the Berkshire Industrial Farm (who are themselves carefully selected, see chapter II) the delinquent groups show, on the average, a very decided degree of emotional instability, indicated by this questionnaire, as compared with unselected New York boys.

Slawson makes an interesting analysis of the specific responses which seem to differentiate the delinquent from the unselected group. In making up her questionnaire, Mathews limited it (with one or two exceptions) to questions to which not more than 30% of the unselected group gave unfavorable answers. Slawson therefore gives particular attention to those questions to which more than 30% of the delinquent boys re-

---

63 Matthews, Ellen: " A Study of Emotional Stability in Children," *Journal of Delinquency*, 8:38–39 (1923).

64 Slawson, John: *The Delinquent Boy* (1926).

sponded symptomatically. These questions follow. The percentages of boys in all three of the delinquent institutions who gave unfavorable responses are indicated after the question, and the percentages of unselected boys who gave unfavorable responses are indicated in parentheses:

Did you ever run away from home?	54%	(4%)
Did you ever want to run away from home?	49%	(13%)
Do you have a light in your room at night?	44%	(20%)
Did you ever have the habit of picking your toes or your nose?	34%	(25%)
Did you ever feel that nobody loves you?	35%	(21%)
Do you ever wish you had never been born?	43%	(20%)
Do you ever wish you were dead?	36%	(13%)
Is it easy to get you cross over very small things?	40%	(33%)
Do you feel that you are a little bit different from other people?	38%	(27%)
Do you ever have the feeling as if you were falling just before going to sleep?	33%	(27%)
Do you feel sort of tired a good deal of the time?	37%	(21%)
Are you ever bothered by a feeling that things are not real?	33%	(22%)
Are you ever troubled with the idea that somebody is following you?	32%	(18%)
Do you ever feel that someone is trying to do you harm?	36%	(16%)
Does it make you uneasy to sit in a small room with the door shut?	33%	(23%)
Do you usually know just what you want to do next?	33%	(25%)
Do you have a hard time making up your mind about things?	31%	(24%)
Did you ever have a strong desire to steal things?	50%	(6%)
Did you ever have a vision?	33%	(26%)
Did you ever feel that you were very wicked?	43%	(20%)

Slawson computed the intercorrelations in the rank given to these various symptoms as determined by the responses of the delinquents and the unselected groups. The coefficients " giving the inter-delinquent institutional relations range from .75 to .85, whereas the coefficients giving the relation between the delinquent institutions and the unselected boys range only from .52 to .58." [65] This means simply that if the questions are ranked for each group from the one to which the

[65] *Ibid.*, 254.

smallest percentage gives unfavorable responses to the one to which the largest percentage gives unfavorable responses, the correspondence in ranking will be closer between any two of the delinquent groups than between any delinquent group and the unselected group. All of which seems to strengthen the evidence that responses to these questions are roughly indicative of tendencies common to delinquents.

Slawson found further that the greater proportion of unfavorable replies given by delinquents was in no way accounted for by social status or nationality. Strangely enough, however, he did not try holding intelligence constant in these comparisons (i.e., by eliminating the intelligence factor from his coefficients of correlation), for it seems probable that certain of these responses (irrespective of actual practices) must be dictated by a knowledge of social conventions, which is probably dependent to a large extent on information, if not on innate intelligence.

Slawson presents a table which seems to indicate very strikingly that this index of emotional instability has more value as a single differentiating index than any of the tests of mental abilities. This table follows:

TABLE 42–A

Comparing the Percentages of Boys at the New York House of Rufuge and the Hawthorne School Who Are At or Below the Median of Unselected Boys in Their Responses on the Psychoneurotic Inventory with the Percentages who Reached or Exceeded the Norms for the National, Thorndike, and Mechanical Tests.

Institution	Psycho-neurotic Inventory	National A + B Test	Thorndike Non-Verbal Test	Stenquist Mechanical Test
N. Y. House of Refuge	8.0	13.6	39.5	49.0
Hawthorne School..	19.0	27.8	44.5	43.8 [66]

It should be remembered that the median score represents the score below and above which 50% of the unselected group falls. " Above median " is favorable in the intelligence and mechanical ability tests

[66] Slawson, John: *The Delinquent Boy*, 236.

because a high score indicates good performance. " Below median " is favorable in the psychoneurotic inventory because a high score indicates a larger number of unfavorable responses than a low score. The " expected " percentage above and below the median for each of these tests would be near 50% (allowing a small margin of error) if the delinquent groups were similar in these respects to the unselected group. We find this 50% approximated in the scores on the mechanical abilities test and approximated, though somewhat less closely, on the non-verbal intelligence test, which means that in these performances there is little difference between these delinquent boys and the unselected boys. On the intelligence test where language is a large factor, we find a large discrepancy between the expected 50% and the actual 14% and 28% found in the two institutions for delinquents, indicating a marked inferiority in the performance of delinquents and unselected boys. This discrepancy becomes even greater in the scores on the psychoneurotic inventory, where instead of the expected 50% we find only 8% and 19% respectively at or below the median. This indicates a decided inferiority in emotional stability as measured by this test.

As Slawson says:

The differences between the mental characteristics of these delinquent boys and unselected boys arrange themselves in the form of a hierarchy, there being the greatest difference in the direction of inferiority between delinquent boys and non-delinquent boys in emotional stability, less difference in verbal abstract intelligence, and the least difference in the ability to handle non-verbal concrete and mechanical situations.[67]

This characterization of delinquents in terms of greater emotional instability is in agreement with other evidence (for example, Healy and Bronner, *Reconstructing Youthful Behavior*), but the most serious question raised by the procedure of Slawson is that the responses of the delinquent boys may be to some extent a reflection of their different experiences and not an expression of psychoneurotic tendencies. For example, the answer to the question about sitting in a small room with the door closed may be a reflection of the boy's juvenile court experience.

There have been a good many studies designed to measure the intellectual aspects of " character." A considerable part of the work done by

---

[67] *Ibid.*, 236.

Raubenheimer and Cady, as well as the work designed specifically to measure " ethical discrimination " and the like have this end in view, but the most complete study of that sort is the recently published monograph on " Testing the Knowledge of Right and Wrong," [68] by Hartshorne and May. They state their problem as follows:

The investigators' interest in what words may reveal of moral knowledge is not based on the assumption that knowledge and behavior are highly correlated. One of our problems is to discover what the relation is between behavior and the knowledge of right and wrong. Furthermore, we do not assume that word behavior and a true knowledge of right and wrong are necessarily correlated. It may be that overt action is a far better indication of what a man really knows about right and wrong than his verbal responses are. If this be the case, there remains the very significant problem of the relation between what he says and what he knows on the one side, and the relation between what he says and what he does or would do, on the other. Words have a social significance that cannot be ignored. The heart of the problem of character lies in the adjustment of persons to one another, and this adjustment is never complete until it has become articulate.[69]

Their aim was to set up tests that would " cover as wide a range of moral experience as possible . . . [and] require the exercise of as many appropriate mental processes as possible."

Thirteen tests, given to a large number of children, are treated statistically. There were three " word " tests: (1) a multiple choice test in which the subject selects the word " most nearly opposite in meaning " to a given word chosen from the field of social relations; (2) a test in which the subject crosses out, from sets of five words, the one word which does not show " similarity " to the others; (3) a multiple choice test in which the subject indicates all the likely consequences, the most likely consequence, the best consequence and the worst consequence of test words (e.g., cheating, betting, etc.). There were eight sentence tests: (1) a true-false test, in which the subject indicates whether a given statement, representing " cause and effect," is true or false (e.g., " Ministers' sons and deacons' daughters usually go wrong "); (2) the subject is asked to indicate whether each of a number of acts is his duty, not his duty, or sometimes his duty and sometimes not; (3) the subject is given multiple choice as to what he would

---

[68] *Religious Education Association, Monograph* No. 1 (July, 1927).
[69] *Ibid.,* 1.

do or say in a given situation (e.g., " if someone steals your lunch: (a) steal another lunch to even it up, (b) report it to the teacher, (c) cry about it, (d) say nothing about it "); (4) the subject is asked to judge whether certain acts are right, wrong, or excusable. The subject matter is chosen in such a way that " the situations named are provocative of responses that are in conflict with ideal modes of response " (e.g., " Helen noticed that nearly everyone in the class was cheating on a test, so she cheated too "); (5) the subject is asked to write down as many consequences, good and bad, as he considers might follow from a given act (e.g., " John accidentally broke a street lamp with a snow ball "). This test is supposed to indicate the subject's " foresight "; (6) the subject is asked to indicate whether given acts are cheating, lying, stealing, " something wrong, but not cheating, lying or stealing," or not wrong at all; (7) the subject is asked to indicate whether certain statements involving " principles " are true or false (e.g., " to master oneself is a greater thing than to win a battle "); (8) the subject is presented with a situation, in which he must act in one of two ways. He is asked to indicate which two of five " principles " apply to the problem, and then indicate which of the two methods of behavior would be " right." The two remaining tests were (1) a social-ethical vocabulary test and (2) a " good manners " test, in which the subject indicates whether given statements are true or false (e.g., " if soup or any liquid is too hot, blow on it slightly to cool it ").

The investigators were confronted with a serious problem in working out a criterion of " right and wrong." They had decided, at first, that some standard must be assumed consistently in order to measure the individual's position with relation to this standard. The criterion used for many of the tests was obtained by the scorings of a class of sixty graduate students in psychology. Generally, a 75% agreement on the part of these graduate students was accepted as validating the tests. But occasionally the investigators were so shocked by the answers given by the majority of the class that they reversed these judgments on the grounds that the judgments were made in the light of convention or prejudice rather than " ethical ideals." For instance, the graduate class made the judgment that it was a duty to " pray at least once a day " in the following proportions: Yes, 64%; Sometimes, 19%; No, 17%. On the basis of a total weighting of 3, these answers would distribute the weights as follows: Yes, 2; Sometimes, $\frac{1}{2}$; No, $\frac{1}{2}$. The investigators,

however, assigned the weights as 2 for No, and 1 for Sometimes and
0 for Yes. A number of the judgments were changed in this way. Occasionally, also, the investigators display an amazing unsophistication in
assuming that questions in which actual data may be obtained may be
" validated " by opinions of this character. For example, they say:
" Of course, the fact that more than 75% of these graduate students say
that it is not true that unemployment is the fault of the laborer does
not make this statement untrue. But it does lend backing to what would
otherwise be the *unsupported personal judgment* of the investigators."
[Italics ours]. In one of these tests it was said that " the decisions of
the graduate class turned out to be so highly conventional that they were
practically ignored as a criterion. . . . For example, in the last illustration given, of the boy who knocked down the bully, 45% of the class
thought it was unqualifiedly right to knock the bully down, 42%
thought it wrong but excusable, and only 13% called it unqualifiedly
wrong. . . . Our own standard gives a value of one to excusable and
of two to wrong." [70] It seems, then, that the investigators accept this
majority opinion in order to lend weight to their " unsupported personal
judgment " whenever this opinion happens to coincide with their judgment, but they throw it overboard when there are marked discrepancies.

The investigators conclude that these tests, thus " validated," are
highly reliable because when they are split into two parts, taking the
odd items in one part and the even items in the other part for each test,
the correlation coefficients range from .52 to .96. (For a discussion of
the way in which the authors arrive at the conclusion that these tests
would finally yield a reliability coefficient of .90 or better, although of
nine actual coefficients only one is above .7, see Appendix). The correlations of each test against the sum of seven of the tests range from
.3 to .7, which is taken as showing that each test measures " moral
knowledge " to some extent (on the assumption that the results on these
seven tests are the best available criterion of the moral knowledge of
the subjects).

The correlations of moral knowledge scores with intelligence are all
relatively high, ranging, however, from .1 to .9. Indeed, the correlation
between the sum of the seven tests, which is taken as the criterion of
intelligence, is .686, which indicates the very large part that intelligence
plays in this whole question. It is very difficult, in the face of this large

[70] *Religious Education Association, Monograph* No. 1:9 (July, 1927).

correlation, and their other ambiguous results, to feel that the authors have done anything more than construct another sort of intelligence test.

In this connection the finding that the score for good manners correlates with each of the tests for moral knowledge significantly is interesting. " The correlations between good manners and vocabulary, age, and intelligence all run higher than most of the corresponding correlations between the separate moral knowledge tests and these three factors. Partialling out intelligence we find a remaining coefficient of .271 between the Good Manners test and the sum of seven tests used as a criterion of moral knowledge. These coefficients indicate that the same factors that lead to a knowledge of right and wrong lead also to a knowledge of etiquette." [71] This probably means that the knowledge of both right and wrong and of etiquette depends on learning, i.e., intelligence plus experience.

Very interesting results were obtained by getting parents, friends, club leaders, public school teachers, and sunday school teachers to take these tests and then working out the correlations between each of their scores and the child's own scores. There was no correlation between the moral knowledge, as represented by these scores, of either the public school or sunday school teacher and the child, and correlations of .14, .35, .55 between the child and his club leaders, friends, and parents respectively. This means that the moral knowledge of a child, as shown by these tests, is not related significantly to that of his teachers, either sunday school or public school, nor to his club leaders. It is related in some degree to that of his friends and to a somewhat greater degree to his parents. How far the common intelligence factor invalidates this comparison is not known, but it is undoubtedly an important factor.

There are few data on the relation between moral knowledge and behavior, but for one group of their subjects they had " in the case of the behavior called cheating . . . available objective measures rather than judgments, procured by a technique which yields a reliability well over .80." [72] (Technique not given in this monograph).[73] The relations found between home cheating and the various moral knowledge tests

---

[71] *Ibid.*, 24–25.

[72] *Ibid.*, 25.

[73] Hartshorne and May have in press a volume, *Studies in Deceit* (Macmillan), in which these techniques will be described in full.

are all very small, usually negative, and none so high as the relation with intelligence, which is —.20. School cheating correlations are somewhat higher, but scarcely high enough to be very significant, ranging from —.05 to —.40. The correlation between school cheating and intelligence is —.39. When moral knowledge is kept constant, the relation between intelligence and cheating becomes almost zero, which suggests to the authors that " it is their superior moral knowledge rather than their intelligence which makes the brighter children cheat less than those less gifted, and that, granted the same amount of moral knowledge, the more intelligent would cheat even more than the dull pupils." The nature of the tests scarcely warrants such a statement.

Further evidence on the relation between moral knowledge and behavior was obtained when the investigators worked out a series of tests for deception. These deception tests, which are not described in any detail in this monograph, but which will be fully represented in a forthcoming publication, are designed to measure behavior, in terms of performance, of the following general kinds:

A. Copying from an answer sheet or dictionary or getting help from someone.

B. Adding to one's work after time is called.

C. Opening the eyes to guide one's pencil when eyes are supposed to be shut.

D. Faking the solution of a puzzle test.

E. Faking a score in a physical ability contest, and so cheating one's school mates.

F. Cheating in parlor games.

G. Stealing money from a puzzle used in a test or from a game at a party.

H. Total number of instances of deception in behaviors A to G.

I. Helpful behavior.[74]

The correlations between these several forms of behavior, as measured by performance, and moral knowledge, were worked out for children in three groups, a suburban school system, an institution for homeless children, and a private school in New York. The negative correlations resulting (except in the case of helpful behavior) were usually smaller than the correlations between mental age and the particular behavior, and when mental age is held constant the correlation is practically wiped out. The authors admit that these figures tend to show that " general moral knowledge as measured by the tests described and

[74] Hartshorne and May: *op. cit.*, 52.

the specific behaviors classified as deception are only slightly related, there being a barely detectable tendency for higher moral knowledge scores to be associated with higher honesty (lower dishonesty) scores." But they then claim that "as this conclusion tends to contradict our common sense judgment in the matter, it would be well to examine our data more closely."

Examination of the data led to the opinion that perhaps the moral knowledge tests were chiefly in terms of the adult rather than the child code. However, when the tests were rescored on the basis of the child's own judgments, i.e., an answer scored "right" if it corresponded to the answers of more than half the children, no appreciable differences in the correlation coefficients resulted. When the tests were examined in detail, certain elements gave very interesting differentiation between the cheaters and non-cheaters. For instance, in the multiple choice test where the question was, "If you make a mistake and put a nickel for a penny in the slot: a. Put in four slugs to even it up; b. Call up the company and tell them about it; c. Smash the thing and get your nickel; d. Report it to the police; e. Do nothing," 100% of those preferring to smash the slot machine to recover the nickel actually cheated on a test. However, it was found impossible to select a group of elements that would consistently differentiate between the honest and the dishonest groups. The dishonest groups seemed to give consistent responses, but there were great differences found between the honest groups tested.

Let us, then, summarize the points brought out in this survey of the different types of approaches to the study of behavior through an analysis of personality, temperament, or the emotions.

This approach has comprised a great variety of attempts to study psychological mechanisms other than the narrowly defined intellectual and in the main has dealt with individual differences in reaction to laboratory situations designed to test some particular trait. A large number of these tests have shown individual differences, but their relationship to the "trait" named is often difficult to find. In fact, it may be generally questionable whether there exist any such traits as some of the tests are designed to measure. Tests have been most successful, from this point of view, when they have been developed with regard to a trait where there is agreement as to diagnosis, where therefore the trait has some objective basis. This is the case in Travis' studies, where the subjects were two groups of abnormals, with symptoms widely different, and there was agreement as to their diagnosis on the part of the psychiatrists. This is the case also in the study of Moore and Gilliland, when the extremes of " aggressiveness " were accepted as subjects, here again there being almost complete agreement as to the diagnosis. But where judges rate great numbers of subjects for a great many or very complicated traits, and all the subjects are included in the experiment, confusion as to meaning must certainly result. This is true in a rating scale such as that of Marston, where the children are rated on a long and complicated scale and the judgments accepted as " validating " the tests.

We feel, indeed, that very few validations based on ratings and estimates of the trait have any worth. What is needed is long-time investigations, in which a specific behavior is related to other sorts of specific behavior and from these data some one type is selected which correlates highly with the other types and may be taken as indicative of the configuration of the " trait " itself. The assumption that the ratings made by judges are actually based on the observation of many specific behavior acts of this sort is probably erroneous. Judgments are apt to be formed on the basis of dramatic episodes rather than by the patient observation and weighting of many specific acts.

The illustrative material we have given in this chapter is probably representative of the best that is being done in this field. It represents almost entirely test situations that give results in terms of overt behavior. These have shown the important individual differences in overt behavior in these test situations. But they have rarely gone far enough. The selection of the test situation by the investigator often depends on chance observation on his part. The most that can be said about the best of the tests is that by some clever " hunch " of the investigator a clue to some of the differentiating elements in behavior has been discovered. This may result in very ingenious situations, which appeal to common sense as indications of the trait that is being measured. It is desirable to have more interrelations in terms of actual behavior.

The tests which purport to show differences in character, to select " potential delinquents," etc., face this same difficulty. How specific a delinquent response of any sort may be is not known. Most of these tests are based on the assumption of a total goodness or badness that will manifest itself in verbal responses to imagined situations as well as to the situations themselves as they arise. Very few of these tests have given any satisfactory results. Cady's come nearest to a prognostic value: tests were definitely selected on the basis of their ability to get differential responses from " incorrigibles " and " corrigibles," as judged by teachers in certain schools. They would have greater validity if a check-up were made of the acts of incorrigibles and corrigibles in the actual school situation. Woodworth's and Downey's tests seem also to offer a clue to some types of delinquency, i.e., certain responses on these tests seem to be associated with delinquent tendencies. The same warning must be given here, however, that was given in regard to the interpretation of delinquency in terms of low intelligence: the great mass of delinquents reacts to these test situations just about as does the great mass of unselected persons. More delinquents are found to give " unfavorable " responses than are found among the unselected persons, indicating a greater instability of the emotions and of " weakness " of character among the delinquents; but, on the other hand, we find large numbers of individuals with " unstable emotions " and " weak characters " among the group unselected for delinquency. That the tendencies indicated by these tests are a factor in delinquency seems undoubted. To accept them as the explanation of delinquency, however, would be absurd.

Almost all these techniques have been shown to have some value as differentiating agents. The responses given on most of them have shown a wide range of individual difference in response. From our point of view, the importance of this lies in the relationship between these differences in test responses and the different personal and social adjustments of individuals. Very few of these tests have been checked up against criteria of successful adjustment outside of the test situation. Where they have been, they seem to give prognoses of success that are less valid than the prognoses given by intelligence tests. Where they have been combined with intelligence tests their prognostic value has often been increased.

This approach appeals quite generally to common sense. Behavior is thought of in terms of the dynamic aspects of personality, of temperament, and of " character." The truth or falsity of this approach has not yet been proved. Certain of the results that we have cited indicate its importance. It must obviously be taken into consideration in any study of behavior. But we must not blind ourselves to the fact that, although the materials dealt with in this approach are probably the most interesting possible, they are intangible and very often lacking in objectivity. Most of the studies that have been made have had grave faults of methodology, and are incomparable one with another because of differences in the units used and lack of standardized procedure.

CHAPTER X
The Psychiatric Approach

IT is an alarming fact that there are more beds for the insane in the hospitals of the country than for all other patients combined. This does not mean that there are more insane patients, because these occupy the beds for a longer time than the surgical and other cases. But there were 267,617 insane patients in hospitals on January 1, 1923, as compared with 40,924 in 1880, or an increase of from 81.6 per 100,000 in 1880 to 241.8 in 1923.[1] This does not mean either that there has been this ratio of increase in insanity, or necessarily any increase, since more of the insane are being gathered into institutions from among the general population, but it does indicate the proportions the problem has assumed.

In addition to the heavy task of treating these patients, and partly as a result of it, the psychiatrists have also a large rôle in the theory and treatment of general behavior problems, although medicine, which was once defined as " a study of the skin and its contents," was in its earlier history far from the study of behavior. Historically " insanity " was treated as a brain disease, or defined as " a symptom of disease of the brain inducing disordered mental symptoms," and the insanities were divided into two classes, the congenital and acquired, containing the idiots and the lunatics. The Kraepelinian system, which was standard until recently, was clinical. It enabled the practitioner to recognize and classify cases on the basis of symptoms, to make a prognosis and apply the treatment indicated in his art. And even in this there was and remains a good deal of confusion. The psychoanalyst Kempf has said that if a certain number of cases were given to a number of

[1] Bossard, J. H. S.: *Problems of Social Well-Being* (1927), 531 ff.

psychiatrists separately for diagnosis and their results were sealed and given to a committee for comparison the whole system would blow up.

Stated very generally, from the standpoint of causation, the present psychiatric view is that mental disturbance represents a failure of the organism to adapt to the conditions of life and of the society in which it lives, that this failure involves the functioning of the organism as a whole, and that no adequate " specificity " can be indicated. Strecker has made the following statement:

Psychiatrists of the present day and generation have been the recipients of many plausible explanations of the origin and phenomena of mental disease. . . . One may have in mind a number of more or less carefully studied cases in which the evidence seems overwhelmingly in favor of physical factors as causative — or, better, precipitating — agents, and another series in which the mental disease seems to have been produced or certainly favored by psychogenic instrumentation. What is one to do when involved in such a predicament? Is it right to abandon a hard-won conviction, even though it may apply to but a single patient? May it not be possible that the difficulty of reconciling two seemingly inimical viewpoints arises not because one is inherently correct and the other inherently wrong, but because, under certain given conditions, they are both true? In other words, may we not find in the last analysis that there is such a thing as multiplicity of causes as applied to mental disease — a non-specific etiology?

In attempting to make clear the premise of the " non-specificity " of mental disease, it may be worth while to turn for a moment to the domain of general medicine. The pathological conditions that can be described as distinctly specific reactions — i.e., always ascribable to well-known and clearly demonstrable causes — are after all quite limited and certainly are easily outnumbered by those morbid states in which the etiology is a matter of doubt and conjecture. Again, one thinks readily of tuberculosis, syphilis, typhoid fever, malaria, and the like, as phenomena that, from the standpoint of causation, have been scientifically tested and proven for all time to come. However, medicine is an art and not a science, and from the criterion of definite cause and unavoidable effect it is not possible to grant, for instance, the absolute specificity of tuberculosis, even though its clinical and pathological limits may be drawn with considerable accuracy and its source is indisputably the bacillus of Koch. It may seem trite to remark that many individuals come into close contact with this organism, but escape consumption, and yet, from this and similar observations, one gains the broader conception of the fallaciousness of thinking in terms of unconditioned specificity. If the presence of the bacillus tuberculosis inevitably meant the development of that disease in an individual, if the pneumococcus, the spirochete pallida, or the bacillus of typhoid fever implied that the necessary outcome must be pneumonia, syphilis, or enteric fever, then indeed it might be profitable, not only in general medicine, but also in psychiatry, to devote exclusive attention to a search for single disease-producing agents. However, in all probability the processes that lead to the development of any morbid condition are immensely complicated and closely related to one another, and disease is almost always the culmination of a long series of more or less detrimental or destructive conditions which eventually become sufficiently strong to break down the barriers of natural and acquired resistance. The tremendous importance of even such general considerations as age, race, climate, nutrition, occupation, hygiene, habits of life, and the like, cannot be overemphasized, and even though it is often true that such general factors would be powerless to produce morbidity in themselves, if the direct mediation of a specific cause were wanting, still it is probably also true that without their predisposing influence, this cause in itself would not exert any harmful effect. These general factors are so well known that we are accustomed to speak of racial, climatic, occupational, adolescent, climacteric, or senile diseases, and the like. By this we do not mean to imply that they are rigidly restricted to certain races, climates, occupations, or age periods, but that these factors in combination with others — among which may be included a more or less clearly understood causal agent — are most frequently encountered in tracing the incidence of the diseases in question. Even such a seemingly simple occurrence as a fracture of a bone may be and often is due to remotely determining circumstances. The age of the individual, the fragility of the bone, or the presence of constitutional disease may in a given instance be much more important and motivating than the actual force of the impact.

It would seem, therefore, that in some sense we are always dealing with total reactions which are the end result of the constant interplay between individual and environment. Furthermore, if it is permissible to speak of the " chances " of contracting any given disease, it is manifestly obvious that there are no two stages in an individual's existence when the " chances " are exactly equal, even though he is at both times in contact with the disease-producing organism. His resistance is either greater or less at one time than at another, and its strength is dependent upon the addition and subtraction of all the upbuilding and deteriorating conditions of his whole life. Thus, at twenty a man may escape tuberculosis, even though he is exposed to the bacillus, because he has led an outdoor, hygienic life and is in excellent physical state, but he may succumb at thirty, owing to reduced resistance due to sedentary occupation, insufficient food, fresh air, and sunshine, and perhaps alcoholic overindulgence. It is even hypothetically plausible to conceive of two human beings who, by reason of previous circumstances of life, are equally protected from or exposed to infection, and yet the one falls ill and the other successfully resists because in the latter hereditary influences are an asset while in the former they are a liability. Heredity may sometimes act directly, as in the instance of inherited syphilis; more often it is non-specific, as when the stock is more distantly weakened by alcoholism or syphilis.

Not only may antecedent factors have a definite value in conditioning the development of disease, but the chronological order of their occurrence sometimes may be decisive. Thus, an individual may go on a debauch and after a period of sobriety be exposed to cold and inclement weather and still continue in reasonably good health, while if the drunkenness and exposure follow each other closely or are simultaneous, pneumonia is apt to be contracted. It is always fascinating to speculate on the considerations that may be responsible for the seriousness or degree of disease after it is actually present. For instance the course of enteric fever may be mild, smooth, and uncomplicated, or it may be severe, stormy, and marked by complications such as hemorrhage, peritonitis, or meningeal symptoms, or finally it may be overwhelming and eventu-ate fatally. It is almost permissible to speak of benign and malignant typhoid fever. We know that the severity of the infection is influential, but surely there are other influences. In the last analysis is it not feasible to weigh in the balance the whole life history of the patient and even to take into consideration remote ancestrally determined strengths or weaknesses of the various systems of the body, such as the cardiovascular or nervous? [2]

Rosanoff [3] had presented an earlier paper in much the same line, based on 1,056 consecutive admissions to the Kings Park State Hospital, indicating the relation of the appearance of psychoses to business troubles, death or illness of relatives, love affairs, sexual episodes, domestic troubles, shock in connection with burglary, assault, fright during a storm, and other critical experiences.

In 1908 Adolf Meyer, present dean of American psychiatrists, defined dementia praecox as the result of bad habit formation, thus bringing a portion of the psychiatric material clearly into the psychological and social fields:

The most serious affections which fill our hospitals for the insane are due to those difficulties of *instinctive and emotional adaptation,* which form both

---

[2] Strecker, Edward A.: "The Non-Specificity of Mental Disease," *Mental Hygiene,* 7:277–81 (1923).

[3] Rosanoff, A. J.: "Exciting Causes in Psychiatry," *American Journal of Insanity,* 69:351–401 (1912).

theoretically and numerically the most important types of psycho-biological problems. We may admit that approximately ten per cent of the admissions to hospitals for the insane suffer from general paralysis or paresis, and about twenty per cent from alcoholic psychoses, that is to say, from disorders with a plainly bacterial or toxic non-mental factor as the exciting link — to be sure also based primarily upon a deviation of instincts, but rather upon an excess of what is considered sane enough to be tolerated as a mere social evil, namely, alcoholism and irresponsible sexual relations entailing risk of venereal infection. But at least thirty per cent of the admissions seem to make up a group of disorders of the more *personal*, instinctive adjustments involving a miscarriage of instincts through lack of balance, — *dementia praecox*. This type of mental disorder is peculiarly liable to lead to permanent collapse, and is one in which the so-called psychogenic factors are especially prominent. . . . Certainly the number of those is increasing who agree with me that the bulk of the manifestations subsumed under the caption of dementia praecox may be most practically expressed as the inevitable and natural development from a deterioration of habits, partly due to developmental defects of the mental endowment, but in part at least to the clashing of instincts and to progressively faulty modes of meeting difficulties, and the disability of a proper balance of anabolism and catabolism which they entail. . . .

A consideration of carefully studied cases of dementia praecox convinces me that in reality we have to do with a perfectly natural, though perhaps unusually persistent development of tendencies difficult to balance. Evolution's method of trial and rejection will lead some children into a reading craze, others into mere day-dreaming of an apparently indifferent, though often fantastic kind, and still others into sexual imagination, which in passing, it may be well to remark, is often as serious if not actually more serious than the often harmless abnormal sexual practices by themselves. All these tendencies are common traits of adolescence, usually offset in one way or another by the more natural and sociable children. The correction comes from more powerful attractions exercised in an opposing direction by better instincts; or the consequences of the failure to meet the requirements of actual life may call for a halt. Here the very habits of the patient, the loss of sense for the real, and the abnormal satisfaction in mere dreaming and good resolutions, encourage a mere dodging of the consequences rather than the giving up of the harmful instincts. To those who meet with failure, there come as further burdens the comparison of themselves with others and the resultant feeling of being at a disadvantage. These feelings are especially strong in those who have ventured or have been hoisted above their level, and they are augmented by a natural irritation at being reminded of the disadvantage under which they labor, — an irritation which is added to that which is the natural outcome of brooding

over disappointments and incapacities. In the real failures, we then find a
covering up, rather than a correction of the harmful yearnings. There develops
an insidious tendency to substitute for an efficient way of meeting the difficulties, a superficial moralizing and self-deception, and an uncanny tendency
to drift into so many varieties of shallow mysticism and metaphysical ponder-
ings, or into fantastic ideas which cannot possibly be put to the test of action. . . . Then, under some strain which a normal person would be prepared
for, a sufficiently weakened and sensitive individual will react with manifestations which constitute the mental disorders constituting the " deterioration
process " or dementia praecox. Unfinished or chronically sub-efficient action,
a life lived apart from the wholesome influence of companionship and concrete
test, and finally a progressive incongruity in meeting the inevitably complex
demands of the higher instincts, — this is practically the formula of the
deterioration process. . . .

Janet has constructed an interesting hierarchy of mental functions. His
study of psychasthenia brings him to the conviction that *complete action* is
the most difficult and highest function. I am tempted to add that completed
action is the first essential for rest and for beginning something new. I thus
come to describe the development of dementia praecox as being essentially a
deterioration of the instincts of action.[4]

In the meantime psychology, pedagogy, anthropology, sociology and
psychoanalysis were working from the standpoint of experience and
habit as determinants in personality formation, and the Pavlovian
and Watsonian work on the "conditioned reflex" added an experimental basis for this approach. Dr. Healy's clinic, in Chicago, dating
from 1909, recognized from the beginning both the social and the organic factors. In this connection a new psychiatric standpoint had been
gradually developed recognizing that many mental disturbances are not
hereditary and inevitable but due to conditions of life and training and
therefore able to be prevented. One of the outstanding results was the
formation in 1909 of the National Committee for Mental Hygiene, an
organization for the promotion of mental health, due directly to a critical experience in the life of Clifford W. Beers, who had been confined
through a temporary mental illness in a hospital for the insane and later
wrote a fascinating volume entitled, *A Mind That Found Itself.*

At this point the interest in psychopathology as related to behavior

---

[4] Meyer, Adolf: " What do Histories of Cases of Insanity Teach Us Concerning
Preventive Mental Hygiene During the Years of School Life? " *Psychological
Clinic,* 2:92–98 (1908).

began to be formulated in two research approaches, the study of the incidence of psychopathic traits in the general population and institutions, particularly prisons and penitentiaries, and the study of the child in the clinic, at first the juvenile court clinic and later the child welfare clinic, which received problem children from homes or schools or any other sources.

In taking up some of these concrete programs for examination we may point out a general source of error to which all specially selected standpoints are liable — the tendency of the mind to work on the basis of its own prepossessions and to weight the data accordingly. This is best shown in connection with the psychology of testimony. The studies of testimony by Gross and the Breslau school show that the witness may perceive elements which are not present but are anticipated and so perceived and believed. The same has been shown of children's lies and phantasies by Stern [5] and his associates. The pathologist and psychiatrist also, whose training was over the dissecting table, in the hospital and the medical clinic, may react in the same way to their cases. It is notorious that medical practitioners in general — surgeons, gland specialists, liver specialists, kidney specialists — are inclined to discover the symptoms of their specialties in the cases which come to them. A representative of the concept of " infection " in the etiology of mental disorders will view every case primarily from that standpoint: " Psychoses arise from a combination of many factors, some of which may be absent, but the most constant one is an intra-cerebral, bio-chemical, cellular disturbance arising from circulating toxins, originating in chronic focal infections situated anywhere throughout the body, and probably to some extent in disturbances of the endocrine system." [6] Other investigators start with the endocrine system and subordinate all other factors to it. The same thing is seen in everyday life, where adherents of political parties and of reform propaganda interpret the total situation from a particular standpoint.

The National Committee for Mental Hygiene has been prominent among the organizations conducting investigations and surveys " to

[5] A good résumé of the work of Gross, Stern and other students of testimony will be found in Bernard Hart, *Psychopathology: Its Development and Its Place in Medicine* (1927), 95–110.

[6] Cotton, H. A.: *The Defective Delinquent and Insane* (1921), 32.

ascertain as far as possible the relationship between anti-social conduct and mental disorder and defect." The figures resulting from these investigations are high and the incidence for mental disturbance is much higher than for mental defect:

Probably the most significant of the studies conducted by the National Committee was the one at Sing Sing Prison in 1916, when several hundred consecutive admissions to that institution were subjected to a careful psychiatric examination. Of 608 men thus studied, 59 per cent were found to be mentally diseased, feeble-minded, or otherwise mentally abnormal. The findings of the psychiatrist and his explanation of these disorders and their bearings upon the anti-social conduct of these prisoners so impressed the New York state authorities inviting the study, that in the reconstruction of the new prison it was decided to build a special structure for a psychiatric clinic as recommended by that study. This clinic, upon its completion, will serve as a center for the reception, classification, study, and treatment of prisoners of this state.

More recently the National Committee has examined and studied approximately 10,000 prisoners in its surveys of penal and correctional institutions in various states, which studies have been financed largely by the Rockefeller Foundation. These surveys have shown that as many as 60 per cent of these prisoners are classifiable in terms of deviation from average normal mental health and are suffering from conditions that appear to bear a causal relationship to their anti-social behavior. Last year, in a study of 3,451 prisoners in the Texas Penitentiary, it was found that only 29.4 per cent could be classified as normal, and of 226 inmates of 18 county jails in that state, only 14.2 per cent were found to be normal. In a recent study of 1,288 prisoners in 34 county jails and penitentiaries in New York state, 76.6 per cent showed a distinct mental deviation along some line.

Other studies have shown large numbers of delinquents to be far from normal in their personality make-up. Of 502 cases studied for the Police Department of New York City in 1917, 58 per cent were reported to be suffering from some nervous or mental abnormality; and of 781 boys and girls studied in the Juvenile Court of New York City, 69 per cent exhibited such conditions. A study of delinquent women in the lower courts of Albany, New York, showed 56 per cent with psychopathic conditions; and of a miscellaneous group of 1,000 offenders in the Municipal Court of Boston, 46 per cent showed similar disorders.[7]

To indicate the method employed we quote some details from one of these studies. This investigation was made of 1,216 inmates of 34 county

[7] " Mental Hygiene and Delinquency," *Mental Hygiene Bulletin*, 3:1 (January, 1925).

jails and penitentiaries in the state of New York " to determine the mental and physical status of the prisoners." The mental diagnoses were made as follows:

Normal [22.9%] designates those who are at least of average intelligence according to psychiatric and psychological tests (I.Q., 90–110), who are free of nervous or mental disease and whose personality development shows no outstanding pathological straits.

Dullard [7.2%] is the diagnosis given to those who are not actually feeble-minded, but who are nevertheless sufficiently below the average in intelligence to be unable to compete with them on an equal basis. In terms of Intelligence Quotient (I.Q.) they usually measure from 80 to 90.

Borderline mental defective [5.4%] includes those who fall in the boundary between definitely recognizable mental deficiency and the dullard. In terms of I.Q. they usually measure from 70 to 80.

Mental defective (feebleminded) [7.6%] is the term applied to those with a definite defect in intelligence which has existed from birth or shortly after, classified as morons, imbeciles or idiots, according to the degree of defect present. In terms of the I.Q. they fall below a rating of 70.

Psychopathic personality [42.2%]. Under the designation psychopathic personality is brought together a group of pathological personalities whose abnormality of make-up is expressed mainly in the character and intensity of their emotional and volitional reactions. The term for this group has been shortened from the older one " constitutional psychopathic inferiority " with which it is synonymous. Individuals with an intellectual defect (feebleminded-ness) are not included.

Personality defect [4.5%] denotes a condition in which pathological traits are so clearly in evidence as to preclude placing the individual in the " normal " group, but not sufficiently marked to warrant the diagnosis of " psychopathic personality."

Psychoneurosis [1.5%] includes those disorders in which mental forces or ideas of which the subject is either aware (conscious) or unaware (unconscious) bring about various mental and physical symptoms; and those disorders of which, while the symptoms are both mental and physical, the primary cause is considered essentially physical (neurosis). Within this group are included hysteria (delusion, stupor, dream states, amnesia); psychasthenia (anxiety and obsessional neuroses, marked fears or phobias, doubts and impulsions); neurasthenia (fatigue neuroses, mental and motor fatigability and irritability, hyperesthesias and parasthesias); hypochondriasis and varying degrees of depression; and other types.

Epilepsy [0.9%] designates those persons who are subject to epileptic seizures or *petit mal* attacks.

Mental disease or deterioration [7.3%] denotes clear-cut mental disorder or a deterioration of mental capacity as a result of disease. . . .

Only 22.9 per cent were found to be normal while 76.6 per cent showed a distinct mental deviation along some line. . . .

Two facts stand out in this survey as of chief importance:

1. That 66 per cent of the prisoners examined were recidivists, i.e., had been arrested previously, the arrests numbering from two to more than fifty.

2. That 77 per cent were psychopathological individuals of well-recognized types.

Along with these two facts should be noted the fall of the percentage of " normal " individuals from 36 per cent for those arrested once to 9.7 per cent for those arrested four or more times; and the rise of the percentage of psychopathology among the recidivists from 63.3 per cent for those arrested once, to 73.8 per cent for those arrested twice, 85.3 per cent for those arrested three times, and 90.3 per cent for those arrested four or more times. . . .

In so far as the prisoners in this study are concerned — and it is believed they are representative of county-jail populations generally — the problem of delinquency is a problem of recidivism, and recidivism is a problem of psychopathology.[8]

This study is a recent representative of several approaches to the determination of a criminal type through the measurement or diagnosing of criminals, all of which fail through defective methods and wrong assumptions, and we may here sketch the development of the whole movement which originated with Lombroso.

Lombroso was an anthropologist, skilled in the use of anthropometric methods. Impressed with the large number of anomalies of an " atavistic " nature found in the skull of a brigand which he was examining, he suspected that the criminal was probably a definite, anomalous human type. He therefore began the measurement of criminals by approved anthropometric methods, and after some shifting of his position, concluded that the " born criminal " could be recognized by certain stigmata or anomalies such as asymmetrical cranium, long lower jaw (prognathism), piglike eyes, scanty beard, low sensitivity to pain, etc. Five or more of these stigmata indicated a complete criminal type; the person with less than three was not a criminal type. Some of the followers of Lombroso claimed that there were subdivisions of the general

[8] National Committee for Mental Hygiene: *Report of a Mental Hygiene Survey of New York County Jails and Penitentiaries, with Recommendations* (1924), 7–9, 142–43.

criminal type, thieves, murderers, sex offenders, to be recognized by particular stigmata.

This theory needed only subjection to a rigorous scientific analysis to show how slight a factual basis it had. This need was supplied by Goring's volume, *The English Convict*. Assisted by Karl Pearson, he studied more than 3,000 consecutive entrants to English convict prisons, employing thirty-seven different measurements of physical characteristics and using the exact methods of anthropometry. By careful statistical analysis he tested the relationship of these characters with the nature of the crime committed and concluded: " If there be any real association between physical characters and crime, this is so microscopic in amount as not to be revealed by the values of our correlation ratios and coefficients of contingency — these values being of almost the same order of magnitude as would have been obtained if, instead of separating them into crime groups, our subjects had, prior to observation, been divided at random into five or six categories of the same numerical proportion as our five or six sub-groups." Criminals were found, however, to be differentiated in physique from the general population to the extent of being somewhat shorter in stature and somewhat lighter in body weight.

Now, in attacking Lombroso's theory of the criminal as an anatomically differentiated type, Goring used quantitative data and scientific methods. His refutation was brilliant, and final — so long, of course, as his data remain unchallenged. It is, therefore, difficult to understand how he could so readily have fallen into the same type of error as Lombroso when he deals, in the second part of his book, with the mental characteristics of criminals as compared with the general population. The general intelligence of the criminals was estimated by a series of impressions " depending on an indefinite number of mental capacities and abilities," giving results which are surely as uncheckable and subject to bias as those of the " anatomico-pathologists," whom he had so scathingly annihilated. All criminals were classified as being intelligent, fairly intelligent, unintelligent, weak-minded and imbecile, and were finally grouped as either weak-minded or not weak-minded. An idea of how far these classifications are from any standards of objectivity is seen from Goring's description of the basis of the weak-minded category. The weak-minded offender is " one who is found to possess low degrees of general intelligence; or to hold extreme disregard for truth, for opinion, and for authority; or to be unteachable, unemployable, profligate, lazy; or to display marked preferences for undesirable company; or to be very impulsive, excitable, restless, uncertain, passionate, violent, and refractory in conduct; or to be careless in business, neglectful of responsibility, false and malevolent in speech, filthy in habits, and nearly always inebriate." It is obvious that a judgment of an offender's intelligence on such a basis is far removed from a measurement of, say, his head length by callipers. No observer's judgment in regard to the former could be free from his own bias and mental set, and any trained observer, with accurate instruments, could objectively determine the latter. There would also necessarily be a wide divergence of opinion as among observers in regard to the former and agreement within narrow, definable limits in regard to the latter. Furthermore, Goring's data for the general population are entirely incomparable with estimates of this sort, that is, he accepted the rather widely challenged estimates of feeblemindedness among the general population made by the Royal Commission on the Control of Feeblemindedness in 1908. It might be thought, therefore, that his conclusion, that " the relationship between mental defectiveness and the committing of all types of crime, with the exception of some kinds of fraud, is an extremely intimate one," could scarcely have been accepted without further attempts at utilizing a more adequate control group.

But the investigators who followed Goring made no serious efforts to apply their tests to a control group. They tested many groups of criminals for feeblemindedness and compared these with their *a priori* conceptions of the amount of feeblemindedness in the general population. In one respect, however, great improvement took place. It became no longer necessary to estimate intelligence by subjective standards such as those used by Goring. Mental tests, of a perfectly objective nature, were devised and continually improved. It was never shown adequately that these tests measured differences in native intelligence, as separate from acquired learning, or that they were free from many sorts of environmental influences. Nevertheless, they have become an exceedingly useful instrument, have had a very wide application, and have, above all else, the virtue of giving checkable results. The interpretations of these tests as applied to criminal groups, however, went far beyond the facts. No adequate groups of the adult population were tested, and standards of adult performance were assumed from the performance of groups of

school children. The " mental age " of the normal adult as determined
by these tests was assumed to be sixteen years. When groups of criminals were tested the assumption was that they were mentally deficient
if they fell below this average, and feebleminded if they were two to
four years retarded. And large proportions of the criminal groups, in
some cases more than fifty per cent, were thus classed as feebleminded.
With such overwhelmingly large proportions of criminals judged feebleminded and the naïve belief that the non-criminal population would
score high on the tests, it was natural that feeblemindedness should be
regarded as the cause of crime. We have seen (p. 364) that Williams
made the astonishing statement that a few children remained whose
delinquency could not be accounted for on the basis of low intelligence
and some other explanation must be sought.

At the same time, the need of an adequate control group was felt by
many psychologists and many criminologists had become skeptical of
the adequacy of the feebleminded explanation. The draft army of
1,726,966 men offered the possibility of such a group for the determination of the validity of the assumption that adults generally graded at
sixteen years on the mental tests. The results were far from expectations
when they showed the average mental age of these adult males to be
between thirteen and fourteen years. Indeed, if the same criteria were
applied to them as had already been applied to the criminal groups,
some forty-six per cent would be shown to be mentally deficient.

These results, even though the draft army could not be considered a
wholly adequate representation of the general population, caused a
thorough reorganization of the theories in regard to crime. If, according
to these standards, just about as large a proportion of feebleminded was
found in the draft army as among the criminals, feeblemindedness could
no longer be looked at as the specific cause of crime.

The criminal type had by this time become firmly established as a
psychological type. And, with the growing feeling in psychological
circles of the inadequacy of attempts to explain behavior differences on
purely intellectual grounds, explanations in the emotional and volitional
field gained favor. The psychiatrists in particular had found antisocial
behavior to be a frequent occurrence among persons of disordered personality and it was therefore assumed that psychopathological traits
would be found very frequently among criminals. Much of this reasoning was in circles, however, because, while psychopathology was looked

to for the cause of crime, criminality in itself was assumed to be a psychopathological trait. That is, certain offenses were taken as *a priori* evidence of mental abnormality and the commission of these offenses gave rise to a diagnosis of abnormality.

In this way we reach the attitude and results of the study we have here taken as an example. Glueck, who examined the Sing Sing prisoners and classified 59% of them " in terms of deviations from average normal mental health," stated: " It is now being universally recognized that the pauper, the prostitute and the criminal classes are primarily the product of mental defect and degeneracy and as such must come within the purview of mental medicine." [9]

These claims have been subjected to no such test as that applied by Goring to the claims of Lombroso, but it should be recognized that no proof has been deduced that psychopathic traits are at the root of crime, and no proof can be deduced until a thoroughly objective attempt is made to classify a control group in these same terms of " deviations from normal mental health."

It is interesting to note that the very scientists who attacked Lombroso's claim of an anatomical criminal type and thoroughly disproved it, were unable to effect a " transfer of learning," and carried over his errors of approach to a further development of claims of a mental type. And, now, with the anatomical and mental type of criminal completely discredited, the idea of a psychopathic type is agitating the criminological world.

All of these attempts to establish a criminal type were, and are, fundamentally unscientific. For this concept of " type " has been based on the idea of some fundamental differentiation from mankind in general, and data regarding even the simplest characteristics of mankind in general have been slow in accumulating. And because there have been no exact data by which a proper statistical characterization of the " normal population " could be made, types have been assumed to deviate from *a priori* concepts of the characteristics of the normal population. It is not surprising, therefore, to find that these concepts have represented idealizations of mankind, and that, in almost every sphere, as data have accumulated, the concepts have had to be scaled down quite radically. There is often considerable resistance to accepting the normal, as shown by data, in lieu of the idealistically conceived normal.

[9] Glueck, Bernard: *Studies in Forensic Psychiatry* (1916), 68.

This was shown, for instance, in the case of certain of the psychologists, who seemed to prefer to consider a large proportion of the population mentally defective rather than give up the idea that the " normal " man has a mental age of sixteen years. Similarly, " normal eye-sight " is assumed to be perfect eye-sight, yet the statistical average, the true norm, of eye-sight in a modern community comes very far from perfection. Hypertrophied tonsils are considered an anomaly, yet they are found in the " average " child. The normal man, as he actually exists, has been found, time and time again, to be very much inferior to the normal man as he is believed to exist.[10]

It should be obvious that the only true norm is the central tendency actually found to exist in any " universe." The norm as the actually known, statistically determined average, is a scientific concept. The norm as an *a priori* determined status is a non-scientific concept. The norm must not be thought of as synonymous with perfection, because defects are universal. The only way the norm can be determined

---

[10] " In 1918, Thomas D. Wood, chairman of the Joint Committee on Health Problems in Education of the National Education Association and the American Medical Association, submitted the following estimates on the physical condition of the school children of the United States:

' At least 5 per cent — 1,000,000 children — have now or have had tuberculosis, a danger often to others as well as to themselves.

' Five per cent — 1,000,000 of them — have defective hearing, which, unrecognized, gives many the undeserved reputation of being mentally defective.

' Twenty-five per cent — 5,000,000 children — have defective eyes. All but a small percentage of these can be corrected, and yet a majority of them have received no attention.

' Fifteen to 25 per cent — 3,000,000 to 5,000,000 children — are suffering from malnutrition [not always due to poverty]. . . .

' From 15 to 25 per cent — 3,000,000 to 5,000,000 — have adenoids, diseased tonsils, or other glandular defects.

' From 10 to 20 per cent — 2,000,000 to 4,000,000 — have weak foot arches, weak spines, or other joint defects.

' From 50 to 75 per cent — 11,000,000 to 16,000,000 — have defective teeth. . . .

' Seventy-five per cent — 16,000,000 of the school children of the United States — have physical defects which are potentially or actually detrimental to health ' . . .

" In 1923, Dr. Wood wrote that he believed these figures were still essentially accurate for the country at large, although he supposed that the percentages would be considerably lower in a few of the cities where rather intensive programs of health care have been undertaken during recent years." — (Moore, H. H.: *Public Health in the United States*, 1923, 56–57.)

is by the careful collection of data regarding the universe to which it is referred.

Returning to the recent claims in regard to a criminal type, it is, therefore, a scientific absurdity to claim, as is done in the report of the Mental Hygiene Survey, that some 77% of the criminals are abnormal, without having any actual norm to which this alleged deviating type can be referred. Little is known as to the incidence of psychopathic traits among the general, unselected population, or, more exactly, among the general population from the same age level, occupation groups, and social classes as the prison population. The most that this 77% can be taken to mean is that certain *a priori* standards of normality, as determined by a group of psychiatrists, are not fulfilled in 77% of the cases in this study. There is no knowledge available as to how far they are fulfilled among the general population.[11] Therefore, these figures are significant only as showing how often certain mental traits occur among these prison inmates. They do not define a type. They show nothing at all with regard to the effect of these traits in producing crime. Such an effect could be adequately shown only by an equally careful examination of a carefully chosen control group. The greatest claims that could logically be put forth as the result of this study would be that psychiatrists generally, as a result of wide experience, *guess* that such a large percentage of mental " deviations " would not be found among such a control group. The weakness of that type of claim was shown in the case of the mental testers, whose concepts of normal mentality were shown by the army tests to have been grossly exaggerated, and the psychiatrists are in an even worse position than the mental testers because their

---

[11] The New York State Hospital Commission in a " Survey of Mental Disorders in Nassau County, N. Y.," reports that in a district intensively studied " 3.6% of the county at large were judged to be mentally abnormal . . . and presumably, up to a certain point, the more active the search the greater will be the number of abnormal persons found." (*Psychiatric Bulletin*, 2:109–231). Commenting on this report Dr. John T. MacCurdy says: " As far as my own experience goes, I have never had extensive knowledge of any family, either socially or professionally, without discovering some mental disease in it. And I do not use this term figuratively. I count only such cases as any group of psychiatrists would include. My conclusion is that today there are few, if any, perfect families from a psychiatric standpoint, and that the only histories which have real significance are those in which are recorded in generation after generation cases of feeblemindedness, epilepsy, alcoholism and flagrant insanity." — (*The Psychology of Emotion*, 1925, 13.)

data are so much less objective. The mental testers went astray in their judgments, even though they had a relatively large mass of quantitative data at their disposal, because these data were not sufficiently representative of the " universe." The psychiatrists have not a fraction of the data that the mental testers had. An even more serious obstacle to the psychiatrists' ability to make a good " guess " or prediction about the incidence of these mental and personality traits in the general population is the lack of agreement among themselves in defining and delimiting the boundaries of these several traits. Their classifications are comparable to Goring's " weak-minded " and " not weak-minded " categories. The IQ, with all its faults, is an instrument for separating subjects into classes with perfectly readily definable characteristics, i.e., the ability to pass certain definite tests at a certain chronological age. The lack of definiteness in categories based on " abnormality . . . in the character and intensity of emotional and volitional reactions " would make it almost impossible to compare studies made by different sets of investigators. Compared with the 59% found abnormal by the Sing Sing study, the work of Healy and Bronner shows 72.5% of their 4,000 repeated juvenile offenders to be " definitely mentally normal," and 13.5% " clearly feebleminded." [12] Slawson, working objectively [13] and employing a control group, places about 15.6% of the delinquents as mentally unstable because they test " at or below the school boy medians as given by Mathews." [14] Healy and Bronner conclude their examination of the question of psychopathic traits as causal factor in delinquency as follows:

To any argument that mental abnormality and not environmental conditions is a predominating cause of crime, the only safe answer is a comparison of one city, Chicago for instance, with other cities. For comparative purposes take London. Psychiatrists know of no statistics which even tend to indicate that there is less mental defect or mental disease there. Yet the vastly smaller amount of crime in London is a subject of constant comment by students of criminology. The murders in London as compared with Chicago are often quoted — in 1920, 15 to 194, that is, 3 per million inhabitants as against 73. Similarly, great differences could be cited between other American communities

---

[12] Healy, W., and Bronner, A. F.: *Delinquents and Criminals* (1926), 150–51.

[13] I.e., employing a standardized test procedure, the Woodworth-Mathews questionnaire (see p. 420 above).

[14] Slawson, John: *The Delinquent Boy* (1926), 234.

and foreign cities, and Chicago itself varies from many other American cities in proportionate amount of crime. But there is not the least reason to suppose that Chicago leads other cities in the amount of mental abnormality among its inhabitants.

Indeed our graphic chart of treatment and outcomes in Chicago and Boston, Chapter VI, bears on this very point. We have shown earlier in the present chapter and in Table 47, that large series of juvenile delinquents in Chicago and Boston show surprisingly similar figures for mental abnormality — and yet there is a tremendous difference as regards the commission of later crime. If 420 juvenile repeated offenders in Chicago produced more than 14 homicides or murders and 39 professional criminals, and 400 repeated delinquents in the same years in Boston produced no homicides and only 2 professional criminals, is the difference likely to be due to mentality — or social treatment?

But we would not neglect abnormal mentality as a factor where it may be shown to exist — particularly in its bearing upon the necessity for adequate treatment of mentally abnormal delinquents. Especially is there need to study outcomes as related to different types of treatment of different groups of the abnormal.[15]

But these criticisms do not destroy the fact that large numbers of the psychopathic, feebleminded and borderline cases spend their lives in and out of institutions, that they are more likely to get into difficulties with the law and be separated out for the institutions than the normal population, in proportion to their numbers, that many criminals would be in psychopathic institutions if they were properly diagnosed before disposition was made of them by the courts, and that this situation has an important bearing on the questions of recidivism and the constitution of the population of penal and reformatory institutions.

In their bearing on these questions certain interrelations brought out in the report we have been considering are highly suggestive. The most important of these is the definite increase in the relative number of psychopathic personalities with the degree of recidivism. Thus, among those arrested only once there were 29.7% of psychopathic personalities, increasing to 36.4% among those arrested twice, to 46.2% among those arrested three times, and to 60.2% among those arrested four or more times. This definite, continuous gradation is undoubtedly significant, especially if taken in conjunction with the fact that those defined as " normal " decrease from 36.0% among those arrested once, to 26.2% among those arrested twice, to 14.2% among those arrested three

---

[15] Healy and Bronner: *op. cit.*, 159–61.

times, to 9.7% among those arrested four or more times. That there is a close connection between psychopathic personalities, as here defined, and recidivism, as shown by the number of times arrested, would seem conclusive from these data except for the possibility that the degree of recidivism itself is used as one basis for the diagnosis of the psychopath.

In interpreting these data it should be remembered that recidivism means repeated known arrests rather than repeated offenses, and it means in part that the general instability of the psychoneurotic and the stupidity of the feebleminded [16] render them less able to avoid repeated arrest than the more intelligent and stable offenders. But the question is more fundamental than this, and a study just completed by Healy and Bronner and their associates (noticed in chapter II) brings out the fact that it is more difficult to make an adjustment in the case of the psychopathic person than in the case of any other class of offender.

It is not entirely appropriate to treat the theory of Cotton, quoted above, as a psychiatric approach to behavior since it represents a bio-chemical standpoint elaborated by a limited circle of psychiatrists and now generally repudiated, but we may nevertheless take it as another example of procedure in the psychiatric field. The following is a more extended statement by Cotton:

Foci of chronic sepsis instead of being limited to the teeth . . . are now found in the tonsils, gastro-intestinal tract, genito-urinary system, and other portions of the body. The danger of chronically infected tonsils is now pretty well known. . . .

For the last eight years we have been interested in this phase of tox-emia. . . . In the majority of our patients we get a history of chronic con-stipation from childhood. At first there are no symptoms as a result of this condition but as the patient becomes older and the constipation becomes more pronounced the stasis and toxemia begin to show their effects on the whole body. Over fifty per cent of our mental cases with pronounced psychoses show disturbance in the colon and this percentage would also apply to the defective and delinquent classes. . . .

For five years we followed [a] method of resecting the colon in mental cases. As a result of this work some three hundred patients were operated upon

---

[16] Healy and Bronner have found a high degree of recidivism among the feeble-minded, which certainly accounts in part for their statement: "The feebleminded appear among serious delinquents from five to ten times more frequently than in the general population." — (*Op. cit.*, 151).

and seventy-five recovered from the surgical procedure and also recovered mentally. The mortality, however, was high, 30% succumbing to operation. While this was justified in chronic insane patients who would never leave the institution, at the same time it was rather alarming to surgeons outside institutional work who rightly did not want to subject their patients to such a high mortality rate. . . .

[With an improved method] over 37% of the patients operated upon recovered mentally and the mortality was only 10%. . . .

In Ohio the rate of cases of mental disease in institutions per 100,000 population is 212. This is not as large as New York and Massachusetts where the rate is 374 and 373 respectively per 100,000 population. We have shown by our work at the State Hospital, Trenton, that all these cases can be restored if treatment of detoxication is instituted early in the course of mental disorder. We have been able to restore 87% of the patients in the so-called functional group in which the recovery rate prior to 1918 was only 27%. In figures this means that 1600 patients have been discharged from the hospital as recovered in the last seven years and that these patients have remained normal during this time. Recurrences have been surprisingly small and there are only about 100 patients in the hospital today who have had a recurrence of mental trouble. If we can accomplish such results after the disease has progressed to the point where serious mental trouble has occurred, it is not unreasonable to assert that had the foci of chronic sepsis been eliminated during the school years these patients would not have developed mental trouble. . . .

While I have spoken largely on the question of chronic sepsis, I do not ignore the question of environment, emotional and mental causes as precipitating factors of mental trouble, but in seven years' experience I have failed to find a single case which was not harboring some foci of infection. Dr. H. H. Mc-Clellan of the State Hospital at Dayton, in examination of some 1200 patients, found over 3000 foci of infection in these cases.[17]

In examining these astonishing claims we should again have to use a method distinguishing between the normal and the ideal. It is assumed here that foci of infection are the cause of mental disease, but the figures of Wood (footnote, p. 449) indicated that from 15% to 25% (3,000,000 to 5,000,000) of our school children have adenoids, diseased tonsils or other glandular defects, and that from 50% to 75% (11,000,-

[17] Cotton, H. A.: "Relation of Focal Infections to Crime and Delinquency," *American Association for the Study of the Feeble-Minded, Proceedings*, 49:66–80, *passim* (1925); cf. also "The Etiology and Treatment of the So-Called Functional Psychoses, Summary of Results Based Upon the Experience of Four Years," *American Journal of Psychiatry*, 2:157–94 (1922).

000 to 16,000,000) of them have defective teeth, and how many of them have toxemic colons is not recorded. That is, foci of infection are widespread in the general population and cannot be a universal cause of mental disease. But for several years these claims agitated the psychiatric world and the interested public. The families of insane persons insisted that if this thing were being done it should be applied to their relatives and made it very uncomfortable for psychiatrists who were not of the Cotton school. Influenced by this situation two psychiatrists, Kopeloff and Kirby undertook a crucial experiment. They selected a group of the insane in a hospital, diagnosed them, paired them, operated half of them by the Cotton method and compared the outcomes in the two groups. We quote from their report:

Because of the difficulties of interpretation inherent in an investigation of this nature, it seemed desirable to reduce the study as nearly as possible to the terms of an experiment. Consequently, all patients were divided into two groups as nearly identical as possible. All members of one group received operative treatment for foci of infection in teeth, tonsils, (and in some female cases) cervix, as indicated, while members of the other group had no surgical interference and could therefore be regarded as controls. In this way, operative treatment might be considered to be the crucial factor in this experiment and an evaluation of its influence on the course of the psychoses might thus be more readily established.

It was realized that rarely, if ever, can one psychotic patient be taken as a perfect control on another having the same diagnosis, yet this method alone permits of the isolation of the single factor of treatment. It might be argued that there was ample control material in the patients of the past and present years who had never been treated from the viewpoint of focal infection. Since it is well-known that any special attention serves to improve the status of a hospital population at any given time, it was considered much more satisfactory to have such a control group made up of patients observed at the same time by the same physicians and under the same living conditions and influences as the patients to be actively treated. The procedure followed therefore, after the diagnostic classification had been made and the infections determined, was to designate automatically that alternate patients be operated. An attempt was made to place in the two different groups, patients comparable as to sex, age, duration of psychosis, diagnosis, prognosis, and infective conditions. . . .

As seen in Table I there were in the control group 62 cases, 41 women and 21 men; the operated cases were 58 in number, 31 women and 27 men. Mental reaction types were classified in the *control* group as 32 dementia praecox,

25 manic-depressive, and five miscellaneous (i.e., psychoneurotic or psychopathic personality); *operated cases,* 33 dementia praecox, 20 manic-depressive, and five miscellaneous. The ages varied from 15 to 57 years in the controls and from 16 to 50 in the operated group.

In the previous report the data have been discussed in detail for what has been called the " first series " and therefore it is unnecessary to repeat what has been set forth there. The present data are concerned with both first and second series complete.

The duration of the psychoses before admission varied in the control group from one week to five years with the exception of one patient (Case 8) with 15 years previous duration. In the operative group the previous duration varied similarly from one week to five years with the exception of three cases which were of longer duration (Cases 78, 94, and 104).

The shortest continuous hospital residence in the control group was six weeks (Case 60), the longest was four and one-half years (Case 39). In the operated group the hospital residence varied from three and one-half months (Case 66) to two years (Case 78) with the exception of two patients who had been in the hospital five years (Cases 73 and 89).

There were in the control group 27 patients with infected teeth and tonsils. Among these, seven female patients had infected cervices. In the operated group there were correspondingly 37, of which six female patients had infected cervices. In the control group there were 23 patients who had infected teeth only. Of this number three female patients had infected cervices and correspondingly in the operated group there were 10 cases. In the control group there were four cases of infected tonsils and negative teeth and there were correspondingly 11 such cases in the operated group. It should be stated that wherever two dates appear for a single type of operation, it was repeated. This occurred frequently for teeth and occasionally for tonsil rests as careful re-examinations were made in order to make sure that all possible foci of infection were eliminated.

There were eight cases in the control group, and one case in the operated group that had neither infected teeth nor tonsils, but the latter case did have an infected cervix.

In the whole control group of 62 patients there were judged to be 189 infected or impacted teeth. From the 58 patients in the operated group 253 teeth were extracted. . . .

It is superfluous to mention that in no case of recovery was the expedient used of changing the classification from the dementia praecox to the manic-depressive group. The percentage of recovery in the manic-depressive operated group is 40 per cent, which is identical with the per cent that recovered in the control group. The total percentage benefited by treatment, i.e., recovered and improved, was 75 per cent in the operated manic-depressive group and 72 per cent in the control group. There is a slightly lower percentage of improvement shown in the dementia praecox operated group than in the control group; that is, 18 per cent as compared with 25 per cent. *On the whole, then, the operated group appears to have improved no more by the elimination of focal infection than the control group which received no operative procedure.* This conclusion is all the more striking in view of the fact that the most resistive and uncooperative cases had to be placed in the control series. (This also accounts for the fact that there were 62 controls as compared with 58 operated cases.) It should also be mentioned that it was necessary to place in the control group, for obvious reasons, the eight patients who showed no evidence of focal infection. However, these could not influence the percentage of improvement in the dementia praecox control group, since two patients improved and two remained unimproved. In the manic-depressive group, however, if these patients are disregarded the percentage of improvement in the control group would be 67 per cent instead of 72 per cent. In other words this negligible difference has not weighted the results unduly, and therefore there is no need for giving this matter further consideration. . . .

Summary: 1. In a series of 120 cases showing manic-depressive, dementia praecox, psychoneurotic, and psychopathic personality reactions, the removal of focal infection in 58 cases did not result in a higher percentage of improvement or recoveries than in a comparable group of 62 cases in which foci of infection were not removed.

2. Reviewing the entire group of operated cases showing recovery or improvement, and comparing the original prognoses with the subsequent course, our observations demonstrate that in every case that recovered, a recovery had been forecast before treatment was started; and that no case recovered in which a poor prognosis had been given. Furthermore, in only one case did an unexpected improvement occur.

3. A critical study of the methods used by Cotton for establishing focal infection has proven them to be unsatisfactory for teeth, stomach, lower intestine, and cervix.

4. It is desirable to eliminate focal infection when adequately demonstrated in psychotic patients in the same way as one should attempt to alleviate any physical disorder in mentally diseased patients. Nevertheless, it has not been shown that focal infection is the etiological factor in the functional psychoses.[18]

The data we have been considering, and the disparity between the ideal and the norm which we have emphasized, indicate that human

---

[18] Kopeloff, N., and Kirby, G. H.: " Focal Infection and Mental Disease," *American Journal of Psychiatry*, 3:151–92, *passim* (1923).

nature and the social order are not so superior as our theories have assumed. Evidently large numbers of persons classed as inferior and committed to institutions are specifications of our society, differing slightly or not at all from a multitude of others who continue to live in society by hook or by crook, often miserably enough but within the law. To exemplify this point we may examine some of the careers of psychopathic, delinquent young women, as recorded in the Psychopathic Hospital of the Bedford Hills Reformatory.

This hospital was a special experimental venture within the reformatory for the intensive study of selected cases — selected, however, not from the several hundred inmates of the reformatory but from the receiving cottage. That is, they were not necessarily the most serious cases in the whole institution. The hospital had a staff of twelve persons, was able to care for eighteen persons at a time and received a total of forty-four girls and women during the two years of its existence. The cases are described as sullen, apathetic, over-active, self-pitying, suicidal, tale-bearing, irritable, opinionated, insolent, fault-finding, loquacious, spitting, dirty, obscene, homosexual, assaultive and homicidal, as the case might be. When the experiment was abandoned, and gradually before that time, they were distributed again among the general outside community. Four years later, in 1922, Dr. Spaulding undertook to look into their subsequent careers. Two were insane, four were dead, five had disappeared from view, eleven were unchanged, that is, remained bad, and twenty-two or half the number had " straightened up," " settled down " and were living inoffensively.

Omitting a number of feebleminded cases included in this report (whose later records usually show a tolerable adjustment) we find that the psychopathic women seem to differ in their delinquencies and not in their psychopathic traits from thousands in the general population whose emotional outbursts, vagaries, whimsicalities and hysterias come to our attention in the public print and otherwise — women with status, protection, greater charm or better luck. In artistic circles they would be classed as " temperamental." The following are the outcomes in these cases:

Mazie L. . . . From October 1 to December, 1920, she was held in jail as witness when an inn in a small New York town was raided. During the following April she was arrested on a charge of vagrancy and sentenced to jail for six months. Since then, however, she has been doing well. One month ago she married a young man who is thought well of in the town in which they both live, and who is said to have been influential in getting her to " straighten up."

Sylvia S. . . . has held a fairly responsible position for several years and has recently changed her occupation to one of even greater responsibility. While her work has been satisfactory, nothing is known of her social life.

Louise D. . . . has had an excellent record since leaving Bedford. She is living with her stepmother and is working steadily.

Martha N. . . . Martha's later history is discouraging. She is no longer in communication with those who tried to befriend her. She has incurred debts which will probably never be repaid and has used a friend's charge account for her own purposes. Nothing has been heard from her since May, 1922. At that time it was felt that she was associating with people who could only prove detrimental to her.[19]

These young women were irritated by their incarceration, many of their " psychopathic " traits as shown in the records were expressions of their resentment, their degree of poor health was " normal " when compared with the figures of Dr. Wood above, after their release and because of the reformatory experience they were living under changed conditions of life, and the scant additional data added by Dr. Spaulding after four years are very instructive as showing the ability of so many of them to make even a precarious and miserable adjustment in a society containing many not unlike themselves.

The home, the school, the church, the law, and all social influences, work with material which is partly defective from the ideal standpoint, and it is important to know the proportions of defective and sound material and the quantity of each kind becoming delinquent. But it would be more instructive and at the same time scientific if a number of factory girls, shop girls, show girls, young wives, gold diggers, etc., living within the law, were taken, from the same social levels as the inmates of a reformatory, and in equal numbers, and diagnosed from a standpoint weighted with the psychopathological concept. We should again probably have in some form a repetition of the experience of the army draft.

In addition to the statistical and hospital work just exemplified, the psychiatrists have approached behavior problems through the child clinic. There had been psychological clinics of a research type for a long time, the first of them established by Dr. Witmer in the University of

[19] Spaulding, Edith R.: *An Experimental Study of Psychopathic Delinquent Women* (1923), 206–355, *passim.*

Pennsylvania in 1896, but the great movement in this direction came with the establishment of the juvenile court clinics, and these were naturally committed to psychiatrists, who were practitioners and had developed the art of diagnosing and treating mental troubles. It would, however, be confusing to speak of a psychiatric approach in these clinics and at the same time identify this with individuals. The work of Dr. Healy and Dr. Bronner, for example, is psychological and sociological rather than psychiatric, and Dr. Thom, a psychiatrist and director of the mental hygiene division of the department of mental diseases of Massachusetts, calls his widely known document, circulated by the Children's Bureau of the government, *Habit Clinics*. The child welfare clinics, serving communities and schools, are now divided between psychologists and psychiatrists. And it must not be forgotten that psychiatrists are themselves emphasizing the " psychogenic " or socially determined causation of mental disturbances. This attitude is now general but not universal among psychiatrists. The consistent representative of organic and bological determinism in behavior is at present not the psychiatrist but the eugenist, one of whom has said, " If you find a bad Italian boy in New York, look for a bad piece of germ plasm in Sicily or Calabria," and, he implies, you will never find anything else.

But there has never been in psychology any satisfactory theory of the mechanism of personality formation, nor in psychiatry any adequate theory of the mechanism involved in mental disease and personality disintegration, and it is on this point — the mechanism of the socially determined mental disturbances — that psychiatrists have been divided into two camps. The psychiatric approach in clinical work may therefore be examined with this in view.

During the early period of the formation of child clinics there appeared a school of psychiatry known as psychoanalysis which not only appreciated the social factors in personality formation and disintegration but brought a definite, complete, opinionated and ingenious theory of the mechanisms involved. This was something very much needed, very useful, if true, and it converted numbers of the psychiatrists of the country, including many of those in charge of the child clinics.

The chief rôles in this theory are given to the " unconscious " and to " repression," and these factors are recognized by the psychologist, but in a different way. The psychologist understands that much " thinking " goes on below the level of consciousness; much determination of action and behavior is located in the nerves, muscles and glands below the brain. This is the type of animal mind, and in humans also only questions not able to be handled below the cortex are passed up. In addition there is in the cortex an immense store of forgotten memories and memories of data that passed in through the receptors and were recorded without the awareness of the subject at the moment, and these memories participate when we are thinking or ruminating, and they continue to work among themselves when we turn our attention to something else or go to sleep. That is why the artist or creative worker does not always know how he gets his results. Often the unconscious brings them to him ready-made. The mathematician Gauss, asked how he was getting along with his work, replied: " I have long had my results but I do not yet know the steps by which I shall reach them." He had still the task of verifying the procedure of the unconscious. The creative artist has not this task of verification and substantiation. His dreamlike creation is offered much as it is, touched up by his conscious technique, and frequently one of its chief charms is that nobody knows how it was done or what it means.

But in the Freudian system the unconscious is pictured as containing elements which have been repressed, pushed back out of consciousness or excluded from the beginning because they represent immodest, immoral and socially intolerable wishes. The wish of the boy for the death of the father because the boy himself loves the mother, the incestuous love of the boy for the mother or the girl for the father are examples. The specific situation is called a " complex." Thus the " fixation " of the boy on the mother is the " Œdipus complex," of the girl on the father, the " Electra complex." These wishes are mainly sexual, dating from early infancy. They are dynamic, seeking to rise into consciousness and kept down by a censorship established by the conscious. This censorship is relaxed during sleep and the unconscious then has its inning, the dream representing symbolically what would never come to consciousness otherwise without the aid of the analyst. Even the dream shows a certain modesty and does not make its meaning quite plain. The repression of the unholy wishes and the conflict of the conscious and the unconscious are then the source of the whole catalogue of mental disturbances — anxiety states, delusions of persecution, compulsive seizures, hysterias, etc. The analyst may interpret the dream, as method of diagnosis, or get the cue from the patient in the course of the analysis. The analysis is a sort of confessional process (called by one of Freud's early girl patients the " talking cure ") which, as one analyst indicates, may require five or six sessions a week for a period of six to eight months or more. The release and bringing to consciousness of the unconscious constitutes the cure. No one can do this, according to Freud, who has not been analyzed by Freud himself or by one in whom he has confidence.[20]

There has been a division in the ranks of the psychoanalysts, Adler espousing the " inferiority complex," Jung introducing the " collective unconscious " and emphasizing the struggle between the " Œdipus complex " and ambition or the " superiority complex," Rank dwelling on the birth trauma and desire of regression to the womb, etc., and these schools rival one another in their fantastic claims. Their grotesqueries would fill a joke book.[21]

---

[20] In a recent treatise (Freud, S.: *The Ego and the Id,* translated by J. Riviere, 1927) the " master " has had another " revelation " and has further complicated but not essentially modified the rôle of the unconscious.

[21] Adler says the first cry of the new born child is an expression of its terror and sense of inferiority at thus being suddenly confronted with reality without an experience in dealing with its problems. Pierce Clark says the child does not grasp the nipple of the mother because of hunger but as the last act of a struggle against being removed from the warm womb, and does not receive the milk as nutriment but as a libido stream from the mother. Rank says that the fear of insects (cockroaches, etc.) is rather an envy, because they can creep into narrow passages and so remind the child of its wish to return to the womb. Freud says the phantasying of children has the function of supplying the racial data of reality lacking in their individual experience, and that a dream of losing a tooth signifies castration as punishment for onanism. Ferenczi, exemplifying Freud's anal-erotic theory, says the impulse to spit or vomit at the sight of disgusting objects is, in fact, an unconscious moral reaction against the wish to take these objects into the mouth. Jung says the historical paintings of the crucifixion, with Christ as the central figure and one thief hanging lower than the other, and likewise the conception of a triune God, are of phallic origin. Sadger says Lady Macbeth's overweening ambition and her walking at night with a lighted candle represent " a reaction formation to infantile bed-wetting." The bed-wetting is erotically pleasurable, it enables the child to dominate the parents, compels them to light a candle and give it attention, and " thus we comprehend precisely why the lady wanders at night with a candle," rehearsing the bed-wetting episodes. A less distingushed contributor to the *Psychoanalytic Review,* writing on the sexual origin of mechanical inventions, gives the bladder and the muscular mechanism for the regulation of the flow of fluid as the origin of the draughtsman's pen, eventually the fountain pen.

In this connection one of the mildest and most distinguished critics of psychoanalysis has said:

As a part of an ingenious and remarkably fertile theory of psychopathology, itself to my mind a product of a one-sided generalization of certain pathological disorders, repression has been made a one-sided explanation of all possible normal common-sense facts. The fact that children do not remember as adults do and that we do not remember much of our childhood is called the product of " repression "; the hysterical person has his or her fits and palsies through " repression." Deny yourself a wish and you will suffer from the " repression." The most remarkable evil effects are laid at the door of various so-called repressions in the sex life. The dream is represented as a labored and camouflaged welling up of repressed topics. Now there is some truth in much of this, enough to justify the advice to the student to search for the facts along this line where real facts suggest such a procedure.[22]

No one questions that mental conflict and repression are important in psychopathology and delinquency. In their very objective studies Healy and Bronner have recorded a number of cases. " We were able," they say, " to discover such conflicts in 6.5% of 4000 cases." [23] The most significant feature of these cases as related to delinquency seems to be that a moral shock, connected with the mention or exploration of taboo questions, especially those of sex, may produce a tendency to motor release which will then express itself in some substitute unsocial activity, representing protest, but not so reprehensible as the one suggested. Thus a boy, learning that his mother receives men in her room, or a girl hearing obscene words, may begin a course of stealing. (See documents 19–21, pp. 44–47).

But repression as a principle is normal. Forms of repression are the most important means of regulating and socializing behavior. Society uses them all the time. The " don't " of the mother and the commandments and the law are examples. The human impulses are motor in tendency, and it is impossible to tolerate in a society their unregulated expression, as in killing, raping, stealing, etc. Lawrence K. Frank [24] has

---

[22] Meyer, Adolf: "Normal and Abnormal Repression," *Bulletin No. 13 of the Progressive Education Association* (1922).

[23] Healy and Bronner, *op. cit.*, 180.

[24] " Physiological Tensions and Social Structure," *Proceedings of the American Sociological Society for 1927:74–82*; "The Management of Tensions," *American Journal of Sociology*, 33:705–36 (1928).

recently pointed out that the organization of individual and institutional life may be stated in terms of physiological tensions and the sustaining of these tensions under conditions prescribed by the social code. The child must learn to sustain physiological tensions in connection with the processes of elimination, hunger tensions between periods of feeding, sex tensions in adolescence, and learn to regulate his approach to the person and property of others. This is all a part of normal life, but it is also true that the failure to sustain the appropriate tensions may lead to crime and mental disease. And of three persons under the same degree of tension one may commit a crime, another go to an insane asylum, and the third make a better adjustment.

We are not taking up in detail the theory of Alfred Adler and his school of psychoanalysis based on " organic inferiority " and the " inferiority complex." Points of physical inferiority are the basis of his system — stammering, strabismus, ugliness, deformities, small stature, defective size and malformations of the genitals, ejaculatio praecox, impotence, enuresis, etc., and he properly associates these defects with psychopathic traits, compensatory strivings and delinquencies. His examples in this field are among the most instructive in the literature of the subject. The defect in this portion of his theory is the limitation of " compensatory strivings " to those afflicted with organ inferiorities. All the behavior manifestations of the constitutionally inferior can be paralleled from the clinical records of children who are organically normal. An " unfair deal," for example (real or imaginary, familial, social or racial), is a frequent source of behavior difficulties. The desire for status, recognition, distinction, is a general trait, found in the whole population.

Moreover, while abandoning the Freudian school, Adler is nevertheless so prepossessed with the sexual standpoint that he employs a remarkable imagination in relating all his data to a sexual background. " The coördination of the inferiority of the sexual apparatus with other organ-inferiorities, though frequently only slightly developed, is nevertheless so often found to exist that I must maintain that there exist no organ-inferiorities without an accompanying defect in the sexual apparatus." [25] It must be understood also that Adler nowhere employs consistency. In his earlier writings he exhausted as far as possible the cases

---

[25] Adler, Alfred: *The Neurotic Constitution* (1917), 6.

of neurotic reactions to inferior organs but introduced many and varied cases of ambitious and compensatory strivings unrelated to organic deficiency. He introduced also (and certainly wrongly) the theory that since the child is always undersized in comparison with his father he feels a sense of inferiority and resentment which is one of the mainsprings of the neurotic traits of childhood. And this point is emphasized in his later writings: " Throughout the whole period of development the child possesses a feeling of inferiority in its relations to both its parents and the world at large." [26] But, on the whole, and apart from his theories, Adler has made an important contribution to the study of behavior through his analysis of the ramifications of the desire for recognition.[27]

In our study of programs we have found that many of the child clinics, probably the majority, if we exclude those connected with nursery schools, are in charge of psychoanalysts more or less prepossessed with one or another of the psychoanalytic standpoints, and we anticipated some strange and terrible consequences from the application of their procedure to the problem children appearing before them. But in this we were mistaken. It has not happened in that way, for a variety of reasons. In the first place, it is not employed extensively in the child clinics; there is a separation of theory and practice. Parents, social workers, visiting teachers, judges, the community, participate in the handling of the case, the social history of the child is investigated and recorded in detail, the proportion of apparently healthy and mischievous children appearing in the clinic is large, many of them have obviously been spoiled by the mothers who bring them in, by the schools which teach them, by the gangs with which they associate. As the child is handled it is found that the clinical picture does not correspond with the Freudian mechanisms, and the psychoanalytic standpoint usually disappears. We have listened, for example, to discussions of cases of truant boys where it was first assumed that the boy had a mother fixation, and inquiries were started as to whether he continued to sleep with the mother, but if it developed that the boy had a reading disability or needed glasses in order to read at all, the first standpoint was abandoned. It is possible, therefore, for the psychoanalyst, in spite of his theories, to handle his cases as well as anyone else in the present rather

[26] Adler, Alfred: *The Practice and Theory of Individual Psychology* (1924), 13.
[27] See, for example, his chapter on " Demoralized Children," *Ibid.*

empirical state of the practice. The very skilfully reported and treated cases of Mildred and Kenneth quoted in documents 16 and 17 (pp. 35–40) were handled by an out-and-out psychoanalyst.

But while psychoanalysis taken as a system of explanation " seems to resemble reality not more than the Greek fates resemble the biological instrumentalities which have replaced them " (C. Judson Herrick), the psychoanalytic movement is to be credited with persistent recognition of the importance of exploring the experiences of the patient and has thus made an important contribution to the technique of securing behavior records. There is also developing, particularly in Europe, a new psychoanalysis which is securing records of children's experiences by the psychoanalytic technique while ignoring or repudiating the explanations of the old masters (Freud, Jung, Adler, etc.).[28] In America the psychiatrist Hamilton has made an important study of this character which we notice in chapter XII (p. 551).

One of the contributions of the psychiatric child clinics to the study of behavior has been the accumulation of a large number of case records prepared with increasing fidelity and completeness. Another result has been the growing appreciation of the psychiatrist himself that his field is not an isolated one, not concerned exclusively with disease, and that personality formation in its normal and abnormal aspects is a very complex matter, bound up with the whole environing social situation. This is the sociological or " situational " standpoint (chapter XII) but it has been very completely stated by Dr. Truitt, a psychiatrist, formerly director of the division on prevention of delinquency (Commonwealth Fund Program) of the National Committee for Mental Hygiene:

Many of the flaws in our psychiatric technic in the delinquency field we have inherited from our work in mental diseases, and not the least of these is the rather narrow and air-tight compartments in which we have worked and an attitude we have assumed in believing psychiatry a self-sufficient science. We fail at times to recognize its limitations, to seek coöperation from allied professional fields and to do the real clinical job necessary actually to get at the underlying causes. . . . For the most part all children's problems originate in the home, school or community, and it is the various ramifications of problems encountered in these situations that handicap us in treatment. . . . When it comes to dealing with the whole problem of preventing delinquency we are actually doing little more than scratching the surface because of our

---

[28] Cf. Freud, Anna: " The Technique of Child Analysis," *Nervous and Mental Disease Monographs,* No. 48.

limited knowledge of other related endeavors and the lack of functional relations with various allied fields. . . . We are not going to do a great deal about methods of preventing delinquency until we recognize that the best methods of preventing it will have to be evolved through fundamental modifications in educational methods, housing plans, social relationships, dealing with the unassimilated alien, court procedures, industrial organization, etc. Our individual case work has taught us that our greatest frustration arises from the fact that we are not pedagogues, sociologists, lawyers, business managers, etc., that we do not understand their jobs and cannot talk their language, see the problems they see and offer constructive suggestions, because they are inclined to regard us as intruders. We need to recognize our limitations and persuade these groups, who after all really control the social system, to let us learn their game. We need to know more about their technics, their aims, the conditions under which they work and then attempt coöperation in a common cause from the inside. We ourselves would have a more effective psychiatry if we had such an interchange with these fields and embodied in psychiatry what they have to offer us and that which they are more responsible for than are we. Many of the roots and remedies for psychiatric problems are in other social fields, and we must recognize this fact even at the expense of our present self-sufficiency. The great problem confronting us is how we can best bring about assimilation of the psychiatric point of view into these agencies and promote the development of their methods in harmony with the psychiatric needs of individuals. After all, psychiatry does not deal with a separate compartment of the person's life but with all those forces which operate to make that life what it is. We cannot take over these other fields but we should be ready to understand enough of their philosophy and working methods to make possible common thinking. . . .

What we need if we are really to evolve methods of preventing delinquency is orientation in the methods of those fields which affect so vitally the adjustive possibilities of every person. There is an undoubted necessity for treating individual cases of yellow fever but we cannot rest content with achievement on this scale and overlook the necessity for eradicating the mosquito. The sources of delinquency are not in psychiatry itself, and if psychiatry is to be preventive it must penetrate those fields that are a part of the normal life of every person.[29]

Chapters XI–XII contain further details on the psychopathic personality and psychopathic behavior, taken from the fields of physiology, morphology, psychology and sociology.

---

[29] Truitt, Ralph P.: "Methods of Preventing Delinquency," *Archives of Neurology and Psychiatry*, 16:613–19, *passim* (1926).

CHAPTER XI

The Physiological-Morphological Approach

THE GENERAL drift of the last chapter was toward the interpretation of behavior reactions in psychological and sociological terms.
There is, however, a hereditary and biochemical basis of life which
cannot disappear from the problem. The chemistry and morphology of
the body are not identical in different persons and we must assume that
these differences will influence the reaction of the subjects to experience.
The materials of Strecker and Rosanoff indicated that certain persons
break under certain critical experiences, and we know that others do
not break under any experiences whatever. The result in either case will
depend in part on preëstablished attitudes, on the way in which the personality has been organized up to that point, but we cannot avoid the
conclusion that constitutional factors play a rôle.

Highly specialized research is under way on the chemistry and morphology of the body and the investigators are so aware of the complica-
tion of their tasks and the incompletude of their findings that they can
often with difficulty or not at all be induced to speak of the behavior implications of their particular studies; frequently they are not aware of
them. The general significance and at the same time the complexity of
the chemistry of life may be appreciated from the following passages:

We shall not be able to proceed far until we have at any rate looked in the
face the problem of individuality. It is only recently that biochemical data
have appeared that indicate the manner in which this problem may one day be
solved. The older writers held out no hopes in this direction, and in a quite
recent book Mathews (*Physiological Chemistry*, 1916) pointed out that it
was very strange that the nucleic acids, the constituents of the cell-nuclei and
the presumable " carriers " of the hereditary constitution of individuals, had

all turned out to be chemically the same. The nucleic acids are, however, united in the body to protein molecules, and this fact gives us perhaps the key to the matter. The class of compounds known as the proteins is indissolubly associated with life, and, together with the fats and the sugars, invariably makes up the material foundations of living organisms. Our knowledge of the constitution of the protein molecule . . . leads to the view that the number of possible varieties in it may be almost infinite.

The protein molecule is made up of a very large number of smaller units, the amino-acids, and each of these can exist in three modifications, differently constructed in space out of the same number of atoms, and therefore rotating polarized light in different directions. The known amino-acids are about twenty in number, and, existing as they do in three modifications, the number of ways in which they can be combined together to form single protein molecules is immensely large, for at least one hundred amino-acid units are required to build up one protein molecule. The molecule of serum albumen may have at least 350,000 million stereoisomers. In this way we can foresee a kind of biochemical individuality, which well might be the physico-chemical manifestation of what we are accustomed to call mental individuality.

Data concerning the individuation of proteins are indeed already to hand. The monumental work of Reichert and Brown and of Reichert succeeded in showing that the hæmoglobins (the protein blood-pigments) of the animal kingdom and the starches of the plant kingdom are quite distinct according to the species from which they are derived. This was a step towards demonstrating chemical differences between individuals. Then the phenomenon of racemization of protein led to some suggestive observations. Dakin and Dudley discovered that by standing in alkali for three weeks proteins would suffer changes in their optical properties, so that subsequent hydrolysis, in showing which amino-acids had been altered, would show which ones had been on the exterior of the molecule and thus give a glimpse of its spatial structure. Dudley and Woodman, following this up, found that the protein of the milk of the sheep was quite different to that of the cow. It has since been found that the blood-proteins differ as between the sexes, and that there are marked individual differences.

The whole tendency of biochemistry hitherto has been to abolish the influence of the individual by taking in any given estimation as many single animals as possible, and thus getting the average figure. In the future a tremendous amount of work will have to be devoted to ascertaining the magnitude and extent of individual differences and their correlation with mental characteristics. . . . The exceedingly minute is now a familiar matter to the physiologist. The infinitesimal amount of vitamine required to maintain a living body in working order, the faint trace of iron necessary for biological oxidations — one ten-thousandth of a milligramme — the almost infinitely small quantity of copper capable of killing plant cells placed in water containing it — one in seventy-seven millions — and the incredible dilution to which certain toxic substances may be subjected while retaining their power: all these instances go to induce an attitude of being surprised at nothing.

Such exceedingly small amounts of chemical substance acting in the individual body have been already much investigated, and even the purest of metaphysicians can hardly have avoided hearing of the name " hormone." I need not dilate upon the extraordinarily profound effects which the glands of internal secretion exert upon the mind and the body; they are already sufficiently well-known. The administration of the active principle of the thyroid gland, for instance, can transform certain types of idiots into normal people in a very few days, and the association between adrenalin and fear is as well marked as anything in physiology. The work of Cannon, though it has been much criticized, has shown that the emotion of fear is associated with liberation of adrenalin from the suprarenal gland, and with a consequent rise in blood-sugar, presumably — if for a debased moment we may allow ourselves to be teleological — to provide for a better functioning of the muscles in the expected fight. The phenomenon of emotional glycosuria is closely connected with this. . . . Apart from the considerable number of modifications which the adrenalin molecule itself may present, the number of possible combinations with other hormones and other substances is innumerable — or rather, let us hope for the sake of our biochemical successors, almost innumerable. The constitution of what Lloyd Morgan speaks of as the " biochemical brew " is really susceptible of a very great number of modifications, and the physico-chemical expression of the emotions may originate in varying percentage relationships of the hormones of the body.[1]

It is generally known that the secretions of the [endocrine] organs are in some obscure way correlated with the general condition of the organism. And it may be sufficient to mention that by this secretion the metabolism of the organism is regulated. This function being of a purely physiological nature will not be discussed in the present lecture. A second function of these organs, which undoubtedly stands in close relation to the one just mentioned, is of greater interest to the morphologist. The endocrine organs control the harmonic development of the body, they are the sources of the directing factors of morphogenesis. The different parts of the body do not develop in an autonomic way, independent of each other, but during development they stand in continuous interrelation. The maintaining of this correlation is that function of the endocrine system which I call their architectonic function. By virtue of

---

[1] Needham, J.: " Lucretius Redivivus " (The Hope of a Chemical Psychology), *Psyche*, 7:10-13 (1927).

this function they are the controlling factors of the development of the body; each morphological feature is subject to their influence. Thus it is clear that these organs are of the utmost significance for the ontogenesis of man. The question, however, which will be treated on in the present lecture, concerns their significance for phylogenesis, the historical evolution of the human body. And I intend to demonstrate to you that the endocrine organs have to a very large extent controlled this evolution also. . . .

That the rate of development generally is regulated by the [endocrine] system is sufficiently demonstrated by experimental researches of late years. Though these experiments are yet in an initial stage, we have already become acquainted with an endocrine organ, able to *accelerate* the development. This organ is the thyroid gland. I mention only the statement that feeding tadpoles with thyroid accelerates the metamorphosis of these animals. But, as far as I am aware, experimental investigations have not yet brought to light any element of the endocrine system able to retard the rate of development. I am convinced, however, that there must be such an inhibitory element in the human organism. And I have a strong belief that this is the pineal gland. This belief is based on the occurrence of well-known anomalous conditions. Every physician is acquainted with the very deplorable cases of so-called premature sexual development. This anomaly occurs in boys as well as in girls, but apparently more frequently in the latter. Several instances of this pathological condition, in which, for example, young girls of six or seven years become pregnant, are dealt with in literature. Now I believe these cases must be explained in this way, that in such individuals the arresting influence of the endocrine system on the function of the genital glands was insufficient, and the check which hindered the maturation of germ cells was removed too early. Considered from this point of view the premature sexual development appears as a physiological atavism. Observations of late years have shown conclusively what endocrine organ is responsible for this anomaly. You know it is the pineal gland.[2] These observations justify my assertion that this organ is, and has been, the regulator of maturation and that it was principally by its agency that the general vital process of man was retarded. . . .

---

[2] This question is still undecided. "The most important and conclusive work on pineal gland extirpation is that recently reported by Dandy on young dogs. Dandy extirpated the pineal body in pups (male and female) ten days to three weeks old and observed their body growth, sex life and mental behavior for eight to fifteen months after the operation. In no case did he find sex precocity or indolence, adiposity or emaciation, somatic or mental precocity or retardation. Dandy concludes that 'the pineal body is not essential to life and seems to have no influence on the animals' well-being at any age'." — (Carlson, A. J.: "Organotherapeutics," in Billings-Forchheimer, *Therapeusis of Internal Diseases*, ed., Blumer, 1:763, 1924).

There exists, as I have mentioned already, a close relation between all internal secreting glands; the whole endocrine system is an organic unit, it is a sort of controlling super-organisation in our somatic organism, an *imperium in imperio*. And this " imperium " fulfils its task in a stimulating or a suppressing manner. The endocrine glands are, so to say, the sense-organs of the autonomic system, sensitive only to chemical stimuli, as the sense-organs of the cerebro-medullar system to physical stimuli. These organs judge the quality and intensity of the chemical substances produced in the body, and regulate the nature and the quantity of the same by means of their hormones. And certainly it is not a mere chance that the principal organs of this system are derived from the epithelium of the foremost part of the alimentary tube. I believe that originally they controlled also the chemical nature of the food, before there were senses of smell and taste. By investigations and observations on the endocrine system during late years we have arrived at a very important point. It seems to me that we have reached a summit, and a large plain and wide perspectives lie open before us.[3]

These statements introduce the problems of temperament and character, of psychological types, of extrovert and introvert tendencies, of the relation of body-build and body chemistry to insanity, criminality and genius, and foreshadow a chemical psychology, with an adequate interpretation of the so-called instincts.

In this connection Hammett has presented the following general theory of the temperaments:

It is evident that . . . the differentiation of the tissues into organs of a predominantly specific function . . . gave rise to new sources of stimuli which we have called the " endogenous " stimuli; these are distributed by the blood and apparently exert their effect through mediation of the nervous system or some of its subdivisions. Among the later developments of this differentiation there arose certain gland-like colonies of cells which produce secretions that have an effect upon the manner in which the organism responds to exogenous stimuli, and hence on instinctive reactions. Such secretions are produced for example by the thyroid, the adrenals, the gonads, the parathyroids, and may be collectively designated as the endocrine stimuli. It is with the appearance of these relatively recent structures that evidence begins to accumulate of the new factor of temperament in animal behavior, and this leads us to relate temperament with the activity of the endocrine glands. It cannot be denied

---

[3] Bolk, L. (Director of the Dept. of Anatomy in the University of Amsterdam and Secretary of the Royal Academy of Sciences): "The Part Played by the Endocrine Glands in the Evolution of Man," *The Lancet*, 201:588–92 (Sept. 10, 1921).

that all the tissues probably participate in modifying the phenomena we recognize as temperamental, nevertheless there is ample support for the idea that these later special cell groups are very important conditioners of reflex activities as expressed in behavior. We see then how instinctive reactions, at first relatively simple reflex responses to changes in the environment, through the fundamental properties of protoplasm of irritability and conductivity, become more and more modified in expression, first by the development of the nervous system and then by the increasing differentiation of tissues, until it becomes a strongly conditioned reflex, on which the factors arising from the bodily constitution and represented largely by endocrine activity exert the dominating and directive forces.

We look on temperament therefore as largely the expression of the influence of the conditioning factors of the endogenous stimuli on instinctive behavior; the nature of this influence being determined by the directive stimuli arising from the products of endocrine activity.

Such a view maintains that bodily constitution plays a significant rôle in the genesis of temperament, but there has been very little experimental evidence presented supporting the idea that the reaction is reversible and should be written " Bodily Constitution $\rightleftarrows$ Temperament."

The studies of Cannon with regard to the possibly greater activities of the adrenal glands resulting from emotional excitation, upon which some doubt has been cast by Stewart and Rogoff, but which the beautiful experiments of Maranon tend to support in principle, were the early indications from the experimental side of alterations induced in the organism as the result of emotion — emotion here being understood to mean the affective aspect of instinct — while quite recently Buscaino has published data which to his mind demonstrate deep-seated changes in structural form of several tissues following induced emotion.

Not only therefore can structural changes in organic constitution be caused by the production of exaggerated emotions, but also it can be shown that far-reaching functional alterations occur, for Hatai and I [4] have demonstrated that while the normal response of the isolated intestinal segment of the albino rat, when suspended in oxygenated Tyrode's solution at body temperature, is a contraction on stimulation by sodium carbonate: yet when the animal from which the segment is taken has been previously frightened or enraged, then the response to the stimulus, instead of being a contraction, is a relaxation. These experiments, however, while showing that the bringing into play of

---

[4] Hatai, S., and Hammett, F. S.: " Four Factors Causing Changes in the Type of Response of the Isolated Intestinal Segment of the Albino Rat (*Mus norvegicus albinus*) to Sodium Carbonate," *American Journal of Physiology*, 53:312–22 (1920).

basal instincts has a marked effect upon bodily constitution, do not afford direct proof that what we designate as temperamental differences are immediately concerned, because any animal can be angered or frightened. Such proof is given, however, by the following two series of findings.

It is a matter of common observation that there are two extremes of temperament to be found, between which all gradations of behavior occur. Among persons there is a group of calm phlegmatic individuals with every evidence of a high threshold and a low irritability in their affective response to excitation; and on the other hand there is a group of excitable persons of low threshold and high irritability, whose reactions are out of all proportion to the importance of the exciting cause. These differences in temperament seem to be associated with differences in the manner in which the respective individuals handle their intermediary metabolism, since it has been found that the total variability of the soluble nitrogenous constituents of the blood as determined by analyses made from week to week is quite markedly different in the two groups.[5] In the unemotional type, there is a tendency for the variability to be low. In the excitable type, on the other hand, the variability of the intermediary metabolism is relatively greater. Hence it is evident that as is one's temperament so is one's intermediary metabolism. Temperamental tone and intermediary metabolism are related. Here we have then a demonstration that temperament can affect bodily constitution.

A prettier proof is afforded by the fact that when the temperament of an albino rat is changed by gentling, from the condition where excitability and irritability are expressed by flight and pugnacity, to a state where the degree of expression of these instincts is reduced almost to insignificance, then the animal becomes markedly more resistant to the loss of the parathyroid secretion. Thus, out of every one hundred animals in which the emotions of fear and anger are conspicuous, some seventy-nine per cent die of acute *tetania parathyreopriva* within forty-eight hours after parathyroidectomy, while when albino rats which have been gentled are similarly deprived of their parathyroids but thirteen per cent fail to survive this period. In addition it has been recently determined, although the results have as yet not been published, that the wild Norway rat, an animal which is still more excitable, is still more dependent upon the secretion of the parathyroid glands for its continued existence than either of the other two groups noted. It is not at all improbable that other factors than temperament in the narrow sense are concerned in the resistance of rats to the loss of the parathyroid secretion, yet from these experiments the conclusion is justified that the differences in mortality are due to differences in temperament.

[5] Hammett, F. S.: "Observations on the Relation Between Emotional and Metabolic Stability," *American Journal of Physiology*, 53:307–11 (1920).

These studies extend the propositions developed by Cannon with respect to the effect of emotion on bodily constitution to include the idea that factors of endogenous origin which give rise to temperament in turn have their function affected by temperamental responses, and the reaction " Bodily Constitution $\rightleftarrows$ Temperament " is reversible and should be written as such.

They also indicate that of the endocrine glands the parathyroids at least play some part in the determination of the nature of the reaction, the exact office of which, however, is as yet uncertain.[6]

Studies of excitability and other manifestations of human subjects by analysis of the products of metabolism have been made by Starr, Rich and others. Available for this purpose are blood, urine, faeces, gastric juice and saliva. Of saliva Starr says:

This fluid is constantly being secreted, swallowed, and passed through the physiological cycle. It may be readily collected for examination at all times and places. It may be regarded practically as transformed protoplasm of the secreting cell, with admixture of salts and other substances virtually dialyzed from the blood, and affected to a greater or lesser degree by the conditions obtaining in the oral cavity and by the constituents of the alveolar air. The glands of secretion have abundant neural connections with both the cranial and the sympathetic nervous systems.[7]

Starr undertook a research " involving about 1,300 salivary analyses and psychological diagnostic judgments . . . the general purpose of which was to investigate the metabolic etiology of stammering and to ascertain the degree of usefulness of the hydrogen ion concentration and concomitant carbon dioxide content of human mixed saliva in psychological examinations." The following is a summary of his findings:

There is one group of stammerers, embracing 73.7% of the stammerers examined in the general survey of those who applied for aid to the Speech Clinic of the University during the scholastic year of 1921–22, who may be denominated as sub-breathers and who have their organisms overloaded with carbon dioxide. As a consequence their mental faculties are dulled,

---

[6] Hammett, Frederick S. (The Wistar Institute of Anatomy and Biology): " Temperament and Bodily Constitution," *Journal of Comparative Psychology*, 1:489–94 (1921).

[7] Starr, H. E.: " The Hydrogen Ion Concentration of the Mixed Saliva Considered as an Index of Fatigue and of Emotional Excitation, and Applied to a Study of the Metabolic Etiology of Stammering," *American Journal of Psychology*, 33:396 (1922).

they are always working in a " fatigued " condition, virtually under pressure. Until the carbon dioxide content of their blood has been reduced more nearly to normal limits it is practically hopeless for them to attempt to break any old habits or acquire any new ones, whether of speech or otherwise. Proper breathing exercises in the open air adapted to the individual's requirements should be of immense value in this connection. A decrease in the carbohydrate content of the diet should also prove of benefit.

Another, and considerably smaller group of stammerers are distinctly psychopathic, — somewhat less than 15.4% of those examined in the present research. These subjects are generally very hyper-excitable. They discharge a disproportionate amount of energy in response to an immediate stimulus, displaying no sense of proportion. A stimulus which would have very little effect upon a normal subject, and none at all upon a typically dulled sub-breather, upsets the " equilibrium " of a psychopath completely. They are practically hopeless subjects for remedial measures, so far as correction of their speech defect is concerned, unless their general psychopathic condition is first cured. For while they may respond with all their power to the stimulus of treatment, in the way of exercise, drill, etc., in the presence of the teacher, there is little if any apperceptive residuum left. Once out of sight of the Clinic, what they have there done and been told to do is speedily eradicated from their minds by fresh stimuli, to which they respond with the same disproportionate display of energy.

Obviously another type of stammerer may be both hyper-excitably psychopathic and a sub-breather. Such a subject in a hyper-excited condition might eject a saliva apparently normal as to pH, inasmuch as his sub-breathing habits would tend to keep his salivary pH low, while his hyper-excited condition would tend to raise it. Between the two contending factors, the salivary pH, at some given moment when the specimen is collected and the determination made, may be occupying a median position approximating that of a normal saliva. An adequate series of determinations, however, should show his predominant tendency, and the series of tests with and without verbal goading will serve to indicate his degree of excitability.

A fourth group of stammerers may not be dulled by defective breathing or other cause of overloading the system with carbon dioxide, resulting in chronic " fatigue " and concomitant lack of energy, nor may they be psychopathic. They may simply be hyper-excitable. Perhaps it is from this class that the psychoanalyst recruits his subjects.

In the light of our findings as to the metabolic etiology of stammering, we may sum up the therapeutic measures indicated by stating that the sub-breathers must be toned up and their systems freed from excessive carbon dioxide by a technique probably involving vigorous breathing exercises and a control of the diet, in addition to the regular drill; the hyper-excitables must be calmed down; and the psychopaths — sent first to a psychiatrist.

As to the hydrogen ion concentration of the mixed saliva in conjunction with determinations of the carbon dioxide content, the present research has found it useful as an index of

(1) the condition of an individual as to fatigue or energy at his disposal, and the breathing habits of the individual;

(2) the degree of emotional excitement under which the subject is laboring at the time of the determination — thus enabling the constantly excited psychopath to be readily detected; and

(3) the degree of excitability of an individual, by means of a series of determinations made before, during and after the application of a definite emotionalizing stimulus.[8]

The progress in this line of research has been recently reported by Rich in a paper giving his own results in the Institute for Juvenile Research in Chicago and indicating sufficiently the findings of other workers:

The chemical determinations [of my experiment] included, among others, the hydrogen-ion concentration of the saliva, the acidity of the urine, the alkali reserve of the blood, the creatinine content of the blood, and the creatinine excretion in the urine. The subjects consisted of undergraduates who were rated by their fraternity brothers, graduate students rated by their fellow workers, and children examined at the Institute for Juvenile Research who were rated by the four workers who saw each child in the clinic. Ratings have been obtained throughout the work upon good-naturedness, aggressiveness and emotional excitability, but definite results have been obtained only in connection with two of these: excitability and aggressiveness.

The earlier part of the study, with university students as subjects, showed a positive correlation between the hydrogen-ion concentration (pH) of the saliva and the emotional excitability of the individual. In one group of 39 persons, it was $+.28$ and in the other, composed of 18 persons, it was $+.45$. In recent months we have evolved a simplified procedure, using the quinhydrone electrode, which can be used with children, and now have data from 134 subjects of the Institute with a correlation of $+.25$. This coefficient has remained relatively constant for some time, differing by only 1% from that obtained from the first 65 cases. These three values may be summed up in an average

---

[8] Starr, H. E.: "The Hydrogen Ion Concentration of the Mixed Saliva Considered as an Index of Fatigue and of Emotional Excitation, and Applied to a Study of the Metabolic Etiology of Stammering," *American Journal of Psychology*, 33:415–17 (1922).

correlation of +.30 on the entire 191 cases, which is over six times its own probable error. There is thus a probability so high as to be almost certainty that, should the determination be repeated, similar results would be obtained. A positive correlation here indicates that the least excitable individuals tend to have the most acid saliva, while those who are more excitable tend toward neutrality or even alkalinity of the saliva.

A further verification of the relationship between body acidity and emotional excitability comes from the urinary determinations. Working with 24-hour samples of urine, which we were able to obtain only from the students, we found correlations of −.25 and −.26, in the two groups of 39 and 18 individuals, respectively, between ratings of excitability and the acid content of the urine was measured by direct titration. It is noteworthy that these two coefficients are of practically the same size as the ones obtained from the salivary determinations. They are of opposite sign merely because pH decreased instead of increasing as a liquid becomes more acid and is therefore a negative measure of acidity. It thus appears that the less excitable persons tend to have a more acid urine as well as a more acid saliva than do those who are rated as excitable. If these two fluids can be taken as adequate samples of the reaction of the entire body, it would seem that there is a definite negative correlation between bodily acidity and emotional excitability. So far as our measurements go we are beyond the possibility of a chance effect, but the human organism is so complex that one must be cautious in extending such findings to other parts of the body.

The negative correlation between excitability and the acidity of the body does not, however, rest solely upon the data which has just been presented. Further evidence has already been accumulated in a number of studies which have been in the literature for some time. Starr, working with types of stammerers, was able to differentiate a lethargic type with a distinctly acid saliva (pH below 6.6) and an excitable type with a neutral or alkaline saliva (pH above 6.9). Expressed in terms of correlation, he found a negative relationship between the acidity of saliva and excitability. Similarly, Ludlum has brought forward some clinical evidence for two types of acute insanity; one excited, with alkaline saliva and alternatingly acid and alkaline urine, perspiration, feces; the other confused, with a generally acid diathesis. Both of these observations were made upon the relatively large variations found in abnormal conditions and were made by contrasting two extreme types. In this experiment, on the other hand, we have taken our subjects at random, running through the range of normality from one end to the other, and have found by the correlation method exactly the same tendencies in more nearly normal individuals. . . .

Since acidity correlates with emotional excitability, it might be expected that any element in the chemistry of the body which varies concomitantly with the acidity would show a similar correlation. Exactly this situation occurs in the case of creatinine. There is a marked parallelism between the excretion of acid in the urine and the excretion of creatinine per kilogram body weight (creatinine coefficient), both between individuals and between the same individual under different conditions. Now, the creatinine coefficient of the urine correlates —.24 and —.23, for the two groups of students, with emotional excitability. In the case of the creatinine of the blood a correlation of —.21 was obtained upon 154 subjects. Here, again, two findings verify one another. The more excitable individuals, it would seem, tend to produce less creatinine than do those who are rated as being less excitable. They therefore show a lower creatinine output in proportion to the amount of metabolizing tissue, and, since the creatinine must be carried in the circulation as a preliminary to elimination, a lower creatinine content of the blood. It is not possible at this time to state whether the variations in creatinine are dependent upon those in acidity, or vice versa, as the concomitance of these two factors is itself a new observation. . . .

It is, after all, not the explanation which is important here, but the fact that there is a definite though low negative correlation between emotional excitability and bodily acidity. The data upon the reaction of the saliva has already accumulated to the point where it is beyond the possibility of being a chance finding. The determinations upon urine support it. Finally the work of such other investigators as Starr and Ludlum is in complete agreement, as is also the effects of ketogenic diets in epilepsy. Our next step is planned to test out whether or not changes in the reaction of the body, acidification or alkalinization, have any effect upon emotional reactions. Since we should then be working with the same individuals, and therefore with a more or less constant past environmental influence upon each person, definite confirmation of our findings is to be looked for, together with indications for their practical utilization.[9]

In another paper, based on the same experiments, Rich says:

The correlations between chemical determinations and personality traits obtained in this study have practically all been relatively low, between .20 and .30. This is about one-half the magnitude of the correlations usually found between a mental test and its criterion. The question naturally arises as to why the coefficients are so low. Doubtless the answer is to be found in several factors. Most important, perhaps, is inadequacy of method. The entire procedure, in view of the lack of previous work of this type, has necessarily followed a method of trial and error. The results thus far clearly show that

[9] Rich, Gilbert J.: " Body Acidity as Related to Emotional Excitability." Read before the 5th annual meeting of the American Orthopsychiatric Association (Feb. 25, 1928). Manuscript. To appear as a publication of the Institute for Juvenile Research.

there is some relation between body metabolism and personality. But it is hardly to be expected that in the first trials we should be so fortunate as to measure those chemical factors which are most closely related to character traits. Nor can it be expected that the first set of traits upon which ratings were made should happen to be those most typically determined by metabolic processes. One may expect to find either of these only after repeated trials. . . .

Perfect correlation between metabolic mechanisms and personality traits, or anything approaching it, is hardly to be expected. It is now generally recognized, save by extremists of one school or the other, that personality is built upon a double foundation of inherent bodily, especially neural, organization and environmental influence. Although not impossible it is highly improbable that the changes in behavior which result from environmental influence can be accompanied by any measureable changes in body chemistry. It is far more likely that the chemical factors here studied are related only to the inherent bodily mechanisms of character and that the part which the latter contribute to personality sets the upper limit for attainable correlations. What this upper limit may be is not known at present. It is even possible that the fact that we consistently obtain correlations between .20 and .30 indicates the maximum part which metabolic processes take in the total make-up of personality. Whether or not this is true can only be determined by further investigation.[10]

Working mainly with insane Swabian peasants Kretschmer [11] has presented a convincing mass of data tending to correlate body-build with the psychic dispositions and the psychoneuroses. He relates the causation of insanity not to brain disorders but to endocrine inadequacies or peculiarities. It is known that the endocrine organs regulate the growth of the body. It is assumed, in fact, that the endocrine substances (hormones) had the architectonic function of developing physical man from the lower forms of life by accelerating and retarding in turn the development of this or that morphological character. The main purpose of the paper by Bolk, quoted above, was to indicate how this happened. Kretschmer assumes in the same connection that body-build is a chemical function, that temperament is related to physique and that different physiques and temperaments are correlated with different types of insanity. He makes three general categories of body-build, the pyknic, the asthenic and the athletic, and finds that the pyknics are

[10] Rich, Gilbert J.: "A Biochemical Approach to the Study of Personality." Manuscript. To appear in the *Journal of Abnormal and Social Psychology*.

[11] Kretschmer, E.: *Physique and Character* (translated by W. J. H. Sprott, Harcourt, Brace & Co., 1925).

much inclined to manic-depressive states (circular insanity) and the asthenics and athletics to schizophrenia (dementia praecox):

The pyknic type, in the height of its perfection in middle-age, is characterized by the pronounced peripheral development of the body cavities (head, breast, and stomach), and a tendency to a distribution of fat about the trunk, with a more graceful construction of the motor apparatus (shoulders and extremities).

The rough impression in well-developed cases is very distinctive: middle height, rounded figure, a soft, broad face on a short, massive neck, sitting between the shoulders; the magnificent fat paunch protrudes from the deep *vaulted* chest which broadens out towards the lower part of the body.

If we look at the limbs, we find them soft, rounded, and displaying little muscle-relief, or bone-relief, often quite delicate, the hands soft, rather short and wide. The joints of the hands in particular and the clavicle are often slim and almost elegantly formed. . . . The pyknic type reaches its most typical form usually early in the riper years between 30 and 40. . . .

When we look at the photographs of old circulars when they were young, it is particularly remarkable that certain men and women exhibited quite a-typical bodies, longish faces, and a narrow build in their twenties, while later on they have developed along distinctly pyknic lines. . . .

A typical pyknic face is the true mirror of the pyknic physique. It has a tendency to breadth, softness, and rotundity. The large skull, therefore, is round, broad, and deep, but not very high. The skin of the face is stretched softly on the unprojecting bony structure, letting the blood-vessels of the skin show through the cheeks and nose having a tendency to redness. . . .

The essential characteristic of the type of the male asthenic is, in a few words, taking the general total impression, *a deficiency in thickness combined with an average unlessened length.* This deficiency in the thickness development is present in all parts of the body — face, neck, trunk, extremities, and in all the tissues — skin, fat, muscle, bone, and vascular system throughout. On this account we find the average weight, as well as the total circumference and breadth measurements, below the general value for males.

We have, therefore, in the clearest cases the following general impression: a lean narrowly-built man, who looks taller than he is, with a skin poor in secretion and blood, with narrow shoulders, from which hang lean arms with thin muscles, and delicately boned hands; a long, narrow, flat chest, on which we can count the ribs, with a sharp rib-angle. A thin stomach, devoid of fat, and lower limbs which are just like the upper ones in character. [The profile is angular, the nose long, the head a shortened egg-shape]. . . .

In the case of *circulars,* among a number of mixed and indefinite forms, we find a marked preponderance of the pyknic bodily type on the one hand, and a comparatively weak distribution of the classical asthenic, athletic, and dysplastic forms on the other.

In the case of *schizophrenes* on the contrary, among a number of hetero-geneously mixed and indefinite forms we find a marked preponderance of asthenic, athletic, and dysplastic types (with their mixtures) on the one hand, and a surprisingly weak distribution of typical cases of the pyknic bodily type on the other.

Thus we can formulate our results straight away.

(1) There is a clear biological affinity between the psychic disposition of the manic-depressives and the pyknic body type.

(2) There is a clear biological affinity between the psychic disposition of the schizophrenes and the bodily disposition characteristic of the asthenics, athletics, and certain dysplastics.

(3) And vice versa, there is only a weak affinity between schizophrene and pyknic on the one hand, and between circulars and asthenics, athletics, and dysplastics on the other.[12]

Kretschmer's differentiation of an athletic type does not appear to be very successful. The bodily proportions are described as similar to those of the asthenic, but the general physique is heavier. It is difficult to dis-tinguish these types and in his later work Kretschmer has included the combined asthenic-athletic builds in a single class called the leptosome group. In addition Kretschmer has described various "dysplastic" types, showing anomalies of development due partly to endocrine dis-orders, and these are classed with the asthenics and athletics, all show-ing schizophrenic tendencies:

PHYSICAL AND PSYCHIC DISPOSITIONS

	Circular	Schizophrene
Asthenic	4	81
Athletic	3	31
Asthenico-athletic mixed	2	11
Pyknic	58	2
Pyknic mixture	14	3
Dysplastic	—	34
Deformed and uncataloguable forms	4	13
Total	85	175 [13]

[12] Kretschmer, E.: *Physique and Character*, 29–50, *passim*.　　[13] *Ibid.*, 35.

Kretschmer employed some measurements, but in general his descriptions give the impression of clinical pictures. He recognizes the provisional character of his work, and makes constant and insistent qualifications and limitations of his theory. There is, he says, a complicated mixture of types, the lines are not clearly drawn, one may find a pyknic head on asthenic shoulders, it is not clear that the asthenic type is the only one in biological correlation with schizophrenic nor the pyknic with circular disorders, etc.:

The important idea about a type is that it possesses a firm center, but not hard and fast boundaries. . . . By " type " we mean a nucleus of more distinct and among themselves quite similar formations which have been deliberately lifted out from a sea of progressive transitions. This holds good, for an anthropological racial type as well as a personality type or a clinical-reaction type.[14]

In his badly organized but wonderfully verbalized pages Kretschmer introduces also a terminology for the temperaments. " We call the members of that large constitution-class from which the schizophrenes are recruited ' schizothymes,' and those that correspond to the circular psychotics are called ' cyclothymes '." These represent in the main healthy or normal persons, while " one may for convenience call the transitional stages between illness and health . . . ' schizoid ' and ' cycloid '." [15] We have therefore one temperament, graded from clinically bad to good: schizophrene, schizoid, schizothyme; and another: circular, cycloid, cyclothyme.

Kretschmer's association of physiological types with the temperaments and the temperaments with social performance may be seen from two of his tables:

THE TEMPERAMENTS

	Cyclothymes	Schizothymes
Psychaesthesia and mood	Diathetic proportion: between raised (gay) and depressed (sad)	Psychaesthetic proportion: between hyperaesthetic (sensitive) and anaesthetic (cold)

---

[14] Kretschmer, E.: *Hysteria* (translated by O. H. Boltz, 1926), x.
[15] Kretschmer, E.: *Physique and Character*, 208.

	Cyclothymes	*Schizothymes*
Psychic tempo	Wavy temperamental curve: between mobile and comfortable	Jerky temperamental curve: between unstable and tenacious alternation mode of thought and feeling
Psychomotility	Adequate to stimulus, rounded, natural, smooth	Often inadequate to stimulus: restrained, lamed, inhibited, stiff, etc.
Physical affinities	Pyknic	Asthenic, athletic, dysplastic, and their mixtures [16]

Special Dispositions

	Cyclothymes	*Schizothymes*
Poets	Realists Humorists	Pathetics Romantics Formalists
Experimenters	Observers Describers Empiricists	Exact logicians Systematists Metaphysicians
Leaders	Tough whole-hoggers Jolly organisers Understanding conciliators	Pure idealists Despots and fanatics Cold calculators [17]

Stimulated by the work of Kretschmer there have appeared a number of German studies, some of them on normal persons, and while there are differences among the results these are not greater than was to be anticipated in view of the indeterminateness of the boundaries between the assumed types and the inevitable differences in the criteria employed in rating the subjects by the different experimenters. The outcomes have in general supported the claims of Kretschmer. In America Mohr and Gundlach have made a study to determine whether the definite physical types described by Kretschmer exist among a prison population, and whether specific performances in intelligence, association, and other tests are associated with these particular types.

In order to get the extremes of the types and to eliminate the mixed types, two processes of selection were gone through. In the first place,

---

[16] Kretschmer, E.: *Physique and Character*, 258.   [17] *Ibid.*, 261.

the men were clinically diagnosed, and subjectively differentiated as to pyknic, asthenic and athletic habitus. This was done in order to exclude the deviates who evidently would not conform by physical measurements. Then physical measurements were computed, and types were arbitrarily determined by a combined measurement, consisting of the sum of the chest, abdomen and hip circumference, and the weight divided by the height. The ranges were then determined in such a way that overlapping cases were arbitrarily excluded. The results showed that it is impossible to recognize recurring (typical) body forms from observation alone. The clinical diagnosis might determine a pyknic type while the anthropometric measurements classed the case as an athletic, etc. In this experiment it was found, for example, that the clinical diagnosis was "right" (corresponded to the anthropometric measurements) in only about half the cases. In order to get cases in which the clinical and physical diagnosis corresponded it was necessary to exclude more than half of the clinical diagnoses.

Six hundred prisoners were examined in order to secure the 89 subjects (19 asthenics, 26 athletics, 44 pyknics) qualifying from both standpoints — clinical diagnosis and physical measurement. This was an arbitrary procedure but instructive and justified also from the main standpoint of the experiment, which was to determine whether clearly marked physical types exhibited mental and emotional deviations.

Nineteen separate performance tests were then applied to these groups. The correlations are all low, the only significant one being a correlation of −.34 with the intelligence test performance, indicating a slight superiority of the asthenics over the pyknics. There is an indication of a difference in speed of reaction between the groups, but no evidence of any significant differences in either attention or learning:

Although the physical types as Kretschmer describes them can be found in a prison population they can not be precisely differentiated by mere inspection. It is found that a number of men classed as *asthenic* have relatively larger chest, hip and abdominal measurements than do many men classed as athletic. The subjectively classified *athletic* men run considerably into the range of the *pyknic* men on the same criteria. The distributions both for the estimate of type and for the physical measurements indicate that we are dealing with a normal distribution constituting a continuous progression from the characteristics that define the extreme asthenic to those that determine the "best" pyknic habitus. . . .

Whatever the exact significance of the physical types may be, there is no doubt that differences in performance of the groups so selected can be demonstrated.

Among the most striking differences obtained between the groups were those on Alpha and the Information test. Such differences have not been previously emphasized. The differences we have found may be due to the selection of the subjects; i.e., it is possible that only the relatively lower-grade pyknic men are found in prisons. . . .

The remaining determined differences indicate (a) that the asthenic subjects show relatively more schizothymic tendencies and (b) the pyknic subjects more cyclothymic tendencies. . . .

Our results support in a general way the Kretschmer theory of physical and temperamental kinds, in that a relationship between physique and character of performance is demonstrated. They tend to modify the theory, however, by breaking down even Kretschmer's loose conception of " types " and insisting on the concept of a general progression both of performance and of physical characteristics. . . .

With a correlation of performance and physical characteristics it is quite reasonable that a *more easily recognized* constellation of physical and psychological attributes should impress the clinical investigator as a " type." The exceptions are so numerous, however, as seriously to impair the validity of this " type " as an entity. Although there is no incompatibility between our results relative to physique and performance and those of Kretschmer relative to physique and temperament, an interpretation of the facts at hand does not require the retention of the concept of " type." [18]

Taking Kretschmer's physical types as a provisional basis, Wertheimer and Hesketh [19] have examined sixty-five male patients chosen from the Phipps Clinic (Baltimore) and the State Hospital for the Insane, at random, without any regard for diagnosis or habitus. These patients were first given psychiatric diagnoses, separately by two individuals, then they were diagnosed deductively according to Kretschmer's methods of defining types, and then a simple anthropological index was computed, in which the relation of leg length to trunk volume was involved. This latter index gave a definition of types inductively. When a comparison was made of the body types obtained from observa-

[18] Mohr, G. J., and Gundlach, R. H.: " The Relation Between Physique and Performance," *Journal of Experimental Psychology*, 10:155–57 (1927).

[19] Wertheimer, F. I., and Hesketh, F. E.: *The Significance of the Physical Constitution in Mental Disease* (1926). [Medicine Monographs, Vol. 10].

tion with the body types obtained inductively, a definite relationship was found to exist, but there was a merging or continuum from one type through intermediate types to the next. Because of the small number of cases no numerical definition of this relationship was possible. There was found a definite age displacement of body types, the pyknic being more frequent with advancing age. A general correspondence was also found between body types and psychoses, but this was very variable.

In chapter IX we have examined the concepts, extrovert and introvert. In Kretschmer we have the corresponding terms cycloid and schizoid. Bleuler, the leading European psychiatrist, recognizes a "syntonic" (tuned together with others) type, corresponding with Kretschmer's cycloid, and agrees with Kretschmer as to the schizoid.[20] He also makes an important identification of "dereistic" (away from reality) thinking of the schizophrene and artistic phantasying.[21] Wertheimer and Hesketh propose the terms "syntropic" and "idiotropic," and have described the corresponding types as follows:

In everyday life personalities are judged usually by the affective attitude toward the environment, especially other individuals and the social group. It seems that with regard to the affective attitude it is possible to distinguish among many individuals two directive tendencies, more or less evident throughout the course of life. Some individuals look for satisfaction in contact with others, the emphasis of their affective experiences and reactions being always on the personal environment. Not only do they react emotionally to the experiences of life, entailing coördination or disagreement with others, but they are always fundamentally in affective contact with the personal and social environment. There are other individuals, on the other hand, who find satisfaction in difference, in detachment and isolation from the personal and social environment. The emphasis of their emotional experiences is much less on the other personalities with whom they come in contact during the course of life, and more on the reactions and ramifications of their own mental experiences, both intellectual and imaginative. One may speak of the first group as the syntropic, because the tendency of the affective attitude of individuals included there is to association and contact with the personal and social environment; the second group, with affective attitude characterized by a satisfaction in difference and separation from emotional relationship with other individuals of their environment, one may speak of as idiotropic. [" From the Greek word *tropos* meaning turn, turn of mind, affective tendency, and from the

[20] Bleuler E.: *Text-Book of Psychiatry* (translated by A. A. Brill, 1924), 177.
[21] *Ibid.*, 45.

Greek *syn-* meaning together with, in company with, and *idios* meaning singular, distinct, separate."] [22]

Working with reference to the psychological research of E. R. Jaensch, and hospitable to the position of Kretschmer, W. Jaensch [23] has made an elaborate attempt to establish types on the basis of the character of the eidetic imagery. He holds that the fundamental psychic structures are less manifold than the varieties of physical (e.g., the endocrine) structures, that not only endocrine factors but ionic, vegetative, peripheral and central nervous factors determine types, that there are two fundamental psychophysiological types, which he calls the T-complex (dependent on the sub-cortex) and the B-complex (dependent on the cortex), and that these fundamental reaction systems may be approached by a study starting with an examination of their optical symptoms, i.e., eidetic images. The psychologist Woodworth has made the following comment on this and other typological studies:

The eidetic image is an exceptionally lifelike visual image, which a proportion of older children and younger adolescents are able to form so vivid as to seem almost like reality. According to W. Jaensch, the total eidetic population falls into two types (plus a mixed type, again). There is the T-type, running off into hallucinatory tetanus as the extreme, and showing itself in milder cases by an insistence and uncontrollability of the eidetic image, as well as by hyperexcitability of the motor nerves. And there is the B-type, running off into Basedowoid conditions, and in milder cases, showing easily controlled and much-liked images, along with bright eye, lively skin reflexes, and respiratory arhythmia. There are great local variations in the incidence of these two types, as well as of eidetic imagery in toto. The T-type seems to be especially prevalent in localities where the drinking water is deficient in calcium, and is relieved by administration of calcium; while the B-type seems to be related to iodine and the thyroid. From a reading of the case material, however, it appears very possible that cases have to some degree been forced into these distinct types.

In this last instance, however, there may be good reason for distinguishing types, since there may be two quite distinct external agents which, acting on the individual, may cause his organism to respond in quite different ways. Where true types exist, I suggest that they are exogenous, originating in the organic response to diverse external agents, such as chemical substances, or infections, or social controls. Truly endogenous types of individuals it is not

[22] Wertheimer and Hesketh: *op. cit.*, 61.

[23] *Grundzüge einer Physiologie und Klinik der psychophysischen Persönlichkeit* (1926).

so easy to conceive or accept. It may be that some such result from the opposite imbalance of antagonistic glands, though even here the end result in
growth, as well as the relative potency of the two internal factors, is likely to
show a continuous gradation rather than actual bimodality.

Often it may be true that a search for types, or for qualitative differences, is
motivated by a very necessary and laudable desire to supplement the comparative barrenness of measurements which are already well in hand, by taking
account of other, not obviously measureable characteristics. So, the gross nutrition of a child can certainly not be adequately stated in terms of his height
and his weight, since, as we may say, some individuals belong to the slender
type and others to the stocky type. Yet this can scarcely be the final statement of the fact. It can scarcely be true, either that the extremely stocky and
the extremely slim individuals are true types of development, or that anything
like a bimodal distribution of stockiness would appear, if we were prepared to
measure this trait. What has been accomplished in calling attention to this
matter of stocky and slender types is the indication of another variable, in
addition to height, which needs to be taken into account, and measured if
possible.

My plea to the psychologist, at least, is to be warned by accumulated experience, which is all against bi-modal distribution and against close correlation of distinct traits, and therefore not to be hasty and facile in the employment of the concept of types.[24]

The scientific determination of the question of morphological types
and their meaning for behavior is dependent not so much on clinical procedure and the measurement of mature subjects as on developmental
studies of growth at every stage of maturation, at every level of physiological age. Some fundamental research of this kind is now in progress,
and in our mention of these programs we have occasion to raise again
the more general question of the concept of the normal and the
abnormal.

In our chapter on the psychometric approach to the study of behavior we traced the development of methods of measuring mental
capacity and growth and gave special consideration to the relationships
between mental states and trends and certain behavior manifestations.
We found that the assumption of a causal connection between behavior
deviations, such as delinquency, and mental deviations, such as feeblemindedness or " subnormal " intelligence, grew largely out of the fact
that the mental tests had not been widely enough applied to give an

---

[24] Conference on Research in Child Development (National Research Council,
Committee on Child Development, May 5–7, 1927), 108–9. (Unpublished).

accurate picture of the mental status and growth of mankind in general. Mental deviations had been measured from an ideal [25] of " general intelligence " to which the statistically determined norm did not approximate. When mental deviations were measured from the statistically determined norm, there was found to be much less connection between these deviations and behavior deviations than had been assumed.

In the physical field, too, we find that an incomplete and narrowly applied system of measurements has resulted in a conception of " normality " that implies physical perfection and absence of defects, and that when physical defects or so-called deviations from normality have been found in association with behavior defects there has been a tendency to assume a causal connection. With the widespread use of certain simple physical measurements, however, it has been found that " defects " are quite the ordinary thing — that the average person from the physical standpoint, quite irrespective of his behavior, has deviations from the ideal in many respects.

We are interested, therefore, in any attempts to determine " normal " development and growth in the physical sphere, because only by the careful development of standards and the widespread use of them can a true conception of the " normal " evolve. From the point of view of behavior analysis, this type of study is important. It is, for instance, quite useless at the present time to make elaborate measurements of any group of behavior deviates because these same measurements have not been widely applied to the general population. We cannot tell to what extent physical deviations are associated with behavior deviations until we have some physical standard from which these deviations may be measured, or until we know to what extent the ideal physical status corresponds to the normal or average. It is quite useless, for instance, to subject a group of criminals to an elaborate series of physical measurements because so little is known about the " normal " development of non-criminal groups of the same age, sex, nationality, etc. Association of physical defect with crime cannot be determined until the amount of physical defect in non-criminals is known. " Normal " physical development and growth must be objectively determined before we can trace out and measure the degree of association of various physical states with various behavior manifestations. It is largely for this reason that we are interested in several recent and important attempts to set up standards

---

[25] This " ideal " had, of course, a statistical base — but a very inadequate one.

of physical growth and development. This work is closely connected with the child welfare research centers and is concomitant with (although as yet usually uncorrelated with) behavior research.

Probably the most outstanding of these attempts is represented by the series of studies brought out by Richard E. Scammon and his associates at the University of Minnesota. Scammon's aim has been to establish population norms regarding the growth and differentiation of the human body and its various organs and parts. The most elaborate of these studies have been made on fetal growth, but there has been a large series on growth from the neonatal period to maturity. Scammon's emphasis has been on the statistical determination of norms. He has collected a large number of very accurate measurements for each age level, usually by months, from about the fourth fetal month. Very interesting results were obtained in the fetal measurements, where it was found that a general " law of developmental direction " could be formulated. This " law " emerged from a study of the growth of 70 external dimensions of the human body in the fetal period and is expressed as follows:

Since all of the dimensions of the body which we were able to analyze in detail are of the straight line type, it follows that the growth in length, girth and diameter of the various external divisions of the body is directly proportional to the growth in total body-length in the fetal period (from at least 3 fetal months to birth). In other words, while each dimension has its own rate of growth with respect to body-length this rate does not change in the period under consideration.[26]

It was also found that the growth in mass of various parts of the body followed the same relationship to the volume of the body as a whole, i.e., was directly proportional to the ponderal growth of the body as a whole. It was found, however, that no such simple interrelationships existed in the growth of various parts of the body in post-natal life. The " laws " of growth found in pre-natal life could not be used to predict post-natal growth, nor could post-natal growth be generalized into any simple proportion of either body-length or mass. The measurements on a large number of organs and parts of the body indicate four general types of growth in post-natal life. The body as a whole and many of its parts

---

[26] Calkins, L. A., and Scammon, R. E.: " Empirical Formulae for the Proportionate Growth of the Human Fetus," *Proceedings of the Society for Experimental Biology and Medicine,* 22:356 (1925).

follow a curve of growth that rises abruptly in infancy, increases less rapidly in early and middle childhood, rises abruptly at about thirteen or fourteen years and shows little growth thereafter. The curve of growth typical of the nervous system (brain, spinal cord, etc.) and the organs of the special senses is hyperbolic in form, i.e., grows very rapidly in infancy and little thereafter. A third form is characteristic of the lymphoid organs, which rise sharply and increase to a maximum at puberty, thereafter declining. A fourth group, representing the genital organs, rises abruptly at puberty. In addition to these four general types of growth to which many organs and parts conform, there are certain organs and parts which follow individual plans of growth.

The main part of Scammon's researches has dealt with this important point of the different plans of growth characteristic of the different parts and organs of the body and the relationship of these different plans to the total growth in length and mass of the body as a whole. Another important point emphasized through Scammon's studies is the shift in the loci as well as the amount and character of growth during the developmental period:

Everyone has noticed the relatively large head and short legs of the young infant, but it is not commonly recognized that these proportions represent the action of a very general principle of growth. This principle is the so-called law of *developmental direction,* a generalization which postulates that the growth of the body is most active first in the head region, then in the trunk, and finally in the limbs. Thus a wave of growth activity passes along the body from head to heel, extending out along the arms and legs and terminating in the hands and feet. While this wave of growth has reached its height before birth, it is still under way in postnatal life.[27]

The findings regarding the different plans of growth of the different parts of the body show how complicated the question of physical abnormality becomes. It may have many different manifestations. It may be brought about by some condition involving a marked deviation from the particular plan of growth of some specific part. Other plans of other organs may or may not be upset by this abnormality. After the specific condition has been corrected, or has run its course, growth may proceed on the normal plan superimposed on an abnormal base, or the

[27] Scammon, R. E.: " The Physical Development of the Child," in *Parent Education,* edited by Richard Olding Beard (1927), 20.

abnormality may affect the entire course of future growth. The extensive data which Scammon has collected and analyzed on normal growth lend themselves to interesting uses in the study of the abnormal. They make possible the study of the abnormal in relation, not only to total growth, but also to the various plans of growth of the various parts of the body, and lead to a determination as to whether a particular defect is limited to a particular region or whether its ramifications extend to other parts. They also make possible the study of the effect of an abnormality upon subsequent growth and development, i.e., whether " normal " laws operate after the abnormality has set in, or whether an " abnormal " plan continues throughout the subsequent course of development.

In Scammon's laboratory, studies of the abnormal are being made in terms of normal growth and are giving interesting results on these points. These studies have taken as their starting point the grossly abnormal — monsters such as anencephalic fetuses. These, because of certain gross deviations which they present, make it possible quite readily to determine wherein the abnormalities lie. The procedure consists in assuming that each part of the monster in turn is normal and comparing the other parts as they are with what they would be if the " normality " extended throughout. It will be assumed, for instance, that the trunk length is normal and the other parts of the body will be computed (from formulae derived from normal data) in terms of the trunk length. The deviations of the parts of the abnormal can then be computed. Similarly, other parts will be assumed to be normal and the normal proportions computed with the deviations of the abnormal from these proportions. The criterion of normality is then expressed in terms of that part which, if conceived to be normal, gives the greatest number of normal interrelationships with other parts. It is possible to apply this technique to the analysis of various groups of abnormals, and it has been planned to proceed from the study of the grossly abnormal through the lesser forms of abnormality. A study of one of the grosser forms of abnormality has been completed and published and is worth quoting in some detail as an example of the possibilities of this sort of analysis. This study is " A Comparison of the Growth of the Body Dimensions of Anencephalic Human Fetuses with Normal Fetal Growth as Determined by Graphic Analysis and Empirical Formulae," by Juan C. Nañagas.[28] A series of

---

[28] *American Journal of Anatomy*, 35:455–94 (1925).

fifty-seven anencephalic fetuses was compared with the data on normal fetuses collected by Scammon. These cases are, of course, immediately marked as abnormal because of the faulty or complete suspension of development of the cranial portion of the head. But there is also " a marked departure from the normal proportions of not only the facial region, but also of the other divisions of the body. . . . This study was undertaken with the object of determining quantitatively the anomalous growth of this type of fetus and the changes in body-form associated with the partial loss or complete absence of the cranial vault and encephalon." [29]

The various measurements obtained on the anencephalic fetuses were each plotted on a graph, curves were fitted to the raw data, and these curves compared with those obtained by the empirical formulae developed from the data on the normal fetuses. These measurements were all expressed in terms of a standard dimension in order to make comparison of the curves of normal and anencephalic fetuses possible, and the standard selected was that of the length of the lower extremity. This was accepted because of the simplicity of measuring it, the smallness of the experimental error (it has as small degree of variability in the anencephalic as in the normal fetus), because its component parts are consistent when plotted against itself or against normal curves, and it is a demension which, when used as a base for calculating crown-heel length by empirical formulae, gives results within a " reasonable range of probability." A great many detailed comparisons were possible on this base and led to the following conclusions:

The quantitative study of the external dimensions of the anencephalus brings out the fact that the most striking departure of this type of anomaly from the normal, aside from the obvious disturbances of the development of the brain and spinal cord and the tissues inclosing them, is the marked disharmony of the proportions of certain regions and segments of the body.

Disregarding the head for the time being, it is found that the external dimensions of the body fall into two main groups as regards their fundamental proportional relationships. In general, the dimensions of the thorax, abdomen, pelvis, and lower extremity show interrelationships which approach fairly closely those of the normal fetus, while the dimensions of the superior extremity are all relatively greater than those of the trunk and legs. In this connection the question immediately arises as to which group of dimensions represents the lesser departure from the normal. In other words, do these cases

---

[29] *American Journal of Anatomy*, 35:455 (1925).

represent a condition in which a dwarfed body is attached to a pair of superior extremities which approach the normal, or do they represent a condition in which a fairly normal trunk, with fairly normal lower limbs, bears a pair of hypertrophied upper extremities? . . .

From a study of the evidence . . . it seems probable that the trunk and the lower extremities approach more nearly the normal condition than do the upper extremities. This conclusion is supported by the following considerations:

1. The dimensions of the trunk and lower extremity form the largest group of measurements of the external dimensions of the body and, as a whole, they show interrelationships which approximate those of the normal fetus.

2. In those instances where it is possible to divide the major dimensions of this group into minor segments it is found that these minor segments are in fairly normal proportions to each other and to the major part. In the case of the upper extremity, the minor segments are not in normal proportion to one another nor to the extremity as a whole.

3. The crown-heel lengths of the anencephalic specimens, when calculated with the empirical formulae from the external dimensions of the lower extremity or of the trunk, are values which are within possible normal limits. If, however, the crown-heel lengths are calculated from the observed upper extremity lengths, the percentage frequencies of very high crown-heel values are far above those of the normal fetuses at term. . . .

4. The state of ossification of the superior tibial epiphysis in the anencephalic material is closely comparable with that found in normal specimens of about the same trunk and leg dimensions, although quite different from that of normal specimens having the same arm dimensions. . . .

The evidence adduced in 1, 2, and 3 throws no light on a second question as to whether the dimensions of the trunk and extremity are normal for age as well as for body-length. However, the study of the ossification centers indicates that these dimensions are probably within the normal limits for age.[30]

This study further shows that at some time in the fetal period something has happened to disturb the relative rates of growth and to cause the body to assume these abnormal proportions, but that thereafter the various parts return to rates of growth corresponding to those of normal fetuses.

This study brings out very clearly the importance of the careful development of norms, such as Scammon has undertaken. The study of individual cases or groups of " abnormals " then becomes a matter of careful comparison. Since every measurement may be expressed in

---

[30] *Ibid.*, 482–84.

terms of every other measurement, it becomes a simple matter to determine wherein the abnormality lies.

This work of Scammon has proceeded on the basis of taking large numbers of cases at each age level (or in terms of each given increment of body length or body mass). The assumption made is that on large numbers of individuals the gross environmental influences will be equalized over a period of time, that is, that the measurements of a group of six-year-olds will correspond, within known limits, to the measurements of a group of five-year-olds taken the following year. The statistical evidence seems to support this assumption. It is claimed by some investigators, however, that a true picture of growth can be obtained only by computing norms on the basis of successive measurements of the same individuals over a period of time. They claim that the measurement of a series of five-year-olds and an equal series of six-year-olds will not give, in the latter case, any necessarily valid prediction of the status of these particular five-year-olds when they reach six years, nor is the five-year group necessarily the equivalent of the present six-year group a year ago. Perhaps the most valuable work of this school has been done by Bird Baldwin, who has accumulated a series of individual growth curves, both for physical and mental measurements.[31] These individual curves are valuable when used in comparison with the population norms. They show, for the individual, how he grows in terms of his own past plan of growth and where he stands in regard to the growth of the group as a whole. It has not been possible to establish norms of population growth by the method of averaging together large numbers of individual curves of growth because the number of such consecutive growth records followed through over a period of time is as yet inadequate.[32] The Child Welfare Station at the University of Iowa is distinguished from the other institutes by the emphasis placed on obtaining these individual growth curves and the

[31] See Baldwin, B. T.: " The Physical Growth of Children from Birth to Maturity," *University of Iowa Studies in Child Welfare*, I, no. I (1921); and Baldwin and Stecher: *The Psychology of the Preschool Child* (1925).

[32] One very obvious difficulty in the way of establishing population norms by this method is the practical one of keeping track of a large number of cases over any period of time. Occupational instability, inter-city migrations, etc., cause a tremendous loss in the number of cases originally selected to follow through. Scammon found this plan totally impracticable in Minneapolis. Buford Johnson, who carried through an elaborate series of measurements on a small group at the Bureau of Edu-

records of Baldwin and his associates have a permanent value which can eventually be analyzed into homogeneous groups. Their individual curves are, of course, also studied in relation to the general distribution obtained by the cross-section method. The longitudinal growth study has also been emphasized at the Bureau of Educational Experiments in New York. Measurements on a small group have been carried through for a number of years.

Various attempts have been made to get a single satisfactory index of anatomical age. One of the most widely studied of these indexes is based on the stage of ossification of the carpal bones. The more recent of these studies depend on two techniques. Baldwin [33] used the exposed area of the carpals as an index of their development. Most other investigators have used radiographs of the wrists as the basis for working out various indexes of development. Outstanding among these studies are those of Bardeen,[34] Woodrow and Lowell [35] and that of Prescott,[36] working in collaboration with Walter F. Dearborn. We shall describe Prescott's work only, since it has certain advantages in objectivity over the work of the other investigators. The significance of studies of this sort from the point of view of determining norms is interestingly brought out:

The criterion of normality is always whether or not an individual measures up to the standard set by the average of people who have lived the same number of years as he. . . . But it would seem that this description of normality should not be made entirely in terms of the individual's position during

cational Experiments in New York, gives the following data on this point: " Despite the hope that stability of patronage might be maintained, the mortality has been great. . . . We have consecutive records for 12 children over a period of five years; 31 children for four years; 55 children for three years; and 70 children for two years, while the total number of individuals examined during that time was 272."— (Johnson, Buford J.: *Mental Growth of Children in Relation to Rate of Growth in Bodily Build,* 1925, 3).

[33] Baldwin, B. T.: " The Physical Growth of Children from Birth to Maturity," *University of Iowa Studies in Child Welfare,* 1, No. 1.

[34] Bardeen, C. R.: " The Relation of Ossification to Physiological Development," *Journal of Radiology,* 2:1–8 (June, 1921).

[35] Woodrow, H., and Lowell, F.: " Some Data on Anatomical Age and Its Relation to Intelligence," *Pedagogical Seminary,* 29:1–15 (1922).

[36] Prescott, D. A.: " The Determination of Anatomical Age in School Children and Its Relation to Mental Development," *Harvard Monographs in Education,* No. 5 (July, 1923).

development, but also in terms of his final level when he has ceased to develop. That is, normality should be determined by the character of the endpoint as well as by the level at any time during growth. For example, there is only one carpal bone ossified at birth among the eight which must finally reach this condition. The last bone is ossified at about the age of thirteen for girls. Between these extremes the other six bones make their appearance, at certain ages on the average. But it is perfectly thinkable for an individual to develop more slowly than the average, to have a smaller yearly increment of growth, and still reach the normal endpoint, having all the bones developed at the age of fifteen perhaps. It would take longer to develop but the result would be normal, yet measured by the average during development, the individual would be judged subnormal. On the other hand, thinking for a moment of mental development, it is certainly true that many individuals, who start out with a smaller yearly increment of growth than is normal, cease growth at the normal time or even before, and are consequently subnormal for life. This fact should not be lost sight of because the character of an individual's training will be increasingly determined by his adjudged normality and if this normality is determined solely upon how long the individual has lived, grave injustices may be done. It should be remembered that both the rate and the duration of development must be considered. . . .

If it should become possible to know, not only the size of the individual's yearly increment of growth, as measured by development to data, but also the probable duration of growth, it would then be possible to know how to train the child because the normality of the endpoint would be known. . . . In the case of the carpal bones, for instance, the number of bones present when development is completed is known, and it is possible to measure the proportionate size of these bones to the final size, taking into consideration the size of the individual. This makes absolute measurement possible. It can be said with assurance when an individual has reached 50% of his total development and, if the position of the individual with respect to the normal is considered, the rate of development can be known and the duration computed. Thus if a boy has reached 50% of his development at seven and one-half years and is exactly normal, it can be foretold that his development will stop at fifteen years if normal development stops there, while if he has reached only 40% of his development at this age, it can be foretold that he will have reached only 80% of his development at fifteen years and may continue to develop for three and three-quarters years longer.[37]

---

[37] Prescott, D. A.: " The Determination of Anatomical Age in School Children and Its Relation to Mental Development," *Harvard Monographs in Education*, No. 5:2-4 (July, 1923).

Prescott worked out a method for determining a satisfactory index of the degree of development from radiographs, and established " norms " by applying this method to about three thousand cases. Samples of cases were taken (averaging about forty in number) and were ranked in order of development by two investigators. Almost perfect correlation of rank resulted. An attempt was then made to work out a logical index, which would rank these cases in the same order, i.e., " some measure which would be significant of carpal development and at the same time be discriminative enough to differentiate the radiographs into their proper rank-order." [38] Several such indexes which were worked out proved satisfactory, and the one was accepted which was simplest to compute:

If the diameter of each of the carpal bones present is measured and the sum of the measurements is divided by the width of the wrist between the points designated, the resulting figure is an index of the anatomical development of the individual, and from it the anatomical age may be determined by comparing it with the median anatomic indices of the various groups.[39]

Distributions of the indexes were formed for six-month age groups from 5 years nine months to 18 years eleven months:

The first evident conclusion to be derived from a consideration of these distributions is the tremendous variability among individuals of the same chronological age. Boys included in the ages 6 years 3 months to 6 years 8 months have indices varying from .50 to 2.20. In terms of anatomic age, this means that the individuals in this group vary in anatomical development from that uually found in four-year-old boys to that usually found in nine and one-half-year-old boys — a range of at least five and one-half years.[40]

An interesting sex difference is found, the girls being " about eighteen months ahead of boys throughout the whole period of growth from years 6 to maturity." [41] The correlations between anatomical age and mental age are significant in that they indicate " that when there is disagreement between chronological age and anatomical development the level of mental development tends to follow anatomical development." [42]

Draper has made an interesting attempt to relate constitutional types to susceptibility to certain specific diseases. He takes the point of view that mankind can more readily be divided into " disease races " than

[38] *Ibid.*, 26.   [39] *Ibid.*, 33.   [40] *Ibid.*, 39.   [41] *Ibid.*, 39.   [42] *Ibid.*, 45.

into the variously described anthropological races, that susceptibility to
a specific type of disease is manifested by a characteristic body-build,
and that persons of varying anthropological races suffering from, or
susceptible to, the same diseases will show greater similarity in structure
than will persons of the same anthropological races not suffering from,
or susceptible to, the same diseases:

> This truth is well illustrated by the instance of 3 cases of perforated gastric
> ulcer lying side by side in the Presbyterian Hospital at the same time. The
> likeness of the 3, one to another, was striking, and anthropometrically their
> measurements and proportions were almost superimposable, yet they had their
> origin in three distinct racial roots — one an Anglo-Saxon, one a Pole from
> middle Europe, and one an Italian from the shores of the Mediterranean
> Sea.[43]

Draper's theory embraces the interrelationships of what he calls the
" four panels of personality," i.e., morphology, physiology, psychology
and immunity:

> We have found that if the four panels of personality are studied and corre-
> lated in each person of a large number of individuals who are affected with the
> same disease, there appears frequent repetition of certain combinations of
> characters. These recurrences are so definite that from a careful analysis of a
> given anatomic panel, for example, it is possible to predicate with great cor-
> rectness the nature of one or more of the other panels.[44]

The published data have not, however, shown any such predictability
as is claimed in the above statement. In his monograph on *The Human
Constitution,* Draper selected patients suffering from six types of disease and tried to trace out the possible relationships between body-build
and disease:

> A set of six diseases was chosen. Each represents about as easily recognizable
> and generally accepted a disease as we know in medicine. Furthermore, the
> group includes expressions of pathology in a wide variety of organs and
> tissues. . . . The group comprises pernicious anemia, pulmonary tuberculosis,
> asthma due to known protein sensitization, nephritis and hypertension, gall-
> bladder disease, and gastric and duodenal ulcer.[45]

---

[43] Draper, G.: *The Human Constitution* (1924), 36.

[44] Draper, G., Dunn, H. L., and Seegal, D.: " Studies in Human Constitution,"
Journal of the American Medical Association, 82: 431 (February 9, 1924).

[45] Draper, G.: *The Human Constitution,* 68–69.

A large number of measurements (over eighty) was made on a relatively small number of cases of each disease category (ranging from 9 males and 11 females in the asthma category to 75 males and 28 females in the pulmonary tuberculosis category) and some thirty-five physical indexes were computed. The seventeen males suffering from gall-bladder disease and the thirty-two males suffering from gastric and duodenal ulcer were selected for special study:

A group of 9 measurements has been selected for the differential recognition of the members of the two disease races. The choice of measurement was made primarily because of a wide divergence between corresponding accumulative percentage curves and secondarily to gain a diverse distribution of the measurements over the whole body.[46]

To select 9 out of a possible 80 measurements was, of course, stacking the cards in favor of bringing out wide differences, since the measurements were definitely selected on that basis. Even so, " the average diagnostic value [calculated by averaging the scores on all 9 elements] of the gall-bladder males was 73.7%; of the duodenal ulcer, 79.5%; and of the gastric ulcer, 74.3% " [47] — by no means a very high predictive value.

A real danger in this type of investigation lies in the fact that, with so many measurements taken, and so few cases used, some of these measurements are almost certain to show statistically " significant " relationships by chance alone. It is questionable whether valuable " discoveries " can be arrived at simply by statistical manipulations of this sort unless independent evidence of the validity of the relationships is established.

Hypotheses of this sort would have to be checked under very strictly controlled conditions, allowing for the factors of race, social status, etc., and related to similar studies of persons with no disease history of these types before they could have any validity.

The difference between studies of this type (the same criticism applies to Kretschmer) and that of Scammon is that these studies are dealing with the abnormal without any point of reference. Elaborate studies are made of the factors associated with the specific abnormal condition, without any real check-up by a statistically determined norm.

---

[46] *Ibid.*, 88.   [47] *Ibid.*, 92.

They are referred to an assumption of a norm or an " ideal." Scammon, in starting out with the study of the unselected and making elaborate measurements on them, gives himself a real point of reference from which to study any particular group of abnormals or extreme deviates.

We mention in passing that in the physiological field also there has appeared a theory of a criminal type based on glandular deficiency, and programs for the elimination of crime on this basis are being elaborated. The following statements are illustrative:

[Having studied] more than twenty thousand cases from every angle, psychologically, neurologically, psychiatrically, physically, chemically and etiologically . . . it would not surprise the writer if investigations were to reveal that a third of all present convicts were sufferers from emotional instability, which is to say gland or toxic disturbances. This does not include feebleminded or insane people.[48]

One striking development of Dr. Timme's research is that twenty-four out of twenty-five " lifers " examined in a New York State prison were " glandular types."

It is now possible, according to the Institute's statement, to recognize at sight certain physical types which are definitely pro-criminal. One such type Dr. Timme describes as having " a Rolls Royce body with an inadequate engine." . . .

" This morning," he said, " I examined consecutively seventeen persons, and of these seventeen four were definitely hypoplastic. Two are in one family, the children of a millionaire drunkard. Another girl I examined lies and steals. The fourth is a boy studying for a profession, yet whose lack of control over himself is a positive menace to society." [49]

We have already discussed the general theory of a criminal type and pointed out the fallacies involved in the attempts to establish such a type. We have noticed also the theory of Dr. Cotton that the insanities are due to a single cause (focal infection) and we have illustrated the varieties of maladjustment in chapter I. We do not, therefore, take up the theory of a glandular criminal type in detail. It is desirable to have scientific research on the glands and on their relation to maladjustment. But the simple expedient of a control group — a number of criminals

---

[48] Schlapp, M. G.: " Behavior and Gland Disease," *Journal of Heredity*, 15:11 (1924).

[49] *New York World* (May 10, 1928).

taken at random and an equal number of citizens taken from their offices and factories and examined by the same method — would probably be sufficient to dispose of the claims just illustrated.

In the foregoing discussion of biochemical factors as correlated with personality it will be noticed that the questions have turned largely on metabolic imbalance, endocrine disturbances, temperaments, physiological, morphological and psychological types, and the materials we have employed seem to converge in the field of psychopathology rather than that of delinquency and criminality. At the same time, it appears, especially in the recent experiment of Healy and Bronner with foster children, that the psychopathic personalities do play a large rôle in delinquency and crime and that they are the most incorrigible of offenders.

But granting that there are wide differences in the constitutional organization of individuals, it is nevertheless necessary to define the meaning of this for behavior studies. The subjects representing these deviations are usually able to live and work with some kind of adjustment as doctors, lawyers, merchants, ministers, laborers, scientists, crooks, etc. The temperament is important occupationally, matrimonially, hedonistically, and valuable from the standpoint of the varieties of creative activity, but it cannot be claimed that behavior or performance ratios are distributed according to temperaments. All temperaments are represented among the normal, the insane and the criminal. The world is a world of deviates, and there are " various standards of normality " (Adolf Meyer). We even find the association of pathological trends, especially in the arts and sciences, with performances which we count as important and even unique values. Many of the prizes go to the psychopaths. Nevertheless, there are evidently problem constitutions as well as problem children.

The physiologists have emphasized the point that the cells of the body live in and constitute an inner environment in contrast with the outer environment in which the organism as a whole lives and moves. The brilliant work of Henderson has consisted largely in exemplifying and determining the mechanism of the following statement of Claude Bernard:

For the animal there are really two environments: an external environment in which the organism is placed, and an internal environment in which the cells live. Life goes on, not in the external environment, air, fresh water, or salt water, as the case may be, but in the liquid internal environment composed of the organic circulating liquid which surrounds and bathes every cell. This medium is composed of the lymph and the plasma, the liquid portion of the blood, which in the higher animals penetrate the tissues and make up the totality of the interstitial liquids. These are the instrument of all the local nutritive processes, the source and confluence of the exchanges of the cells. A complex organism must be considered as a union of simple beings, its cells, which live in the liquid internal environment.

The constancy of the internal environment is the condition of free and independent life. The mechanism which makes possible this constancy assures in the internal environment the maintenance of all the conditions necessary to the life of the cells. Thus we may understand that there can be no free and independent life for those simple beings whose [active] cells are in direct contact with the cosmic environment, but that this form of life is, on the contrary, the exclusive privilege of such beings as have reached the height of organic complexity and differentiation.

The constancy of the environment presupposes such a perfection of the organism that at every moment external variations are compensated and equilibrated.[50]

But while the organism *lives* in the inner environment its behavior takes place in, and is provoked and conditioned by, the outer environment. Given the most perfect glandular and nervous systems conceivable there is yet trouble for the organism if it is not integrated with the outer world and, in human society especially, if it is not integrated with the society of its fellows by a system of learning and habit formation. This approach is developed in the following chapter.

---

[50] Bernard, Claude: *Leçons sur les Phénomènes de la Vie,* 112, quoted by Laurence J. Henderson: "The Physico-Chemical Changes in Blood During the Respiratory Cycle," in Dale, H. H., Drummond, J. C., Henderson, L. J., and Hill, A. V.: *Lectures on Certain Aspects of Biochemistry* (1926), 176–78.

CHAPTER XII
The Sociological Approach

WE are impressed with the existence of constitutional differences dependent on the physiological processes which we have outlined in the preceding chapter. At the same time we are impressed with the fact that life experiences, perhaps a single experience, may so condition the individual that his reactions are or appear to be as pathological as those of the constitutional inferior. Persons may point out that of two children, perhaps twins, even identical twins, one may be daring, the other timid, and they say this must be constitutional, since the children have lived in the same " environment." But Watson has given as example two children who walk with the father on the street, one on the inside and the other on the outside, and one sees the flowers in the yards and the other sees a child crushed by a truck. The children were not in the same environment and the personality configuration of one of them turned largely on the registration (memory deposit) in the organism of an experience. If the fear is excessive the condition is called a " phobia." We have thus an example of a psychopathic trait produced by an experience. The practice of " gentling " rats mentioned by Hammett in chapter XI shows the profound modification of behavior reactions and even of the metabolism made possible through handling or treatment of the subject.

The most important form of procedure used by scientists who work with living material is experimentation with the organism when placed in different situations. This is the method used by the experimental physiologist and psychologist who prepare situations, introduce the subject into the situation, observe the behavior reactions, change the situation, and observe the changes in the reactions. Child [1] rendered one point in the situation more stimulating than others by applying an electric needle or other stimulus and made heads grow where tails would otherwise have grown, changed a part of an organism into a whole organism, restructuralized the whole organism, etc. The situational character of the animal experimentation of the psychologists is well known. The rat, for example, in order to open a door, must not only stand on a platform placed in a certain position, but at the same time pull a string. A complete study of situations would give a complete account of the rat's attitudes, values and intelligence.

The study of behavior with reference to situations which was begun by Vervorn, Pfeffer, Loeb, Jennings, and other physiologists and was concerned with the so-called " tropisms," or the reaction of the small organism to light, electricity, heat, gravity, hard substances, acids, food, etc., was paralleled by the experiments of Thorndike, Yerkes, Pavlov, Bekhterev, Watson, Köhler and others, with rats, dogs, monkeys and babies as subjects, but until quite recently no systematic work from this standpoint has involved the reactions of the individual to other persons or groups of persons. That is to say, the work has not been sociological, but physiological or psychological. The sociological procedure is the study of the individual in social situations.

The present chapter relates to the study of behavior in varieties of situations. The introductory portion deals with the reaction of individuals to a variety of impersonal stimuli (a type of study regarded by Pavlov and his school as physiological and by Watson and the behaviorists as psychological), but the main objective is sociological, that is, the behavior of the individual as determined by his relations to other individuals and to a society. The general method may be called the " situational " or " behavioristic " [2] approach, and only the interaction of personalities is sociological. It will be noticed also that much of the good sociological material, the most of it, in fact, has not been prepared by sociologists but by psychologists, educational psychologists

---

[1] Child, C. M.: *Physiological Foundations of Behavior* (1924), 151 *et passim*.

[2] " Situational " and " behavioristic " are two aspects of a process. We do not identify " behavioristic " completely with " behaviorism," since behaviorism as a school has become characterized by its particular interpretations and denials of mechanisms.

and psychiatrists. The barriers between departments of study break down at this point.

The work of Pavlov, Bekhterev and Watson on the conditioned reflex is foundational for sociology, education and psychiatry, and we shall indicate its importance. In a word the conditioned reflex means that if a dog, for example, is given food, this induces a flow of saliva (a reflex) and if at the same time a bell is sounded, an electric shock applied at any point on the dog's body, an odor presented to his nose, or any other associated stimulus is given, and if this is repeated a number of times, the sound, the odor or the shock will then induce alone, without the presence of food, the same amount of saliva. The reaction to the associated stimulus is called a conditioned reflex.[3] Similarly, a child is not originally afraid of anything it sees, but is frightened by noises. If, then, a child is playing with a white rat and a metallic bar is struck, the child will cry. And if the rat is presented and the bar is struck simultaneously, and this is done repeatedly, the child will cry when given the rat, even if the sound is omitted.[4] In this way fears and prejudices and prepossessions are produced, especially by the behavior of other persons. A single association may be sufficient to produce the reflex. There is on record, for example, the case of a youth who was the subject of an experiment with odors. The odor of roses produced a feeling of fear, and investigation disclosed that the subject had been injured in an automobile accident near a rose garden. A whiff of lavender may recall mother, and tuberoses remind us of death. We have here a most important approach to the formation of personality traits as dependent on situations.

It will be understood that the dog's food depends on his successful response to these experiments — the hunger drive is used — and the experiments may be made very taxing. The dog may have been conditioned to food as associated with the strokes of the metronome at 60 beats. Lying hungry in an upper room, the metronome beating below beside a food box at the rate of 100 the dog will not move, but the moment the rate is changed to 60 beats his saliva begins to flow and he

---

[3] Pavlov, I. P.: *Conditioned Reflexes* (1927).

[4] Cf. Watson, J. B.: *Psychology from the Standpoint of a Behaviorist* (1924), 331.

rushes to the food box. The acoustic powers of dogs are far superior to those of man. They have been trained to discriminate quarter and eighth tones. " Nikiforovsky got a differentiation between sounds of 461 and 435 vibrations per second. . . . Beliakov obtained the highest point of pitch discrimination — that of one-fourth and one-eighth tone interval. His dogs were actually able to recognize the differences between sounds of 800, 812 and 825 vibrations per second respectively."[5] But under these conditions it was possible to demand a degree of discrimination beyond the powers of the dog and cause a neurosis. This is described by Pavlov in connection with another experiment:

The experiments in question were made to determine the limits of the analysis of shapes of different objects [experiments of Dr. Shenger-Krestovni-kova]. A projection of a luminous circle on to a screen in front of the animal was repeatedly accompanied by feeding. After the reflex had become well established a differentiation between the circle and an ellipse with a ratio of the semi-axes 2 : 1, of the same luminosity and the same surface area, was obtained by the usual method of contrast. A complete and constant differentiation was obtained comparatively quickly. The shape of the ellipse was now approximated by stages to that of the circle (ratios of the semi-axes of 3 : 2, 4 : 3 and so on) and the development of differentiation continued through the successive ellipses. The differentiation proceeded with some fluctuations, progressing at first more and more quickly, and then again slower, until an ellipse with ratio of semi-axes 9 : 8 was reached. In this case, although a considerable degree of discrimination did develop, it was far from being complete. After three weeks of work upon this differentiation not only did the discrimination fail to improve, but it became considerably worse, and finally disappeared altogether. At the same time the whole behaviour of the animal underwent an abrupt change. The hitherto quiet dog began to squeal in its stand, kept wriggling about, tore off with its teeth the apparatus for me-chanical stimulation of the skin, and bit through the tubes connecting the animal's room with the observer, a behaviour which never happened before. On being taken into the experimental room the dog now barked violently, which was also contrary to its usual custom; in short it presented all the symptoms of a condition of acute neurosis. On testing the cruder differentia-tions they also were found to be destroyed, even the one with the ratio of the semi-axes 2 : 1. A fresh development of the latter differentiation up to its

---

[5] Anrep, G. V.: " Pitch Discrimination in the Dog," *Journal of Physiology,* 53:367 (1920).

previous exactness progressed twice as slowly as at first, but during the re-establishment of this crude differentiation the animal gradually became quieter, returning finally to its normal state. The development of the finer differentiations now occurred even more quickly than before. The 9 : 8 ellipse at its first application was completely discriminated from the circle, but from the second application onwards no trace of a discrimination was obtained, and the animal again entered a state of extreme general excitation with the same results as before. No further experiments were performed with the animal.[6]

For twenty-five years the Pavlovian experiments were performed mainly with dogs as subjects, but Krasnogorski, an associate of Pavlov, undertook a series of experiments on children resulting in the production of neuroses:

We formed in the child, I. N., aged 6, a conditioned reflex from the metronome. When the reflex was stabilized, we began to differentiate ninety-two from 144 beats. The sound of 144 beats was constantly being accompanied by feeding and occasioned the conditioned motor reflex; the stimulator 92 was inactive, because the child never received food with it. This differentiation was soon formed by the child, that is, after not having been given food six times with ninety-two beats of the metronome. After that, we made differentiations which were more difficult, that is, between 144 and 108 beats of the metronome. This differentiation was also quickly accomplished by the child by means of five nonsupported irritations (104 beats). Then followed the experiment of bringing the active and inactive stimulators still nearer to each other, that is, 144 and 120 beats were applied. This differentiation was formed after four nonsupported irritations, but the conditioned reflex activity of the child had changed. The latent periods of conditioned reflexes had increased in length twice (instead of 0.4 to 0.5 seconds it became 0.8 to 1.9 seconds; experiments performed on May 29 and 31). At the same time we observed an important change in the behavior of the child; having always been easy to deal with and quiet during the experiments, he now became irritable and refused to go to the laboratory. (See pages 510–11 for tables.)

---

[6] Pavlov, I. P.: *op. cit.*, 290–91.

TABLE I. — FINDINGS FOR FOUR MONTHS

Date, 1924	No. of Stimu- lation	Time	Stimulation	Condi- tioned Reflex	Latent Period	Remarks
3/6	91	12:04	Metronome 144	+	0.4	Goes to the experiment
	92	12:07	Metronome 144	+	0.5	quickly and laughing,
	93	12:13	Metronome 144	+	0.4	gets into the apparatus
	94	12:15	Metronome 144	+	0.5	by himself.
4/4	159	3:05	Metronome 144	+	1.2	A calm, well balanced
	10	3:07	Metronome 92	o	—	and quiet child.
	160	3:09	Metronome 144	+	1.5	
	161	3:11	Metronome 144	+	1.0	
	11	3:14	Metronome 92	o	—	
	162	3:17	Metronome 144	+	1.3	
5/21	267	1:09	Metronome 144	+	0.9	After the experiment
	268	1:12	Metronome 144	+	0.9	laughs and talks.
	6	1:15	Metronome 108	o	—	
	269	1:18	Metronome 144	+	...	
5/29	275	2:48	Metronome 144	+	1.2	
	7	2:51	Metronome 108	o	—	
	276	2:54	Metronome 144	+	0.7	
	277	2:57	Metronome 144	+	0.7	
	1	3:00	Metronome 120	+	2.0	
	278	3:03	Metronome 144	+	0.6	
5/31	280	2:01	Metronome 144	+	0.8	Refuses going to the ex-
	281	2:04	Metronome 144	+	0.9	periment; walks and
	282	2:07	Metronome 144	+	0.8	mounts slowly to the
	283	2:12	Metronome 144	+	1.0	apparatus; after the experiment is silent.
6/8	321	12:38	Metronome 144	+	1.2	Goes to the experiment
	322	12:41	Metronome 144	+	0.7	silently and gets into
	4	12:44	Metronome 120	o	—	the apparatus; report
	323	12:47	Metronome 144	+	1.0	from the ward of a
	324	12:50	Metronome 144	+	1.5	change in the patient's
	1	12:53	Metronome 132	+	1.7	behavior, he has be-
	325	12:56	Metronome 144	+	0.9	come taciturn.
6/18	330	12:40	Metronome 144	+	1.2	Is rude, fights with other
	6	12:43	Metronome 120	+	5.3	children; insists on be-
	331	12:47	Metronome 144	+	2.0	ing discharged from
	2	12:50	Metronome 132	+	3.0	hospital; doctor's re-

Date, 1924	No. of Stimulation	Time	Stimulation	Conditioned Reflex	Latent Period	Remarks
	3	12:53	Metronome 132	+	2.0	port from the ward
	332	12:56	Metronome 144	+	0.9	that his behavior is insupportable, he is extremely excited, fights and is disobedient.
6/22	348	1:04	Metronome 144	+	...	
	12	1:07	Metronome 132	+	1.1	
	13	1:10	Metronome 132	+	0.5	Yawns, is sleepy, closes his eyes; at 1:17 falls asleep for the first time after five months of experimenting; at 1:23 awakes from a knock at the door.
	14	1:15	Metronome 132	+	1.4	
	349	1:25	Metronome 144	+	0.8	

Once more we made a differentiation which was still more difficult, that is, 144 and 132. During the work which now began, we were informed from the child's ward that the patient had become nervous; he had always been well behaved; now he cried often, beat the other children and said he wanted to leave the hospital. The experiments had to be discontinued, as not only no new differentiations could be formed, but even the differentiation of June 18 between 120 and 144 beats of the metronome had disappeared (experiment performed on June 18). The inactive stimulation of 132 beats began to cause yawning and sleepiness, and during the fourth stimulation the child went to sleep, which happened for the first time in the course of the whole work of five months (experiment performed on June 22, Table 1).

Thus, the more difficult the differentiation became, the more the balance between irritation and inhibition was disturbed; therefore, the differentiating activity of the child lessened, a general inhibition developed during the experiment (sleep), while the whole behavior of the child was changed.

I observed the same facts with Dr. V. V. Syriatsky while studying on children the difficult differentiations on the skin. When we had formed too many active and inactive places on the child's skin, systematically accompanying by food the first and not the latter, the child became restless; it would refuse to come in for the experiments; the intensity of the conditioned reflexes and the exactness of local differentiations were diminished.[7]

---

[7] Krasnogorski, N. I.: "The Conditioned Reflexes and Children's Neuroses," *American Journal of Diseases of Children*, 30:756–58 (1925).

Experiments were also made on the " delayed " conditioned reflexes:

A conditioned reflex from the metronome was formed in a child, N. S., aged 6, by giving food five seconds after the metronome had started . . . [chart omitted]. When the reflex became stable, we began to delay it. Instead of giving food five seconds after the metronome had started, we began to give it with the thirtieth second. After several such stimulations, the conditioned reflex lost its stability and rapidly disappeared. The child began to yawn and to be sleepy; the development of an intensive inhibition was the result of these experiments.

Then we began to give food again five seconds after the starting of the metronome. Although for five days there was no reflex, for the next three days it was unstable, and not until the eighth day did it become as it had been. . . .

When [after further trials] we had succeeded in delaying the reflex for thirty seconds, we made the conditions of the experiment still more difficult, that is, we began to delay the reflex for sixty seconds. After several such trials the reflex disappeared again; the child began to sleep during the experiments, and refused to go to the laboratory.

All experiments were discontinued for a week, and the child was given full rest. This rest had an excellent effect. When we renewed our work and tried to delay the reflex for sixty seconds, it did not disappear but became delayed for forty and six-tenths seconds . . . also there were no more difficulties in getting the child to go to the laboratory for the experiments.

Thus, as in the case of the differentiating process, so also in the case of forming delayed reactions, as soon as the conditions grew to be more difficult the balance failed and an intensive inhibition developed, which increased to the degree of sleep; at the same time the usual conditioned reflectory activity ceased. It took a whole week of training the reflexes the first time or giving full rest to the child the second in order to free the cerebral hemispheres from this inhibition and restore the normal balance.[8]

The disturbance was still more pronounced in the case of an hysterical child:

S. G., a girl, aged 12, was taken to the Children's Clinic of the Medical Institute with symptoms of globus hystericus and frequent vomiting after the ingestion of food. A year before, the patient had drunk some anisated solution of ammonia by mistake, and after this she began to vomit. She was brought to a hospital, where, however, the physicians did not find any symptoms of poisoning. From that time the patient continued to vomit after eating, when excited. When the patient was excited on an empty stomach, dyspnea, cyanosis

[8] Krasnogorski, N. I.: "The Conditioned Reflexes and Children's Neuroses," *American Journal of Diseases of Children*, 30:758–60 (1925).

and twitching of the muscles of the face occurred, instead of vomiting. Thus the stimulation had two different effects: with a full stomach it radiated to the vomiting center, and with an empty stomach to the respiratory and circulatory centers.

When our patient was first brought to the laboratory, she exhibited an intensive passive-defensive reaction. Usually there is no difficulty in putting the children on the table for experiments, but in this case another child had to be called and placed in the apparatus, before she would lie down.

Then in five minutes we stimulated her by the beats of the metronome. This stimulation produced intensive excitement, which was expressed by dyspnea, cyanosis and convulsions of the muscles of the face. The second stimulation had the same result. The third stimulation caused a weaker reaction, and beginning with the fourth, one new fact was observed. The metronome from the first beats began to cause intense sleepiness in the child. As soon as the metronome began to act the patient closed her eyes, breathed heavily and held a biscuit between her teeth during the whole time of the action of the metronome. One or two minutes after the stimulation with the metronome, the sleepiness passed, and she began to eat the biscuit. Thus the metronome, which at first developed intensive stimulation, now caused inhibition. . . .

Then, together with Professor Pavlov, we decided to make this inhibition conflict with intense excitement. We made the following experiment: we wanted to see what would happen if we applied the metronome, not when the child was having full rest and the innumerable impulses from muscles, ligaments, and articulations were minimal, but in conditions of extreme motor excitement, that is, in dancing. That was easy enough, as the patient thought that she could dance well.

For once we broke our rule of not entering into any conversation with the patient, and in this special case asked her to dance. She began to do so, and when she reached the greatest motor effect, the metronome was put in action. The patient stopped instantly; for a minute or so she stood bending her body slightly to and fro with her eyes fixed on one point; then dyspnea, tremor and cyanosis developed quickly, and she began to sob. When in ten minutes it was possible to put her back into her place, she ceased crying, lay quietly, but refused to take a biscuit. . . .

On the second day, the patient refused to go to the laboratory. The following day, she went, but, as before, showed a strong defensive reaction to the surroundings. However, she lay down in her place and was more or less quiet. As soon as the metronome was set in action she stopped her ears, her respiration became quicker, her face reddened and the muscles of her face twitched. When the metronome ceased she was quiet again. The same thing was observed every time the metronome was started. During the next two days the metronome produced the same effect. On the third day, the reaction of exitement from the metronome gradually began to be less; it did not disappear until the sixth day. But now the metronome has lost its inhibitory power, which it developed so intensively before our experiment with the dance. Our patient did not sleep now, neither did she appear to become excited. We were able to form the conditioned reflex with this stimulator. The reflex was being formed extremely slowly. Only at the one hundred and forty-fifth trial did a slight reflex appear; for a long time it was very unstable, and only at the two hundred and ninety-fifth trial did it become constant. It is interesting that the further study of this reflex showed that it disappeared very slowly; about ten stimulations unaccompanied by food were necessary to cause the conditioned reflex to disappear. The reflex, which was formed with extreme difficulty, was also with difficulty inhibited.

From these experiments we see the difference between the reaction produced by external stimulation in a normal and in a pathological child. The whole activity of the cerebral hemispheres in a normal child is founded on a flexible balance between the irritative and inhibitory processes; here irritation and inhibition regularly and easily replace one another, depending on changing external circumstances. In our pathologic case this flexibility of the balance was lost. We could see that the metronome at first acted for a long time as an intensive inhibitory agent. After that, it produced extreme excitement for five days. Then for a certain time the balance was restored, and we could form the conditioned reflex. However, this reflex could be made to disappear with great difficulty, because now inhibition was lacking. Thus instead of a normal flexibility of the balance, inhibition (sleep) or extreme excitement prevails.

Our experiments show the consequences when intense stimulation conflicts with strong inhibition. An extended and great disturbance of the balance occurs even if such an elementary activity of the cortex as the formation of conditioned reflexes is obstructed. In life such conflicts always take place, but in the normal nervous system a disturbance of balance is quickly restored. However, it acquires a more serious character when several severe conflicts follow one another, or when the child's central nervous system itself shows some pathologic inborn deficiency.[9]

It was found also that in psychopathic children (including a post-encephalitic case) the disturbances had a more lasting as well as a more profound character than in normal children, and Krasnogorski has observed the lasting result of a single experience:

---

[9] Krasnogorski, N. I.: "The Conditioned Reflexes and Children's Neuroses," *American Journal of Diseases of Children*, 30:760–64 (1925).

We have just been observing a child, N. N., aged 8 years, with whom a complete displacement of the balance toward inhibition and an entire change of the whole behavior developed after an attempt to violate her had occurred. Thus, the intensive conflicts between stimuli and inhibition in children sometimes produce a disturbance of the balance which influences the whole behavior of the child and is the cause of the development of serious neuroses.[10]

We do not know whether the explanations of mechanisms offered by Krasnogorski and this school are adequate. We suspect that they are not. But, disregarding for a moment the questions of cortical balance, relation of excitation to inhibition, and all other internal matters, we have in these experiments an exemplification of the most suitable practical method for the study of behavior. And by practical method we mean one that would lead to control.

It was pointed out by Krasnogorski that the tasks were made too hard for the children in two ways, by making the discrimination too difficult and delaying the reactions. The first of these points is significant in connection with, for example, school tasks imposed on children with special disabilities, or at an inappropriate stage of maturation, or out of order from the standpoint of the system of habit formation usual in the group (cases 16 and 17, pp. 35–40). The other point, about delayed reactions, becomes very important when taken in connection with what Frank has called " sustaining and regulating physiological tensions " (p. 561) in the process of learning social adjustments in a society, where delays and strains are multiplied and intensified by various usages and codes.

With these phychological experiments as a background we may examine the present tendencies to study and regulate behavior from the situational standpoint in the fields of education, psychiatry and sociology.

We have already noticed a number of experiments where the child, either for purposes of observation, reform of behavior or improvement of material condition, was placed in a radically different situation. In these cases the family was abandoned as situation favorable to the child and an attempt was made to find a more favorable situation at some point in the community. We have noticed in chapter VIII the experiment of Freeman and his associates who placed about 600 children in

---

[10] *Ibid.*, 767.

foster homes and observed the results of the changed situations. Comparisons were made between results on intelligence tests which had been given before adoption, in the case of one group, and the results after they had been in the foster home a number of years. Another comparison was made between children of the same family who had been placed in different homes, the home being rated on a scheme which took into consideration the material environment, evidence of culture, occupation of foster father, education and social activity of foster parents. Both of these comparisons had held heredity constant, letting the situation vary. A third comparison held environment constant, letting heredity vary, that is, concerning itself with a comparison of the intelligence of the own children of the foster parents and of the foster children. The results, stated in a word, show that when two unrelated children are reared in the same home, differences in their intelligences tend to decrease, and that residence in different homes tends to make siblings differ from one another in intelligence. This study is limited to the question of intelligence as measured by intelligence tests, but it is obvious that a fundamental study of behavior could be made by the same method.

Esther Richards, of the Phipps Psychiatric Clinic in Baltimore, placed psychopathic children in homes and on farms and moved them about until a place was found in which they were adjusted. She discovered that there were whole families of hypochondriacs showing no symptoms of organic deficiency. To be " ailing, and never so well " had become a sort of fashion in families, owing, perhaps, to the hysterical manifestations of the mother. These attempts were rather uniformly successful so long as the parents remained away from the child (see case 30, p. 76).

Harry Stack Sullivan and his associates, working at the Sheppard and Enoch Pratt Hospital, Baltimore, are experimenting with a small group of persons now or recently actively disordered, from the situational standpoint, and among other results this study reveals the fact that these persons tend to make successful adjustments in groupwise association between themselves. The strain on psychopathic and mentally deficient children among a normal and superior group is comparable to that placed by Krasnogorski on children experimentally, where tasks were imposed beyond the powers of the subject. The inferior child is often distinctly relieved and shows improvement when placed in a group of his kind. The recovery of patients in psychopathic hospitals is due to a change of situation. They are removed from home and office strains similar to those placed on the children in Krasnogorski's experiments, and recuperate.

Lurie, of Cincinnati, has one of the most successful clinics for the treatment of difficult children. Dr. Lurie is a neuropsychiatrist and treats the children as though they had organic disorders. But the children are given rest, dieted, removed from exciting causes, kept under observation for a long period in a small selected group of other difficult children, with a carefully chosen matron, and it is impossible to say to what degree the improvement of their condition and behavior is due to the favorable change of situation.

Similarly, it is impossible to say how far the high incidence of psychopathic manifestations among Jews is due to racial and constitutional factors and how far to the fact that historical conditions have placed them in present situations where discrimination forces them to try harder than others in order to gain and maintain status. They also are in the situation of Krasnogorski's children.

Kenneth in case 16 (pp. 35–38) is an example of a boy with a distribution of ability not corresponding with the school curriculum, who attempted to organize his life in a situation of his own choosing. And there are in the records numerous cases which we have been unable to notice where a child escaped from an institution and found a situation in which it was well adjusted. In one case a girl, well dressed and prosperous, returned to the institution to exhibit her success.

The Boston court and clinic have always used the foster home, in preference to the institution, in dealing with delinquent children, but heretofore without conspicuous success. Recently, however, Healy and Bronner and their associates prepared a particularly careful set-up. They took hard cases, " a large number of specially difficult individuals," but at the same time they chose the homes and conducted the supervision with great care. By an examination of a large number of homes they found foster mothers of robust constitution, good nature, expansive personality, and not too particular about noise, dirt and disorder — women better than the ordinary run of mothers for the purpose of interesting and controlling a difficult boy. It was found, in fact, that one of the difficulties to be guarded against was the selection of a home too good from the cultural standpoint:

A person aesthetic by nature and possessed of extremely refined sensibilities will sometimes fail to understand the real nature of a child of coarse fibre, believing him to be more capable than he actually is of conducting himself acceptably in a household of refinement. She may even consider him hopelessly vulgar.[11]

This experiment showed (1) that it was possible to treat children without mental deficiency or psychopathic traits with a high degree of success in these situations (90%); (2) that a certain period of time was necessary for retraining, and that return to the old home and community was disastrous unless there had been a change for the better there in the meantime; (3) that a transfer of the child from family to family, until a suitable situation was found, was often advisable; and (4) that the method was not successful with psychopathic children. Details of this experiment were given in chapter II.

Charlotte Bühler,[12] working with a group of 114 children, not newborn but borrowed from nursing mothers at a milk depot, placing them together in groups of two or more, and giving them toys, found the most various reactions disclosed in the unfamiliar situation. Some were embarrassed and inactive; others were openly delighted; some pounced upon the toys and paid no attention to the children; others explored the general environment; some robbed their companions of all the toys; others proffered, exchanged, or exhibited them; some were furious in the new situation, already, in the first year, positively negativistic. It is impossible to say to what degree these children had been conditioned by association with their mothers and how far the reactions were dispositional. But it is plain that by the end of the first year the most positive personality trends had been established. At this early age the experimenters think they distinguish three main personality types: the dominant, the amiable or humanitarian, and the exhibitionist, or producer.

The growth of interest in behavior, the appreciation of the volume of maladjustment, delinquency and crime, the realization that behavior

---

[11] Healy, Bronner, Baylor and Murphy: *Reconstructing Youthful Behavior: Problem Children in Foster Homes* (in press, Knopf), chap. 17.

[12] " Die ersten Sozialen Verhaltungsweisen des Kindes," *Sociologische und psychologische Studien über das erste Lebensjahr* (Quellen und Studien zur Jugendkunde, 1927), 1–102.

troubles originate at an early age level, that the schools have been inadequate in the control of the development of character and personality, that behavior is largely determined by the process of social interaction, the example of the work of Pavlov and Watson, and the experience of the child clinics, has led to the formation of a number of institutes for the more systematic and controlled study of the behavior of the child. In some of these programs nutrition, physical growth, mental norms and mental development, the establishment of norms for the pre-school levels, etc., have been emphasized, but there has been a growing tendency to concentrate on the study of mental and emotional factors and behavior expressions as conditioned by social relationships, and our discussion of the work of these institutes will center about this approach.

All of these institutes have nursery schools under their control, where young children are available both for controlled experiment and for observation of their spontaneous individual and group activities, and there is opportunity to study individual differences and changes in social behavior as related to the situations in which the behavior occurs, and the further possibility of behavioristic experimentation on the sociological plane through the process of varying the situations.

The most outstanding work of this type has been done at Minneapolis (Institute of Child Welfare) under Anderson and Goodenough. They have at present two main projects under way, a controlled and an observational study. The controlled study (by Marjorie Walker) is a direct outgrowth of the work of Charlotte Bühler, which we have just mentioned, but with better experimental conditions.

The original plan was to make a study of the social interaction in young children with regard to domination and subordination as these aspects of behavior were shown in the nursery school situation, particularly in the undirected play period. It was found, however, that interference by the nursery school teachers in many of the situations of domination and subordination was too frequently necessary to permit this method to give any valid results on this particular problem. So an experimental situation was set up, designed to overcome these difficulties and at the same time be as natural a situation as possible for the children. The experiment was carried on in a small room, bare of furnishings, with a screened window at the back where an observer could watch without consciousness on the part of the children. The children were never, during the whole process of the study, given to understand that they were having anything more than a play period; there was never any experiment-consciousness on their part. Fourteen children were selected for this experiment during the first year, seven boys and seven girls, all in the same age group, and more children were added during the second year. The children were taken to the room, two at a time, and told that there would be some particularly exciting toy there. Everything was done to arouse their anticipation, and great efforts made to have this anticipation realized through having the toys of an interesting and unusual sort. The two children were left alone with one toy in the room. This situation, two children and one toy, no adults around, was designed to produce conflict. The unseen observer recorded the behavior, in specified categories, every five seconds during a six-minute period. A record was made for each child in terms of his behavior as directed towards securing the toy — whether he screamed, pleaded, bargained, threatened, pulled it away deliberately, slapped, pinched or pulled the other child, or relinquished the toy passively; in terms of the type of domination of the successful child, after the outcome of the conflict, i.e., whether he played with the toy alone, controlled it but let the other child participate, or controlled it but let the other child have his turn or share it, and in terms of the unsuccessful child's reactions; in terms of the subsequent behavior of both children — whether the dominant child relinquished the toy, and, if so, whether he still directed the activity, whether either child made a suggestion, and whether it was accepted or rejected by the other child. The fourteen children were paired in all possible combinations, and each combination was given the experiment three times, with three different toys.

The results from this study are not yet worked up for publication, but the method has been validated, and it seems that interesting and consistent behavior differences are shown as between the different children. In two behavior charts it is shown that one of these children used pleading as behavior directed towards securing the toy over two hundred times, the other child not ten times, but the latter child used commanding about as often as the former used pleading. When we consider the great number of combinations from which these computations came, the consistency of behavior is amazing. The pleading child pleaded consistently, whatever other child he happened to be with; the commanding child commanded all other children.

The observational study (by Mildred Parten) is on " The Rôle of Socialization and of the Formation of Social Groups among Pre-School Children " and has extended over two years. The first year included all the forty children in the nursery school. The observation was made during the free play hour, at which time there is a minimum of restriction put on the activities of the children. The procedure consisted in observing each child for one minute each day during this period, rotating the time. The recording included the name of the child, the number of children playing in his group, if there was a group. The child's participation or lack of it in the group activity was recorded under the following headings: Unoccupied (not playing with anything or anybody, and seemingly concerned with nothing); Independent or isolated play; Parallel activity (in a group where others are doing the same thing); Onlooker; Supplementary activity (no organization of activity around any material end, but each child contributing physical or mental effort); and Coöperative play, which included imaginative play and dramatization. If the child was in a group, his type of participation was further noted as to whether he was directing or being directed by others, whether there was a reciprocal relationship, whether he was talking, etc. The interesting thing about this study is the consistency of behavior patterns resulting from these one-minute observations. When the observations were numbered serially and the odd minutes correlated with the even minutes, the coefficient was found to run as high as .9. Here, as in the other study, the individual differences noted are consistent, and give interesting behavior patterns. One child, for instance, talked 90% of the time, another not at all. It was found that a given child participating in play actively with all the other members of the group successively might be leading or dominating in 95% of the situations, whereas another child, under the same conditions, was in the leading position only 5% of the time. That is, within a constant period one child is getting twenty times as much practice in meeting social situations in a given way as a second child.[13] We have here a type of organization of behavior where not only the lack of practice but the habit of subordination will have the most far-reaching consequences in the development of efficiency and personality. Observations will now be undertaken on the effect of the alteration of the composition of groups with the object of giving the less dominant children opportunity to assume

[13] Anderson, John E.: " The Genesis of Social Reactions in the Young Child," in *The Unconscious: A Symposium* (Knopf, 1927), 81.

more important rôles. There is also further testing of this method by observing each child during a long period and comparing this observation with a composite of the one-minute observations.

In the work recently begun at the Institute of Child Welfare Research in Teachers College, Columbia University (Helen T. Woolley, Director, Ruth Andrus, Acting Director), the emphasis has been largely on the development of techniques for the objective recording and study of the behavior of children in groups, and the relation of this behavior to factors of individual and situational differences. As a preliminary to the study of the social behavior of the children, ordinary " diary records " and " personality studies " were utilized. Records of this sort were made on the nursery school children during their various activities. They were found to be valuable as giving a general picture of the varieties of behavior of children in groups, but valueless as materials for objective analysis. Even when these records were made strictly in terms of overt behavior, they were found to be highly impressionistic and dependent upon the idiosyncrasies of the observer. It was found, however, that if complex behavior were split up into certain of its elements, and these elements were in terms of overt acts, almost any observer could record the occurrence of a particular element and this record would correspond to the simultaneous record of the same element taken by other observers.

This led to a number of experiments for testing the validity of techniques (under the direction of Dorothy S. Thomas) and the following procedure is one of the most promising. Floor plans were drawn of the roof and indoor playrooms where the nursery school children spend the first two hours of the day in relatively " free " (in the sense of minimally directed) play activities. In all these rooms, there is a variety of objects, some of which are large and stationary, e.g., jungle-gym, swings, sand-pile, piano, platform and steps, etc.; others may change from day to day, but remain stationary during any particular day, e.g., rabbit cage, box on which nails are hammered, slide, etc.; others are carried about by the children at will, e.g., blocks, doll-carriages, kiddie-kars, and innumerable small toys. The larger, immovable objects are indicated on the floor plans. Records each week have been obtained of the activities of each child of the lower age group by tracing his progress on these floor plans over a five-minute period. Every stop that he made was indicated, and timed, in seconds, with a stop-watch. His approach to and contact with other persons, adults or children, was noted by appropriate symbols, as likewise the contact or approach of other people towards him. Spontaneous activity was indicated, as was also " directed " activity. The time any particular object was in his possession was shown by indicating when he picked it up, and when he dropped it.

Each of these records was made simultaneously by two of four investigators. So far as possible, the selection of a particular child for a particular observation was made by rotation. The investigators worked in every possible combination of pairs. The records which have been obtained on these children are being analyzed as follows, in order that the technique may be evaluated for further work. The consistencies of the various observers with each other are worked up, both with regard to the records of time (as spent by the child on various activities) and the records of gross activity (total amount of space covered). A test of the " validity " of the activity records will be made. The records are being analyzed for consistencies or individual differences between the children themselves. Do these five-minute samplings give consistent behavior patterns, when a sufficient number are taken? The answer to this question can only be indicated, since there are as many as twenty records on only sixteen of the children. This is enough, however, to indicate patterns if they truly exist. It is planned to test, further, how these five-minute records scattered over a period of time compare with records on the same children taken consecutively for, say, a two-hour period. It is not expected that the records now taken will yield results that will show much regarding the social or group behavior of the children, but if the techniques work out satisfactorily they will be applied to the same group of children another year, and also to a new group just entering the nursery school. The records seem to indicate that personality differences in social behavior will emerge from such a study.

Another study on social behavior is being made which is closely related to the study by Miss Parten at Minneapolis. The technique here calls for the recording of every social grouping occurring during a given period, i.e., every time two or more children are together. The time each child comes to and leaves the group is indicated. If possible, the " function " or part played by each child in the group is also indicated briefly, and a check is placed by the child who has initiated the group, if this is obvious. Probably the only data available for statistical purposes are those indicating the time spent by each child in a group, which will make possible the computation of an index of group participation for each child.

On the theory that laughter has a large element of the social in it, a study has also been made of the laughter situations in the nursery school. On a specially prepared blank, every laughter situation is recorded, with the names of the children in the group where the laughter occurred, and checks indicating which of the children " exposed " responded by laughing or smiling. Because of the interest inherent in this study of laughter, it is being made on three separate age groups. Thus, in addition to a laughter index (percentage of laughter to exposure) for each of the nursery school children, which will be used in comparison with the other social data, there is a genetic study of laughter in young children. Several thousand situations have been recorded, and these have been analyzed in their relation to chronological age, mental age, and other variables.

Another study dealing with a phase of social psychology is concerned with the physical contacts of the various children. Data have been obtained which show the relative involvement of each child as the " subject " or active person in physical contacts (under such categories as hits, pulls, pushes, caresses, etc.) and as passive or the " object " of these contacts. The observations cover 180 minutes for each child, the results are highly reliable, and the behavior patterns evolving from the study are consistent and interesting.

These studies, described above, are concerned with various elements in group behavior. The number of children involved in the studies is too small (20 to 50), and the number of observations on each child too limited, to give any adequate study of social behavior. They will be sufficient, however (running from several hundred to several thousand), on the individual studies, to make possible an evaluation of techniques and indicate possible interrelationships.

In chapter I (p. 78) we recorded an amazing difference in behavior of children in the home and the nursery school — defiant, destructive, negativistic behavior in the home and relatively orderly behavior in the school. And in document 42 (p. 88) we had the record of a surprising amount of maladjustment in homes. Some studies have been undertaken from this standpoint, and also with reference to determining how far children may be conditioned by the behavior and habits of their parents. At the Institute of Psychology, Yale University (Arnold Gesell, Director), an investigator spends a whole day once a month in the home of a child and the child is brought to the clinic another day in the month. Thus records of various categories of behavior are obtained in the two situations. At the Teachers College Institute data are being collected on the home backgrounds and social settings, which have so far included records kept every day for a week by about two-thirds of the parents indicating time spent on various social and " cultural " activities and frequencies of such activities. These are giving rough indexes of the social participation of the parents, which are to be compared with the various indexes of social behavior of the children.

At St. George's School for Child Study, University of Toronto, a study of the behavior of the children is being made (under the direction of E. A. Bott and W. E. Blatz) in terms of six types of situation or " services " recurring each day: (1) admitting service, (2) washroom and toilet, (3) playroom and playground, (4) workshop, (5) dining-room, and (6) sleeping-room:

The temporal unity and growth in the life process is one of the most difficult points to take account of and portray systematically in the form of a longitudinal record. In segmenting the life adjustment process for purposes of study, as we do when dealing with the pre-school years, the importance of what has preceded and is to follow must not be forgotten. Moreover even within the daily round of a nursery school further division of periods or services becomes essential and incidents occurring in one service may carry over and affect behavior in another. In short the adjustment process is continuous whether the system of observation is or not.[14]

This research center has a much smaller nursery school than the others — a maximum capacity of only 16 children. A large number of observations have, however, been made on these children in the six situations named. Our concern is with the observations of the " play activities," since this is the period when spontaneous social activity is best observed because least restricted:

---

[14] Blatz, W. E., Chant, N., and Bott, H. (edited by E. A. Bott): " Observation and Training of the Fundamental Habits in Young Children." Manuscript. To be published in *Genetic Psychology Monographs* (June, 1928).

Undirected observations were kept which were carefully analyzed to discover the more readily recordable uniformities in play behavior; next *directed* observations were accumulated in terms of these type reactions in order to test their utility as working concepts; the organization of these results then provided material for a further critique of our procedure before continuing with more extended observations. [9 children are studied: 3 in each age group, 2–3, 3–4, and 4–5 years]. . . .

[From diary records] three types seemed to be clearly indicated: that the child was occupied with (1) the *materials* used in his play, (2) the *adults* in charge in the school, (3) the other children with whom he played.[15]

[The method used was to follow a given child for a period of time, indicating] under the section on *material* (1) the clock time at which a child took a given toy, (2) the name of the toy, (3) what he did with it, (4) the total time to the nearest whole minute that he was occupied with that toy. . . . Our earlier data [on *relations with adults*] had shown that this relationship could conveniently be divided into sub-types and five such categories were selected for trial . . . as follows: Child Asserts, i.e., calls attention to himself; Child Negates, i.e., asks for help or otherwise assumes an attitude of dependence; Child Resists, a special form of assertion but classed separately because of its peculiar interest and frequent occurrence; Adult Stimulates — incites the child to action; Adult Restrains — checks the child in some attempted action. . . .

In the final section relations with other children were entered in the manner shown on the specimen sheet. Here five categories were again selected . . . : (1) Talking, (2) Watching, (3) Interference, (4) Imitation, (5) Coöperation. [An indication was also made as to whether the activity was directed by or towards the child under observation]. . . . Having completed our trial records and training of observers during October and November 1926, the winter months were utilized upon indoor play. As a first study each child was observed on five separate play periods, at irregular intervals and by different workers, extending over December and January. These data were then organized and a second similar set of five indoor occasions was taken for each child during February and March as nearly as possible at weekly intervals. These two bodies of data offered interesting comparisons and the results were finally

---

[15] " The distinction is virtually between persons and things, i.e., social relationships versus those with materials. Our subdivision of the social contacts into those with adults and with other children was an obvious step under the circumstances but is in no sense fundamental simply on the score of age difference because the distinctions which go with age difference apply also among the children themselves in the case of a mixed group such as we had. To distinguish responses made to adults from those to other children, however, seemed worth while as a beginning."

combined for norms regarding the use of toys. The following autumn, October and November, five observation periods for each child on the playground were completed; these outdoor observations were utilized in addition to the indoor for data upon the span of attention. . . .

Our reporting of social activities was incomplete for various reasons. Since three observers dealt only with one child each, the whole group was never covered in one period and considerable time elapsed between the reports for a given child. Absence and variations in behavior due to the time element alone complicated the results. For an adequate picture of social relations in play behavior a record for each child every day which could be combined for the group would seem to be a better procedure. As regards the relations of children with adults this could easily be obtained by assigning one observer for each teacher to cover her relations with all children. But a full record of relations among children is less easy to secure.[16]

The gross frequencies of different types of social activity were found to be as follows:

Relations among Children		*Relations with Adults*	
Talking	406	Child asserts	613
Interference	201	Child resists	16
Watching	111	Child negates	103
Imitation	70		
Coöperation	47		732
		Adult stimulates	471
		Adult restrains	229
			700

While our major interest had been to dissect play into responses to individuals and to materials it was at once evident that all forms of play response were conditioned by the limits of the child's attention. The recorded duration of play incidents may offer some measure of this factor, on the assumption that the length of time a child overtly occupies himself on a unit undertaking is an index of his capacity to attend.

In the determination of times we accepted that, if a child interrupted his activity, e.g., to take another toy, to watch or participate in the activities of other children, this should count as a break in his attention provided the distraction exceeded one minute in length. If he returned to his previous occupation after one minute or longer, this was counted as a new incident, if in less than one minute it was counted as a continuation of his former activity.[17]

---

[16] Blatz, W. E., Chant, N., and Bott, H.: *op. cit.*
[17] Blatz, W. E., Chant, N., and Bott, H.: *op. cit.*

This method, of course, did not take into account the number and variety of responses a child might make. It gave results that the investigators themselves considered unsatisfactory, as evidenced by the following statement:

The main difficulties in timing social responses are: (a) their frequent circularity, brevity and rapidity, (b) overlapping, e.g., talking and imitation may coincide in whole or in part, (c) differentiation, e.g., a momentary occurrence such as accusation by one child of another may be judged profoundly to affect the subsequent play behavior of both so that an arbitrary time unit (viz., one minute) is rendered meaningless as an objective record of the duration of the incident. Moreover the social contacts and conversation of young children are largely of this fragmentary type. In short, social relationships which may overtly be inconspicuous and hard to delineate seem to be powerful in affecting the integration or disintegration of the behavior continuum; in this sense they are the beginnings of a more complex and significant adjustment process than is play with toys. How best objectively to analyze the play continuum in its social aspect is the question.[18]

In Iowa less attention has been paid to socio-psychological investigations than to studies of physical and mental development. Marston's study on "The Emotions of Young Children" (considered in detail in chapter IX) contains a large element of the social. His experiment includes the observation of the child's resistance to a new social situation and corresponds somewhat to Miss Walker's experiment in Minneapolis, but in Marston's experiment the same adult was used with each child, while Miss Walker's report gives a much more complete picture of social reactions, since it includes each child's response to every other child.

In Iowa, also, Ethel Verry made a study of the free play activities in terms of social behavior:

The attempt to unravel the complex design of a personality and discover the nature of the threads which are woven into its pattern, whether these prove to be innate or acquired, is a fascinating line of research; and the loosely knit personalities of pre-school children seem especially to invite such study. During a two-year period, the writer worked closely with two groups of young children in a pre-school laboratory, a situation which offered an excellent opportunity for the study of personality. Recently, sociologists have been pointing out the fallacy of isolating a personality from its social setting and studying it as a

---

[18] Blatz, W. E., Chant, N., and Bott, H.: *op. cit.*

self-contained unit; and they have been directing attention to the importance of status, the social rôle of the individual, his position in the group or groups of which he is a member, in determining his personality. . . . It was with the methodology of such studies in mind that the writer undertook to observe and record the play activities of two groups of pre-school children. Differences in personality were noted as they were expressed in undirected play; then the children were visited in their homes and their parents were interviewed in order to discover whether there were differences in the social experiences of the children corresponding to their personality differences.[19]

The two play groups were organized under the direction of the Iowa Child Welfare Research Station, as a means of providing a laboratory for the study of pre-school children. The younger group was made up of children between the ages of two and three years, the other group of four and five year olds. An attractive play room was furnished for them, and their daily program included stories, music, and occasional formal games, as well as the periods of undirected play during which most of the observations on personality were made. Especial precautions were taken to leave the children as free as possible from supervision and direction during these periods. Usually the writer and an attendant were the only adults in the room, and the children soon learned not to expect attention during free-play.[20]

This study was much more in the nature of ordinary diary-recording and " categories " were later formed from the mass of resulting materials:

At first the play of children two to four years old appears to present simply a mass of unrelated incidents, but it soon becomes evident that many of the social contacts are repeated from day to day in somewhat varied but similar forms. A careful analysis of these forms shows five clearly differentiated types of social attitudes for the data included in this study: (1) treating playmates as objects; (2) assuming an adult attitude; (3) seeking attention; (4) " doing as the others do "; and (5) coöperating with the group. . . . This five-fold classification distinguishes the immediate factors common to the experiences and dispositions of the children which determine certain more or less common modes of social behavior. The concrete expressions of these modes, such as the exact words used, or posture assumed, vary from child to child, and are, of course, explainable in the case of each individual child in terms of its individual

---

[19] Verry, Ethel E.: *A Study of Mental and Social Attitudes in the Free Play of Pre-School Children.* (Thesis for M.A. degree, State University of Iowa, 1923).

[20] Verry, Ethel E.: " A Study of Personality in Pre-School Play Groups," *Journal of Social Forces,* 3:645 (1925).

history. Such a classification points out certain roughly uniform causes which result in distinguishable types of behavior when young children first become members of play groups.[21]

Regarding social development, changes with age were noted, as follows:

[In the 3–4 age group as compared with the younger group] the number and complexity of coöperative activities increased noticeably. Although the five basic attitudes persisted, they seldom appeared in simple situations, but were complex in expression, and broke up into a variety of sub-classes. Individual children could to some extent be characterized by the predominance of one or two of these attitudes over the others. . . . It was possible to pick out characteristic types of response in each child . . . but to group the children as social or unsocial, while still possible, would have been more difficult than with the younger children.[22]

Several minor studies on social behavior are in progress at Iowa. One of these is an observational study of resistance, as related to the various nursery school situations, e.g., free play, relaxation period, eating period and sleeping period. Three-hour observations have been made on each of a small group of children and resistance recorded in terms of its " probable cause," e.g., element of strangeness, activity elements, resistance to suggestion and resistance to thwartings. Another study is on a group of children observed simultaneously from the point of view of what they " want," or seem to want, and conversely, what they seem not to want, or to resist.

At the Bureau of Educational Experiments in New York a full day's diary record is taken of each child each month. In some cases these records have extended over two years. L. D. Anderson is analyzing them into categories in terms of the social behavior of each child.

There has been an attempt, also, to use the psychological test situation as a means of studying the reactions of young children to persons and to things. These test situations have been found to open up rich fields for the study of personality differences of this sort, to show the reactions of the child to an adult whose procedure is consistent from one

[21] Report of Miss Verry's work in Baldwin and Stecher: *Psychology of the Pre-School Child* (1925), 243.

[22] *Ibid.*, 247.

child to another, to give an index of " social resistance," etc. Interesting differences can be studied in the reactions to the Binet tests, involving language, and to the performance tests, involving a minimum of language.

At Minneapolis, in addition to a number of studies which have been made on the relation of the intelligence of the child to various factors, such as nursery school training, parents' occupations, education of parents, order of birth, etc., some attention has been paid to these social factors. Goodenough has noted the effects of emotional attitudes upon intelligence test performance, in her study of the Kuhlman-Binet tests.[23] At the time of testing, ratings were made on each of the children involved in her experiments on various behavior manifestations. There were 300 children, two, three and four years old, who were tested under standard conditions and retested after an interval of 4 to 7 weeks. Ratings were made at the time of the tests on the basis of overt behavior, on shyness, negativism and distractibility. With regard to shyness, the basis of this rating is described as follows:

A rating of 3 [was given] to those children who, on being first brought to the examining room, cried or clung tightly to the mother, refused to look at toys or to speak, and in whom some residual effect of the initial reaction, indicated by mydriasis of pupils, tendency to whisper responses, unwillingness to have mother leave the room or anxiety as to her whereabouts if she did so, persisted throughout the examination. A rating of 2 was given to children who required more than the usual time to adjust to the situation in the beginning, but who showed no indications of real fear, and who, once the preliminary adjustments had been made, talked freely, did not object to having the mother leave the room, and in whom no residual effect of the initial behavior could be observed thereafter. Children who came to the examining room readily without the mother, or who were willing to have the mother leave the room within a moment or two, and who appeared entirely at ease throughout the tests were given a rating of 1.[24]

Ratings in similar terms were made for negativism and distractibility. There were found to be rather slight but consistently positive correlations existing between changes in IQ and changes in the ratings of both shyness and negativism, the coefficients of correlation averaging .4

---

[23] *The Kuhlman-Binet Tests for Children of Preschool Age: A Critical Study and Evaluation* (1928).
[24] *Ibid.*, 105–6.

in both cases. There was no significant correlation between changes in the distractibility ratings and changes in IQ.

A comprehensive study in this field is now being made at the Institute of Child Welfare Research at Teachers College.[25] The total test situation is being studied, with a view to determining the relation of various elements in the " incidental " behavior of the children to their general social behavior, their performance on the tests, etc. The original plan was to have a student concealed behind a curtain in the testing room during each test situation. This student was supposed to record all " incidental " behavior and conversation on the part of both examiner and child. It was expected that this material could then be analyzed in terms of resistance, amount of praise demanded by and given to each child, etc. A check-up on this procedure, however, revealed the difficulties inherent in the taking of diary records. It was impossible for the student to record all the behavior and conversation. The resulting selection turned out to be quite different for two students recording simultaneously. A test situation was set up in which two of the investigators acted as examiner and subject respectively, and the reliability of the various students and the stenographers of the Institute, as well, was tested. The " incidental " behavior and conversation were carefully planned and acted out by the examiner and subject, and the errors of the students and stenographers referred to this standard. It was found that two of the stenographers were exceptionally able to record the conversation accurately, and that the students could record specific behavior elements. The two stenographers were, therefore, incorporated into the set-up, and the plan changed as follows: A stenographer and student were concealed behind the curtain during each examination. The stenographer recorded conversation and the general setting. The student recorded the name of each test, the child's reaction time in taking up materials or responding verbally, each instance of resistance on the part of the child, each instance of demanding a new material, each instance of praise or encouragement on the part of the examiner. These materials are making possible several analyses: (1) A special study of resistance. This includes an analysis of the tests resisted in the total test situation, and the individual tests resisted, whether specific resistances were above or below the mental age level, the relation to the preceding test. It includes also an analysis of the specific manifestations

---

[25] Under the direction of D. S. Thomas and J. F. Nelson.

of resistance on the part of the child, and the handling of the situation on the part of the examiner. The data obtained in this way are compared with ratings made by the nursery school teachers on resistance in the nursery school situation. (2) An analysis of the data on the technique of establishing and maintaining rapport during the psychological examination. This includes analysis of all incidental behavior and conversation on the part of both examiner and child, and involves a study of actual test procedure, i.e., when and how the regular order of tests is varied. In its treatment of rapport in situations involving resistance it overlaps the previous study. (3) An analysis of the amount of praise given by the examiner in relation to the test situation, the individual tests, the mental age level, etc. (4) A study of the reaction time of the child to test material in terms of the response of the group as a whole to the tests, and also the reaction time of all the cases to each part of the tests. Included in this study is an analysis of the relations of individual reaction time to IQ, chronological age and mental age.

This group of studies deals with the relation of the individual child to a fairly well-controlled situation. It shows his reaction to an adult, whose behavior is more or less standardized, to the materials involved in the situation, and to the total situation of adult and materials. The data obtained from this group are on the same children as those obtained in the study of the general social situations mentioned above, and the interrelations of the two sets of data are being worked out.

At the Institute for Juvenile Research in Chicago a study has been made on the resistant behavior of young children in the psychological test situation. These tests were given under relatively unfavorable (" unstandardized ") conditions. The results and conclusions are summarized as follows:

A study of the " resistance " during mental testing was made for seven groups of infants and children in five County Fairs. The criterion for classification was the number of tests taken. Those who could not be induced to take one test of any series were classified in Group I (complete resistance); one or more but not all of any series, in Group II (partial resistance); all tests, in Group III. Nine hundred and eighty-three infants and children were classified in these groups by three examiners working independently. The results were fairly uniform for each group. They were not materially affected by changes made in the technic of testing, by using new tests, by different examiners, or by change in locality. A small group of sixteen used as a control, tested with a new series of tests, in a nursery, and over a longer interval of time, gave practically the same findings. This resistance . . . occurs very frequently for age and sex in a fairly uniform way. It first appears as measured by the method indicated at six months, gradually rises to a high point from which it falls gradually to a low level at 54 months. This high point of resistance for males is highest at 30 months; for females at 18 months. The resistance in the latter group is higher than the males at every age group studied except 30. At 30 months, some form of resistance measured by the test criterion occurred in a majority of cases.

[Conclusion]. The manifestation of resistance by infants and children during mental tests is evidence of some innate behavior pattern. It is typically pronounced at 18 to 23 months in females, and at 30 to 35 months in males. It yields gradually with age in both sexes.[26]

Another important tendency in the study of social behavior centers around the study of language as a social index. This tendency had its impetus from the series of researches carried on at the Jean Jacques Rousseau Institute in Geneva, culminating in Piaget's study.[27] The first part of this study dealt with the complete record of the language of two six-year-old children over a period of a month:

Two of us followed each a child (a boy) for about a month at the morning class at the *Maison des Petits de l'Institut Rousseau*, taking down in minute detail and in its context every thing that was said by the child. In the class where our two subjects were observed the scholars draw or make whatever they like; they model and play at games of arithmetic and reading, etc. These activities take place in complete freedom; no check is put upon any desire that may manifest itself to talk or play together; no intervention takes place unless it is asked for. The children work individually or in groups, as they choose; the groups are formed and then break up again without any interference on the part of the adult; the children go from one room to another (modelling room, drawing room, etc.) just as they please without being asked to do any continuous work so long as they do not themselves feel any desire for it. In short, these school-rooms supply a first-class field of observation for everything connected with the study of the social life and of the language of childhood.[28]

[26] Levy, D. M., and Tulchin, S. H.: "Resistance of Infants and Children During Mental Tests," *Journal of Experimental Psychology*, 6:321–22 (1923).

[27] Piaget, J.: *The Language and Thought of the Child* (1926).

[28] *Ibid.*, 5.

The language of these two children was analyzed into two large classes, the egocentric and the socialized:

When a child utters phrases belonging to the first group, he does not bother to know to whom he is speaking nor whether he is being listened to. He talks either for himself or for the pleasure of associating anyone who happens to be there with the activity of the moment. This talk is ego-centric, partly because the child speaks only about himself, but chiefly because he does not attempt to place himself at the point of view of his hearer. Anyone who happens to be there will serve as an audience. . . . *Ego-centric speech* may be divided into three categories:

1. *Repetition* (*echolalia*): . . . This is a remnant of baby prattle, obviously devoid of any social character.

2. *Monologue:* The child talks to himself as though he were thinking aloud. He does not address anyone.

3. *Dual or collective monologue:* . . . The point of view of the other person is never taken into account; his presence serves only as a stimulus.

In *Socialized speech* we can distinguish:

4. *Adapted information:* Here the child really exchanges his thoughts with others, either by telling his hearer something that will interest him and influence his actions, or by an actual interchange of ideas by argument or even by collaboration in pursuit of a common aim.

Adapted information takes place when the child adopts the point of view of his hearer, and when the latter is not chosen at random. Collective monologues, on the other hand, take place when the child talks only about himself, regardless of his hearers' point of view, and very often without making sure whether he is being attended to or understood. . . .

5. *Criticism:* This group includes all remarks made about the behavior of others, but having the same character as adapted information; in other words, remarks specified in relation to a given audience. . . .

6. *Commands, requests* and *threats.* . . .

7. *Questions.* . . .

8. *Answers.*[29]

The analysis of the language of these two children gives a very interesting result from the point of view of socialized behavior. Piaget computes the proportion of egocentric speech to the total of other spontaneous forms of language (excluding the category of answers) and finds the surprising proportions of .47 and .43 for these two children. He

---

[29] *Ibid.,* 9–10.

checked this " coefficient of egocentrism " by recording the conversations of 20 children between the ages 4 and 7, averaging 6 years:

> The subject of analysis will now be the verbatim report of conversations held, not by one or two specified children, but by the inmates of a whole room, in which they move about from one place to another and which they enter and leave at will. What has been taken down is really the outcome of observations made from a fixed place upon some twenty children on the move.[30]

An interesting confirmation of the coefficient of egocentrism for this age level was found in that the average coefficient for the twenty children was approximately the same as for the two children's language recorded by a different method, i.e., was .45. Piaget accepts this coefficient of egocentrism as an index of social development, and takes the somewhat arbitrary stand that the child becomes genuinely socialized to the extent of really communicating his thoughts between the ages 7 and 8, the age when the coefficient of egocentrism decreases to .25. Obviously, this method gives very interesting data on the social growth and behavior of children.

Several studies in the American institutes have been made as a direct outgrowth of Piaget's study. At the Merrill-Palmer School in Detroit (Edna White, Director), Lelah Crabbs has in progress a study of nine hours' consecutive language on the part of each of a group of children. Her results are giving data on the situations stimulating the child to speech and to action, on the interrelations of speech and action, and the effect of persons upon speech — whether the child's own group is more stimulating than an adult, etc. Activity is being measured by pedometers, and the correlations worked out between the number of words spoken and the number of movements made. A great range has been found both in language and in movements at the same age level, and apparently considerable correlation between the two.

At the Bureau of Educational Experiments a special study is being made of the language factor in social groupings and activities of children. There is a complete record of language for each child one day each month, and it is planned to make other records in connection with social situations.

The most comprehensive study of language is being made at the Institute in Minneapolis. Although this has as its main object a study of

---

[30] Piaget, J.: *The Language and Thought of the Child*, 50.

" The Development of Sentence Formation," the investigator, Dorothea McCarthy, is collecting much information of social importance. Her group of children consisted of 140, from 18 months to 4½ years old, 20 children at each age level of one-half year. The age groups were very carefully selected, so that the average for each group was twenty days before or after this half-year birthday. The group was also selected in such a way that the fathers' occupations were in direct proportion to the occupations of males in Minneapolis. Most of the children were taken from the control group used by the Institute, and all had been given one or more mental tests.

The procedure was to visit the home, taking several toys, which would establish rapport between the investigator and the child and present a standard situation for the reaction of the child. The objects presented were always the same, but the order of presentation was not kept constant, since the children varied in the ease with which they would react to the several toys. Fifty separate, consecutive responses were recorded for each child. The child was addressed as little as possible, but, if so, this was recorded also. The scoring system was a modification of Piaget's classification according to function. Egocentric responses were not common among these children, because the situation presented to them gave very little scope for egocentric response. So the classification was based almost entirely on what Piaget calls socialized speech. This classification follows:

1. Adapted information: The child exchanges ideas with the hearer. The response is directed towards some person.
  (a) Naming objects or toys; (b) Remarks about the immediate situation; (c) Remarks associated with the situation; (d) Irrelevant remarks.
2. Criticism of the actions and behavior of others or of the objects, e.g., toys broken.
3. All emotionally toned responses, such as threats, etc.
4. Questions.
5. Answers to direct questions.
6. Social phrases, such as Goodbye, Thank you, etc., which the child repeats like a parrot, i.e., which are automatic responses.
7. Dramatic imitation, i.e., the children imitate sounds made by animals (stimulated by the pictures in the books), or by adults (one of the toys, the toy telephone, particularly, called this out).

Many of the responses of the younger children were babbling — these were recorded phonetically as nearly as possible.

1. Incomprehensible vocalization: (a) Single sound; (b) Repetition of the same sound; (c) A series of varied sounds.
2. Semi-comprehensible vocalization, usually a keyword missing.

The results of this study will be published. Among the interesting results shown is that simple naming of objects decreases with age, remarks about the immediate situation increase with age, remarks associated with the situation appear relatively late and increase with age, and irrelevant responses occur equally at all age levels. The length of the response was found to correlate significantly with IQ, and very highly with the occupation of the father.

Another important type of study in the child research centers deals with the incidence of various kinds of behavior, particularly " undesirable " behavior, or behavior problems, among unselected groups of school children. These studies have been made both from the cross-sectional and the longitudinal approach. The two main studies in this field have been made at Minneapolis and Toronto. The Minneapolis study was a joint project of the Psycho-Education Clinic of the University, the Institute of Child Welfare, and the Minneapolis Child Guidance Clinic. A report on this project was made by M. E. Haggerty [31] and the data have been further analyzed by Willard C. Olson in a doctor's dissertation.[32]

The findings regarding 800 children were reported by Haggerty as follows:

Each teacher was asked to catalogue, according to a schedule provided, the frequency of occurrence of undesirable behavior in the life of each child in her room so far as such behavior had come to the teacher's knowledge . . . [and] each teacher was asked to rate on five-point scales the several children in her room as regards their standing on each of a list of 37 traits.[33]

Olson's study has included with the 800 children reported by Haggerty the first grade of 15 schools, the pre-school children at the Institute of Child Welfare, and a junior high school, making a total

---

[31] Haggerty, M. E.: " The Incidence of Undesirable Behavior in Public-School Children," *Journal of Educational Research*, 12:102–22 (1925).

[32] Submitted to the University of Minnesota in June, 1927, and to be published.

[33] Haggerty, M. E.: *op. cit.*, 104.

of 2,867 children. His definition of "behavior problem" is made as follows:

No attempts have been made at a standardized terminology in the field. We shall use the term *behavior problem* to represent a discrepancy between the capacities of the individual to adjust on the one hand and the demands of his environment on the other. It follows that the question of what constitutes a behavior problem is dependent upon the environmental demands as well as the reaction possibilities — innate and acquired — of the individual. For a workable definition we must accept as a behavior problem any activity which is objected to by a social group — home, school, or community. A *problem child* is a child manifesting one or more behavior problems.[34]

The results obtained were generally consistent with those of Haggerty's report. Olson is now making a study of nervous habits among public school children. He first went through the clinical literature, and made a list of these habits, which were of such a nature that they could be categorically defined and readily observed. He found fifty-six such habits, and grouped them in several large groups according to geographical location, i.e., oral, genital, etc. He is trying to relate these habits to a variety of factors, and has about 800 cases. His preliminary results show that children who are behavior problems, children of neurotic parents, undernourished children, show a preponderance of these nervous habits. Intelligence is apparently not a factor of any importance. He is investigating the importance of the factor of imitation in the etiology of these nervous habits, and hopes to do something on their physical basis, e.g., their relation to metabolism indexes:

[Analysis of these records showed that] behavior of an undesirable character appeared more or less frequently in 51 per cent of the entire group. . . . As might have been anticipated, *Disinterest in school work* shows the highest frequency and it is closely followed by *Cheating, Unnecessary tardiness,* and *Lying,* while the more serious matters of *Stealing, Masturbation, Truancy,* and *Obscenity* appear the fewest times.[35]

Haggerty includes the following table which shows, in detail, the incidence of the various types of "undesirable" behavior among the 800 children:

---

[34] Olson, Willard C.: Thesis, 6.   [35] Haggerty, M. E.: *op. cit.,* 106.

TABLE I

Frequency of Occurrence of Several Types of Undesirable Behavior

Types of Undesirable Behavior	Number of Children Reported at Each Level of Occurrence				
	Has Never Occurred	Has Occurred Once or Twice but no More	Occasional Occurrence	Frequent Occurrence	Total Occurrence
Disinterest in school work	628	56	73	44	173
Cheating	660	84	42	15	141
Unnecessary tardiness	675	62	38	26	126
Lying	677	77	24	23	124
Defiance to discipline	714	40	29	18	87
Marked overactivity	726	14	27	34	75
Unpopular with children	738	23	18	22	63
Temper outbursts	749	18	24	10	52
Bullying	752	15	21	13	49
Speech difficulties	760	10	8	23	41
Imaginative lying	772	17	7	5	29
Stealing	779	13	4	5	22
Masturbation, suspected	780	9	6	6	21
Truancy	782	7	8	4	19
Obscene notes, talk, or pictures	792	5	1	3	9
Masturbation, actually known .	795	0	1	5	6 [36]

These studies at Minneapolis have dealt with the incidence of behavior problems at a given time in a specific school situation containing various ages, sexes, intelligence levels, etc. At Toronto the study of the incidence of behavior problems is emphasizing the longitudinal approach, i.e., following a number of the same individuals through their public school experience, with a view to exploring the possible changes in relation to various other developmental factors. The plan at Toronto calls for a five-year investigation. Up to the present the study has been concerned largely with developing techniques of recording varying degrees of "misbehavior." A public school representing a good cross-section, with a population of about 1,400 children (31 rooms), representing some 800 families, in a neighborhood where English is the language almost universally used, was selected for the study:

[36] Haggerty, M. E.: *op. cit.*, 107.

The teaching staff have been asked to devote a certain amount of their time to careful observations and the keeping of special records on forms prepared for the purpose, whilst the research staff has made a point of giving such assistance as they could in an advisory way to teachers who requested it. . . . Objective data are required and a continuous record for given children. It was hoped that from a school of fourteen hundred children at the end of five years complete records for perhaps three or four hundred could be obtained. Again, we hesitated to submit a list of behavior acts of our own choosing which might be framed from a standpoint unfamiliar to teachers or in phraseology they might misinterpret. Teachers know behavior first-hand, whatever terms they use to characterize it. . . . We decided to evolve our classification largely from the experience and vocabulary of the teachers in charge.

In order to avoid interpolating any preconceived ideas regarding " good " and " bad " behavior or any explanatory theories of the genesis of abnormal adjustments it was decided to make the study as purely objective as possible. With these ends in view the teaching staff were early gathered together and a general idea of the aims and possible results outlined in a short lecture. This began a series of meetings with the staff which recurred at intervals of about a month and still continue.[37]

The teachers of this school send in weekly reports to the research staff of all " misdemeanors " occurring among the children. The first part of the research program consisted in an attempt to objectify the concept of " misdemeanor." During a preliminary period of six months in 1925

the teachers were asked to refer to the research staff any case which they felt would benefit by a social investigation, psychological and psychiatric examination. A recommendation was then made concerning these cases and follow-up service arranged. From the data thus obtained, including the teachers' description of these sample cases, it was possible at the end of this period to compile a list of misdemeanors.[38]

The main headings under which misdemeanors were finally classified included:

1. Disobedience.
2. Disorder.
3. Dishonesty.

4. Lack of Application.
5. Personal Uncleanliness.
6. Indecencies.

---

[37] Blatz, W. E., and Bott, E. A.: " Studies in Mental Hygiene of Children. I. Behavior of Public School Children — A Description of Method," *Pedagogical Seminary*, 34:558-59 (1927).

[38] *Ibid.*, 560.

7. Emotional. 9. Damage to Property and Persons.
8. Irregularity. 10. Strappings.
11. Unclassified.

Each of these headings was further subdivided, e.g.:

1. Disobedience:
   (a) Petty — slow to respond — reluctant attitude — breaking minor rules of classroom.
   (b) Gross — deliberate refusal to obey commands — resistance to corporal punishment.
   (c) Writing notes.
   (d) Doing work other than prescribed — reading story books — doing homework during lesson.
   (e) Unreliability — general non-compliant attitude.
   (f) Forgetting notes and books.
   (g) Eating candy or fruit or chewing gum.[39]

The justification of this particular method of recording misdemeanors is made as follows:

The next step was to request the teachers in each class to keep a record of the misdemeanors which occurred in their classroom from day to day. A copy of the list was confidentially in the possession of each teacher for reference in recording misdemeanors by number and letter, the record being unintelligible to any one who had not the key. By the end of the year a complete record of the frequency with which any one child interrupted the routine of the classroom and the reason for such interruption would thus be available. This formed our basic raw data, which could readily be organized in various ways, according to grades, age, mentality, sex, etc., and compared with other variables. . . .

The form provides for the date, name of student, type of misdemeanor (by number and letter), with space to check whether the misdemeanor occurred before or after recess in the morning or afternoon. In the last column the teacher is expected to indicate her treatment of the interruption and, in a few words, the result of the measures so taken. This was an attempt to have the teacher formulate her theory or plan concerning treatment of behavior problems in her own class. It was thought by this means to derive a list of methods employed by teachers in the treatment of misbehaving students. And the success or limitations of these methods would be indicated according as future records showed cessation or repetition of the trouble. This would offer an

[39] Blatz, W. E., and Bott, E. A.: "Studies in Mental Hygiene of Children. I. Behavior of Public School Children — A Description of Method," *Pedagogical Seminary*, 34:562–63 (1927).

empirical evaluation of current methods and also of the teacher's judgment of the success or failure of these measures.

The use of a number and letter, signifying class and subheading of the misdemeanor, was a device which, in addition to the advantage of brevity, necessitated the teacher making a careful judgment as to what the particular act itself signified. In the investigation of the previous year it had been found that when a teacher reported behavior descriptively and others attempted to classify it the results were unreliable. Classification of behavior requires facility in crystallizing one's judgment, and because this analytical process is not easy until one has adopted a plan and become proficient in its use, a good many entries appeared at first in the " unclassified " category. To overcome this our revision included more headings under each of the larger categories and also introduced a separate category for the incidence of corporal punishment administered in the school and the reason therefor. This was necessary inasmuch as such punishment was usually meted out by the principal who did not have a class and so was not asked to hand in a weekly report.[40]

The advantage of this method is the continuity of record — the following of children through from class to class, showing the varying incidence from one grade to another with increasing age and mental age, and, perhaps most important, with regard to the changes in the personal situation, i.e., the teacher-pupil relationship. The unobjective nature of the categories of behavior, of course, introduces a tremendous error in this type of longitudinal study.

The authors admit the difficulties in the way of statistical treatment of their data. A most illuminating statement, for instance, is that " during the first year of observation roughly about 40% of the children were not reported for any kind of misdemeanor; with more accurate and systematic recording this figure dropped to approximately 15% in the following year." [41] A variation as great as this must lead to considerable doubt as to the objective nature of the misdemeanors recorded. Many of the " categories " in which the misdemeanors are classified are not in terms of overt behavior, e.g., under " disobedience " as indicated above, such classifications as " reluctant attitude," " unreliability," etc., can readily be conceived as increasing or decreasing according to the teacher's state of mind rather than on any objective basis. Indeed, we may assume that the schedule is devised with a view to measuring the behavior of the teachers quite as much as that of the pupils.

The summary of results, as presented up to the present, is as follows:

---

[40] *Ibid.*, 564–66.   [41] *Ibid.*, 569, footnote.

1. This study presents an attempt to enumerate and later evaluate in an objective manner the behavior of children in a particular social environment, i.e., the public school. The study is organized in parallel with other allied researches which furnish additional knowledge of the situation.

2. The detail of the technique employed for behavior study is elaborated. . . .

3. The frequency of the types of misdemeanors, as classified, is given for the eight grades in the school. The number falls off markedly in the higher grades but at different rates for the various misdemeanors.

4. The number of misdemeanors reported is greater for boys than for girls.

5. The frequency is not closely related to chronological age, the greatest number appearing between ages seven and nine.

6. The frequency of misdemeanors varies inversely with the Intelligence Quotient for boys but not for girls.

7. The data for succeeding years will be analyzed along similar lines in order to present a fuller and more accurate picture of the facts than is possible in this initial stage of the project.[42]

Up to this point we have noticed the behavior of the child mainly in relatively restricted situations — the family and the school. But the family and the school are themselves within other and larger situations — neighborhoods, communities, geographical localities, containing a great variety and disparity of values and stimulations — playgrounds, libraries, settlements, boys' clubs, moving pictures, dance halls, cabarets, gang organizations, etc., and it is desirable to study the contacts of the individual with this congeries of situations and to measure the totality of their influence on his behavior.

Working on the problem of regional differences Park and Burgess and a group of associated sociologists in Chicago are studying the character and composition of urban regions with a view to measuring the social growth of cities and the behavior of individuals as related to regional influences. As a preliminary step the city of Chicago was divided into 500 areas, corresponding to the 500 census tracts of the city, and studies were undertaken to measure the effect on the community of radical expansion:

The center of every city, or the point of dominance in urban growth, is the downtown business district; in Chicago, the loop. As business and light manu-

---

[42] Blatz, W. E., and Bott, E. A.: "Studies in Mental Hygiene of Children. I. Behavior of Public School Children — A Description of Method," *Pedagogical Seminary*, 34:581 (1927).

facturing expand into the residential district surrounding it, there appears a zone in transition, the so-called slum of every English and American city. The skilled worker and his family depart from this area as it deteriorates, and build up the zone of workingmen's homes, not too far away, of course, from the factories in which he works. The professional and clerical groups employed in the downtown offices live still farther out, while those who can afford it and who prize suburban life escape to the commuters' zone. . . . The loop is the business, civic, social work, and cultural center. The zone in transition in Chicago, as in other cities, holds in their most intense and concentrated form the social problems of the city: bad housing, poverty, vice, and crime. It is an area in which flourishes all that is picturesque and arresting in the modern cities: Hobohemia, immigrant colonies like the Ghetto, Greektown, Little Sicily, Bohemia, the Moody Bible Institute, cabarets, and spiritualistic halls. The zone of workingmen's homes is the area of second settlement for the immigrant well on the way to Americanization, already aspiring to enter the residential zone of single family dwellings and apartment houses of the native-born American. . . .

Having worked out this general description of radial expansion, interest at once turns to a feasible method of measuring this process and its effects upon community life. The suggestion was made by Professor Robert E. Park that it would be desirable to work out gradients in city growth. By gradient is meant the rate of change of a variable condition like poverty, or home ownership, or births, or divorce, from the standpoint of its distribution over a given area.[43]

Working then from spot maps along a selected radial on the relation of these areas to behavior, it was found that the incidence of poverty, divorce, delinquency, crime, etc., in the business and slum areas was very heavy and was graduated toward the residential districts:

In the boy-delinquency rate, where the boy population 11–17 years is taken as the base, the most striking differences are obtained as from 443 per 1,000 in the first mile unit, 58 in the second mile, 27 in the third mile, 15 in the fourth mile, 4 in the fifth mile, and none in either the sixth or seventh mile. Note particularly the figures for the first two ¼-mile units of the central business district, where over half the boys were brought into the juvenile court in an 18 months' period.

From the standpoint of the determination of gradients in urban expansion, these figures on boy delinquency, at least for the first four 1-mile unit districts, are very interesting.[44]

---

[43] Burgess, Ernest W.: "The Determination of Gradients in the Growth of the City," *Proceedings of the American Sociological Society for* 1926:178.
[44] *Ibid.*, 181.

Shaw, another representative of this group, is now working out for the Juvenile Research Institute the details of juvenile delinquency from this standpoint for the whole city, and the following are passages from a preliminary paper:

The decided concentration of delinquents in certain areas of the city, the geographical localization of certain kinds of delinquencies, the extremely high frequency of instances of stealing by groups of two or more boys (91 per cent of 6,466 unselected instances of stealing involved two or more participants), and the large number of cases in which the influence of older and more experienced offenders appears as an important factor are findings which seem to reflect community influence. At present, our knowledge of community influences consists of little more than such general impressions as the foregoing ones. There is, therefore, urgent need for a more objective method to evaluate community factors in relation to the development of delinquent careers.

In our general study of male juvenile delinquents in Chicago, we have found that the rate of delinquency is in many respects a valuable quantitative device for studying the community background of the delinquent. This rate is simply the percentage of male juvenile delinquents in the total male population between 10 and 16 years of age, computed upon the basis of the mile-square unit area. It is the purpose of this paper to briefly illustrate the application of this method to the study of male juvenile delinquency.

The first step in the computation of the rate of delinquency was to make a spot map showing the distribution of places of residence of the 9,243 [45] alleged delinquents (10–16 years of age) who were brought into the thirty-seven police stations of Chicago during 1926. The cases in each square-mile area were counted and tabulated. From the Local Community Research Committee of the University of Chicago, which had previously tabulated the 1920 federal census population data of Chicago by one-quarter-mile tracts, we obtained the total 10–16 year male population in each of the 499 tracts of the city. These data were then tabulated by mile-square areas. Thus, having tabulated the number of delinquents and the total 10–16 male population, the rate of delinquency was computed for each of the 181 mile-square areas of the city.

The rate of delinquency, computed by geographical units of uniform size, provided an objective basis for the comparative study of the number of arrested juvenile offenders living in different areas. When such comparison was made (see Map I) it was discovered that a disproportionately large number of delinquents were living in the areas immediately surrounding the Loop — the central business district of Chicago. In these areas approximately 37 per cent of the males between 10 and 16 years of age were brought into police stations on delinquent complaints during 1926. It was found also that the

---

[45] Number of boys involved in 18,916 arrests.

rate progressively decreases toward the boundary of the city, ranging from 37.0, in the areas contiguous to the Loop, to less than 1.0 in the areas near the

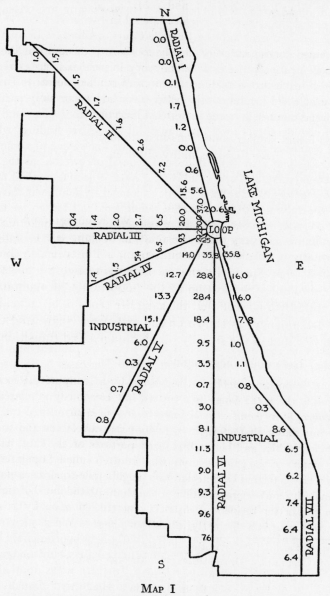

MAP I

RATE OF MALE JUVENILE DELINQUENCY BY SQUARE-MILE AREAS
ALONG LINES RADIATING FROM LOOP

city limits. The rate was found to be relatively high in areas adjacent to such industrial properties as the Union Stockyards and the steel mills of South Chicago (see Map I, radials V, VI, and VII).

The rate of delinquency has been computed in two large series of cases of male delinquents brought into the Juvenile Court of Chicago. In each of these series the rates correspond very closely to those presented on Map I. The decided concentration of cases of delinquency in particular areas of the city, as revealed in each of the three series of cases studied, seems to suggest the probability of a close relationship between certain community backgrounds and the formation of delinquent patterns of behavior.[46]

Burgess found similar conditions in a small city (12,000 population). From one ward three times as many children (per population) were in court as in any other ward and, estimated on the basis of court appearances during a period of two years, half the children in this ward would have been in court between the years of five and seventeen.[47]

In his volume on the gang to which we have referred frequently, Thrasher has made very plain the relation of gang life to delinquency and eventually to crime, and the same point is illustrated in the passage just quoted from Shaw. In the accompanying figure (p. 549) from Thrasher's volume the location of the important Chicago gangs is indicated, and it will be seen that the gang life tends to be coincident with juvenile delinquency, as shown on the map from Shaw, and that both tend to be located in the socially disadvantaged and transitional zones.

Thrasher has called these regions " interstitial " :

The most important conclusion suggested by a study of the location and distribution of the 1,313 gangs investigated in Chicago is that *gangland represents a geographically and socially interstitial area in the city*. . . . The gang is almost invariably characteristic of regions that are interstitial to the more settled, more stable, and better organized portions of the city. The central tripartite empire of the gang occupies what is often called " the poverty belt " — a region characterized by deteriorating neighborhoods, shifting populations, and the mobility and disorganization of the slum. Abandoned by those seeking homes in the better residential districts, encroached upon by business and industry, this zone is a distinctly interstitial phase of the city's growth. It is

---

[46] Shaw, Clifford R.: " Correlation of Rate of Juvenile Delinquency with Certain Indices of Community Organization and Disorganization," *Proceedings of the American Sociological Society for* 1927:174–77.

[47] Burgess, E. W.: " Juvenile Delinquency in a Small City," *Journal of Criminal Law and Criminology*, 6:724–28 (1916).

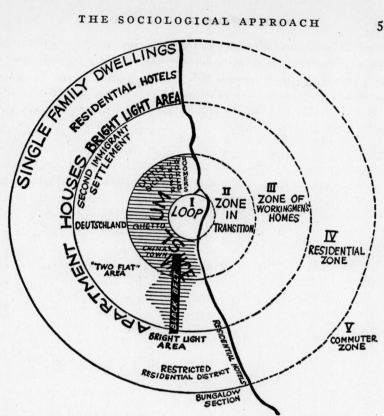

FIG. 1. — THE PLACE OF CHICAGO'S GANGLAND IN THE URBAN ECOLOGY

The shaded portion indicates the approximate location of the central empire of gangland, which has been superimposed upon E. W. Burgess' chart showing urban areas in the development of the city. (See E. W. Burgess, "The Growth of the City," Robert E. Park, et al., The City, p. 55.)

to a large extent isolated from the wider culture of the larger community by the processes of competition and conflict which have resulted in the selection of its population.[48]

The merit of these exploratory approaches is that they tend to bring out causative factors previously neglected and to redefine the problem. Thrasher's study of gangs redefines the crime problem. We have mentioned that Shaw has studied the cases of boys brought before the juvenile court in Chicago for stealing with reference to the number of boys participating, and finds that in 90% of the cases two or more boys were

---

[48] Thrasher, Frederic M.: The Gang, 22–24.

involved. It is certain that many of the boys concerned were not caught, and that the percentage of groupwise stealing is therefore greater than 90%. This again throws a new light on the nature of the problem of crime. Other researches, not yet published, will show that, recruiting from the gangs, criminal life is as definitely organized in Chicago as the public school system or any other department of life, the criminals working behind an organization of " irreproachable " citizens. Studies of this character make it necessary to view hereditary, psychopathic and endocrine factors as items on a more important social background.

In addition to surveys capable of statistical expression, observations have been made of the collective life of the different areas from the standpoint of " social distance," by which is meant the degree of inter-penetration of the lives of the individuals in the same social collectivity and the character of the reciprocal influences of contiguous collectivi-ties. Regions of " anonymity " (e.g., boarding-house areas) are found where no one knows or cares to know anyone else intimately, and regions of " proximity," where all participate in the life of each, etc. Zorbaugh [49] has prepared a study of the Chicago lower north side from this standpoint — a region of the greatest contrasts: poverty and riches, anonymity and proximity in a little space, " a mosaic of little worlds which touch but do not interpenetrate."

The Lynds [50] have made a study of a small, racially homogeneous American city from the standpoint of the relation of various changes and activities to the total situation: the inequalities in change between activities, groups, and members of the same group, and the degree and kinds of interpenetration of groups in the various activities and situations.

These regional studies are, however, able to indicate only the spatial and collective incidence of certain behavior patterns. In order to under-stand the behavior manifestations it is necessary to study the ex-periences of a large series of individuals in a great variety of situations comparatively. The question becomes, what situations provide what ex-periences leading to what behavior? And for this purpose the life-records of individuals are being employed — prepared with as much

---

[49] Zorbaugh, H. W.: *Gold Coast and Slum*. (In press, University of Chicago).

[50] Lynd, Robert S., and Helen M.: *Middletown: A Study in Contemporary American Culture*. (In press, Harcourt, Brace and Co.).

detail and objectivity as possible. At present active experimentation with the making of records is going on. We have referred to the service of the child clinics in the systematic preparation of cases, and we have represented this work and other contributions in chapter I. The Chicago sociologists mentioned above are working systematically in this line. The passage from a case [51] of Shaw in chapter II (p. 97) is representative of this activity. In Philadelphia the workers of the White-Williams Foundation introduce systematic but well considered changes in situations with a view to stabilizing or reorganizing individual and family life (see chapter V) and the records show results over long periods of time. The Philadelphia records are among the most instructive we have found, but we have been unable to represent them among our cases as they are very long and show cumulative effects.

In chapter X we have referred to the psychoanalytic technique for obtaining data. A frequent criticism of the data of the psychoanalysts has been that, although the original case materials are supposedly obtained by recording the subject's free associations, these associations are actually not at all free but are controlled by the analyst's standpoint. This control comes about through the interpolations and interpretations made by the analyst at various points during the process. The fewer the interpretations the better the analyst. But that this occurs even with the best analysts is apparent from a reading of Freud's own accounts of his analyses. The analyst, without necessarily planning to do so, is able to cause the patient to assume the standpoint of the analyst as to the mechanisms involved (e.g., birth trauma, regression to the womb, mother fixation) and to interpret his own case from that standpoint. (L. Pierce Clark claims that he is able to get from his patients a record of their pre-natal " thinking," their " consciousness " in the ambiotic fluid and the birth-canal and their early post-natal ruminations).[52] Even among psychiatrists holding no theories as to specific causes of disorders the procedure is likely to be so variable and the interpolation of weighted standpoint is so probable that the data are unsuitable for research purposes.

Dr. G. V. Hamilton's [53] extensive research into marriage situations

---

[51] To appear as a publication of the Institute for Juvenile Research, issued by the University of Chicago Press, with the title: *The Delinquent Boy's Own Story.*

[52] See *Archives of Psychoanalysis,* I, No. I.

[53] Manuscript.

represents the best attempt to get comparable data from psychiatric case records and to overcome these difficulties. He formulated more than three hundred questions relating to sex life, and these were presented on white cards in a fixed order to the subject. The subject " talked out " his answers to the questions and the psychiatrist recorded what was said, with no comments or interpolations. A body of data collected in this way is obviously valuable for research uses. Its value is, however, dependent on the degree of rapport established with the subjects, the degree to which the questions themselves were " leading," and the equal completeness of understanding and ability for frank expression on the part of the subjects.

In the following chapter we discuss the methodological importance of these personality documents.

CHAPTER XIII
The Methodology of Behavior Study

THE ULTIMATE object of scientific study is prediction, for with prediction we can have control. This is best accomplished by the experimental scientist. The chemist, for example, can predict and control, within limits, because he has learned by experience that certain materials in certain situations always behave in the same way. He can prepare his situations, introduce his materials and get uniform reactions. He is able to measure influence because his materials are stable and he can control all the influences reaching them, or if they change and enter combinations he is able to measure the changes and record the combinations and again predict. The scientist is able to determine a limited number of *laws* — that under given conditions given results will invariably follow. He is not, however, able to give a *complete* causal explanation of any phenomenon. He cannot, for example, explain completely why a certain wild rose bloomed under a certain hedge at a certain moment. In order to do this it would be necessary to begin with the formation of the material world, determine every force and measure every influence in the universe in the order of their reciprocal action down to the present moment.

The complete determination of the causation of any act of human behavior would be a task not less impossible than this. The chemist deals with elements which are relatively simple, while the behaviorist deals with actions which are in turn based on incommensurable physiological conditions — an incredibly complicated integration of endocrines, enzymes, blood chemicals, chromosomes, various nervous systems, behaving as a whole. Moreover, the material of the chemist is static, does not change from time to time, while the material of the behaviorist (the human organism) is itself evolving. The individual is changing, under influences which cannot be measured. His response in situations changes with periods of physical, mental and emotional maturation and as result of experiences in an endless variety of preceding situations. The student of behavior can therefore not hope to establish even the limited number of laws possible in the case of the exact scientist. He may hope to be able to determine that in certain situations certain reactions will usually follow. He will be able to make *inferences* but probably unable to establish *laws*. This would imply, then, not a *complete* but an *adequate* causal explanation of behavior.

It is desirable, therefore, to set up, if possible, a methodological procedure in behavior studies which will fix some limits to the behavior universe, as the scientist fixes some limits to the material universe, and at the same time give data for an adequate prediction and control.

At the close of chapter XI we presented a picture of the "inner [physiological] environment" as drawn by Claude Bernard — the environment in which the organism *lives* — and compared it with the outer environment — the world of outer space in which the organism *behaves*. The physiological system may be regarded as representing what the organism *wants*. If we could read the organism completely in terms of its morphology and chemistry we could predict what it wants. In his epoch-making study of the integrative action of the nervous system Sherrington points out that we cannot understand the reflexes unless we appreciate what they mean for activity. " The reflex action cannot be really intelligible to the physiologist until he knows its aim." [1] The structure represents, then, implicit behavior; the overt behavior is the process of satisfying the wants.

Among all the intricacies of the physiological system there are two major features of far-reaching consequences for behavior. One of them relates to the basic appetites and contains the so-called hunger and sex drives, representing the conditions of organic continuity — nutrition and reproduction. The other relates to the presence in the organism of certain preformed tendencies to behave in specific action patterns, whereby the organism is more or less predestined by its internal structure to behave in given ways. These unlearned action tendencies are the so-called instincts. While we do not wish to emphasize the importance of the " internal environment" for behavior studies — we wish, in fact, to

---

[1] Sherrington, C. S.: *The Integrative Action of the Nervous System* (1906), 236.

minimize it — it is methodologically important to appreciate the rôle of these drives and instincts in their relation to the socially more important field of learned behavior.

In the following description of the gastric contractions of the new-born we see the mechanism of the hunger drive:

We have now made observations on a number of new-born infants, and on two pups, born 8–10 days before term, with results showing that the empty stomach at birth and in the prematurely born exhibits the typical periods of tonus and hunger contractions of the adult, the only difference between infant and adult being the greater frequency and relatively greater vigor of these periods in the young. In the case of the two pups, and in some of the infants, the observations were made before their first nursing. It is thus clear that in the normal mammal the gastric hunger mechanism is completed, physiologically, and is probably active some time before birth.[2]

Psychological interest has recently centered on the relation of the unlearned to the learned factors in behavior. In the scale of evolution below man unlearned behavior is the prevalent form of activity. Insects may be hatched, traverse their life cycle of predestined activities, feed, reproduce and expire within the duration of an hour. In his brilliant work Wheeler[3] has exemplified the complicated unlearned activities of ant societies, and Herrick[4] has shown how several great action systems (insects, birds, mammals, man) approach different termini of structure and activity. Each reaches the limit of efficiency and perfection set by its morphological type and becomes static.

In contrast, man is distinguished in the organic scale by the feebleness of his unlearned action tendencies. He is obliged to learn almost everything and consequently is characterized by a learned habit system developed through his experiences.

Watson was the first to experiment with new-born children, taking them when they were an hour or more old, with a view to determining the presence of unlearned behavior tendencies. He was able to find only three instinctive reactions:

Fear. What stimulus apart from all training will call out fear responses; what are these responses, and how early may they be called out? The principal

---

[2] Carlson, A. J., and Ginsburg, H.: "The Tonus and Hunger Contractions of the Stomach of the New-Born," *American Journal of Physiology*, 38:29 (1915).

[3] Wheeler, W. M.: *Ants* (1910); *Social Life Among the Insects* (1923).

[4] Herrick, C. J.: *The Neurological Foundations of Animal Behavior* (1924).

situations which call out fear responses seem to be as follows: (1) To suddenly remove from the infant all means of support, as when one drops it from the hands to be caught by an assistant . . . (2) by loud sounds. . . . The responses are a sudden catching of the breath, clutching randomly with the hands (the grasping reflex invariably appearing when the child is dropped), sudden closing of the eye-lids, puckering of the lips, then crying; in older children possibly flight and hiding (not yet observed by us as " original reactions "). In regard to the age at which fear responses first appear, we can state with some sureness that the above mentioned group of reactions appears at birth. . . .

Rage. In a similar way the question arises as to what is the original situation which brings out the activities seen in rage. Observation seems to show that the *hampering of the infant's movements* is the factor which apart from all training brings out the movements characterized as rage. If the face or head is held, crying results, quickly followed by screaming. The body stiffens and fairly well-coördinated slashing or striking movements of the hands and arms result; the feet and legs are drawn up and down; the breath is held until the child's face is flushed. In older children the slashing movements of the arms and legs are better coördinated, and appear as kicking, slapping, pushing, etc. These reactions continue until the irritating situation is relieved, and sometimes do not cease then. Almost any child from birth can be thrown into a rage if its arms are held tightly to its sides; sometimes even if the elbow joint is clasped tightly between the fingers the response appears. . . .

Love. The original situation which calls out the observable love responses seems to be the stroking or manipulation of some erogenous zone, tickling, shaking, gentle rocking, patting and turning upon the stomach across the attendant's knee. The response varies. If the infant is crying, crying ceases, a smile may appear, attempts at gurgling, cooing, and finally, in slightly older children, the extension of the arms, which we should class as the forerunner of the embrace of adults.[5]

If we now give our attention to two of these behavior factors, the physiologically based hunger and the psychologically based love, we see that each has eventually far-reaching behavior implications. We may assume that hunger will eventually lead to pursuit of game, manual skill, mechanical inventions, foresight, economy, property, conflicts, war, the state, etc. Similarly the instinct of love, expressing itself first in response between mother and child, will later function as the sex drive and have

---

[5] Watson, John B.: *Psychology, From the Standpoint of a Behaviorist* (1924), 219–21.

a long train of social consequences — courtship, marriage, family — with profound influence on behavior.

We have from Watson's list two other unlearned behavior reactions, anger and fear. He does not name curiosity, but it will appear later with further maturation of the organism, and lead to adventure, exploration, scientific interest, etc. There will also appear a train of other behavior traits which have been called instincts: Gregariousness (the herd instinct), acquisitiveness, instinct for self-preservation, instinct for workmanship, the artistic instinct, instinct for dominance ("will to power"), instinct of rivalry, etc. It would be possible to multiply this list almost indefinitely with the aid of a dictionary (pity, compunction, gratitude, religion, etc.) — a galaxy of psychological entities interacting by some sort of magic. These are probably all learned "attitudes," not instincts, but they are based on organic conditions, body chemistry and maturation of structure. These or the unlearned reactions may not be present today and present tomorrow, when the organism is riper, and they may appear only as a reaction to specific stimuli. Morgan, for example, describes the behavior of a moor-hen chick which had been swimming and practicing for some weeks but had never dived. On the appearance of a rough-haired pup it dived for the first time in its life.[6] Complicating the situation we have the endocrines, the enzymes, blood chemistry, mentioned above, providing a class of endogenous chemical-electrical stimuli. Thurstone [7] has even elaborated the point that, properly speaking, all stimuli are located within the organism itself, that the hunger contraction, for example, not the food, is the stimulus. Finally, we have the question of consciousness, whether it exists, when it appears, whether it is a special endowment or a linking-up of various reflexes, etc.

The traditional interpretations of behavior have worked from this approach and with these data. Focusing on "instincts," "consciousness," "original nature," they attempted to explain why the organism behaves in given ways in view of its internal nature and structure, and the attempt has led to a great deal of controversy and much confusion. On the contrary, we find that all the programs which we outlined in the preceding chapter are behavioristic. They ignore largely questions of

---

[6] Morgan, C. L.: *Animal Behavior* (1900), 89.

[7] Thurstone, L. L.: "The Stimulus-Response Fallacy in Psychology," *Psychological Review*, 30:354–69 (1923); *The Nature of Intelligence* (1924). (The confusion here is not real but due to an inadequate psychological terminology).

the organic causation of behavior, the "*why*" of behavior reactions, and limit themselves to the observation, measurement and comparison of behavior manifestations — *how* the individual behaves in specific situations. This is precisely what the scientist does. He has learned to limit his problems to conditions which he can measure. He does not inquire why his materials behave in given ways but how they behave in given situations.

We are not anxious to discourage behavior studies from the standpoint of the mechanisms of the organism. On the contrary, it is very useful to have the data provided by Carlson on hunger and Watson on the "instincts," etc. In interpretation it is necessary to work with hypotheses, which are heuristic devices employed in the search for meaning — to be abandoned if the data do not provide a sufficient number of corroborations. The hypotheses should be as many as possible and for this purpose the data of the "inner environment," the unlearned and learned "attitudes," "norms," "values," "goals," etc., are useful. Sherrington's work on the nervous system, for example, will hardly be without value to the behaviorist, since the total situation contains the physiological and neurological. (In social studies, as in disputations, the inclination is great toward the "all or none" principle of interpretation.) But if we take a social situation involving the physiologically based hunger, and the psychologically based love of Watson's statement, a situation where a child is placed at birth in his mother's arms, and trace the reactions of both for a period of time, we shall find that *measurable interpretations can be made in terms of the behavior expressions but not in terms of the behavior mechanisms.*

To exemplify this we take some data from a study of new-born children made in Vienna. Working in the hospitals Hetzer and Tudor-Hart [8] divided 126 children into 9 groups of 14 each, the first group containing children 3 days old and under, and the last group containing those 4 to 5 months old, and experimenting with sound-stimuli, they observed the rate at which the child learns to separate out and give attention to the human voice among other sounds. All the children noticed all the sounds (striking a porcelain plate with a spoon, rattling a piece of paper, and the human voice) sometimes, but the reaction of

---

[8] Hetzer, H., and Tudor-Hart, B.: "Die frühsten Reaktionen auf die menschliche Stimme," *Sociologische und psychologische Studien über das erste Lebensjahr* (Quellen und Studien zur Jugendkunde, 5), 107–24 (1927).

the new-born to noises in the first weeks was far more positive than the reaction to the voice, even to loud conversation: 92% of frequency to " ear-splitting " noises and 25% to the excited voice. But in the third week the proportion was about the same, and in the fourth week the reaction was more frequent to the voice. Here we begin to see the behavior of the child humanized by the prominence and function of mother or nurse in the situation. A process of conditioning has been going on — the human voice and feeding simultaneously. The voice has gained a significance over other sounds in the feeding complex, but at first the person speaking or the loudness or softness of the tone makes no difference. The voice has been associated with feeding, and angry tones have not yet been associated with punishment. The first specific reaction to the voice is a puckering of the lips, which appears in the third week. This is a pre-social reaction because it is not associated with any definite person, merely with a voice, any voice — a voice among other noises. The speaking person does not exist for the child. The voice stimulates the saliva reflex and if feeding does not follow the child will cry.

In the meantime the mother or nurse has held the child in her arms, stroked it, changed it, warmed it and made it comfortable, in addition to feeding it, but it is not until the second month that the child recognizes her as a person. At that age he may interrupt his nursing to look at his mother and smile. He has begun to identify the mother and associate her with a feeling of well-being. The authors call the smile the first social reaction of the child.

At this point the mother and child are involved in an intimacy. It is the first social relationship in the developmental history of the child, and it grows out of the hunger contractions and the mother's response. As this intimacy continues it has been observed that some bad habits may have been established — that the child may have become " spoiled." The surprising number of problem children at early age levels and their prevalence in the whole population was indicated in document 42 (p. 88).

Taking up these problems, it will be possible to interpret the behavior of the child at this early age in terms of his " original nature " — the physiologically based hunger and the instinctive love response, leading to a fixation on the mother up to a certain point, but no further. As a result of the intimacy we may have a habit system in which response is overemphasized. It is expressed eventually in clinging to the mother, crying when separated, jealousy, emotional outbursts, etc. The child is then able to use these reactions as power devices to control the mother. Through the tantrum he can secure petting, candy, or anything he wants. We have in mind the case of a child unable to sleep except on his mother's body in a certain position, of another who deliberately crawled on the bed in order to wet it and spite the mother. The birth of another child introduces a crisis and is frequently the occasion of a train of misbehavior to secure attention.

Psychiatrists have located a large class of maladjustments in this field — disappointment, inferiority-feelings, frustrated expectations and ambitions. " Between the bed-wetting and tantrums of childhood at the one extreme and the dilapidated conduct of the senile dement, come a fascinating series of clinical pictures representing the failures to meet the tests of life at each of the seven ages of man." [9] These cases may be interpreted as meaning that the behavior patterns formed on the response level, beginning in the arms of the mother, have persisted beyond infancy and that they have proven unsuccessful means of adaptation to life.

In the meantime the hunger and its satisfaction has resulted in growth and the organism is integrating (musculature, nervous system, glands, etc.) for performances — for the pursuits, explorations, conflicts, skills, goals, careers of adult life in a society containing more enmity reactions than love reactions. As growth and integration progress the motor activities become more diversified, and we have play and curiosity and exploration. At this point there begins to be a hampering of the child's movements by the mother which, as Watson's description has shown, provokes resistance. Consequently some confusion arises in the attempt to trace causation. If " obstinacy," " negativism," " destructiveness," " tantrums " (document 42) are forms of naughtiness designed to hold the attention and provoke the response of the mother, they appear to be also " performance " expressions, a fight with the mother when she attempts to hamper the child's movements in her effort to conform him to a code. We have at this point mixed motives, as when the small boy gave his mother a good-night embrace and at the same time wished he could strangle her. When the attitudes of response and

---

[9] Campbell, C. Macfie: " Psychiatry and the Practice of Medicine," *Boston Medical and Surgical Journal*, 190 (June 19, 1924). Reprint, 24.

resistance coexist and function intermittently we have an " ambivalence " of the emotions. Bleuler, for example, records a hospital case
where a woman wept on hearing of the death of her child, but in the
intervals of her sobbing it was noticed that she was smiling slyly.

It will be seen that it has been possible up to this point to interpret
the child's behavior somewhat successfully from either of the two standpoints, that of " original nature," or that of " situation," but if we
should continue the attempt to interpret his behavior in terms of
" original nature " we should have to fall back on the pseudo-instincts
enumerated above and to assume differences in constitution, in blood
chemistry, in the operation of endocrine organs, in the preponderance
of this or that " instinct " and we should run into endless speculations
and have after all no program of treatment. These speculations formed
the content of the older psychological, sociological and educational
literature.

The behavioristic or situational approach, on the other hand, ignores
or minimizes instincts and original nature and studies behavior reactions
and habit formation in a great variety of situations comparatively. It
assumes that whatever can be learned about original nature will be
revealed in its reactions to these various situations. We regard this approach as the only one capable of giving a rational basis for the control
of behavior which may be a substitute for the common sense, preceptual,
ordering-and-forbidding type of control which has been traditional and
which, to the degree that it had efficiency in the past, has now broken
down.

If we take, for example, the " spoiling " in document 42 we see that
this may originate in a variety of situations. Frank has enumerated some
of the situations relating to the regulation of physiological tensions
which may be the occasion of good or bad habit formation:

The infant is confronted with his first tensional problem shortly after birth,
when physiological hunger appears, in the rhythmic contractions of the
stomach accompanying the fall of blood sugar. These contraction tensions are
usually relieved by the maternal ministrations at recurrent intervals, but the
child must learn to sustain these tensions or to diffuse them (by crying, fret-
ting, or other overt activity) until the feeding period arrives. This problem
demands a physiological adjustment, with a regularization of nutritional
process, uniform utilization of blood sugar over the period between feedings,
and the concomitant functional adjustments, as well as the learning of the

overt activity described. To a considerable extent the child must also learn the unvarying sequence of processes involved in digestion, at least to the extent of developing a straightforward sequence of metabolic processes, a task not so automatic as many assume, as any mother will testify, since only the sucking and swallowing reflexes are prepared. . . .

Indeed, the regularization of the nutritional processes and the management of hunger tensions is a major problem for the infant and young child. The number and variety of " feeding problems," both physiological and psychological, exhibited by young children is ample evidence for this statement and for the importance assigned it in the development of personality.

The hunger tensions and their management are usually made more acute for the child at the time of weaning and of the introduction to solid food. For then the infant is faced with the necessity of learning to use novel stimuli to relieve his hunger tensions. If he is wisely handled at these times, he may achieve a wholesome solution, but the clinical records reveal an astonishing number of children who have made the transition with difficulty. This problem is more or less a prototype of subsequent tensional problems, in that the child, who has learned to use a certain stimulus to relieve his tensions, is now required to relinquish that stimulus and to learn to use other stimuli. This substitution of a novel stimulus for the customary (or biological) stimulus is, of course, one of the essential features of learning, and it describes the physiological learning as well as the psychological. . . .

This process of substituting a new for an accustomed stimulus is difficult largely because the period of learning involves a prolongation of the tensions, the release of which is the focus of the child's activity. In starting a child on solid food, for example, he is offered substances for which he has no learned method of handling; indeed, he scarcely has learned to swallow non-liquid food, and so is inclined to reject it. While he is tentatively tasting and trying to swallow the solid food, the unrelieved hunger tensions increase his irritability toward the strange food and also his efforts to obtain the customary liquids. He must sustain these tensions until he has learned to swallow the solid food and discovered its use as a stimulus to relieve his hunger tensions. This learning can be greatly facilitated by wise handling which assists the child in meeting this trying situation, by giving him such soothing and reassurance as will enable him to endure these prolonged tensions. . . .

The elimination of waste through the urine and faeces occurs as a reflex in the young infant, when the accumulating pressure tensions release the bladder sphincter or the anal sphincter. Sooner or later the parents attempt to teach the child continence and so present him with a new set of tensional problems. He must learn to sustain these accumulating tensions until the appropriate time and place for their release is presented. This learning involves a gradual raising of the threshold of the sphincters so that they will hold against the increased pressures and, more difficult, also learning to use these intravesicular pressures as a stimulus to the overt activity of seeking the appointed place for their release. The child must also learn to regularize his eliminations to a large extent. . . .

As we shall see later, the child is increasingly faced with this problem of learning to respond to present situations in terms of their consequences, which means that his behavior must become increasingly instrumental, or, in other words, he must learn to sustain tensions while he is achieving the duly sanctioned opportunities and means for their release.

In early infancy . . . the infant will [normally], when slightly fatigued, go to sleep, thereby achieving the release of accumulated muscular tension and the restoration of the depleted physiological processes. As the child grows older, however, this almost automatic slumber may, and usually does, disappear, largely because the child cannot readily get rid of the tensions accumulated during waking hours. The child then may have to learn how to release his muscular tensions for sleeping by developing a method of relaxing when put to bed. Not all children do learn this release, especially those who are allowed to become too fatigued. Even when they do sleep, they fail to achieve a wholesome relaxation. We must, therefore, include sleeping in our inventory of tensional problems facing the child. . . .

One process in the child which is functionally complete and efficient at birth is the sympathetic reaction or so-called " emotional response." Under stimulation, such as shock and the blocking of activity, the sympathetic division of the vegetative nervous system is stimulated into action, thus initiating a series of physiological changes: a quick visceral spasm, followed by a progressive relaxation of visceral tone, accelerated pulse and respiration, alternation in circulation from visceral to peripheral, and release of glycogen from the liver into the circulation. All of these changes are in the nature of preparations for the exertion of flight or fight, and they operate to raise the tonicity of striped muscle and to make available the energy resources of the organism. This condition of " panic," however, is inhibitive of any discriminative or adjustive reaction to a situation, and so is rarely useful in social behavior where learned patterns of response must be employed.

The liability to this " panic " and to the release of the suddenly available energy in activities such as retreat from contacts with other persons, violent attacks upon persons or things, and so on, gives rise to tensional problems which we may group under the term " emotional reactions." The essential features of this problem, considered from the viewpoint of the child learning to live in group life, are, first, to inhibit the progressive development of the sympathetic reaction beyond the initial visceral spasm, so that he may escape that cumulative " panic " and its expression in non-sanctioned behavior; second, to learn some form of motor activity more or less adequate to such emotional-producing situations, so that he can deal with those situations whenever they recur. Whatever increased tonicity may be evoked by such situations will then be channeled into some form of overt activity specifically addressed to the requirements of that situation. . . . Moreover, the child does not ordinarily learn either to inhibit his sympathetic reaction (or panic) or to develop an adequate motor pattern, such as a technique addressed to the situation, except with the aid and collaboration of others. For if, concurrently with the emotional stimuli, some soothing or reassuring stimuli, either auditory or tactual or both, are received, the progressive development of the sympathetic reaction may be checked and, with further practice, inhibited or at least restricted to the initial visceral spasm or " start." . . .

The importance of this problem of emotional management arises from the fact that failure to inhibit the " panic " reaction may operate to compromise the child's future learning in situations of the same or similar character as the panic-producing situation. For after a child has once been thrown into panic, a recurrence of the original situation (or portion thereof) will revive the panic and to that extent render learning of motor techniques impossible. So again the intervention of other persons appears necessary to enable a child to escape from his emotional reactions. The threshold to emotional stimuli can be raised by practice, as we see in the various occupations and professions where individuals are taught to handle emotion-producing situations with a specific technique, such as soldiers, firemen, butchers, undertakers, surgeons, nurses, and so on. What we call the secularization of life (or progress) is just this development of techniques for meeting situations which previously evoked reactions of an emotional type. . . .

[Problems arise also when upon weaning the] child will have to learn to use auditory and visual substitutes for the tactual intimacies of infancy, and thereby will be directed to the world of things and people around him, wherein his increasing strength and mobility favor an ever widening exploration. Thus he gradually learns to use these new opportunities for achieving adjustment and so begins the process of his socialization.[10]

We do not enumerate the further steps in " tensional management " which, according to Frank's description, are involved in " the approach to the person and property of others," etc., but in this statement we have a research program in terms of behavior reactions in specific situations, where the effect on behavior formation is measurable when taken com-

---

[10] Frank. Lawrence K.: " The Management of Tensions," *American Journal of Sociology,* 33:707–15 (1928).

paratively. Experimentation and observation (with the use of control groups) would determine the situations favorable to the learning of tensional management.

We have seen that this approach has as yet had a very limited application to human society. The child welfare institutes are working most systematically, the sociologists have made a beginning and we have noted certain important specific projects (Freeman, Richards, Healy and Bronner, etc.). Taken in connection with the whole body of problems and programs which we have been considering this approach suggests certain applications, limitations and extensions, which we shall now consider.

The aim of scientific research is to determine that under certain conditions certain results will follow in certain proportions. We have pointed out above that the student of human behavior is not able to set up a situation in which there is a sufficient degree of control to produce true experimental methods of the type of those in the chemical laboratory. He has not been able to hold other factors constant, while he measures the influence of the variation of some particular factor, and everywhere the complications of the data have led to difficulties in the way of objective analysis. The approaches that have been made from the morphological, physiological and psychometric points of view have attempted to isolate some specific part of the human being from the behavior complex and to relate this specific part to the total remaining part. The isolated factor may be quite simple, as, for example, some product of body metabolism such as the hydrogen ion concentration in the saliva, or quite complicated, as abstract intelligence or mechanical abilities. The measurement of a specific factor, if it be simple enough, can often be done with great accuracy. The investigation of its relationship to other behavior variables, however, becomes a very complicated matter.

Where the total situation is so complicated, the interrelations so numerous and measurement so necessary, the method will evidently be very intimately related to statistical procedure. Although it is impossible to set up real experimental control for the solution of a problem, if groups of individuals roughly similar in a large number of attributes can be studied in varying situations the specific type of behavior resulting may be compared, statistically, for the different situations and inferences drawn as to the relative effects of the situations on the behavior.

A study of this sort may often give results that are very good approximations to the experimental type of situation. This is well illustrated in Freeman's study of foster children (p. 342). A group of children whose IQ's were known at the time of placement had been taken from an environment lacking in certain respects and placed in an environment enriched in these respects. A number of their siblings had been left in the old environment. A number of unrelated foster siblings were brought up with them in the new environment. Inferences were drawn on the basis of the statistical relationship found between the IQ's of this group of children and their own siblings as compared with the relationship found between their IQ's and those of their foster siblings. These data were then referred to the relationship that had been found to exist in other groups of siblings brought up in the same environment. The difficulty of interpreting a study of this kind arises, of course, from the fact that the situation that was allowed to vary was of so complicated a nature. The factors that make for a " good " or a " bad " environment may be largely a matter of judgment and it is impossible to measure an " environment " completely. A more narrowly defined study of the same kind is that of the effect of nursery school training on IQ variability. Here children are selected on the basis of a large number of likenesses in environment and the major difference then becomes nursery school training. The changes in IQ over a period of time for the two groups are compared.

A converse application of statistics in lieu of experimentation is seen in studies of the criminal. Here the problem is to find by how many measurable qualities the criminal is differentiated from those who do not commit crimes. Groups of criminals are matched with groups of non-criminals in certain respects and the significance of any differences found in other measurable respects is determined statistically (Goring). Of course, in all such studies clear-cut, definite results are seldom obtained because of the complexity of what is being measured, and because of the large part that unmeasurable factors play in proportion to those that can be measured. For instance, in the study of the criminal the most adequate approach that has been made, from the point of view of the use of statistics as leading to a situation that approximates experimentation, is a study that compares a group of young delinquents in institutions with boys of the same age, social class, etc., who have not become delinquent. Both groups were given intelligence tests, tests for mechanical aptitudes, tests to determine psychoneurotic responses, and data were collected as to nationality, occupation of parents, size of family, room space per person in the home (Slawson). But it must be obvious that very important aspects of the environment are probably not touched by these measurements, and likewise important aspects of personality make-up are not included. A study of this sort may be quite objective, give verifiable results and lead to guarded and careful inferences as to factors important in the etiology of crime, but it will very probably give a quite inadequate basis for the understanding of crime. In any interpretative study, by selecting out only those factors which are at the moment capable of quantitative expression, there is a necessary overweighting of those factors as against factors not readily expressed quantitatively. With regard to the factors measured, provided they are in a comparable form, an estimate may be made of their *relative* importance as compared with each other. That is, relationships within the group of measured factors will be accurately defined, but factors which cannot be measured readily (or at all) will receive no attention.

In some of the approaches which we have studied this premature quantification of the data is quite obvious, as in the studies that depend on ratings of traits. A large number of persons will be judged on a trait, say, aggressiveness. This may be done by ranking them from the most aggressive to the least aggressive, assigning numerical values for degrees of aggressiveness, or describing, in behavior terms, " degrees " of aggression thought to be equal distances apart, having the judgments made in behavior terms and then assigning values. These methods are all full of pitfalls. The instrument of measurement, i.e., a human " judge," is erroneous and inconsistent. It is never certain how much of the judge and how much of the subject appears in the actual judgment or " measurement." Tabulations resulting from these judgments are difficult to interpret. Statistical manipulations of the data, the application of complicated methods which have definite meaning only when applied to data of a strictly defined and limited character, are absurd. (A good deal of the data in mental measurements, a large part of that in personality and temperament measurement and most of that in psychiatric measurement has this fault in greater or less degree).

Another difficulty often found in these investigations is that one part of the problem can be measured directly, in genuinely quantitative terms, but in the comparisons and correlations that must be made other parts of the problem will be of this pseudo-quantitative sort. For example, a perfectly objective study of individual differences in speed of handwriting may be made. The investigator, however, wishes to study not speed of handwriting, which seems to have little general importance, but general " speed of movement " and " speed of decision " which seem to be weighted with great social significance. Instead, however, of making studies which would show the various relationships of various sorts of speed in the same individuals (which would probably take years of work) this handwriting test will be called a test of " speed of movement," and an attempt will be made to validate it by correlating it with the judgments various people may make of the speed of movement and decision of the individuals taking the tests. This is a short-cut method, based on the assumption that judgments will be made on the basis of recalling observations of " speed of movement " in a large number of natural situations. Assuming that the problem was a good one, that there is a relation between speed of handwriting and speed of decision (which may be doubted) the investigator wants to prove too much in too little time and the results will have little scientific value.

Another variety of this procedure is brought about by an oversimplification of the problems of human behavior. This is frequently seen in persons who have approached the field from another field where high scientific standards prevail, say, from the field of biochemistry. The investigator may have worked out and applied an accurate method of determining certain biochemical states. He assumes (rightly) that personality, temperament, the emotions, etc., have a biochemical base and wishes to work out the relationship of his very accurately determined biochemical index to personality or temperament or " behavior." And in study after study we find him accepting subjective, grossly inconsistent " ratings " of the personality and behavior factors, correlating them with his very accurately defined index and giving interpretations that seem to assume an equally scientific basis for both of the correlatives. This procedure is probably partly due to the naïveté often found in research workers in their approach to the problems of fields other than their own, particularly the more intangible social and psychic fields, but it is partly due also to the lateness of development of objective studies in these fields so that the choice for the investigator from another field is this imperfect sort of correlation or none at all.

Among the approaches which we have reviewed, the psychometric has had the advantage over the others in that it has had two full decades of development during which interest and stimulation in the field have been intense. Not only has the very wide application of intelligence tests resulted in a standardization and development of norms of performance, but it has led to the accumulation of many valuable data on the concomitants of performance on these tests. These concomitants have been found to be occupational, geographical, " cultural " (in the sense of superior material environment), racial and educational (in the sense of the amount of schooling received). This wide application of the tests and the definite knowledge of so many of the concomitants of the results have pointed the way for the development of controls and for the study of probable causation. This has led to the possibility of determining the effect of certain of these concomitant factors on variations in others — notably studies such as Freeman's, where the effect of changed environment on the IQ variability was tested. It has also led to important studies of IQ in relation to delinquency, whereby control has been exercised by equalizing delinquent and non-delinquent groups for certain of these concomitant factors. It will be seen also that so long as the psychometrists clung to the idea that they were dealing with " original nature " in their test results, and that original nature was unmodifiable, that the responses were concomitants of differing original natures, and that being unmodifiable (or so only within narrow limits) original nature was producing the differing responses, very little good behavior material was evolved. When, however, they utilized this knowledge of concomitants to set up controlled experiments, put aside for a moment the question of the unmodifiability of original nature and changed individuals about from one situation to another and recorded the actual changes in their intellectual behavior, interesting light was thrown on " original nature " by the situational study.

This methodological scheme, comprising the development of norms to which deviating groups may be referred, and the study of concomitant factors, has been best worked out and applied in the psychometric field. This means that, for the behaviorists, the materials of the psychometrist are in a much more usable shape than are those of the other fields, although studies of cases, life-histories, etc., indicate that these other fields probably play a more important part in the determination of behavior than does the psychometric.

It is desirable, therefore, that other behavior fields should analyze their materials in terms of the situation. In the personality and psychiatric fields, for example, the difficulty has been that most of the studies have been made from the point of view of the inner life outward, i.e., rather than studying behavior in a variety of situations as a means of inferring drives, instincts, emotions, etc., the instincts, emotions, etc., have been assumed to have a reality of their own and behavior has been studied in terms of them. There has been a tendency to pre-determine what " types " of reactions a set-up would bring out, and obscurity has been the general result. The really fruitful studies have been those that have been based on widespread observation and objective recording of behavior in varying situations, and it is this type of study that leads to the possibility of the development of controls. That is, reactions are first studied in the more " natural " situations and the factors involved in, and concomitant with, these situations are brought out in the behavior study. Then more controlled situations can be evolved which will allow for and rule out as many of the concomitant interfering factors as possible. Through studies of this sort we learn *how* people behave and from them we can then infer *why* people behave as they do.

The studies that are going on in the child welfare research institutes are particularly valuable in this respect because the nursery school represents a variety of situations in which social interaction may be studied, and because the early age level makes possible the study of the beginnings of certain behavior patterns as they are related to the situations conditioning them. It is obvious that there are great gaps in all these studies: children at the earliest age levels are not even yet being studied, from this point of view, or not being studied widely enough to give valuable results. They are not being followed through over long enough periods of time. The " situational " studies are incomplete and uneven — it has been possible to make too few studies of the home situations, for instance.

We are of the opinion that verification, through statistics, is an important process in most of the fields of the study of human behavior. Relationships can be indicated, various processes can be evaluated, if the data are in a form where statistical methods may legitimately be applied, and if the interpretations keep within the limitation of the assumptions on which the methods were based. Probably the greatest distrust of statistics has come through the unwise manipulations of data that are often made, through the expression in terms of great precision of results obtained when complicated formulae are applied to very inexact data, and through the totally erroneous assumption on the part of many statisticians that the statistical results tell all that can be told about the subject.

What is needed is continual and detailed study of case-histories and life-histories of young delinquents along with the available statistical studies, to be used as a basis for the inferences drawn. And these inferences in turn must be continually subjected to further statistical analysis as it becomes possible to transmute more factors into quantitative form. Statistics becomes, then, the continuous process of verification. As it becomes possible to transmute more and more data to a quantitative form and apply statistical methods, our inferences will become more probable and have a sounder basis. But the statistical results must always be interpreted in the configuration of the as-yet unmeasured factors and the hypotheses emerging from the study of cases must, whenever possible, be verified statistically.

The behavior document (case study, life-record, psychoanalytic confession) represents a continuity of experience in life situations. In a good record of this kind we are able to view the behavior reactions in the various situations, the emergence of personality traits, the determination of concrete acts and the formation of life policies, in their evolution. Perhaps the greatest importance of the behavior document is the opportunity it affords to observe the attitudes of other persons as behavior-forming influences, since the most important situations in the development of personality are the attitudes and values of other persons. In the document prepared by Shaw (p. 97) we have seen the determination of behavior partly by institutions, taken as situation, and partly by behavior of others, taken as situation.

It has been strongly objected, especially by the adherents of the school of " behaviorism," that this introspective method has no objectivity or validity. What they mean is that these records will not reveal the mechanisms of behavior, the process of consciousness, what is going on inside of us when we think and act, and with this we are in agreement. But the unique value of the document is its revelation of the situations which have conditioned the behavior, and concerning this there can be no doubt.

There may be, and is, doubt as to the objectivity and veracity of the record, but even the highly subjective record has a value for behavior study. A document prepared by one compensating for a feeling of inferiority or elaborating a delusion of persecution is as far as possible from objective reality, but the subject's view of the situation, how he regards it, may be the most important element for interpretation. For his immediate behavior is closely related to his definition of the situation, which may be in terms of objective reality or in terms of a subjective appreciation — " as if " it were so. Very often it is the wide discrepancy between the situation as it seems to others and the situation as it seems to the individual that brings about the overt behavior difficulty. To take an extreme example, the warden of Dannemora prison recently refused to honor the order of the court to send an inmate outside the prison walls for some specific purpose. He excused himself on the ground that the man was too dangerous. He had killed several persons who had the unfortunate habit of talking to themselves on the street. From the movement of their lips he imagined that they were calling him vile names, and he behaved as if this were true. If men define situations as real, they are real in their consequences.

The total situation will always contain more and less subjective factors, and the behavior reaction can be studied only in connection with the whole context, i.e., the situation as it exists in verifiable, objective terms, and as it has seemed to exist in terms of the interested persons. Thus, the behavior records of the child clinics are contributing important data by including the child's account of the difficult situation, the often conflicting definitions of this situation given by parents, teachers, etc., and the recording of such facts as can be verified about the situation by disinterested investigators.

In the field of psychiatry the context becomes particularly significant, and it is desirable to have here a multiplication of records showing how situations are appreciated and motivate behavior, but the records should be made not without regard to the factual elements in the situation. To the degree that the psychiatric cases are approached from the standpoint of the total situation it will appear that the problems of behavior taken all together assume an aspect of totality. The unfortunate separation of the " abnormal " from the " normal " in behavior studies will disappear, and the abnormal, pathological and criminal behavior reactions will appear not as " disease " but as socially (and individually) undesirable behavior reactions in given situations, and from this standpoint they will lend themselves more readily to study from the behavioristic standpoint.

The situational approach, utilizing statistical methods and the life-record, is capable of throwing light on many problems whose etiology remains obscure. For example, in the literature of delinquency we find under the heading " causative factors" such items as the following: Early sex experience, 18% for boys and 25% for girls; bad companionship, 62% for both sexes; school dissatisfaction, 9% for boys and 2% for girls; mental defect, 14%; premature puberty, 3%; psychopathic personality, 14%; mental conflict, 6.5%; motion pictures, 1%, etc. Now it is evident that many young persons have had some of these experiences without becoming delinquent, and that many mentally defective persons and psychopathic personalities are living at large somewhat successfully without any record of delinquency; some of them are keeping small shops; others are producing literature and art. How can we call certain experiences " causative factors " in a delinquent group when we do not know the frequency of the same factors in a non-delinquent group? In order to determine the relation of a given experience to delinquency it would be necessary to compare the frequency of the same experience in the delinquent group and in a group representing the general non-delinquent population. It is obviously absurd to claim that feeblemindedness or psychopathic disposition is the *cause* of crime so long as we have no idea of the prevalence of these traits in the general population. Similarly, the Œdipus complex (mother fixation) and Electra complex (father fixation) are weighted by the Freudians and made prominent sources of the psychoneuroses and of delinquency, whereas the clinical records show a multitude of cases where children with behavior disturbances are either indifferent to the parents or directly hate them. Again, with regard to economic factors as cause of crime we find, for example, in the records of the White-Williams Foundation of Philadelphia (an organization dealing primarily with non-delinquent children) the same unfavorable economic conditions, broken homes, etc., which are usually assigned as " causative factors " in the studies of delinquency, but in this case without delinquency. The simple expedient of using a control group would aid in clarifying this question of causative factors.

With the same utilization from the situational standpoint of statistical method, life-record and control groups, we can study with advantage the various projects and programs which we have reviewed in these pages, measure their influence and test their claims — juvenile courts, boys' clubs, boy and girl scouts, parent education associations, social agencies, recreations; also the family, the gang, the daily press, commercialized pleasure, etc.

As a more specific example, we have seen that the school is tending to assume responsibility for the " whole child," to be converted, at least for the lower age levels, into a behavior-forming situation. It is taking over the activities formerly carried on by other organizations and performing them better. We have described the varieties of these school programs — those originating externally, as in the child guidance clinics, the projects of some of the community organizations, etc., those originating within the school, as directed towards curriculum and activity changes, the introduction of behavior specialists, and the participation of the teachers in behavior-modification schemes — and it would be possible by a series of surveys to study their efficiency comparatively, let us say, with reference to maladjustment and delinquency.

In the preceding chapter we have seen that the sociologists have made territorial surveys and have determined localities in cities which evidently contain characteristic behavior-forming influences. Their work up to the present has amounted to a preliminary definition of the situation. They know, for example, that in one local area 37% of all boys of juvenile court age have been in the juvenile court (or before the police) and in another area not 1% of the boys. Their further task is to measure, with the aid of personality documents and control groups, the specific behavior-forming situations within these areas.

We have seen also that cities and larger localities differ among themselves as behavior-forming situations. Healy and Bronner estimated, for example, that their failures in Chicago were 50% and in Boston only 21%. The difference is certainly not due in the main to differences in juvenile court procedure, but to differences in the attitudes of the population, and this in turn to differences in the configurations of social influence. We examined in some detail the city of Cincinnati from this standpoint, and have been impressed with Rochester as a characteristic behavior-forming situation, particularly with the prominence of the school in the total configuration of influences. It is desirable that these cities, or others, should be studied comparatively with the aid of the same technique.

With the progress of our studies of the various behavior-forming situations we may hope to approach the still more obscure problem of mass behavior — the participation of whole populations in common sentiments and actions. This is represented by fashions of dress, mob action, war hysteria, the gang spirit, mafia, omertà, fascism, popularity of this or that cigarette or tooth paste, the quick fame and quick infamy of political personalities, etc. We are unable to define this total situation satisfactorily, but it involves the interaction of language and gesture and gossip and print and symbols and slogans and propaganda and imitation, and seems, more than anything else, the process eventuating in the formation of the distinctive character of communities, nationalities and races. The process itself may be described as a series of definitions of situations whereby behavior norms are established.

In the same connection (while we do not advocate anthropological and historical studies as remunerative behavioristic studies in themselves and are of the opinion that the past contains no models on which we may build in the present) it would be useful to extend our studies of this situational character to the large cultural areas, to the contemporaneous races and nationalities, in order to understand the formation of behavior patterns comparatively, in their most general and particular expressions, and appreciate the capacity of human nature to work under various and widely contrasted habit systems. Furthermore, behavior studies within these wide limits may be expected to reveal comparatively and in the most general way the situations within which particular maladjustments (delinquency, crime, the psychoneuroses) tend to appear, and the situations and habit systems unfavorable to their appearance, or, more positively, the situations within which the activities are integrated about particular interests, leading to pursuits, rôles and careers.

Appendix

Appendix

WE have discussed, in some detail, the question of methodology involved in the various approaches in Part III. We have indicated in the last chapter, the importance of statistical analysis as a tool for behavior study, and some of the dangers of an unwise use of statistical methods. We have no intention of discussing the theory of statistics or the mathematical assumptions on which it is based. The reader is referred to such a book as Bowley's *Elements of Statistics* for an appreciation of this very important aspect of the subject. We feel, however, that a brief statement should be made regarding the meaning of some of the statistical expressions most commonly used in the approaches considered in Part III.

The problem of the distribution of the data is an important one and assumes large proportions, particularly in the psychometric and personality testing approaches. When we wish to get a picture of the variability of any factor we form a table indicating the frequency of its occurrence for each unit of measurement. If the range is great, the frequency is noted for equal class intervals, which are multiples of the unit of measurement. The distribution is important as giving a general description of the data which could not be obtained from the scattered individual cases, and as a basis from which we can evolve those necessary summary expressions: the measurement of the central tendency or average, the dispersion of the individual cases about this average, and the symmetry of the dispersion. When the number of cases is very large, and the class interval small, the frequency distribution, when plotted, approximates a smooth curve, and curves can be fit, by means of formulæ, to any frequency distribution. Now, obviously, data might be supposed to fall into a great variety of distributions, but as a matter of fact, most data will approximate one of several readily definable forms. The most frequent of these forms for data in the economic and social sciences is a distribution in which the great number of cases cluster at the average (i.e., the mode and mean approach one another) and taper off towards either extreme, but " skewed " generally towards one extreme or the other. The perfectly symmetrical curve, of the form known as ideal or "normal," is found relatively rarely in practice but is important theoretically. The moderate asymmetry of data in the social sciences is usually taken as evidence of an approximation to the normal curve. This is a legitimate assumption, when it is frankly recognized how divergent the data themselves actually are from the ideal distribution, for it opens up great possibilities for the use of statistical methods which were devised for normally distributed data. It does not give a basis for the supposition, however, that the results can be interpreted as though genuine normal distributions had been dealt with. The results will always be approximate and hedged in with great limitations. If these limitations are recognized valuable inferences will emerge. Unfortunately, however, the normal curve has been regarded or at least implicitly accepted as a law of nature to which various data should, of necessity, conform. Divergences of actual data from the normal curve have not been looked upon as possibly the way these particular data should behave quite in accordance with their own nature, but as due to imperfections in the sample, in the investigator, or some other source, which are leading these data to diverge from the form which would naturally be taken were the " true " or genuine data available. This is an absurd assumption, and has led to the forcing of data of the most diverse forms into a semblance of the normal curve, and, conversely, claiming that data found to conform had some inherent value for that reason. One reason for this is that the investigators were not dealing with data of an immutable, quantitative sort, but were, themselves, forming data in which the personal equation determined the distribution. To find that measured heights, of a large number of individuals, tend to conform to the normal curve is a significant fact, descriptive of a phenomenon. To find that judgments of a trait conform to such a curve means nothing necessarily more than that the basis of judgment predetermined the distribution. For instance, two studies have been made in which groups were rated for extroversion-introversion. In the one study, the judges were given several descriptions to check for each trait, representing each extreme and an intermediate description. In the other study, the judges were given two statements only, one for each extreme, and were asked to indicate an intermediate position only if the case could not be thrown into one or the other of the extremes. It is not to be wondered at that in the first study a " normal " distribution resulted, whereas in the second study a bimodal distribution was formed. Neither of the distributions, however, necessarily indicated the distribution of the trait, extroversion-introversion.

Thus the two great difficulties in regard to the distribution of data are, first, the forcing of data into normal curves where the data do not warrant it, and, second, the validation of pseudo-quantitative data because of their supposed conformity to a normal distribution.

In the use of a control group, which we have emphasized so much in our discussion of methodology, frequency curves are matched for two groups, with regard to various attributes. The usual method is to have, say, the age-distribution and the mental age-distribution the same for the two groups, and similarly other characteristics, then to compute the differences in the frequency curves which result for the factor to be measured. Occasionally, control is exercised by matching each of the cases with another case, similar in regard to certain attributes. This is better, theoretically, but often involves a prohibitive amount of labor. The point that should be emphasized is that there must be a sufficiently large number of cases, usually a matter of a thousand or more, before statistical validity is gained through this method. Otherwise the chance of getting representative data is very slight. In the studies that have been made in this field, there is usually a quite inadequate number of cases, and a false sense of security may be gained through the seeming great accuracy in matching and pairing. This is to be seen, for instance, in one of the studies mentioned, where the attempt is made to have a nursery school population of 40 to 50 children conform, in the distribution of the occupations of their fathers, to the distribution found in a city of several hundred thousand. The chance of getting a " representative " carpenter's child in, say, the case of the one carpenter allowed in the sample, is slight. A carpenter who would send his child to a modern nursery school would possibly approximate in many more characteristics a professional man than he would carpenters generally.

There is also a tendency, in the various studies we have considered, to claim a generality for their results, on the grounds that although the cases they dealt with were not numerous, they were " unselected." What is usually meant is that any case that was available, having, say, certain limitations with regard to age, sex, or race only was accepted. This, however, does not give even an approximation to an " unselected " group in the sense that the statisticians are concerned with random sampling, and in the sense that they can generalize about the universe from the sample because of this random sampling. The factors working towards selection in any group that allows itself to become subjects for any experiment are very definite. A genuinely " random " sample cannot be found in the studies we have cited.

The central problem in most of the studies that we have considered has been one of correlation, i.e., measuring the degree of relationship between variables. The computation of a coefficient of correlation gives a summary figure that is indicative of the degree of relationship. The coefficient commonly computed was devised originally for use with normally distributed biometric data. It varies from plus 1 to minus 1. Plus 1 indicates perfect relationship: when one factor varies the other factor varies in the same direction and proportion. Minus 1 indicates perfect inverse relationship: when one factor varies, the other factor varies in the same proportion but in the opposite direction. A zero coefficient indicates absence of all relationship. The correlation coefficient does not indicate which factor causes the variability in the other. It " tends to be the ratio of the number of causes common in the genesis of two variables to the whole number of independent causes on which each depends " (Bowley: *Elements of Statistics*, p. 356). Coefficients intermediate between zero and one are very difficult to interpret exactly, particularly in the case of data of the sort we have been dealing with. These data are rarely normally distributed, or approximations to the normal distribution. Intermediate values, therefore, cannot be interpreted rigidly, but simply must be taken as indicative of " more or less " relationship, depending on their size. Numerical values of correlation coefficients cannot be taken as directly comparable unless the distributions of the sets of data on which these coefficients are computed are comparable, and unless, of course, the data themselves are equally valid. In a recent publication, for instance, coefficients resulting from the correlation of ratings or judgments of traits are compared with coefficients resulting from correlations of physical measurements of siblings and twins, so that when a correlation of .4 occurs in regard to these judgments, the judges are said to be as alike as siblings, and when a correlation of .8 results, the judges are said to be as alike as twins. This sort of loose interpretation is definitely misleading, and is, from the statistical point of view, perfect nonsense. The use of methods of correlation has great value in the social sciences, as giving a simple index of relationship, free from subjective bias. But this index must always be interpreted, both in the light of what the data themselves mean, and what the method itself means.

Correlation coefficients are often presented with probable errors, indicating the general reliability of the coefficient. Here again, the numerical meaning has an exact interpretation only in the case of normal distributions. An interpretation is often made in terms of probability, i.e., that a given probable error means that the chances are, say, five hundred to one that a given coefficient of correlation could not have occurred by chance alone. With ordinary data, this sort of rigid interpretation on the basis of chance is invalid. The probable error, or better the standard deviation of the correlation coefficient, is a genuine safeguard in interpreting correlation coefficients, since it is a function both of the size of the coefficient and the number of cases used in its computation, but it is a safeguard rather of a negative than a positive sort in most cases of data such as we have been discussing: it indicates what coefficients are probably quite insignificant of any relationship, but it gives very little support to the claims of necessarily " genuine " relationship indicated by correlation coefficients.

In the mental testing and personality testing approaches, much is heard of correlation coefficients corrected for " attenuation." This involves, briefly, an attempt to correct a correlation coefficient, where the data are said to be attenuated because of errors in measurement or observation. It has interesting theoretical implications, but its use is quite generally misleading. It gives a semblance of too great accuracy of measurement to coefficients which are based on data whose very nature is often ill-defined. It is the data themselves that need improving, in practically all the approaches we have considered, if the interpretation is to become clear-cut. Corrections and manipulations made on coefficients and indexes, on purely theoretical grounds, will not contribute much so long as the data are so far from theoretical desirability.

INDEX

INDEX

Abnormal, the, not separable from normal, 572

Absence, cause of, from school, 242; treatment of, in Rochester, 249

Achievement, discrepancy between intelligence scores and, 263

Acidity, of body correlated to excitability, 478

Adams, Elizabeth K., 177

Additon, Henrietta, 214, 216, 221

Adjustment, insanity as representing failure of, to life and society, 436; intelligence as determining factor in successful, to life, 364; measuring, to school in terms of corrigibility, 410; mental ability correlated with ability of, 337; of persons to one another as essence of problem of character, 426; process of, 149; to school, 267; visiting teacher work as stimulating production of, 294

Adler, A., 26, 462, 464, 465, 466

Adler, Herman M., 156, 157

Adolescence, physical changes in, as cause of delinquency, 15 ff.; special studies of, as part of parental education movement, 320

Adoption, insufficient number of children available for purposes of, 124; problem of, 271

Adrenal glands, 472; Cannon on emotional excitation and, 473

Adults, education of, VII, 295 ff.

Adventure, desire for, 11

Aggressiveness, as basis for judgment of person, 567; relation of chemical determination to, 477; specific attempt to measure, 378 ff.; test of, to measure personality traits and behavior types, 371

Allen, Ethel B., 257

Allen, F. H., 27

Allport, F. H., 402, 405, 406

Allport, G. W., 402, 405, 406

Alpha test, 486

Ambivalence, 82, 561

Ambuhl, Frederick, 119, 120

American Association of University Women, 309 ff.

Americanization, problems of, 319

Analysis, of self as pathological tendency, 163

Anderson, J. E., 57, 58, 87, 89, 315, 316, 519, 521

Anderson, L. D., 530

Andrus, Ruth, 522

Anencephalic fetus, growth of, 494

Anger, as unlearned behavior, 556

Anrep, G. V., 508

Approach, personality testing, IX, 370; physiological-morphological, XI, 468; psychiatric, X, 435; psychometric, VIII, 330, 569; sociological, XII, 505

Army, the draft, as psychometric data, 337, 447

Arnold, Judge Victor P., 193

Artistic skill, as means of attracting attention to self, 19; tendency of members of emotionally unstable class toward, 43

Association, measurement of quickness, range, and association of, 333; through contiguity, 31; through similarity, 31

Asthenic type of physique, 480 ff.; characteristics of, 481; and schizophrenia, 482

Asylums, see INSANE ASYLUMS

Athletic type of physique, 480 ff.; and schizophrenia, 482

Athletics, as aid in re-directing a boy's life, 197; in Erasmus Hall High School, 267

Atkinson, Robert K., 187, 192

Attendance, irregular, referred to visiting teacher, 258 ff.

Attention, measuring span and steadiness of, 333

Attitudes, as learned behavior, 557; test of, as measure of affective aspects of personality, 375

Australia, Boys' Club Federation of, 186

B-complex, 488

Bailey, W. B., 107

Baker Foundation, see JUDGE BAKER FOUNDATION

Baldwin, Bird T., 496, 497

Bardeen, C. R., 497

Baylor, E. H. M., 128, 164, 518

Bedford Hills Reformatory, 458

Beers, Clifford W., 440

Behavior, biological determinism in, 460; change in, caused by impairment of nervous system, 63; change in, resulting from environment, not accompanied by changes in body chemistry, 480; conflict studied as, 520; differences of, in home and school, 524; difficulties of, due to emotional life, 42; difficulties of, due to lack of conformity to socially sanctioned patterns, 30; difficulties of, related to mental deficiency; 43; difficulties of, in schools, 232; dishonesty as result of allowing children to report on their own, 283; forms of, accompanying emotional instability, 44; forms of, how normalized, 165; habits, emotions, glands, blood, and nervous system related to, 370; humanized by prominence and function of mother, 559; improvement in, as result of physical care, 330; incidence of various types of, studied, 533 ff.; intelligence related to, 330, 337; knowledge of right and wrong related to, 426, 429; of the mass, 575; methodology of the study of, XIII, 553 ff.; moral, dependent on environment, 361; oversimplifying problems of human, 568; parents' study of technical aspects of problem of, 305; personality differences related to, 370; physical illness related to, 453; playground as offering opportunity to work on, 196; results of Woodworth questionnaire from standpoint of, 419; school's method of handling problems of, 220; significance of criteria of emotionality from standpoint of, 380; study of origins of trends of, 320; study by Strecker and Ebaugh on head injuries causing changes in, 66; teachers' efforts to handle problems of, 255; tests and techniques designed subjectively to measure types of, 371 ff.; troubles of small children widely prevalent, 37

Behavior document, as sociological method, 571 ff.

Bekhterev, V. M., 506, 507

Bennion, D. M., 274

Berkshire Industrial Farm, 115 ff., 122, 138, 422

Bernard, Claude, 503, 504, 554

Bernstein, C., 361

Big Brother and Big Sister Federation, 183

Big Brother organizations, program of, 181 ff.

Big Sisters Association, 361; program of, 181 ff.

Big Sisters Council of Rochester, N. Y., 183

Binet, A., 335, 336, 353, 377

Bingham, W. V., 362, 363

Biochemistry, 468 ff.

Blasphemy, punishable by death, 108

Blatz, W. E., 525, 527, 528, 541, 542, 544

Bleuler, E., 57, 487, 561

Blind, laboratory service for, 271

Blood, alkali reserve of, as measure of excitability, 477; creatinine content of, as measure of excitability, 477; as material for study of excitability, 475; measuring pressure of, in tests, 374; as participating in thinking and behavior, 370; pressure of, as indicative of emotionality, 387; variability of pressure of, in tests, 386

Boarding homes, 139

Boardman, Rhea K., 252

Body, correlation between excitability and acidity of, 478; endocrine glands as regulating growth of, 480, 491; environment as changing behavior but not chemistry of, 480; morphology and chemistry of, 468; temperament and constitution of, 472

Bolk, L., 472, 480

Bond, E. D., 64, 67, 68

Bossard, J. H. S., 435

Boston, abnormality among delinquents in, 452; Boys' Club of, 186; child-helping agencies in, 125; new school curriculum in, 280; number of private charitable corporations in, 166; retarded children in schools of, 236; visiting teacher in, 228; work of Healy and Bronner with agencies in, 127, 131

Bott, E. A., 525, 541, 542, 544

Bott, H., 525, 527, 528

Boy Scouts of America, 171 ff.

Boys, arrested for stealing, 8 ff.; and gang, 5; misbehavior of, as groupwise and predatory, 184; involved in stealing, 8–9; unregulated activity of, 5

Boys' Club Federation, 185 ff., 191, 195

Boys' clubs, effective radius of, 191

Breed, F. S., 360

Breslau School, 441

Bridgeman, Laura, 31, 125

Bronner, Augusta F., 8, 11, 13, 15, 19, 23,

26, 43, 47, 127, 128, 131, 133, 135, 164, 365, 425, 451, 452, 453, 460, 463, 503, 517, 518, 565, 574

Brookline (Mass.), mental tests given to children of, 341

Brooklyn (N. Y.), Catholic Big Sisters of, 183

Brown, V. K., 199

Bruner, Earle D., 123

Bryant, Edythe K., 394, 395

Bühler, C., 518, 519

Bureau of Children's Guidance (New York City), 146, 147, 150

Bureau of Educational Counsel, 161

Bureau of Educational Experiments, 497, 530; study of language as a social index at, 536

Burgess, E. W., 9, 544, 545, 548, 549

Burks, Barbara S., 348, 352, 369

Burt, C., 47, 52, 58, 59, 63, 69, 339, 353, 354, 366

Buscaino, V. M., 473

Cady, Vernon M., 290, 410, 411, 412, 413, 415, 417, 418, 426, 433

Caldwell, Grace M., 2, 79

Calkins, L. A., 491

Cambridge Nursery School, 321

Campbell, C. Macfie, 57, 81, 82, 83, 84, 560

Canada, Boys' Club Federation in, 185, 186

Canal Boat children, intelligence of, 356 ff.

Cannon, W. B., 470, 473

Carbon dioxide, as index of individual's fatigue, emotional excitement, and excitability, 477

Cardiacs, special school programs for, 266

Carlson, A. J., 471, 555, 558

Carpenter, F. L., 392, 393, 394

Case, Emma G., 241

"Case-conference" method in schools, 285 ff.

Catholic Big Brothers League, 141

Catholic Big Sisters League, 141; of Brooklyn, N. Y., 183

Caution, test of, to indicate personality traits and behavior types, 371

Chant, N., 525, 527, 528

Character, attempt to define components of, 370; as dynamic factor for study, 370; education in schools, VI, 273; essence of problem of, 426; exercises for training, 282; factors in forming, 292; handwriting as index of, 389; tests de-

signed to measure intellectual aspects of, 425

Charters, W. W., 359, 361, 363, 364

Chattanooga (Tenn.), Rotary Club of, 203

Chautauquas, as educational agencies, 299; origin of, 300

Chave, Ernest J., 92

Cheating, opportunity given for, in tests, 412; relation between moral knowledge and, 429–430; study of, 283; tests for recognition of, 377

Cheerfulness, technique of measuring, 375

Chemistry of body, 468; differences in, between individuals, 469; factors of, as related to character traits and personality, 475 ff.

Chicago, abnormality among delinquents in, 452; Boys' Club of, 186; child-helping agencies connected with juvenile court in, 125; delinquency in, 191; gangs of boys in, 8; Institute for Juvenile Research of, 154; Jewish People's Institute, Boys' Department of, 186; Juvenile Court of, 95, 134; murder in, 451; plan for handicapped children in, 199; police adjustment of complaints in, 135; regional differences in delinquency in, 544; work of Healy and Bronner in, 131

Chicago Parental School, 98

Child, adoption of, in foster homes, 124; Chicago plan for handicapped, 199; clinics for psychiatric guidance of, III, 144; the constitutionally inferior, 30; the dull-normal, 254; effect of transposition of handedness on, 38; emotional adjustment of, 147; emotions of young, 528; experimental production of neuroses in, 509; the gifted, 340; inferiority feelings of, in relation to parents, 465; in juvenile court, 317 ff.; learning of, 558; manifestation of resistance by, 398, 534; measuring social resistance of, 398; and mental tests, 335; moral code of, 292 ff.; the motor-minded, 31; needing special training, 338; nursery school as benefit for, 320; the pre-school, 305; the problem, 539; personality of, as influenced by home situation and infantile experiences, 79; in public schools, 223; punishment for offenses of, under Connecticut law of 1650, 107; reaction of, to unfamiliar situation, 518; as rural economic asset, 253; study of, in clinic, 441; timing responses of, 528; the underprivileged,

204; unlearned behavior tendencies in new-born, 555; visiting teacher's handling of, 259 ff.; see INFANT

Child, C. M., 506

Child Study Association of America, 305

Child Welfare Research Station, at University of Iowa, 311 ff., 496

Children's Bureau, United States, 460

Children's Morality Code for Elementary Schools, 274

Children's Village, at Dobbs Ferry, N. Y., 117 ff.; comparison with experience of, 128

Cincinnati, treatment of delinquency in, 142, 143; juvenile division of the Court of Domestic Relations of, 134; mental tests given to children in, 341; Vocational Bureau in, 270; work of Jewish Big Brothers of, 183

Citizen, The, published by George Junior Republic, 122

City, gangland as representing a geographically and socially interstitial area in the, 548; social growth of the, 544

Clark, L. Pierce, 462, 551

Clerk, Frederick, 268

Cleveland (O.), establishment of child guidance clinics in, 145; Women's Protective Association of, 167; prostitution in, 167

Clinics, coöperative relationships of, with agencies, 152; development of, in Erasmus Hall High School, 264; as established in various cities, 145; movement to introduce, in schools and colleges, 157; Psychiatric Child Guidance, III, 144; psychiatric, at Sing Sing Prison, 442; psycho-educational, at Yale University, 323; psychological, at University of Pennsylvania, 459; Sheppard-Towner, for infant and maternity welfare, 313; traveling, 153

Code, child as not possessing a uniform generalized moral, 293; superimposing a, 290; where developed, 293

Columbia University, Institute of Child Welfare Research of Teachers College of, 522 ff., 532 ff.

Columbian Squires, of Knights of Columbus, 179 ff.

Colvin, Stephen S., 333, 341, 360, 368

Commonwealth Fund, 250, 252, 254, 257; Program for the Prevention of Delinquency, 144 ff., 150 ff., 253, 466

Community Organizations, IV, 166

Companionship, bad, as cause of delinquency, 573

Complex, the B-, 488; inferiority, 462 ff.; the T-, 488

Compliance, test of as measure of personality traits and behavior types, 371

Conditioned reflex, 507

Conditioned response, 73

Conference on Nursery Schools, Proceedings of the Second, 320

Confidence, test of, as measure of personality traits and behavior types, 372

Conformity, lack of, to socially sanctioned patterns, 30; test of, as measure of personality traits and behavior types, 372

Conklin, Agnes, 264, 265, 266, 268

Connecticut, George Junior Republic at Litchfield, 123; law of 1650, 107; progress of, in traveling clinics, 154; State Reform School Act of 1851 of, 109

Conscientiousness, test of, as measure of personality traits and behavior types, 372

Consciousness, program designed to develop "personality-c.," 161; question of, 557; "thinking" below level of, 461

Constipation, effect of, in inducing psychoses, 453

Control group, in statistical procedure, 446 ff., 573

Cook County (Ill.), Juvenile Detention Home of, 156

Cornell University, child training laboratories at, 321, 326; coöperation of, with George Junior Republic, 124

Correction schools, see INSTITUTIONS

Correspondence Schools, 296 ff.; courses in parental education given by, 314 ff.

Corrigibility, experiments on, 290; measuring adjustment of children to school in terms of, 410

Cotton, H. A., 441, 453, 454, 455, 502

Council of Social Agencies, 137

Courts, cases of stealing before, 8; Chicago movement for juvenile, 95; claim of success for juvenile, in Cincinnati, 141; coöperation of clinics with, 152; countrywide survey of juvenile, 131; establishment of child clinics in juvenile, 144; as giving way to schools in supervising delinquency, 221; juvenile division of Cincinnati Domestic Relations, 134; parent education groups in connection with juvenile, 317; relation of, to schools in Rochester, 248; as representative of conventional standards, 90; in rôle of parent toward child, 96; system of juvenile, poorly developed, 130

Cox, Catharine, 339

Crabbs, Lelah, 324, 536

Creatinine, content of blood and urine as measure of excitability, 477, 479; less produced by excitable individuals, 479

Crime, fallacy of calling feeblemindedness the cause of, 573; feeblemindedness as determining factor in, 364; gangs as leading to professional, 184, 548; incidence of, 545; preventing through socialization of police, 206; reorganization of theories concerning, 447

Criminal careers, originating in gangs, 9

Criminal type, 448

Criminality, relation of biochemistry to, 472

Criminals, characteristics of, 444; as contaminating children in prison, 95; feebleminded as potential, 337

Crowd, problem of behavior of, 575

Culbert, Jane, 222, 251

Curriculum, attempt to make a means of moral instruction of, 280

Cycloid, 487

Cyclothyme, 483

Dallas (Tex.), establishment of child guidance clinics in, 145

Dalton Plan, The, 226

Davenport (Ia.), traveling clinic at, 155

Davis, Katherine B., 94, 214

Davis, W. T., 362, 363

Dawley, A., 366

Deaf, laboratory services for, 271

Dearborn, Walter F., 497

Deardorff, N. R., 221

Deception, tests of, 283, 372, 430

Decision, test of speed of, as indicative of difference between normals and delinquents, 395; test of speed of, as measure of personality traits and behavior types, 372, 568

Delinquency, as approached by Rotarians, 203; boys' clubs as effective in checking, 193; causative factors of, 573; in Chicago, 191; Commonwealth Fund Program for Prevention of, 144; forms of, accompanying emotional instability, 44; gangs as leading to, 9, 548; Healy on sex talk leading to non-sexual, 52; incidence of, 545; indirect incentive to, 463; institutions apparently not checking, 134;

interpretation of, 41; juvenile courts' failure in treating, 130; low intelligence as questionable determining factor in, 364, 365; low rate of, in Hamilton County, Ohio, 141; mental tests as explaining, 338; methods of preventing, 466–467; obscure factors operating in rate of, for Cincinnati, 143; physical inferiority connected with, 464; rates of, 142; relation between feeblemindedness and, 489; relation between will-temperament and, 394; school substituting for court in handling, 221; tests for recognition of, 377; tests of Raubenheimer with purpose of predetermining, 415; treatment of, II, p. 95; treatment of, when arising from home surroundings, 115; unequal mental endowment as factor in, 31; see JUVENILE DELINQUENCY, MISBEHAVIOR, POLYDELINQUENCY

Delusions of persecution, assumed as means of attracting attention to self, 19; caused by repression, 461

Dementia praecox, effect of Travis' test on victims of, 408; Meyer's definition of, 438; victims of, in insane asylums, 439

Denver (Colo.), widowed mothers' class for child discussion in, 318

Depression, technique for measuring, 375

Derrick, Calvin, 119, 120

Des Moines (Ia.), discussion method in schools of, 285; meeting of representatives of parental education at, 313

Detention home, establishment of, 96; influence of, 96; no, connected with Boston Juvenile Court, 125; use of, as clearing house, 113

Detoxication, as cure for mental disease, 454

Detroit (Mich.), activity of women police in, 216; new school curriculum in, 280; parent education work with pensioned mothers in, 318

Disabilities, mental, as related to school curriculum, 37 ff.

Discouragement, effect of, on mental work, 375

Discrimination, between good and evil, 276; effect of, on behavior, 27; test of ethical, as measure of social judgment, 377; of tones, 508

Disease, susceptibility of certain types of physique to, 500

Disease races, Draper's theory of, 500 ff.

Dishonesty, as misdemeanor, 541; relation

between moral knowledge and, 431; as result of allowing children to report on their own tests, 283

District of Columbia, Boys' Club Federation in, 185

Divorce, incidence of, 545

Dixon, Edith D., 314

Dobbs Ferry (N. Y.), Children's Village of, 117

Domination, study of, in nursery situation, 519

Downey, June, 375, 388, 390, 392, 394, 395, 433

Dramatic performances, in Erasmus Hall High School, 267; in reformatories, 109

Draper, G. W., 499, 500

Drives, the physiological, 554 ff.

Duluth (Minn.), parental education courses in, 314

Dunn, H. L., 500

Dynamometer, as used in Johnson's tests, 420

Dysplastic type of physique, 482 ff.; and schizophrenia, 482

Ebaugh, Franklin G., 66, 67

Education, of adults and parents, VII, 295 ff.; character, in schools, VI, 273; democratic systems of, 219; goal of academic, in state schools, 111; "humane," 303; new trends in, 220; pre-parental, in public schools, 324; problem of universal, 272; by university extension work, 296 ff.; for workers, 304

El Retiro, 110, 113

Electra complex, 52, 461, 573

Eliot, Thomas D., 221, 222, 269

Ellis, Havelock, 57, 382

Ellis, Mabel B., 239, 241, 242, 243

Emotions, as causing functional alterations, 473; as having biochemical base, 568; as participating in thinking and behavior, 370; test of, as measure of affective aspects of personality, 373

Emotional instability, associated with sex themes, 52; attempt to discover differences in, between those of normal and abnormal physique, 420; as cause of misbehavior, 30; laboratory technique for measuring, 374; paper and pencil tests of, 374; as shown in Slawson's tests, 425

Emotional life, conditions favoring exploration of, 163

Emotionality, measurement of, 387

Employment, after school, 267; service for specialists, 298

Encephalitis, as accentuating behavior traits, 69; as impairing nervous system and causing change in behavior, 63 ff.

Encouragement, test of effect of, on mental work, 375

Endocrine glands, insanity attributed to peculiarities or inadequacies of, 480; as regulating growth of body, 480; temperament related to, 472

England, Boys' Club Federation in, 186; parental education movement in, 319

English, C. H., 200

Enuresis, case of, 80–81; as part of habit problem, 130; for spite, 560

Environment, ability to adjust to, as measure of intelligence, 333; as causing changes in behavior, 480; emphasis on, in physical approach, 330, 331; intelligence quotient as tending to diagnose differences in, 338; moral behavior as dependent on, 361; two types of, 503; visiting teacher's work in correcting, 243; Whittier Scale as index of, 349

Epileptics, in Erasmus Hall High School, 267; examination of, 271; legislation for, based on mental hygiene surveys, 153

Erasmus Hall High School, treatment of "problem students" at, 263 ff.

Ethical Culture School, 308

Eugenist, view of, of biological determinism of behavior, 460

Euthenics, Vassar Institute of, 328

Evidence, law of, as suggestion for proper human approach, 161

Evolution, architectonic functions of hormones in, 480

Excitability, hydrogen-ion concentration of saliva as index of, 477; studied by products of metabolism, 475; study of saliva and carbon-dioxide content as measure of, 477; as tending to produce less creatinine, 479

Experience, as conditioning life of individual, 505

Expressiveness, facial, as indicative of stability, 387

Extension studies of colleges, 296 ff.

Extroversion, study of personality in terms of, 396 ff.

Eyes, measuring control of, in aggressiveness test, 379

Faeces, as index of insanity, 478; as material for study of excitability, 475

Failures, comparison of, in two cities, 132; correlated with mentality classifications, 129; as evidence of maladjustment, 228; possibility of predicting, in college, 363; relative, of committed and uncommitted, 133; in school as reason for examination, 270; standard for estimating, 130; traits specifically indicative of, 393

Fair-mindedness, test of, as measure of affective aspects of personality, 375

Family, emphasis on, as opposed to institution, 125; historical, as unit, 23; Massachusetts as leader in maintaining, intact, 124; opposition of rural, to physical training, 252; school adopting functions of, 272

Faulkner, Leon, 117

Fear, as unlearned behavior, 555

Federation for Child Study, 305

Feebleminded, at Bedford Hills Reformatory, 458; Binet tests given to, 337; children so called, 31; parole of, 361; proportion of, in draft army, 447; at Sing Sing Prison, 442

Feeblemindedness, as determining factor in crime, 364, 365; fallacy of calling, the cause of crime, 573; incidence of, at Sing Sing Prison, 442; relation between delinquency and, 489; Royal Commission on Control of, 446; what is involved in, 31

Fernald, Mabel R., 270, 366, 377

Fetus, growth of anencephalic, 494

Films, censorship of, 303; see MOTION PICTURES

Fisher, S. C., 114

Focal infection, 453

Foresight, testing, 377

Foster, J. C., 57, 58, 87, 89

Foster home, increase of intelligence in, 345; disadvantages of placing in, 127; experience of Healy and Bronner with, 517; great use of, by Boston Juvenile Court, 126; non-employment of, in Cincinnati, 136; as opposed to institutional plan, 124; results of placement in, 516

Frank, Lawrence K., 463 ff., 515, 561, 564

Freeman, F. N., 333, 340, 342, 348, 350, 352, 354, 369, 565, 566, 569

Freeville, George Junior Republic at, 121; work of parent Republic at, 124

Freud, Anna, 466

Freud, S., 52, 461, 462, 464, 465, 466, 551, 573

Frustrations, as causing desire for personal attention, 19

Galton, Sir Francis, 40

Galvanic reflexes, as measure of cheerfulness and depression, 375

Gangs, as areas of origin of criminal careers, 9; in Chicago, 8, 184; difficulty of converting members of, 188; members' average age, 201; mixed, 9; organization of, very solidary, 187; as problem to playground authorities, 200; as problem in schools, 9; with sexual purposes, 9; of young boys, 9

Gastric juice, as material for study of excitability, 475

Gauss, 461

Geneva, training school for girls at, 157

Genius, relation of biochemistry to, 472; study of early mental traits of, 339

Geographical differences, in delinquency, 9, 544, 550; in intelligence, 368

George Junior Republic, 121 ff.

George, W. R., 121, 122, 123

Germantown Boys' Club of Philadelphia, 186

Gesell, Arnold, 323, 525

Gilliland, A. R., 378, 379, 432

Ginsberg, H., 555

Girls, Business Club of, 113; evolution of training schools for, 110; Geneva Training School for, 157; missing, in Detroit, 217; parole of feebleminded, 361; preparental training of, 325; program for, in reformatories, 110; study of intelligence of delinquent, 366; tabulation of charges against, in Cleveland, 168; Virginia State School for Colored, 112; work done for, in various cities, 231

Girl Scouts of America, 171; disadvantages of program of, 176; program of, 175

Glands of internal secretion, see ENDOCRINE GLANDS

Gleim, Sophia C., 230

Glenview School, The, 136 ff.

Glueck, Bernard, 448

Gonads, the, 472

Goodenough, Florence, 352, 369, 519, 531

Gordon, Hugh, 354, 356, 358, 368

Goring, C., 445, 446, 448, 451, 566

Greene, E., 361

Gregariousness, 557

Gross, H., 441

Growth, curves of, 496; law of, 491; measurement of physical, 330; studies of, 330

Gruenberg, S. M., 306, 308, 309

Gullette, R., 384, 385, 386, 388

Gundlach, R. H., 484, 486

Habits, data on formation of, 43, 89, 130, 276, 319, 324

Hæmoglobin, as differing according to species from which derived, 469

Haggerty, M. E., 367, 538, 539, 540

Hallam, Oscar, 143

Hall-Quest, A. L., 298, 299

Hamilton County (O.), 135, 183; Court, 139

Hamilton, G. V., 466, 551

Hammett, F. S., 472, 473, 474, 475, 505

Handedness, left- and right- as factors in throwing child into confusion, 38

Handicap, effect of physical, on child, 199 ff.

Handwriting, as material for indirect personality test, 388

Hanover Conference of 1925, 363

Hart, B., 441

Hartford (Conn.), visiting teacher in, 228

Hartshorne, H., 174, 283, 292, 293, 371, 378, 392, 426, 429, 430

Hatai, S., 473

Haviland, Mary S., 283

Hawaii, Boys' Club Federation in, 185

Hawthorne School, The, 422

Hayes, M. H. S., 366

Head injury, as impairing nervous structure and causing change in behavior, 63; studies of Strecker and Ebaugh on, 66

Healy, William, 8, 11, 13, 16, 19, 23, 26, 43, 44, 47, 48, 52, 127, 128, 131, 133, 135, 143, 164, 365, 425, 440, 451, 452, 453, 460, 463, 503, 517, 518, 565, 574

Heart disease, clinics for, 313; see CARDIACS

Henderson, L. J., 503, 504

Henmon, V. A. C., 334

Herrick, C. J., 466, 555

Hesketh, F. E., 486, 487, 488

Hetzer, H., 558

Heurtin, Marie, 31

Hilcrest School, The, 136 ff.

Hoffman, Frederick L., 142

Hoffman, Judge Charles W., 135, 136, 137, 139

Hogendyk, C. E. G., 213

Holland, Boys' Club Federation in, 186

Holzinger, Karl J., 342, 354

Home-making, courses in, 308

Home situation, as basis of discrepancy between intelligence scores and school achievement, 263–264; effects of urbanization and commercialized recreation on, 280; influence of, on personality of child, 79; referred to visiting teacher, 258; study of, at Teachers College Institute, 525

Homicide rate, for various cities, 142 ff.

Honesty, as an entity, as indicated by test, 371; incentive to, 275; moral knowledge related to, 431; testing, as indication of personality traits and behavior types, 372

Hormones, 470, 480

Howe, Samuel Gridley, 125

Hull House Social Settlement, 95, 156, 184, 192

Hunger, Carlson on, 558; as drive, 554

Hutchins, William J., 274

Hydrogen-ion concentration of saliva, as measure of excitability, 477

Hygiene, education for agencies in mental, 127; National Committee for Mental, 144; survey of mental, as basis for legislation, 153

Hyperkinesis, consequent on encephalitis, 67

Hyperkinetic, automatic handwriting as showing, tendencies, 390; the, as member of emotionally unstable class, 44

Hypoplastic types, 502

Hysteria, caused by repression, 461; characteristics of, 406

Idaho, placing state schools under state board of education in, 111

Idiotropic, 487

Illinois, parole in, 133

Illinois Children's Home and Aid Society, 343

Illinois Institute for Juvenile Research, 8, 154; behavior documents prepared for, 96

Illinois State Reformatory, 103; mental hygiene surveys in, 154

Illiteracy, attempt to decrease, 303

Imagination, measurement of facility in, 333

Incorrigibility, experiments on, 290; test of, as measure of personality traits and behavior types, 372

India, Boys' Club Federation in, 186

Industry, connection of, with school, 272

Infant, study of care of, as part of pre-parental education in public schools, 235; see CHILD

Infection, focal, 453

Inferiority feelings, 19, 26, 462, 464, 465

Information test, 486

Insane, care of, by legislation based on mental hygiene surveys, 153; number of, in hospitals, 435

Insane asylums, characteristics of those admitted to, 439; neurotic cases in, 85; number of patients in, 435; tendency of members of emotionally unstable class toward, 43–44

Insanity, biochemistry related to, 472; endocrine peculiarities related to, 480; nature of, 436; physiques and temperaments related to different types of, 480

Insight, as test of personality, 402

Instability, criteria of, 387; laboratory technique for measuring general emotional, 374; paper and pencil tests of emotional, 374; Slawson's tests of emotional, 425

Instincts, criticism of theory of, 557 ff.; test of, as measure of affective aspects of personality, 373

Institut Rousseau, research in, 534 ff.

Institute for Child Guidance (N. Y.), 150 ff.

Institute for Child Welfare Research (Teachers College), research in, 522 ff., 532 ff.

Institute of Child Welfare (Minneapolis), research in, 519 ff., 531 ff., 536 ff.

Institute for Juvenile Research (Chicago), 5, 8, 96, 106, 154, 156, 157, 161, 533 ff.

Institute of Psychology (Yale University), research in, 525

Institutions, 95 ff.; distrust of, in Boston, 126; facilities of, limited in Cincinnati, 143; incidence of psychopathic traits in, 441; non-employment of, in Cincinnati, 136, 140; when preferable to foster homes, 130

Intellect, aspects of, in character, 425

Intelligence, behavior related to, 330; cheating related to, 430; determination of, in criminals, 445; nature of, 332; physical types related to, 484; prognostic value of, 359; study of relation between dynamic factors and, 370; symposium on, 332; as test of personality, 402

Intelligence quotient, 335; defense of low, 362; proportions contributed to, by na-ture and by nurture, 348; value of, in diagnosis, 336 ff.

Interests, test of, as measure of affective aspects of personality, 375, 376

International Association of Policewomen, 214

Interstitial regions, 548

Introversion, study of personality in terms of, 396 ff.

Iowa, Child Welfare Research Station at University of, 311, 529; mobile clinic of State Hospital of, 153; movement for parental education in, 311; nursery schools in, 320; State College of Agriculture, 312

Iowa City (Ia.), Children's Hospital in, 313

Irwin, E. A., 223, 225

Isserlis, L., 339, 342

Jacobsen, C., 384, 385, 386, 388

Jaensch, E. R., 488

Jaensch, W., 488

Jail, criminals as contaminating children in, 95; employees of, in relation to child, 106; indenture system as obviating confinement in, 124; physical conditions of life in, 108, 109

James, William, 43

Janet, P., 440

Jennings, H. S., 506

Jews, incidence of psychoneuroses among, 517

Jewish Big Brothers Association, 141, 183

Jewish Big Sisters Association, 141

Jewish People's Institute, Boys' Department, 186

Johnson, Andrew G., 115, 122

Johnson, Buford, 419, 420, 421, 496, 497

Johnston, J. B., 363

Joint Committee on Methods of Preventing Delinquency, 38, 40

Judge Baker Foundation, procedure of, 126

Judgment, Cady tests for moral, 413; tests designed to measure social-ethical, 376

Jung, C. G., 84, 462, 466

Juvenile court, Chicago movement for, 95; child welfare agencies connected with Boston, 125; in Cincinnati, 134; establishment of child clinic in, 144; the Los Angeles, 109; parent education groups in connection with, 317; schools as replacing, in handling juvenile delinquency, 221; survey of, in whole country,

131; system of, generally poorly developed, 130, 442

Juvenile delinquency, regional variations of, in same city, 9; see DELINQUENCY

Juvenile detention home, see DETENTION HOME

Juvenile Protective League, 140

Juvenile Psychopathic Institute of the Jewish Hospital, 137, 139

Juvenile Research, Illinois Institute for, 5, 8, 96, 106, 154, 156, 157, 161, 533 ff.

Keller, Helen, 31
Kempf, E., 435
Kenny, Edward J., 183
Keppel, Frederick P., 295, 296
Kerns, Harry N., 160
Kings Park State Hospital, 438
Kirby, G. H., 455, 457
Kirchwey, George W., 107
Kirk, John R., 285
Kirkland, J. B., 124
Kirkland, W. W., 185, 192, 193
Kirksville (Mo.), character education program of State Teachers College at, 284
Kiwanis International, 202, activities of, in various states, 204 ff.
Klees, Robert D., 189
Knapp, Pearl M., 15
Knighthood of Youth, 281 ff., 290
Knights of Columbus, 179 ff.
Köhler, W., 31, 506
Kohs, Samuel C., 222
Kopeloff, N., 455, 457
Krasnogorski, N. I., 509, 511, 512, 514, 515, 516, 517
Kretschmer, E., 480, 482, 483, 484, 486, 487, 488, 501

Landis, Carney, 380, 383, 384, 385, 386, 388
Language, as social index, 534 ff.; see SENTENCE FORMATION; SPEECH
Laughter, as social index, 524
La Salle-Peru-Oglesby Township High School, 156, 160 ff.
Lawrence (Mass.), Boys' Club of, 186
Learned behavior factors, 555
Lee, Porter, 146, 149
Left-handedness, see HANDEDNESS
Legislation, child labor, 195; mental hygiene surveys as basis for, 153; method of advancing, 303
Leptosome type of physique, 482 ff.
Levy, D. M., 534

Life-record, as sociological method, 571 ff.; in the field of psychiatry, 572
Lindsey, Judge B. B., 318
Lions International, 202, 206
Loeb, J., 506
Lombroso, C., 444, 445, 448
Los Angeles, Business and Professional Women's Club of, 114; establishment of child guidance clinic in, 145; Girls' Business Club in, 113; Juvenile Court, 109; new school curriculum in, 280; parent education groups in connection with juvenile court in, 317; Raubenheimer's tests of children in, 418
Love, as unlearned behavior, 556
Lowell, F., 497
Lowrey, Lawson G., 151, 153
Ludlum, S. D., 478
Lundberg, Emma O., 131
Lurie, L. A., 517
Lyceums, as educational agencies, 299
Lyday, June F., 156
Lying, pathological, 47 ff.
Lyman School, 133
Lymphoid organs, 492
Lynd, Helen M., 550
Lynd, Robert S., 550

Macleod, Annie L., 328
MacPhail, A. H., 360
Magdalen Society of Philadelphia, 230 ff.
Maine, Sir Henry, 40
Maison des Petits de l'Institut Rousseau, 534
Maladjustment, as affected by social stratum, 254; treatment of, in schools, V, 219 ff.; varieties of, I, 1 ff.
Manual training in reformatories, 109
Marks, L. A., 223, 225
Marston, Leslie R., 396, 397, 398, 399, 401, 432, 528
Mass behavior, 575
Massachusetts, compulsory examination of backward children in, 154; laws of, as particularistic, 132; as leader in maintaining families intact, 124; parole in, 133; rate of cases of mental disease in, 454; returns made to Public Welfare Department of, 125
Mathews, A. P., 468
Mathews, Ellen, 420, 422, 424, 451
May, Mark A., 174, 283, 292, 293, 363, 371, 378, 391, 392, 394, 395, 396, 426, 429, 430
McAdoo, William, 94

McCarthy, Dorothea, 527

McClellan, H. H., 454

Measurement of physical growth, 330, 490

Meek, Lois Hayden, 309, 310, 311

Mental age, 447

Mental capacity, correlated with behavior, 337; measurement of, 331

Mental characteristics, biochemical differences correlated with, 469

Mental clinics, see CLINICS

Mental conflict, critical experience as causing, 80; delinquency caused by, 573; Healy's treatment of, 44; importance of, in delinquency and psychopathology, 463; inhibited reprehensible forms of behavior in, 44; sex talk as causing, 52

Mental deficiency, case of, 43; delinquency caused by, 573; factors involved in, 31; habit formation related to, 30; history of culture related to, 30; misbehavior caused by, 30; offenses as evidences of, 448; as result of failure to form important habit, 38; school curriculum related to, 30; segregation of those with, as solution of behavior difficulties, 330; successful placement of those with, 128; theoretical and experimental side of, VIII, 330; see FEEBLEMINDEDNESS

Mental disease, non-specificity of, 436 ff.

Mental disturbance, as result of failure of organism to adapt itself, 436; socially determined causation of, 460

Mental hygiene, department of, at Yale University, 157; mobile clinic for, of University of Iowa, 313; National Committee for, 144; surveys in various localities, 153 ff.

Mental testing, approach, 330 ff.; in Erasmus Hall High School, 263; in Rochester Public Schools, 240; value of, in diagnosis, 336 ff.

Mentality classifications, success and failure correlated with, 129

Merrill-Palmer School, 322 ff., 351 ff., 536

Meredith, Lois A., 254

Mertz, Elizabeth R., 183

Metabolism, personality and excitability related to, 475 ff.

Methodology, of Behavior Study, XIII, 434, 553 ff.

Meyer, Adolf, 67, 283, 438, 440, 453, 503

Miller, M. L., 324

Mindedness, measurement of various types of, 375 ff.

Minneapolis (Minn.), Institute of Child

Welfare of, 519 ff., 531 ff., 536 ff., parental education courses in, 314 ff.

Minnesota, nursery schools in, 320

Misdemeanor, attempt to objectify concept of, 541 ff.; headings under which, may be classified, 541

Mitchell, Blythe C., 342

Mobile Clinic of Iowa State Hospital, 153

Mohr, G. J., 484, 486

Monmouth County (N. J.), visiting teacher in, 252

Mood, test of, as measure of affective aspects of personality, 375

Moore, H. H., 449, n.

Moore, H. T., 378, 379, 432

Morgan, C. Lloyd, 470, 557

Morons, capacity for work of, 168 ff.

Morrison, Harry C., 37, 38

Morse, Fannie, 112

Motherhood, pre-parental education as preparation for, 325

Motion pictures, censorship of, 303; delinquency caused by, 573; used in testing, 374

Movement, test of speed of, 568

Multiple choice test, 376, 425

Murchison, C., 338, 365

Murphy, J. P., 128, 164, 518

Nañagas, Juan C., 493

Nash, Jay B., 201

National Child Welfare Association, 282 ff.

National Committee for Mental Hygiene, 144, 151, 153, 441, 466; origin of, 440; study of Sing Sing by, 442 ff.

National Committee on Nursery Schools, 320

National Congress of Mothers and Parent-Teacher Associations, 302

National Council of Parental Education, 305

National Probation Association, 215

National tests, 424

Negativism, 80; changes in intelligence quotient correlated with changes in ratings of, 531

Nelson, J. F., 532

Nervous habits, Olson's work on, among school children, 539

Nervous structure, behavior changed by impairment of, 63; curve typical of growth of, 492; studies of Ebaugh and Strecker on head injuries as affecting, 66

Neuroses, experimental production of, in child, 509

New Trier Township High School, 268

New York, nursery schools in, 320; rate of cases of mental disease in, 454; traveling clinics in, 153

New York City, Boys' Club of, 186, 195; Bureau of Children's Guidance in, 146; experiment to determine requirements of different types of children in, 223; Institute for Child Guidance in, 150 ff.; police department of, 442; Public Education Association of, 229; visiting teachers in, 228, 253

New York House of Refuge, 422

New York Probation and Protective Association, 361

New York School of Social Work, 146, 151

New England, Boys' Club Federation in, 186

Noffsinger, John S., 296, 297, 298, 299, 300, 301

Norm, definition of, 450; method of determining, 450; statistical determination of, 491

Normal, compared with the ideal, 448 ff., 457

Nucleic acids, 468

Nurses, and parental education movement, 323

Nursery schools, parental education movement connected with, 320; Proceedings of the Second Conference on, 320

Nutrition, studies of, 330

Oakland (Cal.), pageants in, 201

Occupation, relation of child's intelligence to father's, 340; relation of drafted men's intelligence to their, 339–340

Œdipus complex, 52, 461, 573

Ogburn, William F., 107, 109

Ohio, Humane Society of, 141; rate of cases of mental disease in, 454; traveling clinics in, 153

Olson, W. C., 538, 539

Oppenheimer, J. J., 230

Originality, test of, as measure of behavior types and personality traits, 372

Orphanages, coöperation of clinics with, 152

Otis tests, 341

Overstatement, tests as emphasizing individual's tendency to, 413, 417

Pageants, 201

Parathyroid glands, 472, 474

Parents, attempts of, to live in and through their children, 85; child's feeling of inferiority in relation to, 465; children of neurotic, as exhibiting nervous habits, 539; knowledge of child related to that of his, 429; work in educating, VII, 295 ff.

Parent-Teacher Association, 302 ff.

Park, Robert E., 544, 549

Parole, of feebleminded children under institutional care, 361; in Massachusetts, 133; of prisoners in custody of police, 207, 521 ff.

Parten, Mildred, 521, 523

Partridge, G. E., 64, 67, 68

Pasadena (Cal.), child guidance service organized in, 145

Pathfinders of America, The, 280 ff.

Pavlov, I. P., 73, 440, 506, 507, 508, 509, 519

Pawtucket (R. I.), Boys' Club of, 186

Pearson, Karl, 445

Pennsylvania, George Junior Republic at Grove City, 123; traveling clinics in, 153

Pennsylvania School for Social Service, 239

Perkins Institute, 125

Perkins, Nellie L., 321, 327

Perry, Chesley R., 202

Perseverance, test of, as measure of personality traits and behavior types, 373

Perseveration, test of as measure of personality traits and behavior types, 373

Persistence, test of, as measure of personality traits and behavior types, 373

Personality, attempt to measure differences in, 370; biochemical base of, 568; categories into which analysis of, falls, 402; change in auditory threshold as index of type of, 406; differences in, measured in terms of differential conduct, 410; as dynamic factor for study, 370; experiments on correlating chemical determinations with traits of, 500; fallacy of isolating, from social setting, 528; handwriting as index of traits of, 389; problems of, in studies of Healy and Bronner, 130; problems of, at Yale University, 159; program designed to develop consciousness of, 161; study of, in terms of introversion and extroversion, 396; testing approach, IX, 370; tests and techniques designed objectively to measure traits of, 371; tests of various aspects of, 369

Peterson, Leroy, 207, 209, 210, 212

Philadelphia (Pa.), child guidance clinic

established in, 145; Germantown Boys' Club of, 186; Magdalen Society of, 230; number of helpful organizations in, 166; retarded children in schools of, 236; White-Williams Foundation of, 230; working certificates in, 233

Phipps Psychiatric Clinic, 486

Physical defects, of school children in U. S., 449 n.

Physical deficiency, intelligence quotients of victims of, 356 ff.; school retardation related to, 235

Physiological drives, the, 554 ff.

Physiological-Morphological Approach, The, XI, 468 ff.

Physique, categories of, 480 ff.; defects of, as cause of mental trouble, 453 ff.; glands as affecting, 470; indicative of emotionality, 388; psychic dispositions related to, 480; study of relation between dynamic factors and, 370; susceptibility to disease manifested by characteristic, 500; tests to discover differences in emotional stability between those of normal and abnormal, 419 ff.

Piaget, J., 534, 535, 536

Pigeon, Helen D., 214

Pilpel, C., 307

Pineal glands, 471

Pintner, R., 334, 361, 362

Pitch, discrimination of, 508

Placement, problem of, 271; see FOSTER HOMES

Play activities, observation of, 525; study of free, 528

Playground (a periodical), 195

Playgrounds, movement for, 195

Poffenberger, A. T., 392, 393, 394

Police, and crime prevention, 206; as organization for oversight of problem children, 206 ff.; as parole officers, 207 ff.; as probation officers, 140; as welfare officers, 211 ff.; children's, 213; junior, 209

Policewomen, 213 ff.; International Association of, 214

Polydelinquency, percentage of success with those engaged in, 129

Praise, measuring effect of, on increase in mental output, 375

Pratt, Anna B., 231

Prediction, as object of scientific study, 553

Preferences, test of, as measure of affective aspects of personality, 375

Prejudices, eliciting expression of, as test of fair-mindedness, 375; test of, as measure of affective aspects of personality, 375

Prescott, D. A., 497, 498, 499

Pressy, S. L., 340, 368, 374, 385, 386

Prison, see JAIL

Prisoners, Binet tests given to, 337; incidence of psychopathic traits among, 441; paroled in custody of police, 207–208; psychiatric examination of, 442; study of physical types among, 484; as victims of defective glands, 502

Probation, developed in Massachusetts, 125; emphasis on local regulations concerning, 303; members of Kiwanis Clubs as officers of, 204; survey of, in Cincinnati, 140 ff.

Proceedings of the Second Conference on Nursery Schools, 320

Prospect Club, 167

Prostitute, as product of mental defect, 448

Prostitution, in Cleveland, 167; in Detroit, 216

Protestant Big Brothers Club, 141

Protestant Big Sisters Club, 141

Providence (R. I.), Boys' Club of, 186; discussion method in schools of, 285

Psychiatric Approach, The, X, 435 ff.

Psychoanalysis, criticism of theory of, 460 ff.; grotesque claims of, 462 n.; in child clinics, 465

Psychoanalytic theory, repression in, 460, 463 ff.; the unconscious in, 460 ff.

Psycho-Educational Clinic (Yale University), 323

Psychometric Approach, The, VIII, 330 ff.; compared with other types of approach, 569

Psychoneuroses, Cady tests designed to uncover, 413; constipation as factor in producing, 453; effect of Travis' tests on victims of, 408; Electra complex as source of, 573; high incidence of, among Jews, 517; interpretation of, 41; Œdipus complex as source of, 573; physical disturbances related to, 453; physique correlated with, 480; prevalence of, 450, n.; sex talk as leading to development of, 52; Woodworth tests designed to uncover, 419 ff.

Psychopathic personality, results of study of, 128

Psychoses, among criminals, 447; relation between other troubles and, 438

Puberty, delinquency as caused by premature, 573

Public Education Association of New York City, The, 229, 249, 253, 254

Pyknic type of physique, 480 ff.; characteristics of, 481; and schizophrenia, 482; tendency to circular insanity of those possessing, 481

Rage, as unlearned behavior, 556

Ralston, R., 340, 368

Rank, O., 462

Ratliff, Beulah A., 87

Raubenheimer, Albert S., 415, 416, 417, 418, 426

Reaction time, in tests, 386; increased by emotional disturbance, 388

Reading, Paul M., 285, 287, 288

Reamer, J., 361, 362

Recidivism, among the psychopathic, 452 ff.

Recreation, facilities for, in combating delinquency, 203; playgrounds as form of, 195 ff., 201

Reflexes, conditioned, 507; measurement of psycho-galvanic, 374

Reformatories, see INSTITUTIONS

Repression, in psychoanalytic theory, 460, 463 ff.

Reproval, testing effect of, on increase in mental output, 375

Resistance, lack of, to suggestion, 164; material analyzed in terms of, 532; measuring child's social, 398; observational study of, 530; test of social, as measure of personality traits and behavior types, 373

Rich, G. J., 475, 477, 479, 480

Richards, Esther Loring, 73, 74, 76, 87, 163, 516, 565

Richmond (Va.), child guidance service organized in, 145; visiting teacher work in, 255

Right-handedness, see HANDEDNESS

Rippin, Jane D., 176

Rochester (N. Y.), school system and visiting teacher movement in, 239 ff.

Rock Springs (Wyo.), visiting teacher work in, 255

Rôle, conception of, 41

Rosanoff, A. J., 438, 468

Rotary International, 202 ff.

Rousseau, Jean Jacques, Institute in Geneva, 534

Royal Commission on the Control of Feeblemindedness, 446

Sadger, I., 462

St. Charles, training school for boys at, 157

St. George's School for Child Study, research in, 525 ff., 540

St. Louis (Mo.), child guidance clinics established in, 145

St. Paul, child guidance clinics established in, 145; parental education courses in, 314

Salem (Mass.), Salem Fraternity of, 186

Saliva, and carbon-dioxide content as measure of excitability, 477; insanity correlated with alkaline, 478; as material for study of excitability, 475

Samarcand Manor, 110

San Francisco (Cal.), policemen in, 215

Sanborn, F. B., 125

Sanders, Clare, 319

Sauk Center (Minn.), 112; state school at, 111

Scammon, Richard E., 491, 492, 493, 494, 495, 496, 501, 502

Schizophrenia, characteristics of, 406; responses to visual and auditory tests by victims of, 409; relation between physique and, 482

Schizothymes, 483

Schlapp, M. G., 502

School, adjustment to, 267; adjustment to, measured in terms of corrigibility, 410; as assuming entire responsibility for child, 574; back-to-school campaigns, 202; cause of absence from, 242; character education in, VI, 273 ff.; court as replaced by, 220; court related to, in Rochester, 248; intelligence quotient as related to length of attendance at, 353; intelligence test emphasized in, 334; maladjustment treated in, 539; movement to introduce mental clinics into, 157; nervous habits among children in, 539; pre-parental education in, 324; racial composition of, in Rochester, 244; recreational programs developed in, 177; slow response of, to demands of a changing society, 328

School children in U. S., physical defects of, 449, n.

Seegal, D., 500

Self-assertion, measuring degree of, 400; test of, as measure of personality traits and behavior types, 373

Self-assurance, test of, as measure of personality traits and behavior types, 373

Self-estimation and evaluation, test of, as

measure of personality traits and behavior types, 373, 402

Sentence formation, study of development of, 537; see LANGUAGE, SPEECH

Sepsis, as cause of mental disorder, 454

Sex, as drive, 554; as source of mental conflict, 44 ff., 463 ff.; premature development of, 471; psychoanalytic view of, 52, 464 ff.

Shaw, Clifford R., 8, 9, 106, 546, 548, 549, 551, 571

Sheldon, Rowland C., 183

Sheppard and Enoch Pratt Hospital, 516

Sheppard-Towner Clinic for infant and maternity welfare, 313

Sherrington, C. S., 554, 558

Shyness, changes in intelligence quotient correlated with changes in ratings of, 531

Sing Sing, study of, by National Committee for Mental Hygiene, 442 ff.

Slawson, John, 365, 366, 422, 423, 424, 425, 451, 567

Sleighton Farms, 111

Smith, Carrie W., 111

Smith College School for Social Work, 151

Social perception, test of, as measure of personality traits and behavior types, 373

Social resistance, measuring child's, 398; test of, as measure of personality traits and behavior types, 373

Sociological Approach, The, XII, 505 ff.

Spaulding, Edith R., 458, 459

Speech, see LANGUAGE, SENTENCE FORMATION

Stability, criteria of, 387; Slawson's tests for disclosing, 422; Slawson's tests as showing decided lack of emotional, 425; tests to discover degrees in emotional, between those of normal and abnormal physique, 419 ff.

Stammering, 475 ff.

Starr, H. E., 475, 477, 478

Stealing, by boys in groups, 8 ff., 549; cases of, before Chicago Juvenile Court, 184; study of, 283

Stearns, M. M., 179, 226, 269, 270

Stenquist, John L., 362

Sterling House, 167, 168

Stern, L. W., 441

Strayer, George D., 239

Strecker, E. A., 66, 67, 436, 438, 468

Stowe, L. B., 123

Student government, at Clinton Farms, 111; at George Junior Republic, 123

Studiousness, test of, as measure of personality traits and behavior types, 373

Subordination, study of, in nursery situation, 519

Suggestibility, test of, as measure of personality traits and behavior types, 373

Suggestion, lack of resistance to, 164

Sullivan, Harry Stack, 516

Susceptibility, relation of specific diseases to constitutional types of, 499

Syntonic type, 487

Syntropic type, 487

T-complex, 488

Taft, Jessie, 30, 89, 90

Taylor, Marianna, 86

Teachers College Institute for Child Welfare Research, 321, 522 ff., 532 ff.

Temperament, as dynamic factor for study, 370; endocrine glands related to, 472, 473; as having biochemical base, 568; test of, as measure of affective aspects of personality, 375

Tensions, regulation of behavior through sustaining of physiological, 463 ff., 515, 561 ff.

Terman, L. M., 334, 335, 337, 338, 339, 340, 341, 342, 348, 368

Tests, for personality traits and behavior types, 371 ff.; SEE ALLPORT; ALPHA; BINET; BROOKLINE; DELINQUENCY; DISCRIMINATION; DOWNEY; DYNAMOMETER; ELLIS; EMOTIONAL INSTABILITY; ENCOURAGEMENT; EYES; FORESIGHT; HART'S TEST; INFORMATION TEST; MAY; MENTAL TESTING; METRONOME; MOTION PICTURES; MULTIPLE CHOICE TESTS; NATIONAL TESTS; OTIS TESTS; PERSONALITY; PRESSEY; REACTION TIME; SCHIZOPHRENIA; STABILITY; STEALING; TERMAN; TRUE-FALSE TEST

Testimony, studies of, 441

Thom, D. A., 86, 460

Thomas, Dorothy S., 522, 532

Thorax, measurement of, 494

Thorndike, E. L., 332, 506

Thrasher, Frederic M., 7, 8, 9, 10, 184, 187, 188, 190, 193, 548, 549

Threshold, change in auditory and visual, as index of personality type, 409

Thurstone, L. L., 557

Thyroid gland, as accelerating physical development, 471

Titration, acid content of urine measured by, 478

Toledo (O.), discussion method in schools of, 285; Rotary Club of, 203

Tonsils, chronic sepsis of, related to psychoses, 453; removal of diseased, resulting in improved behavior, 330

Toronto (Ontario, Canada), incidence of behavior problems in, 540

Toxemia, as cause of mental disorder, 453

Trabue Completion Sentences, 412

Training schools, evolution of, for girls, 110

Traits, see CHARACTER, PERSONALITY

Traveling clinics, 153

Travis, Lee E., 406, 408, 409, 431

Travis, Roland C., 409

Trought, T. W., 213

Truancy, emphasis on local regulations concerning, 303; as result of poor home conditions, 266; treatment of, in Rochester, 249

True-false test, 426

Truitt, Ralph P., 466, 467

Trustworthiness, test of, as measure of personality traits and behavior types, 373

Tudor-Hart, B., 558

Tulchin, S. H., 534

Type, criminal, 448

Unconscious, the, in psychoanalytic theory, 460 ff.

Union League Boys' Club (Chicago), 188 ff.

University Women, American Association of, 309 ff.

Unlearned behavior factors, 555 ff.

Urbanization, effect on home life of, 280

Urine, acidity of, as index of excitability, 477; creatinine content of, as measure of excitability, 477; as index of insanity, 478; as material for study of excitability, 475

Utah, state schools placed under state board of education in, 111

Utah Character Education Outline, 274

Van Waters, Miriam, 93, 109, 113, 317

Vassar Institute of Euthenics, 328

Verry, Ethel, 528, 529, 530

Visiting teacher, 125; in Rochester, 239 ff.; measures employed by, 259 ff.; origin of work of, 228; primary functions of, 258; problems of, in rural districts, 252 ff.; progress in increasing numbers of, in various states, 256 ff.; promotion of, movement, 255; reasons for referring child to, 258; work of, 228 ff.; work of, in conjunction with visiting mother, 309

Vocational Bureau, in Cincinnati, 270

Voelker, P. F., 412, 415

Vollmer, August, 212

Walker, Marjorie, 519, 528

Washburne, C., 179, 226, 269, 270

Watson, John B., 73, 106, 291, 440, 505, 506, 507, 519, 555, 556, 557, 558, 560

Weeks, Ila D., 302, 303

Weet, H. S., 240, n., 241

Wembridge, Eleanor R., 170

Wertheimer, F. I., 486, 487, 488

West, James E., 172

West Point, mental hygiene at, 157

Wheeler, W. M., 555

White, Edna, 322, 536

White-Williams Foundation, 230 ff., 254, 551, 573

Whittier Scale, as index of environment, 349

Whittier State School, The, 364, 394, 414, 418

Williams, George, 230

Williams, J. Harold, 364, 365, 447

Winnetka (Ill.), 177, 225 ff., 268

Witmer, L., 31, 35, 459

Women police, see POLICEWOMEN

Women's Protective Association (Cleveland), 167

Wood, T. D., 449, n., 454, 459

Woodrow, H., 497

Woods, Arthur, 206, 207, 209, 211, 212

Woodworth, R. S., 386, 413, 419, 420, 421, 433

Woolley, Helen T., 69, 73, 82, 270, 328, 329, 351, 352, 353, 369, 522

Worcester (Mass.), Boys' Club of, 194

Wright, J. F., 280

Yale University, mental hygiene department at, 157 ff.; Psycho-Educational Clinic at, 323

Yerkes, R. M., 506

Young Men's Christian Association, 170, 174, 187, 191, 195, 296

Youtz, May P., 312

Zorbaugh, H. W., 550